CORRUPTING THE YOUTH

James Franklin

Corrupting the Youth

A history of philosophy in Australia

MACLEAY PRESS
Sydney

First published 2003
Macleay Press
PO Box 433
Paddington NSW 2021
Australia

Edited by George Thomas
Cover design by Reno Design Group, Sydney
Printed in Australia by Southwood Press, Marrickville

National Library of Australia
Cataloguing-in-Publication entry

Franklin, James, 1953– .
Corrupting the youth : a history of philosophy in Australia.

Bibliography.
Includes index.
ISBN 1 876492 08 2.

1. Philosophy - Australia - History. 2. Philosophy -
        Australia.

199.94

Contents

Abbreviations

ACR	*Australasian Catholic Record*
ADB	*Australian Dictionary of Biography*
AJP	*Australasian Journal of Philosophy*
AJPP	*Australasian Journal of Psychology and Philosophy*
SMH	*Sydney Morning Herald*

Preface

DOES life have a meaning, and if so what is it? What can I be certain of, and how should I act when I am not certain? Why are the established truths of my tribe better than the primitive superstitions of your tribe? Why should I do as I'm told? These are questions it is easy to avoid, in the rush to acquire a water frontage. Even for many of a more serious outlook, they are easy to dismiss with excuses like 'it's all a matter of opinion' or 'let's get on with practical matters' or 'they're too hard'. They are questions that may be ignored, but they do not go away.

A small proportion of the population pursue the answers to these questions through philosophy. Philosophy doubts whether rushing ahead with practical matters is a good idea, in advance of deciding which practical matters are important, and which direction is forward. It believes that some opinions are better than others, and that it is possible to give logical reasons as to why. It inquires as to the value of water frontages, vis à vis the range of other goods proper to human nature.

Those who cultivate philosophy fall into two groups. They are the youth, and philosophers.

In the small window between the end of unquestioning childhood and the onset of the terminal busyness of working life, the inquiring young are willing for a year or two to examine their fundamental assumptions, and perhaps take on new ones. Their search may be ill-directed or incompetent, but can be intense for a time, and adults offering philosophical or religious opinions find a ready audience. In the normal course of psychological development, some world view or lack of it is found serviceable and workaday reality supervenes. But a few discover in themselves a special aptitude for the way of ideas, and become professional philosophers. They become the teachers and writers who provide the next generation with its smorgasbord of options.

The emotional charge of the big questions that philosophy examines makes the relationship between philosophy teachers and their students a powerful one, irrespective of whether the teachers are any good (or good). When the citizens of Athens condemned Socrates to death in 399 BC on a charge of corrupting the youth, they recognised the power of ideas to change what the rising generation might believe, and how they might act. When the New South Wales Parliament in 1943 condemned Professor John Anderson's statements on religion and education as 'calculated to undermine the principles which constitute a Christian State', they were well aware that the state's future schoolteachers had access to philosophical ideas almost entirely through him. When German disabled persons in wheelchairs prevented the Australian philosophy professor Peter Singer from speaking in 1991, it was because they feared his views on the permissibility of killing babies might come to be accepted — and with some reason, since his book *Practical Ethics* is widely used in university courses.

This is the story of Australian philosophers, both in their thinking and in how their thought and action influenced their students. It is a story of some remarkable achievements, of insights and arguments that truly advanced understanding of perennially difficult questions. David Armstrong's work on laws of nature, and Rai Gaita's on the foundations of ethics in the preciousness of human life, are among permanent contributions to understanding reality at the most abstract level.

Not all is sweetness and light, however. Because philosophy deals with fundamentals, to which the human mind is not very well adapted either through evolution or education, there is always disagreement about what counts as good philosophy and what as bad. Philosophy is peculiarly susceptible to an illusion like white-out in the Antarctic, where the horizon seems to be just beyond what one can see. Consequently, almost everyone who has heard of philosophical questions thinks he can judge philosophy. So philosophical reputations are often decided by popular vote, for example by totalling the adulation of undergraduates. The book contains, therefore, as well as admirable thinkers, some fast-talking charlatans and some gullible disciples, and between the two, an extraordinary quantity of overheated air.

We begin the story with the arrival of John Anderson in 1927 as Professor of Philosophy at Sydney University. Although there was an older tradition of Idealist philosophy, and long before that an Aboriginal philosophy of the land (which will be treated in their place), Anderson's arrival marked a sharp break which set Australian philosophy on its characteristic course. His philosophy was realist (in the sense of being concerned with the ways of working of real things in the world, rather than having our ideas as the central focus of philosophy), materialist, atheist and more interested in criticism than in synthesis or moral uplift. Sydney philosophy, especially but not uniquely, has maintained those biases.

There were of course alternatives to the Andersonian style. There was Catholic philosophy — also realist, indeed more so when it came to the objectivity of ethical truths; though it had little impact in universities, it later inspired the High Court judges in the Mabo case to draw from the ethical underpinning of the law a reason for overturning the doctrine of *terra nullius*. Melbourne also resisted the Andersonian trend. The old Idealism survived longer there, and merged with the influence of an overseas guru, Wittgenstein, to produce a distinctive style of philosophy more attuned to ethics, commentary on public issues and history than the hard-edged and scientific thinking of Sydney. The University of Tasmania's efforts to keep out of the orbit of Sydney atheism led it to appoint a third-rate Christian philosopher from Melbourne, Sydney Sparkes Orr, whose affair with a student created a scandal that grabbed headlines for a decade.

But philosophy does not exist only in the classroom and adjoining offices, conference rooms and cloisters. Many of those who come into contact with philosophers in their youth take away fundamental reorientations about what is important, and follow life courses that are to one degree or another implementations of philosophical ideas. So before moving to more recent times, we examine a number of issues where the reach of philosophical ideas extends deep into ordinary life. First, the libertarian excesses of the celebrated Sydney 'Push' were a living out of at least one interpretation of the ethical views of their teacher, John Anderson, and were at the leading edge of 'The Sixties'. The second of these issues is the mind, a traditional topic of philosophy and more recently of psychiatry, psychology, literature and artificial intelligence. The theory of 'Australian materialism', that the mind is nothing over and above the brain and its workings, has been common among philosophers and some medical practitioners, but others have emphasised how unique and unlike matter the ways of the mind are. A last topic is even further from academic life. The Australian colonies were planned foundations of the age of Enlightenment, in which there was never an established church. Secular education therefore sought a replacement for religion, a philosophy to inspire the youth in the paths of virtue. It adopted a series of ideas — the Empire, the ancient classics, the Anzacs, sport, improving literature — which have moulded Australian ways of thinking in deep but unacknowledged ways.

In later chapters, as the story of professional philosophy moves beyond the small and comparatively coherent world of the mid-century, there is inevitably a certain fragmentation, as specialised, sometimes inward-looking schools have taken up particular issues. Australian achievements in realist philosophy of science have been outstanding, though little known to the public. Feminism and environmental philosophy have been at least popular. Ethics, though, has had the highest profile in recent years, as befits the importance of its subject matter. Peter Singer became Australia's best-known philosopher as a result of unusual views such as the permissibility of infanticide. Argument over euthanasia still turns more on essential philosophical disagreements than on differing estimates of the practical consequences of changing the law.

As these examples make clear, fundamentals are dangerous, in that changes in them have consequences that reach far into the depths of thought and conduct, and far into the future. That is why philosophy matters, and why knowledge of a country's philosophical past is the surest guide to where it is going.

The book has two unusual features. It is long on quotes, and it is full of footnotes. Philosophers are word-oriented people and at their best write very well. With careful selection, a book on philosophy can bring readers face to face with the thing itself: raw and well-written philosophy, without the need for dilution or homogenisation by clumsy paraphrase. The many footnotes are not for reading. They are a window into the huge mass of material that has been written in Australia on important ideas. For one thing, since a reference in this book is the only chance for many of those ideas to avoid oblivion, there is an ethical requirement to give them their opportunity. And some of the stories to be told would hardly be believable but for the invitation to consult the source. But the main reason for supplying so many footnotes is to avoid the narrowness of so many books on Australian ideas. At the very time when internet-skilled readers are used to a network of links to further information, book publishers press authors to prune footnotes to a minimum, and authors respond with a mass of poorly-supported opinions on a familiar range of topics. A real book on ideas does not hide the sources from its readers, but displays them.

PART ONE:
JOHN ANDERSON'S SYDNEY AND ALTERNATIVES

Chapter 1   Anderson and the State

John Anderson had an answer to every conceivable question. It was "No".
— *James McAuley* [1]

A S Professor of Philosophy at Sydney University from 1927 to 1958, John Anderson was Sydney's best-known academic. He dominated the higher reaches of Sydney intellectual life for those thirty years. His students played a leading role for another thirty, not only in academia, but in politics, law, journalism and teaching. Many of them made impressive contributions to their fields, but Anderson's own concerns were not with positive achievements, honours or the good of society. His position was one of opposition:

> The work of the academic, qua academic, is criticism; and whatever his special field may be, his development of independent views will bring him into conflict with prevailing opinions and customary attitudes in the public arena and not merely among his fellow-professionals. [2]

And that was not just hot air. Generations of academics have justified their tenure on the grounds that they *might* want to criticise the powers that be, someday, but how many have actually done it? Anderson did so, and did it loudly enough to goad the authorities into action.

When the University of Sydney advertised its chair of philosophy in 1926, it received two applications. John Anderson was selected on the strength of two discussion articles in *Mind*, a book on logic in

---

[1] J. McAuley, quoted by D.M. Armstrong in R. Bogdan, *D.M. Armstrong* (Dordrecht, 1984), pp. 6–7; one version of the original in *Bulletin* 30/6/1962, p. 29.
[2] J. Anderson, 'The place of the academic in modern society', in J. Anderson, *Education and Inquiry* ed. D.Z. Phillips (Oxford, 1980), p. 214.

mind, and glowing testimonials from two of Scotland's leading philosophers.[3] What these references failed to mention was that Anderson
was a political radical, and had become more so with the failure of
the British General Strike of 1926 to develop into the hoped-for
Revolution.[4] Persistent rumours that the warmth of the testimonials
was caused by the desire of the writers to speed Anderson's passage to
the most distant regions possible[5] may be true, or may just be a standard motif of academic politics. In any case, with no other professor
of philosophy within 500 miles, Anderson was at last free to do things
his way.

He settled into his office at the University, acquired a house in
leafy Turramurra on Sydney's exclusive upper North Shore, with
maid and gardener, and called on the city headquarters of the Communist Party to offer his services.[6] Though he did not become a Party
member, he was given the status of 'Theoretical Adviser' to the Party,
and in the next few years wrote a number of articles for its various
organs.[7] They are jargon-ridden, but there are a few points of interest
in the personal spin that Anderson put on some of the Marxist ortho-
doxies. He had no patience with the 'class view of truth', according
to which ideas are a function of the class position of whoever holds
them, and hence have only a relative claim to truth. As befits an expert in logic, Anderson was for absolute truth.[8] For much the same
reasons, he was not prepared to accept a purely economic motivation
for the struggle of the workers: 'the incentive to revolution', he says,
'is a moral one. This does not mean that it is altruistic or that it is

[3] Anderson's application is printed in *Dialectic* (Newcastle University) 30
(1987): pp. 144–5.
[4] A.W. Bishop, 'John Anderson 1931–1935', *Sydney Libertarians Broadsheet* 91
(June 1977): pp. 3–6; some of Anderson's earlier occasional writings on
radical themes reprinted in *Heraclitus* 28 (Sept 1992); 30 (Mar 1993); 31
(May 1993); 32 (Aug 1993); on Anderson in Scotland, B. Kennedy, *A
Passion to Oppose: John Anderson, Philosopher* (Melbourne, 1995), chs 1–5; A.J.
Baker, 'Anderson's intellectual background and influences', *Heraclitus* 33
(Oct. 1993): pp. 4–12; Anderson archives listed in
www.usyd.edu.au/arms/archives/anderson_john .
[5] ASIO file on Anderson (Australian Archives series A6119/43 item 389, p.
8, report of 17/7/1950).
[6] Kennedy, *A Passion to Oppose*, chs 6–7.
[7] Summaries in A.J. Baker, *Anderson's Social Philosophy* (Sydney, 1979), pp.
48–63, 80–9; M. Weblin, *A Passion for Thinking* (to appear), ch. 3; writings
of 'Comrade Spencer', summarised by S. Cooper in 'When Anderson and
Reich were good Stalinists', *Sydney Libertarians Broadsheet* 61 (July 1970): pp.
6–7 and 69 (July 1972): pp. 5–6, and following articles (see below).
[8] J. Anderson, 'Some obscurantist fallacies', *Freethought* no. 2 (Nov 1932): pp.
10–12, summarised in Baker, *Anderson's Social Philosophy*, p. 52.

obligatory; it means that it is a demand for a particular way of living, broadly describable as freedom.'[9]

'Freedom' was a tricky concept to deploy in Marxist circles, and it was on this issue that Anderson departed most forcefully from his comrades. The *Workers' Weekly* of 14 November 1930 printed a long letter from Anderson under the heading 'Workers Have Right to All Public Buildings: Capitalist Class Have Not All the Brains'.[10] It protested against the denial of the use of Sydney Town Hall for celebrations of the thirteenth anniversary of the Russian Revolution. 'It is intolerable', he wrote, 'that the [Sydney City] Council should set itself up as a censor of views to be expressed at Town Hall meetings.' Anderson was not unaware of the view expressed in some quarters that certain classes in the Soviet Union suffered similar restrictions on liberty. He had some advice to the Friends of the Soviet Union on this matter:

> It seems to me to be an important part of the work of your organisation to show that nothing corresponding to this disenfranchisement exists in Russia ... Meanwhile the economic position of the 'kulaks' gives them a special political status, and the reserving of entry into the Soviets and other organisations for the rest of the community really makes for political equality. If anything like this, fragmentary as it is, is a part of your position, I think you would do well to state it as clearly and forcibly as possible.

Excellent theoretical advice from a master of the art of argument, but not in accord with Party policy. The page opposite Anderson's letter had an article, 'Imperialist agents receive just deserts: death sentence executed', reprinted from *Pravda*, which rejoiced in the 'liquidation of the kulak as a class'. The *Workers' Weekly* added the editorial comment: 'Workers in U.S.S.R. — exterminate more of these vile enemies of the working class.'

This letter of Anderson's caught the attention of Australia's rudimentary security services. In the files later inherited by ASIO, the first reference to Anderson was a request that investigations be made concerning the letter 'purported to have been received by the "Friends of Soviet Russia".' It requested:

[9] 'Comrade Spencer' [i.e., Anderson] 'The moral factor in the proletarian revolution', *The Communist* (Feb 1928), repr. in M. Weblin, ed, *A Perilous and Fighting Life: From Communist to Conservative: The Political Writings of John Anderson* (Sydney, 2003), pp. 16–20.
[10] *Workers' Weekly* no. 375 (14/11/1930), p. 5; full text in *Labor Daily* 12/11/1930; reply in T. Walsh, *Sydney 'Varsity Professor Goes Red: An Open Letter to Professor Anderson* (pamphlet, Sydney, 1931, copy in Anderson papers, Sydney University Archives).

John Anderson: photo submitted with his application to University of Sydney, 1926 (Anderson papers, University of Sydney Archives)

Will you please find out if there is a professor at the University of this name and whether you could possibly verify the truth of the statement.

If there is any truth in it one cannot but view with alarm the sympathy expressed by one who is in a position to effectively spread the doctrines as evinced in his letter to the Secretary referred to. DIRECTOR[11]

Alas, verified it was.

There is a Professor John Anderson at Sydney University, his Chair bein [*sic*] Philosophy; he is described as a young man of enthusiasms in some directions and representative of school of thought evidenced in the letter to the paper mentioned. He is stated not to be regarded very seriously by his colleagues some of whom have already spoken to him regarding the present matter.[12]

Despite this initial alarm, Anderson does not seem to have been re-garded seriously by security either. The only other mention of him in the 1930s (or 1940s) in the file is a note of late 1931 that he has 'very recently been in personal consultation with principal members of the C.P.A. at the Communist Hall, including MOXON lately returned from BOURKE.'[13] But an article in *N.S.W. Police News* did take exception to one of Anderson's Freethought addresses, in which he claimed that there was no political freedom and that the evidence of one policeman counted for more than many denials by non-police-men. The article observed, with some prescience, that many a man has been made famous by public censure of his views, and has then with age 'moderated his opinions and finally reversed them, after get-ting the true philosophical point of view.'[14]

Whether Anderson was in fact using his position to spread Com-munist doctrines among the students is unclear. A speech of his at an 'anti-war' rally in 1933 suggests there was little neutrality about his position. 'University students are a breeding ground for Fascism', he said. 'It is among these people that a great deal of valuable work can be done ... Many university students are taking up a class position. They could be organised and brought together, only that the powers that be will prevent such a movement.'[15]

Events in Moscow were to destroy Anderson's special relationship with the Party. With the rise of Stalin, previous policies of co-opera-tion between the Communist parties of all countries and other far left parties were forbidden. Relentless Communist criticism of former

[11] ASIO file on Anderson, p. 3 (21/11/1930).

[12] ASIO file, p. 4 (24/11/1930).

[13] ASIO file, p. 5 (23/11/1931).

[14] 'Professor Anderson and the police', *N.S.W. Police News* 11 (8) (15/8/1931), p. 6.

[15] *SMH* 10/4/1933, p. 13.

allies, now branded 'social fascists', weakened the left opposition everywhere (notably in Germany, easing Hitler's rise to power). Australia was a significant country in international theory, in this very connection. It had been the scene of the world's first 'reformist' (Labor) governments, and Lenin himself had expressed the rage of the true revolutionary at workers proving themselves satisfied with the gains won by reformist parties.[16] Orders came from Moscow to overthrow the comparatively easy-going leadership of Jack Kavanagh and replace it with the hardline Stalinism of Lance Sharkey and Herbert Moxon. The Party Conference of 1929 accepted the directive.[17] Kavanagh made the mistake of attacking the manifesto of the agent sent from Moscow to clean up the Party, apparently under the impression that it had been written by Anderson,[18] and was promptly expelled for 'rightist deviationism'. Anderson, as a man committed to theory, supported the new Stalinist line ('with a naivete and enthusiasm that might seem unbecoming in a mind generally acknowledged by philosophers as first rate.'[19]) Anderson's position had been entirely against reformism, with its trading of material gains for compromise on principle. ('The merely utilitarian pursuit of the workers' "interests" is suitable for Labour opportunists. But to express the sickness of society in terms of the poverty of the masses is not the position of revolutionists';[20] 'the humanitarian objection to violence is an objection to emancipation.'[21]) But whatever Anderson's zeal, there was no place for fellow-travelling intellectuals in the new order, and he was forced to resign when an article of his, on the theme that the fear of

[16] V.I. Lenin, 'In Australia', *Pravda* no. 134 (13/6/1913); see R. Kuhn, 'Lenin on the ALP: The career of 600 words', *Australian Journal of Politics and History* 35 (1989): pp. 29–49; background in J. Tampke, '"Pace setter or quiet backwater?"—German literature on Australia's Labour movement and social policies, 1890–1914', *Labour History* 36 (1979): pp. 3–17.

[17] B. Curthoys, 'The Communist Party and the Communist International (1927–1929)', *Labour History* 64 (1993): pp. 54–69; B. Penrose, 'Herbert Moxon, a victim of the "Bolshevisation" of the Communist Party', *Labour History* 70 (1996): pp. 92–114; L.L. Sharkey, *An Outline History of the Australian Communist Party* (Sydney, 1944), pp. 21–3.

[18] F. Farrell, *International Socialism and Australian Labour* (Sydney, 1981), p. 182.

[19] Farrell, *International Socialism and Australian Labour*, p. 224.

[20] 'Comrade Spencer' [i.e., Anderson] 'The moral factor in the proletarian revolution'.

[21] 'Comrade Spencer', 'Reformism and class consciousness, part II', *The Communist* (June 1928), repr. in Weblin, *A Perilous and Fighting Life*, pp. 21–4; see 'Edna Ryan on Anderson and C.P. Secretary Moxon', *Heraclitus* 64 (Apr 1988): p. 11.

spontaneity was a sign not of leadership but of bureaucracy, was suppressed by the new Party leadership.[22] Like Heidegger's involvement with the Nazi party,[23] the relationship came to an end at the initiative of the Party, not the philosopher.

IN THE meantime Anderson's relentless criticism troubled a larger pond than the diminutive Central Committee of the Party. Anderson had set up at the University the Freethought Society, giving himself as President a permanent platform. His first presidential address, of 9 July 1931, was on 'Freethought and Politics'. It made him famous overnight, mainly for the statement, 'War memorials are political idols.' No complete record of it exists,[24] but it seems that the most controversial points were correctly summarised in the motion of censure moved in the NSW Legislative Assembly by the leader of the Country Party, Mr Bruxner. Lieutenant-Colonel Michael (later Sir Michael) Bruxner, DSO, chevalier of the Legion of Honour, had been severely wounded at Gallipoli, commanded the 6th Australian Light Horse in the Sinai, and had been in charge of supply to the right flank of Allenby's advance on Damascus.[25] He had therefore known more than a few of those commemorated on the war memorials. He moved in the Legislative Assembly:

> That, in the opinion of this House, the statements made on Thursday, 9th July, by the Professor of Philosophy at the Sydney University, namely, Professor Anderson, when speaking as the president of the Free Thought Association, to the effect that such terms as 'the State,' 'the country,' and 'the nation' were superstitious notions; that such terms as 'your King and Country need you' were appeals to prejudice and superstition; that 'loyalty' was a kind of superstition, that war memorials were idols, and that the keeping up of religious celebrations connected with them were fetishes which only served the purpose of blocking discussion — are

---

[22] S. Macintyre, *The Reds* (Sydney, 1998), pp. 230–1; Farrell, *International Socialism and Australian Labour*, p. 224; Baker, *Anderson's Social Philosophy*, p. 89; the offending article, 'Censorship in the working-class movement', repr. in Weblin, *A Perilous and Fighting Life*, p. 49.

[23] B. Hindess, 'Heidegger and the Nazis', *Thesis Eleven* 31 (1992): pp. 115–30.

[24] Summaries in Baker, *Anderson's Social Philosophy*, pp. 90–1; Weblin, *Passion*, ch. 5.

[25] D. Aitkin, *The Colonel: The Political Biography of Sir Michael Bruxner* (Canberra, 1969), pp. 23–32; 'Bruxner, Michael', *ADB*, vol. 7 pp. 468–9; 'Celebrities of the A.I.F. no. 71: Lieut.-Col. M.F. Bruxner, DSO', *Reveille* 9 (11) (July 1936): pp. 8–9.

against the best interests of the community, and are not in accord with the national sentiment of the people of this State.[26]

The motion was debated on and off for a couple of months, but not passed, as the Lang Labor government was still in power, and its minister for education supported Anderson at least to the extent of defending his freedom of speech. Among the more interesting arguments were those of Albert Henry, Member for Clarence and another ex-serviceman. These and later public reactions to Anderson cast light on something normally hidden in obscurity: what the 'dominant ideology' of Australia really has been. As often observed, tradition works best when it is not justified, but presumed, so that all take it to be natural and thus to admit of no serious alternative. As Anderson put it, 'Tradition itself invites criticism, because it represents certain things as worth while but is unable to give any account of their value.'[27] When someone like Anderson challenges the status quo, the ruling class — to use that term in as noncommittal way as possible—is forced to look for arguments to defend itself. The results are revealing. Henry expressed a philosophy of education diametrically opposed to Anderson's.

> Mr. HENRY: If we spend £6,500,000 in New South Wales upon education then such a thing as patriotism, which is not upon the curriculum of the University of Sydney or of our schools, is a sentiment and an inspiration in regard to civil duties and responsibilities which we cannot overlook. What is the use of educating a man in mathematical science or in academic matters unless at the same time we instil into him the fundamental principles of citizenship, civic responsibility and noble ideas?[28]

Henry went on to discuss a question rarely debated on the floor of the New South Wales Parliament: what is philosophy itself for?

> This man is a professor of philosophy. I believe in philosophy; it is a necessary study, and gives one an outlook upon life which is of great consolation to persons who possess the elasticity of mind necessary to adjust themselves to changing thought and conditions. But when a man stands up and traduces in unbridled terms institutions that are revered, and that appeal to the highest sentiments and the noblest motives in the community, he transgresses the reasonable bounds of propriety and all the canons of decent conduct. For instance, why did not this professor go farther, and say that religion is a fetish—that churches ought to be razed

---

[26] *New South Wales Parliamentary Debates*, 14 July 1931 (2nd series, vol. 128 pp. 4266–7); the text has 'mocking' for 'blocking'.
[27] J. Anderson, 'Socrates as an educator', repr. in *Studies in Empirical Philosophy*, pp. 202–13, at p. 207.
[28] *NSWPD*, 8 Sept 1931 (vol. 129 pp. 5995–6).

to the ground, and that people went to church on Sunday only because they believed in a superstitious doctrine? Because he did not dare to attack religion openly.[29]

SINCE that sums up rather well a certain view of society, it is time to consider what Anderson's own philosophy was. Anderson never wrote a short summary of it, but there is an excellent one by his student John Mackie. It makes clear how his politically contentious views of 1931 follow from his general philosophy:

His central doctrine is that there is only one way of being, that of ordinary things in space and time, and that every question is a simple issue of truth or falsity, that there are no different degrees or kinds of truth. His propositional view of reality implies that things are irreducibly complex, and we can never arrive at simple elements in any field. Anderson rejects systematically the notion of entities that are constituted, wholly or partly, by their relations: there can be no ideas or sensa whose nature it is to be known or perceived, no consciousness whose nature it is to know, no values whose nature it is to be ends or to direct action. Knowledge is a matter of finding what is objectively the case; all knowledge depends on observation and is fallible; we do not build up the knowledge of facts or laws out of any more immediate or more reliable items. Ethics is a study of the qualities of human activities; there can be no science of what is right or obligatory, and the study of moral judgements would belong to sociology, not to ethics. Similarly aesthetics can only be a study of feelings or judgements and not a source of directives for artists. Minds, like anything else, are complex spatio-temporal things: they are societies of motives or feelings, and there is no ultimate self to which the motives belong. Similarly a society is a complex of movements which both co-operate and compete; it has no inclusive social purpose, but neither is it reducible to its individual members. And all things have their regular causal ways of working.[30]

---

[29] *NSWPD*, 1 Sept 1931 (p. 5819).
[30] J.L. Mackie, 'The philosophy of John Anderson', *AJP* 40 (1962): pp. 265–82, at pp. 265–6; other short statements of Anderson's philosophy are in Baker, *Anderson's Social Philosophy*, pp. 5–7; A.J. Baker, 'Anderson, John', in *Routledge Encyclopedia of Philosophy*, ed. E. Craig (London, 1998), vol. 1, pp. 266–9; S. Grave, *A History of Philosophy in Australia* (St Lucia, 1984), ch. 3; S. Körner, 'Anderson's philosophy of experience', *Quadrant* 7 (2) (Autumn 1963): pp. 69–71; J. Passmore, 'Anderson, John', in *Encyclopedia of Philosophy*, ed. P. Edwards (New York, 1967), vol. 1, pp. 119–21; M. Weblin, 'Anderson and social inquiry', *Australian Journal of Anthropology* 3 (1–2) (1992): pp. 80–99; Weblin, *Passion*, ch. 4; T. Overend, 'Social realism and social idealism', *Inquiry* 21 (1978): pp. 271–311; a popular introduction in G. Souter, 'Our one and only guru', *SMH* 5/3/1977, p. 13; bibliography of works by and on Anderson up to 1984 in G. Suter, 'Bibliographic study of

It is clear why Anderson was in direct conflict with Henry's 'highest motives and noblest sentiments': he believed nothing is or can be higher or nobler than anything else. Nor are there 'civil duties and responsibilities', since there is no purpose to society, but only conflicting interests. Nor are there 'canons of decent conduct'. And as to 'consolation', no-one ever suspected Anderson of offering that. Some of the corrosive implications of the more central tenets of his philosophy are clear, some will become clearer in the following chapters.

The University Senate, 'while asserting the principle of free speech in universities,' severely censured Anderson for using 'expressions that transgress all proper limits' and required him to abstain from such utterances in future.[31] Anderson was unrepentant, and issued a statement to the effect that 'the fight for freedom of thought and speech does not stop.'[32] When he entered his logic class, there was a sustained demonstration in his favour. Visibly moved, he said, 'I will not insult the intelligence of this class by asking it to put the Senate's resolution into logical form.'[33]

As to the claim in Parliament that he did not dare to attack religion openly, that was, as the saying goes, 'asking for it'.

Following the Communists' rejection of him, Anderson joined the Trotskyists, the home for a number of other individuals unappreciated by the Party. He largely paid for their printing press, and contributed articles. The Workers' Party (Left Opposition) was, like any Trotskyist group, so small that it is a surprise to find more than one person of significance in it. But there was another, Laurie Short, later a central figure in the fights of the 1950s against Communist control of the trade unions. Short recalled, 'Anderson came to a little meeting in Jack Sylvester's home in early 1933. I was only a boy of seventeen, I had never met a university professor, and here was this tall, dignified looking character with a hooked pipe, and a slight stammer in his voice, and of course I thought he must be very wise because of this

the philosophy of John Anderson', *Australian Historical Bibliography*, Bulletin 10 (Sept 1984): pp. 1–60;
many texts at setis.library.usyd.edu.au/oztexts/anderson.html .
[31] *Minutes of the Senate* 20/7/1931; *SMH* 21/7/1931; summary in C. Turney, U. Bygott & P. Chippendale, *Australia's First: A History of the University of Sydney*, vol. 1 (Sydney, 1991), pp. 501–2; Baker, *Anderson's Social Philosophy*, p. 92; J. Passmore, *Memoirs of a Semi-Detached Australian* (Melbourne, 1997), pp. 119–21.
[32] Baker, *Anderson's Social Philosophy*, p. 93.
[33] W.H.C. Eddy, 'Adult education and its intellectual environment', *Quadrant* 17 (1) (Jan/Feb 1973): pp. 49–60, at pp. 49–50; Bishop, 'John Anderson 1931–1935', pp. 3–6.

bent pipe and this profound look. He impressed me enormously'.[34] During the rest of the 1930s, Short often visited Anderson in his office at the University, talking and borrowing books. Under Anderson's influence, he became converted to a view of society as pluralist, where various forces contend for power but where there may be overall stability.

Anderson split the Workers' Party at its 1937 conference, arguing that Trotsky was wrong to see the Soviet Union as a true workers' state merely suffering temporarily from Stalinism. His disillusionment with the USSR proceeded rapidly thereafter. By the time of his 1943 paper, 'The servile state', Anderson was one of the harshest critics on the Left of the Soviet Union, then being viewed at its rosiest as a result of its resistance to Hitler's invasion.

The second major public controversy in which Anderson was involved concerned a public lecture he gave in 1943 in a series on 'Religion in education'. His view was that 'As with the subject of snakes in Iceland — one could say "There is no religion in education". In other words, education is necessarily secular.'[35] Religious teaching as usually understood, he argued, was not part of education but opposed to it, as it limited inquiry instead of encouraging it. Teachers, he concluded, 'would be well advised to endeavour to keep the clergy out of the schools.'[36] Anderson was particularly angered by students arriving at University and immediately joining religious societies to 'safeguard themselves in

[34] L. Short, quoted in S. Short, *Laurie Short: A Political Life* (Sydney, 1992), p. 26; also L. Short, 'John Anderson as a Trotskyist', *Heraclitus* 35 (May, 1994): pp. 1–3; Passmore, *Memoirs*, p. 176; Weblin, *Passion*, ch. 8; B. Nield, 'The Andersonians: Their radical past', *Century* 13/2/1959, p. 6; D. Horne in *Daily Telegraph* 14/9/1946, p. 15; cf. 'Trotsky defended', *SMH* 12/7/1935, p. 15; and reports of addresses by Anderson on Trotsky and on the Moscow trials (1935–6), 'Intellectualism versus Bolshevism and Trotskyism' (1939), repr. in Weblin, *A Perilous and Fighting Life*.

[35] J. Anderson, 'Religion in education', in *Religion in Education* (five addresses), published by the New Education Fellowship (Sydney, 1943), pp. 25–32, at p. 25 (copies in G.F. McIntosh papers, Mitchell Library MSS. 5103 and in Stout papers, item 273); repr. in *Education and Inquiry*, pp. 203–13 and in *Dialectic* (University of Newcastle) 14 (1977): pp. 1–8; discussed in Baker, *Anderson's Social Philosophy*, p. 118 and Weblin, *Passion*, ch. 12; *SMH* 7/4/1943, p. 6, 14/4/1943, p. 4, 22/4/1943, p. 7; *Daily Telegraph* 7/4/1943, p. 5, 8/4/1943, p. 7; 14/4/1943, p. 5; reprise in 1947, in L. Rumble, 'Question Box', *Catholic Weekly* 13/2/1947, p. 12.

[36] Summary in A.R. Walker, 'Public controversies and academic freedom', *Dialectic* (Newcastle University) 30 (1987): pp. 11–23, p. 16; also *Honi Soit* 15 (10) (9/4/1943), p. 1; 15 (11) (16/4/1943), p. 1; 15 (13) (29/4/1943), p. 1.

advance against learning anything.'[37] There was an outcry in the newspapers and pulpits. Reversing what had happened in 1931, the State Parliament condemned him, *nem. con.*, declaring that his statements were 'unjustified, inasmuch as they present a travesty of the Christian religion and are calculated to undermine the principles which constitute a Christian State.'[38] The attack was led by the Reverend Donald Macdonald, MLA for Mosman, a Presbyterian minister and former military chaplain. His collected sermons on marriage had had a certain vogue among 'those who would retain the highest ideals in regard to Marriage, Home, and Family Life.'[39] He held the same university degree as Anderson (MA, Glasgow). He delivered an impressive piece of oratory. Philosophy, he made clear, was a good thing:

> If I know anything at all of philosophy, its principles date right back to the Greek schools where it was set out originally by Aristotle as an elaboration of Socrates and Plato, that the main principles of philosophy could be propounded by way of the syllogism. They pointed out that thereby two given ideas can be presented at the same time, and one could 'think together' consistently along certain lines. The Greek word used was συνοπτικως. Synthetically one can, as Browning [*sic*] put it, by a syllogism, 'see life steadily, and see it whole.'

In a statement whose content is not far from Anderson's own opinions, he said, 'Universities were never meant to be filling-up stations to fill the students' minds with a conglomeration of facts, but they were meant to be institutions where the inquiring mind might develop'. But an inquiring mind, he said, is not developed by turning a lecture desk into a soap box.

Then he got down to the business of what was wrong with Anderson's philosophy:

> Philosophy has many vagaries, many avenues of inquiry and many strange words, terms and symbols—abstract and concrete. May I quote just in passing the terms 'ideational' and 'sensate', used by Professor Sorokin, as probably the most modernised terms in the vocabulary of philosophy. I submit that Professor Anderson takes the sensate view, and dismisses the

---

[37] Anderson, letter to *Honi Soit* 2/7/1942, quoted in Baker, p. 118.

[38] Baker, *Anderson's Social Philosophy*, p. 120; Protestant objections in 'Canon T.C. Hammond exposes false attitude of Professor Anderson', *The Watchman* 3 (5) (June 1943): pp. 5, 9, 11, 19; and T.C. Hammond, *Abolishing God: A Reply to Professor Anderson of Sydney University* (pamphlet, Melbourne, 1944?); on Hammond, B. Dickey, *Australian Dictionary of Evangelical Biography* (Sydney, 1994), pp. 150–3; W. Nelson, *T.C. Hammond, Irish Christian* (Edinburgh, 1994).

[39] D.P. Macdonald, *Your Marriage* (Sydney, 1930), p. 3; G. Souter, *Mosman: A History* (Melbourne, 1994), p. 177.

ideational. The things that are seen are only part of the whole; the things that are believed, that cannot be expressed, are the deeper part of man's being and of man's hope. The ideational is something that may not be demonstrated—like this desk—the idea that lies beyond this desk is the growing tree; and the elements and mystery of nature and the mystery of creation. But the sensate view says: 'This is just a wooden desk.' A primrose is just a primrose to one man while to another it conjures up thoughts too profound for words or tears:

> A primrose by a river's brim,
>
> A yellow primrose was to him,
>
> And it was nothing more.[40]

Macdonald's references make it clear that his opposition to Anderson was not based on philosophical thin air. He was a representative of the philosophical school of Idealism. Now almost forgotten, Idealism was of immense influence a century ago. It included the first professional philosophers in Australia, and inspired great projects from the British Empire to the Australian Conciliation and Arbitration Court. It will be described in chapter 6.

Anderson was far from understanding any of this, thought Macdonald. He might be strong in logic, but knew little of ethics. And what about the youth? Macdonald continued:

We know the student mind; we know how impressionable and malleable 'freshers' are, and how inclined to hero-worship of their professors during the first year—though they get over it in a year or two—and surely Professor Anderson has a greater task to do than merely making himself popular and appearing very clever before a group of immature students. We are awaiting for their instruction a positive contribution from Professor Anderson. We are still awaiting a textbook on logic that will surpass in value the textbooks of John Stuart Mill, or Jevons or Mellone. Here is an opportunity for a positive work, instead of all this destructive, negative criticism that is emanating from an accredited professor of our university.[41]

Since Anderson's book on logic was no closer to publication in 1943 than it had been in 1927, this was a direct hit. The book never did appear.[42] What was missing from Macdonald's speech, though,

---

[40] *New South Wales Parliamentary Debates*, vol. 171 p. 2173 (the phrase attributed to Browning is from Matthew Arnold).

[41] *NSWPD*, vol. 171, p. 2071

[42] See B. Nield, 'The Andersonians: Anderson's masterpiece', *Century* 26/3/1959, p. 6; an extract in *Heraclitus* 72 (Mar 1999): 2; the full typescript in Anderson archives, Sydney University; on Anderson's published views, W.A. Merrylees, 'Some features of Professor Anderson's logic', *AJPP* 7 (1929): pp. 130–8, reply pp. 138–45.

was any evidence that Anderson had travestied Christianity, in the sense of misrepresenting it.

Lieut.-Col. Bruxner rose to read from Hansard of 1931, and regretted that he had not then commanded the powers of rhetoric of the honourable member for Mosman. He hoped that this time there would be no hitches in getting rid of Anderson. 'I do not know of a better way of spending public money than to pay him for all the remaining years for which he has been engaged to serve as teacher and to pay his fare to any place where he may care to go.'

Others joined in. J.J. Cahill, Minister for Public Works and a future Premier, complained that the *Sunday Telegraph* had responded to his criticism of Anderson by saying that 'it would be as ridiculous for Professor Anderson to give his opinion on bulldozers or gutters'. The member for Kurri Kurri asserted that in attacking religion, Professor Anderson was attacking the fundamental structure on which the British Empire was built. 'What man is there here', he asked, 'who has not the happiest memories of the days when he attended Sunday-school and received religious instruction?' None disagreed. The member for Yass congratulated Macdonald on his range of knowledge in philosophy and the mysteries of religion, 'matters of which we do not hear enough in this Chamber'. The member for Phillip, the electorate in which Sydney University lay, protested that the motion did not go far enough, since it did not instruct the Senate of the University as to what exactly to do. 'The time is due for an overhaul of University matters generally. I find from certain weekly religious papers that the University is being charged with drifting into atheism, communism and materialism'. Several other members spoke, all in favour of the motion condemning Anderson, and it was passed.[43]

A week later in the Legislative Council, a similar motion was introduced by Sir Henry Manning, the Council's representative on the University Senate. The preamble to the University and University Colleges Act stated that the purpose of founding the University of Sydney was 'for the better advancement of morality and religion and the promotion of useful knowledge', which implied, according to Manning, that Anderson had signed a contract to advance those aims. But not all was plain sailing, as it had been in the lower house. A Labor member said the motion reeked of bias and prejudice, and would be ruled out of order if it had come before the Ironworkers Union:

> Hon. members when battling for votes pose as champions of democracy. Their jaws, which in most cases are the strongest parts of them, reach dislocation point in their advocacy of freedom from fear, freedom of

speech, and freedom of thought. But once they get off the soap-box and public platform and reach the soft, seductive couches of Parliament, they forget all they said ... Millions of men throughout the world to-day are opposed to the Axis Powers and are fighting to give the human race that very freedom of thought and speech that members of Parliament evidently want to deny to Professor Anderson.

Support for Anderson did not come only from the left. A reasoned defence of free speech was mounted by Sir Norman Kater, a medical graduate of Sydney University and president of the New South Wales Sheepbreeders' Association. He had taken part in the opposition to Lang, and was regarded by the left as a key figure in the capitalist Establishment.[44] While admitting that Anderson's remarks had been unfortunate, he believed that Anderson must have really been merely advocating a less literal interpretation of the Bible, of which Sir Norman said,

> I look on the Bible as one of the greatest works in English literature. I can say this with some knowledge, for though I cannot say that I have read every word of the Old Testament, I have read the bulk of it, and I have read some of the books many times. I have read the whole of the Apocrypha, including that very interesting book entitled 'Bel and the Dragon'.

This extensive reading had convinced him that there was nothing wrong with a certain amount of non-literal interpretation, and that heresy hunts were bad for the advance of science. 'Science is always advancing, and it may be that certain opinions which now may be considered unorthodox may be proved later to be absolutely correct. Take the case of Galileo, who was born in the year 1364 [*sic*] ...'[45]

The resolution was passed in the Council, though not over-whelmingly. It was forwarded to the Senate of the University of Sydney, but the Senate sent back to the Parliament a reply pointing out that the University Act laid it down that 'no religious test shall be applied to the teachers or the students of the University', and added, 'remembering, as it does, the results that have followed the regimentation of universities in other parts of the world, it is also strongly of the opinion that nothing but harm would follow the stifling in the University of the spirit of free inquiry.'[46] It could have been written

[44] A. Moore, *The Secret Army and the Premier* (Sydney, 1989), pp. 64, 99, 210; Arthur Calwell in House of Representatives, 13/11/1941, in *Commonwealth of Australia, Parliamentary Debates* vol. 169 p. 415.

[45] *NSWPD*, vol. 171 pp. 2316–26; D.S. Macmillan, *The Kater Family, 1750–1965* (Sydney, 1966), pp. 96–9.

[46] Baker, *Anderson's Social Philosophy*, pp. 120–1; W.F. Connell *et al.*, *Australia's First: A History of the University of Sydney*, vol. 2 (Sydney, 1995), p.

by Anderson himself. By this time, the controversy had turned into a full-scale hue and cry on the theme of freedom of speech—even though, as a Catholic commentator sourly pointed out, what Anderson had actually called for was *restriction* of freedom of speech, by excluding clergy from schools.[47] In a meeting of the Freethought Society shortly afterwards, Anderson said, 'The theorist cannot recognise any limitation of freedom of speech and academic freedom, and has the right to be as blasphemous, obscene and seditious as he likes, whatever offence may be sustained by vested interests'.[48] That is about as far as you can go. Free speech had won total victory. Anderson, and any other academic, was in a position to say virtually whatever he liked. Neither Anderson nor anyone else, as it happened, chose to go any further than Anderson had already gone.

IN THE heat of the debate, Anderson was attacked from the opposite direction. The background to the dispute was the takeover of the Workers' Educational Association, or at least its section dealing with political matters, by Andersonians, especially Percy Partridge. Evening lectures were an important part of intellectual life at a time when a very small proportion of the population could afford to go to university. When postgraduate study was almost unknown, they also gave an opportunity for graduates to pursue intellectual interests while working. John Kerr, for example, a young lawyer in the city in the mid-thirties, enthusiastically attended Partridge's WEA lectures on political and social philosophy.[49] Partridge was the first true member of the Andersonian school, having studied with Anderson in his first years in Australia, and soon becoming lecturer in philosophy in Anderson's department. He was later Professor of Social Philosophy at ANU — appointed in preference to Karl Popper[50] — served on various commissions, and was Chancellor of Macquarie University.[51] In his WEA lectures, he repeated Anderson's denunciations of the Soviet Union and its

28; also D. Wetherell & C. Carr-Gregg, *Camilla: A Life* (Kensington, 1990), pp. 131–2.

[47] E. O'Brien, 'The Professor is intolerant', *Daily Telegraph* 9/4/1943, p. 6.

[48] *Honi Soit* 29/4/1943, quoted in Baker, *Anderson's Social Philosophy*, p. 121; a later round in *Honi Soit*'s 'blasphemy' issue, 12/7/1945, on which see A. Barcan, *Radical Students: The Old Left at Sydney University* (Melbourne, 2002), pp. 160–5; *SMH* 20/7/1945, p. 4.

[49] J. Kerr, *Matters for Judgement* (2nd ed, Melbourne, 1988), p. 45.

[50] W.G. Osmond, *Frederic Eggleston* (Sydney, 1985), pp. 273–4.

[51] Obituaries of Partridge in *Political Theory Newsletter* 1 (1989): pp. 54–7; Grave, *History*, pp. 84–5; an appreciation of Anderson by Partridge in 'Anderson as educator', in Anderson, *Education and Inquiry* pp. 3–10.

crimes. The author of the pamphlet *The WEA Exposed* [52] was Anderson's old enemy, Lance Sharkey. Sharkey was still firmly in control of the Communist Party and had had a decade to refine his Moscow-line prose style:

> Anderson, as Professor of Philosophy at the University, is receiving a big salary to teach the opposite of Dialectical Materialism, i.e., metaphysical, bourgeois philosophy ... After a period, Anderson 'renounced' the Trotskyites and formed what he called the 'University Free Thought Society', with himself as high priest and generalissimo. Anderson's 'free thought' is as jumbled a hotchpot of ideas as Hitlerism, which it further resembles in that its main motif is counter-revolution ...[53]

Anderson, he said, had transformed the WEA into a nest of 'free-thought' and Trotskyism, dedicated to blackening the name of the Soviet Union under the 'slogan of "free inquiry" and "discussion".' Sharkey gave free rein to his imagination, in considering what Anderson deserved for his fascist treachery:

> When a counter-revolutionary murderer is dealt with in Soviet Russia, the Andersons rush to the defence of the criminal and denounce Soviet justice, in chorus with the Trotskyites, and counter-revolutionaries the world over. The existence of the revolution requires the crushing of the enemy — 'the weapon of criticism gives way to the criticism of weapons', as Marx wrote ... Soviet justice is the finest system of justice in the world ... It does punish criminals, spies and provocateurs, just as the great French Revolution and every other historical movement had to suppress enemies of progress, just as every revolutionary movement has had to deal drastically with spies and provocateurs and every trade union with scabs ... Anderson's creed in the absolute links Anderson with Hitler, Goebbels, Archie Cameron and the blackest reactionaries the world over.[54]

When Sharkey was gaoled in 1949 for claiming that if Soviet troops were to invade Australia, Australian workers would welcome them, Partridge was one of the few public figures to protest.[55]

THE LATE 1940s saw the polarisation of Australian politics, with the Communist victories in Eastern Europe and China

---

[52] L. Sharkey, *The WEA Exposed* (Sydney, 1944); summary in R. Gollan, *Revolutionaries and Reformists* pp. 135–6; also L.L. Sharkey, 'The W.E.A. and the "inherent lie" ', *Communist Review* no. 22 (June, 1943): pp. 69–70.

[53] L.L. Sharkey, 'Prof. Anderson — a counter-revolutionary humbug', *Communist Review* no. 21 (May 1943): pp. 54–6, partly quoted in P. O'Brien, *The Saviours: An Intellectual History of the Left in Australia* (Melbourne, 1977), p. 52; cf. 'Anderson has no message: Rotten anti-Soviet views', *Tribune* no. 119 (21/4/1943): p. 3; also no. 122 (12/5/1943): p. 1.

[54] O'Brien, *The Saviours*, p. 53.

[55] *SMH* 3/11/1949, p. 3.

prompting the secret manoeuvres of B.A. Santamaria's Movement and Menzies' efforts to ban the Communist Party. Anderson, like many others, moved sharply to the right, and shocked former leftist colleagues and many students by supporting Chifley's use of troops to break the coal strike of 1949. He now saw Marxism as one of an array of dangerous Utopian illusions and regularly spoke against it. He never went so far as to approve of the suppression of free speech that Menzies's proposed ban on the Communist Party would have involved, but he at least said that any argument against the ban should start with recognising Communism as the greatest threat of the day.[56] Writers who enjoy discoursing on Sydney–Melbourne differences are inclined to attribute to Anderson the absence in Sydney of an intellectual left in the 1950s — Sydney Communists, it is said, organised but could not argue.[57] Sydney anti-Communism, on the other hand, disposed of considerable argumentative resources. The leading figures associated with *Quadrant*, Australia's main anti-Communist magazine, were Eastern European refugees and three of Anderson's students, James McAuley, Peter Coleman and John Kerr. All three had made the journey from left to right under Anderson's influence.[58]

By 1950, Anderson was regarded as a reactionary by all on the left, a sad case of decline in intellectual powers and in commitment to the cause. The view from Melbourne, where the rage was maintained, was recorded by Manning Clark:

> As a Melbourne man, I was suspicious of Anderson as the man who had betrayed the Left, a man who had gone over to the other side. Melburnians wanted Anderson to answer a simple question: was he or was he not interested in the fact that some were very rich and some very poor? Anderson replied that we were all bothered by different things. That finished him with the Melburnians. Out of his own mouth Anderson had shown himself to be wrong-headed and walnut-hearted. Exit John Anderson, the Fascist bastard, ha, ha, ha!

> I heard John Anderson speak in Canberra at the philosophy conference in 1951, and was enchanted. Melburnians had warned me to be on my guard lest he get me in. The man, they said, was a mesmeriser, a man who got you in by giving you in the first five minutes of his talk high-

[56] Baker, *Anderson's Social Philosophy*, pp. 130–3.

[57] Gollan, *Revolutionaries and Reformers*, pp. 200–1.

[58] P. Coleman, *The Heart of James McAuley* (Sydney, 1980), pp. 6, 62; P. Coleman, *Memoirs of a Slow Learner* (Sydney, 1994), p. 40; P. Coleman, 'John Anderson', *Bulletin* 30/6/1962, pp. 27–8; J. Kerr, *Matters for Judgement*, p. 43; R. Hall, *The Real John Kerr* (Sydney, 1978), pp. 33–4; see J. Docker, 'Sydney versus Melbourne revisited', in J. Davidson, ed, *The Sydney–Melbourne Book* (Sydney, 1986), pp. 159–67, at p. 163.

minded reasons for wanting to 'kill' your father. Be on your guard, Melburnians said, the bastard will convince you that if you do what you want to do you will not feel guilty. Yes, be careful, or he will persuade you that everything is allowable.

Well, I was carried away, though I did not know why. I disagreed with everything he said, but enjoyed the act he put on. Maybe it was the Scottish accent; maybe it was the capacity to toss off the right word or the lively image; maybe it was the man wearing Scottish tweed suits in sunny Australia, a man wearing a tie when most of his colleagues in philosophy and other intellectual sports were dressing much more casually. I was already convinced that the Bohemians of the heart wore suits, and that the new conformists stripped off all formal gear; maybe it was the thumbs under the waistcoat, and the twiddling fingers that explained the attraction; or maybe it was the light in the eye, a sign that there was a man within who was still alive.[59]

Clark may have picked up a few clues on how to dress like a prophet, but his admiration of the great man did not last long. At a conference party, Anderson gave one of his famous renditions of blasphemous songs,[60] and Clark was shocked to the depths of his manse-sodden soul. 'I thought of him later as a man of vast gifts who, for some reason I did not understand, devoted the last half of his life to swimming upstream against the great river of life.'

But there were limits to Anderson's fame as an anti-Communist. In 1952, the recently formed ASIO conducted a wide-ranging series of inquiries into subversion at all Australian universities.[61] One of the sixteen staff listed under 'Communist Activities at Sydney University' was John Anderson, whose file had been added to in 1950. The 1950 report on Anderson has three pages. One page notes his signature on a letter to the newspapers protesting at the Communist Party Dissolution Bill.[62] The second is a handwritten note that 'He proposes the Communist doctrine to friends while travelling from the city by train.' The final page has more information:

My informant is a senior member of the University staff, and knows him well. I reproduce what he told me below:

---

[59] M. Clark, *The Quest for Grace* (Melbourne, 1990), pp. 193–4.
[60] Versions more or less as sung by Anderson in D. Laycock, *The Best Bawdry* (Sydney, 1982), pp. 23–6; *Sydney Libertarians Broadsheet* 24 (Feb 1962), p. 5. There is also a tape.
[61] D. McKnight, *Australia's Spies and Their Secrets* (Sydney, 1994), pp. 146–50.
[62] 'University and Anti-Red Bill', letter, *SMH* 22/5/1950, p. 2; the 33 signatories include, besides Anderson, the Andersonians Partridge, Stout, Mackie, Rose and Foulkes.

Although some of Professor ANDERSON's activities — e.g. the Free Thought Society — may seem rather ridiculous to outsiders, it would be a great mistake not to take him seriously. He is a very lucid, plausible and convincing speaker who makes a great appeal to students of the intellectual type, and his influence on them, which is great, is entirely a bad one. My friend had no evidence of subversive activity, or association, against Professor ANDERSON, but said such evidence would be practically impossible to get as ANDERSON was too clever to give himself away.[63]

ASIO apparently remained entirely unaware of Anderson's anti-Communism, although the letter to the papers referred to begins 'we are wholly opposed to the aims and methods of the Communist Party', and the front page of the *Herald* said that the left regarded him as 'the greatest intellectual force against Communism in the country.'[64]

While anti-Communism was a common enough position by 1950, Anderson had not run out of less popular targets. After 1945, the gravy train started rolling for intellectuals in Australia. Though there were no sudden attempts to restructure society from top to bottom on the advice of intellectuals, as happened overseas under Roosevelt and Attlee, there was a gradual acceptance that the role of government should expand, in areas like the welfare state, housing and education, free milk for schoolchildren and the like.[65] It was further accepted that planning, advising and policy-making in these areas could benefit from people with university training. While there was no Australian Keynes, there were men of wide intellectual training like 'Nugget' Coombs, who came to have a large role in planning the new society. Even the new Liberal Party was convinced by its in-house intellectuals that a reasonable dose of welfarism was a good thing.[66] In the late 1950s, Menzies himself came to accept that university education was something Australia needed a lot more of, and money was found for a large increase in the size and number of Australian universities.

To all these developments, Anderson had the same attitude. It was 'No'. His article of 1943, 'The servile state', already appreciated that wartime planning was an indication of the widespread planning and regimentation to come.

---

[63] ASIO file, p. 8 (17/7/1950).

[64] *SMH* 22/5/1950, p. 1 column 8.

[65] S. Cornish, 'Keynesian revolution in Australia: Fact or fiction', *Australian Economic History Review* 33 (1993): pp. 42–68; T. Rowse, *Nugget Coombs: A Reforming Life* (Melbourne, 2002).

[66] J.R. Hay, 'The Institute of Public Affairs and social policy in World War II', *Historical Studies* 20 (1982): pp. 198–216.

Even if the *word* freedom is used, 'freedom from want' and 'freedom from fear' are simply the *sufficiency* and *security*, the desire for which marks the servile mentality ... And those persons who expect 'sufficiency' to be provided for them, will find themselves worse off in relying on what the State deems sufficient than in making their own organised efforts for the provision of materials they require ... But the second and more vital point is that the pursuit of security and sufficiency is itself a low aim, that the maintenance of a high level of culture depends on the existence of a plurality of movements which take their chance in the social struggle, instead of having their place and their resources assigned to them from a supposedly all-embracing point of view.[67]

He went on to oppose the 'planned society', 'service to the community', 'such demagogic slogans as "equal opportunity for all"', education for 'the needs of industry' and '"social unity", (i.e., established interests)'. All these philanthropic ideas, he said, were merely sectional interests masquerading as the good of society, something which does not exist.

Like many academics approaching retirement, he took to protesting about the decline in 'standards'.[68] In a single talk of 1958, he attacked expansion of universities (as there were already more students than could cope with real university work), lower failure rates (for the same reason), tutorials (which dealt with the students' problems, when students ought to be dealing with the problems of the subject), specialist training generally and 'universities' of technology in particular, and religious university colleges.[69] In his last published article, 'Classicism', of 1960, he looked back almost with nostalgia to the standards of the Golden Age, when education was pure inquiry (whenever that was: Glasgow in 1912?).

---

[67] J. Anderson, 'The servile state', *AJPP* 21 (1943): pp. 115–32, repr. in *Studies in Empirical Philosophy* (Sydney, 1962), pp. 328–39, at pp. 334–5; an early version in J. Anderson, 'Social service', *Freethought* no. 3 (May, 1936): pp. 2–7; similar in P.H. Partridge, 'Some thoughts on planning', *AJPP* 19 (1941): pp. 236–52; discussion in J. Docker, *Australian Cultural Elites* (Sydney, 1974), ch. 8; Coleman, *Memoirs*, p. 33; D. Horne, *Confessions of a New Boy* (Ringwood, 1986), pp. 158–9; P. Stavropoulos, 'Conservative radical: The conservatism of John Anderson', *Australian Journal of Anthropology* 3 (1–2) (1992): pp. 67–79; P. Beilharz, 'John Anderson and the syndicalist movement', *Political Theory Newsletter* 5 (1993): pp. 5–13.

[68] *SMH* 29/3/1955, p. 16; also *Honi Soit* 14/10/1954, p. 5.

[69] D.J. Ivison, 'Report of Anderson on education', *Sydney Libertarians Broadsheet* 3 (May 1958), repr. in *The Sydney Line*, ed. A.J. Baker & G. Molnar (Sydney, 1963), pp. 105–6.

John Anderson at his home in Turramurra, 1960 (Anderson papers, University of Sydney Archives)

Concentration on what serves one's purposes, satisfaction with the 'just as good' or the 'good enough to get there', exists even more strikingly and influentially in public life at present than it did in Arnold's time, and it has penetrated more and more deeply into education, promoting shoddy thinking and slipshod language in the name of social equality and amelioration and other 'inadequate ideas' which have less and less critical intelligence applied to them ... the function of education at the present time is substantially that of turning the populace into Philistines.[70]

The classical theme of the decline of the present age was strong:

The classicist recognises the natural opposition between disinterestedness and interestedness, between concern with the working of things themselves and concern with what we can get out of them. He will certainly note the special weakness of the objective outlook at the present time; he may even decide that our modern intellectual age, dating from the Renaissance, is on the verge of collapse and that a new barbarism is imminent; he can hardly fail to note the resemblance between current conditions and the decline of classical Greece, with the replacement of the solid thinking of the preceding time by a woolly-minded cosmopolitanism and humanitarianism.[71]

The article included a final tough-minded 'No' to the style of protest that emerged in the late 1950s. The Sixties would, like Anderson, be against just about everything, but the 'protest' of the Sixties was far from the 'criticism' that Anderson advocated:

A topical example of such salvationist thinking is to be found in agitations for peace, in which, leaving aside any attempt to determine the objective conditions either of the occurrence of international conflicts themselves or of the discovery of truth concerning them, it is assumed that anything that is 'undesirable' can, by a sufficiency of protests or 'appeals to reason', be eliminated.[72]

It was all a long way from the imminence of the Revolution and the criticism of everything.

Anderson died in 1962, aged 68, after collapsing at his home from a stroke brought on by a furious bout of woodcutting.

[70] J. Anderson, 'Classicism', in *Studies in Empirical Philosophy*, pp. 189–202, at p. 191; comment in Kennedy, *A Passion to Oppose*, introduction, and W. Morison, 'Classicism broad and narrow', *Heraclitus* 28 (Sept 1992); similar complaints in R. Menzies, *Speech is of Time* (London, 1958), pp. 223–4; comparable views from the Melbourne Professor of Philosophy, A. Boyce Gibson, in J. Poynter & C. Rasmussen, *A Place Apart* (Melbourne, 1996), pp. 2–4 & 176.

[71] Anderson, 'Classicism', at p. 199.

[72] Anderson, 'Classicism', at p. 190.

Chapter 2   Anderson and the Youth

As regards students, Anderson contended that the morality of criticism would reject the current talk of their "corruption". If this "corruption" means a departure from established views on the part of students, then the job of the university is to corrupt the youth.[1]

T HE main reason for being interested in Anderson, after all these years, is the huge impact he had on several generations of students. The power and immediacy of that impact are caught in the most famous account of it, by Donald Horne:

On the day I first arrived at the university I saw Anderson walking along the cloisters in the Quad: someone pointed him out as the Scottish radical who was the university's main rebel, a renowned atheist, not long ago a communist, censured in the New South Wales Parliament and by the university Senate. Anderson seemed the most important person at the University. When he walked by, my skin might stiffen and my hair prickle at the roots. He was in his forties, very tall, stooped, gangling, striding loosely past in a brown suit and a green hat with an upturned brim, usually sombre, with his pipe jutting out from between his teeth. He seemed an embodiment of what was grave and constant in human suffering, but sometimes he would wave an arm at a student, loosely, as if it were a puppet's, and smile, strong teeth bursting out beneath his full black moustache. His huge, sad brown eyes seemed to sag right down into his face, pulling the cheeks down with them, lost in wisdom. Sometimes he seemed very tired, both tough and fragile, bearing a great load, but still walking briskly. Then he would laugh, or raise his arm. I was gripped by the need to know him.

---

[1] A.R. Walker, discussing a speech by Anderson on the Orr case, 25/8/1958, in A.R. Walker, 'Public controversies and academic freedom', *Dialectic* (Newcastle University) 30 (1987): pp. 11–23, at p. 19.

Light came into the philosophy lecture theatre, where the Literary Society held its meetings, through leaded glass windows, and on either side of the blackboard there were murals, one of classical and one of modern philosophers. There was the sense of an inner temple about this room when early in term Pritchett and I sat in it to hear Anderson give his annual address to the Literary Society, of which he was president. When he began speaking in an urgent Glaswegian sing-song the room seemed stilled by significance. Most of the time he spoke strongly, but occasionally his voice hovered and fluttered while he stuttered for words, by this hesitation building up a pressure that then burst through into a confident and sustained high note. The style of his address was intensely serious, but lightened now and again with a wisecrack, or with sarcasm ... when the discussion was over, he made a triumphant ending, flowing strongly again, correcting errors and confusions and bestowing agreement like a final blessing. It took only an hour, but we felt that we had just witnessed an important new contribution to the theory of aesthetics.[2]

Horne's experience, though not universal, was a common one. Peter Coleman, a rather different kind of mind, but one also to be long a follower of Anderson, describes the same scene a few years later, at the end of the War. He was unimpressed with the ambience and decor, but not with the speaker:

On the walls were crude paintings of great philosophers — Plato, Bacon, Descartes and so on. I do not know how many students were turned away from philosophy by this mural *kitsch*, but at the time I ignored it. A number of *dévots* walked in, dropping their voices, pocketing pipes. Finally the Master — tall, stooped, pop-eyed, waistcoated — took up his position at the dais and began speaking in a high-pitched, Glaswegian stammer.

He took us on a *tour d'horizons*, which shocked as much as it fascinated me ... I was still not prepared for the full blast of Anderson's impiety. The world was going downhill fast. It was an age of socialism, religion, communism, rationalism. Abroad President Roosevelt had delivered Central Europe to communist gangsters. In Australia Labor and Liberal parties were both committed to destroying freedom and independence. The Churches and the Rationalists, the universities and newspapers, were all servile to the spirit of the times.[3]

[2] D.R. Horne, *The Education of Young Donald* (2nd ed, Ringwood, 1988) pp. 173–4; on Horne as young Andersonian see B. Nield, 'The Andersonians: Careers in the making', *Century* 3/4/1959, p. 6; Horne's first Anderson article: 'John Anderson: University's stubborn No-man', *Daily Telegraph* 14/9/1946, p. 15, on which see D. Horne, *Confessions of a New Boy* (Ringwood, 1986), pp. 267–8; later in *Observer* 29/11/1958, pp. 652–3, on which see B. Nield in *Century* 17/4/1959, p. 6; transcripts of a number of Anderson lectures are at setis.library.usyd.edu.au/anderson .
[3] P. Coleman, *Memoirs of a Slow Learner* (Sydney, 1994), p. 40; further in *Australian* 28/10/1995, p. R9; similar in J. Passmore, *Memoirs of a Semi-*

Anderson is outstanding in Australian academic life for the extraordinary impact he had on students, and the length of time for which his influence lasted. What he proposed to do with the youth, once he had them in his hand, is explained in his early article, 'Socrates as an educator'.

> Socrates did not deny, but rather gloried in the fact, that he had striven by example and precept to inculcate the spirit of criticism, to encourage the questioning of received opinions and traditions; and nothing that the Athenians could do, he declared, would prevent his pursuing this task while he lived. 'The unexamined life is not worth living'; to lead such a life is to be in the lowest state of ignorance, ignorant even of one's own ignorance. And therefore he would not cease to call upon the Athenians to give an account of their lives, as the facts of life would compel them to do even if they got rid of him.
>
> The Socratic education begins, then, with the awakening of the mind to the need for criticism, to the uncertainty of the principles by which it supposed itself to be guided ... There is no virtue in being an Athenian, no peculiar and superior Athenian brand of goodness, but goodness is the same wherever it occurs, and what passes as good at Athens may not be really good at all. It requires the most careful scrutiny, and until this process of examination has begun, education has not begun. To see the full force of this criticism, we may substitute Australia for Athens, and imagine Socrates saying, 'You think there is some virtue in being Australian, and that a good Australian is better than a good Greek or Italian, but what you call goodness is just your own ignorance.' Clearly such talk would be infuriating, clearly also it would be very hard to answer.[4]

If we are to substitute Australians for Athenians, there are no prizes for guessing who is down to play the role of Socrates. First-year students, who began Philosophy I with Anderson's lectures on the trial of Socrates, needed no more than the first lecture to pick up the point. 'Before it was half over I already had the bull by the foot; I was young and foolish, and I was not sure which was Socrates and which was John Anderson. One was short, strikingly ugly, and wore a sort of toga; the other was tall, strikingly handsome, and wore a blue suit.

Detached Australian (Melbourne, 1997), p. 93; P. Anderson, *Elwyn Lynn's Art World* (Sydney, 2001), pp. 7–12.

[4] J. Anderson, 'Socrates as an educator', *Journal of the Institute of Inspectors of Schools*, NSW, 12 (3) (Nov 1930) and 13 (1) (June 1931), and *AJPP* 19 (1931): pp. 172–84, repr. in J. Anderson, *Education and Politics* (Sydney, 1931), pp. 29–52, and in *Studies in Empirical Philosophy*, pp. 203–213; quotation from pp. 206–7; see A. Barcan, 'The evolution of Andersonian views on school pedagogy', *Melbourne Studies in Education* 39 (1998): pp. 69–89; A. Barcan, 'The Andersonians and progressive education', *MSE* 41 (2000): pp. 91–114.

But these differences were superficial. They were great men, and men of the same kind.'[5]

Socrates, as everyone knows, is famous for his difficulties with the State, which eventually led to his execution on a charge of corrupting the youth. Every academic since that time who has received criticism from outside the university, especially if it concerns his effect on his students, has taken the earliest opportunity to compare himself to Socrates. Since this motif will recur several times in the present story, it is as well to state at the outset that the charge that Socrates corrupted the youth is absolutely true. The Sophists, Socrates says indignantly, offer the youth knowledge in exchange for money. It would be a lot better, he thinks, if the wise handed on knowledge in exchange for sexual favours.[6] Especially memorable in Plato's account of the matter is the phrase, 'philosophical talk which clings more fiercely than a snake when it gets a hold on the soul of a not ill-endowed young man',[7] suggestive as it is of the real seductiveness of the *quid pro quo* on offer, to appropriately inclined minds.

Those to whose souls Andersonian philosophical talk clung acquired two gifts. The first was the Andersonian world picture, and the second was a method of argument, especially negative argument. The method of critical argument comes from Socrates, but Anderson's vision is very different from the one that Socrates had. Socrates, in Anderson's view, was too sentimental:

> That there is in his doctrines a streak of romanticism or mysticism (even though this can often be treated as merely a trimming around a realist or empiricist core) is clear enough from his belief in 'ultimates', entities standing above the actual movement of things. This is in striking contrast with the thorough-going objectivism of his predecessor, Heraclitus, who was unremitting in his attack on subjectivist illusions, on the operation of desire or the imagining of things as we should like them to be, as opposed to the operation of understanding or the finding of things (including our own activities) as they positively are, with no granting of a privileged

---

[5] P. Shrubb, in *Bulletin* 30/6/1962, p. 29; another account in W.L. Morison, 'Anderson and legal theory', *Dialectic* (Newcastle University) 30 (1987): pp. 40–9.

[6] Plato, *Symposium* 209a–212c, 216d–219e, 184b–185c; for Anderson's mention of this see W. Morison, 'Causation and moral responsibility', *Heraclitus* 38 (1994): pp. 1–5; for its relation to later Australian academic approval of pedophilia see T. Leahy, 'Positively experienced man/boy sex: The discourse of seduction and the social construction of masculinity', *Australian & New Zealand Journal of Sociology*, 28 (1992): pp. 71–88, at p. 82; what Socrates really said in J. Finnis, 'Law, morality and "sexual orientation"', *Notre Dame Law Review* 69 (1994): pp. 1049–76, at pp. 1056–61.

[7] *Symposium* 218a.

position in reality to gods, men or molecules, with conflict everywhere and nothing above the battle.[8]

And Anderson's style of teaching was eminently suited to recommending so austere a vision. In him, form and content were one. This complex of views is behind the impression of him noted by a visiting philosopher at the Australasian Philosophy Conference in 1951:

> As to his 'atheism', there is no doubt about this. But when I first saw the man — he was chairing the first meeting of the congress — another observer whispered as he was talking that he was exactly like a Presbyterian clergyman. And so, indeed, he is (there is much more in it than a Scottish accent); though of a type which is now dying out. The leader of some fairly small dissenting Scottish sect, scorning mere 'conventional religion', reverencing nothing but his God, dominating his flock and yet honestly appealing for (and sometimes evoking) independence of mind and action. And there are still more definite echoes of Calvinism in his creed. Strict determinism, for one thing. Asked at the congress whether we would have an obligation to assist a wounded man lying before us, he replied that we would have none, except in the sense that we might feel good impulses striving within us with bad; if the good prevailed, we would help the man, and if not, not. He also has a deep and obvious distaste for anything that smacks of the hierarchical, even in quite abstract realms. All facts, for example, are of the same order — there are not 'deeper' truths and more superficial ones; what is the case is the case and there's an end on't. Professor Ryle, of Oxford, in a recent critical article in the association's journal, sums up the Andersonian position in the sentence, 'There are only brass tacks'.[9]

---

[8] J. Anderson, 'Classicism', in *Studies in Empirical Philosophy*, pp. 189–202, at pp. 193–4; for Anderson and Heraclitus, see I.F. Helu, 'Anderson, Heraclitus and social science', *Australian Journal of Anthropology* 3 (1–2) (1992): pp. 22–31 (on Helu and Andersonianism in Tonga, see *Australian* 4/2/1998, p. 39); on the influence of these ideas in Australian anthropology, K. Maddock, 'The temptation of Paris resisted: An intellectual portrait of a Sydney anthropologist', in *Scholar and Sceptic: Australian Aboriginal Studies in Honour of L.R. Hiatt*, ed. F. Merlan, J. Morton & A. Rumsey (Canberra, 1997), ch. 4.

[9] A.N. Prior, 'This quarter', *Landfall* 6 (1952): pp. 49–53, at p. 51; for Anderson's later criticisms of religion, A. Olding, 'John Anderson and religion', *Philosophical Investigations* 6 (1983): pp. 200–13; J.A.B. Holland, 'A system of classical atheism', *Scottish Journal of Theology* (Aug, 1973): pp. 271–4; 'John Anderson on religion', *Honi Soit* 2/7/1942, repr. in *Sydney Libertarians Broadsheet* no. 87 (Mar 1976): p. 7; *Honi Soit* 23 (15) (12/7/1951) and succeeding issues; on which see Weblin, *A Passion for Thinking* (to appear), ch. 16; Sydney evangelical Anglicanism accused of agreement with Anderson in E.F. Osborn, 'Realism and revelation', *Reformed Biblical Review* 9 (1960): pp. 29–37, which answers D.B. Knox, *Propositional Revelation, The*

*Students in Sydney University Quad outside Philosophy Room, 1940s
(photo by Frank Hurley, National Library of Australia)*

For how this struck students, especially the ones soaking it up as
fast as they could, Donald Horne is again the ideal witness:

> The first freethinkers I met in the Quad were mere outriders of Ander-
> sonianism, but they were such zealots that after I had spent my first after-
> noon with them I felt skinned. For weeks afterwards I nevertheless sub-
> jected myself to their logic and bullying ... '*Ah!*' I was learning to say in
> the Andersonian fashion, 'but what do you *mean* by that?' Pouncing on a
> careless phrase and tearing at it for meaning — 'relative terms' were par-
> ticularly good for this purpose — could jolt almost any conversation to a
> stop. If definitions were offered it was easy to shoot them down from the
> hip. Or one could detect a 'confusion' in an opponent's argument, as if
> pointing to contradictions settled the matter, or restate the argument as a
> 'position' in terms that made it simple to get rid of. I hoped to become a
> laconic analyst, clarifying discussion, sorting out confusions, clear-headed,
> objective ... scientific. But I also enjoyed attack, and the Andersonian
> weapons seemed irresistibly strong.[10]

Only Revelation (pamphlet, Newtown, 1960); an Andersonian/Platonist view
of religion in G. Stuart Watts, *The Revolution of Ideas: Philosophy, Religion and
some 'Ultimate Questions'* (Sydney, 1982).

[10] Horne, *Education of Young Donald*, 2nd ed, p. 179.

There is a truth about philosophy generally here, not just about Andersonianism. The cast of mind attracted to the subject is especially one that loves the cut and thrust of argument, the tendency to see questions in terms of 'positions', 'confusions', definitions, refutations. Anyone who fails to understand why logic is central to philosophy has not understood what philosophy is about; Horne's 'as if pointing to contradictions settled the matter' shows he is not going to become a philosopher.

As Horne hints, there was something emotionally difficult, perhaps arid and cruel, in the relentless 'criticism' of the Andersonian school. The atmosphere is caught in an unlikely place, a story of conversion to Catholicism. It is by Helen Fowler, an Andersonian student of the early thirties. Like many female students she experienced an emotional antipathy to bullying with logic, but being married to one of the most enthusiastic Andersonians,[11] she saw it all at close range:

> Living, as I did, on the fringe of the circle of Realist philosophers of which the Central Influence of my life was the leader, I knew full well that anyone who had not had the advantage of learning the philosophy we knew could not be supposed to be on our intellectual level.

> One knew they couldn't argue intelligently and that any ideas they had about anything at all must be wrong; if they showed a particular brilliance in any of the arts or sciences we dismissed them as mere technicians, and at the views of other philosophers we simply laughed pityingly. Catholics, however, were away below, at the very bottom of the scale, because in addition to their stupidity they were, as well, vicious and dangerous, for they had at times publicly attacked both the Realist philosophy and its exponents.

> All these things I accepted as true, and I tried hard, for the sake of the C.I., to be an earnest Realist; this was, however, a little difficult for me, for I had somehow never really accepted the position, and, what is more, I had just never liked many of the Realists I knew — neither their company, their behaviour, their conversation, their manners nor their moral outlook. Though I laughed when they did, it was often hollow laughter, and though I frowned with them, it was with a conscious contraction of the brows. And this, though I tried hard to conceal it, was, I am sure, apparent to the Realists and but for the C.I., who many times censured

---

[11] See A. Barcan, *Radical Students: The Old Left at Sydney University* (Melbourne, 2002), pp. 46–7; F.W. Fowler, 'A criticism of conventional morals', reported in *Union Recorder*, 15/10/1931, repr. in *Heraclitus* 44 (Oct 1995): p. 5; F.W. Fowler, 'Anderson in the 1930s', *Heraclitus* 33 (Oct 1993): pp. 1–4; M. Mackie, 'Frank Fowler, Harry Eddy and the Teachers' College', *Heraclitus* 92 (Nov 2001): p. 6; obituaries of Fowler in *Heraclitus* 57 (Apr 1997): pp. 1–4, *Australian*, 20/3/1997, p. 12; Fowler's notes of Anderson's lectures in Mitchell Library, MLMSS 6457.

me severely on the matter, I think they would never have tolerated me. And, of course, it was of supreme importance for me to remain in the Realist world, for I knew no other.[12]

One surprising feature, to those who know academic life, is that Anderson cared what she thought. Coleman rightly comments on how unusual it was that Anderson might speak to one in the Quad to express his disappointment about one's logic exercise.[13] It is not a negligible cause of Anderson's influence.

Things were perhaps happier for those at a little distance from the central turmoil, who had the opportunity to take a small dose of Anderson while experiencing a range of other ideas. It prevented the brain being flooded. One such was John Ward, later Vice-Chancellor of Sydney University and leader of the Vice-Chancellors in their campaign against the Dawkins reforms of the 1980s aimed at making universities more 'efficient' and 'relevant'. 'It was Anderson', Ward said, 'who taught me that academic policy should be criticised and examined systematically' — but only by those who know what they are talking about, namely, academics.[14] Another who had the luxury of picking and choosing which Andersonian ideas to take on was John Kerr, who recalled:

> It was not until I reached university and came to know a number of people who had studied Arts and read Philosophy that I discovered much about the world of ideas and art in its various forms ... Later, whilst at the Bar, I was overcome by a strong desire to experience Anderson as a teacher. He was so obviously a teacher of impressive psychic impact that I felt I should have at least some experience of this. I enrolled as a student, not proceeding to a degree, in Philosophy I in Arts. The subject was logic. I had heard so much about Anderson's teaching methods that I approached the experience with eagerness and I was not disappointed. I did not sit for the examination at the end of the year and did not attempt to master the subject as taught by him. My desire was simply to listen.[15]

At an even greater distance were students who were not impressed with Anderson at all. They included, naturally, those who had no interests beyond getting a professional qualification. But there were others.

---

[12] H.M. Fowler, 'Things make sense now', in *Roads to Rome*, ed. P.A. O'Brien (London, 1955), pp. 166–180, at p. 168; cf. P. Shrubb, *Family Matters* (Sydney, 1988), pp. 132, 194–5, 213–4; G. Kelly, *There Is No Refuge* (London, 1961), pp. 137–9.

[13] Coleman, *Memoirs*, pp. 40–1.

[14] J.M. Ward, 'Some recollections of a student's view of the 1930's', *Teaching History* 9 (1) (Mar 1975): pp. 22–9, at p. 26.

[15] J. Kerr, *Matters for Judgement* (2nd ed, South Melbourne, 1988), p. 43.

What did it take for an intelligent student *not* to fall under the spell of Anderson? An interesting case is Gough Whitlam, a student involved in many campus activities in the late 1930s. He attended a few lunchtime lectures by Anderson, but did not need Anderson to persuade him that most Christian and vice-regal rituals were archaic. His family background meant he was not shocked by Anderson's ideas, in the way that many students from more intellectually sheltered backgrounds were.

He does not remember Anderson saying much about Ethiopia, India or Manchukuo or the Aborigines or Papuans. He believes that Anderson would have understood the University's motto to mean 'I may have come to a different hemisphere but I have not changed my ideas'. He found that Anderson was more interested in State politics than Federal politics.[16]

Whitlam is correct about Anderson's attitude to the notion of changing his ideas merely because of coming to Australia. In an address of 1937 on 'Australian literature', Anderson said, 'There is no more an Australian literature than an Australian philosophy or mathematics. There is a world literature to which Australians contribute.'[17] In a short piece for a newspaper of about the same time, headed, 'Is there an Australian philosophy?' he went further:

> It can scarcely be doubted that utilitarianism, the passion for 'results' whether it be racing results, athletic or scholastic successes, or the ordinary worldly benefits, is more deeply rooted in the Australian mentality than is the case in communities which have had time to develop a speculative tradition as part of a broad culture ... At present the Australian has much of the mental lethargy of the mere athlete and the schoolboy's domination by catchphrases. If and when a vigorous philosophy flourishes in the land, it will be the clearest possible sign of national maturity.[18]

Helen Fowler's piece, especially, draws attention to the question of the *moral* impact of Anderson's teaching. His views on ethics were much attacked by clergy and 'moralists' everywhere, but what exactly were they? There are two aspects to Anderson's ethics, both of them unusual, and both arguably having a tendency to deprave and corrupt the youth. The first is that what he takes to be good differs from what other people take to be so. The second is that even when one has decided what is good, that has no impact on what one ought to do.

The second of these is perhaps the more amazing, and it is the one he insists on most strenuously:

[16] Author's text as amended by E.G. Whitlam, 1/5/1995.

[17] *Honi Soit* 13/10/1937, repr. as 'Australian culture', in *Art & Reality: John Anderson on Literature and Aesthetics*, ed. J. Anderson, G. Cullum & K. Lycos (Sydney, 1982), p. 254.

[18] J. Anderson, 'Is there an Australian philosophy?', *Sun* (Sunday ed, called *Sunday Sun and Guardian*) 24/3/1935, p. 21; repr. in *Heraclitus* 23 (1991).

The most obstinate confusion obstructing the growth of ethical knowledge lies in the assumption that ethics teaches us how to live or what to
live for, that it instructs us in our duty or in the approach to the moral
end.[19]

It is in fact a standing obstacle to the acceptance of ethics as a positive science that people simply will not be persuaded that, when we say 'X is
good', we are not urging them to promote X or to exhibit activities of
the character X — that there is no more advocacy in our statement than
in the statement 'X is red.'[20]

The very conceptions of a 'moral end' or of 'intrinsic value' are, he
says, 'relativist confusions': there cannot possibly be anything whose
very nature means that it is someone's duty to bring it about. Hence
there is no such thing as 'obligation':

Historically considered, obligation can only mean constraint or compulsion, and this, it will be admitted, at least *frequently* prevents instead of
promoting goods. It is better, therefore, to drop the term 'right' from
ethical theory, and it is necessary emphatically to reject the view that
goodness has anything to do with obeying commandments.[21]

And there is nothing in what he says elsewhere to qualify the
opinion that whatever may be good, its being good does not require
any action of anybody. But what then is this 'good'? 'We may thus
approach a *definition* of good. Goods, we may say, are those mental
activities, or those social activities, which are "free" or enterprising,
which exhibit the spirit of enterprise.'[22] ('Free' is in quotation marks
here because Anderson is of course a determinist, believing that all
events, including human actions, are causally determined, and that
free actions, in any sense that is incompatible with determinism, are
therefore impossible.[23]) So what activities, exactly, are 'free' and
enterprising? No surprises here: 'Inquiry is the good which I find

---

[19] J. Anderson, 'Realism versus relativism in ethics', *AJPP* 11 (1933): pp. 1–
11, repr. in *Studies in Empirical Philosophy*, pp. 238–47, at p. 239.
[20] J. Anderson, 'The meaning of good', *AJPP* 20 (1943): pp. 111–140, repr.
in *Studies in Empirical Philosophy*, pp. 248–67, at. p. 263.
[21] 'Realism versus relativism', at p. 242; similar discussion in E. Kamenka,
The Ethical Foundations of Marxism (2nd ed, London, 1972), ch. 9.
[22] 'The meaning of good', at p. 267; see B. Birchall, 'Anderson's positive
ethics', *Dialectic* (Newcastle University) 3 (1969): pp. 46–61; R. Volpato,
'John Anderson and environmental philosophy', in *Australian Philosophers*, ed.
P. Dowe, M. Nicholls & L. Shotton (Hobart, 1996), pp. 5–24.
[23] J. Anderson, 'Causality and logic', *AJPP* 14 (1936): pp. 309–13, in *Studies
in Empirical Philosophy*, pp. 122–5.

myself most frequently taking as an example, and there may be special reasons for that choice.'[24]

That is not to say that he, Anderson, *recommends* or *advocates* that students, or anyone else, should inquire. Students will catch the habit of inquiry, or not, depending on their predispositions, and that is all there is to say about it. Other good activities named are artistic appreciation and creation.

It may be argued that the activities Anderson names are indeed good, and even that they are goods under-recognised in the general scheme of ethical training. What is lacking in his view of good is any sense of the restraint of conscience. 'Thou shalt not' is not in it anywhere, as that would be a sign of a 'servile' mentality. Anderson was completely open about his view that conscience is simply part of the 'fraud of moralism':

> Moralism, the doctrine of conscience and 'moral necessity', exemplifies the natural causality of repressed motives. There *are* acts which are performed under a sense of obligation, but what they exhibit is not communication but compulsion. Freud has informed us of the elaborate performances which compulsion-neurotics feel bound to go through. They are simply 'the thing to do'; they are 'right' but not good, forced, not spontaneous. The spontaneous action of a motive seeking its objective cannot be induced by compulsion. Compulsion can only induce conformity. And the motives which will incline a man to conform, to do a thing because he is obliged, are, speaking generally, fear and that desire for self-abasement which, in sexual theory, is called 'masochism'.[25]

It is natural to ask whether lecturing to the youth about their lack of moral obligations will cause them to believe, or behave as if, they have no moral obligations. The link between Andersonian theory and his students' behaviour was a direct one, according to David Stove, an Andersonian student who was to become one of Australia's best-known philosophers:

> What did strike home to students was the negative side, the critique of 'moralism' as he calls it. There he claims to show that there is intellectual confusion, even inconsistency, in the very idea of moral obligation, i.e. in the ordinary serious moral use of words like 'ought'. Whether or not this thesis is any less incredible than the 'positive' one, its effect on students was simply immense. And, as may easily be imagined, one effect of the

---

[24] J. Anderson, 'Ethics and advocacy', *AJPP* 22 (1944): pp. 174–87, in *Studies in Empirical Philosophy*, pp. 279–87, at p. 283; see P. Hager, 'John Anderson and critical thinking', *Educational Philosophy and Theory* 26 (1) (1994): pp. 54–70.

[25] J. Anderson, 'Determinism and ethics', *AJPP* 6 (1928): pp. 241–55, in *Studies in Empirical Philosophy*, pp. 214–26, at p. 225.

acceptance of such a theory on a student was a sort of paralysis of the active or practical side of his nature.[26]

Stove confessed that his circle of Andersonian students shoplifted under Anderson's influence.[27]

But it was not just the 'negative' side of Anderson's ethics that was a danger. The general tenor of Anderson's 'positive' morality approached the Nietzschean 'artist is above morality' stance that Sydney had already seen something of in Norman Lindsay. Manning Clark actually wrote of Lindsay and Anderson as forming a Nietzsche 'group', dedicated to attacking Clark's own *bêtes noires*, philistinism and puritanism.[28] That is ridiculous, in that there was no connection between Lindsay and Anderson, or their circles. But there is some similarity in their points of view, as well as in the attempts of both to found a one-man classic tradition by cutting themselves off from all developments in their field in the outside world. One of Anderson's earliest articles attacked the same censorship that made Lindsay a byword.

> The important point is that education, properly so-called, is not preceptive or moralistic but aesthetic; only so can it be co-operative and creative ... Seize hold of things, hammer out the issues, abjure dilettantism in any shape. This is the true attitude of the artist, whose mind is superior to the squirming refinements and sensitive shrinkings of the 'aesthete', the *arbiter elegantiarum*, and who permits no ideals or taboos to come between him and a direct handling of the things themselves ... 'This ought not to be, therefore avoid it', says the moralist. 'This is, therefore grasp it,' says the artist.[29]

And again, 'freedom in love is the condition of other freedoms ... there can be no culture without it.'[30]

If parents of Anderson's students had read his works, as few did, they might well have felt moved to institute some activity of inquiry

---

[26] D. Stove, 'John Anderson and cultural freedom in Australia', *The Free Spirit* 7 (1) (May/June 1962): pp. 6–7; also D.C. Stove, review of A.J. Ayer's *Philosophical Essays*, *AJP* 34 (1956): pp. 60–5; to the contrary, Janet Anderson, letter, *SMH* 3/4/1963, p. 2.

[27] D.C. Stove, 'The force of intellect', *Quadrant* 21 (7) (July 1977): pp. 45–6; more in R.J. Stove, 'The prime of Mister Jean Brodie', *Annals Australia* Oct 1996, pp. 28–34; cf. J. Ogilvie, *The Push* (Sydney, 1995), pp. 80–1.

[28] M. Clark, *A Short History of Australia* (New York, 1963), p. 215.

[29] J. Anderson, 'Censorship', *Schooling* 11 (4) (1928), repr. in J. Anderson, *Education and Politics* (Sydney, 1931), pp. 14–28, at pp. 19–20; cf. Horne, *Education*, p. 186.

[30] J. Anderson, 'Art and morality', *AJPP* 19 (1941): p. 255; repr. in *Art & Reality*, pp. 83–93, at p. 90; see D.J. Ivison, 'Anderson as a liberator', *Dialectic* (Newcastle University) 30 (1987): pp. 7–9.

themselves. What, for example, was the connection between Andersonian moral theory and his own activities? As the citizens of Hamelin failed to ask about the Pied Piper, was this the man to be trusted with our sons and daughters?

That might depend on what was filling their minds when Anderson's impact began. A first-year student of 1934, Ruth Walker, recorded some of her earlier daydreams, at Anderson's request:

> The earliest ones ... all deal with a wicked young damsel who goes through a long list of punishments (I decline to give you the details here) and who finally emerges good, purified or what not. Sometimes she runs away from home, comes to a hill, enters therein, and then the fun begins, the hill being a sort of little hell specially provided for such as she ... Most of these dreams are just plain erotic after this. What with Arabian sheikhs (generally dwelling in castles), slaves, captured princesses whose resistance is about on the point of breaking when the tormentor manages to fall in love with them, and so on, and so on.[31]

In August 1935, Anderson approached Ruth, then a second-year student in philosophy and English, in the Quad, and invited her to his study for 'a small talk about her essay'. Discussion widened to criticism of the beliefs of Ruth's mother, a Christian Scientist. During subsequent meetings, Ruth came to accept Anderson's ideas on religion, communism and free love, and an affair developed. Ruth graduated with First Class honours and the University Medal in Philosophy — Anderson announced the good news: 'Annuntio vobis magnum gaudium, as the bird said to the Jew'.[32] She was appointed a part-time 'correcting assistant' in 1937, and a full-time assistant lecturer in 1941, enabling her to afford a flat in which the Professor and his friends could be entertained.

There were naturally some, including herself, who wondered if she had got there solely through her intellectual merits.[33] Her professional publications amounted only to a few book reviews on Freudian and similar topics in the *Australasian Journal of Psychology and Philosophy* (editor, John Anderson), and an article of 1960 explaining some

---

[31] Ruth Walker to Anderson, 26/6/1936, in Walker papers, Sydney University Archives, P.158 series 1.

[32] Anderson to Ruth Walker, 18/12/1936, in Walker papers, Sydney University Archives, P.158 series 2. 'I announce to you great joy' refers to the story of the Annunciation, Luke 1:28.

[33] B. Kennedy, *A Passion to Oppose*, ch. 10, based on private diary of Ruth Walker, and letters of Anderson to Walker in Walker papers; Weblin, *Passion for Thinking*, chs. 9, 11; also M. Weblin, 'A philosophical affair: Letters from John Anderson to Ruth Walker' *Heraclitus* 48 (Apr 1996): pp. 11–14 & 53 (Oct 1996): pp. 8–12.

aspects of Anderson's logic.[34] There are also two articles by her on Anderson's influence on students (one entitled 'Anderson and the student body') and his involvement in public controversies.[35] Admittedly, the phenomenon of failure of early promise to flower after permanent appointment is common enough in academia, and was particularly evident, according to some, among Anderson's appointments. As to her teaching, some who remember it name her as the worst lecturer they ever had; others believe the competition for that honour is too fierce but allow that she was a contender. It seems reasonable to conclude on the evidence that Australia's first woman lecturer in philosophy benefited — if that is the right word — from positive discrimination, before that phrase was current.

Ruth's continuing affair with Anderson remained the centre of her life. 'It seems some sort of violation of the soul', she wrote to him, 'when you even hypothetically consider our proceeding more lightly.'[36] In 1950, she suffered a breakdown and, when it became apparent that nursing in the Andersons' home would not be sufficient to cure it, her family were called in. On medical advice, they admitted her to a hospital for drug and shock treatment. It was successful enough at least to overcome the worst symptoms, which included serious memory loss, delusions, ravings about a pregnancy, and an obsessive fear of betraying Anderson. The other members of the department were organised by Anderson to take over her teaching load and keep quiet about everything. She was able to resume teaching in 1951, and, despite a recurrence of the problem and more shock treatment in 1956, continued teaching until her retirement in 1972. Before her death in 1986, she gave a sum of money towards a collection of essays in honour of Anderson.[37]

It is possible to see after 1950 a greater circumspection in Anderson's expressed views, but not a change in his position. By that time, a group of Libertarians later called the 'Push' had come into being who claimed to be following an Andersonian lifestyle; more of them in Chapter 8, but a Catholic view of 1950 conveys the general trend

[34] A.R. Walker, Review of J.R. Unwin, *Sexual Relations and Cultural Behaviour*, *AJPP* 16 (1938): pp. 85–8; others in 18 (1940): pp. 161–80; 20 (1942): pp. 151–60; 21 (1943): pp. 152–62; 'Observations on the distribution and "significance" of terms in propositions', *AJP* 38 (1960): pp. 120–36; also 'Katherine Mansfield', report in *Union Recorder* 5/5/1938, repr. in *Heraclitus* 42 (July 1995): pp. 2–3.

[35] A.R. Walker, 'Professor Anderson and the student body', *Honi Soit* 1/5/1963, pp. 3–4; 'Public controversies and academic freedom', *Dialectic* (Newcastle University) 30 (1987): pp. 11–23.

[36] Ruth Walker to Anderson, 15/2/1947, in Walker papers, series 1.

[37] Published as *Dialectic* (Newcastle University), number 30 (1987).

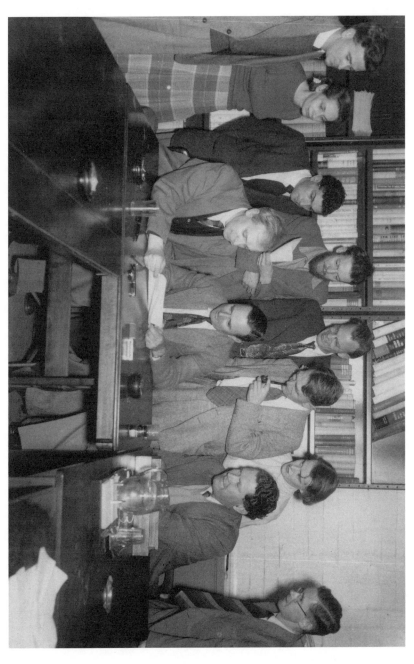

Anderson's disciples, Newcastle, 1954. Standing, from left, R. Walters, Ruth Walker, Milo Roxon, Sandy Anderson, W.H. Eddy, D.H. Monro, Barbara Roxon, John Mackie; seated, John Anderson, A. Bussell, Tom Rose (Anderson papers, University of Sydney archives)

of what was to come: 'It is notorious that the immoral views Professor Anderson preaches are practised at philosophy conferences at Newport, where the nights are filled with lewd promiscuity, which was justified and rationalised in pseudo-philosophical chatter earlier in the evening. It is notorious that a large number of philosophy students rebel against parental authority, leave home, and live in the back streets of Kings Cross.'[38] Anderson had no sympathy with any students who drew those conclusions. In a 1951 paper on James Joyce, he rejected the 'illusion involved in the attempt to lead the untrammelled life, the negative attitude of disbelief traditionally called Libertarianism',[39] and in another address rejected the suggestion that there was any link between freethought and particular ways of living: 'There is no need to link views with activities or to say that the holder of certain views must practise certain things. This itself is superstitious and makes it another religion.'[40] As a meditation on the relation between theory and practice, it is far from the young man who admired Marxism for its close relation of theory to practice: 'true theory is that in the light of which we *transform* things, and which we arrive at only by being active.' None of this, however, is in any sense an act of repentance on his part, as is clear from his remarks on the Orr case, of which also more in the next chapter. Some thought he was playing with fire with his view that 'Professor Orr's answer to the question whether a professor who seduced one of this students should be dismissed — "Yes, of course, he should" — seems to me, while it is understandable enough, to confuse the issues ... no evidence was offered that Professor Orr's work as a teacher had been affected by his relations to any student.'[41]

If there was a lack of knowledge of this darker side of Anderson, there was one sin of his which was well-known, and commented on by everyone. It was that criticism, doled out to all and sundry, was not allowed to apply to himself. That was the case in class, where objections and critical questions were not welcome. 'I don't like classes that talk back', he wrote to an intimate.[42] It applied to his

[38] 'M. Cusack', 'The big bad wolf', *Honi Soit* 8/6/1950 ('M. Cusack' may be a pseudonym of Dr P.J. Ryan: Barcan, *Radical Students*, p. 368 n. 88).
[39] *Honi Soit* 20/9/1951, quoted in A.J. Baker, *Anderson's Social Philosophy* (Sydney, 1979), p. 134.
[40] D.M. McCallum, 'Anderson and Freethought', *Australian Highway* (Sept 1958), pp. 71–5, at p. 75.
[41] J. Anderson, 'The Orr case and academic freedom', *Observer* 28/6/1958, p. 293.
[42] Anderson to G.F. McIntosh, 28/5/1953, in G.F. McIntosh papers, Mitchell Library MSS 5103.

refusal to engage with new trends in philosophy overseas, which led to Sydney philosophy developing into a small and isolated pond, where grew strange and antique forms no longer found in the open sea. When the leading Oxford philosopher Gilbert Ryle wrote a rare article discussing Anderson's views,[43] Anderson claimed not to have bothered to read it, and never replied.

It applied too in appointments to his department, and to the two other departments of philosophy in New South Wales, those in the university colleges at Armidale and Newcastle, where appointments were effectively under his control. Strict toers of the Andersonian line, however second-rate, were preferred to independent thinkers. And even those loyal followers were discouraged from writing expansions of the Andersonian position, lest it be more than a parroting of the revealed truth.[44] All the surveys of the students of Anderson who became well-known in philosophy — David Armstrong, John Passmore, David Stove, John Mackie, Percy Partridge, Eugene Kamenka — have noticed their need to fight their way out of the scorched-earth zone immediately surrounding the great man.[45] No doubt the struggle did them a lot of good, but it may be that the payoff for Australian philosophy was a long time coming.

In one of the most direct attacks on him by a student in his own lifetime, David Armstrong wrote:

> His real intellectual weakness lies in his desire to make disciples, his encouragement of the growth of an Andersonian orthodoxy, his unwillingness to take criticism seriously. By a tragic paradox, his work in arousing in so many students some real feeling for the Western intellectual tradition, and his considerable achievement in the field of pure philosophy, have been largely stultified by his encouragement of an Andersonian provincialism in place of those other provincialisms he so vigorously attacked in the name of culture.[46]

---

[43] G. Ryle, 'Logic and Professor Anderson', *AJP* 28 (1950): pp. 137–53; see J. Mackie, 'Logic and Professor Anderson', *AJP* 29 (1951): pp. 109–13; L. Cumming, 'Ryle on "Logic and Professor Anderson"', *Dialectic* (Newcastle University) 30 (1987): pp. 109–16; Melbourne views in P. Herbst, 'The nature of facts', *AJP* 30 (1952): pp. 90–116.

[44] A.J. Baker, 'Anderson in retrospect', *Heraclitus* 39 (Jan 1995): pp. 1–3; A.J. Baker, 'Anderson and Andersonians: A history and analysis', *Heraclitus* 92 (Nov 2001): pp. 7–14.

[45] E. Kamenka, 'The Andersonians', *Quadrant* (July 1987): pp. 60–64; J.J.C. Smart, 'The philosophical Andersonians', *Quadrant* 20 (1) (Jan 1976): pp. 6–10; [G. Munster], 'Prophet in a gown', *Nation* no. 9 (17/1/1959), pp. 10–13.

[46] D.M. Armstrong, 'Educating Sydney?', *Observer* 19/4/1958, p. 152; similar in D.M. Armstrong, 'The Andersonians', *Observer* 4/10/1958, p. 535;

Anderson even admitted privately, 'It's at least an arguable matter how far I've produced the sort of provincialism he speaks about, but certainly some of my pupils have little interest in, or ability to tackle, doctrines other than mine.'[47] But he regarded Armstrong as 'a chap with whom I should never have got beyond strictly *formal* relations' and shared with Ruth Walker the farcical misjudgement, 'The fact is that both David's are weak in logic — D.C.S[tove]. because he doesn't have the training, D.M.A[rmstong]. congenitally.'[48]

Still, what was there to Anderson's influence, beyond mere criticism? What, in the end, was that man for? The secret is in the recollections of Anderson's best students, those who became the leaders in the next generation of philosophy. According to Partridge,

> He was still very young when he came to Sydney: between 1927 and 1937, he was thinking strenuously, still developing his 'position'. And consequently those of us who studied with him (or later worked with him) had the experience of being associated with a thinker engaged in the work of creating a very impressive intellectual construction ... He commanded few of the usual arts and skills of the 'good teacher'; he was never popular, spectacular or 'interesting'. But he was one of the few original and systematic thinkers who have worked in this country (perhaps, in the field of the humanities, the only one). And his closest pupils at least were in touch, therefore, with an ambitious project of intellectual construction going forward: they could observe at first hand what intellectual creation is like.[49]

And David Stove, a student twenty years later than Partridge, and as severe a critic of Anderson as any, wrote:

> The influence Anderson exercised was purely, or as purely as a human influence can be, purely intellectual. I never felt anything like the force of his intellect. Disagreeing with Anderson was (to compare it with something most people have experienced), like playing chess against someone altogether above your own class. Your strongest pieces are, you cannot tell how, drained of all their powers, while on his side even pawns can do unheard-of things; and as though by invisible giant fingers, you are quickly crushed ... He was in love with philosophy himself, and he communicated the love of it to others so effectively that many will have it while they live. This is the greatest service he did.

---

see also S. Thiele, 'Anderson and authoritarianism', *Australian Journal of Anthropology* 3 (1–2) (1990): pp. 100–19.

[47] Anderson to W.H.C. Eddy, 9/6/1958.

[48] Anderson to Ruth Walker, 1952, quoted in Weblin, *A Passion for Thinking*, ch. 15.

[49] P.H. Partridge, 'Anderson as educator', *Australian Highway* 1958, repr. in *Education and Inquiry*, pp. 3–10, at pp. 4–5; also P. Harris, 'John Anderson's legacy', *Quadrant* 43 (12) (Dec 1999): pp. 11–18.

Yet for every person whom he made a philosopher he left ten people, I should say, with a respect for philosophy, and a recollection of what it is like to wrestle in earnest with desperately difficult intellectual questions. This may not sound much, but I think it is much. Whoever can remember what serious thinking is like, is to some extent armed against all the enemies of education. He is armed against the acknowledged leaders of the war against education, the educationists. He is armed against educational levellers of every kind. And he is armed against systems, such as Marxism, which pretend to answer every question out of a little holy catechism, and which just for that reason often act like a revelation on unfurnished minds.

In this way, Anderson leavened the lump of middle-class life in Australia; for, because of him, there is a teacher or a doctor here, a librarian or a lawyer there, who can remember what serious thinking is like.[50]

A STRANGE postscript to the story of John Anderson was the 'Bertrand Russell, Andersonian' affair. Russell was one of the few famous philosophers to actually visit Australia. Though aged 78 at the time, he undertook a gruelling two-month tour of Australia in 1950. A reporter thought he looked like a 'koala who has just thought of a funny joke'; he in turn thought the Australians 'cordial but uninteresting'.[51] In Sydney, Anderson attended his talk, perhaps the last time Anderson came in contact with a leading overseas philosopher.[52] Ideological Melbourne turned on a characteristic performance, with both the Communists and Archbishop Mannix denouncing Russell. Mannix said that the USA had refused Russell entry on account of his immoral views, and Australia should have done the same. The factual part of this was not exactly true, and Russell extracted from Mannix a rare public apology.[53]

---

[50] D.C. Stove, 'The force of intellect', pp. 45–6; more on Anderson's students in A.J. Baker, 'Anderson and Andersonians, a history and analysis', *Heraclitus* 91 (Oct 2001): pp. 1–8.

[51] C. Moorehead, *Bertrand Russell: A Life* (London, 1992), pp. 461–2.

[52] Anderson's notes, G. Suter, 'Bibliographic study of the philosophy of John Anderson', *Australian Historical Bibliography*, Bulletin no. 10 (Sept 1984): pp. 1–60, items 243–4; some comments by Anderson on Russell in Kennedy, *Passion*, pp. 171–2.

[53] N. Griffin, 'Russell in Australia', *Russell* 16 (Winter, 1974–5): pp. 3–12; B. Russell, *The Autobiography of Bertrand Russell*, vol 3 (London, 1969), pp. 26–7, picture with koala opposite p. 48; R.W. Clark, *The Life of Bertrand Russell* (London, 1975), pp. 510–11; R. Monk, *Bertrand Russell* (London, 2000), vol. 2, pp. 326–8; 'Bertrand Russell puts case for White Australia', *SMH* 4/7/1950, p. 2; P. Coleman, *Memoirs*, p. 50; further papers on the visit in National Library, MS 2512; on Russell's subjectivist ethical views, D.H. Monro, 'Russell's moral theories', *Philosophy* 35 (1960): pp. 30–50; C.

Bertrand Russell and friend, Australia, 1950 (from Autobiography of Bertrand Russell)

The tour left Russell with an Australian admirer, Anderson's student Paul Foulkes. Strangely, Foulkes' connection with Russell appears in one of Anderson's few recorded dreams:

> I wandered into an empty Church and thought I'd like to mount the pulpit and read a 'lesson' of some sort, but there were no Bibles around. I wondered if, instead, I'd recite the epilogue to 'Asolando' ('One who never turned his back but marched breast-forward' etc.) or Henley's 'unconquerable soul', but knew I wasn't letter-perfect in either. So I went outside and met P. Foulkes who said he had something suitable in his rooms not far away; he dashed off and came back with a volume of *Principia Mathematica*. So my pulpit-reading didn't come off.[54]

In 1959 there appeared a handsomely illustrated book, *Wisdom of the West*, by Bertrand Russell. Or more exactly, according to the title page, by 'Bertrand Russell, [in small print] editor, Paul Foulkes'. It was well received, sold well, and there were at least a dozen transla-

James, 'Bertrand Russell struggles after heaven', in *Even As We Speak* (London, 2001), pp. 90–109; S. Candlish, 'Russell and Wittgenstein', in *Wittgenstein and the Future of Philosophy*, ed. R. Haller & K. Puhl (Vienna, 2002), pp. 21–29.

[54] Anderson to Ruth Walker, 5/9/1952, quoted in Kennedy, *Passion*, p. 168.

tions. Reviewers said, 'This book could not have been written by anybody but Russell ... A certain personal imaginative quality which appears on the page as dry wit is related to a whole humane background, a whole way of life', and again, 'written in Russell's inimitable, clear, and often fascinating style.' In Australia, however, there were doubts. David Armstrong wrote, 'Those who are familiar with Andersonian thought will find that topics dealt with, and the views expressed, are often much closer to Anderson than to Russell'; in a review of another book by Russell, he said, 'A book called *Wisdom of the West* was recently published under his name, although it is clear he had little to do with it.'[55] David Stove's review, headed 'Bertrand Russell, Andersonian', said:

> The oddest thing about the book is that it bears the unmistakable impress of Professor John Anderson of the University of Sydney, under whom Dr Foulkes took his first degree in philosophy. Perhaps Russell was nodding, or needed the money. Anyway, those who know will detect this influence, both in matters of overall emphasis ... and in a hundred points of detail. The most amazing example is the detailed treatment given to a few of the Socratic dialogues of Plato. Those who heard Anderson's lectures to first-year students on 'Phaedo' and the rest will be gratified to learn how very large those lectures bulk in the wisdom of the west.[56]

Stove and Armstrong were right. Foulkes had written the lot, including the foreword thanking him for his help. Foulkes had visited Russell a few times, by arrangement with the publishers; Russell had made a few minor comments on the text, but it is far from clear whether he had read it all, let alone written any of it. The suggestion that he needed the money was also true, as he had by then three granddaughters to support. The deliberate deception was more on the part of the publishers than Russell himself — Russell urged that Foulkes be given 'appropriate acknowledgement' on the title page, and threatened to reveal the truth live on television. But he allowed himself to be fobbed off by the publisher's reasoning as to why such a gesture would not be opportune, legally desirable, or in accordance with normal publishing practice.

There the matter stood until revealed by research in the Russell archives in 1986. At the time, no notice was taken by the overseas public of the reviews in Australia, and the book was undoubtedly the best-selling work of Australian philosophy up to that date. The only

---

[55] D. Armstrong, 'Russell the sage', *Observer* 2 (24) (28/11/1959): p. 31; D. Armstrong, 'Chopped sage', *Bulletin* 5/8/1961: pp. 32–3.
[56] D. Stove, 'Bertrand Russell, Andersonian', *Nation* 16/1/1960: pp. 22–3.

known reaction to the reviews came from the publishers. They sacked Foulkes.[57]

---

[57] C. Spadoni, 'Who wrote Bertrand Russell's *Wisdom of the West?*', *Papers of the Bibliographical Society of America* 80 (1986): pp. 349–67, summary in L. Cumming, 'A remarkable philosophical hybrid', *Quadrant* 33 (1/2) (Jan/Feb 1989): pp. 61–2.

Chapter 3 Gross Moral Turpitude: the Orr Case

S YDNEY Sparkes Orr studied at Queen's University, Belfast, in the late 1930s. His application for the chair of philosophy at the University of Tasmania in 1952 recorded that he won prizes in logic, philosophy, ethics, political philosophy, metaphysics, history of philosophy, Greek and mathematics, and that he was awarded an MA with first class honours. None of that was true. He was awarded a pass MA. His PhD thesis, on 'The Socratic theory that virtue is knowledge', was twice rejected by the examiners, and never completed. In 1944 he was made temporary assistant lecturer at the University of St Andrews, with the understanding that the following year he would be confirmed in a lectureship. This did not take place, after difficulties over complaints from female students and failing to follow the syllabus. After some time on unemployment benefits, he took the Antipodean exit traditional for men in his situation.[1] He was appointed to a temporary vacancy in philosophy at Melbourne University in 1946, and became permanent when the American philosopher appointed to the post was found shot dead in Brisbane.

When Orr's wife arrived in Melbourne to join him, she found him living with a 21–year-old social worker he had met at a Student Christian Movement conference. The three agreed to live together, and the arrangement continued until the second 'wife' became pregnant and Orr demanded she live elsewhere. She soon left perma-

---

[1] C. Pybus, *Seduction and Consent: A Case of Gross Moral Turpitude* (Melbourne, 1994), pp. 35–8; summary also in J. Teichman, 'Sophists, frauds and madmen: C.E.M. Joad and S.S. Orr', in *Philosophers' Hobbies and Other Essays* (Melbourne, 2003), pp. 37–40.

nently; Mrs Orr stayed on.[2] Orr alienated his professor and students, who resented his ravings about Communists and his frequent references to his belief that he was the illegitimate son of Edward VIII.[3] His standing at Melbourne University is clear in a report later provided to the security services by the Registrar:

> Disposition: Peculiar. Not a good mixer with equals — opportunist, very mercenary, attitude towards students aggressive and uncharitable, particularly when marking papers. Very emotional. Always talking, often to his own ultimate disadvantage. Frequently sought concessions over fellow lecturers. Quite selfish. Egotistical. Probably schizophrenic ... Was in charge of "CLEAR THINKING" section of lectures. Was placed last in list of preference for promotion to Senior Lecturer. When informed over 'phone that he had not obtained the Senior's posting, fainted.[4]

Around the time he came to Australia, Orr wrote two philosophical articles. The first was an attack on the logical positivist and linguistic tendencies of current English philosophy, a rambling work with a excess of exclamation marks.[5] It appeared in the *Australasian Journal of Psychology and Philosophy* adjacent to John Mackie's article, 'The refutation of morals', whose conclusion is in no sense less extreme than its title suggests, and is an example of the tendencies Orr saw himself as combating. The second, a contribution to a discussion on the metaphysics of Plato's *Republic*, is a much superior work. It again establishes Orr's opposition to the relativist currents of the day. The concern of the true thinker, he says, is 'to reproduce the nature of cosmic order in his own environment, and not merely to amuse himself by *clearing up concepts* ...' [6] These two articles proved to be his last published philosophical works. He continued to promise a book reinterpreting Plato's theory that 'virtue is knowledge'. This saying is correct, Orr said, only if it is understood that Plato intended 'knowl-

---

[2] Orr's version in his seven-part exclusive in *Pix* 46 (1) (8/6/1957), pp. 6–10; 46 (2) (15/6), pp. 10–13; 46 (3) (22/6), pp. 12–15; 46 (4) (29/6), pp. 12–15; 46 (5) (6/7), pp. 12–15; 46 (6) (13/7), pp. 49–51; 46 (7) (20/7), pp. 42–3.

[3] Pybus, *Seduction and Consent*, pp. 38–41; J.B. Polya & R.J. Solomon, *Dreyfus in Australia* (Erskineville, 1996), p. 71.

[4] Australian Archives, series A1533/33 item 1956/3736; more favourable recollections of Orr as lecturer in V. Buckley, *Cutting Green Hay* (Ringwood, 1983), p. 62, and W.H.C. Eddy, *Orr* (Brisbane, 1961), ch. 27.

[5] S.S. Orr, 'Some reflections on the Cambridge approach to philosophy', *AJPP* 24 (1946): pp. 34–76, 129–67.

[6] S.S. Orr, 'The alleged metaphysics in the *Republic*', *Aristotelian Society Supplementary Volume* 19 (1945): pp. 207–29, p. 222.

edge' to cover a far wider field than is commonly supposed (in particular, it bears a close relation to Love).[7]

This is the background to Orr's appointment as first professor of philosophy at the University of Tasmania in 1952.

The University was autocratically ruled by its Chancellor, Sir John Morris, who was also Chief Justice of Tasmania. He wanted no moral relativists or atheists in the chair. He was contacted by Sir Frederic Eggleston, the grand old man of Australian liberalism and author of a book on political philosophy of which little notice had been taken by professional philosophers.[8] Eggleston believed there was a conspiracy to fill all the chairs in Australian philosophy with men who had replaced the traditional weighty concerns of philosophy with 'mere logical techniques'. They were analysts of language only, 'arid, neutral and relativist on all great moral and intellectual issues'. What was wanted instead was a philosopher 'capable of displaying some qualities of intellectual leadership in these critical times', and filling the moral vacuum that would otherwise be occupied by Communism.

The general idea that a certain kind of technical philosophy leaves a moral vacuum which tends to be filled by irrational and emotionally charged movements may be a defensible one, but Eggleston's proposed remedy was not a happy choice. Through the Student Christian Movement, he believed he knew a man of honesty and courage who fitted the bill, Sydney Sparkes Orr. Further, he could give advice on the other three candidates, Kurt Baier and Quentin Gibson of the Melbourne linguistic school, and the Sydney Andersonian, John Mackie. 'Have you read Mackie's paper on the refutation of morality?' he wrote. 'It is a typical example of the superficial way in which present day students dispose of questions of such importance.' Other advice on Orr was, indeed, not so favourable. In particular, his head of department at Melbourne, Alexander Boyce Gibson, ranked him well below the other three candidates, and added that Orr could not work with those who did not agree with him, and was deficient in both discretion and dignity.

But it was too late. Morris's mind was made up, and Orr's appointment went through.[9] It was reported that a 'down-town' member of the selection committee had asked Orr whether he thought businessmen had something to learn from philosophy; not much, he

---

[7] *University of Melbourne Report of Research and Investigation* 1950, p. 115; J. Tate, 'Note on the Platonic studies of Mr. S.S. Orr', in Eddy, *Orr*, pp. 691–4; Polya & Solomon, *Dreyfus*, p. 91.

[8] W. Osmond, *Frederic Eggleston: An Intellectual in Australian Politics* (Sydney, 1985), pp. 273–4; F.W. Eggleston, *Search for a Social Philosophy* (Melbourne, 1941).

[9] Pybus, *Seduction and Consent*, pp. 203–7.

said, but he had found that philosophers had a lot to learn from businessmen.[10] As a joke of the time had it, Orr was the only candidate with the necessary disqualifications.[11]

On taking up his duties, Orr proceeded to alienate most of his students. He fought with the man he appointed as the only other member of the Philosophy Department, a Serb Kantian named Milanov[12] whom he had also made use of as his personal psychoanalyst. And of course he fought the administration. He joined an already existing opposition to his benefactor Morris, and wrote on their behalf an extreme letter in the Hobart *Mercury*, demanding a Royal Commission into the affairs of the University. The Commission was set up and reported, calling for change in the personnel running the University. That did not happen.

During 1955 Orr began an affair with a student in his second year ethics course, Suzanne Kemp. Her diary, later tendered in court, describes Orr's technique:

> Someone had told him — jokingly — that I had a crush on him, and that had made him decide to say something to me. It was his duty to tell me, in case he was leading me on unconsciously. He should tell me and so free me — that was what was moral in it. Because he believed in my maturity — a deep questioning behind my eyes — that I was past crushes. That he believed something more than the desire to discuss philosophy was behind his relationship with me. I gave him peace &c., he was emotionally involved — what had never happened to him before ... Then he talked of his mother, who he said, didn't love him ...[13]

By the beginning of 1956, the University authorities were considering various complaints against Orr, notably from Milanov and from a student who claimed Orr had implied that good marks would only be forthcoming in return for help with the design and decoration of his house.[14] Then Suzanne told her father about the affair. Up to this

[10] John Anderson to Ruth Walker, 18/4/1952, in Walker papers, Sydney University Archives, P.158 series 2.

[11] D.M. Armstrong, 'The strange case of Sydney Sparkes Orr', *Quadrant* 37 (4) (Apr 1993): pp. 82–3.

[12] Pybus, *Seduction and Consent*, pp. 44–6, 53–5, 137–41; Polya & Solomon, *Dreyfus*, pp. 51–7; bibliography of Milanov in A.G. Price, ed, *The Humanities in Australia: A Survey* (Sydney, 1959), p. 305; his statements in Eddy, *Orr*, pp. 699–704; his ASIO file in Australian Archives series A6119/84 item 1854.

[13] *The Dismissal of S. S. Orr by the University of Tasmania* (Hobart, 1958), p. 35.

[14] Pybus, *Seduction and Consent*, pp. 50–2, 56–7; on the student's Wittgenstein-inspired art, see B. Reid, 'Maker and signmaker — some aspects of the art of Edwin Tanner', *Art and Australia* 9 (1971): pp. 213–23.

point, the story has similarities with that of Anderson and Ruth Walker, but Reg Kemp was a different kind of man from Ruth's father, of whom nothing was heard. Accompanied by Suzanne's boyfriend, he went round to Orr's house and assaulted him. Orr fell to the floor, then pulled himself onto a chair and denied everything. Kemp, he said, was a brute who had reduced his daughter to a mental state bordering on schizophrenia, for which he, Orr, was treating her. He accused Kemp and the boyfriend themselves of sexual relations with Suzanne, and threatened writs for assault and defamation the next morning.[15] Kemp complained to the University. Orr tendered his resignation, though denying that any affair had taken place. The University Council, at a meeting at which Reg Kemp was allowed to speak but Orr was not present,[16] refused to accept it and insisted on dismissing him instead. After further internal hearings confirmed the Council's decision, he appealed to the Tasmanian Supreme Court. Miss Kemp stood up well to four days of cross-examination. The Court found for the University. Orr appealed to the High Court of Australia, and lost.[17]

The subsequent long-drawn-out history of the Orr case is of little concern to the history of Australian philosophy, and there are three books[18] on it already in addition to the vast amount of print expended on it at the time. Most academics on the mainland took the case to be more about questions of the correct procedures for dismissing academics, and whether the relation of universities to academics was that of master to servant. Orr himself was an embarrassment to both sides. His opponents were wrong-footed by his earlier attack on the administration, which gave credence to the view that his dismissal was a payback by his enemies. And his supporters were continually embarrassed by his outrageous behaviour, and revelations about his earlier private life and his lying about his qualifications. They found themsel-

---

[15] Pybus, *Seduction and Consent*, pp. 14–6.

[16] *The Dismissal of S.S. Orr*, p. 12; Polya & Solomon, *Dreyfus*, p. 117.

[17] Pybus, *Seduction and Consent*, ch. 4; R. Davis, *Open to Talent: The Centenary History of the University of Tasmania, 1890–1990* (Hobart, 1990), pp. 147–59; W.D. Joske, 'Orr', *ADB* vol. 15, pp. 543–4; P. McPhee, *'Pansy': A Life of Roy Douglas Wright* (Melbourne, 1999), pp. 115–29, 143–4; Orr *v.* University of Tasmania, *Tasmanian State Reports* 1956, pp. 155–61; Orr *v.* University of Tasmania, *Commonwealth Law Reports* 100 (1958–9): pp. 526–31.

[18] One good—that by Pybus (fn. 1) and two bad (those of Polya and Solomon, fn. 3, and of Eddy and Orr, fn. 25); not counting R.D. Wright's unpublishable *roman à clef*, 'The Cuckoo', on which see McPhee, *'Pansy'*, pp. 125–6.

Sydney Sparkes Orr leaves the High Court of Australia building, 22 May 1957 (Newspix)

ves suppressing evidence of his sexual abuse of students years earlier in Scotland.

The involvement of philosophers in the affair was substantial. Most supported Orr, though not all for the same reason. Anderson, as we saw, believed Orr should not have been dismissed even if he had seduced his student,[19] and Ruth Walker suggested in all seriousness that the *Australasian Journal of Philosophy* ought to publish something 'of a philosophic character' as to why dismissal for seduction was wrong.[20] The Sydney 'Push' philosopher George Molnar maintained

[19] J. Anderson, 'The Orr case and academic freedom', *Observer* 28/6/1958, p. 293; speech by Anderson on the Orr case, 25/8/1958, reported in A.R. Walker, 'Public controversies and academic freedom', *Dialectic* (Newcastle University) 30 (1987): pp. 11–23, at p. 19; P. Coleman, *Memoirs of a Slow Learner* (Sydney, 1994), pp. 78–9.
[20] Ruth Walker to Anderson, 16/4/1960, in Walker papers, series 1; also Walker letter, *Nation* 25/1/1964, p. 17.

Orr should have taken a principled stand on sexual freedom. The issue ought to have been 'the freedom to behave sexually as one is moved, without interference and persecution by moralists who administer public institutions.'[21] Unusually, the 'moralists' provided a coherent explanation of what was supposed to be wrong with Orr's behaviour. The Tasmanian Vice-Chancellor stated his case in the context of a clear philosophical view about education, a conservative alternative to the Andersonian ideal of academic life as constant 'criticism':

> The act of seduction seems to me especially despicable if a professor misuses his position as a teacher to aid him in his purpose, as it is clear from Miss Kemp's diary that Orr did in their private discussions on the subject of free love ... [A university] must afford young men and women every opportunity within its command not only to stretch their mental powers but, both by formal study and by rubbing shoulders with each other and with mature and emotionally-balanced teachers, to learn to understand, and enshrine in their own lives, the highest principles of human behaviour, and thus to become in themselves mature human beings capable of living in a progressive free society with integrity and respect for the rights of others. In their main duty, which is the search for truth, academics must certainly be prepared fearlessly to assess ethical values as part of truth. But it is not enough that they should do this as an intellectual exercise: in carrying out their grave responsibility to their students — in all their personal relations with them — they are under obligation to be strictly moral in their own actions, and careful not to desecrate their trust.[22]

But most philosophers believed in Orr's innocence. In this they showed themselves markedly inferior to the legal profession as evaluators of evidence on matters of fact. Besides the careful work by counsel and judges in the two court cases, the evidence was considered in detail by the lawyers John Kerr and Hal Wootten. Their report revealed that Orr's 'reasons' for demanding a reopening of his case were all gross misrepresentations of the evidence submitted in court. They ended by suggesting that the courts were 'at least entitled not to have their decisions and actions grotesquely misrepresented by people who claim moral and intellectual leadership in the community.'[23] The Tasmanian Vice-Chancellor also commented on the

---

[21] G. Molnar, 'Sexual freedom in the Orr case', *Australian Highway* 41 (3) (June 1960): pp. 54–5; more Push comment in 'The wild colonial don', *Combined Universities Songbook* (Sydney, 1965), p. 17.

[22] K.S. Isles, in *The Dismissal of S.S. Orr*, pp. 2–3; similar values in *Report of the Committee on Australian Universities* (Murray Report) (Canberra, 1957), p. 9.

[23] J.P. Kerr & J.H. Wootten, 'Re-opening the Orr case', *The Free Spirit* 4 (10) (Aug 1958): pp. 3–15, replies in 4 (11) (Sept/Oct 1958); see J.

'many philosophers, including teachers of logic and scientific method' who had chosen to believe Orr on little more than a cursory glance at a fraction of the evidence.[24]

Despite this, philosophers and many other academics maintained that the evidence of his guilt was at least insufficient, and hence that he had been denied natural justice. The usual comparison with Socrates was of course not neglected.[25] The Australasian Association of Philosophy declared the Chair black.[26] There were some efforts to find Orr a job elsewhere, but, whatever could be said of their evaluation of matters of fact, philosophers were fully aware of Orr's incompetence in philosophy. David Stove recalled:

> I knew him, but only in the sense that everyone in the (then small) profession knew him. That is, they knew enough to put on an appearance of being in deep conversation with someone else if, at a conference, they saw Siddie coming. He was an *absolute pariah*, before he became a martyr. Stupid, devious, boring, and, to add to his charms, a Christian of the purest "creeping Jesus" kind. He had the kind of Scotch-Irish accent which some women find irresistible, and which makes all men feel for their wallet, to make sure it is still there.'[27]

David Armstrong at one point proposed to offer Orr a tutorship at Sydney University, but his colleagues jumped on the idea.[28] Philosophy teaching in Tasmania was undertaken by several visiting lecturers, and by Milanov, who stayed at the University for some years, working on such topics as 'Punishment as a form of social control'.[29]

Orr died in 1966, shortly after accepting a monetary settlement from the University of Tasmania.

The tragedy of the Orr case affected a remarkable range of people. Being Orr cannot have been very enjoyable. Neither can being one of his relatives or partners. Beyond those most immediately affected, a large number of well-intentioned people wasted a vast amount of time, energy and money supporting Orr. Among the worst affected was the Sydney philosopher Harry Eddy, who had the misfortune to

McLaren, *Writing in Hope and Fear* (Cambridge, 1996), pp. 89–90; J. Kerr, *Matters for Judgement* (2nd ed, Melbourne, 1988), pp. 175–6; another legal event in R. Coleman, *Above Renown* (Melbourne, 1988), ch. 23.

[24] Isles, in *The Dismissal of S.S. Orr*, p. 6; further on this document in *Orr v. Isles, Weekly Notes (N.S.W.)* 83 (1965–6) vol. 1 pp. 303–34.

[25] Eddy, *Orr*, pp. 631–2.

[26] Pybus, *Seduction and Consent*, pp. 127–30; A.K. Stout, W.J. Ginnane & S.S. Orr, *Report to the A.A.P. Council on the Moves for a Settlement of the Orr Case* (Sydney, 1964).

[27] D. Stove to author, 15/10/1991.

[28] Pybus, *Seduction and Consent*, pp. 186–7.

[29] *University of Tasmania Research Report* 1957, p. 68.

have Orr living in his house for a year while Orr wrote most of the huge book on the case to which Eddy put his name.[30] Eddy came to believe that Orr was a victim of a conspiracy by Communists, a good indication of how hard it was for so many to believe the alternative hypothesis, that the universe could contain someone as appalling and deceptive as Orr.

Still, the universe has ways of dealing with such people, a truth expressed well by none other than Orr himself, in his early article on Plato:

> The principle which ensures that the perfection of the whole is subserved by every detail is conceived as the principle of Cosmic Justice ... Any deviation from the balance is automatically compensated by counterdevelopments, moral and physical, elsewhere in the whole. The aggressiveness of any element in physical nature, as well as in human thought or society, is treated in general as a disturbance of the balance. And the word which Plato here uses to describe it is the same as that which he used in the *Gorgias*, where he also indicated that licentiousness, the lust for power or possessions, or, in general, immorality, is not merely wrong from the ethical point of view, but a violation of the very principle upon which the universe is constructed.[31]

There remains one mystery about the Orr case. Was Orr in fact the illegitimate son of the Prince of Wales, later Edward VIII? Orr's claim was always treated as a joke, and certainly the fact that Orr claimed it is no reason whatever to believe it. Still, given the Prince's known habits, and the undoubted facial resemblance between the two, there is nothing implausible about it. Both men were a notably short five feet five inches.[32]

The story might become more probable than not, if it were established that the Prince did visit Belfast nine months before Orr was born. It is difficult to discover if he did, despite the glare of publicity in which the Prince habitually moved. Officially, he did not visit that city in April 1914. Ulster in early 1914 was no fit place for an official Royal visit of any kind, since extreme loyalists were distributing arms in anticipation of the declaration of Home Rule and military action was expected at any moment. Part of the government's response to the crisis was to have a number of naval vessels 'exercising' in the

---

[30] Pybus, *Seduction and Consent*, pp. 156–62; M. Eddy, 'Andersonian by marriage', *Heraclitus* 58 (May 1997): pp. 1–4; P. Coleman, 'Competing legends', *Sydney Review* 52 (Apr 1993): pp. 11–12; on Eddy's work, *ADB* vol. 14, pp. 75–6 and O. Harries, *Liberty and Politics* (Sydney, 1976), pp. 1–6, 149–51; another dupe in W.T. Southerwood, *The Wisdom of Guilford Young* (George Town, Tas, 1989), pp. 350–4, 407–8.

[31] S.S. Orr, 'The alleged metaphysics in the *Republic*', at pp. 212–3.

[32] Security file on Orr (fn. 4); C. Higham, *Wallis* (London, 1988), p. 55.

strait between Ireland and Scotland. Among them was the battleship
Collingwood, on which the Prince of Wales spent a week in late April.
He is reported visiting several locations on the Scottish coast opposite
Ulster.[33] The blockade was made more difficult by the fact that the
crews, especially the younger officers, were enthusiastic supporters of
the Loyalist volunteers. It is reported of some of the ships supposedly
enforcing the blockade, 'The vessels were saluted by the Volunteer
signalling stations and their officers were regaled on shore with typical
Ulster hospitality by the local Loyalist residents.'[34] Whether the crew
of the *Collingwood* were able to participate in these displays of loyalty
remains unknown.

[33] *Times* 23/4/1914, p. 8; 24/4, p. 11; 25/4, p. 11; 27/4, p. 10; 28/4, p. 7.
[34] M.H. Hyde, *Carson* (London, 1953), pp. 364–5; rumours of other
Australian offspring of HRH quashed in M. Davie, *Anglo-Australian Attitudes*
(London, 2000), pp. 80–8.

Chapter 4 The Catholic Scholastics

I N HIS autobiography, B. A. Santamaria recalled his schooldays at Melbourne's St Kevin's College.

The type of Catholic "apologetics" which was the strength of religious teaching at St Kevin's prepared my mind for John Henry Newman and later C.S. Lewis, who both provided confirmation of my religious beliefs. To the professional philosopher, Newman and C.S. Lewis might appear to be no more than popularizers of other men's ideas. Yet I do not despise the popularizer, since it seems that there are few new objections to religious belief. What one normally encounters are new formulations of the old objections—except, of course, for those contemporary philosophic systems which, in complete self-contradiction, pretend to prove the uselessness of reason as a mechanism in the search for truth ... In the last analysis, the "apologetics" we absorbed could not lift religion above dependence on an act of faith, but an act of faith sustained by, and consonant with, reason. It was not an act of faith standing, as it were, unsupported or contrary to reason ... Sheehan's *Apologetics and Christian Doctrine* provided me, as a schoolboy at matriculation standard, with the rational justification for my act of faith in Catholic Christianity. When I examine what so many Catholic students at the same level are offered today, I stand appalled not merely at the intellectual poverty of the offering but at the ease with which so many so-called teachers of religion dismiss the intellect as a convincing support for religious belief in favour of highly subjective "religious experience". I can understand why so few students believe anything at all: for that which reason does not sustain rests on most unsubstantial foundations when confronted with the challenges of the "new morality" (which, as someone remarked, is only the old immorality writ large).[1]

---

[1] B.A. Santamaria, *Santamaria: A Memoir* (Melbourne, 1997), p. 8.

Santamaria here recalls a time when Catholic intellectual life, from primary school up, was informed by a complete official philosophy, the scholasticism of St Thomas Aquinas. Thomas Keneally's memoirs at the corresponding point also describe the impact of the 'nifty' arguments for the existence of God in Sheehan's *Apologetics*, and represent the author as briefly inspired to combat the evil forces of atheistic Sydney University philosophy.[2] The Catholic childhood of legend was more than guilt and incense, and one of the essential extra ingredients was philosophy.

The Catholic Church has always been more hospitable to philosophy than other religious bodies. It has taken the view that if 'reason' is a danger to faith, as it obviously is, then the solution is not less reason but more. It is true that the Australian Church has always had at least its fair share of anti-intellectuals, and some leaders of the local church have regarded the pursuits of the mind as an irrelevance and a nuisance, but others argued the opposite, as a response to the pluralism of a colonial society. According to a writer of 1896:

> The simple rudimentary Christian knowledge which was sufficient for the poor exile of Erin while yet in his own saintly island village, where his humble home was perhaps sheltered by the ivy-clad ruins of some ancient church or monastery, where he saw 'books in the running brooks, sermons in stones, and good in everything,' did not suffice when he found himself in a land where both press and pulpit teemed with calumny against his Holy Faith, and where there were then few shepherds to ward off the wolf from the fold.[3]

In any case, decisions on such matters were made in Rome. Official policy was to ensure that even primary school children understood their faith as clearly as possible, through instruction in the Catechism. At a time when tertiary and even upper secondary education was a rarity, the Catechism was the text that did most to create a difference between a Catholic and a secular education. It began on an abstract note:

Q. Who made the world?

A. God made the world.

Q. Who is God?

A. God is the Creator of heaven and earth and of all things and the Supreme Lord of all.

[2] T. Keneally, *Homebush Boy* (Melbourne, 1995), pp. 37, 43, 45; similar in *Sweet Mothers, Sweet Maids*, ed. K. & D. Nelson (Ringwood, 1986), pp. 168–9.

[3] M.J. Treacy, 'The necessity of being able to give a reason for the faith that is in us', *ACR* 2 (1896): pp. 412–24, at pp. 415–6.

Q. How do we know that there is a God?

A. We know that there is a God by the things that He made ...

Q. If God be everywhere, why do we not see Him?

A. We do not see God, because He is a pure Spirit, and therefore cannot be seen by us in this life ...

Q. Had God a beginning?[4]

And that is just part of the first page. The later parts of course do not deal in such abstract and philosophical issues, but the precision of the definitions is notable throughout. They are a philosophical education for those with an ear for such things:

Q. What is man?

A. Man is one of God's creatures, composed of a body and soul, and made to God's likeness.

Q. How do you know that you have a soul?

A. I know that I have a soul because I am alive, and because I can think, reason and choose freely.[5]

Q. What is sin?

A. Sin is any wilful thought, word, deed or omission contrary to the law of God.[6]

Q. What is presumption?

A. Presumption is the expectation of salvation without making proper use of the means necessary to obtain it.[7]

Q. What is a lie?

A. A lie is the saying of anything that we believe to be false.[8]

---

[4] *Catechism of Christian Doctrine: Adapted for Australia by 2nd and 3rd Plenary Councils* (4th ed, Sydney, 1944), p. 11; almost identical, but lacking the third question, in *Catechism: Approved for General Use by the Cardinal Delegate, Archbishops and Bishops* (Sydney, 1905), p. 9; see M. Sheehan, 'Some remarks on the catechism problem', *ACR* 14 (1937): pp. 182–9; recollections in J. Redrup, *Banished Camelots: Recollections of a Catholic Childhood* (Sydney, 1997), pp. 127–8.

[5] *Catechism*, 1944, p. 12.

[6] *Catechism*, 1905, p. 25, 'actual sin' in 1944, p. 29.

[7] *Catechism*, 1944, p. 34.

[8] *Catechism*, 1944, p. 38; cf. A. Coady, 'The morality of lying', *Res Publica* 1 (2) (Winter, 1992): 6–9.

As an intellectual training, it was not without effect either. Little girls came up with curly questions like 'How could Our Lady have free will if she couldn't sin?' [9] and 'How could a God of intrinsic goodness create evil?'[10] The risk in relying on argument, of course, is that the audience may not be convinced. 'I remember Sister Amard who tried to teach me the philosophical proofs of the existence of God, and thereby destroyed my faith completely because she didn't know them; rather, she did know them but they weren't valid', says Germaine Greer. She adds 'the nuns were dreadfully incompetent at teaching Catholic philosophy. The Jesuits on the other hand were very good at it, and if I'd been taught by Jesuits I'd probably still be a Catholic.'[11] The reputation of the Jesuits for increasing the validity of arguments is no doubt exaggerated.

The passage from Santamaria refers to the two central themes of Catholic philosophy, the consonance of faith and reason, and the objectivity of ethics. The Church has welcomed the search for arguments for the existence of God,[12] and has tried to resolve the apparent incompatibilities of faith and reason, such as conflicts between science

---

[9] Nelson, *Sweet Mothers, Sweet Maids*, p. 130; a serious answer to a similar question in T. Muldoon, 'Christ's free will and the Father's command', *ACR* 23 (1946): pp. 169–85; also on the Cathechism as intellectual training, R. McLaughlin, 'Humanity', in *On Being Human*, ed. V. Nelson (Melbourne, 1990), pp. 127–140, at p. 127.

[10] J. Arnold, *Mother Superior Woman Inferior* (Melbourne, 1985), p. 101, cf. pp. 143–4.

[11] G. Greer in *There's Something About a Convent Girl*, ed. J. Bennett & R. Forgan (London, 1991), pp. 88, 92; also in C. Packer, *No Return Ticket* (Sydney, 1984), p. 88.

[12] Arguments for the existence of God in the apologetic style in L. Rumble, *Radio Replies in Defence of Religion* (Sydney, 1936), ch. 1; L. Rumble, *Questions People Ask About the Catholic Church* (Kensington, 1972), ch. 1; L. Dalton, *Can We Prove There Is A God?* (Kensington, 1939); P.J. Ryan, *The Existence of God: The Argument from Design*, (Kensington, 1950); analysis in T.A. Johnston, 'A note on Kant's criticism of the arguments for the existence of God', *AJP* 21 (1943): pp. 10–16; C. Roberts, 'St Thomas's world and his "ways"', *ACR* 27 (1950): pp. 311–6; P.A. Hutchings, 'Necessary being', *AJP* 35 (1957): pp. 201–6; for contrary views see G. Stuart Watts, 'The Thomist proofs of theism', *AJP* 35 (1957): pp. 30–46; C.B. Martin, *Religious Belief* (Ithaca, N.Y., 1959), ch. 9 (Thomist criticism of which in J.M. Finnis, 'Theology and criticism', *On Dit* 19/9/1961, pp. 5–8); M. Scriven, *Primary Philosophy* (New York. 1966), ch. 4; G.C. Nerlich, 'Popular arguments for the existence of God', in *Encyclopedia of Philosophy*, ed. P. Edwards (New York, 1967), vol. 6 pp. 407–11; A. Olding, *Modern Biology and Natural Theology* (London, 1991); G. Oppy, *Ontological Arguments and Belief in God* (Cambridge, 1995); A. Witherall, *The Problem of Existence* (Aldershot, 2002).

and religion, and the problem of evil. It has also been committed to natural law ethics. The reason murder is wrong, on this view, is neither an arbitrary command of God (or of society, or of our genes), nor a free-floating rule, nor some fact about the greatest happiness of the greatest number, nor its failure to be 'free and enterprising' in John Anderson's sense, but the intrinsic worth of persons, which makes their destruction wrong.

> Ultimately, then, the morality of human acts is not to be explained by the civil legislation, public opinion and tradition, nor the authority of great men, nor mere utility, nor by gradual evolution from brute beginnings, nor their relation to the production of the super-man, but by their conformity to the law of God, founded in the nature and essential relationships of things, and known by reason. On the other hand, the morality or immorality of our acts does not depend wholly on God's will. In other words, a thing is not always bad because God forbids it; God forbids it because it is bad.[13]

The two themes themselves stem from a more basic doctrine, also mentioned by Santamaria. Thomas Aquinas inherited from Aristotle an unusually optimistic view of reason's ability to know important truths. While sense knowledge may be subject to manifold errors, the human mind, it was believed, has an ability to understand with certainty important matters of principle, like mathematics, philosophy and ethics. It is this capacity to understand objective general facts about the world that grounds both our reasoning about God and our ethical conscience.

While these positions have been part of Catholic tradition at all times, the Church went further in the period of about ninety years from 1880. It officially adopted a very particular philosophy, the scholasticism of Aquinas, taught it to all seminarians and anyone else who would listen, and based school education on it as far as possible. There had been very little attention to Aquinas or other medieval

---

[13] P.J. Ryan, 'The fundamental tenets of scholasticism', *Catholic Press* 17/5/1934, p. 12 & 7/6/1934, p. 6; cf. H.B. Loughnan, 'Scholasticism versus realism in ethics', *AJPP* 11 (1933): pp. 141–53; other introductions to scholastic philosophy: T.V. Fleming, *Foundations of Philosophy* (Sydney, 1949) (on Loughnan and Fleming, D. Strong, *Australian Dictionary of Jesuit Biography* (Sydney, 1999), pp. 107–8, 198–9); a more popular introduction: E. Gryst, *Talk Sense!: A Pilgramage Through Philosophy* (New York, 1961); M.R. Leavey, 'The relevance of St Thomas Aquinas for Australian education', *Melbourne Studies in Education* 1963, pp. 83–200, at pp. 131–93; briefly in R.A. Naulty, 'The philosophy of Aquinas', *Colloquium* 28 (1996): pp. 53–63; G. Oppy, 'On the lack of true philosophic spirit in Aquinas', *Philosophy* 76 (2001): pp. 615–24; H. Ramsay, 'Conscience: Aquinas — with a hint of Aristotle', *Sophia* 40 (2) (2001): pp. 15–29.

thinkers earlier in the nineteenth century. When the first Catholic Bishop and Archbishop of Sydney, John Bede Polding, taught metaphysics before coming to Australia, it was Scottish 'commonsense' realism that formed its basis, Aquinas being then little known north of the Alps.[14] But in the obscure recesses of the Vatican, changes were under way.[15] One of the earliest enthusiasts for the new order was Roger Bede Vaughan, author of the first biography of Aquinas in English and later second Archbishop of Sydney and leader in the fight against secular education.[16] Sydney did not get a philosopher Archbishop again, though it came close in 1940, when the Sheehan whose *Apologetics* so impressed the young Santamaria and Keneally almost succeeded to the see. He had been appointed Coadjutor Archbishop with right of succession some twenty years earlier, but the survival of the incumbent Archbishop to the age of 90 prevented realisation of his right.[17] Much the same happened in Melbourne, where the scholastic philosopher Justin Simonds[18] was Coadjutor to Daniel Mannix until the latter's death at 99.

[14] W.B. Ullathorne, *From Cabin-Boy to Archbishop: The Autobiography of Archbishop Ullathorne* (London, 1941), pp. 38, 41; T. Suttor, 'Polding's intellectual formation, *ACR* 54 (1977): pp. 360–70; on the philosophy degree of the first bishop of Brisbane, see G. Roberts, 'James Quinn's Roman background', *ACR* 37 (1960): pp. 11–16.

[15] Brief accounts in E.J. Howley, 'Neo-scholasticism', *ACR* 19 (1913): pp. 403–9; N.M McNally, 'Scholasticism', *Austral Light* 13 (1912): pp. 775–84.

[16] J.T. Donovan, *The Most Reverend Roger Bede Vaughan* (Sydney, 1883), pp. 24–6, 35–41; R.B. Vaughan, *The Life and Labours of Saint Thomas of Aquin* (2 vols, London, 1871–2); also R.B. Vaughan, *Science and Religion: Lectures on the Reasonableness of Christianity and the Shallowness of Unbelief* (Baltimore, 1879); *Arguments for Christianity Delivered in St Mary's Pro-Cathedral* (Sydney, 1879); Address at St John's College, Sydney University, 1878, in R.B. Vaughan, *Occasional Addresses Delivered in New South Wales* (Sydney, 1881), pp. 38–44; G. Haines, 'The Catholic mind of Roger Bede Vaughan', *Tjurunga* 25 (1983): pp. 133–46; A.E. Cahill, 'Archbishop Vaughan and St John's College', *Journal of the Australian Catholic Historical Society* 14 (1992): pp. 36–47; 'Philosophy lectures delivered by Archbishop Vaughan, St John's College, Sydney University', student notes (Fisher Library, Sydney University, Rare Book Library uncatalogued mss, single ms. no. 139.)

[17] G. Byrnes, 'Archbishop Sheehan — a biographical sketch', *Journal of the Australian Catholic Historical Society* 14 (1992): pp. 24–35; M. Sheehan, *Apologetics and Catholic Doctrine* (Dublin, 1926, 4th ed, Philadelphia, 1951; 6th ed, ed. P.M. Joseph, London, 2001), (review in *ACR* 7 (1930): pp. 272–5); M. Sheehan, *The Origin of Life: The Case For and Against Evolution* (Dublin, 1952).

[18] M. Vodola, *Simonds: A Rewarding Life* (Melbourne, 1997), pp. 8–16; *ADB* vol. 16 pp. 243–4; M. Vaughan, 'The philosopher archbishop of Melbourne', *Bulletin* 30/11/1963, pp. 28–31; J.D. Simonds, 'Laughter',

The advantage of running a Church through a centralised bureaucracy is that when change comes, it comes quickly; what was forbidden yesterday is permitted today and may be compulsory tomorrow. An 1879 encyclical made St Thomas Aquinas philosopher By Appointment to the Catholic Church, and study of his philosophy was instituted in seminaries everywhere. That applied even in distant Australia, and especially to Manly seminary, Australia's largest. The seminary continued to teach long courses in philosophy to all its students, though the production of genuine enthusiasts for the subject was probably low.[19] The seminary's official journal records formal debates in Latin in 1923 and 1924 on such topics as 'That God knows himself and knows all other things through himself' and 'There exists in man an intellective faculty which is inorganic and immaterial.'[20] An effort was certainly being made.

The difficulty for seminary philosophy perhaps lay not so much in its content as in its being compulsory. Philosophy, in Latin, for people whose interests lay primarily in getting to parish work as soon as possible, was an uphill task;[21] philosophy is not an ideal choice as a compulsory subject in any circumstances. The student's sensation of an incoherent jumble of terms is well caught in the recollections of Gerard Windsor, a Jesuit seminarian in the 1960s, one with a mind more literary than philosophical:

> I heard a confident, unprepared burble about Ethics or a detached, alienated display of Metaphysical Psychology. Principles and tags and maxims and terms bobbed past. None of them seemed to possess or be possessed of any urgency. They floated on, in a rolling, half exposed way, doing the circuit of some river of tradition where every seminarian, as far back and as far forward as imagination reached, paddled fitfully and then stepped

ACR 8 (1931): pp. 289–96; 'Evolution and theology', *ACR* 10 (1933): pp. 12–19; 'Free will and modern psychology', *ACR* 10 (1933): pp. 289–93; 'Einstein and the Prima Via', *ACR* 11 (1934): pp. 11–16; 'Maurice de Wulf', *ACR* 11 (1934): pp. 353–6; 'A new theological series', *ACR* 36 (1959): pp. 78–81; another Louvain philosophy graduate in K. Coen, *Monsignor John Leonard and the Catholic Youth Organisation* (Strathfield, 2000), pp. 19, 31–2.
[19] F.P. Kissane, 'A plea for philosophy', *Manly* 5 (2) (1936): pp. 73–8; F.P. Kissane, 'St. Thomas Aquinas and Aristotle', *Manly* 6 (1) (1939): pp. 53–7.
[20] *Manly* 2 (2) (1923): p. 192 and 2 (3) (1924): pp. 266–7; content of Melbourne seminary philosophy c. 1960 described in V. Noone, 'Post-war Catholic intellectual life: A view from a seminary', *Footprints* 16 (1) (June 1999): pp. 2–28.
[21] J. Hill, 'Philosophy and the priesthood', *Metaphilosophy* 10 (1979): pp. 215–26; also J. Rheinberger, 'The teaching of ethics in seminaries', *ACR* 47 (1970): pp. 242–5; H. Ramsay, 'Philosophy, teaching and the academic vocation', *ACR* 78 (2001): pp. 131–40.

out. The mind was forever being dipped in the magical stockpot of the Church's Styx.[22]

The scholastic industry in seminaries had virtually no impact on Australia's universities. There were a few Catholics among the university philosophy staff, but they were not of a scholastic orientation. The only official post in scholastic philosophy at a university was created at the University of Queensland in 1953, when the Archbishop leaned on the University Senate.[23] The appointee, Father Durell, was not welcomed with open arms by the philosophy department, and experienced difficulty in having credit given to his courses.[24] There was a scholastic philosopher briefly appointed at Sydney University in the same period — accidentally, according to rumour, as he confused everyone by knowing about modern symbolic logic as well as scholastic philosophy.[25]

As with any live intellectual movement, scholasticism was subject to a number of schisms, feuds and long-drawn-out wars between opposing camps. Like the Marxists of the same era, the scholastics naturally arranged themselves on a continuum from 'left' to 'right'.[26] The 'left' included such figures as Bernard Lonergan, who sought some kind of *rapprochement* with modern thought, by which they under-

---

[22] G. Windsor, *Heaven Where the Bachelors Sit* (St Lucia, 1996), p. 117; similar in C. Geraghty, *Cassocks in the Wilderness* (Melbourne, 2001), pp. 102–5, 110–5; C. Geraghty, *The Priest Factory* (Melbourne, 2003), pp. 37-42; J. Hanrahan, *From Eternity to Here* (Melbourne, 2002), pp. 69, 139–40, 173–4; G. Dening, *Performances* (Melbourne, 1996), pp. 17–19; I. Guthridge, *Give Me a Child When He Is Young* (Melbourne, 1987), pp. 47–66, 76–80; on Jesuit philosophy teaching, see the articles in *Australian Dictionary of Jesuit Biography* on Daniel, Egan, Fleming, Flynn, Fynn, Gleeson, Gryst, Hehir, Keane, Loughnan, McEntegart, McEvoy, McInerney, Murphy, O'Brien, O'Neill and Stormon.

[23] T.P. Boland, *James Duhig* (St Lucia, 1986), p. 345; T. Truman, *Catholic Action and Politics* (Melbourne, 1960), p. 61.

[24] 'University course in scholastic philosophy', with complaint by Durell to Duhig, c. 1959; I am grateful to T.P. Boland for providing a copy.

[25] 'New philosophy lecturer on university standards', *Honi Soit* 23 (14) (5/7/1951), p. 3; *One Hundred Years of the Faculty of Arts* (Sydney, 1952), p. 31; J.J. Wellmuth, 'Philosophy and order in logic', *Proceedings of the Catholic Philosophical Association* 17 (1941): pp. 12–17; J.J. Wellmuth, 'Some comments on the nature of mathematical logic', *New Scholasticism* 16 (1942): 9–15; summary of his thesis in *Dissertation Abstracts* vol. 3 no. 2 (1941), pp. 72–3; also J.J. Wellmuth, *The Nature and Origins of Scientism* (Milwaukee, 1944).

[26] Overseas background in G.A. McCool, *From Unity to Pluralism: The Evolution of Modern Thomism* (New York, 1989); H.J. John, *The Thomist Spectrum* (New York, 1966).

stood mainly post-Kantian continental philosophy. While Lonergan was studied in Jesuit circles, this stream of scholasticism has not been strongly represented in Australia.[27] There have been few followers of the 'Trotskyist' Scotist, Ockhamist and Suarezian splinter groups that occasionally appeared in Europe.[28] The scholastic 'centre' was represented by two French laymen, Jacques Maritain and Etienne Gilson. While Maritain was part of the general European Catholic thought that inspired the Campion Society in Melbourne,[29] and Gilson was also widely read in the English-speaking world, Australian scholasticism has been almost exclusively of the 'right'. The far right was strongest among ecclesiastics, especially those at the Gregorian and Angelicum universities in Rome. Its dominant figure was the Genghis Khan, so to speak, of the Thomist spectrum, Réginald Garrigou-Lagrange, professor of theology and philosophy at the Angelicum University in Rome from 1909 to 1960. Late in life, Garrigou-Lagrange supervised the doctoral thesis of Karol Wojtyla, later Pope John Paul II and the world's most famous philosopher (even if not most famous *qua* philosopher). The isolationism to which ecclesiastical institutions are prone made this an inward-looking brand of Thomism, which regarded virtually all philosophical thought since 1600 as a mistake and saw even the scholastic 'left' as sadly deluded semi-Kantian deviationists. It was this milieu that produced Sydney's

[27] But see W. Ryan, 'The philosophy of Aquinas', *AJPP* 2 (1924): pp. 272–82; 'McEvoy, Patrick', in *Australian Dictionary of Jesuit Biography*, pp. 220–2; on Lonergan, *Lonergan and You: Riverview Reflections 1985* (Pymble, 1987); *Australian Lonergan Workshop*, ed. W.J. Danaher (Lanham, 1993); W.J. Danaher, *Insight in Chemistry* (Lanham, 1988); Windsor, *Heaven Where the Bachelors Sit*, p. 116; Dening, *Performances*, pp. 22–3.

[28] E.J. Stormon, 'Scotus redivivus', *ACR* 19 (1942): pp. 24–37; F.A.R. Misell, 'Francis Suarez', *Newman* (Newman College, Melbourne) 1943, pp. 38–41; complaints of Ockhamist persecution of Thomists in D.D. Smith, 'A report on philosophical teaching given at St Paschal's Franciscan College, Box Hill, Melbourne, Australia, in the year 1947', typescript (copy in Ryan Archives, St Paul's Seminary, Kensington); the Ockhamist's ideas in S. Day, *Intuitive Cognition: A Key to the Significance of the Later Scholastics* (St Bonaventure, NY, 1947); cf. J. Fox, 'Truthmaker', *AJP* 65 (1987): pp. 188–207.

[29] Santamaria, *Santamaria*, p. 11; C.H. Jory, *The Campion Society and Catholic Social Militancy in Australia 1929–1939* (Sydney, 1986), p. 33; meeting of Kevin Kelly and Maritain, with comments on Maritain's influence in Australia in the 1930s in K.T. Kelly to M. McInerney, 26/1/58, comments in A. Calwell to G. Heffey, 20/6/1958 (in possession of Kelly family), also B. Duncan, *Crusade or Conspiracy?* (Sydney, 2001), pp. 40–4, 385; for Brisbane see G. Harwood, *Blessed City* (Sydney, 1990), pp. 152, 193, 205, 241, 244, 246, 252.

most remarkable scholastic philosophers, two priests who, in different ways, brought their philosophy out of the seminary and into the 'world'. They were Dr P.J. ('Paddy') Ryan of Kensington, and Dr Austin Woodbury of the Aquinas Academy.

In Sydney in the 1930s and 1940s, in contrast to the vigorous Catholic intellectual life in Melbourne, Catholic philosophy, apologetics and controversy was almost a one-man show. The man was Father Paddy Ryan. If it was a question of attacking Communists, or replying to objections on radio, or debating atheist philosophers, or setting up Catholic adult education, or writing a pamphlet to prove the existence of God, one contacted the Sacred Heart fathers at Kensington and got Father Ryan on the job. Born near Wodonga in 1904, he had studied at the Gregorian University in Rome, earning in 1929 doctorates in theology and philosophy with the highest honours.[30] He taught philosophy, of a strictly scholastic orientation, at the Kensington seminary thereafter.

His ability as a controversialist was first widely recognised in a debate with John Anderson at Sydney University in 1936.[31] Anderson and Ryan met again in 1939, in a symposium with two biologists on 'The origin of life'. The largest hall in the University was packed with 500 people; others were turned away. Ryan defended one of the most controversial assertions of mid-century scholasticism, that the evolution of life from the non-living is impossible, whether now or in the distant past, for purely philosophical reasons.[32] Though Catholic

---

[30] P. Ryan, *De via morali quam ad Deum cognoscendum proposuit Eduardus le Roy*, thesis, 1932; similar in 'God in contemporary non-Catholic philosophy', typescript, 1937; a fuller account of Ryan in J. Franklin, 'Catholic thought and Catholic Action: Dr Paddy Ryan MSC and the Red Peril', *Journal of the Australian Catholic Historical Society* 17 (1996): pp. 44–55; summary in *ADB*, vol 16, pp. 156–8; also Duncan, *Crusade or Conspiracy?*, pp. 60, 67–9, 180–2, 209–11, 240–1; A. Caruana, *Monastery on the Hill: A History of the Sacred Heart Monastery, Kensington, 1897–1997* (Sydney, 2000), pp. 226–31.

[31] O.U. Vonwiller, J. Anderson & P.J. Ryan, 'Symposium on science, philosophy and Christianity', *Science Journal* (Sydney University), Michaelmas 1936: pp. 24–36.

[32] 'Symposium on "The Origin of Life"', *Catholic Press* 20/7/1939, p. 27; *Catholic Freeman's Journal* 20/7/1939, p. 30; D. Horne, *The Education of Young Donald* (2nd ed, Ringwood, 1988), pp. 179–80; similar earlier in S. Bourke [i.e. Burke], 'The Darwinian theory', *ACR* 6 (1900): pp. 173–89; on the author's philosophy teaching at Manly, K.T. Livingston, *The Emergence of an Australian Catholic Priesthood, 1835–1915* (Sydney, 1977) pp. 198–200; F. Mecham, *'John O'Brien' and the Boree Log* (Sydney, 1981), p. 49.

philosophy generally gave up the fight against evolution by the 1940s,[33] Ryan did not.

There is a sense of the cut and thrust of live argument in the report of a debate Ryan held, also in 1939 at Sydney University, on freewill. His opponent was A.G. Hammer, later Professor of Psychology at the University of New South Wales. An audience of 500 was again estimated. Hammer claimed that 'all our decisions are as necessary as the explosion of a bomb', and asserted that 'we can predict all human acts with absolute certainty, granted a sufficient knowledge of a man's heredity, environment, and other factors extrinsic to the will.' Ryan took his stand on the 'clear and unmistakable testimony of consciousness that it is very often in his power to choose freely amongst various actions which he has motives to perform.' He was reported, in perhaps a moment of overkill, as having 'proceeded to prove that the testimony of consciousness is absolutely reliable'. Some interesting exchanges during the discussion were reported, which give some sense of Ryan's ability to argue on his feet — as well as the style of vigorous trading of certainties that once played such a part in the tradition of public debate:

> Mr O'Neill, an ardent determinist: Dr Ryan assumes the 'self' or 'ego' to be an abiding reality. But as a mere succession of states, the 'ego' could not be self-determining.

> Dr Ryan: My appeal is to facts of experience. We have the direct and immediate experience of the 'self' as an abiding reality and the subject of successive states quite distinct from it. The facts cannot be explained away by futile indulgence in metaphysical speculations concerning the nature of the 'ego'.

> Mr O'Neill: Your proof from the validity of consciousness means that all illusions are impossible. Yet there are illusions.

> Dr Ryan: How do you know that there are any illusions except from your consciousness of them?

The chairman of the debate, John Passmore, perhaps less well-informed about the history of philosophy than he was later to become, then intervened with a historical point. 'Relinquishing his duties as chairman', he accused Ryan of reviving Descartes' philosophy, and 'attacked the notion of a self-determining principle, declaring it to be

---

[33] F.A. Mecham, 'Evolution and man', *ACR* 26 (1949): pp. 19–28, 262–8; J. Burnheim, 'Biology versus Catholic philosophy: A new approach', *ACR* 27 (1950): pp. 267–71; also B. Smith, *The Boy Adeodatus* (2nd ed, Melbourne, 1990), p. 206; an earlier pro-evolutionary article in J. Flynn, 'On organic evolution', *ACR* 6 (1900): pp. 342–88.

absurd.' Ryan pointed out that Descartes's philosophy was not the same as Aristotelico–Thomistic philosophy.

Mr Passmore: The only person other than Descartes who adopted Dr Ryan's line of approach was St Augustine, a man not regarded as a philosopher by anyone outside a certain religious organisation.

Dr Ryan: Not one word of that is correct.[34]

Ryan's interest in Sydney University continued in the ensuing years. His campaign against Andersonians at the associated Sydney Teachers College seems to have been responsible for two of them being sent off to the classroom 'to gain more teaching experience.'[35] In one of his radio broadcasts, he claimed:

I personally have argued for hours with graduates of Sydney University in a futile endeavour to convince them of their own existence, — so deeply had their very reason been undermined by scepticism and sophistry …

In defending self-evident truths like one's own existence and personality, or easily demonstrable truths like the existence of God, we are merely defending the foundations without which all talk of justice and injustice is so much meaningless twaddle.[36]

[34] *Catholic Freeman's Journal* 27/5/1939, p. 20; another scholastic treatment in H.B. Loughnan, 'Determinism and responsibility', *AJPP* 14 (1936): pp. 216–28; earlier work in 'Philalethes' [S.O. Lovell], *Free Will and Determinism* (Hobart, 1893); later in R.L. Franklin, *Freewill and Determinism* (London, 1968); P. O'Sullivan, *Intention, Motives and Human Action: An Argument for Free Will* (St Lucia, 1977); R. Young, *Freedom, Responsibility and God* (London, 1975); R. Young, 'The implications of determinism', in *A Companion to Ethics*, ed. P. Singer (Oxford, 1991), pp. 534–42; W.R. Boyce Gibson, 'Freedom and evil', *AJPP* 3 (1925): pp. 91–8; P. Herbst, 'Freedom and prediction', *Mind* 66 (1957): pp. 1–27; P. Edwards, 'Hard and soft determinism', in S. Hook, ed, *Determinism and Freedom in the Age of Science* (New York 1958), pp. 104–13; P. Forrest, 'Backwards causation in defence of free will', *Mind* 94 (1985): pp. 210–7; see S. Grave, *A History of Philosophy in Australia* (St Lucia, 1984), pp. 134–8.
[35] A. Barcan, *Radical Students: The Old Left at Sydney University* (Melbourne, 2002), p. 48; reports on A.G. Hammer, W.H.C. Eddy and Dr Woodward, in Ryan archives, St Paul's Seminary, Kensington, section Articles, folder Teachers' College Reports, with letter of M.D. Forrest MSC to NSW Director of Education, 14/12/1939; Dr Rumble, Question Box, *Catholic Freeman's Journal* 19/10/1939, p. 10; also 2/11/1939, p. 6; 16/11/1939, p. 6; 23/11/1939, p. 6; 30/11/1939, p. 6; 7/12/1939, p. 6; 14/12/1939, p. 12; 21/12/1939, p. 6.
[36] P. Ryan, Question Box, *Catholic Freeman's Journal* 3/7/1941, p. 8; his university debates of the War years in *Honi Soit* 15 (12) (22/4/1943), p. 1; also *Honi Soit* 15 (24) (26/8/1943), p. 1; reply by Doug Everingham, later

Donald Horne had the opportunity to tangle personally with Ryan in 1941, when, as editor of the student newspaper *Honi Soit*, he was a representative at a 'Youth Parliament' which saw a clash between Stalinists and Catholics. Horne recalled, 'In the evening I drank beer with some of the Stalinists, infuriated by the unscrupulous red-herring tactics of the clerical fascists, who were not concerned with the constructive work of the Youth Parliament but with disrupting it by obscurantist Gestapo methods ... Whenever the name "Catholic Action" was mentioned I would fall quiet with hate.'[37] The Catholic resolution which particularly disturbed the 'Parliament' was one affirming 'its complete adherence to the principles of democracy; its repudiation of the Totalitarian ideologies whether Nazi, Fascist or Communist.' As Ryan said, it was hard to see why any genuinely democratic Australian would not be in favour of such a motherhood resolution, so it was fair to ask why the 'Youth Parliament' rejected it. 'Characteristic in this respect', Ryan added, 'is the Mr D.R. Horne, published in "Honi Soit" issue of June 27, 1941. Mr Horne writes with deep emotion — with more heat than light. I gather from the references to the "unbalanced priest" who speaks over Radio 2SM, "the vaporisings of Dr Ryan", the "Catholic papers" and sundry threats of Blitzkriegs to come, that he is making some sort of attack on me.'[38]

Ryan was employed by the Church in a huge range of activities during the thirty years from about 1932 to 1962. At various times in the late 1930s, during the hierarchy's periodic wringings of hands over the loss of young Catholics after they left school, lecture courses on apologetics and social theory were instituted, with Ryan as director and provider of study material.[39] After the War, he headed a 'Workers' School of Social Reconstruction'.[40] In 1954, the problem was as unsolved as ever ('There is practically no such thing in Australia as the Catholic mind', according to Ryan[41]) and an Adult Educa-

minister of health in the Whitlam government, in *Honi Soit* 15 (26) (30/9/1943), p. 3.

[37] Horne, *Education*, pp. 262–4.

[38] 'The cat got out', in Dr Ryan's Question Box, *Catholic Freeman's Journal* 10/7/1941, p. 8; Horne letter in *Honi Soit* 13 (14) (27/6/1941), p. 2.

[39] 'Catholic Action: Educational lectures inaugurated', *Catholic Press* 19/3/1936, p. 10; C. Jory, *Campion Society*, p. 105; B.F. Duncan, *From Ghetto to Crusade: A Study of the Social and Political Thought of Catholic Opinion-Makers in Sydney During the 1930s* (PhD thesis, Dept of Government, Sydney University, 1987), ch. 10.

[40] *Catholic Weekly* 5/9/1946, p. 3; P.J. Ryan, 'Vested interests challenged', *Social Survey* 1 (2) (Oct 1951): pp. 2–5.

[41] Quoted in N. Turner, *Catholics in Australia: A Social History*, (Melbourne, 1992) vol. II p. 111; P.J. Ryan, 'The Catholic mind: As it is in Australia

tion Institute (Director, Paddy Ryan) was set up in the city to offer courses in apologetics, theology and public speaking. Another outlet for his arguments was provided by radio; in a single broadcast of 1941 he dealt with the permissibility of moderate consumption of alcohol, the idiocy of chain letters ('shows the depth of absurdity to which people can fall when they lack genuine religion') and the responsibility of H.G. Wells for the War ('If people teach, as Mr Wells does teach, that the Ten Commandments are so much junk, they have no right to complain if Hitler presents them with a working model of their own philosophy.')[42]

It was the Red Peril, however, that came to take up most of Ryan's energy. While many Australians took a favourable view of the USSR at the time when Stalin was on the same side during the war, and membership of the Communist Party of Australia reached a peak in 1944, Catholic circles remained solidly hostile. In 1943, Ryan answered one of the most effective leftist writings of the day, *The Socialist Sixth of the World* by the 'Red Dean' of Canterbury, Hewlett Johnson. This was the book which had converted to Communism the young Frances Bernie, hitherto active in Catholic youth organisations; one result was her leaking of papers from Dr Evatt's office to the Communist Party, and eventually her appearance before the Petrov Royal Commission.[43] Ryan's answer, concentrating on the lack of freedom of religion in Russia, sold some 45,000 copies.[44] There was a reply by the indefatigable Communist General Secretary, Lance Sharkey, at this time also busy with 'exposing' Anderson's Trotskyism. Sharkey says that Lenin is as much in favour of a moral way of life as Father Ryan. But the fact that employers and their press laud the strikebreaker as a hero, while the workers regard him as a scab ('the most immoral creature on earth') 'refutes Father Ryan's stand-

today', *The Newman* (Newman Catholic Graduates Association) 1 (2) (June 1955): pp. 5–7.

[42] *The Southern Cross* 2/5/1941, p. 5; 'Rev Dr. Ryan's Question Box' appeared weekly in the *Catholic Freeman's Journal* from 7/3/1940 to 18/12/1941; on the radio work of Ryan's colleague Dr Rumble, see E. Campion, *Australian Catholics* (Ringwood, 1987), pp. 134–6; *Observer* 17/9/1960, pp. 6–8; *SMH* 15/11/1975, p. 14; biography in *Who is Father Rumble?* (pamphlet, St Paul, Minnesota, n.d.); *ADB* vol. 16 pp. 150–1.

[43] *Royal Commission on Espionage: Transcript of Proceedings* (Canberra, 1955), vol. 3 p. 1329; the Dean's visit to Sydney University in *Honi Soit* 27/4/1950.

[44] P.J. Ryan, *Dean Hewlett Johnson's Socialist Sixth: A Commentary*, (Sydney, 1943); similar in anon, *A Catechism of Communism for Australian Youth* (Melbourne, 1936); L. Dalton, *Red Menace in Australia* (Melbourne, 1937); L. Dalton, *Notes on Communism* (Kensington, 1945); F.J. Sheed, *Communism and Man* (London, 1938); Campion, *Australian Catholics*, p. 133.

point that there is a general, fixed system of morals that applies to all conceivable conditions.'[45]

Ryan's finest hour came with a public debate at the Rushcutters Bay Stadium on September 23, 1948, on the topic 'That Communism is in the best interests of the Australian people.' His opponent was Edgar Ross, a member of the central committee of the Party. Despite rain, 30,000 turned up, clogging the trams. Ross complains in his memoirs that the front rows were flooded with priests and nuns, though the other side also did their best, rounding up members of the Eureka Youth League and the New Housewives Association.[46]

Ross opened with a quotation from Pope Leo XIII on the need to find a remedy for the misery and wretchedness of the working class. He went on to condemn monopoly capitalism, imperialism, atomic bombs, American bases. 'Against this, the Soviet Union stood strong, secure, stable and prosperous (applause and boos).' 'The family was the bulwark of Soviet society (Laughter). In no country of the world were human rights so explicitly acknowledged. The Catholic Church in Russia enjoyed complete freedom of activity. (Dr Ryan scribbles furiously and waves a gently protesting hand to shush the audience).'

Ryan then spoke. He alleged Communism was based on a degraded philosophy of life, that its program necessarily involved ruthless and unlimited dictatorship, and that the Australian Party had no loyalty to God or country, but only to Moscow. 'The audience broke out into coughing as Dr Ryan went measuredly into the influence of the philosopher Hegel on the thought of Karl Marx', but perked up when he moved on to the possibility of getting a divorce in Russia simply by sending a card through the post to the registrar. Even more shockingly, he alleged that workers in Russia were forbidden to strike.

Ross, in reply, 'claimed that Dr Ryan had given a lot of generalisations on philosophy, a few lies about the Soviet, but nothing about the practical tasks confronting the worker in the real situation today.' Catholic preaching about the evils of society was like trying to cure cancer with an Aspro. To Ryan's claim that all the Catholic bishops in Russia were dead, in exile or missing, Ross replied that the

---

[45] L.L. Sharkey, *Reply to Father Ryan* (1943), summarised in *The Sharkey Writings*, ed. L.H. Gould (Sydney, 1974?), pp. 159–62; also L.L. Sharkey, 'Marxism and morals: Dr. Ryan answered', *Tribune* 2/10/1948, p. 7; 'official' Communist view on morality in V. Kolbanoski, *Communist Morality*, with foreword by L.H. Gould (Sydney, 1947); Ryan's reply in the pamphlet, *Said Comrade Sharkey* (Sydney, 1944).

[46] E. Ross, *Of Storm and Struggle* (Sydney, 1982), p. 113; *News Weekly* 15/9/1948, reported in ASIO file on Catholic Action, Australian Archives series A6122/30 item 1222.

churches were open 'in thousands' in Russia. 'To the laughter he shouted, "Do you think I would pull the wool over your eyes?" One solitary shrill feminine voice shouted: "Yes".' Ryan asked what reliance could be placed on Ross's word, when 'according to Lenin, Communist morality was wholly subordinated to the class struggle of the proletariat.' 'In saying that the Catholic Church supported Fascism, Mr Ross was (again the quiet unimpassioned voice) a liar. The Catholic Church was the deadliest enemy of Fascism, and of Red Fascism, too (Wild applause).'[47]

Ryan's wish to spend some of his time on such an abstruse matter as Hegel's influence on Marx is a perfect example of what Frank Knopfelmacher was later to call the 'seminarian-deductive' attitude to political doctrines. It is characterised, according to Knopfelmacher, by a 'naive' kind of intellectualism, which is pre-Freudian and pre-Marxist in believing in the 'authentic force and causal efficacy of intellectual convictions.'[48] Ryan certainly did believe that, though whether it is naive is arguable. In any case, Australia might well be grateful for the 'intellectualism' that meant that the Cold War was fought here, not with the widespread killings of many other countries, but by nothing much worse than Dr Ryan lecturing the Communist housewives of New South Wales on Hegel.

Ryan continued to speak against Communism to large audiences, notably at the time of the coalminers' strike and during the campaign for Menzies' anti-Communism referendum of 1951.[49] These speeches, and Ryan's study materials, are the prototypes of the thousands of 'Evils of Communism' speeches in emotion-charged church halls that are such a well-remembered element of Catholic myth. He was the founder in Sydney of the 'Movement' that ran cells of anti-Communists in the unions. Unlike B.A. Santamaria, who ran the parallel operation in Melbourne, he maintained official contacts with the security services (the forerunners of ASIO).[50]

---

[47] 'Stadium's record crowd hears political debate, with big anti-Communist majority', *SMH* 24/9/1948, pp. 1, 3; 'Huge stadium crowd shows wide interest in Communism', *Tribune* 29/9/1948, p. 8; full text in *Catholic Weekly* 30/9/1948, pp. 1–4, 19–20.

[48] F. Knopfelmacher, *Intellectuals and Politics* (Melbourne, 1968), pp. 76–7.

[49] Listed in Franklin, 'Catholic thought and Catholic action'; Sydney University speeches in *Honi Soit* 14/9/1950, 4/10/1951, 9/10/1952.

[50] Early theory in P.J. Ryan, *An Outline of Catholic Action* (Kensington, 1935); summary in Duncan, *From Ghetto to Crusade*, pp. 158–60; see the regular 'Secretariate of Catholic Action' page in the weekly *Catholic Freeman's Journal*, 1939 to mid-1941; Ryan's founding of the Movement in P. Ormonde, *The Movement* (Melbourne, 1972), p. 3; Santamaria, *Santamaria*, p. 73; G. Williams, *Cardinal Sir Norman Gilroy* (Sydney, 1971), p. 51; G.

Dr P.J. Ryan (centre) at a wedding, September 1948 (St Paul's Seminary, Kensington, Archives)

A significant issue of applied moral philosophy arose in connection with these activities: may one vote at meetings of organisations of which one is not a member? That is, could the Movement stack meetings? This became an issue for students at Sydney University, where the Movement had spectacular success in 1951–2 and controlled all major student organisations;[51] the editorship of *Honi Soit* went to Movement activist Edmund Campion.[52] Students reported that Ryan positively encouraged Arts and Engineering students to vote at Medical students' meetings, and vice versa. The chaplain at Sydney University recalled that 'Dr Ryan had once come back from the Vatican and reported to him and some Movement people that he had consulted some top moral theologians at the Gregorian and Lateran Universities and they had advised that Catholics were morally justified in doing anything that Communists did.'[53] Views such as these, understandable enough in the context of, say, Czechoslovakia,

Henderson, *Mr Santamaria and the Bishops* (Sydney, 1982), p. 26; J. Kane, *Exploding the Myths* (North Ryde, 1989), p. 23; R. Murray, *The Split* (2nd ed, Melbourne, 1972), p. 46; Hanrahan, *From Eternity to Here*, p. 148; security contacts in ASIO file on Catholic Action, as above; D. McKnight, *Australia's Spies and Their Secrets* (Sydney, 1994), pp. 202–3; further in Franklin, 'Catholic thought and Catholic Action'; exposed by Communists in *Tribune* 27/8/1949, p. 3; also 7/9/1949, p. 6.
[51] Barcan, *Radical Students,* pp. 254–63; *Honi Soit* 16/10/1952.
[52] E. Campion, *Rockchoppers* (Melbourne, 1982), pp. 104–7.
[53] Ormonde, *The Movement*, p. 43.

were less acceptable in Australia. Many Catholics were not prepared to lie on demand and left the Movement over such tactics.

Ryan's operation was taken over by the Melbourne Movement, which disagreed with what Santamaria called Ryan's 'cowboys and indians' tactics.[54] There was ill feeling on both sides. Ryan was a key speaker at the meetings in 1956 at which the vast majority of New South Wales Movement men decided to accept the Sydney bishops' policy of staying with the Labor Party instead of joining their Victorian and Queensland colleagues in what later became the Democratic Labor Party.

An earlier student from the same Roman milieu as Ryan was a Marist priest from the Hawkesbury Valley of New South Wales, Dr Austin Woodbury.[55] A student of Garrigou-Lagrange in Rome in the 1920s, he founded the Aquinas Academy in Sydney in 1945[56] and headed it for thirty years. It was primarily an evening school, aimed principally at the laity, and was for long a remarkably successful operation. In 1961, for example, it was running nineteen classes a week, with a total enrolment of some 500.[57] Like his counterpart and rival a few miles away at Sydney University, John Anderson, 'the Doc' was a charismatic classroom teacher. The artist John Ogburn recalls

> Frequently Woodbury would send me to the canvas with his answer and I responded to this as a miner greets the fresh air after working a double shift underground. Through the teaching of these two men [Woodbury and the artist Orban] I had at last found the source of that clear stream of

[54] B.A. Santamaria to author, 7/11/1996.

[55] 'Friend of philosophy', *Catholic Weekly* 15/2/1945, p. 9; *ADB* vol. 16 pp. 580–1; obituary in *SMH* 6/2/1979, p. 4; brief summary of his philosophy in A.M. Woodbury, 'What is metaphysics?', *Catholic Weekly* 14/2/1946, pp. 11, 21; introduction to Academy philosophy in J. Young, *Reasoning Things Out* (booklet, Parramatta, 1975, repr. Fort Worth, 1981).

[56] 'School of philosophy to be opened here in March', *Catholic Weekly* 25/1/1945, p. 1; 1/3/1945, p. 2; 1/3/1945, p. 6; 21/6/1945, p. 1; 27/3/1947, p. 6; courses detailed in *Catholic Weekly* 3/4/1947, p. 2 and 8/5/1947, p. 6; on the Academy's teaching on the philosophy of economics, see H.G. Pearce, *Value, Normal and Morbid: An Exposition of Economic Value* (Sydney, 1948, 2nd ed, Eastwood, 1987); D.G. Boland, *Economics and Justice* (to appear); cf. J.P. Kelly, *Aquinas and Modern Practices of Interest Taking* (Brisbane, 1945); A.J. Walsh, *A Neo-Aristotelian Theory of Social Justice* (Aldershot, 1997); on Thomist economic principles and the Cain government's policies, see M. Simons, 'Hard times for local heroes', *Eureka Street* 1 (2) (Apr. 1991): pp. 13–15.

[57] *The Academician* 2 (5) (June 1961), p. 3; 2 (10) (Nov 1961); further in 'The dream that came true: The story of the Aquinas Academy', *Catholic Weekly* 28/4/1960; 400 normal at the start of most years, J. Ziegler to author, 12/4/1995.

loveliness and beauty, the Being from which or in which all other beings are. I could now start to paint seriously.[58]

The historian and theologian Tim Suttor also writes of the immediate impact of a single evening of Woodbury's lecturing, which freed him from dissatisfaction with modern philosophers and oriented him towards Thomism.[59]

Also like Anderson, Woodbury became after his return to Australia rather isolated from the world scene. Again like Anderson, he never published a book summarising his thought — though there were a few pamphlets and many volumes of lecture notes — and he did not tolerate dissent, discussion or questions. His opinion of Anderson's philosophy was much the same as Anderson's of his, an opinion he expressed freely and often in his lectures. The cold war between the Academy and Anderson's department entered a brief hot phase in 1952, when Woodbury claimed publicly, 'The department of philosophy in the University of Sydney is a cancer at what ought to be the heart of the scholastic life of this city. It is a disgrace to the University of Sydney, and would be a disgrace to any university anywhere. I would warn students, and the parents of students, that a grave risk to their future intellectual and moral life is incurred by students who follow the course of philosophy at the University of Sydney without at the same time taking courses at this academy.' Anderson deigned to reply, at least briefly, describing Woodbury's attack as 'sheer rubbish and propaganda'. 'Dr Woodbury not only knows nothing about philosophy, but he knows nothing about the department of philosophy at the University.'[60] As for debate between the two positions, none was forthcoming.

This skirmish was only a curtain-raiser to the later 'Gough–Kinsella affair', to be described in the next chapter. The Aquinas Academy entered the limelight briefly once more in 1966 at the time of the 'Mother Gorman affair', a confused scuffle over the television appearance of an American nun of 'advanced' views,[61] but generally simply

---

[58] N. Turner, *Catholics in Australia: A Social History* (Melbourne, 1992), vol. II, pp. 286.

[59] T. Suttor, 'Austin Mary Woodbury', *ACR* 55 (1978): pp. 142–50, at pp. 149–50; cf. T. Suttor, introduction to Thomas Aquinas, *Summa Theologiae*, vol. 11 (London, 1970).

[60] *Catholic Weekly* 13/3/1952, p. 1; also 'Atomic age no threat to perennial philosophy', *Catholic Weekly* 13/3/1952, p. 15; reply in *Sun* 9/3/1952, p. 12; Anderson to Ruth Walker, 14/3/1952, in Walker papers, Sydney University Archives, P.158 series 2; a recollection in McLaughlin, 'Humanity', at pp. 128–9.

[61] 'Dr Muldoon and Mother Gorman', *Nation* 10/12/1966, pp. 9–10; Campion, *Rockchoppers*, pp. 172–6.

pursued its teaching role in the background. Attendance waned as Dr Woodbury's health failed in the 1970s. After Woodbury's death in 1979, the Academy was continued for some time by his followers, but then fell to a coup by Jungians, who changed the character of its teaching entirely. The defeated party set up and still maintains a small Centre for Thomistic Studies, which preserves whole and unreconstructed the authentic deposit of ancient days.[62]

One other scholastic philosopher gained some prominence in the fight against the godlessness of university philosophy. Father Farrell, a Dominican and brother of the historian of Catholic Australia, Patrick O'Farrell,[63] took the unusual step of submitting an article to the 'enemy' journal, *Mind*; *Mind* took the even more unusual step of printing it.[64] It was a reply to an article by John Mackie of Sydney University on the problem of evil. It is recognised by most religious philosophers that the problem of evil is the most serious rational objection to religion: how can a good God cause, or even allow, evil in the world he creates? Or at least, how can a good God allow the never-ending tragedies that actually exist in this world: if people have an obligation to prevent evil when they can, why not God?

The problem is a very obvious one. In the only philosophical interlude in Albert Facey's *A Fortunate Life*, he writes, 'Anyone who has taken part in a fierce bayonet charge (and I have), and who has managed to retain his proper sanity, must doubt the truth of the Bible and the power of God, if one exists.'[65] The thought is reasonable, even inevitable. Still, experiences of great evils have been interpreted very differently by those with different philosophical ideas. Mackie posed the problem in its traditional form: how can it be held simultaneously that God is omnipotent, that God is wholly good, and that evil exists? For surely if he were good and had the power to remove the evils, he would do so? Are there then any excuses that can be made on God's behalf? Mackie argued that various excuses offered by believers all amount to implicitly denying one of these three propositions. For example, the idea that evil is due to human will, or that the universe as a whole is better with some evil, or that

---

[62] J. Ziegler, 'A brief history of the CTS'; *Universitas* 3 (1) (1999) (www.cts.org.au/1999/ctshistory.htm); support for Thomism also from Opus Dei in P. Grant, 'Metaphysics', *ACR* 63 (1986): pp. 412–5.

[63] P. O'Farrell, *The Catholic Church and Community in Australia: A History* (Melbourne 1967, rev. ed. 1977); *Vanished Kingdoms* (Kensington, 1990), pp. 99–100, 185–196; occasional writings in *Current Affairs Bulletin* 22 (9) (1958), 30 (6) (1962), 31 (1) (1962).

[64] P.M. Farrell, 'Evil and omnipotence', *Mind* 67 (1958): pp. 399–403; further in 'Freedom and evil', *AJP* 36 (1958): pp. 216–21.

[65] A.B. Facey, *A Fortunate Life* (Fremantle, 1981), p. 317.

evil is necessary as a means to good, he argued to be incompatible with true divine omnipotence, as a truly omnipotent God would be able to remove the evils, but retain the goods.[66]

Father Farrell replied that designing universes is not as easy as Mackie makes it sound. If the universe is not to be extremely simple, the result must be an interconnected whole in which what happens in one part necessarily restricts what can happen in another. The corruption and decay of living things is an evil, for example, but it is simply impossible for God to create corruptible goods like living things, in such a way that they do not corrupt. So omnipotence is compatible with evil because, though it is not obvious to us, eliminating evils while retaining goods is logically impossible. No doubt the abstractness of the treatment may give an impression of lack of feeling in the face of suffering. On the other hand, the problem posed was an abstract one, and the alternative to an abstract treatment is to start speculating on reasons for the existence of particular evils, which is bound to end in farce. Fr Farrell shows himself aware of the pitfalls by mentioning that the point of the existence of 'certain groups of bacteria, e.g.' in the divine plan remains obscure to us. Plainly, whatever necessities there may be connecting the parts of creation, we cannot expect to discern them with any confidence. But it is just the *possibility* of such necessary interconnections that explains why one can consistently believe all three of the propositions: God is omnipotent, God is wholly good, evil (even a great deal of it) exists. There is no better excuse for anything than absolute necessity; nor will anything less do as an answer.

The same line of reasoning had been developed for a more popular audience in Sheehan's *Apologetics*: 'The notion that there are defects in the work of God is due, not to the imperfect character of His design, but to our imperfect understanding of it.' He appears at first to overstep the mark in offering to explain God's design, on such questions as why there are so many useless things in the world. 'if the animals called labyrinthodonts which belong to the early geological ages had been endowed with intelligence, they might have made a strong case against the wisdom of Providence from the lavish waste of fern spores.' Yet, all that vegetable waste has given us our coal. The animals would have judged wrongly 'from their not being able to

---

[66] J.L. Mackie, 'Evil and omnipotence', *Mind* 64 (1955): pp. 200–12, repr. in *The Philosophy of Religion*, ed. B. Mitchell (Oxford, 1971), pp. 92–104; Farrell is unmentioned in Mackie's later *The Miracle of Theism*, but there is a brief mention in J.L. Mackie, 'Theism and utopia', *Philosophy* 37 (1962): pp. 153–8, and a polemical reply in *Prospect* 5 (3) (1962): p. 23.

foresee events of what was to them an incalculably remote future.'[67] The example is bizarre but the point is a fair one: it is the abstract possibility of long-range trade-offs in the design of the universe that is being argued for, rather than the explanation of this or that evil.[68] The same thought on the necessary interconnection of evils was advanced, though in a more political context, by John Anderson: 'It is only in the struggle with evil that goods exist, and the attempt to eliminate evils ... could lead, at its most successful, only to a drab existence which would emphatically be evil.'[69]

In 1961 Farrell took the fight to the public, publishing in the Catholic newspapers an attack on the academic standards of Mackie

[67] Sheehan, *Apologetics and Catholic Doctrine*, pp. 41–2; other arguments on evil and necessity in F. Mora, 'Thank God for evil?', *Philosophy* 58 (1983): pp. 399–401; B. Langtry, 'Can God replace the actual world by a better one?', *Philosophical Papers* 20 (1991): pp. 183–92; E.J. Khamara, 'In defence of omnipotence', *Philosophical Quarterly* 28 (1978): pp. 215–28; E.J. Khamara, 'Mackie's paradox and the free will defence', *Sophia* 34 (1) (1995): pp. 42–8; M. Levine, 'Must God create the best?', *Sophia* 35 (1) (1996): pp. 28–34; J. Franklin, 'Two caricatures, II. Leibniz's best world', *International Journal for Philosophy of Religion* 52 (2002): pp. 45–56.

[68] Other work on the problem of evil: M.B. Ahern, *The Problem of Evil* (London, 1971); H.J. McCloskey, *God and Evil* (The Hague, 1974); J. Cowburn, *Shadows and the Dark* (London, 1979); C. Roberts, 'God and evil', *ACR* 26 (1949): pp. 11–18; G. Schlesinger, *Religion and Scientific Method* (Dordrecht, 1977), Part I; G.N. Schlesinger, *New Perspectives on Old-time Religion* (Oxford, 1988), ch. 2; K. Campbell, 'Patterson Brown on God and evil', *Mind* 74 (1965): pp. 582–4; M. Scriven, *Primary Philosophy* (New York, 1966), pp. 158–64; A. Olding, 'Finite and infinite gods', *Sophia* 6 (1967): pp. 3–7; P. Edwards, 'Difficulties in the idea of God', in *The Idea of God*, ed. E.H. Madden *et al.* (Springfield, Ill, 1968), pp. 43–77; R.J. Pargetter, 'Evil as evidence against the existence of God', *Mind* 85 (1976): pp. 242–5; P. Kelly, *Searching for Truth: A Personal View of Roman Catholicism* (London, 1978), pp. 67–71; C.B. McCullagh, 'Evil and the love of God', *Sophia* 31 (3) (1992): pp. 48–60; B. Langtry, 'God, evil and probability', *Sophia* 28 (1989): pp. 32–40; B. Langtry, 'Some internal theodicies and the objection from alternative goods', *International Journal for the Philosophy of Religion* 34 (1993): pp. 29–39; B. Langtry, 'Eyeballing evil: Some epistemic principles', *Philosophical Papers* 25 (1996): pp. 127–37; M.P. Levine, 'Pantheism, theism and the problem of evil', *International Journal for Philosophy of Religion* 35 (1994): pp. 129–151; J. O'Leary-Hawthorne, 'Non-organic theories of value and pointless evil', *Faith and Philosophy* 9 (1992): pp. 387–91; P. Bilimoria, 'Duhka and kharma: The problem of evil and God's omnipotence', *Sophia* 34 (1) (1995): pp. 92–119; J.J.C. Smart & J.J. Haldane, *Atheism and Theism* (Oxford, 1996), pp. 66–73, 183–5; P. Forrest, *God Without the Supernatural* (Ithaca, N.Y., 1996), ch. 8.

[69] J. Anderson, *Studies in Empirical Philosophy* (Sydney, 1962), p. 338

and certain other university philosophers. Mackie's article, he claimed, was defective in claiming to have refuted all existing attempted solutions to the problem of evil, while ignoring those put forward by Aquinas. He complained further about a later article by another Melbourne University philosopher,[70] which had agreed with Mackie's article but not referred to Farrell's or considered the kind of argument he had put forward. Since university philosophers were attacking Christianity while ignoring its counter-arguments, Farrell concluded, the public ought to complain and Catholic students should avoid philosophy at universities.

The debate dragged on inconclusively for months, with the Catholic philosophers of Melbourne and elsewhere being mostly concerned to draw a *cordon sanitaire* around Farrell and any like-minded Dominican inquisitors.[71] Parents were assured that studying philosophy at respectable universities like Melbourne was no danger to their children's faith. Max Charlesworth, a philosopher in the liberal tradition of Melbourne Catholicism, was goaded into expressing his real opinion of scholastic philosophers: 'If we were to apply Father Farrell's test of philosophical competence to contemporary scholastic philosophers' treatment of modern philosophical positions, we would be forced to declare the majority of them to be flagrantly "incompetent".'[72] Another university Catholic philosopher involved was Selwyn Grave, whose story of conversion to Catholicism appears to provide a counterexample to the theory that no-one is converted by pure argument.[73] Grave had himself written an answer to Mackie.[74] His opinion of the scholastics is evident in his later *History of Philosophy in Australia*, which gives them not so much as a single footnote. No mention was made during the debate of the fact that, except for Fr Durell's tenuous position in

[70] H.J. McCloskey, 'God and evil', *Philosophical Quarterly* 10 (1960): pp. 97–114.
[71] *Advocate* 26/10/1961: p. 18; 2/11: p. 18; 9/11: p. 18; 16/11: p. 18; 23/11: p. 18; 30/11: p. 18; 7/12: p. 18; 21/12: p. 12; 14/12: p. 18; *Catholic Weekly* 12/10/1961: pp. 12–13; 16/11: p. 20; 30/11: p. 13; 21/12: p. 22; 11/1/62: p. 12; *Prospect* 5 (1962): p. 26; J. Kovesi, 'The temptation of absolute truth', *Twentieth Century* 16 (1962): pp. 216–22; R.M. Gascoigne, 'A comment on a controversy', *Twentieth Century* 17 (1962): pp. 17–24; J. Kovesi, 'An answer', pp. 25–41; cf. T. Suttor, 'Australian Catholic culture', *Manna* 4 (1961): pp. 122–36.
[72] M. Charlesworth, 'Academics and Christianity', *Advocate* 30/11/1961: p. 18.
[73] S. Grave, 'A discovery of the Church', in *Treasure Hidden in a Field*, ed. M. Elliott (Melbourne, 1971), pp. 149–58.
[74] S. Grave, 'On evil and omnipotence', *Mind* 65 (1956): pp. 259–62.

Queensland, none of the Catholic philosophers employed in Australian universities were scholastics. The Sydney University philosophers did not join the debate, and there was no substantial discussion of Farrell's actual charges against Mackie.

As Grave's case shows, not all converts to Catholicism have been enthusiastic about scholastic philosophy, thinking perhaps that they have taken on board quite enough new doctrines already. James McAuley, on the contrary, understood that in a sense Catholicism with its philosophy asked for less belief than the faith alone, since the philosophy provided a few principles from which a great deal follows. The Christian tradition, he says, is 'confined to a few bare principles of natural law and a meagre deposit of revealed teaching'.[75] After phases of Marxism, Andersonianism and anarchism in youth,[76] he was converted to Catholicism and was happy to buy the whole package. He admired Gilson in particular,[77] though he was distressed that both Gilson and Maritain were admirers of modern art.[78] McAuley expressed his own view of the essence of Catholic philosophy in a well-known passage in *The End of Modernity*:

> While the Greco-Christian tradition remained intact, it was possible to give an intelligible account of human personality and show in what its eminent dignity and worth consist. To be a person means to be capable of reason and choice; able therefore to apprehend objective values and become a bearer of those values. What the Renaissance did was to begin to

[75] J. McAuley, *The End of Modernity* (Sydney, 1959), p. 12.

[76] 'McAuley and Anderson', ch. 4 of M. Cook, 'James McAuley's Encounter with Modernism', PhD thesis, Sydney University, 1993; J. McAuley, 'Realist aesthetics', reported in *Union Recorder*, 1/10/1936, repr. in *Heraclitus* 41 (May 1995): p. 6; 'Metaphysical poetry', *Union Recorder* 2/7/1936, reported in *Heraclitus* 40 (Mar 1995): pp. 4–5; G. Balzidis, 'James McAuley's radical ingredients', *Meanjin* 39 (1980): pp. 374–82; Horne, *Education of Young Donald*, pp. 200–1.

[77] Cook, 'McAuley's Encounter', pp. 274–82; J. McAuley, letter, *Australian Quarterly* 24 (2) (1952): pp. 76–8; J. McAuley, 'A small testament', *Quadrant* 20 (12) (1976), repr. in *James McAuley*, ed. L. Kramer (St Lucia, 1988); with comment in *Quadrant* 25 (9) (Sept 1981): p. 79 and 25 (11) (Nov 1981): p. 76; N. Rowe, 'James McAuley and the grammar of existence', *Australian Journal of Law and Society* 9 (1993): pp. 107–17; G. Melleuish, *Cultural Liberalism in Australia* (Cambridge, 1995), pp. 181–6.

[78] J. McAuley, 'A note on Maritain's views', in *The End of Modernity*, pp. 111–6; also J. Wright, 'Art and tradition — a rejoinder', *Australian Quarterly* 24 (1) (Mar, 1952): pp. 73–6; cf. A. Boyce Gibson, reviews of *Art and Faith: Exchange of Letters between Jean Cocteau and Jacques Maritain*, *AJP* 27 (1949): pp. 70–2 and of Gilson's *Dante the Philosopher*, *AJP* 28 (1950): pp. 43–50; and A. Boyce Gibson, 'The French spirit in philosophy', in *Light Out of France*, ed. J.G. Stanbury & A.R. Chisholm (Sydney, 1951).

fritter away this conception of man as a rational being oriented to real values, in favour of a cult of individualism and personal idiosyncrasy. To-day our publicists deafen us with proclamations of the 'value' or 'sacred-ness' of 'personality'; but which of them can give us a rational account of these terms? Scientism, the contraction of science to empirical knowledge, presents us with an impoverished reality in which *persons* have no theo-retical charter to exist. In its rigorously determinist from, scientism leaves no room for free will, values, or rational judgement itself. As Etienne Gilson says: 'This is the reason why, for want of a rational metaphysics by which the course of science could be regulated, the liberal philosophers had no other choice than to attack science itself and to weaken its abso-lute rationality. The source of modern agnosticism is the fear of scientific determinism in the hearts of men who, by breaking metaphysical ration-alism, had broken the very backbone of human liberty.' The notion of the value of personality, whose banishment the totalitarians have gladly ac-cepted from the hands of scientism, survives for the liberals only as an irrational sentiment, and under these circumstances the very meaning of personality is corrupted.[79]

He also drew some lessons for poetry. In particular, he thought, the common exaltation of imagination over intellect by poets is a mis-take: 'deep waters of feeling are stirred, and imagination induced to disclose its hidden treasures, only under the regnant star of intellectual ideas.'[80]

Remarkably, A.D. Hope, McAuley's rival as the leading poet of his generation, also had some connections with medieval philosophy. Though remaining closer to Anderson and classicism, and never a Catholic, he wrote an early article expressing substantial criticism of Anderson's ethics.[81] He proposed to write a thesis on Ockham, until prevented by Anderson,[82] and wrote an article on 'The esthetic theory of James Joyce', which is really about Thomas Aquinas' aesthetics.[83]

---

[79] 'The loss of intellectuality', in *The End of Modernity* pp. 86–9, at pp. 88–9; cf. p. 35; similar in J. McAuley, 'Friend of permanent things', *Quadrant* 14 (2) (Mar/Apr 1970): pp. 40–3; discussion in C. Pybus, *The Devil and James McAuley* (St Lucia, 1999), pp. 139–40; his views on university philosophy in 'A letter to John Dryden', *Collected Poems* (Sydney, 1994), pp. 104–17.

[80] McAuley, *End of Modernity*, preface, p. vii.

[81] A.D. Hope, 'The meaning of good', *AJPP* 21 (1943): pp. 17–26.

[82] A.D. Hope, *Chance Encounters* (Melbourne, 1992), p. 52; see 'A.D. Hope in his Sydney years', *Heraclitus* 82 (2000): p. 8.

[83] A.D. Hope, 'The esthetic theory of James Joyce', *AJPP* 21 (1943): pp. 93–114; further on the same theme in 'Three faces of love', in A.D. Hope, *The Cave and the Spring* (Adelaide, 1965), on which S. Moore, 'A.D. Hope's "Three faces of love"', *Australian Literary Studies* 10 (1982): pp. 389–91; cf. Anderson, *Art and Reality*, p. 260; recollection of Hope at this time in D. Horne, 'Portrait of an un-Australian', *Observer* 4/10/1958, pp. 517–8; on

The aspect of scholastic philosophy with the widest impact on ordinary life, and the source of its most widespread controversies, was moral philosophy and its offshoot, the 'science' of casuistry. The promise of objectivity in ethics, combined with the expectation that confessors should provide detailed and consistent advice on any matter that penitents cared to raise, created a vast body of reasoning on the application of moral principles to particular 'cases'.[84] As we saw, Dr Ryan sought opinions from experts on the morality of matching Communist tactics, and Dr Woodbury used to tell the story of Franco asking his advisers in moral theology whether it was permissible to make war on the Spanish republic, to which the answer was, 'not only licit but obligatory'. During the Vietnam War, too, Catholics created some bemusement among outsiders by debating whether the conflict fulfilled the traditional conditions for a just war.[85] Some of the stranger cases of conscience arose from complications in Church rules, rather than from natural law, but even those were supposed to be solved as reasonably as possible. May one deliberately confess to a deaf priest? (Of course not, since that defeats the essential purpose of confession.)[86] Is an excommunicate obliged to attend Mass? (A more realistic case than it looks, as there were many who considered themselves Catholics but who had incurred automatic excommunica-

Hope and Anderson also E. Fell, 'John Anderson is alive and well and treasured by a generation', *Financial Review* 23/7/1982, p. 35.
[84] J. Franklin, *The Science of Conjecture: Evidence and Probability Before Pascal* (Baltimore, 2001), ch. 4.
[85] V. Noone, 'Melbourne Catholics and the 1965 increase in Australian military intervention in Vietnam', *Journal of Religious History* 16 (1991): pp. 456–81, section III; M. Charlesworth & V. Noone, 'Christians, Vietnam and the theory of the just war', in *War: Australia and Vietnam*, ed. K. Maddock & B. Wright (Sydney, 1987), pp. 148–59; J. Fox, 'Can war ever be justified?', in *Catholics in Revolution*, ed. P. Ormonde (Melbourne, 1968), pp. 113–8; opposite Catholic view in Bob Breen, *First to Fight* (Sydney, 1988), p. 23; V. Noone, ed, *Catholics and Nuclear War*, (Melbourne, 1982); also *Critical Philosophy* 3 (1986), special issue on nuclear armaments; S.I. Benn, 'Deterrence or appeasement', *Journal of Applied Philosophy* 1 (1984): pp. 5–19; C.A.J. Coady, 'The leaders and the led', *Inquiry* 23 (1980): pp. 275–91; C.A.J. Coady, 'Deterrent intentions revisited', *Ethics* 99 (1988): pp. 98–108; C.A.J. Coady, 'Objecting morally', *Journal of Ethics* 1 (1997): pp. 375–97; D. Oderberg, *Applied Ethics: A Non-Consequentialist Approach* (Oxford, 2000), ch. 29.
[86] J.J. Nevin, 'Purposely confessing to a deaf priest', *ACR* 20 (1943): pp. 258–9 (on the author: K.J. Walsh, *Yesterday's Seminary: A History of St Patrick's Manly* (Sydney, 1998), pp. 190–218; cf. J. Passmore, *Memoirs of a Semi-Detached Australian* (Melbourne, 1997), p. 45; P. Mullins, 'Looking back on the way we were', *ACR* 75 (1998): pp. 264–70.

tion by marrying in another Church: Ben Chifley, for example.[87] The answer is tricky.[88]) The most important cases, though, were ones involving matters of ethical principle, which ought to apply equally to everyone, whether Catholic or not. Outside the Catholic (and Jewish) tradition, there has been a general feeling that it is not appropriate to confine ethical principle to such detailed 'rules',[89] but this perhaps rests on a misunderstanding of casuistry. Moral dilemmas, like legal cases, come up of their own accord, each with its own collection of properties and circumstances. To decide what is right in those circumstances, there is hardly any choice but to look at how all applicable ethical principles bear on the case, and perhaps conflict with one another. And the answer is surely applicable to all other relevantly similar cases, and can thus be called a rule.

The crunch for casuistry came, as far as the general Catholic population was concerned, with the prohibition of the Pill, on the grounds that artificial contraception defeats one of the essential purposes of sexual activity. Since the subtle deductions of casuistry did permit sex for the infertile as well as contraception by the rhythm method, the boundary between the licit and the illicit was a very thin one, and the reasoning did not carry the conviction hoped for, even among experts.[90] The large number of Catholics who ignored the Pope's 1968 encyclical on the Pill tended to blame and reject the whole apparatus of casuistry and confession. They did not usually respond to the arguments.

[87] D. Day, *Chifley* (Sydney, 2001), pp. 92–4; P. Hasluck, *The Chance of Politics* (Melbourne, 1997), p. 29.

[88] J.J. Nevin, 'Is an excommunicate bound to go to Mass on Sunday?', *ACR* 22 (1945): pp. 232–5; on the relevant metacasuistical principles, see H. McDermott, 'Probabilism vindicated', *ACR* 12 (1905): pp. 374–84; Walsh, *Yesterday's Seminary*, pp. 133–4; T.F. Roche, 'St. Alphonsus' probabilism', *ACR* 19 (1942): pp. 146–53.

[89] E.N. Merrington, *The Possibility of a Science of Casuistry* (Sydney, 1902); Anon, *Roman Catholic Morality as Inculcated in the Theological Class-Books Used in Maynooth College* (3rd ed, Dublin, 1836, repr. Sydney, 1839).

[90] Earlier Catholic views in S. Siedlecky & D. Wyndham, *Populate and Perish* (Sydney, 1990), pp. 15–16; J.C. Thompson, *Lectures on Medical and Legal Ethics Given at St John's College, University of Sydney* (Sydney, 1933); later debate in J. Finnis, 'Natural law in Humanae Vitae', *Law Quarterly Review* 84 (1968): pp. 467–71; N. Ford, 'Humanae vitae — twenty-five years on and beyond', *ACR* 70 (1993): pp. 139–60; N. Tonti-Filippini, 'Postpartum contraception', *ACR* 71 (1994): pp. 82–8; J. Young, *Catholic Thinking* (Merrylands, 1990), pp. 104–5; F. Mobbs, *Beyond its Authority? The Magisterium and Matters of Moral Law* (Sydney, 1997); G. Gleeson, 'The scope of the Church's moral teaching', *ACR* 75 (1998): pp. 264–70.

On the surface, scholasticism has virtually disappeared. After the Second Vatican Council of the 1960s, much of Catholic opinion lost sympathy with systems of thought identified with the *ancien regime*. Circles eager for change, in which 'before the Council' became a term of abuse, were hardly likely to approve of an intellectual structure that dated from before the Council of Trent. It was certainly true that scholasticism had in some ways left itself in a weak position to survive the onslaught, by taking little notice of so many developments in modern thought. It had made little attempt to come to terms with scientific thought, for example.[91] That was despite the fact that modern science itself grew out of a scholastic matrix, which gave it its initial vocabulary, set of questions and methodology. (These matters were one of the themes of the Australian expatriate Alistair Crombie, from his widely read *Augustine to Galileo* of 1952 to his monumental *Styles of Scientific Thinking in the European Tradition* of 1994.[92]) By contrast, new ideas in general were the weak point of modern scholasticism. It was said that the way to stop the charge of a man-eating Thomist was to ask what questions not dealt with by Aquinas Thomists were about to work on.[93]

Catholic philosophy since the 1960s has gone through a 'post-scholastic' phase, which rejects the details of scholasticism but hopes to preserve a distinctively Catholic orientation. This means that a concern for objective morality and the general reliability of reason has been grounded on a synthesis, or attempted synthesis, of some of the basics of scholasticism with ideas from modern philosophy.[94] There

---

[91] Some Australian attempts in G. Ardley, *Aquinas and Kant* (London, 1950); G.W.R. Ardley, 'Prolegomenon to any natural science which can be called philosophical', *Modern Schoolman* 32 (1955): pp. 101–13; V.A. Garten, 'Physics and the goodness of creation', *Divus Thomas*, no. 4 of 1985, pp. 276–88; D. Rockey, 'Some fundamental principles for the solution of terminological problems in speech pathology and therapy', *British Journal of Disorders of Communication* 4 (1969): pp. 166–75; J.B.T. McCaughan, 'Capillarity — a lesson in the epistemology of physics', *Physics Education* 22 (1987): pp. 100–6.

[92] J.D. North, 'Alistair Cameron Crombie', *History of Science* 34 (1996): pp. 245–8; bibliography in A.C. Crombie, *Science, Optics and Music in Medieval and Early Modern Thought* (London, 1990); originally in A.C. Crombie, 'Scholastic Logic and the experimental method', *Actes du Ve Congrès International d'Histoire des Sciences, Lausanne, 1947* (Paris, 1948), pp. 45–50; also on this theme, J. Franklin, 'Mental furniture from the philosophers', *Et Cetera* 40 (1983): pp. 177–191; J. Franklin, 'The genius of the scholastics and the orbit of Aristotle', in Franklin, *The Science of Conjecture*, pp. 343–9.

[93] F.J. Sheed, *The Church and I* (London, 1974), p. 104.

[94] Examples in R. Gascoigne, *Freedom and Purpose: An Introduction to Christian Ethics* (Sydney, 1993); N. Brown, *The Worth of Persons: A Study in Christian*

have continued to be defenders of the need to base Catholic education on a commitment to intellectual values, though, as Santamaria said, the results have not always been evident in Catholic schools.[95] Similar motives lie behind the project by Catholics of varying degrees of orthodoxy to develop, or discover, an 'Australian spirituality'.[96]

All these attempts are interesting, and not without their successes. From the scholastic point of view, though, they are like trying to have one's cake after eating the ingredients. Or perhaps more exactly, they are like trying to have Euclid's theorems without the axioms.

In some ways, the demise of scholasticism has been much exaggerated. Survivals of it are everywhere. Casuistry is back, for example, and not just in Catholic circles. It is now called 'applied ethics', and is performed by committees. It will be treated briefly in the last chapter. Distinctively Catholic views on ethics are also visible in the recent debates on such topics as euthanasia, as will also be described in the last chapter. There are other issues on which most Catholics still maintain views which descend from the core doctrines of the old moral philosophy. A properly conducted sociological study of Australians' attitudes to abortion showed that opposition to abortion depended strongly on 'deductive moral reasoning from basic Christian beliefs', and little on such attitudes as obedience to the Pope or ('contrary to received wisdom') a desire to keep women tied to the

Ethics (Manly, 1983); and in *ACR* 64 (1987): pp. 167–81; N. Ford, 'The meaning of intrinsic moral norms for persons', *ACR* 60 (1983): pp. 186–97; J. Hill, 'Natural sanction and philosophical theology', *Sophia* 17 (1978): pp. 27–34; J. Hill, 'Christian moral education', *Journal of Religious Ethics* 9 (1981): pp. 103–17; J. Hill, 'The methodology of *Veritatis splendor*', *ACR* 71 (1994): pp. 145–61; J. Hill, 'Can we talk about ethics anymore?', *Journal of Business Ethics* 14 (1995): pp. 585–92; E. Hepburn, *Of Life and Death: An Australian Guide to Catholic Bioethics* (Melbourne, 1996).

[95] E. D'Arcy, 'The intellectual apostolate', *ACR* 62 (1985): pp. 349–58. J. Franklin, 'Australian Catholics', *Quadrant* 32 (1/2) (Jan/Feb 1988): pp. 114–6; B. Tobin, 'The Catechism of the Catholic Church and the role of cognition in Christian life', *ACR* 71 (1994): pp. 411–8.

[96] J. Thornhill, *Making Australia* (Newtown, 1992); J. Thornhill, *Sign and Promise* (London, 1988); Tony Kelly, *A New Imagining: Towards an Australian Spirituality* (Melbourne, 1990); V. Brady, *Caught in the Draught* (Sydney, 1994), esp. ch. 5; E. Stockton, *The Aboriginal Gift: Spirituality for a Nation* (Alexandria, 1995); R. Cameron, *Karingal: A Search for Australian Spirituality* (Homebush, 1995); less orthodox but in the same vein, D.J. Tacey, *Edge of the Sacred* (Melbourne, 1995); D. Tacey, *Reenchantment* (Sydney, 2000); Thomist reaction in T. Rowland, *Culture and the Thomist Tradition after Vatican II* (London, 2003).

kitchen sink.[97] In the philosophy of religion, there have also been several substantial books by Catholic philosophers who added to rather than subtracted from the scholastic legacy.[98]

Even more surprisingly, just as scholasticism was being consigned by most Catholics to the scrapheap of history, the realist metaphysics at its core was becoming respectable in mainstream philosophy, and nowhere more so than in Australia. The main event in its acceptance was the publication in 1978 of David Armstrong's *Universals and Scientific Realism*, which defends a strongly and explicitly Aristotelian position in the old scholastic debate, the problem of universals.[99] The story will be described in chapter 12. As a result, the *Australasian Journal of Philosophy* has welcomed articles on topics like substances, universals, dispositions and haecceities, previously regarded as the among the most obscure and meaningless items of decadent scholasticism.[100]

[97] J. Kelley, M.D.R. Evans & B. Headey, 'Moral reasoning and political conflict: the abortion controversy', *British Journal of Sociology* 44 (1993): pp. 589–612; work on the topic from a Catholic orientation in J. Finnis, 'The rights and wrongs of abortion', in M. Cohen *et al.*, eds, *The Rights and Wrongs of Abortion* (Princeton, 1974), pp. 85–113; N. Ford, *When Did I Begin?* (Cambridge, 1988); A. Fisher & J. Buckingham, *Abortion in Australia* (Blackburn, 1985); B.F. Scarlett, 'The moral status of embryos', *Journal of Medical Ethics* 10 (1984): pp. 79–80; P. Drum, 'Hylomorphism and abortion', *Australian Journal of Professional and Applied Ethics* 2 (1) (2000): pp. 71–4; T. Keneally, *Three Cheers for the Paraclete* (Sydney, 1968), pp. 110–3; Les Murray, 'Who's Ignatius, whose Loyola?', *Kunapipi* 1 (2) (1979): pp. 149–54
[98] P. Forrest, *God Without the Supernatural: A Defense of Scientific Theism* (Ithaca, N.Y., 1996); discussion in M. Wynn, 'In defence of "the supernatural" ', *American Catholic Philosophical Quarterly* 73 (1999): pp. 477–95; also P. Forrest, *Speculation and Experience: The New Metaphysics* (inaugural lecture, Armidale, 1987); B. Miller, *A Most Unlikely God* (Notre Dame, 1996), especially ch. 9; cf. R.J. Kearney, 'Analogy and inference', *New Scholasticism* 51 (1977): pp. 131–41 earlier B. Miller, *The Range of Intellect* (London, 1961); *From Existence to God* (London, 1992).
[99] D.M. Armstrong, *Universals and Scientific Realism* (Cambridge, 1978); see esp. vol II p. 75 n. 1; Catholic view in D. Gallery, 'Nominalism and realism', *ACR* 10 (1904): pp. 145–51.
[100] *AJP*, special number on universals 64 (1) (1986); M.M. Tweedale, 'Aristotle's universals', *AJP* 65 (1987): pp. 412–26; B. Ellis & C. Lierse, 'Dispositional essentialism', *AJP* 72 (1994): pp. 27–45; M.C. LaBossiere, 'Substances and substrata', *AJP* 72 (1994): pp. 360–70; J.L. Kvanvig, 'The haecceity theory and perspectival limitation', *AJP* 67 (1989): pp. 295–305, etc; also D.S. Oderberg, 'Form and matter', *Ratio* 11 (1998): pp. 209–13; D. Brown, 'Immanence and individuation: Brentano and the scholastics on knowledge of singulars', *Monist* 83 (2000): pp. 22–46.

Chapter Five   The Gough–Kinsella Affair

ALTHOUGH John Anderson and Austin Woodbury never came face to face in debate, a war by proxy between them briefly captured the attention of the public at the time of the 'Gough affair' of 1961. Dr Victor Kinsella, a Sydney surgeon, wrote in his *The Mechanism of Abdominal Pain*, 'pain from the alimentary tract is typically central, deep and diffuse'[1] and that describes accurately enough his gut reaction to Andersonian philosophy after a course of study with Woodbury at the Aquinas Academy. Kinsella eventually became a part-time lecturer in philosophy at the Academy.[2] In 1958 he privately printed and distributed widely a pamphlet, *Empiricism and Freedom*, attacking the philosophy being taught at Sydney University. Its language is vigorous; the following extract gives a flavour of its invective (and indeed of Woodbury's lectures, on which it is based):

> It has been rightly said of empiricism that it is the philosophy of the gutter, for it admits only sense-knowing — peering, sniffing, nosing, cocking the ears, etc. And now, Professor Anderson shows that lining the empiricist gutter there are posts, but no propters ... The empiricist rejects 'agencies and the like', i.e., causes. For him, 'there are only facts, i.e., occurrences,' and no causal link can be admitted between them ... Having denied to man any knowing faculty whereby he can read within the externals of things and know something of their natures, the empiricist must reject the moral law. As Professor Anderson tells the school children coming to the University in Orientation Week — 'intelligence' (for him a sorter of sense-images) 'does not recognise such concepts as lack of obscenity or sedition.'[3]

---

[1] V.J. Kinsella, *The Mechanism of Abdominal Pain* (Sydney, 1948), p. 209.
[2] *Academician* 6 (1) (Apr 1965), p. 7.
[3] V.J. Kinsella, *Empiricism and Freedom* (Killara, 1958), p. 5.

(Kinsella was quite wrong in saying that Anderson denied causality, but, as we saw, the claims about not recognising such concepts as obscenity were correct.)

The pamphlet provoked little reaction at the time, but an opportunity to publicise it arose a few years later when the NSW Government set up the Youth Policy Advisory Committee.[4] Its chairman Judge (later Sir) Adrian Curlewis was the son of the author of *Seven Little Australians*, a work on the education of youth with, it is fair to say, a philosophy diametrically opposed to Anderson's. He had been strongly involved in promoting healthy outdoor activities for the young, like surf lifesaving, Outward Bound, and the Duke of Edinburgh's Award Scheme.[5] He had earlier chaired the NSW Government's Shark Menace Advisory Committee,[6] after which there were very few shark attacks in Sydney. Could he repeat the performance? Although he did not state publicly his views on those who threatened the morals of society, it is clear what they were from extracts from a speech by Sir Patrick (later Lord) Devlin that he sent to an inquirer. It is worth quoting these views for their insight into the thinking of some of the more extreme (by later standards, at least) of the defenders of society's mores:

> Societies disintegrate from within more frequently than they are broken up from external pressures. There is disintegration when no common morality is observed and history shows that the loosening of moral bonds is often the first stage of disintegration, so that society is justified in taking the same steps to preserve its moral code as it does to preserve its government and other essential institutions. The suppression of vice is as much the law's business as the suppression of subversive activities; it is no more possible to define a sphere of private morality than it is to define one of private subversive activity ... there can be no theoretical limits to legislation against immorality ... Christian morals are the basis of the criminal

---

[4] G. Sherington, 'Youth, state and community: The report of the Curlewis Youth Policy Advisory Committee in New South Wales', in *Australian and New Zealand History of Education Society Twenty-First Annual Conference Proceedings*, Adelaide, 1992, vol. 2 pp. 125–38; D. Macpherson, *The Suffragette's Daughter: Betty Archdale* (Sydney, 2002), p. 245.

[5] Obituary of Curlewis in *Australian Law Journal* 59 (1985): p. 581; *Australian* 16/12/1970, p. 3; his work as 'Dean' of a 'University' in Changi in P. Poole, *Of Love and War: The Letters and Diaries of Captain Adrian Curlewis and His Family, 1939–1945* (Sydney, 1982), p. 128; H. Nelson, *P.O.W.: Prisoners of War* (Sydney, 1985), p. 26.

[6] A.H. Curlewis et al., *Report of the Shark Menace Advisory Committee* (Sydney, 1935).

law and ... without the support of the churches the moral order, which has its origin and takes its strength from Christian beliefs would collapse.[7]

Kinsella included his pamphlet in a submission alleging that the empiricist philosophy and psychology taught at both Sydney's universities were corrupting the morals of the youth. The inquiry considered the matter at some length, assisted by the expertise of its member Monsignor Leonard, holder of a doctorate in scholastic philosophy from the University of Louvain. It eventually found that there was insufficient evidence to support the charge,[8] and confined its recommendations to such schemes as the expansion of cadet units in schools and drawing the attention of the US ambassador to the TV programs from his country which gave the youth the impression that brutalising or serious crime was normal there.[9]

But in the meantime Curlewis had sent a copy of Kinsella's pamphlet to Dr Hugh Gough, the Anglican Archbishop of Sydney and Primate of Australia. Gough, the only supporter among the English bishops of the Billy Graham crusade of 1954, had found in Sydney a diocese of even more Evangelical tenor than himself, and had settled into regular condemnations of immorality and Communism, evils some thought he did not distinguish very clearly.[10] He warned the press to expect something sensational from his sermon in St Andrew's Cathedral on 6 July 1961, and the reporters were not disappointed.

After warming up with some remarks on how the 'seeds of the corruption of the moral consciousness of the Nazis was sown away back in the 19th century by various German philosophers, who taught first agnosticism and then atheism', he attacked the 'worse and greater threat in the world-wide challenge of Communism', the basis of which is atheism. Then he got to the point. 'Even in Sydney', he said, 'we have those who are shamelessly teaching in our universities the same soul-destroying philosophies. I am not saying that such lecturers are Communists, but they are teaching ideas which are break-

---

[7] P. Devlin, extracts in A. Curlewis to A. Carey, 29/3/1962, in Stout papers, Sydney University Archives, item 908; text in P. Devlin, *The Enforcement of Morals* (Oxford, 1965), pp. 13–4, 23; context in D. Hilliard, 'Church, family and sexuality in Australia in the 1950s', *Australian Historical Studies* 28 (1997): pp. 133–46.

[8] *Report of the New South Wales Youth Policy Advisory Committee, 1962* (Sydney, 1963), p. 32.

[9] *Report*, pp. 168, 162.

[10] *Nation* no. 73 (15/7/1961): pp. 8–10; *Bulletin* 15/7/1961, p. 11; 12/8/1961, pp. 12–14; S.B. Babbage & I. Siggins, *Light Beneath the Cross: The Story of Billy Graham's Crusade in Australia* (Kingswood, 1960), p. 156; M. Loane, *Men to Remember* (Canberra, 1987), pp. 78–89; obituary in *Australian* 27/11/1997, p. 17.

ing down the restraints of conscience, decrying the institution of marriage, urging our students to pre-marital sexual experience, advocating free love and the right of self-expression.'[11] What made university folk everywhere put the wagons round in a circle was his call for State action: 'If it is true that empires and nations have fallen because of moral corruption which has sapped the mental vitality and physical strength of the people, is it not the duty of governments to take note of this decline in morals and to take action? This is an unpopular and even dangerous question to ask. Any suggestion which raises the slightest suspicion of interference with freedom immediately arouses wrathful opposition.'[12]

True enough. The press was full of it for weeks. Various university figures professed themselves astonished at the idea that anyone at universities should be in favour of free love; Sydney University's Vice-Chancellor claimed that 'the morals of students are higher today than ever before' and threatened a libel action.[13] *Pix*, leading human-interest-and-cheesecake pictorial, sent its investigative team to interview students at both Sydney universities on their attitude to free love; most were against it, except possibly for other people. A pensive president of the University of New South Wales Students' Representative Council, John Niland, was pictured beside his opinion that 'Maybe it's all right for the few, but free love wouldn't fit in with civilised living for the majority.'[14]

Kinsella followed up with a long letter to the Youth Committee denouncing, in addition, the University of New South Wales Philosophy Department, the Sydney Libertarian Society, and the textbook by John Hospers used at Sydney, and demanding that the University should be called on to show cause why it should not lose its Royal Charter.[15] *Pix* made Dr Kinsella's attack on Hospers' textbook

---

[11] Sermon printed in full: copy in Sydney University Archives, Stout papers, item 871; extract in *Southern Cross: The Magazine of the Diocese of Sydney* 1 (3) (Aug 1961): pp. 3, 11 (also editorial p. 1); 'University professors deny charge of immoral teachings', *SMH* 7/7/1961, p. 4; *Anglican* 14/7/1961, pp. 1, 12; P. Coleman, *Memoirs of a Slow Learner* (Sydney, 1994), pp. 155–9; A.J. Baker, *Anderson's Social Philosophy* (Sydney, 1979), pp. 141–3.

[12] *Nation* no. 73 (15/7/1961), p. 10.

[13] 'Allegation "outrageous" ', *SMH* 7/7/1961, p. 4; D.R.V. Wood, *Stephen Henry Roberts* (Sydney, 1986), p. 87 (a large collection of the newspaper cuttings is in the Stout papers, item 864).

[14] 'Do you believe in free love? University students speak out', *Pix* 62 (8) (29/7/1961), pp. 54–5.

[15] *Telegraph* 10/8/1961; *SMH* 10/8/1961, p. 13; 'Who put the arsenic in the chocolate?', *Bulletin* 19/8/1961, p. 6; also Kinsella letter, *Bulletin* 5/8/1961, p. 24.

PIX

SEPTEMBER 16 1961

Sophia Loren &
Rome scandal

WORLD'S TOP
LUXURY CARS

Groucho Marx's
tilt at Royalty

'EVIL'
UNI.
TEXT
BOOK
—EXTRACTS

1/6

Cover of Pix *magazine, 16 September 1961*

its cover story ('Raised eyebrows at the uni text book belong to lovely 16–year-old model Elizabeth Thomas. The book is called "evil" by a well-known doctor. Elizabeth is not called evil by anyone.') Kinsella explained that the author was too cunning to advocate free love explicitly, but that his denial of the objectivity of morals and caricaturing of traditional arguments for the existence of God inevitably led to it.[16] Channel 7 wheeled out the usual suspects for a stoush: the Liberal parliamentarian W.C. Wentworth claimed students believed that to pass they had to write what their lecturers liked, while Labor's Dr Jim Cairns said that universities, far from being the centre of too much criticism, did not ask nearly enough embarrassing questions.[17] The Communists demanded a meeting with the Archbishop to deny that immorality had anything to do with them.[18] Prime Minister Menzies, then facing his toughest electoral test, bowed to Gough at a dinner and said, 'I am pleased to see his Grace here. Nothing brings so much balm to the spirit as to see a man who, like himself, is in trouble.'[19]

Perhaps the only reaction that gave the impression of being anchored in experience was a letter to the press from 'Concerned mother' of Neutral Bay. It is interesting for its recognition that more than a clash of opinions is under way:

> Sir, — I write as the parent of an honours graduate of Sydney University, who has completed his course comparatively unscathed (if one could assume complete loss of religious faith previously held as 'unscathed').
>
> My child (now adult) is surrounded by graduate and other university friends who are either living at times with the mate of the moment or, having married young, are eking out an existence in the accepted matrimonial state, with both partners in a perpetual state of nerviness, bordering on neurosis.
>
> Both of course are employed in some way outside the home, and in few cases is the home more than a substitute for that worthy institution. One young woman university student whom I have befriended sees no wrong in bringing an illegitimate child into the world and a short time ago demonstrated this very fact. Her friends rallied to her assistance, and she wanted for nothing. Other young women I have known have aborted in their first university year …
>
> Where then is this unrest and this disturbing influence on the emotions coming from?[20]

John Anderson wrote in a letter to the press:

> It's no use having to ask the Archbishop's opinion every time you want to suggest a new theory. In my thirty-two years at Sydney University, I never heard a Philosophy teacher advocate free love or pre-marital ex-

---

[16] 'This textbook is unspeakably evil', *Pix* 63 (2) (16/9/1961): pp. 7–9.

[17] *SMH* 31/7/1961, p. 6.

[18] *Mirror* 13/7/1961.

[19] *SMH* 14/7/1961, p. 1.

[20] Letter, *SMH* 12/7/1961, p. 2; cf. 'Parents fear of uni. ideas', *Sun* 10/7/1961.

perience in the lecture-room. What he expresses in private is his own business and not the Archbishop's or Dr Kinsella's.[21]

The dispute occasioned Anderson's last major public appearance, when the retiring president of the students' union, Peter Wilenski, invited him to speak at his old university. He defended himself in some detail against Kinsella's charges, while denying both Kinsella and the Curlewis committee any standing or competence in judging his philosophy. On Kinsella's charge that empiricism had an unhealthy monopoly on university positions in philosophy, Anderson replied that 'if you give students all sorts of views, you are not encouraging a real grasp of philosophy.'[22] Anderson also spoke at the University of New South Wales, and made it clear that there was no mistake about the conflict between his views and Gough's. 'The academic world has to attack any religion which tries to lay down requirements not in accordance with reality. In any university the fight between secularism and religion is intense ... church-going minds are childish. We are dealing with people who are not really adults.'[23]

This drew a reply from Bishop Muldoon, a Catholic bishop who had written on scholastic philosophy,[24] who suggested that a teacher who felt so vehemently could hardly have failed to communicate his scorn and contempt to his students.[25] Kinsella himself lobbed onto campus, to heated objections, telling the students, 'You're not the culprits, you're the victims.'[26]

The three professors at Sydney University attacked by Kinsella, Alan Stout, John Mackie and William O'Neil, also gave their views publicly. From the point of view of Kinsella's claims, all had interesting histories.

Strangely, Stout owed his appointment in part to agitation by scholastics. In the late 1930s, complaints about Anderson had begun to make an impact on the University Senate. In 1937, Catholic circles believed they had convinced Sir John Peden, Professor of Law and a

---

[21] *Sun* 7/7/1961, quoted in Baker, p. 142.

[22] *SMH* 15/7/1961, p. 5; 'John Anderson on "Academic autonomy and religion"', *Sydney Libertarians Broadsheet* (Aug 1961): pp. 2–6; *Honi Soit* 33 (17) (27/7/1961): p. 4; Coleman, *Memoirs*, pp. 163–6; Anderson's further opinions in J. Anderson, 'Religion and the university', *Australian Highway* 42 (3) (Nov 1961): pp. 50–54.

[23] *SMH* 21/7/1961, p. 5.

[24] T. Muldoon, *De Deo Uno* (Rome, 1958); review in *ACR* 36 (1959): pp. 78–81; see K.J. Walsh, *Yesterday's Seminary* (Sydney, 1998), pp. 265–6; the burning of these books in C. Geraghty, *The Priest Factory* (Melbourne, 2003), pp. 141-51.

[25] *SMH* 31/7/1961, p. 5; *Catholic Weekly* 3/8/1961, p. 1.

[26] *Honi Soit* 33 (18) (7/9/1961): p. 1.

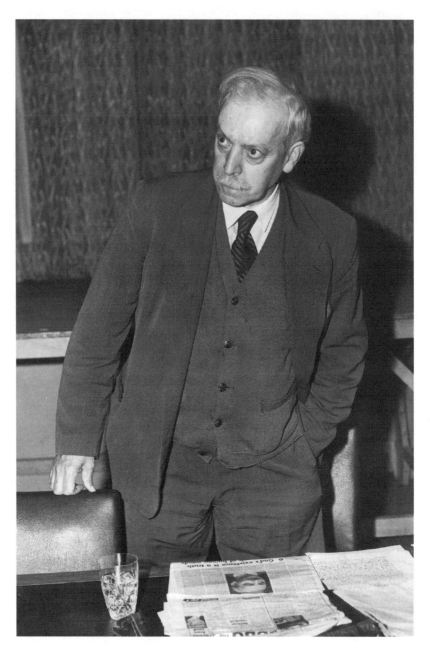

John Anderson speaking to University of New South Wales students at the time of the Kinsella affair, 1961 (Fairfax Photos)

dominant figure on the Senate, that the appropriate solution was a chair of scholastic philosophy. Sources of money for the proposed chair were spoken of, along with methods of ensuring that the appointee was an orthodox scholastic, and could be removed if his scholasticism failed to remain orthodox.[27] A certain misunderstanding of the idea of academic freedom in a secular university seems to be involved here.

In a rare display of Christian unity, the Anglican Archbishop and bishops signed a petition to the University Senate complaining that philosophy at the University was taught exclusively from an anti-theistic viewpoint, which, 'if it be not exposed to effective criticism from within the University itself, is, in our opinion, deeply prejudicial to the best interests of students, and particularly to those of the students who are contemplating service in the Christian ministry ... we believe that the most valuable kind of religious faith is one which has thought its way through all the arguments which can be adduced against it. But we have the strongest possible objection to the negative view being the only view which is officially represented in the teaching of the University.'[28] The Senate agreed that these complaints were correct, but decided it could not be seen to be influenced by outside criticism of the University. It eventually agreed on a 'compromise'. To counterbalance Anderson, there would be a separate chair of Moral and Political Philosophy, but it would be advertised openly in the usual way.[29]

Anderson was too fast for the opposition, and during his sabbatical overseas in 1938, encouraged Stout, then at Edinburgh, to apply. Stout promptly became a crony of Anderson, and is reported as saying, doubtless in jest, 'Of course, it made no difference to John. He went on corrupting the youth just as much as before, and damn it all, he corrupted me too!'[30] He supported Anderson publicly in the 1943

---

[27] Correspondence of Monsignor King to Archbishop Sheehan, in Paddy Ryan archives, St Paul's Seminary, Kensington.

[28] University of Sydney Senate, minutes 12 Oct 1936, in Sydney University Archives; reply to the Archbishop in minutes of 2 Nov.

[29] University of Sydney Senate Minutes, 12 Oct & 2 Nov 1936, summarised in C. Turney, U. Bygott & P. Chippendale, *Australia's First: A History of the University of Sydney*, vol. 1 (Sydney, 1991), p. 607; see S. Grave, *A History of Philosophy in Australia* (St Lucia, 1984), p. 89.

[30] D.H. Munro, obituary of Stout, *AJP* 61 (1983): pp. 337–9; other obituaries, *Australian Academy of the Humanities Proceedings* 1982–3: pp. 107–9, *The Times* 23/7/1983. There is a film of Anderson and Stout playing tennis, c. 1939: Stout Papers, item 284.

'religion in education' controversy,[31] and it was not long before the Catholics were complaining that his corruption of the youth was real enough.[32] Anderson's ASIO file reported in 1950, crudely but not inaccurately,

> Professors Anderson, Elkin and Stout form a sort of triangle ... Stout is completely under Anderson's influence and always ready to step in and cover his tracks. Anderson has the brains of the trio.[33]

Stout's views on ethics emphasised a 'moral commitment' in the absence of reasons,[34] but did not reach the austere extremity of Anderson's. A student of 1960 recalls:

> Ethics classes were more entertaining. Professor Alan Stout, short, passionate and a little on the stout side, sometimes bounced up and down on the platform in his excitement. He had greying hair, a waistcoat buttoned up higgledy-piggledy and, when he was really bouncing, his half-moon glasses swung around him on a black chain ... 'I am, in many senses, the last of the objectivists,' he announced. 'I believe in good and evil, I am quite prepared to point to the good, whatever the difficulties of defining goodness. The preservation of the foreshores is good. The Nazi persecution of the Jews was evil. It is no mere matter of, "Preservation of the foreshores — hooray!" and "Killing the Jews — boo!"'[35]

He did very little philosophy after arriving in Australia, but put a great deal of energy into being a public intellectual. He was a member of the National Morale Committee during the War, and enjoyed himself immensely as chairman of Sydney University's Air Raids Precaution Committee.[36] By the late 1940s he was president of the Prison Reform Council, on the National Film Board, active in drama and ballet, and so on.[37] Later he was a leading supporter of Sydney Sparkes

---

[31] *Honi Soit* 15 (11) (16/4/1943), p. 1; *SMH* 27/11/1946, p. 2; further in Stout's obituary of Anderson, *Australian Humanities Research Council, Annual Report* no. 6 (1961–2): pp. 26–8.

[32] Dr Rumble, 'Question box', *Catholic Weekly* 9/5/1946, p. 12; 16/5/1946, pp. 12–13; 30/5/1946, p. 12; 5/12/1946, p. 2; Dr Rumble was also a student of Garrigou-Lagrange: *Who is Father Rumble?* (pamphlet, St Paul, Minnesota, n.d.), p. 29.

[33] Australian Archives, series A6119 item 389, p. 9.

[34] A.K. Stout, 'Morality without religion', in *A Humanist View*, ed. I.S. Edwards (Sydney, 1969), pp. 31–43.

[35] P. Nelson, *Penny Dreadful* (Sydney, 1995), pp. 133–4.

[36] W.F. Connell, G.E. Sherington, G.H. Fletcher, C. Turney & U. Bygott, *Australia's First: A History of the University of Sydney*, vol. 2 (Sydney, 1995), pp. 9–10, 15; C. Pybus, *The Devil and James McAuley* (St Lucia, 1999), p. 24.

[37] *Daily Telegraph* 19/7/1947; A.K. Stout, 'Films in Australia: My 35 years' saga', *Media Information Australia* 6 (Nov 1977): pp. 14–20; details on theatre, ballet, music and the ABC in Stout papers, part VII.

Orr and involved in the anti-nuclear and anti-Vietnam War causes, and with the Council for Civil Liberties.[38] It is probably Stout who is referred to in Gough's hint, 'I am not saying such lecturers are Communists, but ...' ASIO had him down as a 'possible sympathiser', on the evidence that he was associated with the Sydney Film Society and the Youth Carnival for Peace, both allegedly full of fellow-travellers, that his name was 'in a list found in the Marx House raid of 1949' and that his son was once seen visiting the Soviet Embassy.[39]

Stout achieved a brief public prominence at the time of the Melbourne Peace Conference of 1959. The Conference, with many distinguished international invitees, was regarded by the right as a Communist front. ASIO, not without a certain prescience, suspected that the peace movement might be the conduit whereby far left ideas would again infect wider sections of society. Stout, one of the Conference's sponsors, was personally visited by Charles Spry, the director of ASIO, to convince him of the dangers of being a Communist dupe. Stout did withdraw his sponsorship, but also revealed publicly the visit from Spry. A minor scandal ensued, with Garfield Barwick and W.C. Wentworth savaged in Parliament over their role in sending Spry to see Stout, and Labor parliamentarian Eddie Ward asking Menzies if he could have a personal visit from Spry too, to learn the 'truth' about the Conference.[40] (In the event, the truth about the conference *was* revealed, when it failed to pass a motion in support of imprisoned Hungarian writers, and the most famous overseas attendees withdrew their support.[41]) In response to Kinsella, Stout claimed he had only been joking in putting forward on television arguments

[38] C. Pybus, *Seduction and Consent*, pp. 74, 110, 210–11 & ch. 9; *Honi Soit* 34 (5) (27/3/1962): 4; 'Censorship', *Tribune* 24/3/1964; *Australian* 16/7/1964, 27/11/1964, p. 8; 'Battler in search of the quiet life', *SMH* 30/10/1967, p. 6 (Stout retired to Lambert Ave, Sandy Bay, the street in which the Kemp family lived.)

[39] Commonwealth Investigation Service report, 19/11/1948, in ASIO file on Stout, Australian Archives, series A6119/64 item 484.

[40] P. Summy & M. Saunders, 'The 1959 Melbourne Peace Congress', in *Better Dead Than Red*, ed. A. Curthoys & J. Merritt (Sydney, 1986), pp. 74–95; D. McKnight, *Australia's Spies and Their Secrets* (Sydney, 1994), pp. 115–7; D. Marr, *Barwick* (Sydney, 1980), pp. 147–9; Pybus, *The Devil and James McAuley*, pp. 175–6; P. Kelly, 'Peace movements in Australia', *Bulletin* 23/6/1962 (copy in second ASIO file on Stout, Australian Archives series A6119/79 item 1363); Stout papers, items 909–943, especially letter of P.R. Heydon, Acting Secretary, Dept of External Affairs, to Stout on red dangers, item 924; *Nation* 4/7/1959, p. 6; *Observer* 26/12/1959, pp. 26–9; *Sunday Telegraph* 25/10/1959, p. 9; 'The Spry-Stout confab', *Sun Herald* 22/11/1959.

[41] Coleman, *Memoirs*, pp. 127–9.

in favour of trial marriages. He denied he was a member of Anderson's school, and claimed he knew of no case of immoral conduct in the University.[42] His lectures went further. 'Ripping into Gough's undistinguished academic record at Cambridge, he told us, "The Archbishop, ladies and gentlemen, has *two Thirds*".'[43]

At the end of the year of the controversy, Stout was appointed chairman of Sydney University's Board of Studies in Divinity. A churchman hoped this meant he had 'come on side with Christ at last'. Stout said, 'I think he's got a cheek.'[44]

John Mackie was an entirely different proposition. His father, Alexander Mackie, a philosophy graduate from Edinburgh, had been the first Principal of Sydney Teachers' College and Sydney University's first Professor of Education; that is, in control of teacher education in New South Wales. His views on education as an intellectually respectable profession dominated education in the state for decades after his death.[45] John Mackie fell under the Andersonian spell early, and was to be found in the 1930s voicing strict Andersonian views[46] and, according to reliable reports, doorknocking for communist candidates.[47]

His article, 'The refutation of morals', achieved some notoriety, since it meant what it said; it accepted the negative part of Anderson's ethics while denying the positive. It ended, 'We have shown that the great mass of what is called moral thought is, not nonsense, but error, the imagining of objective facts and qualities of external things where there exists nothing but our feelings of desire and approval.'[48] On the

---

[42] Stout to Curlewis, 10/7/1961, in Stout papers, item 872; *SMH* 13/7/1961, p. 4; A.K. Stout, 'The Archbishop and the philosophers', *Vestes* 4(3) (Sept 1961): pp. 34–7.

[43] Nelson, *Penny Dreadful*, p. 136.

[44] 'Prof. Stout "for Christ", cleric says', *Telegraph* 16/3/1962.

[45] A.D. Spaull & L.A. Mandelson, 'The college principals — J. Smyth and A. Mackie', in C. Turney, ed, *Pioneers of Australian Education*, vol. 3 (Sydney, 1983), ch. 2; H. Wyndham, 'Retrospect: Professor Alexander Mackie', *Forum of Education* 43 (2) (1984): 3–11.

[46] J.L. Mackie, letter, 'Social service', *Honi Soit* 8 (13) (2/7/1936), p. 5; cf. 'Social service "a mistake": Professor Anderson's views', *Honi Soit* 8 (3) (1/4/1936), p. 1; on Abyssinia, *Union Recorder* 19/9/1935; J.L. Mackie, 'The theory of the comic', reported in *Union Recorder* 18/7/1936, repr. in *Heraclitus* 40 (Mar 1995): p. 1; other reprints in *Heraclitus* 46 (Jan 1996): 4 and 47 (Feb 1996): p. 6; see B. Nield, 'The Andersonians: Worship of their hero', *Century* 24/4/1959, p. 6.

[47] D.C. Stove, unpublished recollection of Mackie, 1982; cf. J. Mackie, 'Revolution at Rome from the Gracchi to Augustus', talk reported in *Union Recorder* 29/4/1937, repr. in *Heraclitus* 46 (Jan 1996): pp. 2–3.

[48] J. Mackie, 'The refutation of morals', *AJPP* 24 (1946): pp. 77–90.

one hand, it was far enough from Anderson's views to bar him from admittance to the inner circle of the great man's disciples;[49] on the other, it prevented Mackie gaining the chair in philosophy in Tasmania that went instead to Orr.[50] No suggestion of moral impropriety attached to him; on the contrary, all spoke of his helpfulness and honesty. But many remarked a certain lack of emotional warmth. David Stove recalled:

> I think I was as close to being a friend of John's as anyone was, but that is not saying much. When I was with him I always felt I had to supply warmth for two, his as well as my own. I didn't grudge the effort, because he was such a good chap really; but oh, so *cool!*[51]

After some time in New Zealand, Mackie succeeded Anderson in the Challis Chair of Philosophy at Sydney University in 1959, and let some fresh air into that enclosed atmosphere. He left permanently for England in 1964. Before his death at a comparatively young age in 1981, he completed six well-regarded books, including *Ethics: Inventing Right and Wrong*, which repeats unattenuated his earlier sceptical views on ethics, and the anti-religious *The Miracle of Theism*.[52] Mackie had tangled briefly with Gough in 1960, when the Archbishop advocated the compulsory wearing of seatbelts. Mackie had protested against this moralistic intrusion on liberty with the words, 'If, however, Christianity can be summed up in the principle, "Everyone else must put up with what I like," as Dr Gough's other remarks on morality, censorship, and religion in schools would seem to indicate, then surely Christian driving is exactly what we have too much of already.'[53] At the time of Kinsella's campaign, he replied to the one aspect of the attack that had gained acceptance, the opinion that philosophy teaching at Sydney University was one-sided.[54] Mackie said that while a diversity of views in philosophy departments might be in

---

[49] Stove, recollection; Grave, *History*, p. 90.

[50] Pybus, *Seduction and Consent*, pp. 206–7.

[51] D.C. Stove to G.L. Cawkwell, 2/2/1982.

[52] Obituaries in *The Times* 15/12/1981, p. 12; *AJP* 60 (1982): p. 105; memorial addresses and bibliography in T. Honderich, ed, *Morality and Objectivity: A Tribute to J.L. Mackie* (London, 1985), pp. 215–28; also J.D. Goldsworthy, 'God or Mackie? The dilemma of secular moral philosophy', *American Journal of Jurisprudence* 30 (1985): pp. 43–78.

[53] Letter, *SMH* 20/10/1960, p. 2; similar from Libertarians on Gough on breathalysers in D.J. Ivison, 'Another outbreak of virtue', *Sydney Libertarians Broadsheet* 9 (Nov 1960), repr. in *The Sydney Line*, ed. A.J. Baker & G. Molnar (Sydney, 1963), pp. 15–17; a serious treatment of such issues in J. Kleinig, *Paternalism* (Totowa, NJ, 1984), ch. 4.

[54] Editorial: 'Archbishop Gough and the philosophers', *SMH* 15/7/1961, p. 2; 21/9/1961, p. 4.

principle desirable, it was certainly not the business of any outside authority to 'secure such diversity in order to reduce the risk of offending those who are hostile to the critical spirit.'[55]

Bill O'Neil's early work was distinctly Andersonian,[56] and he later saw his work of that time as a first attempt at the 'Australian materialism' that later became popular in the philosophy of mind (to be described in chapter 9). [57] Like several leading Andersonians, he was the product of a Catholic education, his views on which appear in his paper, 'The advantages of a Catholic education' in the second number of Anderson's *Freethought*. He complained that though Catholic students were told their faith was in accord with reason, they were not equipped with the arguments to refute objections. Further, despite too little attention by the Brothers to things intellectual and too much to swotting, he still didn't get good exam marks.[58] His appointment to the Sydney University chair of psychology in 1945 was attacked in the *Catholic Weekly* on the grounds of his materialism.[59]

Like Mackie, he was a thinker of independent mind. But he admired, in particular, Anderson's generally materialist point of view, and accepted his opinion on the lack of unity of the mind — the insistence on 'the plurality of feelings which interact within an economy or society of mental processes.' He admitted 'his [Anderson's] influence upon my own basic psychological views has been greater than that of any psychologist I have encountered, either in the flesh or through the printed page.'[60] It was O'Neil who gave the address at Anderson's retirement, praising him as the 'modern version of Socrates, the Athenian philosopher who was condemned for corrupting the

---

[55] J.L. Mackie, 'The place of philosophy in the universities', *Vestes* 4 (3) (Sept 1961): pp. 38–43, at p. 43.

[56] W.M. O'Neil, 'The experimental investigation of volition', *AJPP* 11 (1933): pp. 300–7; 'Mind as feeling?', *AJPP* 12 (1934): pp. 280–7, with note by Anderson, pp. 287–8; *Heraclitus* 40 (Mar 1995): p. 3.

[57] W.M. O'Neil, 'Psychology: another view', *Dialectic* (University of Newcastle) 30 (1987): pp. 60–2.

[58] W.M. O'Neil, 'The advantages of a Catholic education', *Freethought* 2 (Nov 1932): pp. 9–10.

[59] Editorial, *Catholic Weekly* 26/7/1945, p. 4; also L. Rumble, 'Question Box', *Catholic Weekly* 11/12/1947, p. 12.

[60] W.M. O'Neil, 'Some notes on Anderson's psychology', *Australian Highway* (Sept 1958): pp. 69–71; also obituary of O'Neil in *Bulletin of the Australian Psychological Society* 13 (3) (July 1991): pp. 2–3, and recollections of him in 14 (5) (Oct 1992): pp. 9–11 & 15 (2) (Apr 1993): pp. 11–28. There is a short and psychologically unrevealing autobiography in *Conceptual Analysis and Method in Psychology: Essays in Honour of W.M. O'Neil*, ed. J.P. Sutcliffe (Sydney, 1978), pp. 195–206.

youth.[61] The Andersonian influence meant that the Sydney Psychology Department was one of the few in the world where mention of philosophy was permitted. In most places, academic psychology was still trying to put as much distance as possible between itself and philosophy, in the interests of maintaining its status as a true experimental science, free of waffle. At Sydney, on the other hand, it was permissible to suggest that claiming to be free of philosophical assumptions is merely to adopt some long-refuted simplistic philosophical view, and one could say things like 'a great proportion of psychological research has been misdirected, to pseudo problems on which no conceivable data could throw any light.'[62]

The actual range of philosophical views, however, was not wide. No doubt there was some exaggeration in Kinsella's belief that 'in these matters the two departments are indistinguishable; the Psychology Department acts as an annexe of the Philosophy Department',[63] nevertheless, the differences between their position and Anderson's were perhaps more evident to insiders than to outside observers, and on the points that mattered, there was a good measure of agreement.[64]

T HE Gough 'affair' died down, but flared up briefly twice again in 1962. Kinsella was invited to orientation week at the University of New South Wales to debate Dr Peter Kenny, a psychologist with connections to the Sydney University Psychology Department[65] and self-styled sexologist. Kenny duly shocked everyone with his views

---

[61] *SMH* 31/12/1958, p. 4.

[62] J.R. Maze, *The Meaning of Behaviour* (London, 1983), p. iv; cf. P.B. Bell & P.J. Staines, *Logical Psych* (Kensington, 2001).

[63] 'Stout hits back at Kinsella', *Honi Soit* 34 (5) (27/3/1962), p. 1.

[64] J.J. Furedy, 'On the relevance of philosophy to psychological research: Some autobiographical speculations concerning the influence of Andersonian realism', *Australian Psychologist* 24 (1989): pp. 93–100; more on Andersonian and similar views in the Sydney Psychology department in T. McMullen, 'A critique of humanistic psychology', *Australian Journal of Psychology* 34 (1982): pp. 221–9; T. McMullen, 'John Anderson on mind as feeling', *Theory and Psychology* 6 (1996): pp. 153–68; J.R. Maze, 'The concept of attitude', in *Conceptual Analysis* ed. Sutcliffe, pp. 3–14; J. Michell, 'Maze's direct realism and the character of cognition', *Australian Journal of Psychology* 40 (1988): pp. 227–49. J.P. Maze, 'John Anderson: implications of his philosophic views for psychology', *Dialectic* 30 (1987): pp. 50–9; McMullen, Maze & Michell on 'The life of John Anderson' in *Metascience* 10 (1996): pp. 6–16; D.J. Ivison, 'Orgasm theory', *Libertarian* 3 (1960): p. 18; D.J. Ivison, 'Anderson as a liberator', *Dialectic* (Newcastle University) 30 (1987): pp. 7–9; A. Coombs, *Sex and Anarchy* (Ringwood, 1996), pp. 117, 122, 130, 189–90.

[65] See P. Kenny, 'Determinism and free will', *Pluralist* no. 5 (1965): pp. 28–32.

on sexual freedom, and Kinsella denounced him to the Curlewis committee, as evidence of the depths to which immoral philosophy had led.[66] Later in the year, Kinsella's letter was used as publicity for a talk by Kenny at the University of Queensland, leading to the student editor of *The Freethinker*, Humphrey McQueen, being suspended and given a sound talking to by the Vice-Chancellor on the need for morality.[67]

Gough and Kinsella lost the battle comprehensively. It was widely agreed that Gough had been misled by Kinsella's allegations, and even Gough came to suspect he had been sold a dud. All the same, a few on the other side harboured private thoughts that their victory was not altogether deserved. David Stove, then recently appointed to Sydney University, wrote privately to David Armstrong concerning Armstrong's letter criticising 'the attempt to link the names of Professors Anderson, O'Neil and Stout with any kind of impropriety':[68]

> I didn't like your letter on the Archbishop etc a bit. Unless you're privately redefining 'impropriety' it is neither silly nor scandalous to impute an influence for impropriety to Anderson, but just obviously true. But I won't start on this. Alan [Stout] has nearly driven us mad by his reluctance to shut up. In my opinion he's playing with fire, as well as being plainly and repeatedly dishonest.[69]

He was known to say, many years later, 'I hate to agree with an idiot like Kinsella, but he was absolutely right.'

Peter Coleman, then beginning to achieve some success in the literary world with books like *Obscenity, Blasphemy, Sedition*, which attacks those notions as strongly as Anderson, recalled the Sydney University speech as something of a turning-point in his views, which were rapidly becoming more conservative:

> The great philosopher could not see that the crowds now shouting tally-ho shared none of his austere, stoic and classicist values. These were the forward scouts of all the creeds of the sixties against whose coming he had spoken so eloquently — the liberationism, the relativism, the irrationalism. Next week they would be cheering his enemies again. But this scourge of religious moralists, patriotic blowhards, philistine censors and

---

[66] Kinsella's letter reprinted in *Sydney Libertarians Broadsheet* 26 (Apr 1962), p. 3; *Telegraph* 21/3/1962; 22/3/1962, p. 44; *SMH* 22/3/1962, p. 5; 23/3/1962, p. 10; *Honi Soit* 34 (8) (17/4/1962); C. Wallace, *Greer: Untamed Shrew* (Sydney, 1997), pp. 95–7.

[67] *Sydney Libertarians Broadsheet* 27 (July 1962); McQueen on Anderson in H. McQueen, *Gallipoli to Petrov* (Sydney, 1984), pp. 93–6.

[68] D.M. Armstrong and nine others, letter, 'The allegations of Dr Gough', *SMH* 10/7/1961.

[69] D.C. Stove to D.M. Armstrong, July 1961.

leftwing bullyboys was overwhelmed by the flattery of the multitude and could see no tincture of truth in the charges of his critics.

Here then was Australia as the 1960s began. The head of the only Church with which I had any bond had raised important issues far beyond his grasp. The head of an old conservative family and publisher of a leading newspaper had taken sides against the teacher who had done most to expose the humbug of our times. That philosopher was now paying grateful homage to the shock troops of the new dark age against which he had warned.[70]

Dr Kinsella later gave philosophy lessons in several Marist Sisters schools, which are remembered as stimulating by some of the better students.[71] These lessons, and his primer for philosophy in schools,[72] make him a pioneer of the lately fashionable philosophy for schools movement.

The author of the offending textbook, John Hospers, became a genuine danger to other countries, if not Australia. He was Presidential candidate for the Libertarian Party, advocating the dismantling of government services, in the US Presidential Election of 1972, and was later involved in a secessionist coup in the New Hebrides.[73]

Gough was not so lucky, and became a victim of the new age against which he had fought. Allegations that he was sacked for adultery on a cruise liner[74] are apparently untrue; he was not sacked, nor were the allegations of adultery established. But it was certainly the case that a romantic attachment of some kind to a member of the church led to rumours taken advantage of by his enemies, by then numerous.[75]

The mainstream press did the right thing and carried the usual 'ill health' stories when he suddenly resigned,[76] but *Oz* magazine, representing those condemned by Gough in 1961, made the most of the opportunity: 'Let OZ state quite categorically that it cannot believe such stories in view of Hugh's well known and forthright public

---

[70] Coleman, *Memoirs*, p. 165; similar thoughts in Stove, 'Force of intellect', at p. 46.
[71] Sr J. McBride SM to author.
[72] V. Kinsella, *Philosophy for Schools* (48 pp., printed by Erica Press, Huntingdale, Vic, n.d.).
[73] *Age* 4/6/1980, p. 11; *Bulletin* 17/6/1980, pp. 97–103.
[74] R. Neville, *Hippie Hippie Shake* (Melbourne, 1995), p. 105.
[75] A. Gill, 'A "shabbily treated" archbishop', *SMH* 27/10/1987, p. 3; S. Judd & K. Cable, *Sydney Anglicans* (Sydney, 1987), p. 274; A. Gill to author, 1/11/1995, K. Cable to author, 8/11/1995, S. Judd to author, 21/11/1995.
[76] *SMH* 25/5/1966, p. 1.

statements on the true morality.'[77] Gough was packed off to be vicar of Freshford, Somerset (population 600).[78]

---

[77] 'Whatever happened to Hugh?' *Oz* no. 28 (1966): pp. 2–3.
[78] *SMH* 19/1/1967, p. 6.

Chapter 6   Idealism and Empire

When the hysterical vision strikes
The facade of an era it manifests
Its insidious relations.
— *Ern Malley*[1]

HOW far can philosophy diverge from common sense? This is a question, of course, for philosophy, and one that has produced a range of divergent opinions.[2] Some regard the deliverances of common sense as data that philosophy can explain, but not deny. Others dismiss common sense as so much Stone Age metaphysics, incorporating the confusions of the Cave Man in the street in much the same way that ordinary language includes antique science like 'The sun rises in the east.'

Now, if departures from common sense are allowed, how far can you go? Surely there is a limit. David Armstrong's first year lectures on Descartes included this joke: A philosophy lecturer noticed one of his students looking more and more worried as the course progressed. The student was absent for a while, then staggered in unkempt, dirty, obviously unslept. 'Professor, Professor,' he said, 'You've got to help me. *Do I really exist?*' The Professor looked around and said, 'Who wants to know?'

[1] Ern Malley, *Collected Poems* (Sydney, 1993), p. 36.
[2] K. Campbell, 'Philosophy and common sense', *Philosophy* 63 (1988): pp. 161–74; cf. P. James, 'Questioning the evidence of commonsense', *Melbourne Journal of Politics* 14 (1982/3): pp. 46–57; J. Kennett & M. Smith, 'Philosophy and common sense: The case of weakness of will', in M. Michael & J. O'Leary-Hawthorne, eds, *Philosophy in Mind: The Place of Philosophy in the Study of Mind* (Dordrecht, 1994), pp. 141–57.

The point of Descartes' dictum, 'I think, therefore I am' is that, if you really try, you can doubt the existence of everything outside your own mind at least in principle. But there is no denying the existence of yourself, at least if 'yourself' means only the thinking being that you directly experience.

The most determined school of philosophy in pushing doubt to this theoretical limit is idealism. The best-known version of idealism is that of George Berkeley, the eighteenth-century Irish bishop who maintained that there were no physical objects outside the mind at all. Instead, he thought, God causes directly the play of (apparent) perceptions on our psyches. Hector Monro's *Sonneteer's History of Philosophy*, one of the shorter introductions to the subject, summarises Berkeley's position as follows:

> 'The scientific cosmos', grumbled Berkeley,
> 'Is, once you penetrate beneath the patter,
> Made up of something mystical called Matter.
> It's not just that you see it through glass darkly,
> You cannot see the stuff at all. It's starkly
> Devoid of scent and sound and colour, flatter
> And duller than a garden party's chatter.
> We're all bamboozled by the learned-clerkly
> Romantic balderdash. Reality
> Is surely what we touch and hear and see.
> If what our senses yield is in the mind,
> Then so's Reality.' At once maligned,
> Good Berkeley's universe, because it's mental
> Is labelled thin, ethereal, transcendental.[3]

Needless to say, it is not a widely held opinion. Indeed, it invites jokes about why anybody who holds it should be concerned to express it: who does he think he is talking to? The significance of Berkeley lies actually more in his arguments than in his conclusions. The colonial poet Charles Harpur wrote:

> His logic puzzles so, it don't convince.
> So wide his arguments, we half suspect them
> Of aberrations though we can't detect them.[4]

---

[3] D.H. Monro, *The Sonneteer's History of Philosophy* (Melbourne, 1981), p. 20; also in *Philosophy* 55 (1980): pp. 363–75 (repr. with permission of Dugald and Gordon Monro); comments on the causes of such opinions in H. Caton, 'Pascal's syndrome: Positivism as a symptom of depression and mania', *Zygon* 21 (1986): pp. 319–52.

[4] Quoted in *Between Two Worlds: 'Loss of Faith' and Late Nineteenth Century Australian Literature*, ed. A. Clark, J. Fletcher & R. Marsden (Sydney, 1979), p. 18.

This is quite wrong, as Berkeley has an exceptional ability to make gross mistakes clearly, and is therefore in regular use as target practice for philosophy undergraduates — as David Stove said, an undergraduate course without Berkeley is like a zoo without elephants.[5] He is important not only for students: David Armstrong's early works, in which he refined the rigorous style of argumentation that became his hallmark, are on Berkeley.[6]

The only sign of Berkeleian idealism being taken seriously in Australia was an event in 1936, when the Sydney Anglican Church wheeled out the Lord Archbishop of Armagh and Primate of All Ireland, the Most Reverend C.F. D'Arcy, to give a talk at Sydney University. The Archbishop said that Berkeley's doctrine, although it had been attacked severely, had not, in his opinion, been overthrown. 'The principles of his philosophy supplied a great spiritual need at the present time.'[7] No doubt there was a spiritual need, especially with John Anderson firmly in the chair of philosophy, but Berkeleian idealism is a cure surely at once worse than the disease, and necessarily ineffective.

The Primate's suggestion that the point of idealism is to pervade the universe with a general tone of moral uplift, amenable to religion, is even more evident in the other variant of the theory, Absolute Idealism. This is a late Victorian construction with some resemblance to the wedding-cake architecture beloved of the period. It is possibly too alien a thought-world to understand at this distance, but the general idea is that, while the physical world may exist, its nature is essentially mental rather than (what we take to be) material. Everything is interconnected, and is a manifestation of the Absolute, which is something like God, but less crudely personal, and also less distant from oneself.[8] Absolute Idealism in its heyday — around the 1890s — became the first and only philosophy to be accepted as orthodoxy in

---

[5] D.M. Armstrong, Course submission for 1974.

[6] D.M. Armstrong, *Berkeley's Theory of Vision* (Melbourne, 1960); *Berkeley's Philosophical Writings*, ed. with an introduction by D.M. Armstrong (New York, 1965); Berkeley, the Push and Australian painting in H. McQueen, *Suburbs of the Sacred* (Ringwood, 1988), pp. 29–31.

[7] *SMH* 12/6/1936, p. 10; some parallels in Christian Science: R. Dessaix, *A Mother's Disgrace* (Sydney, 1994), pp. 79–81.

[8] J. Passmore, *A Hundred Years of Philosophy* (London, 1957), chs 3–4; S. Candlish, 'The status of idealism in Bradley's metaphysics', *Idealistic Studies* 11 (1981): pp. 242–53; S. Candlish, 'Idealism and Bradley's logic', *Idealistic Studies* 12 (1982): pp. 251–9; S. Candlish, 'Bradley, F.H.', in *Routledge Encyclopedia of Philosophy,* vol. 1 pp. 857–63; J. O'Leary-Hawthorne, 'Anti-realism, before and after Moore', *History of Philosophy Quarterly* 12 (1995): pp. 443–67.

the whole learned world (Paris, Heidelberg, Edinburgh, Peking, Adelaide ...). Then it simply evaporated. John Anderson always regarded idealism as the prime enemy, but by his time there were hardly any live idealists left to devour — in the philosophical world, at least, though as we saw in chapter 1, there were some in the New South Wales Parliament. The importance of idealism for Australia is that all of the first philosophers in Australian universities were adherents, including, for example, Australia's only philosophical knights, Sir Francis Anderson at Sydney and Sir William Mitchell at Adelaide.[9] In his memorable attack, 'Idealism: A Victorian horror story', David Stove writes,

> Nineteenth-century idealism, accordingly, provided an important holding-station or decompression chamber, for that century's vast flood of intellectual refugees from Christianity; or at any rate, for the more philosophically inclined among them. The situation of these people was truly pitiful. The burden of their biblical embarrassments had become intolerable ... The problem was how to part with the absurdities of Christianity, while keeping cosmic consolation: no one dreamt of parting with the latter as well (it should hardly be necessary to say), or at any rate no philosopher did.[10]

An idealist, he says, is one of a philosophical turn of mind, who can no longer stomach the raw barbarisms of popular religion, but 'in whom, nevertheless, the religious determination to have the universe congenial is still sovereign.' This was a period in which a wide variety of remedies were tried by the less philosophical, including the Wisdom of the East, theosophy, spiritualism, and so on,[11] as well as relig-

[9] S. Grave, *A History of Philosophy in Australia* (St Lucia, 1984), ch. 2; J. Passmore, 'Philosophy', in *The Pattern of Australian Culture*, ed. A.L. McLeod (Melbourne, 1963), pp. 131–69; obituary of Mitchell in *AJP* 40 (1962): pp. 261–3; W.M. Davies, *A Mind's Own Place: The Life and Thought of Sir William Mitchell*, (Lewiston, NY, 2003); account of Francis Anderson's philosophy in G. Melleuish, *Cultural Liberalism in Australia* (Cambridge, 1995), pp. 87–95; W.M. O'Neil, 'Francis Anderson', in *ADB*, vol. 7 pp. 53–5; obituary in *AJPP* 19 (1941): pp. 97–101; 'Francis Anderson: Professor and citizen', *Hermes* 27 (3) (Nov 1921); Francis Anderson's papers in Sydney University Archives listed at www.usyd.edu.au/arms/archives/anderson.htm ; a late example of idealism in G. James, *Philosophy: A Synopsis* (Brisbane, 1957).

[10] D.C. Stove, *The Plato Cult and Other Philosophical Follies* (Oxford, 1991), pp. 87–8.

[11] Jill Roe, *Beyond Belief: Theosophy in Australia, 1879–1939* (Kensington, 1986); R. Dixon, *Writing the Colonial Adventure* (Cambridge, 1995), ch. 6; H. Green, *Ulysses Bound* (Canberra, 1973), pp. 355–6, 528–41; 'Spirit-rappin'', in *Henry Lawson: Autobiographical and Other Writings*, ed. C. Roderick (Sydney, 1972), pp. 260–1; J. Curtis, *Rustlings in the Golden City:*

ion substitutes like the 'religion of humanity', socialism and Australian nationalism,[12] and attempts to find a non-dogmatic common core of Christianity. As the Catholic Archbishop Vaughan said, 'the troubled air resounds with Pan-Christianities, Pantisolatries, Eirenica, the fraternization of Churches, and the amalgamation of sects.'[13] And as one of those he attacked was happy to admit, 'our thought is eclectic, our method is elastic.'[14] But for those who demanded philosophy, there could be only one possible answer, idealism. 'That is,' (Stove says)

> something like Berkeley's pan-spiritualism, as long as it could be freed from its embarrassing implication of universal hallucination. If Berkeley's too gaseous world could be solidified (so to speak), or at least 'jellied', by being passed through a strong field of Kant-Hegel radiation; *that* would be the very thing. Let the refugees from Christianity be told, on the highest possible philosophical authority, that Nature *is* Thought, that the Universe *is* Spirit, that the Absolute is experience, that the dualism of matter and mind, like the related dualism of fact and value, is a superficial one, and 'ultimately' (as the Hegelians loved to say) even a self-contradictory one. That should buck them up, as nothing else could.[15]

Stove's diagnosis is confirmed by the poet Christopher Brennan's reaction to Francis Anderson's lectures at Sydney University. After leaving the Jesuit Riverview College, the undergraduate Brennan experienced the doubts customary in these cases. 'Religion began to worry me in my 19th year ... The next Christmas I experienced a sudden collapse of all the barriers and entered the philosophy class in March 1890 a ripe agnostic, already beginning to elaborate a special epistemology of the Unknowable, which was the Absolute. The year

Being a Record of Spiritualistic Experiences in Ballarat and Melbourne (Ballarat, 1890?)

[12] P. Morgan, 'Australian nationalism as a religion substitute', in *Between Two Worlds*, ed. Clark, Fletcher & Marsden, pp. 53–72; F.S. O'Donnell, 'Socialism and religion', *Austral Light* 6 (1905): pp. 352–61; cf. J.E. Poole, 'Marcus Clarke: "Christianity is dead"', *Australian Literary Studies* 6 (1973): pp. 128–42; R.D. Jordan, 'Adam Lindsay Gordon and the religion of Australia', *Westerly* 43 (2) (Winter 1998): pp. 27–42.

[13] R. Vaughan, *Hidden Springs* (Sydney, 1876), p. 38.

[14] A.B. Camm, *Phases of Unitarianism, Orthodoxy and Freethought in Sydney* (Sydney, 1885), p. 2; also A.B. Camm, *Liberal Religion in the Higher Current Literature* (Sydney, 1883); D. Scott, *The Halfway House to Infidelity: A History of the Melbourne Unitarian Church, 1853–1973* (Melbourne, 1980); S. Magarey, *Unbridling the Tongues of Women* (Sydney, 1985), ch. 3; R. Ely, 'The tyranny of amenity and distance: The religious liberalism of Andrew Inglis Clark', in *An Australian Democrat*, ed. M. Haward & J. Warden (Hobart, 1995), pp. 98–118.

[15] Stove, *The Plato Cult*, pp. 88–9; some primary evidence in J.G. Stewart, 'The philosophy of religion', *Victorian Review* 7 (1883): pp. 29–36.

I spent in open conflict with F.A.'[16] Brennan has caught on to one of
the defining tics of Absolute Idealism, its plague of Capital Letters.
The caricature some still have of philosophers, as men spouting vapid
and implausible generalities about Truth and Wisdom and the Absolute, is perhaps the last vestige of the reign of Absolute Idealism.

In Melbourne, idealism actually constituted itself as an institutional
religion, in the Reverend Charles Strong's Australian Church. Strong
took modern philosophy and science to have rendered outmoded the
myths of the Old Testament, and to have shown the way forward to
'the idea of a universe that lives and moves and has its being *in* God
... Ultimate Reality is not to be found outside but *inside* us, in our
own minds and natures.'[17] The Church, formed after Strong's
persecution by his own Presbyterian Church, was a success for some
years. A typically idealist project was Strong's leadership of the Melbourne Peace Society; he believed that Australia could lead the way
towards the resolution through arbitration of conflict between
nations, as it had for the conflict between labour and capital.[18] Francis
Anderson was assistant minister in the Church before leaving for Sydney University,[19] and Alfred Deakin and the poet Bernard O'Dowd
were staunch supporters.[20]

Idealism also had its political significance, arising from its tendency
to reify abstract concepts and endow them with claims on people.
History and Progress were favourites. The Mind that permeates the
world ought to express itself in History, which is thus a cosmic process with a direction rather than a statistical result of individual human
actions or just one damned thing after another. The universe, Francis
Anderson said, was in constant evolution, a never-ending progressive
unfolding towards a higher stage of development; 'History is a great

[16] C. Brennan, 'Curriculum vitae', in *Christopher Brennan*, ed. T. Sturm
(Brisbane, 1984), p. 177; Brennan's version of idealism in 'Fact and idea'
(1898), in Sturm, pp. 187–96; discussion in Melleuish, *Cultural Liberalism*,
pp. 97–101; selections from Brennan's dissertation 'The Metaphysic of
Nescience' reprinted in R.B. Marsden, 'New light on Brennan', *Southerly* 31
(1971): pp. 119–35.
[17] 'The Immanent God of modern philosophy', sermon of 1898, in C.R.
Badger, *The Reverend Charles Strong and the Australian Church* (Melbourne,
1971), pp. 271–7.
[18] M. Saunders, 'The origins and early years of the Melbourne Peace Society,
1899–1914', *Journal of the Royal Australian Historical Society* 79 (1993): 96–
114; cf. C. Strong, 'The tercentenary of George Fox', *AJPP* 2 (1924): pp.
283–5.
[19] See *The Australian Church: Report MDCCCLXXXVII and sermons preached
by Chas. Strong and Francis Anderson* (Melbourne, 1887).
[20] See B. O'Dowd, 'To Immanuel Kant', in *The Poems of Bernard O'Dowd*
(Melbourne, 1944), p. 166.

Professor (later Sir) Francis Anderson, c. 1902 (National Library of Australia)

adventure in which man sets out to discover himself and the secret of his personality.'[21] Religion, of a non-sectarian sort, was also approved of, as promoting an 'advance to a further and higher phase of

[21] F. Anderson, *Liberty, Equality and Fraternity* (Sydney, 1922), p. 22, quoted and discussed in Melleuish, *Cultural Liberalism*, p. 88 and G. Melleuish, 'Liberal intellectuals in early twentieth century Australia', *Australian Journal of Politics and History* 35 (1989): pp. 1–12, at p 3; D.C. Band, 'The critical reception of English neo-Hegelianism in Britain and America, 1914–1960', *Australian Journal of Politics and History* 26 (1980): pp. 228–41; J. Docker, 'The origins of Paddy McGuinness', *Arena Magazine* 3 (Feb/Mar 1993): pp. 21–24.

development, under the guidance of the spirit of Truth.'[22] One of the leading British idealists was Sir Henry Jones, John Anderson's main teacher in philosophy; the pupil's views on the state, religion, and technical philosophical questions are diametrically opposite to Sir Henry's. Jones visited Francis Anderson in Sydney in 1908, giving a series of lectures later published as — note the title — *Idealism as a Practical Creed*. His farewell lecture concluded with a marvellously Edwardian piece of orotund condescension towards the colonials:

> I cannot forget the greatness, and the difficulties of your enterprise — a new people amidst the lonely silence of a vast continent. Material prosperity you will attain, I have no doubt; and it is worth attaining. Perhaps power among the nations of the world awaits you, which is also worth attaining. But a kingdom founded upon righteousness, a life amongst yourselves sanctified in all its ways by this faith in man, in the world and in God, is greater far than all these things. I can form no higher wish for you than that it may be your destiny to try by actual experiment how far this faith of the Idealists will stand the strain of a nation's practice.[23]

John Anderson later recalled with a degree of horror Jones forcing himself to spell out the optimistic idealist faith of Robert Browning while suffering the pains of advanced cancer.[24] The incident does something to explain the tremendous emotional force behind John Anderson's reaction to anything that smelt of a sentimental attachment to another world, or of consolation or uplift.

If Sydney was only mildly responsive to such 'practical idealism', Melbourne saw one of its boldest experiments. There, the unique Australian scheme for the settlement of industrial disputes by an Arbitration Court was undertaken under the presidency of the idealist

---

[22] F. Anderson, 'The present religious situation', *AJPP* 1 (1923): pp. 216, 219–22, also in Melleuish, 'Liberal intellectuals'.

[23] H. Jones, *Idealism as a Practical Creed: Being the Lectures on Philosophy and Modern Life Delivered Before the University of Sydney* (Glasgow, 1910), pp. 298–9, quoted and discussed in B. Kennedy, *A Passion to Oppose* (Melbourne, 1995) pp. 76; similar in F. Anderson, 'A modern philosopher — Green of Balliol', *Union Book of 1902* (Sydney, 1902), see Melleuish, *Cultural Liberalism*, p. 88; 'Philosophy and modern life', *Hermes* 14 (3) (July 1908): pp. 54–6; more generally, M. Sawer, 'The ethical state: Social liberalism and the critique of contract', *Australian Historical Studies* 31 (2000): pp. 67–90 .

[24] [G. Munster], 'Prophet in a gown', *Nation* no. 9 (17/1/1959), pp. 10–13, at p. 10; for Jones on Browning see H. Jones, *Browning as a Philosophical and Religious Teacher* (Glasgow, 1891); for Browning as an answer to Darwin, M.W. MacCallum, *Browning after a Generation* (Sydney, 1924), pp. 8–13; cf. D. Stove on '*horror Victorianorum*' in *Against the Idols of the Age* (New Brunswick, 1999), pp. 25–32.

Henry Bournes Higgins. He wrote of the purpose of arbitration in typically idealist prose:

> Though the functions of the Court are definite and limited, there is opened up for idealists a very wide horizon, with, perhaps, something of the glow of a sunrise ... Give them [the workers] relief from their materialistic anxiety; give them reasonable certainty that their essential material needs will be met by honest work, and you release infinite stores of human energy for higher efforts, for nobler ideals, when 'Body gets its sop, and holds its noise, and leaves soul free a little'.[25]

The quotation is from Browning, on whose thought Higgins had written.[26]

To appreciate fully the victory of idealism in its day, one needs to understand that a student would not avoid it simply by failing to take philosophy. At the time Francis Anderson was serving as Sydney University's first professor of philosophy, the occupants of the new chairs of Modern Languages and of History were giving their students much the same message. Mungo MacCallum had studied the same idealist philosophy at Glasgow as Francis Anderson, and had produced a long idealist interpretation of the Arthurian legend.[27] And George Arnold Wood in History proclaimed a similar optimistic doctrine of progress driven by spiritually active men[28] — demonstrated, he thought, nowhere better than in the history of Australia, from its foundation by noble convicts to its apotheosis at Gallipoli and Flanders.[29]

A secular version of these notions appears in *What Happened in History?*, a work of immense worldwide popularity written by Francis Anderson's student, V. Gordon Childe. It is resolutely about the Progress of Man: 'history may still justify a belief in progress in days of

---

[25] H.B. Higgins, *A New Province for Law and Order* (London, 1922, repr. London, 1968), pp. 37–8; see P.S. Callaghan, 'Idealism and arbitration in H.B. Higgins' New Province for Law and Order', *Journal of Australian Studies* 13 (1983): pp. 56–66.

[26] H.B. Higgins, *Robert Browning: His Mind and Art* (Melbourne, 1906); also H.B. Higgins, 'Australian ideals', *Austral Light* 3 (1902): pp. 9–19.

[27] M. MacCallum, *Tennyson's Idylls of the King and Arthurian Story from the XVIth Century* (Glasgow, 1894); Melleuish, *Cultural Liberalism*, pp. 82–5; L. Dale, *The English Men* (Toowoomba, 1997), pp. 27–32.

[28] R.M. Crawford, *A Bit of a Rebel: The Life and Work of George Arnold Wood* (Sydney, 1975), pp. 135–42; B.H. Fletcher, 'History as a moral force: George Arnold Wood at Sydney University, 1891–1928', in *The Discovery of Australian History, 1890–1939*, ed. S. Macintyre & J. Thomas (Melbourne, 1995), pp. 10–27; Melleuish, *Cultural Liberalism*, pp. 85–7.

[29] G.A. Wood, 'Convicts', *Journal of the Royal Australian Historical Society* 8 (1922): pp. 177–208.

depression.'[30] Something similar occurred in Melbourne, where the idealist views of history of the philosophy professor W.R. Boyce Gibson had an impact on the overblown style of history associated with Melbourne University.[31] At their best, doctrines of historical evolution towards a better world could inspire reasonable projects of reform. Francis Anderson himself spent a great deal of effort on reforms of the public education system and mental health services, and wrote controversial pamphlets on such subjects as 'The Root of the Matter: Social and Economic Aspects of the Sex Problem'. 'The end of teaching', he said, 'is to produce self-active pupils',[32] and unlike some who have expressed similar opinions, he meant it. 'An inspirer of youth to action in the interests of daring and adventure', [33] he had an impact on, among other students, H.V. Evatt (who gained a University Medal in philosophy and tutored in the subject), the anthropologist and architect of policy on Aborigines, A.P. Elkin, and Ernest Burgmann, the 'Red Bishop'.[34]

And since the idealists had taken charge of reforms of the school curriculum as well, it was not just the small number of university-trained intellectuals who were being fed idealism. Donald Horne is here describing his *primary* school education:

---

[30] Melleuish, *Cultural Liberalism*, pp. 126–36; G. Melleuish, 'The place of Vere Gordon Childe in Australian intellectual history', in *Childe and Australia*, ed. P. Gathercole, T.H. Irving & G. Melleuish (St Lucia, 1995), pp. 147–161.

[31] D. Watson, *Brian Fitzpatrick: A Radical Life* (Sydney, 1979), pp. 14–15.

[32] F. Anderson, *On Teaching to Think* (Sydney, 1903), p. 4; recollections of his teaching in G.V. Portus, *Happy Highways* (Melbourne, 1953), pp. 62–7, 176–8; A.R. Chisholm, *Men Were My Milestones* (Melbourne, 1958), pp. 41–2; on his work on education reform, A.R. Crane & W.G. Walker, *Peter Board* (Melbourne, 1957), pp. 13–19, 153–4, 286–7 and J. Roberts, *Maybanke Anderson: Sex, Suffrage and Social Reform* (Sydney, 1993), ch. 6.

[33] E. Morris Miller, 'The beginnings of philosophy in Australia and the work of Henry Laurie. I', *AJPP* 7 (1929): pp. 241–51, at p. 250; on Morris Miller and his idealism, M. Roe, *Nine Australian Progressives* (St Lucia, 1984), ch. 10 (Miller got his start by working his way up through the ranks of the Moonee Ponds Mental Improvement Society); J. Reynolds and M. Giordano, *Countries of the Mind* (Hobart, 1985); also E.M. Miller, 'McKellar Stewart: a contemporary's appreciation', *AJP* 32 (1954): pp. 169–84.

[34] T. Rowse, *Australian Liberalism and National Character* (Malmsbury, Vic, 1978), ch. 2; P. Crockett, *Evatt: A Life* (Melbourne, 1993), pp. 46, 49; K. Buckley, B. Dale & W. Reynolds, *Doc Evatt* (Melbourne, 1994), pp. 10–12; T. Wise, *The Self-Made Anthropologist: A Life of A.P. Elkin* (Sydney, 1985), pp. 18–20; P. Hempenstall, *The Meddlesome Priest: A Life of Ernest Burgmann* (Sydney, 1993), pp. 43–6; also G. Barwick, *A Radical Tory* (Sydney, 1995), p. 12.

We were offered a view of life based on an optimistic belief in inevitable progress, a progress that would proceed of necessity, without our doing anything in particular about it. It was the officially expressed belief of the New South Wales Department of Public Instruction that there was a natural 'sense of growth and development' in human affairs, and that 'the human race ... was developing towards better and happier conditions of life'. This meant that one of our schoolroom views of mankind was optimistic, progressive and radical. We were on the side of revolution, exploration and innovation. We were for the barons against King John; for Wat Tyler against Richard II; for Sir Thomas More against Henry VIII, and for Henry VIII against the Pope ... Human history was a predictable progress of discovery and reform; innovation served the welfare of the ordinary people in a sure evolution from serfdom to having a good time playing tennis at Muswellbrook.[35]

Horne is speaking of 1933, at the end of the twenty years from the Somme to the Depression.

Also given a capital letter and endowed with moral standing were the State and the Empire. The State was not adored in the way it was in some European countries, if only because Australia had barely established itself as a nation. The Empire certainly was. As an entity to inspire loyalty, the Empire had several useful and remarkable properties. On the one hand, it was abstract, but on the other, it was right where you were. In fact, you were part of it. Its ability to be in many places at once, and to unite the emotional high points of all of them, made it the sort of entity the Absolute Idealists were proud of. It was itself not a mere person, but was strengthened by personal devotion to the monarch. All creeds could unite in praying for its welfare. And its successful defence against its many enemies made for stirring stories. All in all, it was a perfect focus for loyalty in the armed forces and for idolatry in schools.[36] Those who had charge of its implementation in schools were careful to avoid making the Empire an excuse for simple jingoism. Something morally superior was aimed at. A circular from Peter Board, Francis Anderson's chief ally in school reform, on the celebration of Empire Day in 1906 instructs: 'It is not intended that there should be any encouragement of an exaggerated sentiment arising out of a mere glorification of the British

---

[35] D. Horne, *The Education of Young Donald* (2nd ed, Ringwood, 1988), p. 67.

[36] S.G. Firth, 'Social values in the New South Wales primary school 1880–1914', *Melbourne Studies in Education 1970* (Melbourne, 1971): pp. 123–59; N. Townshend, 'Philosophy of history in the School Magazine of New South Wales, 1916–1922', *Journal of Australian Studies* 11 (1982): pp. 36–53; B. Bessant & A. Spaull, *Politics of Schooling* (Melbourne, 1976), ch. 1; hostile philosophical comment in D.H. Monro, 'The concept of myth', *Sociological Review* 42 (1950): pp. 115–32.

races by the disparagement of other peoples, but that the interest in the Empire should rest on a knowledge of what it is, and on an appreciation of the higher qualities that have played a part in its progress. By this means, also, pupils may be encouraged to become worthy citizens of their own native country, feel a pride in its progress, and an obligation to advance its interests.'[37]

During the rest of the year, the Empire and its virtues occupied a large part of the syllabus, especially in history. As to the particular higher qualities for which the Empire was to be admired, the view of a typical textbook is that of *A Story of the English People*, by K.R. Cramp, later the historian of the New South Wales Freemasons.[38] 'For British rule, in spite of a mistake here and there, has brought peace, justice, liberty and prosperity in its train wherever it has been established. And the size, wealth and population of the Empire is a kind of guarantee that those ideals of Peace, Justice, Liberty and Prosperity must be respected. For they endear British rule to the native races.'[39]

Between the Wars, Empire Day retained a place alongside Anzac Day, and became an occasion for student practice in giving talks on the moral destiny of the Empire.[40] Though not as deeply significant as Anzac Day, students were told, it was celebrated more widely.

On that day, in almost every school in the Empire, children are reminded, not so much of the greatness and wealth of the Empire, but of the need to

---

[37] P. Board, 'Empire Day Celebration', circular, *Public Instruction Gazette* (N.S.W.) 1 (1905–7): p. 78; F.B. Boyce, *Fourscore Years and Seven* (Sydney, 1934), ch. 10.

[38] On the author see 'K.R. Cramp OBE, BA, FRAHS', *NSW Freemason* 46 (1951): pp. 446–7; *ADB* vol. 8 p. 135.

[39] K.R. Cramp, W. Lennard & J.H. Smairl, *A Story of the English People: Issued by the Department of Public Instruction for Use in Schools* (Sydney, 1919), p. 408; at greater length in Walter Murdoch, *The Australian Citizen: An Elementary Account of Civic Rights and Duties* (Melbourne, 1912), ch. 8. also ch. 27 on 'liberty'; L. Alston, *The White Man's Work in Asia and Africa* (London, 1907), esp. ch. 2, 'Christian ethics and philosophy in relation to the lower races'; further in Partington, *Australian Nation*, pp. 162–4; G. Souter, *The Idle Hill of Summer* (Sydney, 1972), pp. 46–7; on the moral aspects of university history teaching, see *One Hundred Years of the Faculty of Arts* (Sydney, 1952), pp. 65–8; Irish Catholic scepticism about British 'freedoms' in 'The struggle for freedom', *Austral Light* 10 (1909): pp. 687–701.

[40] R. Hall, *The Real John Kerr* (Sydney, 1978), p. 12; R. Cracknell, *A Biased Memoir* (Melbourne, 1997), p. 10; H.L. Rubinstein, 'Empire loyalism in inter-war Victoria', *Victorian Historical Journal* 70 (1) (June 1999): pp. 67–83; M. French, 'The ambiguity of Empire Day in New South Wales, 1901–21', *Australian Journal of Politics and History* 24 (1978): pp. 61–74.

Empire Day, Coopers Glen Public School, near Bega, 1913 (Bicentennial Copying Project, State Library of NSW)

keep it bound together by ties of good will and love. This can be done by helping one another, and being fair to one another... In a small way, even a boy may become an Empire builder, for so long as he works honestly, strives for the right, and keeps his mind clean, he is adding something to the greatness and glory of our Empire.[41]

There is no point in trying to force a naturalistic interpretation on this passage. An Empire which is bound together by ties of love and can be benefited by a boy's keeping his mind clean is an idealist entity. It is the same language as used by a real idealist, Sir Francis Anderson, who spoke of the 'moral bonds of union' which, with the person of the King, unified the Empire more than economic self-interest or military fears.[42] Sir Henry Jones, too, said that in performing

---

[41] G.T. Spaull, *New Syllabus English and Australian History for Fifth Classes, with Civics and Moral Stories* (Sydney, 1937), pp. 214–5; on Spaull's enthusiasm for Francis Anderson and Peter Board's reforms, S.H. Smith & G.T. Spaull, *History of Education in New South Wales* (Sydney, 1925), pp. 195–200.

[42] F. Anderson, *The Empire and the League* (League of Nations Union, Leaflet series no. 7, Sydney, 1937?); more religious aspects in R. Ely, 'The forgotten nationalism: Australian civic protestantism in the Second World War', *Journal of Australian Studies* 20 (1987): pp. 59–67; R. Frappell, 'Imperial

his duty to the state an individual was building his own character, 'at the same time he is a humble hod-bearer on the walls of a greater and more permanent edifice than his own character; he is building the State.'[43] Even the very young John Anderson took some part in this, at the very time when the Great War was beginning to make it look as though History might have lost the plot.[44]

THE ideology of Empire was not simply imposed on an unwilling mass of children, either. Boys were spending their own pennies freely enough on English magazines full of Public School ripping yarns. The Melbourne University archivist recalled how common it was to find among the papers left by a distinguished scientist or judge copies of the *Magnet* or *Gem*, tucked furtively away.[45] These were not simply entertaining stories, but models that encouraged imitation of a certain ideal. Donald Horne says, 'At other times I miserably contemplated how I was not living up to the standards of the Billy Bunter stories or acting like the son of a trooper in the Australian Light Horse.'[46] How this ideal could appear to one who absorbed it fully is perfectly expressed by one of the Empire's personifications in later life, Robert Menzies:

> To many people the British Commonwealth is a curious machine that has worked; looking to the outsider rather like a Heath Robinson invention; but relied upon by mankind twice during this century, to their great deliverance. But what does it mean to you? I think I know what it means to me. May I break through our usual polite reticences and tell you?
>
> To me it means (and here you will find a curious jumble in both time and place) a cottage in the wheat lands of the North-West of the State of Victoria, with the Bible and Henry Drummond and Jerome K. Jerome

fervour and Anglican loyalty 1901–1929', ch. 4 of *Anglicanism in Australia: A history*, ed. B. Kaye (Melbourne, 2002).
[43] H. Jones, *Principles of Citizenship* (London, 1919), quoted and discussed in J. Morrow, 'British idealism, "German philosophy" and the First World War', *Australian Journal of Politics and History* 28 (1982): pp. 380–90.
[44] J. Anderson, essay 'Is the state a moral agent?' (1916), discussed in Kennedy, *A Passion to Oppose*, pp. 57–59; A.J. Baker, 'Anderson's intellectual background and influences', *Heraclitus* 33 (Oct 1993): pp. 4–12.
[45] I. Britain, 'In pursuit of Englishness: Public School stories and Australian culture', *University of Melbourne Library Journal* 1 (4): (1994/5): pp. 11–17, at pp. 13–14; also M. Lyons & L. Taska, *Australian Readers Remember* (Melbourne, 1992): pp. 92–3; J. Redrup, *Banished Camelots* (Sydney, 1997), p. 203; for girls: A Woollacott, '"All this is the Empire, I told myself": Australian women's voyages "home" and the articulation of colonial whiteness', *American Historical Review* 102 (1997): pp. 1003–29.
[46] D. Horne, *Education of Young Donald*, p. 87.

and *The Scottish Chiefs* and Burns on the shelves. It means the cool green waters of the Coln as they glide past the church at Fairford; the long sweep of the Wye Valley above Tintern, with a Wordsworth in my pocket; looking north across the dim Northumbrian moors from the Roman Wall, with the rowan trees on the slope before me, and two thousand years of history behind; old colour and light and soaring stone in York Minster. It means King George and Queen Mary coming to their Jubilee in Westminster Hall as Big Ben chimed out and Lords and Commons bowed, and, as they bowed, saw beyond the form of things to a man and a woman greatly loved ... It means, at Canberra, at Wellington, at Ottawa, at Cape Town, the men of Parliament meeting as those met at Westminster seven hundred years ago; at Melbourne the lawyers practising the Common Law first forged at Westminster. It means Hammond at Sydney, and Bradman at Lords ... It means the past ever rising in its strength to forge the future.

Is all this madness? Should I have said, as clever, modern men are wont to do, that the British Commonwealth means an integral association of free and equal nations, whose mutual rights and obligations you will find set out in the Balfour Formula, the Statute of Westminster, and later documents: Or should I have watered it down, as some would have us do and define it in terms of friendship, or alliance, or pact, as if we were discussing an Anglo-Portuguese treaty?

A plague take such notions. Unless the Commonwealth is to British people all over the world a spirit, a proud memory, a confident prayer, courage for the future, it is nothing.[47]

Menzies had unfortunately to eulogise here not the Empire, which undoubtedly did exist, but the British Commonwealth, whose actuality was by no means obvious. This was despite some fancy footwork and play with mirrors by Arthur Balfour — no mean philosopher, though a prime minister. (John Anderson's first piece in the *Australasian Journal of Psychology and Philosophy*, printed shortly after his arrival in Sydney in 1927, was a dismissive note on one of Balfour's books.[48]) Balfour had been one of the first English statesmen to appreciate that the dominions could no longer be regarded as colonies, and had urged the attendance of the Duke of York, later George V, at the inauguration of the Commonwealth of Australia to cement a necessary personal bond in place of the constitutional one.[49] Some thought Balfour's attempt to define the essence of the British Com-

---

[47] R. Menzies, lecture of 1950, in R.G. Menzies, *Speech is of Time* (London, 1958), pp. 3–20, at pp. 19–20; cf Menzies's diary of his first visit to Britain, in M. Davie, *Anglo-Australian Attitudes* (London, 2000), pp. 121–7.

[48] J. Anderson, note on A.J. Balfour, *Familiar Beliefs and Transcendent Reason*, *AJPP* 5 (1927): p. 233; see also D.C. Stove, *The Plato Cult* (Oxford, 1991), p. 107.

[49] K. Young, *Arthur James Balfour* (London, 1963), p. 194, cf. pp. 450–2.

monwealth in words was a mistake, and it would have been better to muddle through with implicit understandings in the fashion of Britain's unwritten constitution. Menzies succinctly explained why the inarticulateness of tradition is a positive virtue:

> One of the great current difficulties of creating a happy, mutual understanding between the British and the other great Powers arises from the fact that our intellectual tradition is inductive — trial, error, trial, success, a precedent — so that we sometimes appear to the onlooker to have no principles; while deductive minds elsewhere sometimes seem to us to be so occupied by pure syllogisms that common sense and human values seem to disappear. Perhaps it was because of our instinctive reluctance to write things down that the Balfour formula, which seemed in the first enthusiasm to solve everything, ended up by leaving most things unsolved.[50]

But the Empire had itself left a number of problems unsolved, most notably the moral justification of its own existence. Its elevated rhetoric on the Liberty of Peoples was its undoing. The Empire that survived Hitler had no answer to Gandhi. There was to be no British Dien Bien Phu.

Its success in justifying the existence of its servants, or providing them with meaning for their lives, was more mixed. One might die alone and unknown, but one could still enjoy the satisfaction of knowing one had been of some service to the Empire — been with Younghusband to Lhasa, brought law to the Barotse, or stood firm against Nasser over Suez — one had been part of some greater Whole. Not many of the secular ideologies that have succeeded the Empire can say as much.

A T THEIR worst, doctrines of the inevitable evolution of historical forces led to the deportation to Siberia of millions believed to be standing in the way of the March of History. Marx's 'dialectical materialism' was a kind of reversal of Hegel's idealism, and meant that the moral restraints of idealism were discarded but the inevitability of historical development retained. As a result, orthodox Marxism was always on the lookout for 'Idealist' deviationism. The results included grave suspicion in the Soviet Union over quantum mechanics and relativity; locally, the Party leader Kavanagh, in a bizarre misunderstanding of John Anderson's position, reported to the Central Committee:

---

[50] R. Menzies, 'The ever-changing Commonwealth', *The Times*, 1956, repr. in Menzies, *Speech is of Time*, pp. 21–32, at p. 24; again pp. 38–9; further on Menzies' view of Empire in J. Brett, *Robert Menzies' Forgotten People* (Sydney, 1992), pp. 129–55.

In 1929 I had an argument with him over this very question, in 395 Sussex Street. He denied that his ideas of things were the result of sense impressions. I asked him if a table that was in the hall was on the floor or in his mind. He said that the table was in his mind and not an impression of it. I pointed out that if that was the case there must be two tables because it was also in my mind.[51]

That is all many years ago. Is idealism as dead as it seems? Another point of interest in Stove's attack is his identification of an argument at the bottom of idealism, which is at once so bad and so pervasive as to encourage despair in the philosophical enterprise. Stove calls it the 'Gem',[52] and exhibits it in all its appalling simplicity in Berkeley. The argument is: You cannot think of trees-outside-the-mind, without having them in mind. Therefore, trees cannot be outside the mind. Stove finds this argument many times in the nineteenth-century British idealists whose followers founded philosophy in Australia. A general version of the argument is the winner of Stove's Competition to Find the Worst Argument in the World. Here is his 'Judge's report' on the 'competition':

> Ten candidate-arguments were submitted. All of them had some merit, and some of them were very interesting indeed. But none of them is worse than the argument I had in mind when I started the competition. Consequently none of them wins the prize.
>
> Three dimensions, it will be recalled, entered into overall degree-of-badness as here understood: (a) the intrinsic awfulness of the argument; (b) its degree of acceptance among philosophers; (c) the degree to which it has escaped criticism.
>
> The argument — really a family of arguments — which I had in mind as the worst, was the following:
>
> > We can know things only:
> > • as they are related to us
> > • under our forms of perception and understanding
> > • in so far as they fall under our conceptual schemes, etc
> > So, we cannot know things as they are in themselves.
>
> If there is a worse argument than this, I am still to learn of it. This argument has imposed on countless philosophers, from Kant to the present hour, yet it is very hard to beat for awfulness ...[53]

---

[51] Kennedy, p. 89; Anderson's true views on the question in 'Marxist philosophy', in J. Anderson, *Studies in Empirical Philosophy* (Sydney, 1962), pp. 292–313, at pp. 299–300.

[52] Stove, *Plato Cult*, p. 140.

[53] D.C. Stove, 'Judge's report on the competition to find the worst argument in the world', January 1986, repr. in D.C. Stove, *Cricket versus Republicanism* (Quakers Hill, 1995), pp. 66–7.

As we will see in chapter 15, 'to the present hour' is no exaggeration, as the argument underpins the modern form of linguistic idealism known as postmodernism.

Stove, idiosyncratic in so many of his views, was typical of Australian philosophy at least in his defence of realism, the view opposed to idealism which admits that reality exists in the way we ordinarily believe it does. Work in favour of realism is even something of an Australian specialty. Michael Devitt wrote, 'I have always been a realist about the external world. Such realism is common in Australia. Some say that Australian philosophers are born realists. I prefer to attribute our realism to nurture rather than nature.'[54] ('Nurture' means, of course, in large part John Anderson, however oddly the word applies to him.) John Passmore writes in similar vein;

> Australian philosophy, broadly considered, is direct, clear, forceful, blunt, realist, naturalistic, secular, interested in the world rather than in language and certainly unprepared to identify the two, respectful of science, unwilling to draw a sharp distinction between the conceptual and the empirical, not conspicuous for its subtlety.[55]

It is true that 'broadly considered' means here 'except for those who disagree with myself', and that it is an old Andersonian speaking, but outsiders say much the same thing, at least regarding realism. According to a survey paper on realism, 'Australia, out of the loop evolutionarily, continues as stronghold of realists and marsupials.'[56] A long line of graduate students going from Australian universities to the top American philosophical schools have experienced more than a little culture shock at the anti-realist tendencies they have found themselves expected to take seriously.

There is also a British school of anti-realism, one of whose members wrote (under the impression that Australia was discovered in

---

[54] M. Devitt, *Realism and Truth* (Princeton, 1984), p. vii; also M. Devitt, 'Aberrations of the realism debate', *Philosophical Studies* 61 (1991): pp. 43–63; J. Wright, *Realism and Explanatory Priority* (Dordrecht, 1997); something less realist in H. Price, *Facts and the Function of Truth* (Oxford, 1988); H. Price, 'Metaphysical pluralism', *Journal of Philosophy* 89 (1992): pp. 387–409; R. Sylvan, 'Language, thought and representation of "the" world', *Revue Internationale de Philosophie* 41 (1987): pp. 64–96.

[55] J. Passmore, 'Australian philosophy or philosophy in Australia?', in *Essays on Philosophy in Australia*, ed. J.T. Srzednicki & D. Wood (Dordrecht, 1992), pp. 1–18, at p. 13.

[56] J. Heil, 'Recent work in realism and anti-realism', *Philosophical Books* 30 (1989): pp. 65–73, at p. 65; cf. H. Putnam, 'Reflections on Goodman's *Ways of Worldmaking*', *Journal of Philosophy* 76 (1979): pp. 603–18, at p. 611; L. Reinhardt, 'Anti-anti-realism', *Quadrant* 44 (1–2) (Jan-Feb 2000): pp. 44–7.

1683) that, 'I can allow no sense to the idea of the existence of Australia before 1683'.[57] This should be a joke, something along the lines of the one perpetrated by Oxford linguistic philosophers in 1958 ('Now it is clear that "Australia" is not a real place; or better, that "Australia" is not a name. The words "in Australia" are used simply to signify that the contradictory of what is stated to be the case "in Australia" is in fact the case. Thus we say "In Australia there are mammals that lay eggs" (meaning that there are none in reality); "In Australia there are black swans" (meaning that all real swans are some other colour) ...'[58]). But it is not a joke. That is not exactly to say that the average American, British or French philosopher literally thinks the physical world does not exist. But somehow, it seems that few in those places are prepared to say so bluntly. Or if there are in fact many realists, the climate of thought in the academic world they inhabit hides their views behind those who take every opportunity to class anything they can as a 'construction'. American philosophy has a century-old tradition of self-indulgence in this area,[59] which puts a premium on enormous books about the power of ideas, words and things starting with 'soc'.

It is questionable whether one should attempt to *argue* against idealism. It might be thought that idealism denies so much that there is no place left to argue *from*, and that there is nothing to be done but to say: knowing that the world is there is where I start from; what could be more basic? But there is another possibility. Devitt argues that realism about any entity, including the whole 'external' world, can be supported by showing it gives the best explanation of experience.[60] There are possibilities in the argument, but it does have an air of conceding too much to the opponent. Berkeley has *an* explanation of experience, and it may be a tough business showing it is not as good as the realist hypothesis.[61]

---

[57] M. Luntley, *Language, Logic and Experience* (London, 1988), p. 249; further shocking quotes in Devitt, *Realism and Truth*, 2nd ed, ch. 13, and Stove, *The Plato Cult*, ch. 2.

[58] L. Sturch, in *Why?*, quoted in D. Armstrong, 'Black swans: The formative influences in Australian philosophy', in *Rationality and Irrationality*, ed. B. Brogaard & B. Smith (Vienna, 2000), pp. 11–17, text at www.ditext.com/armstrong/swans.html .

[59] Stove, *Plato Cult*, p. 31; on the earlier American tradition, P.H. Partridge, 'The social theory of truth', *AJPP* 14 (1936): pp. 161–75.

[60] Devitt, *Realism and Truth*, especially 2nd ed (Oxford, 1991), p. 108.

[61] J. Franklin, 'Healthy scepticism', *Philosophy* 66 (1991): pp. 305–324; 'Scepticism's health buoyant', *Philosophy* 69 (1994): pp. 503–4; other views in S.C. Hetherington, *Knowledge Puzzles* (Boulder, 1996), ch. 18; S.C. Hetherington, *Epistemology's Paradox* (Savage, Md, 1992), ch. 2.

Some more detailed Australian realist work, concerning the reality of particular kinds of entities, will be discussed in chapter 12 on the philosophy of science.

Chapter 7   The Melbourne Spectrum

I T IS an old saying that philosophy begins with a sense of wonder. That is *a* source of philosophy, but there is another one, the sense that 'that's all bullshit (and I can explain why)'. Different philosophers draw on these sources in differing proportions. An uncritical sense of wonder leads one out of philosophy altogether, into the land of the fairies, to start angels from under stones, find morals at every turn and hug the rainforest. A philosopher near the other extreme — or one, like David Stove, actually occupying the extreme — will at least still be doing philosophy, but it will consist entirely of criticism of others.

In the Australian intellectual tradition, the wonder/criticism mix varies not only according to individuals but according to cities. At least, it has since 1927, when John Anderson arrived in Australia and Sydney and Melbourne set off on different paths. Various writers, mainly from Melbourne, have discoursed at some length on the contrasts between the two cities in their styles of thought, and with all due allowance made for the hot air factor, there is undoubtedly some distinct difference to be identified. Where Sydney intellectuals, following Anderson, tend to be critical, pessimistic, classical and opposed to 'meliorist' schemes to improve society, Melbourne's unctuous *bien pensants* are eager to 'serve society', meaning, to instruct the great and powerful how they ought to go about achieving Progress and the perfection of mankind.[1] Manning Clark — and it is characteristic of

---

[1] J. Docker, *Australian Cultural Elites: Intellectual Traditions in Sydney and Melbourne* (Sydney, 1974); V. Buckley, and J. Docker in *The Sydney–Melbourne Book*, ed. J. Davidson (Sydney, 1986), chs 10–11; J. Quinlem, 'The rule of saints?', *Observer* 16/5/1959, pp. 303–4; B. Kingston, 'Letter from Sydney', *Australian Historical Studies* 116 (2001): pp. 141–5; Sydney

optimistic, pompous Melbourne that its guru should be a historian rather than a philosopher — saw a difference in the secular faiths of the two cities: 'Sydney because of its different historical situation came under the influence of Nietzsche, just as Melbourne became a child of the Enlightenment.'[2] By this he meant that Melburnians strive to build a secular Jerusalem, or at least advise on how to do it, while Sydney thinkers do not care about the poor, and sit around admiring their own ability to criticise and to live free from illusions.

Philosophical idealism, as we saw in the last chapter, was the dominant tradition in philosophy in the late nineteenth century, and Melbourne has never broken with it quite as decisively as Sydney. It was represented first by Henry Laurie, a journalist with Scottish philosophical training who campaigned for the first position in philosophy in Australia and was offered the job he had created. He later wrote a sound book on Scottish philosophy and an interesting article in *Mind* on inductive logic.[3]

His successor was W.R. Boyce Gibson, appointed in 1911. One of his referees assured the University, 'Melbourne will both obtain a safe man and yet avoid the danger which is very real in the case of colonial universities which import their professors from the home country, viz, that of having foisted on it a second-rate representative of a declining school, simply because the other men who belong to it are well known by name and have commended him.'[4] Gibson's position was a 'personal idealism', a version of idealism more Christian than the usual Absolute Idealism, in holding that human life is not a mere 'incident in the life of God'.[5] 'A sweet old scholar, redolent of the

---

scepticism about perfectibility in J. Passmore, *The Perfectibility of Man* (London, 1970).

[2] M. Clark, 'Melbourne: An intellectual tradition', *Melbourne Historical Journal* 2 (1962): pp. 17–23, at p. 19; further in M. Clark, 'Faith', in *Australian Civilization*, ed. P. Coleman (Melbourne, 1962).

[3] S. Grave, *A History of Philosophy in Australia* (St Lucia, 1984), pp. 14–16; E. Morris Miller, 'The beginnings of philosophy in Australia and the work of Henry Laurie. I', *AJPP* 7 (1929): pp. 241–51; H. Laurie, 'A plea for philosophy', *Victorian Review* 5 (Nov, 1881): pp. 76–89; H. Laurie, *Scottish Philosophy in its National Development* (Glasgow, 1902); H. Laurie, 'Methods of inductive inquiry', *Mind* 2 (1893): pp. 319–38.

[4] F.C.S. Schiller, quoted in Grave, *History*, p. 31.

[5] Grave, *History*, pp. 28–31, 41–5; *ADB* vol. 8 pp. 659–60; obituary in *AJPP* 13 (1935): pp. 85–92; papers in University of Melbourne Archives no. 756; recollections in K. Fitzpatrick, *Solid Bluestone Foundations* (Melbourne, 1983), pp. 169–70; *More Memories of Melbourne University*, ed. H. Dow (Melbourne, 1985), pp. 6–14; A. Chisholm, *Men Were My Milestones* (Melbourne, 1958), pp. 107–8; R. Priestley, *The Diary of a Vice-Chancellor*, ed. R. Ridley (Melbourne, 2002), pp. 5, 35.

nineteenth-century days when Germans had their poets, philosophers and dreamers instead of jack-booted militarists',[6] he kept students abreast of the latest developments — on the Continent as well as in England and America, which is more than could be said of most Australian philosophers then or later. As will be noted in chapter 9, he visited Husserl and translated his work.

At his death in 1935, he was succeeded in the chair by his son Alexander (Sandy) Boyce Gibson. By that time, idealism itself was becoming untenable, but Sandy continued in general his father's personalist and Christian themes.[7] Another contrast with Anderson's Sydney lay in Boyce Gibson junior's presiding over rather than ruling his department. He did not appoint clones of himself. As a matter of principle, he favoured balance, hoping it would lead to 'a fruitful tension of opposites'.[8] In the 1950s, he even appointed a Sydney Andersonian, David Armstrong, who stayed for a few years until appointed Professor at Sydney.

Earlier, when the department threatened to become dominated by linguistic philosophers in the tradition of Wittgenstein, Boyce Gibson made an effort to achieve balance by appointing an anti-Wittgensteinian with views similar to his own. The unhappy result was that he had Sydney Sparkes Orr on his staff. One of Orr's two publications in philosophy was a long article on 'the Cambridge approach to philosophy', taking Wittgensteinians to task for ignoring the extent to which scientific knowledge and even sense knowledge are intellectual and, so to speak, philosophical.[9] It was rumoured that Boyce Gibson gave Orr a glowing reference to get rid of him, but later research showed that on the contrary he nobly warned the University of Tasmania what it was in for.[10]

[6] G. Hutton, in Dow, *More Memories*, p. 28.
[7] Grave, *History*, pp. 70–5; *ADB* vol. 14 pp. 264–5; papers in University of Melbourne Archives no. 7417; recollections in E. D'Arcy, 'Christian discourse', *Australian Biblical Review* 14 (1966): pp. 3–8; J. Hanrahan, *From Eternity to Here* (Melbourne, 2002), p. 125; Priestley, *Diary of a Vice-Chancellor*, pp. 345, 383; obituary in *Australian Academy of the Humanities Proceedings* (1973): p. 39; A.B. Gibson, *Theism and Empiricism* (London, 1970); *The Challenge of Perfection: A Study in Christian Ethics* (Melbourne, 1968); *The Religion of Dostoevsky* (London, 1973); 'The riddle of the Grand Inquisitor', *Melbourne Slavonic Studies* 4 (1970): pp. 46–56; radio talk transcripts at Australian War Memorial AWM series 80 items 1/178 & 11/287.
[8] Grave, *History*, p. 74.
[9] S.S. Orr, 'Some reflections on the Cambridge approach to philosophy', *AJPP* 24 (1946): pp. 34–76, 129–67, on Wittgenstein at pp. 140–1, 162–3.
[10] C. Pybus, *Gross Moral Turpitude* (Melbourne, 1993), p. 207.

Melbourne University Philosophy Department, 1950. Back row, left to right, Douglas Gasking, 'Camo' Jackson, Sydney Sparkes Orr, Barbara Coates, Olga Warren, Don Gunner, Kurt Baier. Front row, Peter Herbst, Dan Taylor, Prof. A. 'Sandy' Boyce Gibson, Charles Ogilvie (Melbourne University Philosophy Department)

The result of his policy of diversity was a gradual divergence in philosophical style between Sydney and Melbourne, partly reflecting and partly causing the wider intellectual differences between the two cities. Melbourne philosophers were broader in outlook, more ready to see religion as a serious option. Politically, they supported the development of the welfare state, if not positions much further to the left.[11] A typical Melbourne view of Sydney was 'the philosophy there seemed to an outsider [i.e. Melburnian] to be not only inbred and impervious to outside developments, but narrow, doctrinaire and negative into the bargain.'[12] The difference in style was evident at the annual Australasian philosophy conferences, where papers could be given under either 'Melbourne rules' or 'Sydney rules'. Sydney rules meant that Anderson read a paper, then members of the audience could make comments, followed by Anderson's reply to such points as he chose. Under Melbourne rules, a single point could be discussed

---

[11] A. Donagan, 'Introduction', in *Contemporary Australian Philosophy*, ed. R. Brown & C.D. Rollins (London, 1969), pp. 15–19.
[12] W. Ginnane, 'John Anderson's book', *Bulletin* 20/10/1962, pp. 36–7.

by everyone until it was finished with, leading to a much more spontaneous and focused discussion.[13]

In the 1940s, a generation of remarkable Melbourne students who were to become prominent in the US — notably Alan Donagan, Michael Scriven and Paul Edwards — were joined by a group of Germans deported on the *Dunera* to Australia early in the War — Kurt Baier, Peter Herbst and Gerd Buchdahl.[14] Buchdahl lectured on Plato and Aristotle during the horror voyage, and he and Herbst wrote on a toilet roll the '*Dunera* Constitution' which provided a political framework in the internment camps in which the deportees found themselves.[15] Buchdahl was involved after the War in the foundation of the History and Philosophy of Science Department at Melbourne, one of the earliest of such attempts to bridge the 'Two Cultures' gap between the sciences and the humanities.[16]

Unlike Sydney, Melbourne did not grow, or import, its own replacement for the great men of idealist days. Instead, it looked to several overseas philosophers as the founts of wisdom. The main one was Ludwig Wittgenstein.

The central idea of the later Wittgenstein was that careful attention to how language is used will show that the traditional problems of

---

[13] J.J.C. Smart, 'Australian philosophers of the 1950s', *Quadrant* 33 (6) (June 1989): pp. 35–9.

[14] S. Toulmin, 'Alan Donagan and Melbourne philosophy', in A. Donagan, *Philosophical Papers*, ed. J.E. Malpas (Chicago, 1994), vol. 1, pp. vii–xiii; V. Buckley, *Cutting Green Hay* (Ringwood, 1983), p. 63.

[15] C. Pearl, *The Dunera Scandal* (London, 1983), p. 39; Peter Herbst tapes, National Library, ORAL TRC 3021.

[16] S. Toulmin & G. Buchdahl, 'History and philosophy of science: An Australian experiment', *Australian Journal of Science* 19 (1956): pp. 91–8; G. Buchdahl, 'History and philosophy of science: some anecdotal memories', *Studies in History and Philosophy of Science* 20 (1989): pp. 5–8; obituaries of Buchdahl in *Times* 24/5/2001, *Studies in History and Philosophy of Science* 32 (2001): pp. 401–5; D. Dyason, 'After thirty years: History and philosophy of science in Australia, 1946–1976', *Melbourne Studies in Education 1977*: pp. 45–74; R.D. Wright, 'The origin of the teaching of history and philosophy of science at the University of Melbourne', in *Patients, Practitioners and Techniques*, ed. H. Attwood & R.W. Home (Melbourne, 1985), p. 216; A.M. Turtle, 'History and philosophy of science at the University of Sydney: A case study in non-innovation', *Historical Records of Australian Science* 7 (1987): pp. 27–37; Y.E. Cossart, M.A. Pegler & R.C. Givney, 'Back to the future: History and philosophy of medicine experiment at Sydney University', *Medical Education* 30 (1996): pp. 349–52; R.W. Home & R. MacLeod, 'History and philosophy of science', in Academy of the Social Sciences in Australia, *Challenges for the Social Sciences and Australia* (Canberra, 1998), vol. 1 pp. 141–6.

philosophy are not real, but result simply from misuses of language. 'Philosophical problems arise when language *goes on holiday*.'[17] Non-admirers of Wittgenstein naturally think this is anti-philosophy, though of course his emphasis on the primacy, subtlety and difficulty of language has made him a favourite among poets.[18]

How his method works can be seen in a 1938 article by the man who shortly afterwards introduced Wittgenstein's thought to Melbourne, George Paul. The topic is Lenin's theory of perception. According to Lenin, the fundamental question is 'Are our sensations copies of bodies and things, or are bodies complexes of our sensations?' The copy theory, he thinks, is the true materialist theory that is accepted by workmen, housewives and scientists, while the opposite, idealist, theory is a fantasy spun by bourgeois professors and religious zealots. Lenin thus has a *representative* theory of perception. Standard treatments of perception, like David Armstrong's *Perception and the Physical World*, treat representative theories as one of the serious options, and contrast them with, on the one hand, idealist theories like Berkeley's which hold that no real world exists behind the experience, and on the other hand direct realist theories, which hold that the mind registers reality not via internal representations or copies but directly, in much the same way as a thermometer directly registers temperature. These theories are all taken to be perfectly coherent, and reasons are adduced for favouring one or other of them.[19]

---

[17] W. Ginnane, 'The unspeakable', *Arna* (1962): pp. 116–24; also G.A. Paul, 'Wittgenstein', in *The Revolution in Philosophy* (London, 1960), pp. 88–96; J. Passmore, 'Ludwig Wittgenstein', *Current Affairs Bulletin* 21 (1957–8): pp. 99–112, and in *A Hundred Years of Philosophy* (London, 1957), ch. 18; K.E.M. Baier, 'Ludwig Wittgenstein', *Meanjin* 19 (1960): pp. 84–7; J. Teichmann, 'Wittgenstein on persons and human beings', in *Understanding Wittgenstein*, ed. G. Vesey (London, 1974), ch. 9; R. Haack, 'Wittgenstein's pragmatism', *American Philosophical Quarterly* 19 (1982): pp. 13–71; B. Garrett, 'Wittgenstein on the first person', *AJP* 73 (1995): pp. 347–56; F. Rizvi, 'Wittgenstein on grammar and analytic philosophy of education', *Educational Philosophy and Theory* 19 (2) (1987): pp. 33–46.
[18] A. Hoddinott, 'Gwen Harwood and the philosophers', *Southerly* 41 (1981): pp. 272–87; A. Hoddinott, *Gwen Harwood* (Sydney, 1991), pp. 142–64; G. Harwood, 'A note on Noel Stock's note on Wittgenstein's *Tractatus*', *Poetry Australia* 67 (1978): p. 79; A.B. Palma, *Stones in Summer* (Sydney, 1981), pp. 9–11, 86–8; B. Hill, *The Best Picture* (Melbourne, 1988), pp. 65–101, 251–4; D. Anderson, 'Monks demonstrates how things stand with Ludwig', *SMH* 30/11/1991, p. 50.
[19] D.M. Armstrong, *Perception and the Physical World* (London, 1961), introduction; F. Jackson, *Perception: A Representative Theory* (Cambridge, 1977), introduction; J.B. Maund, 'The representative theory of perception', *Canadian Journal of Philosophy* 5 (1975): pp. 41–55; J.B. Maund,

Lenin is unusual in being apparently unaware of the direct realist option.

But Wittgensteinians believe there is something wrong with the way the whole problem is set up, and that it will be seen to dissolve with due attention to language. Lenin is misled, Paul says, by thinking of the question 'How do people see things outside themselves?' as like 'How do people see things out of submarines?' Hence, they are tempted to give an answer like 'by having an image inside which is an accurate reflection of the things outside'. But the two cases are not alike. There is no possibility of holding up the internal image and checking it against the thing of which it is supposed to be a copy (as there is in the case of the image in a periscope's mirror). And if it is answered (as Lenin attempts to do) by saying that we are successful in practice in assuming that our internal sense perceptions are indeed faithful copies of what is outside, it can be answered that the success is explained in terms of our perception telling us the truth about what is there in the world, but nothing about copies or images comes into this story.[20] If this still leaves us craving an account of what *does* go on inside when we perceive, Paul, like any Wittgensteinian, is not interested in telling us. Any constructive theory is left for science, philosophy's job being done when the confusions produced by language have been exposed.

Paul makes some moves of the same kind in arguing that all talk about sense data or internal experience is meaningless, on the grounds that language is public and only adapted to talking about the public world, and in attempting to dissolve by similar linguistic considerations the presumed conflict between free will and determinism.[21]

These ideas created great excitement, and not only among philosophers. A student recalls the period around the end of the War:

> Meanwhile, there were extraordinary things going on in the Philosophy school. George Paul, a graduate of St Andrews and Cambridge, was expounding with an all conquering charm the linguistic approach to philosophy that had derived from the work of Wittgenstein and Wisdom.

'Representations, pictures and resemblance', in *New Representationalisms*, ed. E.L. Wright (Aldershot, 1993); A. Gallois, 'Sense-data', *Routledge Encyclopedia of Philosophy,* vol. 8, pp. 694–8.

[20] G.A. Paul, 'Lenin's theory of perception', *Analysis* 5 (1938): pp. 65–73; further in E.P. Edwards, 'Are percepts in the brain?', *AJPP* 20 (1942): pp. 46–75; a similar 'dissolution' theory in P. Slezak, 'The tripartite model of representation', *Philosophical Psychology* 15 (2002): pp. 239–70.

[21] G.A. Paul, 'Is there a problem about sense-data?', *Aristotelian Society Supplementary Volume* 15 (1936): pp. 61–77, repr. in *Logic and Language* (first series), ed. A. Flew (Oxford, 1951), pp. 101–16; G.A. Paul, 'The problem of guilt', *Aristotelian Society Supplementary Volume* 21 (1947): pp. 109–18.

Paul's exposition was subtle, sophisticated and wildly exciting. His enrolled students were few, but his lectures in Logic and History of Philosophy were packed with those of other courses. Staff members from such diverse departments as English, History, Science and Commerce sat at his feet as he expounded an approach to philosophy through an exact examination of language and terms. Historians began to have doubts about the concept of causation in history and to wonder whether the use of such words as 'imperialism' and 'democracy' was valid (after all, what did they *mean*? What role did they play in language?). The wave of scepticism hit the English school where teachers began to doubt the validity of critical judgements they had been making for years; it swept across the lawn to the commerce building where students began re-reading their texts and seeing them as blends of tautologies and sentences aiming at ethical persuasion. In Chemistry, there were doubts about the conservation of matter.[22]

Max Crawford, newly appointed to the Chair of History, had Paul lecture to honours classes in history. '"What do you do?" was his repeated question, a genuine one, for he wanted to know; and it was a question which made us in turn look to our practice with a closer, if somewhat anxious, scrutiny.' His lectures on logic of 1944 were attended by all the full-time teaching staff in history, and stimulated a long-running debate on the philosophy of history.[23] Paul left Melbourne in 1945 for a fellowship in Oxford. He did not shine there, possibly because the tutorial style of teaching did not supply the rewards of Melbourne's large lectures.[24] He died at no great age in a boating accident in the Lake District.[25]

His successor as leader of the Wittgensteinian school, and eventually Boyce Gibson's successor as Professor at Melbourne, was Douglas Gasking.[26] Gasking's best known article — and the first article in the new analytic style to appear in Australia — was an attack on mathe-

---

[22] K. Gott, 'Student life: The forties', *Melbourne University Magazine* (Spring 1961), pp. 23–7, at p. 24.
[23] R.M. Crawford, 'The school of prudence', *Melbourne Historical Journal* 2 (1962): pp. 3–16; R.M. Crawford, 'History as a science', *Historical Studies* 2 (1944–9): pp. 153–75 (on which D. Gasking, 'The historian's craft and scientific history', *Historical Studies* 4 (1950): pp. 112–24; A.L. Burns, 'Ascertainment, probability and evidence in history', *Historical Studies* 4 (1951): pp. 327–39; G. Buchdahl, 'Logic and history', *AJP* 26 (1948): pp. 94–113; A. Donagan, 'Explanation in history', *Mind* 66 (1957): pp. 145–64.
[24] J. Passmore, *Memoirs of a Semi-Detached Australian* (Melbourne, 1997), p. 250.
[25] *Age* 26/4/1962, p. 2.
[26] D. Gasking, *Language, Logic and Causation*, ed. I.T. Oakley & L.J. O'Neill (Melbourne, 1996); obituaries in *Australian* 17/5/1994, p. 15; *Australian Academy of the Humanities Proceedings* 1994: pp. 57–9.

matics which takes Wittgensteinianism virtually as far as it can go. The idea is that one might make 2 + 2 equal to 5 by suitably changing one's conventions of measurement. It is not easy to make this idea work, given the interconnectedness of mathematical facts. Gasking was persistent in following through the changes that would have to be made, but in the end even he was not convinced he had succeeded.[27]

Perhaps the best aspects of Wittgensteinian thought are evident in Gasking's 1960 article on 'clusters'. A cluster of ships may be defined, let us say, as any group of ships which are serially in radio contact with each other (each one close enough to be in radio contact with one other, but perhaps with no more than one). Or a forest may consist of the trees such that each is serially within twenty yards of another (so, one may create two forests from one by making a firebreak). In such cases, facts about the cluster relate to facts about the individuals in it in rather subtle ways. The cluster of ships is in the Atlantic if a sufficient number of its members are, but not any particular ones: the odd straggler might not quite be there. And different people can have conceptions of the cluster that differ, within reason, but still have sufficient commonality for communication: I may think of the cluster as ships A, B, C and anything serially in contact with those; you may think of the cluster as B, C, D, E and anything serially in contact with those, and we will have no trouble in identifying the same cluster. Our communication will survive, indeed, a small proportion of mistakes in knowledge as to which ships are actually in the cluster. 'A cluster can be thought of as an entity and given a name only if it is stable enough for the probability of a slightly erroneous conception to be not high and for that of a wildly erroneous full conception to be negligibly small.' Gasking suggests that ship clusters are a simple model for thinking about more complicated and philosophically important cases where a 'higher-order' entity has a subtle dependence on the 'items' that go to make it up. Material bodies, for example, are clusters of serially contiguous spatial (and temporal) parts, and can remain the same with some (but not too much) variation in their parts, and the relation between a high-level theoretical statement in science and the observation statements that support it is similar.[28]

[27] D.A.T. Gasking, 'Mathematics and the world', *AJPP* 18 (1940): pp. 97–116, repr. in P. Benacerraf & H. Putnam, eds, *Philosophy of Mathematics* (Oxford, 1964), pp. 390–403; Grave, *History*, pp. 80–2; similar views on logic in D.A.T. Gasking, 'Mr Williams on the a priori', *Analysis* 6 (1938): pp. 69–78.
[28] D. Gasking, 'Clusters', *AJP* 38 (1960): pp. 1–36, repr. in *Language, Logic and Causation*, pp. 144–85; other notable articles of the Melbourne linguistic

These matters are by no means minor linguistic subtleties, irrelevant to 'real' life. As Gasking points out elsewhere, legal reasoning in doubtful cases is much the same. Deciding whether something rather different from the examples originally thought of is or is not a 'charitable trust' involves the same kind of reasoning as deciding whether an outlying ship is in a cluster.[29]

Gasking also applied his linguistic skills to understanding John Anderson, and succeeded in showing that Anderson's ideas on logic had a close similarity to some of the conclusions of the early Wittgenstein.[30] No-one thanked him for it.

If Gasking looked to the 'clear' Wittgenstein, the 'deep' Wittgenstein was represented by the only close student of his who was a native Australian, A.C. (Cameron or 'Camo') Jackson, who studied in Cambridge in the late 1940s.[31] Of all the members of the school, he most took to heart Wittgenstein's sense of the vast complexity of the relation between language and reality. The result was a teaching style that led students to think hard, but prevented him from publishing any substantial books or articles (though he did manage to finish a Cambridge doctoral thesis on causation). Vincent Buckley recalls:

> He [Jackson] summed up what was diffused by several others; and what he summed up was all very aristocratic, in a way. One was in no doubt that one was in close (if ambiguous or unformulated) relation to a most élite élite. The good side of this was that it associated thinking, the discussion, earthing, uncovering and demystifying of philosophical issues

school: S.E. Toulmin & K. Baier, 'On describing', *Mind* 61 (1952): pp. 13–38; K. Baier, 'The ordinary use of words', *Proceedings of the Aristotelian Society* 52 (1952): pp. 47–70; B.S. Benjamin, 'Remembering', *Mind* 65 (1956): pp. 312–31; (obituary of Benjamin in *AJP* 41 (1963): p. 1); P. Herbst, 'The nature of facts', *AJP* 30 (1952): pp. 90–116; W. Ginnane, 'Thoughts', *Mind* 69 (1960): pp. 372–90.

[29] D.A.T. Gasking, 'Types of questions', *Melbourne University Magazine* 1946: pp. 4–6; similar in J. Glover, 'Wittgenstein and the existence of fiduciary relationships', *University of New South Wales Law Journal* 18 (1995): pp. 443–63; also B.J. Garrett, 'Best-candidate theories and identity', *Inquiry* 31 (1988): pp. 79–85.

[30] D. Gasking, 'Anderson and the Tractatus Logico-Philosophicus', *AJP* 27 (1949): 1–26; Grave, *History*, pp. 92–4.

[31] G. Marshall, 'Wittgenstein and the analytic tradition', in *Essays on Philosophy in Australia*, ed. J.T.J. Srzednicki & D. Wood (Dordrecht, 1992), pp. 19–37; Smart, 'Australian philosophers of the 1950s'; R. Dahlitz, *Secular Who's Who* (Melbourne, 1994), pp. 152–3; obituary in *AJP* 68 (1990): p. 253.

with style: style of mind and even of body, comic or irritating as *some* bodily mannerisms might be.[32]

The less sympathetic David Stove, of Sydney, mocked the 'micro-Wittgensteins', who gave talks punctuated with silences during which they wrestled with the difficulty of expressing just what we would say in this or that situation. Interruptions during these supreme moments of philosophising were not allowed. Jackson's only publication was a recollection, written with Gasking, of their teacher, which explains where they learned this style of philosophising. 'At times, Wittgenstein would break off, saying, "Just a minute, let me think!" and would sit for minutes on end, crouched forward on the edge of a chair, staring down at his upturned palm. Or he would exclaim with vehement sincerity: "This is as difficult as *hell!*"' They say, nevertheless, that despite some difficulty in following the overall plan of a Wittgenstein lecture, 'Nearly every single thing said was easy to follow and was usually not the sort of thing anyone would wish to dispute' — a claim that came as a surprise to others who had attended.[33]

Buckley too had a complaint: 'Yet philosophers often develop skills (in analysis, interrogation, setting things up) which, though awesome to those who do not possess them, they use too much on too trivial matters. I have heard philosophers in pubs devoting the most sophisticated thinking to the most banal problems — and having their views contested by counter-analysis no whit less subtle. It is like the man who boasts into late middle-age about the state of his muscles and supports his boast by showing his bicep to total strangers.'[34] On the face of it, this is not a reasonable criticism. Surely philosophers are entitled to their time off, just as mathematicians are entitled to play chess to relax. But it does point to a deeper problem. Philosophy in the style of Wittgenstein, which aims to analyse problems away and 'leave everything as it is' is in grave danger of degenerating into triviality.

The Wittgensteinians brought from Cambridge their guru's political commitments as well as his philosophy. Wittgenstein had been an admiring visitor to Stalin's Russia in the 1930s — 'straight Stalinist' according to Jackson[35] — until it was suggested to him that he would

---

[32] Buckley, *Cutting Green Hay*, pp. 63–4.

[33] D.A.T. Gasking & A. C. Jackson, 'Ludwig Wittgenstein', *AJP* 29 (1951): pp. 73–80, repr. in K.T. Fann, ed, *Ludwig Wittgenstein: The Man and His Philosophy* (New York, 1967), pp. 49–55; also A.C. Jackson, review of N. Malcolm, *Ludwig Wittgenstein*, *Mind* 69 (1960): pp. 269–70.

[34] Buckley, *Cutting Green Hay*, pp. 64–5.

[35] A. Flew to author, 6/6/1995.

be more useful to the cause back in Cambridge.[36] His view that philosophy was mostly a collection of pseudo-questions tended to remove any intellectual obstacles to giving political commitment free rein.[37]

While there were plenty of other sources of Melbourne leftism, Paul's importation of Wittgenstein's influence certainly added to it, especially in view of his impact on historians as well as philosophers. When John Passmore visited Melbourne in 1938, he was familiar enough with the fellow-travelling and Trotskyism common in Sydney, but the optimistic card-carrying Communism of Melbourne came as a shock. 'In Melbourne I was dealing with full members — although I did not realise this at the time — of the Communist Party, experienced in its intrigues and confirmed in their faith to a degree that made my pessimism seem nothing short of ridiculous. I was amazed to meet very intelligent philosophers who were optimistic not only about the remote future, but even the immediate future — in 1938!'[38]

Among the most radical of the Communists he met was George Paul's wife Margaret, a sister of both the philosophical wunderkind Frank Ramsey and of a later Archbishop of Canterbury. She was a driving force in organising the Australian Student Labour Federation.[39] Passmore recalls her fear that a purse lost in the street contained incriminating documents; when returned by the police, however, these turned out to be only the constitution of the Melbourne University Conservative Society. Her zeal was nearly matched by the later left politics of 'Camo' Jackson, not a Party member but, according to his ASIO file, 'accepted as being at least pink if not more'.[40] More than one inquirer found him still a Soviet apologist

---

[36] Some embroidering on the basic facts in K. Cornish, *The Jew of Linz* (London, 1998), ch. 2; on the philosophy studies of Australia's leading Communist spy, Ian Milner, see R. Hall, *The Rhodes Scholar Spy* (Sydney, 1991).

[37] F. McCutcheon, 'The pursuit of perspicuity — Wittgenstein on the goal of philosophy', *Philosopher* 1 (3) (1996): pp. 14–20; also F. McCutcheon, *Religion Within the Limits of Religion Alone: Wittgenstein on Philosophy and Religion* (Aldershot, 2001).

[38] J. Passmore, *Memoirs*, pp. 180–3.

[39] A. Barcan, *Radical Students: The Old Left at Sydney University* (Melbourne, 2002), p. 114; Royal Commission Inquiring into the Origins, Aims, Objects and Funds of the Communist Party in Victoria, Transcript, pp. 1635–6, 7558; ASIO file on Margaret and George Paul, Australian Archives series A6119/89 item 2299.

[40] ASIO file on A.C. Jackson, Australian Archives series A6119/89 item 2288; Gasking's files (A6119/89 items 2311 and 2312) record only mild interest in a Peace conference.

after 1968.[41] ASIO's perception that the departments of history and philosophy at Melbourne were hotbeds of subversion was not far from the truth.[42] The matter of the objectivity of lecturing by such people came up at the 1949–50 Royal Commission on Communism in Victoria, where a witness gave evidence on the teaching of philosophy:

A. ... I said how did that [the putting forward of Party policy] square up with their jobs — one as tutor and one as lecturer (i.e. Mabel Eloise TAYLOR and Daniel TAYLOR) when it was the duty of a lecturer in the tutoring of philosophy to give an impersonal explanation of the various philosophies to the students and leave them to evaluate for themselves and she (Mabel Eloise TAYLOR) said that that was a lot of claptrap.

Q. Go on?

A. That was a lot of claptrap, that everyone has an axe to grind and that you need any means available for the grinding of your axe and that lecturers and tutors were in an excellent position for influencing students towards their point of view, and she said that a lot depended on the personality and that her husband had the personality which was attractive to students and which made them amenable to his points of view. She gave as an example of the work a lecturer could do to change a student's point of view, a Miss Anne HURLEY, whom she said had come from a typical bourgeois conservative family when she came to the University but she said 'When we had finished with her she was a good little Leftist and ...'

(Objection to evidence not sustained)

Q. ... Have you finished what she told you about Miss HURLEY?

A. That she had married a Mr. Cameron JACKSON.[43]

The most famous outcome of this thoughtworld was no doubt Manning Clark's celebrated remark that Lenin was 'Christ-like, at least in his compassion'.[44] Clark, however, was among the historians least impressed by the wave of philosophy. Some contemporaries, he said, 'having withstood the temptation to become sceptics and mockers, they, the [history] students, found themselves confronted with the

---

[41] P. O'Brien, *The Saviours: An Intellectual History of the Left in Australia* (Richmond, Vic, 1977), pp. 78–9; some anti-Soviet jokes by Jackson ('W.H.F.') in *Melbourne University Magazine* 28 (1934): p. 19.

[42] F. Capp, *Writers Defiled* (Ringwood, 1993), p. 98; also S. Murray-Smith, *Indirections* (Townsville, 1981), pp. 23–8; C. Lowe, *Report of the Royal Commission Inquiring into the Origins, Aims, Objects and Funds of the Communist Party in Victoria* (Melbourne, 1950), p. 100.

[43] Royal Commission, transcript, pp. 1633–5, quoted in ASIO file on Jackson; Taylor's appointment in Priestley, *Diary of a Vice-Chancellor*, pp. 146, 159.

[44] M. Clark, *Meeting Soviet Man* (Sydney, 1960), p. 12.

enormous temptation to seek recognition for their subject from the philosophers ... a most terrible mistake', and they 'sometimes succumbed to the darker temptation to talk about what it would be like to write history, supposing one were to write history, rather than to write history. Not all lost their way ...'[45]

PHILOSOPHERS are popularly supposed to spend a lot of time thinking about the meaning of life. On the other hand, no-one ever seems to think of asking them what it is. Philosophy departments do not receive letters asking for advice on the subject, and Caroline Jones' radio series, 'The Search for Meaning', elicited the opinions of environmentalists, artists' models, former prime ministers, herbalists and so on, but not of any philosophers.[46] It is true that the Sydney intellectual atmosphere does not lend itself to work on the question. 'No-one in Sydney ever wastes time debating the meaning of life — it's getting yourself a water frontage', says a character in David Williamson's *Emerald City*.[47] It is Melbourne graduates who have been to the fore in discussions of the meaning of life.

In choosing 'The meaning of life' as the theme of his inaugural lecture as Professor of Philosophy at Canberra University College in 1957, Kurt Baier was making a major departure from normality. After giving a few reasons for rejecting religious explanations of the universe and asserting instead that 'science is in principle able to give complete and real explanations of every occurrence and thing in the universe', he argues that this does not mean that life is without purpose, or meaningless. The reason is, simply, that like any value judgement, the judgement as to whether a life is worthwhile must be made by the relevant criteria. The appropriate criterion is: the average of the kind. Someone is said to be tall if he is taller than average for people; a life is said to be worthwhile if it is as good as average by the measures we normally use, such as its balance of happiness, or the happiness it has created for others. There is no further purpose, in the sense that there would be if humans were a kind of robot or watch-dog, manufactured by God for some end of his own. And, he asserts, 'this conclusion is innocuous': if one remains dissatisfied, it is because

---

[45] M. Clark, 'Melbourne: An intellectual tradition', *Melbourne Historical Journal* 2 (1962): pp. 17–23, at p. 22.

[46] C. Jones, *The Search for Meaning* (Crows Nest, 1989, book 2, 1990).

[47] D. Williamson, *Emerald City* (Sydney, 1987), p. 2 ('in Melbourne all views are equally depressing, so there's no point.'); see also on Melbourne existentialism, H.F. Dosser, 'Melbourne's non-existent society', *The Melburnian* 11 (6) (Aug/Sept 1996): pp. 27–9; A. Boyce Gibson, 'Existentialism: An interim report', *Meanjin* 7 (1948): pp. 41–52.

one has judged life by some inappropriate standard, perhaps by comparing it with a supposed perfect future life.[48]

The printed version of Baier's lecture became one of the exhibits in Father Farrell's campaign to prove the bankruptcy of the intellectual standards of analytic philosophy, noted in chapter 4. Baier's claim that Christianity was against pleasure, in particular, was according to Farrell a 'gross parody'. and he dismissed the whole piece as 'a propagandist pamphlet'.[49] Certainly, Baier does caricature the view of Christians in picturing them as arguing, 'There is a transcendent purpose, therefore things matter here on earth', when it would be more accurate to see them as saying something like, 'Things matter here on earth, and there must be an explanation for that — so there must be a transcendent purpose.'[50]

An answer to Baier came from Bill Joske, a Melbourne graduate who succeeded to the chair in Tasmania left vacant for many years by the boycott over the Orr case. He pointed out that if lives are by definition worthwhile if they are better than average for lives, then half of us are living lives that are not worthwhile. 'I would not accuse a man of undue concern if he deplored that state of affairs.' Worse, 'Baier's account of evaluation has the paradoxical consequence that a man can raise himself above the average and make his life worthwhile, not only by improving himself, but also by increasing the balance of misery in the lives of other people.' He takes it as clear that there is a possibility that life, like other activities, could be futile, in the sense that the state of the universe is such that it makes the fulfilment of important goals impossible. Squaring the circle is an impossible goal, and pursuing it is futile; life would be similar, he says, if certain philosophical views about the nature of the universe were true. For example, if humans were just naked apes, wholly determined by biology, 'we cannot but be cynical concerning the superstructure of justification associated with many of the most memorable human activities ... we can no longer regard as meaningful the gloss of reasoning and argument which men use in an attempt to show that their undertakings are reasonable.' He is less sure about what relevance moral relativism and atheism have for the question. On the latter, he says, 'I believe that although atheism does not render life meaningless,

---

[48] K.E.M. Baier, *The Meaning of Life* (Canberra, 1957), partly repr. in M. Weitz, *Twentieth Century Philosophy* (New York, 1966); Grave, *History*, pp. 180–1.

[49] P.M. Farrell, 'Philosophy and Christianity in Australian universities', *Catholic Weekly* 12/10/1961, pp. 12–13.

[50] J. Teichman, 'Humanism and the meaning of life', *Ratio* 6 (1993): pp. 155–64; J. Bacon & J. Richters, 'What shall we live for? A dialogue', in *On Being Human*, ed. V. Nelson (Melbourne, 1990), pp. 9–17.

it *opens* for us the possibility of discovering that it is futile.' For these reasons, he concludes, 'the contemporary attempt to establish the bland neutrality of philosophical views is not successful; philosophy is indeed dangerous stuff, and it is fitting that it should be approached with fear.'[51]

A substantial treatment of the same topic is found in Paul Edwards' article on 'Life, meaning and value of' in his *Encyclopedia of Philosophy*. The *Encyclopedia*, the standard encyclopedia of philosophy for thirty years, is a large work which made a special effort to include serious treatments of all schools of philosophy, and thus owes a good deal to the broad Melbourne background of its editor, Edwards.[52] Edwards himself was something of a crusading atheist. As an undergraduate, he founded a Freethought Society at Melbourne University in 1942, and later edited one of Bertrand's Russell's most popular books, *Why I Am Not a Christian*.[53] He did not have to actually write it, as Foulkes did with *Wisdom of the West*, as it consists of reprints of earlier Russell pieces.

His treatment of the meaning of life starts with a presentation of the pessimistic views of Schopenhauer, according to whom life and all its hopes are a cruel joke. As he quotes Schopenhauer, 'The present may be compared to a small dark cloud which the wind drives over the sunny plain: before and behind it all is bright, only it itself always casts a shadow.' But the past no longer exists, and all hopes for the future will be frustrated in the long run by death. Edwards, though conceding something to this line of reasoning, argues that Schopenhauer, like the religious, has made too much of what happens in the distant future, which is only mildly relevant to meaning in the here

---

[51] W.D. Joske, 'Philosophy and the meaning of life', *AJP* 52 (1974): pp. 93–104; comment in F.C. White, 'The meaning of life', *AJP* 53 (1975): pp. 148–50.

[52] *The Encyclopedia of Philosophy*, ed. P. Edwards (New York, 1967); Grave, *History*, p. 84; A. Donagan, 'The Encyclopedia of Philosophy', *Philosophical Review* 79 (1970): pp. 83–138; P. Edwards, 'Statement concerning the supplementary volume of the Encyclopedia of Philosophy', *Philosophy* 73 (1998): pp. 122–4; an online encyclopedia, also with strong Australian content, is under way in the *Stanford Encyclopedia of Philosophy*, at plato.stanford.edu ; there is much Australian content also in T. Mautner, *A Dictionary of Philosophy* (Oxford, 1996) and in F. Jackson & M. Smith, eds, *The Oxford Handbook of Contemporary Analytic Philosophy* (Oxford, 2003); also A.W. Sparkes, *Talking Philosophy: A Wordbook* (London, 1991).

[53] Gott, 'Student life', at p. 26; Edwards to author, 19/5/1998; B. Russell, *Why I Am Not a Christian*, ed. P. Edwards (London, 1957), with introduction and appendix by Edwards; also P. Edwards, 'Tribute to Bertrand Russell', *Humanist* 85 (1970): pp. 102–4; P. Edwards, articles 'Atheism', 'Russell, Bertrand', 'Why' in *Encyclopedia of Philosophy*.

and now. 'If bliss in the next life is not in need of any further justification, why should any bliss that there might be in the present life need justification?' He then falls back on Baier's idea that the pessimist has set up unreasonably high standards. Humans are on occasions in pursuit of attainable goals that seem to them worthwhile, and if the pessimist is still unhappy about that, he is trying to impose without justification standards of evaluation much more demanding than those of most ordinary people.[54]

Interesting as all these considerations are, they will inevitably be found disappointing by anyone who is seeking answers to the question of the meaning of life. These authors concentrate rather on the question of whether we should be worried by finding that life has no meaning, in the normally understood sense. That is a reasonable question, but one would think that philosophy might have first put forward a range of possible positive answers as to what the meaning of life might be, and evaluated them.[55]

Naturally, religions believe they are doing better on this front. Even so, the standard presentations of the major religions have not made their answer to this important question as clear as one might wish. The Catholic Church's Catechism said:

Q. Why did God make us?

A. God made us to know, love and serve him here on earth; and to see and enjoy him Him forever in Heaven.[56]

That is clear enough as far as it goes, but surely there is something incomplete. The following pages contain plenty of detail on how to serve God, in the sense of what commandments to obey. But there is no very clear theory as to what makes these commandments, rather than others that might have been chosen, the ones that make human life meaningful. What is the relation between self-development, the realisation of one's talents, and serving God? How does 'making a better world' relate to obeying commandments? Is one actually helping God in the task of universe-making? No doubt answers to these questions can be extracted from the works of Thomas Aquinas, or

---

[54] P. Edwards, 'Life, meaning and value of', in *Encyclopedia of Philosophy*, ed. P. Edwards (New York, 1967), vol. 4 pp. 467–77; similar in G. Weiler, 'Wittgenstein — a reasonable pessimist', *Quadrant* 9 (4) (July/Aug 1965): pp. 44–9; also M. Levine, 'Camus, Hare and the meaning of life', *Sophia* 27 (3) (Oct 1988): pp. 13–30; F. Mathews, 'Value in nature and meaning in life', in R. Elliot, ed, *Environmental Ethics* (Oxford, 1995), ch. 8.

[55] Some objectivist but abstract speculations in R. Routley & N. Griffin, 'Unravelling the meanings of life?' (Discussion Papers in Environmental Philosophy no. 3, ANU, 1984).

[56] *Catechism of Christian Doctrine* (Sydney, 1944), p. 13.

even from the New Testament, but it is hard to find Christian writings that have taken the trouble to extract the answers and lay them out.

One could even come to feel a momentary sympathy for the point of view of the Nietzscheans, who recommend creativity, including the creation of one's own values, as the right aim in life. It is an attitude that has appealed especially to artists like Norman Lindsay and Brett Whiteley, gifted with an excess of energy and an ambition to direct it into unconventional channels. [57] Others will think that the hundred years since Nietzsche have seen all too much of the inventing and imposing of new values, and that nothing but harm can be expected from an invitation to 'transcend' normal moral standards.[58] Still, the Nietzscheans have put on the table a coherent answer to the question, 'What is the meaning of life?' It is more than their rivals have managed.

One would like to see more explanation, too, of the role work plays in a meaningful life,[59] and on the significance of personal auton-

[57] For Lindsay and Nietzsche see N. Macainsh, *Nietzsche in Australia* (Munich, 1975), pp. 137–42; Docker, *Australian Cultural Elites,* ch. 2; *The Antichrist of Nietzsche: A new version in English,* by P.R. Stephensen, with illustrations by Norman Lindsay (London, 1928); N. Lindsay, *My Mask* (Sydney, 1970), p. 124; N. Lindsay, *Creative Effort: An Essay in Affirmation* (Sydney, 1920; London, 1924); J. Lindsay, 'Zarathustra in Queensland', *Meanjin* 7 (1948): pp. 211–25; C. Munro, *Inky Stephensen* (Melbourne, 1984), pp. 65–7; also D. Shteinman, 'Tribute to a Dionysian free spirit: The Brett Whiteley retrospective', *Philosopher* 1 (3) (1996): pp. 9–13; R. Baker, 'Christina Stead: The Nietzsche connection', *Meridian* 2 (1983): pp. 116–20; Enoch Powell on Nietzsche in Passmore, *Memoirs,* p. 146; more academic work in E.E. Sleinis, *Nietzsche's Revaluation of Values* (Urbana, 1994); T. Sadler, *Nietzsche: Truth and Redemption* (London, 1995); J. Teichman, 'Friedrich Nietzsche', in *An Introduction to Modern European Philosophy,* ed. J. Teichman & G. White (Basingstoke, 1995), ch. 7.
[58] M.A. Casey, *Meaninglessness: The Solutions of Nietzsche, Freud and Rorty* (Melbourne, 2001).
[59] R. Sworder, *Mining, Metallurgy and the Meaning of Life* (Quakers Hill, 1995); R. Gaita, *Romulus, My Father* (Melbourne, 1998), pp. 97–100; J. Carroll, *Ego and Soul: The Modern West in Search of Meaning* (Sydney, 1998), ch. 2; K. Campbell, 'Technology and the philosophy of work', *Australian Academy of the Humanities Proceedings* 13 (1984–6): pp. 57–71; A.J. Walsh, 'Meaningful work as a distributive good', *Southern Journal of Philosophy* 32 (1994): pp. 233–50; S.A. Cohen, *Commonplace Moraliser* (Lanham, Md, 1993), pp. 63–76; M. Deutscher, *Subjecting and Objecting* (St Lucia, 1983), ch. 11; K. Blackburn, 'The Protestant work ethic and the Australian mercantile elite, 1880–1914', *Journal of Religious History* 21 (1997): pp. 193–208.

omy.[60] And one would like to know whether the health of the young is being affected by a lack of meaning in life. If philosophical worries are characteristic of adolescence, then a lack of sustenance in that area could have results as lethal as lack of love does to infants. Some have suggested that the appalling rate of youth suicide in Australia has some connection with a lack of philosophical meaning in life. It is hard to evaluate this suggestion, but if there is anything in it, there is no point in expecting the problem to be solved by programs that concentrate on employment, firearms, drug education, depression and so on.[61]

It is clear that there are certain difficulties in the way of the Wittgensteinian scheme of dissolving the big questions by talk of the 'criteria we would use', as Baier and Edwards attempt. Boyce Gibson accused the analytic philosophers of double vision. 'They want to be guiltless of ontology (a serious crime in their culture group), and at the same time to say that the data of religion, properly sifted, are merely fraudulent. But they cannot have it both ways. Either they restrict themselves to clarification, and in that case they must not question their data; or they can question their data, and then they are up to their neck in ontology.'[62] It was an embarrassment, too, when later biographical research on Wittgenstein revealed he had been a mystic himself. 'The old boy had us tricked', Gasking said.[63]

MELBOURNE philosophy has also been the home of many Catholic philosophers, with views less hostile to modern philosophy than those of the scholastics. Most but not all have been loosely 'left' in politics, left Catholicism being, indeed, a phenomenon common enough in Melbourne but rare in Sydney.

[60] R. Young, *Personal Autonomy* (London, 1985); R. Young, 'The value of autonomy', *Philosophical Quarterly* 32 (1982): pp. 35–44; C. Mackenzie & N. Stoljar, eds, *Relational Autonomy in Context* (New York, 2000); cf. R.J. Haack, 'Education and the good life', *Philosophy* 56 (1981): pp. 289–302.

[61] R. Eckersley, 'Failing a generation', in *The Written World: Youth and Literature*, ed. A Nieuwenhuizen (Melbourne, 1994), pp. 29–47; R. Eckersley, 'Killer cults and the search for meaning, *AQ* 72 (1) (Feb-Mar 2000): pp. 16–19; T. Sprod, 'Philosophy, young people and well-being', *Youth Studies Australia* 18 (2) (June 1999): pp. 12–16; R. Black, 'Age of meaninglessness is a killer', *Age* 28/6/1999.

[62] A. Boyce Gibson, 'Natural theology and philosophy of religion', *Proceedings of the XIth International Congress of Philosophy* (Amsterdam, 1953), vol. 11, pp. 45–9, at p. 47; more fully in A.B. Gibson, *Theism and Empiricism* (London, 1970), chs 1–3.

[63] Smart, 'Australian philosophers', p. 36; see I. Kesarcodi-Watson, 'Wittgenstein and the "mystical"', *Journal of Studies in Mysticism* 22 (Spring 1979): pp. 52–9.

Among the best-known, and certainly one of the most prolific and wide-ranging writers in Australian philosophy is Max Charlesworth. His liberal brand of Catholicism was confirmed by his PhD studies at Louvain University, a centre of the reforming tendencies that led to the Second Vatican Council as well as of scholastic philosophy.[64] His first book was an examination of Wittgenstein and other linguistic philosophers from a broadly scholastic point of view,[65] but in Australia he soon distanced himself from the scholastics. Though he translated a volume in the standard translation of Thomas Aquinas, taught a course on medieval philosophy and wrote a book on Saint Anselm,[66] he was, as we saw in chapter 4, severe in rejecting criticism by scholastics of the state of university philosophy. In the 1960s, he was a leader in Melbourne campaigns against the 'Movement' and Australian involvement in Vietnam.[67]

He contributed to the diversity of Melbourne philosophy as one of the founders of the journal of philosophy of religion, *Sophia*, in which appeared, for example, a number of the papers on the problem of evil considered in chapter 4. He has promoted investigation and acceptance, as far as possible, of the claims of all religions, including those of Australian aborigines.[68] He became Dean of Humanities at Deakin University, and Director of the National Institute for Law, Ethics and Public Affairs. He has been prominent in the developing field of bioethics, described in chapter 16, and a member of various ethics committees, and accepted the role of public intellectual and commentator

---

[64] J. Hawley, 'Growing up Catholic', *Age* 14/6/1986, supp. p. 3.

[65] M. Charlesworth, *Philosophy and Linguistic Analysis* (Pittsburgh, 1959); briefly in 'Analytical philosophy', *New Catholic Encyclopedia* (Washington, 1967), vol. 1, pp. 470–3; a similar line in V.I. Rice, 'Necessary being', *Sophia* 3 (2) (July 1964): pp. 28–31.

[66] Thomas Aquinas, *Summa Theologiae* (Cambridge, 1964–81), vol. 15; M. Charlesworth, 'The study of medieval philosophy in Australia', *Twentieth Century* 16 (1961): pp. 131–7; M. Charlesworth, trans, *St Anselm's Proslogion*, with commentary (Oxford, 1965); also M. Charlesworth, 'Questions about natural law', *Australian Biblical Review* 14 (1966): pp. 9–23.

[67] M. Charlesworth, 'Australian Catholic intellectuals: The *Catholic Worker* and the "Movement"', in *Intellectual Movements and Australian Society*, ed. B. Head & J. Walter (Melbourne, 1988), pp. 274–88; M. Charlesworth, 'Conditions for dialogue with Communists', in *Catholics in Revolution*, ed. P. Ormonde (Melbourne, 1968), pp. 19–39.

[68] M. Charlesworth, *Religious Inventions* (Cambridge, 1997); *Philosophy and Religion: From Plato to Postmodernism* (Oxford, 2002); introductions in *Religion in Aboriginal Australia*, ed. M. Charlesworth *et al.* (St Lucia, 1984); see A. Olding, 'Religion as smorgasbord', *Quadrant*, 42 (5) (May 1998), pp. 73–5.

on such matters as ethics, religion, science and the state of universities.[69]

A similar tradition has been maintained at Melbourne University, where philosophers such as Tony Coady are associated with the Centre for Applied Philosophy and Public Ethics, which publishes the high quality journal *Res Publica*.[70] It includes articles on such subjects as euthanasia, the limits of multiculturalism, business ethics and voluntary unionism.

A combination of Catholic positions much less usual than Charlesworth's is represented by Eric D'Arcy, an admirer of linguistic philosophy, but conservative in theology and politics. He achieved early and unwanted fame when a letter by him, leaked to the press in 1955, provided the public with the first hard evidence of the existence of the Movement. The letter, sent to carefully chosen Catholics in business and professional spheres to call a meeting to raise money for the Movement, said,

> The next few weeks will see either a great victory or a great defeat for the men working so stoutly to defend the Church in Australia.

> Whichever God sends, victory or defeat, it will not be the end of the fight. It will be the beginning of a new phase. At this meeting you will hear the person best qualified to explain the present crisis. He will seek your endorsement of measures already taken and your support for other proposals in the future ... I hate melodrama but you will agree that this gathering demands the highest security ... STRICTLY NO ADMITTANCE WITHOUT THIS LETTER ...

> Sincerely yours in Domino,

> Eric D'Arcy (Rev.), Chaplain.

The revelations about the operations of 'The Movement' created a furore and the Labor Split was on in earnest.[71] D'Arcy joined the philosophy department at Melbourne University, and achieved a more

---

[69] M. Charlesworth, 'The house of theory for the liberal ideal', *Meanjin* 50 (1991): pp. 463–78; 'What the top thinkers think', *Bulletin* 16/5/1989, pp. 49–50; criticism in R. Gaita, 'Intellectuals: "speaking the truth to power"', *Quadrant* 36 (9) (Sept 1992): pp. 26–8.

[70] www.philosophy.unimelb.edu.au/cappe ; A. Coady, 'The public philosopher', *Meanjin* 50 (1991): pp. 479–92; C.A.J. Coady, 'Messy morality and the art of the possible', *Proceedings of the Aristotelian Society, Supplementary Volume* 64 (1990): pp. 259–79; A. Coady & M. O'Keefe, eds, *Terrorism and Justice* (Melbourne, 2002); on philosophical issues for schools, M. Laverty, *What's in an Issue?* (Melbourne, 1997).

[71] T. Truman, *Catholic Action and Politics* (Melbourne, 1960), pp. 170–1.

satisfactory recognition with his book on freedom of conscience.[72] His method owes much to the linguistic philosophy then current, but uses it to defend characteristically Catholic moral positions. He recommends theologians study Wittgenstein to acquire clarity, instead of turgid Germans. [73] He eventually became head of the Philosophy Department but moved on to a more conventional ecclesiastical career. His skills in language proved most useful many years later, after he had become Archbishop of Hobart. The major new *Catechism of the Catholic Church* was sent to the United States for translation into English, but embarrassingly came back in 'gender-free' language. D'Arcy was entrusted with the delicate task of taking the gender freeness back out again.[74]

Then there is Eastern philosophy. One extreme opinion on the subject is that of Sydneysider Clive James, that 'human reason as we know it in the West is the only kind of thought there really is, and that the Wisdom of the East, to the extent that it exists at all, is at least partly and perhaps largely responsible for the fact that India can't provide a decent life for the majority of its people.'[75] Naturally, Melbourne has been more hospitable.[76]

[72] E. D'Arcy, *Conscience and its Right to Freedom* (London, 1961); trans. as *La conciencia y su derecho a la libertad* (Madrid, 1963) and *Plaidoyer pour la liberté de la conscience* (Paris, 1964); summary in 'Freedom of religion', *New Catholic Encyclopedia* (Washington, 1967), vol. 6 pp. 107–14 and 'Conscience', *Journal of Medical Ethics* 3 (1977): pp. 98–9; Thomas Aquinas, *Summa Theologiae* (Cambridge, 1964–81), vols 19–20 translated by D'Arcy; E. D'Arcy, *Human Acts: An Essay in Their Moral Evaluation* (Oxford, 1963); some similar issues in M. Charlesworth, *Church, State and Conscience* (St Lucia, 1973); some scepticism from colleagues on the Catholic record on freedom in M.J. Charlesworth, 'Catholics and the free society', and H.J. McCloskey, 'The myth of Catholic liberalism', in *Catholics and the Free Society*, ed. H. Mayer (Melbourne, 1961); F. Knopfelmacher, *Intellectuals and Politics* (Melbourne, 1968), ch. 4.

[73] E. D'Arcy, 'Towards the first golden age?', *ACR* 73 (1997): pp. 294–306.

[74] C. McGillion, 'Doctoring the catechism', *Tablet* 248 (21/5/1994): pp. 624–5.

[75] C. James, 'The Bagwash speaks', in *Glued to the Box* (London, 1983), pp. 215–6.

[76] P. Bilimoria, 'Comparative and Asian philosophy in Australia and New Zealand — introduction', *Philosophy East and West* 45 (1995): pp. 151–69; symposium in *AJP* 73 (1) (1995); P. Bilimoria & P. Fenner, eds. *Religions and Comparative Thought: Essays in Honour of the Late Dr. Ian Kesarcodi-Watson* (Delhi, 1988); P. Bilimoria, *Hinduism in Australia* (Melbourne, 1989); R.A. Hutch & P.G. Fenner, eds, *Under the Shade of a Coolibah Tree: Australian Studies in Consciousness* (London, 1984); P. Fenner, *The Ontology of the Middle Way* (Dordrecht, 1990); P. Fenner, *Reasoning into Reality: A System-Cybernetic Interpretation of Middle Path Analysis* (Boston, 1993); P. Fenner, *The*

In Sydney, the philosophy departments at the second and third universities have had a low profile, but it has been otherwise in Melbourne. Monash and La Trobe have both had large and distinguished philosophy departments. La Trobe was founded with a few large departments, one of them philosophy, and big plans for expansion. These were mostly not realised, as the climate of opinion about tertiary education moved to renaming colleges of advanced education as universities instead of founding or expanding real universities. Nevertheless, some of the characteristically Australian work in philosophy of science and universals, to be considered in chapter 12, has been done by philosophers at La Trobe and Monash. More recently, Monash has been famous, or notorious, for the activities of Peter Singer and his school in ethics, described in chapter 16.

To Sydney eyes, the story of Melbourne philosophy is a worthy one, but perhaps lacks a certain sense of excitement. Undoubtedly, the present book is Sydneycentric. If anyone can write a book on *Why Melbourne Philosophy is Interesting After All*, I am all for it.

In one respect, Melbourne has succeeded in projecting its vision a long way forward into the future, through its influence on Canberra. The Australian National University has actually had two philosophy departments on the same campus, one in the former University College, a normal department that teaches undergraduates, and the other a pure research institute. The former especially had strong Melbourne connections in its early years. The first full-time lecturer in philosophy there (in 1945) was Quentin Gibson,[77] the younger brother of Sandy Boyce Gibson. A political background similar to John Anderson's is revealed in a Communist Party source: 'expelled for Trotskyist tendencies ... shows signs of becoming nasty and exposing our people.'[78] Peter Herbst and Kurt Baier from Melbourne soon joined.

Edge of Certainty (York Beach, Maine, 2002); A. Sharma, *The Philosophy of Religion: A Buddhist Perspective* (Delhi, 1995); J.P. McKinney, 'Can East meet West?', *Philosophy East and West* 3 (1953): pp. 257–67; M. Lu, 'Was Mencius a true successor of Confucius?', *Philosophy East and West* 33 (1983): pp. 79–85; K. Lai, *Moral Cultivation, Self and Community: Learning from Confucian and Daoist Philosophies* (Aldershot, 2003); A.K. Stout, 'The East-West Working Party of philosophers', *Hemisphere* 2 (5) (May 1958): pp. 10–13; papers of the Working Party in Stout Papers, Sydney University Archives P.088, part VIII; see also the journal *Religious Traditions*.

[77] Q. Gibson papers in National Library MS 6937; Q. Gibson, *Facing Philosophical Questions* (Melbourne, 1948); Q. Gibson, *The Existence Principle* (Dordrecht, 1998); obituary in *ANU Reporter* 32 (18) (2001).

[78] ASIO file on Q. Gibson at Australian Archives 6119/418 (digitised on www.naa.gov.au), p. 21.

At the Research School, the Melbourne influence was not so dominant. The Sydney Andersonians John Passmore, Percy Partridge and Eugene Kamenka were early leaders, but as their work was in social and political philosophy and the history of philosophy, more central areas of the subject did not come under Sydney domination. Work in those areas has been led by Frank Jackson, the son of Camo Jackson, and Jack Smart from Adelaide, both known for their work on the philosophy of mind to be described in chapter 9.[79] The dominant trend of philosophy there has followed the 'Canberra plan', which adds some of Sydney's realism and materialism to a project with remote origins in Wittgenstein: of defending 'the platitudes', or leaving everything as it is — in maintaining, for example, that there is nothing fundamentally mysterious in the mental or the moral realms.[80] With active research in logic, environmental philosophy, political philosophy and other areas, ANU has been notably successful in attracting outstanding staff and visitors and in placing its PhD graduates in university positions. It is listed well ahead of all other Australian philosophy departments in the *Philosophical Gourmet Report*. The accolade is deserved.[81]

[79] Departmental history at philrsss.anu.edu.au/history.php3 .
[80] J. O'Leary-Hawthorne & H. Price, 'How to stand up for non-cognitivists', *AJP* 74 (1996), section VI; P. Menzies, 'Probabilistic causation and the preemption problem', *Mind* 105 (1996): pp. 85–117, section 3; web.syr.edu/~dpnolan/philosophy/Credo.html .
[81] www.philosophicalgourmet.com ; *Australian* 3/12/1997, p. 48.

PART TWO:
THE WIDER SPHERE OF PHILOSOPHY

Chapter 8   The Push and Critical Drinkers

A CCORDING to some, including many former members, the
Sydney Push was a drunken gang of logorrhoeac poseurs, that
no-one could take seriously — in Barry Humphries' words, 'a
fraternity of middle-class desperates, journalists, drop-out academics,
gamblers and poets *manqués*, and their doxies'.[1] Feminists of various
schools have been keen to say what a lot of sexist bastards they were.
Undoubtedly it is all close to the truth. But if the queue to bag them
is so long, surely they must have had something going for them? The
reason why they are still of more interest than the many other cliques
of Bohemian loudmouths that have infested Sydney pubs since the
Rum Corps is that they have some claim to a role in bringing about
'the Sixties'. If it is pointed out that the Sixties happened all over the
world and could not have been caused by a minute group at the
bottom end of the planet, that of course must be admitted. Still, certain essential aspects of the Sixties, even overseas, were in part the
creation of two late hangers-on of the Push, Richard Neville and
Germaine Greer.

The reason for interest in them in a history of philosophy is that
the Push really was, up to a point, a realisation of Anderson's ideas.
The particular Andersonian production to which their activities most
closely related was not any of his published work, but a paper handed
around in typescript to those considered ready for it from 1940. The
title was 'Obscenity'. It breezily asserted, in the combination of 'objectivity' and sex for which the Push was to become famous:

> It is noteworthy that the use of obscene words is comparatively rare
> among women; and this is connected with the anti-feminine tendency
> (the contemptuous or sadistic attitude towards women) in obscenity. Thus

[1] B. Humphries, *More Please: An Autobiography* (Melbourne, 1992), p. 169.

the commonest or, at least, the 'most obscene' of obscene words, the words for the sexual act and for the feminine organ [there follow several obscene words, the printing of which here would simply advance Andersonian interests] ... this is more so in English than in other languages ... Is there here something typical of the English character — is English energy, English 'empiricism' (their prosaic outlook, their mechanical way of doing things) connected with an obsessional attitude to sex?

There are then a few pages of Freudian speculation, and a suggestion that the alternative to sentimental or brutal sex is 'comic copulation'.[2]

The origin of the Push as a movement distinct from Andersonianism is usually dated to the split in Freethinking circles occasioned by Anderson's support for most of the Menzies Government's anti-Communist policies. One must distinguish four entities: the Freethought Society, the Anti-Conscription Committee, the Libertarian Society, and the Push. Each grew out of the preceding one, and the first three were largely run by philosophers; the Push was a wider movement of which the Libertarian Society was a core and source of ideology. The Freethought Society, as we saw, was a vehicle for Anderson's talks to students, already some twenty years old in 1950. Its members were surprised when Anderson supported Chifley's use of troops to break the coal strike in 1949, and the last straw came in 1950, when the Korean War led to conscription proposals, and students formed the Anti-Conscription Committee. The president was David Stove, and prominent members were David Armstrong and Eric Dowling, all later philosophers.[3] Opposition from the University authorities, allegedly because the University's donors in the business community would be displeased, was not unexpected.[4] Nor was opposition from more conservative students; law student William Deane (later Governor-General), for example, argued 'identical principles underlie compulsory taxation and conscription, whereas if they were to oppose the former they would be working merely for the economic ruin of their country instead of for the much more disas-

---

[2] J. Anderson, 'Obscenity', 1940, repr. in Sydney Libertarians Broadsheet 73 (May 1973): pp. 7–10 and in Heraclitus 49 (June 1996): pp. 4–5; cf. R. Neville, Play Power (London, 1970), pp. 274–8.
[3] Honi Soit 20/7/1950, p. 1; 27/7/1950, p. 2; 3/8/1950, p. 3; D. Stove, 'Liberals, democracy and the anti-Communist bill', 4/5/1950, p. 5; P. Coleman, 'Nothing but the bill', 18/5/1950, p. 4; P. Coleman, 'Democracy v. conscription', 20/7/1950, p. 2; R.E. Dowling, 'Your home in the Army', 14/9/1950, p. 3, also 5/10/1950, p. 2; 28/9/1950, p. 1; A. Barcan, Radical Students: The Old Left at Sydney University (Melbourne, 2002), ch. 8.
[4] Honi Soit 14/9/1950, p. 3; 21/9/1950, p. 1; 28/9/1950, p. 1; 5/10/1950, p. 2.

trous consequences which would probably follow if, by any wild freak of fate, their present campaign were to be successful.'[5] What hurt was the opposition of Anderson himself. At a meeting of the Freethought Society on 2 August 1950, attended by over 250 students, Anderson said that freethought was not against compulsion as such. 'To be political is to have the power of deciding on what front we are going to fight — to have a sense for what is an immediate and important issue.' The largest issue being the threat of Russia, anti-conscription was in comparison a slight matter. Not one speaker supported him. Armstrong suggested that the role of social adjuster was a new one for Anderson, Stove that he had sold out on the task of criticism.[6] For freethinkers, Anderson's thesis that criticism had to be restricted to certain subjects was unacceptable. 'This was news to old freethinkers, who had always taken it to be a feature of freethought to fight on all fronts at once, not to look for allies, but to criticize superstitions, illusions and encroachments on liberty wherever they were found.'[7] Finally — and it had taken a long time — Anderson was subjected to criticism.

As long-term president of the Freethought Society, Anderson claimed a right to veto anything he did not like, and that Society died. The left wing of the opposition constituted itself as the Libertarian Society at Sydney University. The first meeting was chaired by Jim Baker, lecturer in philosophy, who stated that 'the aim of the society was to conduct an inquiry into the fields of political, sexual and religious authoritarianism.'[8] In distinction from normal Bohemian movements, papers were given regularly from 1956, in the Philosophy Room after Anderson's retirement in 1958.[9] In summary,

> The libertarian standpoint is that of opposition, in every field of human activity, to authoritarian forces and to their social and political demands. Concurrent with this is support for non-servile, co-operative and free activities. On this basis, libertarians are found to be atheists, supporters of

---

[5] *Honi Soit* 21/9/1950, p. 6.

[6] [D. Waters], 'Fathers and sons – Anderson betrayed', *Honi Soit* 7/9/1950, p. 3, repr. in *Heraclitus* 59 (July 1997): p. 3; reply in J. Anderson, 'The right to be wrong', *Honi Soit* 21/9/1950, p. 2; on Waters, F. Moorhouse, *Days of Wine and Rage* (Melbourne, 1980), pp. 26–8; obituaries in *Australian* 2/5/97, p. 16; *SMH* 8/5/1997.

[7] A.J. Baker, 'John Anderson and Freethought', *Australian Quarterly* 34 (Dec 1962): pp. 50–63, at p. 62; A.J. Baker, *Anderson's Social Philosophy* (Sydney, 1979), pp. 132–4; J. Ogilvie, *The Push* (Sydney, 1995), pp. 69–73.

[8] *Honi Soit* 17/4/52, p. 5; A. Coombs, *Sex and Anarchy: The Life and Death of the Sydney Push* (Melbourne, 1996), pp. 66–7; 'Libertarian Society history', *Sydney Libertarians Broadsheet* 93 (Oct, 1977): p. 6.

[9] Coombs, *Sex and Anarchy*, p. 52.

sexual freedom and opponents of repressive institutions, particularly that great destroyer of independence and initiative, the political State.[10]

The Sydney Libertarians and their associates thereafter constituted a recognisable entity in the Sydney scene until the late Sixties.[11] Anderson himself entirely repudiated their opinions. But two leading members, Baker and George Molnar, were at various times lecturers in philosophy at Sydney University, and philosophical issues maintained a presence in their newssheet, the *Sydney Libertarians Broadsheet*. One of the issues they debated was whether it was necessary to take up Anderson's philosophical ideas in order to be a true Libertarian. Molnar held that strictly speaking it was not, but that it certainly helped.[12] In any case, it is clear that those who felt any need to justify libertarian behaviour intellectually looked directly to Anderson's thought:

> Not only were we rid of theism but of any sense of obligation inherited from family or society. There is nothing whose nature it is to be obeyed, and the categorical imperative is a fraud of moralism unless it can be spelt out in hypothetical terms, indicating the hidden assumption (e.g., 'if you wish to please God, you should go to church' rather than, 'You should go to church'), an assumption which can then be challenged as not reflecting your interests ('But I do not wish to please God').[13]

Apart from the general Andersonian emphasis on criticism, the Push's most distinctive philosophical position was an opposition to 'moralism'. Baker and others promoted the Andersonian view that moral opinions are projections of interests and preferences, dressed up

---

[10] *Sydney University Orientation Handbook*, 1958, quoted in A.J. Baker, 'Sydney Libertarianism and the Push', *Broadsheet* 81 (Mar 1975): pp. 5–10; also in A.J. Baker, 'Sydney Libertarianism', *Broadsheet* 10 & 11 (Dec 1960 & Jan 1961), repr. in *The Sydney Line*, ed. A.J. Baker & G. Molnar (Sydney, 1963), pp. 27–32 and at www.takver.com/history/aia/aia00026.htm

[11] General views, besides Coombs' *Sex and Anarchy*: W. Harcourt, 'The Push', *National Times* 3–8/2/1975, pp. 28–31; with reply by J. Baker, 'Sydney Libertarianism and the Push', *Sydney Libertarians Broadsheet* 81 (Mar 1975): pp. 5–10 and letters in no. 82 (May, 1975); P. White, 'Sydney Libertarianism: A History and Critique', BA (Hons) thesis, Dept of Government, Sydney University, 1980.

[12] G. Molnar, 'Libertarianism and philosophy', *Broadsheet* 35 (1964): pp. 4–6.

[13] D.J. Ivison, 'Anderson as a liberator', *Dialectic* 30 (1987): pp. 7–10; consequences for 'free love' in D.J. Ivison, 'What is this libertarianism anyway?' *Honi Soit* 30/9/1964, p. 5, quoted in C. Wallace, *Greer: Untamed Shrew* (Sydney, 1997), pp. 80–1; earlier in *Honi Soit* 29/6/1950, p. 1, with partial denial in next issue; R. Pinkerton, 'The ideology of chastity', *Libertarian* 1 (1957): pp. 22–32.

as 'Thou shalt's.[14] Molnar's article, 'The nature of moralism', attributed it more to a dogmatising search for universally true rules, an 'itch
for generalisation':

> The moralist is full of shibboleth. As a rule he is attached to principles
> which he is seldom shy of waving about for everybody to hear. By princi-
> ples the moralist means universal moral truths; strict, potent measures of
> all conduct ... The falsity of the moralist's principles is simply the falsity of
> universal propositions which are subject to exception: as if someone were
> to say 'All men are Caucasian.' I think we can, sometimes at least, make
> definite sense out of what someone intends when he says that intercourse
> between young people is always bad. Perhaps he means that it always has
> certain debilitating effects on character or on human relations. So under-
> stood, the proposition is just not true. One knows of very many cases of
> promiscuity which fall outside the principle, which falsify it. Moralists are
> typically lightminded in their disregard of evidence which tells against
> them. Think here of the dogmatic ease with which it is said that obscene
> publications, or the depiction of violence on the screen, lead to certain
> effects. Or when it is asserted, with a confidence proportional to the ab-
> sence of evidence, that certain beliefs are the foundations of our society
> and any questioning of them will lead to our mutual ruin.
>
> The reason for the moralist's cavalier attitude towards the facts is that he
> has a false picture of the nature of moral thought. He thinks that univer-
> sally valid principles are needed for any moral judgement to stand up. Be-
> cause of this he is committed to seeking principles, and he finds them
> where there are none. His itch for generalisation is powerful.[15]

Molnar drew the conclusion that Sydney Sparkes Orr should have
insisted on his right to sexual freedom, unconstrained by the persecution of moralists.[16]

---

[14] J. Baker, 'The illusions of moralism', *Libertarian* 1 (1957): pp. 14–21
(Coombs, *Sex and Anarchy*, p. 133); A.J. Baker, 'Morals: The Libertarian
view', *Sydney Libertarians Broadsheet* 60 (June 1970): pp. 1–3; cf. A. Skillen,
Ruling Illusions (Hassocks, Sussex, 1977), ch. 4.

[15] G. Molnar, 'The nature of moralism', *Sydney Libertarians Broadsheet* 48
(May 1966): pp. 1–4; also G. Molnar, 'The sexual revolution', *Sydney
Libertarians Broadsheet* 39 (Sept 1964): pp. 1–5; 'The straightforward sexual
relationship', Libertarian Soc talk, 1959, text in Molnar papers, Mitchell
Library MLMSS 6978, box 2; similar ideas later in P. Petersen, *Morality,
Sexual Facts and Fantasies* (Moorooka, 1999); P. Petersen, review of I.
Primoratz, *Ethics and Sex*, *AJP* 80 (2002): pp. 122–4; debate on whether
'anything goes' in G. Priest, 'Sexual perversion', *AJP* 75 (1997): pp. 360–72;
D. Baltzly, 'Peripatetic perversions: a neo-Aristotelian account of the nature
of sexual perversion', *Monist* 85 (2003): pp. 3–29.

[16] G. Molnar, 'Sexual freedom in the Orr case', *Australian Highway* 41 (3)
(June 1960): pp. 54–5.

George Molnar, 1970s (Carlotta McIntosh)

In one way Molnar's account is unfair to those who hold an objective theory of morals, since it is hardly central to any such theory whether rules are exceptionless or not. If there are conflicting objective values, then one would expect the conflict to show itself as exceptions to rules: a rule attempting to implement one value would have an exception because some other value conflicted with it. On the other hand, actually existing morality, circa 1960, did tend to express itself as a set of rules, often unaccompanied by the reasoning behind them, and was vulnerable to the criticism the Libertarians made.

Descended from Anderson's promotion of 'permanent criticism' was the Libertarians' lack of 'activism' in the sense of the later Sixties. While they were against the State, they had no intention of provoking it or working towards its downfall. Much less did they expect it to change. Demonstrating in the streets or organising for political action was regarded as succumbing to illusions.[17] Their opposition to 'morality' expressed itself in their own lifestyles rather than in proselytising. The *Sydney Libertarians Broadsheet*, for example, was distributed to those who asked, but there was never any suggestion that it might appear on newsstands to alarm the citizenry. That was all to change with the younger Push generation. By the mid-Sixties there was a certain amount of activity in support of causes especially concerned with freedom, such as the Council for Civil Liberties — founded after the police broke into a bedroom being used by George Molnar — hiding draft resisters, and anti-psychiatry.[18] More visible activities were to come later.

An ASIO assessment of them resulted from an agent's interview with Jim Baker in 1959. After a brief outline of Libertarian Society history, the report says their general philosophical line is controlled by ex-Communist Party members like Molnar, and adds Baker's assertion that they include 'a few anarchists who wouldn't hesitate to drop a bomb on the Sydney Harbour Bridge or de-rail a train'. The source comments:

> At first meeting with these people one is inclined to regard them as an offshoot of the 'beatniks', but after knowing them a short while it becomes obvious that they are well above the average 'beatnik' intellectually. Their knowledge of Marxism is surprising and their ability to discuss this subject on levels not encountered in the C. P. of A. is both stimulating and educational.

> With the exception of Jim BAKER, the Libertarians have absolutely no standard of ethics. Their behaviour and conversation in mixed company would be regarded as 'shocking' even in 'modern' society.

---

[17] Coombs, *Sex and Anarchy*, ch. 4, esp. p. 54; I. Davison, 'The failure of Australian Bohemia', *Australian Humanist* 3 (Spring 1967): pp. 13–16.
[18] Coombs, *Sex and Anarchy*, pp. 186–7, 236, 278.

They have no respect for property and live entirely within their own periphery of standards, which can only be described as obscure ... The Libertarians should not be underestimated despite their base outlook.[19]

Publicity was not sought by the Push, and was unwelcome in the only case where it was seriously threatened. Before the 'We're all Libertarians now' position truly took hold, the public had one last chance to salivate over lurid revelations of the doings of intellectual folk. And it wasn't students. On New Year's Eve, 1962, CSIRO technician Geoffrey Chandler and his wife Margaret attended a party. As befitted a fringe Push member, Chandler, 'unable to accept the petty rules and regulations of society', in his own words,[20] approved of 'open' marriages. He had given his wife to understand that she was free to have an affair with Gilbert Bogle, a leading young CSIRO research physicist,[21] who was also to attend the party. Chandler and his girlfriend, a secretary in the Sydney University Psychology Department, went on to a Push party.[22] The bodies of Bogle and Mrs Chandler were found the next morning beside the Lane Cove River. The cause of death was never definitively established. The mystery surrounding the deaths and the connections of those involved made it one of Australia's best-known murder cases. Reporters invaded the Push pub, the Royal George Hotel, but almost everyone refused to speak to them. Chandler was grateful to a number of Push people who hid him from the pack.

Why did the youth fall for any of this simplistic and self-serving tripe? It is a fair question. Answering it would cast a good deal of light on a period whose sudden changes are still poorly understood.

The first source of the Push's appeal was simply that it was an island of excitement in a sea of dullness. By the time the 1950s were well under way, the moralists had been so successful they had created a landscape of cultural monotony. As we will see in chapter 10, the deprivations of the Depression and the War had helped create favourable conditions for the triumph of 'moralism', which had used its strength both to impose its views by law and to excuse itself from giving a reasoned defence of its positions. Institutional persecution of homosexuality was still universal in the 1950s, while Federal Cabinet

---

[19] ASIO file on Libertarians, Sydney University, Australian Archives series A6122/39 item 1311, folio 10; repeated in file on Molnar, A6119/79 item 989.

[20] G. Chandler, *So You Think I Did It?* (Sydney, 1969), p. 55.

[21] G.S. Bogle, 'Masers', *Australian Scientist* 1 (1961): pp. 128–32, 'Lasers', pp. 188–91; B. Toohey, 'Bogle-Chandler: New ASIO link', *National Times* 24–30/10/1982, p. 4.

[22] Coombs, *Sex and Anarchy*, pp. 163–4.

decided to retain the ban on *Lady Chatterley's Lover* as late as 1965. For some, it was almost impossible to breathe.[23]

In those circumstances, the Push had appeal simply because there was something going on. A first-year pharmacy student ventured into the Royal George in 1962: 'I spoke to no-one all evening and no-one spoke to me until just before closing time when I went outside ... and two policemen seized me. I was flung into the back of a Black Maria and driven to the back of Darling Harbour ... They tipped me out into the cold night air and gave me a lecture: "Look, son, don't you go near that pub again – it's full of loose women, social diseases and drugs." I thought "Terrific!" and was back there next night.'[24] How it looked to one not admitted to the circle is evoked by Bob Ellis in one of his longest sentences:

> To an outsider, and many of us were outside the Push, unable because of our tentative personalities to break through the strong, royal curtain into their loving affections, they loomed as homeric giants, whose life was one long bland adventure, night after night, party after party, race meeting after poker session and tragic love after tragic love, following only the minute's need or desire, following it for its own sake, with no ulterior goal in view, following their own soul's odyssey through all its incarnations with granite amusement, delivering their papers on sex and death and Reich and Christ and Phar Lap, arguing and drinking far into the night, taking round the hat for incidental abortions, offering no rebuff to anyone who showed up at midnight and wanted to sleep on the floor, but calmly putting up with him for as long as he wanted to stay, conducting their ritual contests, inventing their savage games, and having their parties, parties, parties, all the parties I missed.[25]

What that does not evoke is how boring afternoons in pubs could be. Some of the later phrases do call attention to another source of the Push's appeal, especially for some of its more central and outrageous members. It was a kind of substitute family for some people from emotionally difficult backgrounds. Many of them had lost their fathers in one way or another — through broken homes, mental ill-

---

[23] A good account in E. Morris, 'The patriarchal Push', *Quadrant* 23 (1) (Jan/Feb 1979): pp. 74–7; see also E. Morris, 'John Anderson, splitter', *Nation Review* 19–25/5/1977, p. 747.

[24] S. McInerney, 'The Push revisited', *SMH* 22/10/1983, pp. 33–4; similar in R. Neville, *Hippie Hippie Shake* (Melbourne, 1995), p. 18; C. Pybus, *Till Apples Grow on an Orange Tree* (St Lucia, 1998), p. 10; S. Ryan, *Catching the Waves* (1999), pp. 57–8.

[25] Bob Ellis, 'The book that never came', *Nation Review* 9–15/3/1973, pp. 634–5; reply in *Sydney Libertarians Broadsheet* 72 (Apr 1973): p. 12; cf. R. Weiner, 'Dynamics of the Push', *Honi Soit* 25/6/1963, p. 9.

ness or death.[26] For them, the friendship, often practical, was all that was on offer in place of family. 'The Push looked after its own. They visited the hospital or passed the hat ...'[27] The significance of friendship is the source of the central idea in one of the few books on philosophy to come out of the Push, *Morality and Modernity*, by Ross Poole,[28] a lecturer in philosophy at Macquarie University. He laments in familiar terms the fragmenting effect of modern life, and argues in good Libertarian fashion that any external standard of duty is a voice outside us that cannot give us any reason why we should obey it. As a partial solution, he recommends attention to the meaning of friendship. 'We seek and often achieve recognition from others whose independence we recognise ... the demands of those friendships are not external: the needs of our friends are our needs, and the reason of friendship is our reason ... If we enter into a relationship with another just in order to gain certain pleasures, the relationship is not one of friendship, and whatever we get out of it, we do not obtain the specific pleasures of friendship.'[29]

The urge for youthful rebellion that provided some of the motivation for seeking out the Push would in earlier years have been satisfied by joining the Communist Party. But the demise of Communism in splits and its discrediting after Hungary and Khrushchev's speech on the horrors of Stalinism meant that by the early 1960s there was little appeal in traditional left-wing politics. With the Communists marginalised and Labor split, the Push to some extent filled an ideological vacuum.[30] Compared to the 'grubby Marxist leaflets and hand-me-down rhetoric' of the Old Left's aging Leninists, it was at least colourful.[31]

Worth considering too are some of the reasons given by the right for the general phenomenon of the 'youth revolution of the Sixties'. ASIO's theory was that the whole thing was just another Communist

---

[26] Coombs, *Sex and Anarchy*, p. 206; G. Greer, *Daddy, We Hardly Knew You* (London, 1989).

[27] K. Jennings, *Bad Manners* (Melbourne, 1993), p. 55.

[28] Coombs, *Sex and Anarchy*, pp. 72–3, 153, 202–3.

[29] R. Poole, *Morality and Modernity* (London, 1991), pp. 143–4; earlier, R. Poole, 'The freethought movement', *Honi Soit* 27/7/1967, pp. 10–11; other treatments in D. Cocking & J. Kennett, 'Friendship and the self', *Ethics* 108 (1998): pp. 502–27; R. Langton, 'Sexual solipsism', *Philosophical Topics* 23 (2) (1985): pp. 149–87.

[30] J. Docker, 'Sydney intellectual history and Sydney Libertarianism', *Politics* 7 (1972): pp. 40–7; on which J. Baker, 'Sydney Libertarianism: A reply', *Sydney Libertarians Broadsheet* 75 (Aug 1973): pp. 7–9.

[31] K. Windschuttle on Neville's *Play Power* in *Old Mole* no. 5 (31/8/1970): pp. 12–13.

front, like the youth and women's organisations of the Thirties and Forties and the peace movement of the Fifties. There was, they thought, a worldwide Soviet-led plot to undermine the West by corrupting its youth.[32] Though not a ridiculous theory, intense efforts failed to turn up much evidence. Technological developments had more to do with it. Modern pharmacology produced the penicillin that cured VD, and the Pill, which removed the most obvious reasons for not behaving like the Push. Chemical wizardry also produced a choice of drugs. B.A. Santamaria mentioned another invention in his 1973 article, 'Philosophies in collision'. He saw three major philosophies in competition for the soul of West: Christianity broadly understood, Soviet Communism, and secular humanism or libertarianism, meaning the assertion that anyone can do what they like. Television, he thought, as well as the Pill, had given the last philosophy the edge, since it beamed the value structure of advertising and 'anything goes' right into homes.[33] Santamaria gamely went on the Box himself, not without success, but few of those who agreed with him had the ability to make argument into memorable television.

Last but not least, the strictly intellectual appeal of the Push, as a group that actually took ideas and argument seriously, should not be underestimated. In theory, of course, academic life introduces the student to teachers who love and share ideas. In practice, over and above the strategies academics have to adopt to cope with the flood of students, and their simple fatigue, there is an inevitable cognitive mismatch between the young and the old brain. Youth interested in ideas must always find one another. Robert Hughes, a fringe member, wrote, 'I certainly heard the basic message of Sydney libertarianism loud and clear — that you should never believe anything someone says merely because he/she is saying it. This has been of fundamental value to me as a writer. It was not, of course, invented in Sydney in the late 1940s, but in Athens about 2300 years before that. Nevertheless I first encountered it in Sydney through the medium of the Push.'[34] Clive James too recognised the significance of theory in the Push, though he was less high-minded about its effects: 'Endorsing Pareto's analysis of sexual guilt as a repressive social mechanism, the Libertarians freely helped themselves to each other's girlfriends.'[35]

[32] D. McKnight, *Australia's Spies and Their Secrets* (Sydney, 1994), chs 18–19.

[33] B.A. Santamaria, 'Philosophies in collision', *Facts* (National Civic Council) no. 37 (May 1973), repr. in *Man, How Will He Survive?*, ed. J.N. Santamaria (Melbourne, 1973), pp. 22–39.

[34] R. Hughes, quoted in Coombs, *Sex and Anarchy*, p. x; his relation to the Push, p. 157.

[35] C. James, *Unreliable Memoirs*, p. 137; on James and the Push, pp. 132, 137–9; Coombs, *Sex and Anarchy*, p. 157; I. Britain, *Once an Australian*

Hanging around the Push could be a training in how to speak and write as well as how to think. Germaine Greer said, 'Australians speak over-emphatically. Just listen to any of them: listen to Barry Humphries, listen to Clive James, listen to Robert Hughes, they all have this "over the top" rhetorical power. It's one of the ways Australian language is spoken. I actually like it; I think it's rather good stuff.'[36] But it isn't Australians in general who speak or write like this — or if it is, only a small group have the knack of packaging it for print. Besides those just named, and at her best, Germaine herself, one could mention David Stove,[37] and perhaps a few later humorists like Patrick Cook and Mike Carlton. Where the style came from, and why it arose at the fringes of the Sydney Push, remains a mystery, but the reading and viewing public in Australia and elsewhere has been vastly entertained by it.

Germaine Greer arrived from Melbourne in 1959 and immediately gained a central position in the Push. Though she soon moved on to other circles, Libertarian philosophising had an important place in her education. 'When I first encountered the dingy back room of the Royal George, I was a clever, undisciplined, pedantic show-off. My conversation was all effect — entertaining enough, I dare say — but emotional and impressionistic. In the flabby intellectual atmosphere of the Melbourne Drift, I had been encouraged to refrain from ungainly insistence upon logic and the connection of ideas, to be instead witty, joking together heterogeneous notions ... In Sydney, I found myself driven back, again and again, to basic premises, demonstrable facts. The scrupulosity that I had missed in my irreligious life was now a part of my everyday behaviour ... If ever, of anyone, I desired a good report, I desire it of them, my guides, philosophers and friends, the Sydney Libertarians.'[38] 'I found out that in Sydney there were at least intellectually rigorous people and that they could teach me something. At least they could teach me about the way I already thought. I was already an anarchist. I just didn't know why I was an anarchist.

(Melbourne, 1997), pp. 102–3; Ellis, 'The book that never came'; Les Murray's connections in P.F. Alexander, *Les Murray: A Life in Progress* (Melbourne, 2000), pp. 97–9.

[36] Germaine Greer, in R. Koval, *One to One* (Sydney, 1992), p. 15.

[37] J. Franklin, 'Lit crit and non-fiction: Or, the development of an Antipodean style', *Quadrant* 28 (10) (Oct 1984): pp. 41–4.

[38] G. Greer, 'The strongest influence on my life', BBC Radio 4 talk, 28/5/1975, quoted in Coombs, *Sex and Anarchy*, pp. 114, 304 and A. Coombs, 'Pushy women', *Independent Monthly* (Apr 1994): pp. 50–6, at p. 53, similar in J. McGreevy, *Cities* (New York, 1981), p. 152; a similar reaction later in A. Summers, *Ducks on the Pond* (Melbourne, 1999), pp. 294–7.

They put me in touch with the basic texts and I found out what the internal logic was about how I felt and thought.'[39]

It did not take her long to learn how to write in the required style herself. In the 1961 *Libertarians Broadsheet*, she responded to an attack on libertarian attitudes with:

> Libertarians are not bound together by an all-consuming interest in freedom of inquiry, but are also interested in political, social and sexual freedom, with varying intensity and emphasis, based on a common philosophical background of realism and determinism ... [libertarians] are not committed to beer-drinking; there is no *a priori* reason why libertarian women should be a null class.[40]

Andersonian jargon has been got in the right order there.

Using argument to 'expose illusions', in the Andersonian sense, is an exact description of *The Female Eunuch*. It is set apart from the mainstream of feminist writing by its libertarian line. Most of it is criticism, and the positive suggestions in the last two pages are also of a distinctly Andersonian cast, with the sole addition that women are mentioned specifically. 'The surest guide to the correctness of the path that women take is *joy in the struggle*.' 'Joy' means not so much a simple emotion, as a concatenation of Andersonian keywords: 'it does mean the purposive employment of energy in a self-chosen enterprise. It does mean pride and confidence. It does mean communication and cooperation with others.' It does not mean organising or reforming — 'meliorism' in Anderson's jargon. 'Privileged women will pluck at your sleeve and seek to enlist you in the "fight" for reforms, but reforms are retrogressive.'[41] Anne Coombs writes in her book on the Push, 'The Libertarian legacy shines through *The Female Eunuch* — revolutionary but not utopian, smashing icons but not erecting new ones, self-reliant without being self-blaming, attacking the conventional family while not opposing motherhood or sexuality or men.'[42] Reformist American feminism never forgave Greer for her opposition to equal rights amendments, for her love of argument for its own sake, for the counter-suggestibility that had her praising earth mothers and trashing women poets when the Sisterhood was still 'consolidating gains',[43] for her refusal to belong to any school of theoreticians. 'When I have to explain where I'm coming from to the English, who see that I'm not a proper Marxist, or a proper

---

[39] In C. Packer, *No Return Ticket* (Sydney, 1984), p. 94.

[40] G. Greer, 'Pontifications', *Sydney Libertarians Broadsheet* 20 (Oct 1961): pp. 8–9.

[41] G. Greer, *The Female Eunuch* (London, 1970), pp. 330–1.

[42] Coombs, *Sex and Anarchy*, p. 265, also p. 259.

[43] Wallace, *Greer*, pp. 193, 217, 328, 193.

Marcusian, or a proper Freudian or a proper anything else, then I have to invoke that kind of ad hoc training that used to be meted out to me in the beer-stained purlieus of the Royal George.'[44] And as to morality, she was against the existing set of rules, but also against replacing them with any other set.[45]

THE backwaters of history are full of 'movements' which thought they were going to change the world, and made no impression whatever. The Push never expected to change anything, and even had a theory about why it couldn't. Then it found the world changing to its values overnight. One Push member, isolated for some years in Peru, wrote: 'When, in September 1968, I went to the US as a grad student at the University of Illinois, you can imagine my reaction — Shit, the bloody Push has extended over the whole world ... the late 1960s and early 1970s were like a Libertarian dream come true: we *are* gonna change the world!'[46] The hard-core Push were not so impressed by the spread of 'Utopian illusions', but the younger crowd began to be gripped by a wild surmise that real change might be possible.

The degree to which the Push itself was responsible for 'the Sixties' is hard to gauge. George Molnar's opinion was, not at all. Of course, the influence of overseas gurus like Marcuse, Reich, Kinsey and so on was important, as was the impact of the Vietnam War. A lot of the Sixties was, obviously, an American (and British and European) production, swallowed whole in their Australasian colonies. Still, there were two Australian exports that had great international impact, at the libertarian end of the Sixties spectrum. One was Greer's *The Female Eunuch*. The other was Richard Neville's London magazine, *Oz*.

Sydney *Oz* magazine and its London successor were the creation of the colourful offshoot of the Libertarians at the University of New South Wales. Richard Neville took his cue from Eric Dowling — in Neville's memoirs 'the bonking philosophy professor', later the author of a book on the philosophy of love with preface by Blanche D'Alpuget.[47] Neville was impressed also by the Push economics lecturer Paddy McGuinness (a 'professional antagonist', dirty in appear-

---

[44] Greer, interview with Liz Fell, quoted in Wallace, *Greer*, p. 256.
[45] G. Greer, 'Sex and society — whose rules?', *Sunday Times* 27/2/1972, repr. in G. Greer, *The Madwoman's Underclothes* (London, 1986), pp. 102–4.
[46] J. Earls, quoted in Coombs, *Sex and Anarchy*, p. 175.
[47] E. Dowling, *Love Passion Action: The Meaning of Love and its Place in Life* (Melbourne, 1995); another treatment of the topic: R. Brown, *Analyzing Love* (Cambridge, 1987).

ance but extremely intelligent and shrewd, according to ASIO[48]) and the *Libertarians Broadsheet*.[49] Unlike the *Broadsheet*, *Oz* had pictures and was sold to the public. *Oz* number 6 contained, among other items designed to offend the class of persons usually offended by such items, a fictional first-person narrative of a gang rape. An enraged magistrate handed out sentences of six months hard labour.[50] The editors were luckier in their appeal case before the more liberal Judge Levine, which produced one of those learned discussions of philosophical points the law does so well. Heavyweights appearing on Neville's side included the Andersonians John Kerr as counsel for Neville, James McAuley, who testified to *Oz*'s literary merit, and the leading psychiatrist John Ellard,[51] who gave his opinion that one of the classes of persons who would allegedly tend to be depraved and corrupted by *Oz*, 'persons of weakened personality structures', were typically unaffected by what they read. Levine was disposed to quash the convictions, but before doing so referred the case to the Supreme Court for guidance on a number of legal points, notably one concerning the kind of evidence that should be admitted to prove that a publication 'tended to deprave and corrupt'. The general question of what evidence is relevant to showing the existence of a tendency or disposition is recognised in philosophy as a difficult enough one, but there are special complications in the case at hand. Levine's view involved some subtleties concerning both strengths of tendencies and the class in which the tendency occurs: 'whilst the prosecution does not bear the burden of proving that any particular person has been depraved, and need only prove that the publication charged as obscene has a tendency to do so, it does carry the burden of establishing not some mere theoretical, nebulous or fanciful tendency, but a real and practical tendency to deprave not a theoretical group of unidentified persons but persons or groups whom the court in judgement can refer to as those likely to be affected.'

The learned judges of the Supreme Court held that this was quite wrong. No identifiable class of persons need be named, and expert opinion is not in any case relevant. 'Ordinary human nature, that of people at large, is not a subject of proof by evidence, whether sup-

---

[48] ASIO file on Libertarians, folio 55; McGuinness as Andersonian in J. Docker, `The origins of Paddy McGuinness', *Arena Magazine* 3 (Feb/Mar 1993): pp. 21–24.

[49] Neville, *Hippie*, p. 17.

[50] K. Buckley, *Offensive and Obscene* (Sydney, 1970), ch. 2; the magistrate's objectivist moral views in O. Ajala, 'Mr Locke, S.M.', *Nation* 3/10/1964, pp. 5–6; the earlier similar *Tharunka* trial in *Obscenity* no. 1 (1964).

[51] On Ellard and Anderson: J. Ellard, *Some Rules for Killing People* (Sydney, 1989), p. 228; J. Ellard, *Anatomy of Mirages* (Sydney, 1994), p. 219.

posedly expert or not', but instead something that judges are presumed to know. It by no means follows, however, that if the judges
find themselves uncorrupted by the literature in question, they should
conclude that it has no tendency to corrupt others. 'The court will be
entitled to look in a broad way at the whole of the community, rec-
ognizing that there are people of varying degrees of intelligence and
moral fibre ... it would be sufficient if the court took the view that
the publication had a tendency to corrupt those who were susceptible
to corruption or to deprave those who were receptive to wicked influences.' With these distinctions made, the matter was sent back to
Levine, who again decided that the convictions should be quashed.[52]

Soon after, Neville took the show to London, founding London
Oz. It was more of the same: all hippie, all psychedelic, all obscene,
all radical. But its radicalism did not have the edge of violence associated with the American revolutionary left. 'I was and still am a liberal', Neville says. 'Sometimes then I was a bit embarrassed by it, because I thought I ought to be a little more revolutionary, but I've
always completely loathed violence and bloodshed and every time I
dived into Marxism all I could think of was Lenin shooting the anarchists. I could never come to terms with the Big Idea. I come from
libertarianism.'[53]

The trial of London Oz was the last great media censorship battle
in England, which only ten years earlier had given the world the classic of the genre, the trial of Lady Chatterley. The Sixties began, on one
reckoning, on 20 October 1960, when counsel for the prosecution
asked an English jury, 'Is it a book that you would even want your
wife or servants to read?'[54] and the jury laughed. By 1971, the censorship battle was nearly over, but not quite. 'Schoolkids Oz', an issue
mostly edited by a group of schoolchildren, had its turn at the Old
Bailey. The trial was said to have provoked more letters to The Times
than the Suez crisis.[55]

No-one will have trouble guessing which dead philosopher made
an appearance. John Mortimer QC concluded his opening speech,
'Members of the Jury, those of you familiar with history may have
heard of the Greek philosopher Socrates. Socrates also stood trial and

[52] Neville, Hippie, pp. 52–6; Oz, Oct 1964; Weekly Notes (N.S.W.) 83
(1965–6) Part 1 pp. 501–27; C. McGregor, People, Politics and Pop (Sydney,
1968), pp. 85–90.
[53] R. Neville, quoted in N. Fountain, Underground: The London Alternative
Press, 1966–74 (London, 1988), p. 57.
[54] C.H. Rolph, ed, The Trial of Lady Chatterley (London, 1961), p. 15; Push
comment in G. Molnar, 'Their fair lady', Sydney Libertarians Broadsheet 10
(Dec 1960), repr. in Baker & Molnar eds, The Sydney Line, pp. 18–19.
[55] G. Robertson, Obscenity (London, 1979), p. 6.

The editors of London Oz, from left, James Anderson, Felix Dennis and Richard Neville, outside the Old Bailey during their obscenity trial, 5 August 1971 (Newspix)

his trial resulted in his death. And the charge on *his* indictment was that he had corrupted the morals of young persons. And the reason he was so charged, was his unfortunate habit of continually asking why. And we who defend in this case believe that we do so in the interests of everyone, whatever age or sex or class or education, to question and ask, why.'[56] Dead philosophers are much safer in court than live ones, but the Australian Rhodes Scholar co-ordinating the defence, Geoffrey Robertson, conceived the idea that there was no precedent that prevented live philosophers being called as expert witnesses.[57] Among the last witnesses, along with the comedian Marty Feldman, was the Professor of Jurisprudence at Oxford, Ronald Dworkin. He explained that his work dealt with the relation between private and public morality. Neville asked whether he thought *Oz* did, in fact, debauch or corrupt public morality. The Professor distinguished at some length between two senses in which one might tend to corrupt

[56] T. Palmer, *The Trials of Oz* (London, 1971), p. 14; Neville, *Hippie*, p. 284; J. Mortimer, 'The time was out of joints', *Spectator* 13/5/1995, p. 35.
[57] G. Robertson, *The Justice Game* (London, 1998), p. 17.

public morality, and was in the process of giving his opinion that in neither sense did *Oz* do so, when the judge interrupted, 'This is not a lecture theatre.' After a pause, Dworkin gave his further opinion that the prosecution was, in his second sense, a corruption of public morals, and added that the prosecution would be unconstitutional in the United States in virtue of the First Amendment.[58] The last witness for the defence was Richard Wollheim, Grote Professor of Mind and Logic at the University of London, author of *The Nature of Law* and *The Limits of State Action*. Wollheim praised the quality of moral argument in *Oz* and asserted that the prosecution of it was a grave attack on 'the morality of toleration which is a large part of the morality of a society like ours', and was in danger of leading to the polarisation of society.[59]

The judge believed the *Oz* three were a front for a worldwide conspiracy of pornographers, and that his armed guard was very necessary.[60] In his summing up, he made clear his views of 'so-called experts'. The jury found the defendants guilty of publishing obscenity, though not guilty of the more serious charge of conspiracy to corrupt the morals of the public. The judge handed down stiff gaol sentences — fifteen months for Neville, with a recommendation for deportation since he was an Australian. After a unpleasant week in Wormwood Scrubs, the three were released pending appeal. Judging the appeal, the Lord Chief Justice held that the judge in the lower court had seriously misdirected the jury in not calling attention to defence counsel's 'aversion defence' — that the drawings and prose were so disgusting as to turn the reader off the practices represented.[61] The English were thereupon free to print more or less whatever they wanted.

In any case, Rupert Murdoch had already bought the London *Sun*, and declared that the 'permissive society' was no longer an opinion but a fact and that 'Anyone – from the Archbishop of Canterbury to Mick Jagger — is entitled to put forward his own moral code.' Not many column inches were actually allocated to Mick or the

---

[58] Palmer, *The Trials of Oz*, pp. 165–7; Neville, *Hippie*, pp. 305–7; Robertson, *Justice Game*, pp. 32–3; also in Robertson's 1991 BBC TV film, 'The Trials of Oz', starring Hugh Grant as Neville.

[59] Palmer, *The Trials of Oz*, pp. 178–81.

[60] M. Argyle, 'O no John! No John! No John! No', *Spectator* 20/5/1995, p. 27.

[61] Neville, *Hippie*, pp. 328–58; Fountain, *Underground*, ch. 14; *Weekly Law Reports* 1971 vol. 3 pp. 939–50; G. Greer, '*Oz* trial post mortem', *The Madwoman's Underclothes*, pp. 60–1; P. Dobrez, *Michael Dransfield's Lives* (Melbourne, 1999), pp. 341–3.

Archbishop to expound their views on ethics. It wasn't philosophies the *Sun*'s page three girls put forward.[62]

Back in Australia, there was one round still to go. The most spectacular action in pursuit of Libertarian ends was undertaken by one of the last women to join the Push before it lost its identity, Wendy Bacon. Like Greer, she had come from Melbourne and noticed a difference in the intellectual air.[63] She too learned something about how to think from the Libertarian philosophers, especially Baker. 'As an analytical person libertarianism was appealing — it made sense. It was clear-thinking, expressed in simple language. I liked the way it critiqued notions of morality, the "should". That's what I had grown up with — a fairly heavy load of Presbyterianism. The Libertarians gave me a framework.'[64] She welcomed the decay of assumptions underlying notions of 'depravity' and 'corruption', now that 'more people recognised that moral views are connected to social movements and must be seen in that context; that no one set of views is inherently preferable to another. Seen in this light, depravity and corruptions cease to have any meaning.'[65]

Molnar and a number of other older Libertarians helped with the production of the 1970 issues of the University of New South Wales student newspaper *Tharunka*, edited by Wendy Bacon and two others.[66] Its best-known issue printed the words of the old sex fantasy ballad, 'Eskimo Nell', along with a piece by George Molnar on 'Drugs and freedom', and a reprint of Anderson's 1943 address on 'Religion and education'.[67] Summonses started arriving. A substantial demonstration was arranged for the court hearing, including women in nun's habits distributing copies of the offending material, and a gorilla with trainer. Wendy Bacon displayed on her habit the slogan, 'I have been fucked by God's steel prick.' The obscenities that

---

[62] G. Munster, *A Paper Prince* (Melbourne, 1985), p. 135; M. Leapman, *Barefaced Cheek* (London, 1983), p. 58; on Murdoch, founding member of Oxford's Voltaire Society: N. Chenoweth, *Rupert Murdoch* (New York, 2001), pp. 41–2.

[63] D. Horne, *Time of Hope* (Sydney, 1980), pp. 19–20, 31; interview with Wendy Bacon, *UNSW Alumni Papers* (Winter 1988): pp. 14–7.

[64] Coombs, *Sex and Anarchy*, p. 233; also W. Bacon, 'From P.L.C. to Thor', in W. Bacon et al., *Uni Sex* (Dee Why, 1972), pp. 43–65, at p. 46.

[65] *Censorship: Wendy Bacon versus Peter Coleman* (Melbourne, 1975), p. 23.

[66] F. Moorhouse, 'The story of an underground paper', in F. Moorhouse, *Days of Wine and Rage* (Melbourne, 1980), pp. 4–13; on Moorhouse and the Libertarians, see G. Kinross Smith, 'Liberating acts: Frank Moorhouse, his life, his narratives', *Southerly* 46 (1986): pp. 391–423, at pp. 402–4.

[67] *Tharunka* 16 (3) (18/3/1970); Anderson's 'Art and morality' repr. in 16 (4) (26/3/1970): pp. 4–6.

Anderson had quietly circulated in typescript and sung at parties were flaunted in the open. It remained to be discovered whether the perpetrators would get away with it.

Bacon was arrested and charged with exhibiting an obscene publication, viz, the slogan. She based her defence on the contention that obscenity is not a real quality in a text but exists only in the eye of the beholder. In court she attempted to argue the point with reference to Socrates' dialogue *Euthyphro*. In the dialogue, Socrates, himself leaving court, poses the problem: do the Gods love what is pious because it is pious, or does something become pious when the Gods love it? Bacon began to elaborate on the parallel between piety and obscenity — does the average man object to a publication because it is obscene, or does it become obscene because the average man objects to it? Unfortunately the judge (Levine again) ruled that philosophy had no place in the trial: 'The comments of Socrates are not relevant to New South Wales law.'[68] A jury of average persons returned a verdict of guilty. Bacon spent a week in prison on remand.[69]

After leaving the editorship of *Tharunka*, Bacon was involved in the production of the similar but freelance *Thorunka*, with even more rude pictures. Bacon conducted her own defence at the ensuing trial, to make it a 'confrontation' free of legal niceties. George Molnar appeared, Germaine Greer testified to *Thorunka*'s literary merits and was told by the judge, 'You are not on a platform now', a nice example of a self-refuting statement.[70] Bacon was sentenced to a fine and bond. On appeal to the Supreme Court of New South Wales, presided over by Chief Justice John Kerr, the convictions were overturned. The Court had to consider a number of conceptual issues. Counsel for Bacon argued that *Thorunka* was neither a book, a magazine nor a periodical, as it was a newspaper-like entity with only a single issue. The Court dismissed this with the loosely Wittgensteinian reasoning that an item need not possess quite all of the features of a definition to be in the relevant class. 'A publication which has all the other features of a magazine will be called a magazine in New South Wales despite the fact that it has, and is intended to have,

---

[68] Bacon, 'From P.L.C. to Thor', at pp. 53, 57; F. Moorhouse, 'Wendy Bacon v. the Commonwealth', *Bulletin*, 13/2/1971, repr. in *Days*, pp. 13–18.

[69] W. Bacon, 'An editor in jail', in Moorhouse, *Days*, pp. 18–21.

[70] *Nation* 4/3/1972, pp. 12–13; *SMH* 10/2/1972, p. 8; *Australian* 10/2/1972, p. 3; *Bulletin* 26/2/1972, p. 22 & 4/3/1972, pp. 26–7; *Censorship: Wendy Bacon versus Peter Coleman* (Melbourne, 1975) (Anderson quoted at p. 16); P. Coleman, *Obscenity, Blasphemy, Sedition* (2nd ed, Sydney, 1974), pp. 62–4; later activism by Bacon and Push associates in *Scrounge* no. 1 (1973)–no. 16 (1974).

only one single issue.' But the Court did agree that the judge had seriously misdirected the jury in telling them that a publication obscene in a part was obscene as a whole.[71] A new trial was ordered, but the authorities had had enough.

Where to, when there are no more worlds to conquer? Gay Liberation was still to come (one of its world leaders, Dennis Altman, first promoted it in Wendy Bacon's *Tharunka*[72]) and the Sydney Gay Mardi Gras is as purely libertarian an event as any still in existence. Women's Liberation was not a continuation of the Libertarian movement, however, except in Germaine Greer's unique interpretation. Quite the opposite.

> Liberation seems to me to have come much more fully to the male, our wandering Casanovas, who no longer need fear the 'shotgun wedding' or the maintenance order. They are now entitled to expect that their more-or-less willing victim will have got the Pill on the National Health. If she was silly enough to be 'careless', to use their jargon, they can refer her to a newly-legal abortion clinic. *She* is not 'liberated' from the inconveniences of the Pill, or the traumas of abortion. But who can deny that *his* 'liberation' is complete? [73]

This particular way of expressing things is by Santamaria, a writer not much read in libertarian circles, but many of the women in the Push were coming to substantially the same conclusion by themselves. Most of the published writing on the Push has been by women some thirty or forty years later. The substance of it has been that Push men were beasts. Some writers maintained that, as women, they lacked a language to complain about it.[74] Whatever the truth, Push women found their voice quickly when Women's Liberation did arrive, and were the core of at least the second wave of Sydney feminism.[75] In London, some of the Australian women who had answered the phones, poured the tea and rolled the joints on London *Oz* set up

[71] R. *v.* Bacon, *New South Wales Law Reports* 1973, vol. 1 pp. 87–104; *Bulletin* 28/10/1972, p. 22.
[72] D. Altman, *Defying Gravity* (Sydney, 1997); cf. S. Soldatow & C. Tsiolkas, *Jump Cuts* (Sydney, 1996), pp. 43, 50–1.
[73] Santamaria, 'Philosophies in collision', at p. 32.
[74] Morris, 'The patriarchal Push'; Coombs, *Sex and Anarchy*, ch. 5; on which E. Morris, 'The authorized version of the Push Bible?', *Heraclitus* 52 (Sept 1996): 7–10; Ogilvie, *The Push, passim*; J. Ker Conway, *The Road from Coorain* (London, 1989), pp. 220–2; J.K.M., 'Sexism in the Push', *Sydney Libertarians Broadsheet* 71 (Feb 1973): 1–3; contrary in L. Segal, *Is the Future Female?* (London, 1987), pp. 76–7.
[75] Coombs, *Sex and Anarchy*, ch. 14; Summers, *Ducks on the Pond*, pp. 300–5.

Spare Rib, the leading English women's liberation magazine of the Seventies.[76]

Total victory is pleasant, but the winners always face an alliance between the defeated party and those among themselves unhappy with the actual outcome.

Among the first and most coherent to have second thoughts was the old Andersonian Peter Coleman. He had written a largely historical book on censorship, *Obscenity, Blasphemy, Sedition,* in 1960, which argued along Andersonian lines for the meaninglessness of these terms and for the abolition of censorship. But no sooner was it published than he began to have doubts.[77] By the 1970s he was a leading supporter of some form of censorship of pornography. Like many others, he saw pornography, on the scale then being produced, as 'the racism or anti-semitism of the male chauvinist', degrading especially to women, and tending to coarsen, de-individualise and degrade human relationships. It had political significance, he believed, since 'the pornographic life-style is the rejection of restraint, reticence, and what it might call "false shame", and the espousal of a view of human nature most appropriate to dictatorship. It is part of the advanced guard of the politics of servitude.' At a deeper level, he complained that pornography is an attack on sexual privacy or reticence.[78]

The poverty of Push philosophy is shown by the fact that it cannot even understand the terms in which Coleman is speaking. It can do nothing except dismiss them as more 'moralising'.

[76] Fountain, *Underground,* pp. 169–74; Introduction, in *Spare Rib Reader,* ed. M. Rowe (Harmondsworth, 1982), pp. 13–22.
[77] P. Coleman, *Memoirs of a Slow Learner* (Sydney, 1994), p. 146.
[78] *Censorship: Wendy Bacon versus Peter Coleman,* pp. 45–7, 52–3; some admissions in Moorhouse, *Days of Wine and Rage,* pp. 7, 11.

Chapter 9   Mind, Matter and Medicine Gone Mad

THE Bogle–Chandler murder case mentioned in the previous chapter briefly opened a window not only on the Push, but on the implicit philosophical views of a section of the medical establishment. This arose from the involvement in the case of unknown 'substances'. At the time, the range of possible undetectable substances that could have caused the deaths without leaving a trace was regarded as too wide for any conclusions to be drawn. Still, the hypothesis that *some* substance that the couple took killed them seemed very likely, in the absence of any probable theory of another sort. In hindsight, experts thought of one substance in particular which would have evaded the forensic tests of the time, and was commonly available in the scientific circles in which Dr Bogle moved. It was LSD.[1]

The wide availability of LSD in some quarters is now little remembered, but the drug was widely promoted by its makers until its sudden withdrawal in 1964 when it was realised how extensive its recreational use had become. Some thought LSD was useful in bringing on the 'liberation of the Sixties.'[2] It was also one of the substances used in CIA experiments to try to crack the secrets of Communist brainwashing at the time of the Korean War.[3] In the medical profes-

---

[1] *SMH* 20/1/1996, pp. 1, 10; but doubts in *Who Weekly* 19/2/1996, p. 16; *SMH* 22/5/1989, p. 12; *Sun-Herald* 29/5/1994, pp. 16–17; W. Jenkings, N. Lipson & T. Barnao, *As Crime Goes By* (Randwick, 1992), ch. 13.

[2] J. Murphy, 'Bill Dwyer and LSD', *Sydney Libertarians Broadsheet* 59 (Apr 1970): pp. 1–3; K. Windschuttle, 'The drop on LSD', *Nation* 21/10/1967, pp. 13–14; P. Dobrez, *Michael Dransfield's Lives* (Melbourne, 1999), pp. 194–8.

[3] *Brain-washing: A synthesis of the Communist textbook of psychopolitics*, with introduction by Eric Butler, Victorian League of Rights pamphlet

sion the idea emerged that LSD could be the wonder drug that would speed up the painfully slow process of psychoanalysis, breaking down the patient's defences and allowing him to experience consciously the release 'consequent upon a temporary disintegration of ego control of repression.'[4] It was widely recommended in the medical literature that the therapist should experience the drug himself, with a series of at least twenty to forty sessions of it. This is one theme of an article that appeared in the same number of the *Australian Scientist* as an article by Dr Bogle on his work on masers. It was written by W.H. (later Sir William) Trethowan, then Professor of Psychiatry at Sydney University. He wrote:

> Perhaps the most remarkable aspect of LSD-25 is its ability to produce psychotic symptoms in normal individuals even when administered in minute amounts ... Not unnaturally this discovery led to considerable speculation as to the possibility of some naturally occurring agent, perhaps resembling LSD, as a cause of schizophrenia ... If nothing else, the administration of lysergic acid to experimental subjects has at least allowed psychiatrists to share some of the experiences of their patients.[5]

In raising the question of the mental effects of physical substances, Trethowan was beginning to trespass on old philosophical territory, the problem of the relation of the mind to the body. It is ground that has been subject to a demarcation dispute between philosophers and medical men from time immemorial. We will look shortly at the doctors' contributions, but let us first consider the philosophers.

'Central-state materialism', sometimes known as 'Australian materialism' or the 'identity theory of mind', became in the 1960s the first home-grown, distinctively Australian philosophical theory to be taken

---

(Melbourne, 1956) (actual U.S. story in G. Thomas, *Journey into Madness: The True Story of Secret CIA Mind Control and Medical Abuse* (New York, 1989), especially pp. 99, 159–63; J. Marks, *The Search for the "Manchurian Candidate": The CIA and Mind Control* (London, 1979), chs. 4–6; M.A. Lee & B. Shlain, *Acid Dreams: The CIA, LSD and the Sixties Rebellion* (New York, 1985) ch. 1).

[4] LH. Whitaker, 'Lysergic acid diethylamide in psychotherapy', *Medical Journal of Australia* 51 vol. 1 (1964): pp. 5–8, 36–41; I. Martin, '"Ritalin" and "sodium amytal" an alternative to LSD 25 as an adjunct to psychotherapy', *Medical Journal of Australia* 53 vol. 2 (1966): pp. 1264–7; cf. I.H. Martin, 'The nature of man', *Australian Rationalist* 3(1) (1973): pp. 11–14; also *Medical Journal of Australia* 44 vol. 1 (1957): pp. 178–9; review in *Australian and New Zealand Journal of Psychiatry* 4 (1970): pp. 64–7, 170–3; U.S. background in S.J. Novak, 'LSD before Leary', *Isis* 88 (1997): pp. 87–110.

[5] W.H. Trethowan, 'Drugs which affect the mind', *Australian Scientist* 1 (1961): pp. 115–20, at p. 120.

seriously on the world stage.[6] It holds that there is no mind, or any sort of mental entities, over and above the brain and its physical processes. Experiences, hallucinations, after-images, perceived colours, consciousness and so on, it is maintained, have been discovered by science to be identical to certain brain processes. An English commentator remarks superciliously, 'Detractors called it the belief that thinking and physical activity were one and the same, adding that Australia was the only place where it was true.'[7]

In one way, this is an old theory, something like it being assumed by a long line of atheist doctors. Anderson's philosophy incorporated something of the idea, without arguing at length for it. Anderson did not deny the reality of the internal world — 'The doctrine of "realms" or "worlds" is itself a phantasy (as Heraclitus was the first to point out); and the supposed hard-headedness of believers in an "external world" (as contrasted with an inner world of thought) is simply theoretical muddlement'[8] — but he did believe that the inner and outer worlds were the same kind of (material) thing. Anderson and other precursors of the identity theory did not make very precise what the theory actually was, nor did they argue for it in detail, or reply to the long-standing philosophical objections to it.

Those tasks were first seriously undertaken in the 1956 paper which U.T. Place developed during his time at Adelaide, 'Is consciousness a brain process?'[9] Place argued that there was no room in physics for mental entities, such as 'phenomenal properties'. To suppose there was, he thought, was due to a logical mistake, the 'phenomenological fallacy': 'the mistake of supposing that when the sub-

---

[6] Overviews in S.A. Grave, *A History of Philosophy in Australia* (St Lucia, 1984), ch. 6; W. Joske, 'The mind-body problem', in J.T.J. Srzednicki & D. Wood, eds, *Essays on Philosophy in Australia* (Dordrecht, 1991), pp. 39–51.
[7] 'Science does it with feeling', *Economist* 20/7/1996, pp. 75–7.
[8] J. Anderson, 'Classicism', in *Studies in Empirical Philosophy*, pp. 189–202, at p. 200; also J. Anderson, 'The non-existence of consciousness', *AJPP* 7 (1929): pp. 68–73, repr. in *Studies*, pp. 60–7.
[9] U.T. Place, 'Is consciousness a brain process?', *British Journal of Psychology* 47 (1956): pp. 44–50; summary in Grave, *History*, pp. 113–4; this and other papers repr. in C.V. Borst, ed, *The Mind–Brain Identity Theory* (London, 1970) and in D.J. Chalmers, ed, *Philosophy of Mind: Classical and Contemporary Readings* (Oxford, 2002); also L. Stubenberg, 'Austria vs Australia: two versions of the identity theory', in *Austrian Philosophy Past and Present*, ed. K. Lehrer & J.C. Marek (Dordrecht, 1997), pp. 125–46; U.T. Place, 'Thirty years on: Is consciousness still a brain process?', *AJP* 66 (1988): pp. 208–19.

Three materialists: from left, U.T. Place, J.J.C. Smart, D.M. Armstrong,
Leeds, 1997 (D.M. Armstrong)

ject describes his experience, when he describes how things look,
sound, smell, taste or feel to him, he is describing the literal properties
of objects and events on a peculiar sort of internal cinema or television screen.' So there is no logical reason against saying that consciousness can be identified with a physical brain process, if scientific
investigation makes that a reasonable conclusion. It is similar to identifying lightning with an electrical discharge in the clouds: one does
not know they are the same thing to begin with, but scientific investigation can show that they are.

Place was soon supported by his colleague at Adelaide, J.J.C.
Smart, who emphasised how gross an anomaly a mental consciousness
would be in a world otherwise physical: 'There does seem to be, so
far as science is concerned, nothing in the world but increasingly
complex arrangements of physical constituents. All except in one
place: in consciousness.'[10]

---

[10] J.J.C. Smart, 'Sensations and brain processes', *Philosophical Review* 68
(1959): pp. 141–56; Grave, *History*, pp. 114–5; discussions mostly of Smart's
views in *The Identity Theory of Mind*, ed. C.F. Presley (St Lucia, 1967, 2nd
ed, 1971); bibliography of Smart's works to 1986 in *Metaphysics and Morality:
Essays in Honour of J.J.C. Smart*, ed. P. Pettit, R. Sylvan & J. Norman
(Oxford, 1987), pp. 198–207; his account of the development of his ideas in
'My semantic ascents and descents', in *The Owl of Minerva*, ed. C.J.
Bontempo & S.J. Odell (New York, 1975), pp. 57–72; Smart papers are in
Australian National Library, MS 7740; further responses in J. Teichmann,
'The contingent identity of minds and brains', *Mind* 76 (1967): pp. 404–15;

Australian materialism culminated in one of the most influential books of Australian philosophy, David Armstrong's *A Materialist Theory of the Mind*, of 1968.[11] Armstrong accepts the arguments of Place and Smart, but places them in a wider analysis of mental concepts, which emphasises their causal role. A mental state, he argues, is just whatever it is — whether it turns out to be physical or immaterial — that is apt for bringing about certain sorts of behaviour. It is then a scientific question as to what fills that causal role, just as it is a scientific question as to what entities fill the causal role of the gene, that is, the causing of inheritance of characteristics.[12] The gene turned out on scientific evidence to be identifiable as the DNA molecule; similarly, says Armstrong, the total weight of the scientific evidence suggests that the cause of complex adaptive behaviour is the physical states and processes of the brain.

The remainder of the book offers physicalistic analyses of various mental concepts, including some that most materialists have tended to avoid. Consciousness, for example, is said to be the perception or scanning by one mental state of other mental states, thus explaining the feeling of 'self-awareness' associated with being conscious.[13] Mental images, whose very existence was denied by some materialists, are said by Armstrong to be mental states similar to those normally found in perception, but not attended by beliefs about the external world.[14]

J. Teichman, *The Mind and the Soul* (London, 1974), chs 5–7; S. Candlish, 'Mind, brain and identity', *Mind* 79 (1970): pp. 502–18; R. Elliot, 'Materialism and Occam's Razor', *Philosophy* 54 (1979): pp. 233–4; recent survey in D. Braddon-Mitchell & F. Jackson, *The Philosophy of Mind and Cognition* (Cambridge, Mass, 1996), ch. 6; earlier historical background in P.S. MacDonald, *History of the Concept of Mind* (Aldershot, 2003).

[11] D.M. Armstrong, *A Materialist Theory of the Mind* (London, 1968, revised ed, New York, 1993), trans. *Materialistyczna Teoria Umysu* (Warsaw, 1982); further in D.M. Armstrong, *The Nature of Mind and Other Essays* (St Lucia, 1980); *The Mind–Body Problem: An Opinionated Introduction* (Boulder, 1999); origins of his views in D.M. Armstrong, 'Self-profile', in *D.M. Armstrong*, ed. R. Bogdan (Dordrecht, 1984), pp. 3–51, at pp. 20–3.

[12] The particular example in this context in B. Medlin, 'Materialism and the argument from distinct existences', in *The Business of Reason*, ed. J.J. Macintosh & S. Coval (London, 1969, but written 1962), pp. 168–85; Armstrong, *Mind–Body Problem*, p. 86.

[13] Armstrong, *A Materialist Theory*, pp. 92–113; further in D.M. Armstrong & N. Malcolm, *Consciousness and Causality* (Oxford, 1984); 'What is consciousness?', in Armstrong, *The Nature of Mind and Other Essays*, ch. 4; Armstrong, *Mind–Body Problem*, ch. 10; also A. Gallois, *The World Without, the Mind Within* (Cambridge, 1996).

[14] Armstrong, *A Materialist Theory*, ch. 13; other discussions in B. Smith, *Memory* (London, 1966), chs 6–7; K. Lycos, 'Images and the imaginary', *AJP*

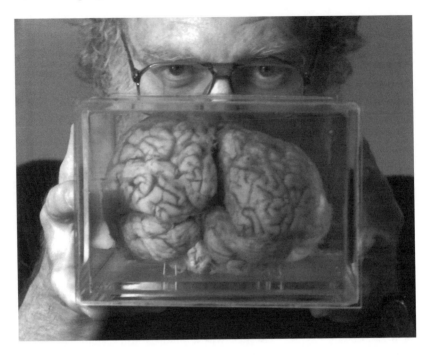

U.T. Place's brain, bequeathed by him to Adelaide University (with philosopher Chris Mortensen), 5 June 2001 (Newspix)

Not everyone has been so willing to explain away the inner world. There are two approaches to defending the non-physicality of the mental, a purely philosophical one that argues that internal experience is not the sort of thing that could possibly be reduced to something purely physical, and a scientific one that tries to counter the scientific arguments that materialists rely on. Of course, many people have a gut feeling that looking at inner experience scientifically, 'from the outside', somehow misses the point, and leaves out the essential thing about the mental. It can be a strong intuition, but how can it be expressed in a communicable way? Argument, in the strict sense, is dif-

43 (1965): pp. 321–38; G. Currie, 'Visual imagery as the simulation of vision', *Mind and Language* 10 (1995): pp. 25–44; S. Candlish, 'Mental imagery', in *Wittgenstein and Contemporary Philosophy of Mind*, ed. S. Schroeder (London, 2001), pp. 107–28; P. Slezak, 'The imagery debate: Déjà vu all over again?' *Behavioral and Brain Sciences* 25 (2002): pp. 209-10; J. Franklin, 'Diagrammatic reasoning and modelling in the imagination: the secret weapons of the Scientific Revolution', in *1543 and All That: Image and Word, Change and Continuity in the Proto-Scientific Revolution*, ed. G. Freeland & A. Corones (Dordrecht, 2000), pp. 53–115; dangers of doing philosophy the same way in M. La Caze, *The Analytic Imaginary* (Ithaca, NY, 2002).

ficult, since there is so little to argue from: how could one be closer to conceptual bedrock than in deciding what experience is like? Perhaps the best that can be done is to dramatise intuitions with examples. Frank Jackson, then at Monash and later professor at ANU, invented one of those colourful and simple examples that gain a life of their own in philosophy, and take some of the edge off its abstractness. This is the example of 'What Mary Knew':

> Mary is a brilliant scientist who is, for whatever reason, forced to investigate the world from a black and white room *via* a black and white television monitor. She specialises in the neurophysiology of vision and acquires, let us suppose, all the physical information there is to obtain about what goes on when we see ripe tomatoes, or the sky, and use terms like 'red', 'blue' and so on. She discovers, for example, just which wavelength combinations from the sky stimulate the retina ... What will happen when Mary is released from the black and white room or is given a colour television monitor? Will she *learn* anything or not? It seems just obvious that she will learn something about the world and our visual experience of it. But then it is inescapable that her previous experience was incomplete. But she had *all* the physical information. *Ergo* there is more to have than that, and Physicalism is false.[15]

If one does find this line of reasoning appealing, one will soon run into difficulties in explaining how mental entities fit into the causal story about perception and behaviour. It is not always clear what causal role is envisaged for purely mental entities by those who believe in them. Armstrong writes: 'if one accepts an account of mental states in terms of their causal relations to behaviour; and at the same time one agrees that physical operations of the brain are adequate to

---

[15] F. Jackson, 'Epiphenomenal qualia', *Philosophical Quarterly* 32 (1982): pp. 127–36, at p. 130; repr. with postscript in P.K. Moser & J.D. Trout, *Contemporary Materialism* (London, 1995), pp. 180–9; further in F. Jackson, 'What Mary didn't know', *Journal of Philosophy* 83 (1986): pp. 291–5, repr. in F. Jackson, ed, *Consciousness* (Aldershot, 1998), pp. 95–9; both in F. Jackson, *Mind, Method and Conditionals* (London, 1998); reply in J. Bigelow & R. Pargetter, 'Acquaintance with qualia', *Theoria* 56 (1990): pp. 129–47; symposium on the resulting debate in *Dialogue* (Canada) 32 (1993), no. 3; novelised in D. Lodge, *Thinks...* (New York, 2001), p. 53, ch. 16; also J. Garfield, 'Casting out demons and exorcising zombies: Exposing neocartesian myths in Frank Jackson's philosophy of mind', in *Australian Philosophers*, ed. P. Dowe, M. Nicholls & L. Shotton (Hobart, 1996), pp. 55–95; J. Hawthorne, 'Advice for physicalists', *Philosophical Studies* 109 (2002): pp. 17–52; recent survey in Braddon-Mitchell & Jackson, *Philosophy of Mind and Cognition*, ch. 8; a more general survey in P. Forrest, 'Difficulties with physicalism, and a programme for dualists', in *Objections to Physicalism*, ed. H. Robinson (Oxford, 1993), pp. 251–69; also M. Deutscher, *Subjecting and Objecting* (St Lucia, 1983), ch. 10.

bring about all human behaviour; and yet one still wants to resist the identification of mental states and brain states; there seems to be only one position one can adopt. One must say that physical processes in the brain give rise to mental processes of a non-material sort which in turn give rise to behaviour. The mental processes must be inserted into the causal chain at some point, although the chain unfolds in exactly the same way that it would unfold if there was no such insertion.'[16] This, he says, is a trivial logical possibility, like the possibility that a DNA molecule acts via an immaterial principle, which has effects identical to the usual chemical effects. There is no reason to believe such an unnecessarily complicated story.

Anti-materialists will reply that the two cases are not similar, since one observes the mind from the inside and DNA from the outside. But that does not provide the causal story that Armstrong is insisting must be provided. Nevertheless, some philosophers have argued that even that anomaly has to be put up with, as the evidence for the unique and non-physical nature of the mind makes it a price well worth paying. On the purely philosophical front, there were such books as Keith Campbell's *Body and Mind*,[17] which argued that the mind was a kind of 'epiphenomenon' of brain activity, caused by it but having no action back on it. The latest and most successful such book is *The Conscious Mind*, by David Chalmers, formerly an Australian mathematician and now a philosopher in Arizona. He argues that causal analyses like Armstrong's tell us about the psychological aspects of mind, but say nothing about the phenomenal nature of felt qualities: consciousness is exactly what they leave out. 'We know consciousness far more intimately than we know the rest of the world, but we understand the rest of the world far better than we understand consciousness.'[18] The phenomenal concept of mind, he says, is that based on the way the mind *feels*; it is quite different to the psychological concept of mind, based on what it *does* — so different that it could in principle turn out that the two minds were quite different entities. In support of this he advances such arguments as that from

[16] Armstrong, *A Materialist Theory of the Mind*, p. 365.

[17] K. Campbell, *Body and Mind* (London, 1971; 2nd ed, Notre Dame, Ind, 1984); trans. *Il corpo e il mente* (Rome, 1976); discussed in E.R. Kraemer, 'Imitation-man and the new epiphenomenalism', *Canadian Journal of Philosophy* 10 (1980): pp. 479–87; also A. Olding, 'Going mental', *Quadrant* 44 (7-8) (July-Aug 2000): pp. 54–9.

[18] D. Chalmers, *The Conscious Mind: In Search of a Fundamental Theory* (New York, 1996), p. 3; summary in D.J. Chalmers, 'The puzzle of conscious experience', *Scientific American* 273 (6) (Dec 1995): pp. 80–86; symposium in *Explaining Consciousness: The Hard Problem*, ed. J. Shear (Cambridge, Mass, 1997); also B. Garrett, *Personal Identity and Self-Consciousness* (London, 1998).

Frank Jackson (left) and David Chalmers at Australian National University, 2002 (David Chalmers)

What Mary Knew, and that from the possibility that two people should be physically identical but see the colour spectrum in the opposite order,[19] but his favourite argument is from zombies. It is logically possible for there to be zombies — beings physically identical to humans, whose behaviour is also identical, but who have no inner experience: there is nothing 'it is like to be a zombie'.[20] It follows that phenomenal experience is nothing like a case it is sometimes compared with, life, which was also once thought irreducible to physics: if physical processes explain how living beings grow, reproduce and so on, they have explained life, but if physical processes can explain why animals react as they do to stimuli, there is still something left over, namely, phenomenal experience. Chalmers goes on to develop a theory of mind according to which the laws of nature imply that zombies are naturally impossible (though logically possible): anything that has the same organisation as a human develops the same experiences, as a matter of scientific law. His theory seems to have the odd consequence that my experience of red is not part of the cause of my say-

[19] Also in M.C. Bradley, 'Sensations, brain-processes and colours', *AJP* 41 (1963): pp. 385–93; Armstrong, *A Materialist Theory*, pp. 256–60.
[20] Chalmers, *The Conscious Mind*, ch. 3; cf. F. White, 'David Armstrong and the return of metaphysics', in *Australian Philosophers*, ed. P. Dowe, M. Nicholls & L. Shotton, pp. 39–54.

ing that I am experiencing red. But, as he says himself, you can't have everything. No theory of mind is plausible all through.

The What Mary Knew and colour spectrum reversal examples can be regarded not as isolated curiosities, but as indications that it may be possible to describe experience from the inside in some detail, without, for the moment, worrying about how it relates to the world outside. Some would argue that this topic belongs to psychology, not philosophy, but since most psychologists are hard-headed and scientific and don't want it, it remains philosophy at least for the time being. The project of describing 'pure' experience, so to speak, is pursued by the school of phenomenology, stemming from Husserl and Heidegger. The school has had a marketing problem in that these founders described inner experience in German, and the translations that have been undertaken have not universally been regarded as meaningful English. The massive task of translating Husserl was attempted by W.R. Boyce Gibson, the Professor of Philosophy at Melbourne University, inspired by his visit to Husserl and Heidegger in Freiburg in 1928.[21] Little was heard of phenomenology in Australia in the mid-century, but it reappeared in the 1960s as one of the multitude of continental trends then imported, and promoted with a great deal of complaining about the hegemony of anglophone analytic philosophising.[22]

---

[21] E. Husserl, *Ideas: General Introduction to Pure Phenomenology* (London, 1931); W.R. Boyce Gibson, 'The problem of real and ideal in the phenomenology of Husserl', *Mind* 34 (1925): pp. 311–27; discussion in J. McKellar Stewart, 'Husserl's phenomenology', *AJPP* 11 (1933): pp. 221–31 & 12 (1934): pp. 62–72; see 'From Husserl to Heidegger: Excerpts from a 1928 Freiburg diary by W.R. Boyce Gibson', *Journal of the British Society for Phenomenology* 2 (1971): pp. 58–83.

[22] M. Harney, 'The contemporary European tradition in Australian philosophy', in Srzednicki & Wood, eds, *Essays on Philosophy in Australia*, pp. 125–51; P. Bilimoria, 'Phenomenology in Australia', in *Encyclopedia of Phenomenology*, ed. L. Embree & J.N. Mohanty (Dordrecht, 1997); M. Harney, *Intentionality, Sense and the Mind* (The Hague, 1984); papers from Australian phenomenology conferences printed in *Dialectic* (University of Newcastle) 20 (1983), 23 (1984), 26 (1986), 28 (1986), 29 (1987), 31 (1988); *Thesis Eleven*, special issues 36 (1993) & 37 (1994); M. Tapper, 'The priority of being or consciousness for phenomenology: Heidegger and Husserl', *Metaphilosophy* 17 (1986): pp. 153–61; P. Carpenter, 'The phenomenology of Husserl', *Forum of Education* 37 (2) (June, 1978): pp. 32–44; R. Small, 'Uses and abuses of phenomenology in education', *Educational Philosophy and Theory* 19 (1987): pp. 12–17; L.C. Ehrich, 'Untangling the threads and coils of the web of phenomenology', *Educational Research and Perspectives* 26 (2) (1999): pp. 19–44; A. Bartjes, 'Phenomenology in clinical practice', ch. 12 of *Towards a Discipline of Nursing*, ed G. Gray & R. Pratt (Melbourne, 1991);

It survives to the present, but it remains a minority position among both philosophers of mind and among psychiatrists,[23] another group who have in a different way sought descriptions of inner experience. Perhaps one of its problems is that it does not postulate hidden causes of mental activity accessible only to professionals. What is the point of being an expert on the mind if one knows no more about it than the novelist in the street?

The idea of concentrating on experience in isolation has suggested some unusual phenomenological approaches to subjects like geography, architecture and town planning. These disciplines deal with the ways humans change the environment in order to change the experiences of other humans, so that an approach that merely studies physical rocks and houses is too narrow and misses the point of the actions on the environment. The feminist geographer Louise Johnson argues that since the 'lifeworld' is the way we experience our environment, geographers will have to study it, instead of keeping to 'scientistic' perspectives appropriate to subjects like biology.[24] Her article does not include any applications, but what one would be like is indicated by Meaghan Morris's well-known article on the 'cultural meaning' of Sydney Tower. The Tower is just another tall building in a big city, but from the moment of its design, it began to be invested by its promoters and the media with a meaning as 'Centrepoint', 'the Heart of the City', a symbol of Sydney's progress and growth, which would make Sydney 'a world city in the real meaning of the word'. And the people converging on the wonder would then look out to see the city itself converted into spectacle.[25] These 'features' of the building exist not as properties of the physical tower, but in the minds of those who think about it. They are not therefore unreal; on the contrary they have the causal power to generate, for example, profits for the

L.J. Paul, 'Phenomenology as a method for the study of informal care', *Journal of Family Studies* 5 (1999): pp. 192–206; D. Byers, 'Edmund Husserl: Philosopher of infinite tasks', *Philosopher* 1 (2) (Winter 1995): pp. 9–15; T. van Gelder, 'Wooden iron? Husserlian phenomenology meets cognitive science', *Electronic Journal of Analytic Philosophy* 4 (1996).

[23] Exceptions in P.E. Mullen, 'A phenomenology of jealousy', *Australian and New Zealand Journal of Psychiatry* 24 (1990): pp. 17–28; P.J.V. Beumont, 'Phenomenology and the history of psychiatry', *ANZJP* 26 (1992): pp. 532–45.

[24] L. Johnson, 'Bracketing lifeworlds: Husserlian phenomenology as geographical method', *Australian Geographical Studies* 21 (1983): pp. 102–8.

[25] M. Morris, 'Sydney Tower', *Island* 9/10 (Mar 1982): pp. 53–61; sequels in M. Morris, 'Metamorphoses at Sydney Tower', *Australian Cultural History* 10 (1991): pp. 19–31 and M. Morris, *Great Moments in Social Climbing: King Kong and the Human Fly* (Sydney, 1992).

Tower's owners. Examples like this show that architecture is a ideal case for applied phenomenology, since experiencing architecture is unavoidable, and the failure of architects to consider what their works will be like for the experiencers has led to some unpleasant results.[26]

It is true that traditional town planning and architecture leave some room for people's perceptions of the environment they have to live in. Eliciting people's opinions by questionnaire is a common procedure with any planning decision. But one of the phenomenologists' points is that a large proportion of 'perceptions' are normally beyond the reach of language, being instead coded in some semi-pictorial form at the edge of conscious awareness. As Rolf Harris says:

> I'm a very calm man. But the thing that drives me into a rage is walking up or down a set of steps and finding the last one is a couple of inches higher or lower than the rest. It is in the nature of things that one's body, without conscious direction, immediately adjusts itself to the exact regular height of each riser, and to suddenly, unexpectedly drop an extra inch or so, to be stopped with a sickening, spine-jarring jolt, is nearly as bad as coming to a shattering stop two inches before you expected to. I clench my teeth and imagine the terrible things I would do to the designer or builders of such steps.[27]

It is the body that adjusts, but the expectation of where the next step will be is a mental entity, even though in the normal course of events one that is not attended to.

These considerations bring us close to the more traditional kind of aesthetics, the philosophy of art. That branch of philosophy has been little studied in Australia, and the most famous item remains John Passmore's article of the 1950s explaining why aesthetics is boring.[28]

---

[26] B.H. Slater, '"Experiencing" architecture', *Philosophy* 59 (1984): pp. 253–8; P.R. Proudfoot, 'Phenomenology: A model for architectural education?', *Architectural Science Review* 32 (1989): pp. 95–100; A. Snodgrass & R. Coyne, 'Is designing hermeneutical?', *Architectural Theory Review* 2 (1) (Apr 1997): pp. 65–97; M. Elkan, 'Readings in phenomenology: Experiencing the Walker house at Bilgola by Rick le Plastrier', *ATR* 3 (1) (1998): pp. 104–9; *Phenomenography: Philosophy and Practice*, ed. R. Ballantyne & C. Bruce (Canberra, 1994); something more radical in E. Grosz, *Architecture from the Outside* (Cambridge, Mass, 2001); on ethics and architecture, R. Boyd, *The Australian Ugliness* (2nd, ed, Ringwood, 1980), ch. 8.

[27] *SMH, Good Weekend* 24/2/1996, p. 11; cf. R. Light & R. Fawns, 'The thinking body: Constructivist approaches to games teaching in physical education', *Melbourne Studies in Education* 42 (2) (Nov 2001) pp. 69–87; J. Malpas, *Place and Experience: A Philosophical Topography* (Cambridge, 1999).

[28] J. Passmore, 'The dreariness of aesthetics', *Mind* 60 (1951): pp. 318–35; Anderson's views, mostly on literature, in J. Anderson, *Art & Reality* (Sydney, 1982); also D.H. Rankin, *The Development and Philosophy of Australian Aestheticism* (Melbourne, 1949), part III; J. Passmore, *Serious Art*

If there is one art form that cries out for phenomenological treatment, it is television. Watching TV needs a host of mental processes to be active just at the edge of consciousness. One has a 'horizon of expectation', as the theorists say, about what will happen next. The notion applies especially well to the formulaic soap operas and game shows that Australia has exported so successfully: there are strong expectations as to what the characters will say, what will appear if the camera moves, what is presumed to have happened off-screen between scenes. Some characters one is supposed to 'identify' with, some endings are expected, some not. These facts about audiences will be much better known through introspection than by surveys. And woe betide any producer who makes a mistake about what the audience expects.[29] Perhaps, too, a closer look inside will reveal some Freudian items among the mental paraphernalia of the couch potato. An article in the final number of the late lamented *Australian Journal of Screen Theory* connected daytime soaps, not unreasonably, with Freud's 'compulsion to repeat',[30] while the Melbourne psychiatrist Ronald Conway maintained that the nation's fascination with Kylie Minogue's paint-stripping characterisation of Charlene in *Neighbours*, 'an abruptly discourteous, metallic-voiced, bossy, bad-tempered little broad', was a symptom of wimpish Australian men's unhealthy relationship with their overbearing mothers.[31]

A phenomenological entity held more or less in common, if it exists at all, is the Thylacine of the mind, the much hunted but rarely glimpsed 'Australian identity'. In his celebrated article introducing the notion of the Cultural Cringe, A.A. Phillips explained the subtlety of the inferences to other minds involved in one attempt to bring into being the Great Australian Identity, though what he writes could as well apply to many attempts at literary criticism. 'A Jindyworobak

(London, 1991); recent work in *Literature and Aesthetics: The Journal of the Sydney Society of Literature and Aesthetics*; P. Thom, *For an Audience: A Philosophy of the Performing Arts* (Philadelphia, 1993); H. Grace, ed, *Aesthesia and the Economy of the Senses* (Kingswood, 1996); G. Currie, *Image and Mind: Film, Philosophy and Cognitive Science* (Cambridge, 1995); G. Currie, *An Ontology of Art* (Basingstoke, 1989); G. Currie, articles on 'Art works, ontology of', 'Artistic forgery', 'Film, aesthetics of', 'Narrative', 'Photography, aesthetics of', in *Routledge Encyclopedia of Philosophy*; J.A. McMahon, 'Beauty', in *Routledge Companion to Aesthetics*, ed. B. Gaut (London, 2000), pp. 227–38; P. Forrest, 'Aesthetic understanding', *Philosophy and Phenomenological Research* 51 (1991): pp. 525–40.

[29] Tony Wilson, *Watching Television: Hermeneutics, Reception and Popular Culture* (Cambridge, 1993).

[30] J. Davies, 'The television audience revisited', *Australian Journal of Screen Theory* 17–18 (1984): pp. 84–105.

[31] R. Conway, 'Neighbours', *Quadrant* 32 (6) (June 1988): pp. 50–2.

writer uses the image "galah-breasted dawn". The picture is both fresh and accurate, and has a sense of immediacy because it comes direct from the writer's environment; and yet somehow it doesn't quite come off. The trouble is that we — unhappy Cringers — are too aware of the processes in its creation. We can feel the writer thinking: "No, I mustn't use one of the images which English language tradition is insinuating into my mind; I must have something Australian: ah, yes —". What the phrase has gained in immediacy, it has lost in spontaneity."[32]

In any case, inferring what is in other people's minds is essential in all walks of life. The old philosophical 'problem of other minds' asks how one can tell that other people have a mind at all, when all one can observe is their outward behaviour.[33] It is easy for poets, according to A.D. Hope, who wrote, 'Once we realize that all our perceptions reach the brain in the form of coded information, the idea of looking into someone else's mind presents no more intrinsic difficulties than the idea of looking into his kitchen', and '[a poem's] effect is to create states of consciousness that can be directly perceived.'[34]

At a more day-to-day level, inferring intentions from outward marks is a crucial part of what lawyers do when they read legislation. In the 1970s, the High Court under Garfield Barwick kept to a strictly literal approach to the interpretation of tax law. Artificial tax schemes proliferated. 'The citizen has every right', Sir Garfield held, 'to mould the transaction into which he is about to enter into a form which satisfies the requirement of the statute ... the freedom to

[32] A.A. Phillips, 'The cultural cringe', *Meanjin* 9 (1950): pp. 299–302, at p. 302; cf. J.D. Blomfield, 'Phenomenology and cultural crises: An attempt to situate "critical self-reflection" in Australian culture', in *A Hundred Years of Phenomenology*, ed. R. Small (Aldershot, 2001), pp. 175–86.

[33] A. Hyslop, *Other Minds* (Dordrecht, 1994) (summary in *Routledge Encyclopedia of Philosophy* vol. 7 pp. 170–3); F. Jackson, 'The analogical inference to other minds', *American Philosophical Quarterly* 9 (1972): pp. 168–76; R.J. Pargetter, 'Scientific inference to other minds', *AJP* 62 (1984): pp. 158–63; P. Gerrans, 'The theory of mind module in evolutionary psychology', *Biology and Philosophy* 17 (2002): pp. 305–21; psychiatric aspects in M. Harney, 'Psychoanalysis and hermeneutics', *Journal of the British Society for Phenomenology* 9 (1978): pp. 71–81; M. Harney, 'Philosophical aspects of psychotherapy', *Australian and New Zealand Journal of Psychiatry* 13 (1979): pp. 309–13; G. McDonell, ed, *Interpretive Psychology, Medicine, Philosophy* (Kensington, 1993); in literature, S.L. Goldberg, *An Essay on King Lear* (London, 1974), p. 37; on animal minds, L.J. Rogers, *Minds of Their Own: Thinking and Awareness in Animals* (Sydney, 1997); contrary view in P. Harrison, 'Do animals feel pain?', *Philosophy* 66 (1991): pp. 25–40.

[34] A.D. Hope, 'Perception and poetry: or the new Cratylus', *Meanjin* 26 (1967): pp. 385–95.

choose the form of transaction into which he shall enter is basic to the maintenance of a free society.'[35] To the contrary, Lionel Murphy raged, 'It is universally accepted that in the general language it is wrong to take a sentence or statement out of context and treat it literally so that it has a meaning not intended by the author ... In my opinion, strictly literal interpretation of a Tax Act is an open invitation to artificial and contrived tax avoidance. Progress towards a free society will not be advanced by attributing to parliament meanings which no one believes it intended so that income tax becomes optional for the rich while remaining compulsory for most income earners.'[36] In the short term, Parliament's intentions were subverted, but Murphy won in the long run. The crucial section 15AA was added to the Acts Interpretation Act in 1981. It provided:

> In the interpretation of a provision of an Act, a construction that would promote the purpose or object underlying the Act (whether that purpose or object is expressly stated in the Act or not) shall be preferred to a construction that would not promote that purpose or object.

In 1984, the revolutionary section 15AB was added, allowing recourse to external evidence such as Hansard as evidence of the legislators' purposes.[37] Australia's tax avoidance industry, hitherto a world leader, never recovered from the blow.[38]

---

[35] Barwick CJ in *FCT v Westraders Pty Ltd*, *Australian Law Reports* 30 (1980): pp. 353–73, at p. 355; G. Barwick, *A Radical Tory* (Sydney, 1995), p. 276.

[36] Murphy J (dissenting), at p. 371; see D.C. Pearce and R.S. Geddes, *Statutory Interpretation in Australia* (3rd ed, Sydney, 1988), pp. 176–7.

[37] See Mr Justice Bryson, 'Statutory interpretation: An Australian judicial perspective', *Statute Law Review* 13 (1992): pp. 187–208; D. Lyons, 'Original intent and legal interpretation', *Australian Journal of Legal Philosophy* 24 (1999): pp. 1–26; T. Macleod, *The High Court and the Interpretation of Statutes* (Sydney, 1924); J. Goldsworthy & T. Campbell, eds, *Legal Interpretation in Democratic States* (Aldershot, 2002); A. Glass, 'Interpretive practices in law and literary criticism', *Australian Journal of Law and Society* 7 (1991): pp. 16–26; some European-style philosophical theory on the topic in B. Christensen, *Intentionality and Language* (Würzburg, 1991); C.B. Christensen, 'Sense, subject and horizon', *Philosophy and Phenomenological Research* 53 (1993): pp. 749–79; K. Hart, *The Trespass of the Sign: Deconstruction, Theology and Philosophy* (Cambridge, 1989); J. Begley, 'Modern theories of interpretation', *ACR* 73 (1996): pp. 81–91; J. Franklin, 'Natural sciences as textual interpretation', *Philosophy and Phenomenological Research* 44 (1984): pp. 509–20; P. Thom, *Making Sense: A Theory of Interpretation* (Lanham, 2000).

[38] 'Interpreting statutes — a new challenge to accountants and lawyers', *The Chartered Accountant in Australia* 52 (2) (Aug 1981): pp. 42–3; M.L. Perez, 'Wielding the axe on Australia's tax laws', *Australian Business Law Review* 20 (1992): pp. 362–71.

Is the inwardness of phenomenology altogether healthy? Wallowing in the world of inner experience is all very well, but like drugtaking, it can lead to one's becoming excessively cut off from the bracing world of the great outdoors. Overmuch indulgence in the delights of living inside can even lead to the question, *Is there anything out there at all?* If phenomenology is the marijuana of the philosophical world, the heroin that beckons the percentage of hardy souls who are always on the lookout for boundaries to transgress is idealism. Idealism is the doctrine that *all is ideas*: there is no truly physical world out there at all. As we saw in chapter 6, this initially bizarre idea has had a sub-surface presence much more widespread than one would think.

THE tendency of medical practitioners to speculate about physical causes of mental effects has been irrepressible, running from phrenology and mesmerism[39] through craniometry and the effect of lost sexual organs[40] to claims about small parts of the brain even less accessible to empirical study.[41] The attempt to explain the mental, including the spiritual, in terms of the physical is seen at its most entertaining in an article by Trethowan in the Sydney University Arts magazine, later reprinted in his colourful *Uncommon Psychiatric Syndromes*, on the theme that possession by demons must have been caused by psychoactive ingredients in ointments.[42] Despite this, Trethowan's own view of the relation of mind and body was reasonably balanced. He complains elsewhere

[39] M. Roe, *The Quest for Authority in Eastern Australia, 1835–1851* (Melbourne, 1965), pp. 161–4; 'On some recent experiments on the brain', *Quadrilateral* (Hobart) 1 (1874): pp. 35–7; 'Matter, science and the ego', *Quadrilateral* 1 (1874): pp. 204–7.

[40] M. Cawte, 'Craniometry and eugenics in Australia', *Historical Studies* 22 (1986): pp. 35–53; K. Hogg, 'An introduction to the relation of female pelvic organs to insanity', *Australasian Medical Congress, Transactions* 1908, vol. 3, pp. 281–6.

[41] W.A. Lind, 'The physical basis of insanity', *Medical Journal of Australia* 9 (1922) vol. 2 pp. 465–72; W.A. Lind, 'On insanity', *Medical Journal of Australia* 13 (1926) vol. 1 pp. 315–24; F.N. Manning, 'The causation and prevention of insanity', *Journal and Proceedings of the Royal Society of New South Wales* 14 (1880): pp. 340–55; J. Bostock, 'The "composite" point of view on the causation of mental disorders', *Australasian Medical Congress, Transactions*, 2nd session, 1927, pp. 110–3; comment in A.T. Edwards, *Patients Are People* (Sydney, 1968), pp. 153–4; S. Garton, 'Freud versus the rat: Understanding shell shock in World War 1', *Australian Cultural History* 16 (1997/8): pp. 45–59.

[42] W.H. Trethowan, 'Demoniacal possession', *Arna* (1962): pp. 66–75; cf. Trethowan, 'The demonopathology of impotence', *British Journal of Psychiatry* 109 (1963): pp. 341–7.

It is disturbing to observe that a first-year medical student may start his career with a mind more perceptive to the facts of human nature than he will have after completing his preclinical course. As a rule, during this part of his career, he becomes indoctrinated with a scientific attitude largely evolved, not from the study of the behaviour of living organisms interacting with their environment, but from the physical sciences. One result of this is the propagation of the absurd mind-body dualism which so strongly colours the thinking of the average medical practitioner. The essentially materialistic nature of the early years of medical training strongly fosters this dualistic attitude.[43]

One medical student who did not find anything absurd about mind-body dualism was John Eccles. While studying medicine at Melbourne University, he read the philosophical and psychological literature on the subject, and finding it dogmatic and scientifically ill-informed, resolved to devote his life to research in neuroscience to clear the matter up.[44] He is a rare Australian example of a kind of scientist like the founders of quantum theory, common in Europe early in the century, who were inspired to do science by a desire to solve big philosophical questions. After research at Oxford, he feared his career was at an end when it turned out that he had picked the wrong side in the controversy over whether synapses communicate electrically or chemically. Fortunately, he was by this time in New Zealand with Karl Popper, who convinced him that it was a virtue in a scientific theory to be refuted.[45] Recovering his equilibrium, he conducted a decade of ground-breaking research at ANU, which resulted in his sharing the 1963 Nobel Prize for Physiology or Medicine. He later wrote with Popper a book, *The Self and its Brain*, arguing against materialist theories of mind.[46] This line of reasoning

---

[43] Trethowan, 'Psychiatry and the medical curriculum', *Medical Journal of Australia* 47 (1960) vol. 1 pp. 441–5, at p. 443.

[44] J. Eccles, 'Under the spell of the synapse', in *The Neurosciences: Paths of Discovery*, ed. F.G. Worden, J.P. Swazey & G. Adelman (Cambridge, Mass, 1975), pp. 159–79, at p. 159; J. Eccles, 'My scientific odyssey', *Annual Review of Physiology* 38 (1977): pp. 1–18, at p. 17.

[45] J.C. Eccles, *Facing Reality* (New York, 1970), pp. 104–8; J. Eccles, 'My living dialogue with Popper', in *In Pursuit of Truth*, ed. P. Levinson (Atlantic Highlands, NJ, 1982), pp. 221–36.

[46] K.R. Popper & J.C. Eccles, *The Self and its Brain* (New York, 1977), also J. Eccles, *The Human Mystery* (Berlin, 1979); *The Human Psyche* (New York, 1980); earlier J. Eccles, *The Neurophysiological Basis of Mind* (Oxford, 1953), ch. 8; another physiologist's plan in M.R. Bennett, *The Idea of Consciousness: Synapses and the Mind* (Amsterdam, 1997), ch. 3; further science-based ideas in D. Hodgson, *The Mind Matters: Consciousness and Choice in a Quantum World* (Oxford, 1991); D. Hodgson, 'Nonlocality, local indeterminism and consciousness', *Ratio* 9 (1996): pp. 1–22 (profile in *Australian Financial Review*

was not looked on favourably by the central-state materialist philosophers, who had been counting on neuroscience to help them explain the mind away, but it was always possible to attribute views like Eccles' to the well-known philosophical naivety of scientists. Armstrong spoke of Eccles' 'lack of philosophical sophistication', and regarded his theory of consciousness as merely a re-badging of Armstrong's own theory that consciousness is no more than one brain process scanning another.[47]

Psychiatry was the medical discipline that raised mind-body problems most urgently. How was it to establish itself as a reputable branch of the medical profession? Perhaps the laconic Australian temperament cannot be expected to support the population of shrinks that New York does, but a 1960 article by Trethowan suggested some more philosophical reasons for the slow emergence of the field. 'The development of psychiatry in Australia,' he said, 'like that of some of the patients whom it endeavours to treat, is still at a somewhat immature stage.' Part of the problem lay in the narrowly biological training of medical students. 'It is now to be seen that social isolation, loneliness, the psychological problems of ageing, the stresses and strains of modern living, marital disharmony, the waning of religious interests, psycho-sexual immaturity, uncertainty as to the future and other anxieties of many different kinds are just as much the causes or harbingers of ill-health as are trauma, bacteria and other physically noxious influences.' A system of medicine based on 'a philosophy of science and derived from certain physical disciplines' would not make any progress in these areas, and would cause the paying customers to go to 'those who are, in other ways, less properly qualified to deal with these matters.' He meant psychologists as much as alternative healers. To combat such a grave threat to the income of the medical profession, students ought to be trained in the anatomy of personality. While there was, he thought, some truth in the claim that Freudian theory was unscientific, he said, 'it must be remembered that before Freud much of human behaviour and very many of the symptoms of mental disorder were quite inexplicable other than in terms of morality and degeneracy, both of which have proved to be sterile con-

27/4/2001, p. 58); Z. Torey, *The Crucible of Consciousness* (Melbourne, 1999); G. O'Brien & J. Opie, 'The disunity of consciousness', *AJP* 76 (1998): pp. 378–95.

[47] D.M. Armstrong, review of Popper and Eccles, *Times Literary Supplement* no. 3960 (17/2/1978), pp. 183–4, repr. in *Quadrant* 22 (7) (July 1978): pp. 18–22.

cepts.' 'It seems more often than not that the investigation of man's nature is the area of medicine's main neglect.'[48]

Even an extreme materialist view of human nature does not necessarily result in medical inconveniences, in its place. One of the most successful outcomes of a rigidly materialistic approach to mental illness was the Australian discovery of lithium treatment for bipolar disorder (manic depression) by John Cade.[49] The discovery took many years to be accepted, partly at least because it was published in the *Medical Journal of Australia,* not a widely-read journal in the centres of medical power in the United States and Europe.

Then again, one should not necessarily believe everything printed in the *Medical Journal of Australia.* In 1973, it published — over the substantial objections of the only traceable referee[50] — a paper on 'The control of affective illness by cingulotractotomy',[51] by Harry Bailey and co-workers. A certain amount of concern arose from the fact that this group was performing half the leucotomies in Australia. It was pointed out that the papers reported an unbelievably high rate of improvement, failed to compare the treatment to less drastic ones or to any control group, did not systematically evaluate at progressive follow-up periods, and operated on homosexuals and people facing criminal charges in circumstances suggesting consent was not wholly voluntary.[52]

Bailey represents the downside of the materialist attitude to mind. A man 'philosophically and intellectually attracted to a belief that

[48] W.H. Trethowan, 'Psychiatric teaching and practice in Australia', *Vestes* 3 (4) (1960): pp. 29–34.
[49] F.N. Johnson, *The History of Lithium Therapy* (London, 1984), ch. 3; J.F.J. Cade, 'The story of lithium', in F.J. Ayd, *Discoveries in Biological Psychiatry* (Philadelphia, 1970), pp. 218–29 and J.F.J. Cade, *Mending the Mind: A Short History of Twentieth Century Psychiatry* (Melbourne, 1979), ch. 11.
[50] B. Bromberger & J. Fife-Yeomans, *Deep Sleep: Harry Bailey and the Scandal of Chelmsford* (Sydney, 1989), p. 89.
[51] H.R. Bailey, J.L. Dowling & E. Davies, 'The control of affective illness by cingulotractotomy: A review of 150 cases', *Medical Journal of Australia* 60 (1973) vol. 2 pp. 366–371; also H. Bailey, J.L. Dowling, C.H. Swanton & E. Davies, 'Cingulotractotomy in the treatment of severe affective illness', *Medical Journal of Australia* 58 (1971) vol. 1, pp. 8–12; diagrams of the bits cut in *Medical Journal of Australia* 60 (1973) vol. 2, p. 1101.
[52] R. Winkler, 'Current psychosurgery in Australia: Local concerns', in *Psychosurgery and Society: Symposium Organised by the Neuropsychiatric Institute, Sydney, 26–27 September 1974*, ed. J.S. Smith & L.G. Kiloh (Oxford, 1976), pp. 91–8; later discussion of such issues in J. Kleinig, *Ethical Issues in Psychosurgery* (London, 1985), pp. 70–1.

mental illness involved physical abnormalities',[53] he was excited by the many reports in the 1950s, the time of his graduation, of wonder cures by ECT, deep coma insulin, lobotomies, LSD and the like.[54] Cade suggested lobotomy was actually discovered accidentally by an Australian medical officer at Gallipoli, who observed that a depressed major who survived shooting himself through the frontal lobes with his service revolver was thereafter composed, even complacent.[55] Its medical use dates from the late 1930s, but such brain operations were treatments of last resort and were generally replaced by drug treatments from 1959, except in Bailey's group.[56]

It was in this atmosphere of a frontier discipline where bold men could make big strides that Bailey travelled overseas in 1954–6 to meet the world experts. In Montreal he had contact with the work of Dr Ewen Cameron, which involved the use of heavy sedation and ECT; a number of Cameron's experiments were funded by the CIA and given without the patients' consent, leading to large compensation payouts many years later to some of the surviving victims.[57] In London he visited William Sargant, another world leader in 'physical psychiatry'. While Sargant thought Cameron's experiments had gone too far, he was one of the last to continue using induced sleep therapy, and his account of it in his textbook on physical treatments in psychiatry[58] was to play an important role in Bailey's later defences of his actions. Sargant's views on the mind are best known from his gripping popular book, *Battle for the Mind*, which deals with brainwashing, religious and political conversions, the eliciting of confes-

---

[53] Bromberger & Fife-Yeomans, *Deep Sleep*, p. 6; a forerunner of Bailey in Edwards, *Patients Are People*, pp. 26–30.

[54] Described in Cade, *Mending the Mind*, ch. 6; also R.S. Ellery & D.C. Lear, 'Schizophrenic patients treated by induced convulsions', *Medical Journal of Australia* 25 (1938) vol. 1, pp. 779–81; Edwards, *Patients Are People*, pp. 141–7; R.S. Ellery, *Psychiatric Aspects of Modern Warfare* (Melbourne, 1945), pp. 37–8, 90–1; US background in E.S. Valenstein, *Great and Desperate Cures* (New York, 1986).

[55] Cade, *Mending the Mind*, p. 57; a similar case in *Medical Journal of Australia* 44 (1957) vol. 2, pp. 632.

[56] Cade, *Mending the Mind*, ch. 9; K. C. Bradley *et al.*, 'Modified leucotomy: report of 100 cases', *MJA* 45 (1958) vol. 1, pp. 133–8.

[57] Bromberger & Fife-Yeomans, *Deep Sleep*, p. 11; Thomas, *Journey into Madness*, chs. 6, 11; Marks, *'Manchurian Candidate'*, pp. 131–41; A. Collins, *In the Sleep Room: The Story of the CIA Brainwashing Experiments in Canada* (Toronto, 1988).

[58] W. Sargant & E. Slater, *An Introduction to Physical Methods of Treatment in Psychiatry* (5th ed, Edinburgh, 1972), ch. 11; in Australia: D. Moore, 'The use of sleep therapy in psychiatric treatments', *Medical Journal of Australia* 45 (1958) vol. 1, pp. 9–11.

sions under torture, and so on, in terms of brain physiology. Its tenor
is well represented by a passage which Sargant quotes with approval
from Aldous Huxley's *Devils of Loudun*:

> No man, however highly civilized, can listen for very long to African
> drumming, or Indian chanting, or Welsh hymn singing, and retain intact
> his critical and self-conscious personality. It would be interesting to take a
> group of the most eminent philosophers from the best universities, shut
> them up in a hot room with Moroccan dervishes or Haitian Voodooists
> and measure, with a stop-watch, the strength of their psychological resis-
> tance to the effects of rhythmic sound. Would the Logical Positivists be
> able to hold out longer than the Subjective Idealists? Would the Marxists
> prove tougher than the Thomists or the Vedantists? What a fascinating,
> what a fruitful field for experiment! Meanwhile, all we can safely predict
> is that, if exposed long enough to the tom-toms and the singing, every
> one of our philosophers would end by howling and capering with the
> savages.[59]

Across the board, Sargant disparaged 'generalized philosophies
about the need to treat and heal the "whole man"', and 'Freudian and
other metaphysical beliefs.' It was time, he thought, for psychiatry to
catch up with the rest of medicine, and rely on simple physical treatments like drugs and ECT.[60]

Bailey's travels took him on to Louisiana, where he observed the
pioneering work of Robert G. Heath, who implanted electrodes into
the 'pleasure centres' of the human brain, and connected the electrodes to a box which the brains' owners could carry around with
them and use to give themselves 'shots' of pleasure.[61] It was probably
not true, as Bailey later claimed, that Heath's experiments were done
on humans because 'it was cheaper to use niggers than cats'.[62]

These bold researchers found an eager listener in Harry Bailey.
Back in Australia, he determined to lead Australian psychiatry out of
the wilderness. He is reported to have experimented on himself and
others with LSD and a range of other drugs, though the truth of this
is hard to establish,[63] and he extracted a very large sum of money from

---

[59] W. Sargant, *Battle for the Mind* (Baltimore, 1957), p. 148.

[60] W. Sargant, 'Psychiatric treatment in general teaching hospitals: A plea for
a mechanistic approach', *British Medical Journal* 1966 vol. 2, pp. 257–62.

[61] *SMH* 20/8/1988, p. 1; 8/10/1988, p. 11; US background on Heath in
A.W. Shaflin & E.M. Opton, *The Mind Manipulators* (New York, 1978), pp.
334–8.

[62] 'Dr Bailey's staff lecture', *Report of the Royal Commission into Deep Sleep
Therapy*, vol. 12, pp. 531–54, at p. 544.

[63] Bromberger & Fife-Yeomans, *Deep Sleep*, p. 19; *SMH* 20/8/1988, p. 1;
Report of the Royal Commission into Deep Sleep Therapy, vol. 2, pp. 59–62;

the state government to build a Cerebral Surgery Research Unit.[64] He had established himself as a man at the cutting edge of research. It seemed his rise would be unstoppable, but his career underwent a hiccup when allegations he made against his staff at Callan Park Mental Hospital led to a Royal Commission. Though a few of his complaints were vindicated, he was forced to resign.[65] He went into private practice, where his 'research' proceeded, free from any constraints that a public hospital system might have imposed.

The kind of research he chose to do stemmed from his views on mind and brain. As the later Royal Commission into his activities described them:

> Dr Bailey's idea of mind and brain was very limited. The naivety may not have been unique to him but its extreme manifestations as noted in his lecture and practice must be condemned. His description of electric brain stimulation of the pleasure centres and the experiences of pleasure and orgasm give some understanding of the simplicity in which he believed. His approach ignored completely the richness of the human person and the relationships which surround it. These frequently were reduced to his crude comment that the patient needed a good physical sexual experience; something that he himself provided at times.[66]

The last sentence refers to another of Bailey's 'treatments', of which the *Medical Journal of Australia* was also happy to publish an account. His article 'Treatment of the depressed, frigid woman' describes his procedures at Crown Street Women's Hospital. He recommends 'a very direct incisive approach, uncluttered by "hang-ups" in verbalization.' The treatment itself involves injections of hormones and an intensive course of antidepressants. For patients revealing poor mammary development, implants are in order, the psychological advantages of which are claimed to be 'extreme'.[67] Patients recalled that the 'uncluttered' approach meant that Bailey would often begin a consultation with 'How are things in the fucking department?' One patient at the Royal Commission said that it was not unusual for him to suggest, 'What you need is a good fuck, and I am just the person

H.R. Bailey, J.S. Blow & S.G Sandes, '"Siqualine" (fluphenazine) in psychiatric practice', *Medical Journal of Australia* 47 (1960) vol. 1, pp. 885–7.

[64] Bromberger & Fife-Yeomans, *Deep Sleep*, p. 16.

[65] Bromberger & Fife-Yeomans, *Deep Sleep*, pp. 25–34; C.J. Cummins, *A History of Medical Administration in New South Wales, 1788–1973* (Sydney, 1979), pp. 121–6; *SMH* 8/9/1961, p. 1; 'Dr Bailey quits public service: A martyr, says Askin', *SMH* 13/9/1961, p. 1.

[66] *Report of the Royal Commission into Deep Sleep Therapy*, vol. 3 p. 23.

[67] H. R. Bailey, 'Treatment of the depressed, frigid woman', *Medical Journal of Australia* 60 (1973) vol. 1, pp. 834–7; on the general issues, see D. Russell, *Women, Madness and Medicine* (Cambridge, 1995).

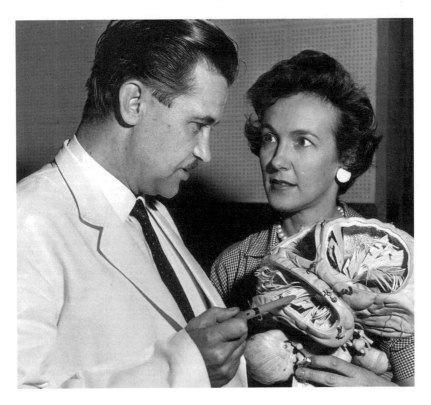

Dr Harry Bailey explains the workings of the brain to Mary Rossi, ABC TV, 1961 (Australian Broadcasting Corporation)

to do it.'[68] Any impression that all this has something to do with 'the Sixties' is only strengthened by Bailey's activities on the editorial board of the sex-oriented journal *Forum*, and his drinking with the Push.[69]

In the end it was neither for his sex therapy nor his brain excavations that Bailey was finally called to account, but for his deep coma insulin treatment. As with his brain operations, Bailey was using a version of a treatment that had been tried and superseded in Australia years earlier. Full coma insulin treatment for schizophrenia had been used in the 1940s and 1950s, but given up because of the occasional irreversible comas resulting, and because of the availability in the

[68] Bromberger & Fife-Yeomans, *Deep Sleep*, pp. 68–9.
[69] *Forum: The International Journal of Human Relations* 1 (8) (1973), p. 3, etc; A. Coombs, *Sex and Anarchy* (Melbourne, 1996), p. 278; but Bailey called 'sexist butcher' in S. Soldatow, 'Psychiatric liberation', *Scrounge* no. 8 (23/8/1973), pp. 15–22.

mid-1950s of suitable drugs. About 1100 patients had deep sleep treatment at Bailey's Chelmsford Hospital. There were perhaps 30 deaths probably attributable to the therapy from 1964 to 1978.[70] Many others suffered brain damage or a worsening of their psychiatric conditions.

It took a long time for anyone to complain, but reports slowly leaked out. The evidence of wrongdoing gradually became impossible to ignore, and a Royal Commission was set up. Bailey committed suicide in 1985 as the Royal Commission was closing in, leaving a note saying 'the forces of madness have won'.[71]

I N THE medical arena, the main anti-materialist current of thought was Freudianism. The meaning of Freud's legacy is not easy to grasp. The matter is confused because Freud himself believed in a materialist theory of mind, and his medical background enabled him to present his theory as 'hard science', undoubtedly a factor in its wide acceptance. The second cause of confusion is that Freudianism had an existence outside its use as a therapy, and its meaning in the wider sphere of philosophy, literary criticism, art and so on is only loosely related to actual psychotherapy.

Interest in Freud in Australia began early. Freud himself sent, by invitation, a short introductory paper on his work to the Australasian Medical Congress of 1911;[72] in his more depressed moments, he had fantasies of emigrating there himself.[73] A reaction of 1913 already points out that even if Freud is sometimes right about the causation of mental problems by childhood trauma, he ignores the fact that certain well-defined mental illnesses are known to have physical causes.[74] A heated debate in the *Medical Journal of Australia* in 1936, prompted by the assertion by Sydney's first psychoanalyst that most physical illnesses had psychological causes,[75] was only the most prominent inci-

---

[70] *Report*, vol. 5 pp. 134–5.

[71] Cf. H.R. Bailey, 'Sedatives and suicide', *Medical Journal of Australia* 51 (1964) vol. 1, p. 393.

[72] S. Freud, 'On psycho-analysis', *Australasian Medical Congress*, 9th session, Sydney, 1911 (Sydney, 1913), vol. 2 pp. 839–42; there are accompanying papers by Jung and Havelock Ellis. On Havelock Ellis's sojourn in Australia, V. Brome, *Havelock Ellis: Philosopher of Sex* (London, 1979), ch. 2; P. Grosskurth, *Havelock Ellis* (London, 1980), chs 2–3.

[73] E. Jones, *The Life and Work of Sigmund Freud*, vol. 1 (New York, 1953), pp. 179, 181.

[74] Review of E. Jones, *Papers on Psychoanalysis*, *Australasian Medical Gazette* 33 (1913): p. 233.

[75] R.C. Winn, 'Psychoanalysis and general medicine', *Medical Journal of Australia* 23 (1936) vol. 1, pp. 293–99; also pp. 323–6, replies pp. 342–3, 383, 485–6, 629, 728–30; further 35 (1948) vol. 1, pp. 588–93; 37 (1950)

dent in a long-running debate. 'True' psychoanalysis — that is, therapy practised by a training analyst in apostolic succession from Freud — did not begin in Australia until the arrival of a Hungarian refugee analyst in 1940,[76] but Freudian methods were already well-known, both inside and outside the medical profession. The first volume of the *Australasian Journal of Psychology and Philosophy*, of 1923, had five articles on psychoanalysis, on such topics as its relation to traditional psychology, religion, medicine and education. The articles already assume some familiarity with the subject, and, like most writing by other than hard-line Freudians, are very concerned to give a 'judicious' assessment: 'there's something in it, and it is probably of use when other ideas fail' could summarise much of the writing on psychoanalysis. Meanwhile, it is very convenient for providing a structure for comment on art,[77] literature, civilization, and so on, without there being any necessity to inquire into the details of the clinical evidence as to whether Dr Freud's theory is actually true.[78]

Undoubtedly one of the reasons for the early interest in Freud was that a great deal of writing was already taking place on topics to do with the mind, in areas later parcelled out into subdisciplines, of which psychoanalysis was one. (Indeed, since the unity of the mind is one of its prime and most mysterious attributes, it would be of great benefit to recover the unified study of the mind as it existed early in the century, before it became fragmented into the disciplines of experimental psychology, psychoanalysis, neuroscience, philosophy of mind, phenomenology and artificial intelligence; unfortunately, how these points of view may be combined to yield again a coherent picture remains completely obscure.) The range of these early writings is extraordinary. At the more philosophical end, they included, for example, the two massive and famously incomprehensible books on the

vol. 2, pp. 946–7; obituary of Winn, 51 (1964) vol. 1, pp. 333–4; also S. Garton, *Medicine and Madness* (Kensington, 1988), pp. 82–4; D.W.A. Arnott, *Fifty Years in Psychiatry* (Sydney, 1980), pp. 28–9, 54–6, 101–3.

[76] J. Dingle, 'The entrance of psychoanalysis into Australia', in *Papers of the Freudian School of Melbourne, 1980* (Bundoora, 1980), pp. 23–38; O. Zentner, 'Antecedents of a foundation', *Papers of the Freudian School of Melbourne, 1988*, pp. 1–9; S. Gold, 'The early history', *Meanjin* 41 (1982): 342–51; C.L. Geroe, 'A reluctant immigrant', *Meanjin* 41 (1982): pp. 352–7; C. Geroe, 'First annual report of the Melbourne Institute for Psychoanalysis for the year 1941', *Psychoanalytic Quarterly* 11 (1942): pp. 613–5; obituary in *ANZJP* 14 (1980): p. 223.

[77] E.g. E.T. Lovell, 'Psycho-analysis and art', *Art in Australia* 3rd series no. 5 (Aug 1923).

[78] S. Garton, 'Freud and the psychiatrists: The Australian debate 1900 to 1940', in B. Head & J. Walter, eds, *Intellectual Movements and Australian Society* (Melbourne, 1988), pp. 170–187.

mind by Sir William Mitchell, the Professor of Philosophy and later
Vice-Chancellor at Adelaide University and centenarian,[79] and the
book on *The Soul* by David Syme, the proprietor of the *Age* and a
major figure in Victorian politics.[80] At the more medical end of the
spectrum, where Freud himself worked, one of many doctors interested in such topics as the use of hypnosis and suggestion and the
power of the subconscious was J.W. Springthorpe. Now best known
for the elaborate funerary monument he erected to his wife,[81] he was
a critic of the details of Freud's theory. A paper of his of 1922 recalled
that he had published on 'The psychological aspect of the sexual appetite' in 1884, well before Freud's contributions to that topic. Nevertheless, he wrote, the blot on Freud's theory is the claim that *all*
neuroses are the result of infantile sexual repression. The Freudian
singling out of the role of the unconscious 'is probably true in childhood, when higher representations are not yet possible; but to regard
this definition as applicable to the adult also is to subordinate facts to
fancies, intelligence to instinct and morality to its absence. Such a
view also would place eastern civilization in advance of western,
which, as Euclid says, is absurd.'[82]

John Anderson admired many aspects of the Freudian theory: its
large scale that unified diverse phenomena, its naturalism, its emphasis
on the complexity of the mind and its drives, especially drives in con-

[79] W. Mitchell, *Structure and Growth of the Mind* (London, 1907); *The Place of
Minds in the World* (London, 1933); see Grave, *History*, pp. 22–3, 26–7; M.
Davies, 'Sir William Mitchell and the new mysterianism', *AJP* 77 (1999): pp.
253–73; W.M. Davies, *A Mind's Own Place: The Life and Thought of Sir
William Mitchell* (Lewiston, NY, 2003); also 'Lovell, A.T.', *ADB* vol. 10, pp.
155–6; W.M. Kyle, *Mind and Experience* (Brisbane, 1956).

[80] D. Syme, *The Soul: A Study and an Argument* (London, 1903); see C.E.
Sayers, *David Syme: A Life* (Melbourne, 1965), p. 260; Syme's Hegelianism
in D. Veitch, *David Syme: The Quiet Revolutionary* (Melbourne, 2001), chs 8,
30.

[81] C. Spicer, 'Love evermore: The history of the Springthorpe memorial',
Historic Environment 6 (1) (1987): pp. 39–46.

[82] J.W. Springthorpe, 'Psychology: Its basis and application', *Medical Journal of
Australia* 9 (1922) vol. 2, pp. 461–4; J.W. Springthorpe, 'On the
psychological aspect of the sexual appetite', *Australasian Medical Gazette* 4
(1884): pp. 8–14; also J.W. Springthorpe, *Therapeutics, Dietetics and Hygiene:
An Australian Textbook* (Melbourne, 1914); J.W. Springthorpe, 'Psychotherapy in practice', *Australasian Medical Congress, Transactions* 1923 (Sydney,
1924), pp. 448–51; other such work listed in R.C.S. Trahair & J.G.
Marshall, *Australian Psychoanalytic and Related Writings, 1884–1940: An
Annotated Bibliography* (Bundoora, 1979).

flict.[83] The latter idea, he thought, was not carried far enough: does not the possibility of righteous indignation against an authority figure show that the superego is itself complex?[84] On the other hand, Anderson objected to the internalism of the Freudian theory. Where Freud regarded psychic life as generated by internal drives that have a fixed course of normal development, and then saw the emergence of co-operation between people as a problem, Anderson believed 'Man is *not* confronted with the task of living with his fellows, but is social all along.' Freud, he said, had no sense of the individual 'as a "vehicle" of social forces, as a member of movements which are just as real, just as definite as he is.'[85]

Interestingly, there is a Freudian theory on why the influence of Anderson and his school was not wide.

> John Anderson was the 'ideal father' — the Freudian 'fairy godfather' who absolved many from guilt, not merely by agreeing with their 'revolutionary' thoughts, but by showing that they could be derived by consistent argument ... we find at times a 'backlash' because Anderson (and a consistent application of his theory) did *not* agree with all the notions and purposes to which these students adhered — and more than a suggestion of that irrational anger that arises when 'imperfections' are found in a 'fairy godfather'. The antagonism of such disappointed neurotics, added to the antagonism John Anderson's beliefs aroused directly in other people, may well have inhibited students of his work who otherwise would have been disposed to follow him more closely.[86]

The writer is John Anderson's son, so he should know. It is widely agreed that his life was made miserable by living in the shadow of the great man.[87] Other devoted disciples likewise felt themselves oppressed by Anderson's opposition to their publishing anything that developed his views.[88]

---

[83] J. Anderson, 'The Freudian revolution', *AJP* 31 (1953): pp. 101–6, repr. in *Studies in Empirical Philosophy*, pp. 359–62; earlier, 'John Anderson: Psychoanalysis' (1931), repr. in *Heraclitus* 35 (Mar 1994): pp. 3–4; also J. Passmore, 'Sigmund Freud', *Current Affairs Bulletin* 10 (4) 1952.

[84] J. Anderson, 'Psychological moralism', *AJP* 31 (1953): pp. 188–205, repr. in *Studies*, pp. 363–74, at p. 369.

[85] J. Anderson, 'Freudianism and society', *AJPP* 18 (1940): pp. 50–77; discussion in I. Dilman, *Freud and Human Nature* (Oxford, 1983), pp. 78–9, 146–8.

[86] A.J. Anderson, 'Following John Anderson', *Dialectic* 30 (1987): pp. 129–143, at p. 133.

[87] Obituaries of Sandy Anderson in *Australian* 18/9/1995, p. 13; 28/10/1995, p. R9; *Heraclitus* 43 (Sept 1995): pp. 4–9; M. Mackie, 'John Anderson as I saw him', *Heraclitus* 47 (Feb 1996): pp. 12–13; S. Watts, 'The Andersons en famille', *Heraclitus* 58 (May 1997): pp. 4–6.

[88] A.J. Baker, 'Anderson in retrospect', *Heraclitus* 39 (Jan 1995): pp. 1–3.

The impression gained from Freud that sexual activity is a good in itself, more important than others, was also in line with Andersonianism. In her first publication, a review of a Freudian-inspired book on culture, Ruth Walker maintained that 'the state of sexual opportunity within a society is itself an index of its cultural position ... just as we recognise a man's literary activities as having "intrinsic value", so it may be with his sexual activities.' Her further view that another index of cultural progress is the 'penetration of the sacred by the profane' indicates the conflict then developing between Freud and religion.[89]

Donald Horne put his finger on what Freudianism was *for*, to the undergraduate of 1939:

> I considered myself well on the way to becoming a Freudian. Freud was not a normal part of intellectual discourse in Australia, but John Anderson and his followers had taken him up and there was a lot of talk about psycho-analysis in the Quad, which seemed to provide an opportunity to be bitchy while also being scientific. Once again, people were not what they seemed: look hard enough at them and you would find they would give their *real* selves away by some word or action, thereby revealing that they *really* possessed the anal character or showed signs of substitute oral eroticism. Our prime hunt was for signs of repressed homosexuality. After someone read that green was a homosexual's colour, when we saw anyone in the Quad wearing even the slightest touch of green we would smile knowingly. Although I had hardly any idea what unrepressed homosexuals did with each other, I was afraid that, by some accident of dress or gesture or slip of the tongue, I might be accidentally mistaken for a repressed homosexual.
>
> This gossipy side of Freudianism extended to literature. Literary works were examined as if they were reports of dreams in a psycho-analyst's notebook. *Kubla Khan* was obviously an intra-uterine phantasy, *Hamlet* a phantasy of the Oedipal situation (we always spelt 'fantasy' with a 'ph'). Again, nothing was what it seemed. In this shadow play of opposites we Freudians alone could see through the screen with our analytic vision to what went on inside.[90]

The pleasures of 'deconstructing' (as it would now be called) a literary work by showing it to be surface play of hidden forces, visible only to the critic, were pursued in one of Peter Coleman's earliest articles, 'A Freudian view of Hamlet'. His accompanying article 'I would have Olivier whipped' enthusiastically attacked Olivier's film version for botching the Oedipal aspects of Hamlet's relation with

---

[89] A.R. Walker, review of J.R. Unwin, *Sexual Relations and Cultural Behaviour*, *AJPP* 16 (1938): pp. 85–8.
[90] D. Horne, *The Education of Young Donald* (2nd ed, Ringwood, Vic, 1988), p. 177; Andersonian original in J. Anderson, 'Psycho-analysis and romanticism', *AJPP* 14 (1936): pp. 210–5.

Claudius.[91] A.D. Hope was a critic of such attempts, arguing against, for example, the *Kubla Khan* as intra-uterine phantasy theory, which had been put forward by John Passmore.[92]

Ethics as much as aesthetics felt the disembowelling touch of Dr Freud's scalpel. A 1943 article by Hope in the *Australasian Journal of Psychology and Philosophy* explained the point exactly. While Hope did not agree with all the details of the Freudian theory, he accepted the central role of the unconscious and believed that an account of the mind based on consciousness and introspection was now as outmoded as Ptolemaic astronomy. This undermined, he said, the theory of G.E. Moore (here close to that of Anderson) that there is an intuition or direct apprehension of goodness. 'It might be maintained that the quality of good was in fact only a rationalisation by the Ego of its attitude to conflicting demands in the Unconscious mind: what Freud calls "projection". And it is a fact that the conviction of goodness and badness is a common feature of neurotic compulsions and obsessions, and that when these are removed by analysis the act of object or situation which seemed before obviously qualified as good or bad seems to become quite natural and to lose this quality though the only operative change has affected the patient and not the object.'[93] In simple terms, this means that Freudianism explains morality away. One sees the point of the remark of Anderson's predecessor, Sir Francis Anderson, that psychology was 'eating the morals out of his classes.'[94]

On what it meant for students vis à vis their own lives, Horne writes,

> As well as Freudianism, a few of us in the Quad, women and men, also talked some of the language of sexual freedom. This had nothing to do with love, of which we were inclined to be scornful because, like everything else, love wasn't what it seemed. Nor did it have anything to do with our actual behaviour — with each other, or with anyone else.

---

[91] P. Coleman, 'A Freudian view of Hamlet' and 'I would have Olivier whipped', *Honi Soit* 5/8/1948, p. 4; opposite view in A.J.A. Waldock, *Hamlet* (Cambridge, 1931), pp. 50–6; also J. Wiltshire, 'Freud and the scientific imagination', *Critical Review* 23 (1981): pp. 82–8.

[92] J.A. Passmore, 'Psycho-analysis and aesthetics', *AJPP* 14 (1936): pp. 127–44; A.D. Hope, 'Psycho-analysis and poetry', *Southerly* 1 (1) (1939): pp. 25–9.

[93] A.D. Hope, 'The meaning of good', *AJPP* 21 (1943): pp. 17–26, at p. 21; cf. Hope's review of Anderson's 'Art and morality', *AJPP* 19 (1941): pp. 253–66, with debate in *Honi Soit,* Oct 1943; a 1942 poem on Freudians in A.D. Hope, in *Collected Poems, 1930–1965* (Sydney, 1966), pp. 18–21.

[94] K. Letters, *History Will Out: F.J.H. Letters at the New England University College* (Armidale, 1998), p. 92.

Occasionally, women and men together, we might discuss 'seduction' ...
We talked about repression as if it had nothing to do with our own situation and about sexual experiment as if it did.[95]

The meaning of Freudianism as undergraduate theory-of-every-
thing is in many ways the direct opposite of its significance to thera-
pists. In particular, if anything like Freud's picture of the normal
stages of early child development is correct, then growing up in a
more or less normal family is absolutely crucial for later psychic
health.[96] Those who took Freudianism to be a licence for sexual experimentation and the general casting aside of 'repressions' in sexual
matters have been among the last to praise settled family life, or provide it for their children.

Another consequence of Freudians' all-or-nothing approach has
been an attempt to explain away opinions on philosophical and religious topics by finding causes for them. Catholics were among the
first to recognise the ambitions of Freudianism in this regard. Not
only did it usurp the role of confession, it purported to offer a complete explanation — if not of the world, then of opinions about the
world.[97] Their suspicions were justified. For the Freudian, religion is
indeed an illusion, but — and this is the truly offensive thing for philosophers — no more so than rationality. A typical Freudian writes:

> Although psychoanalysis is able to afford no evidence as to the validity or
> non-validity of the belief in the existence of the soul after death, it affords
> evidence as to the nature of this belief under different circumstances, and
> the motives which give rise to it. Working in accordance with the tech-
> nique already described, the canon which the analyst applies to such
> beliefs when he comes in contact with them in the course of his work is
> not 'whether or not they seem plausible', but rather 'whether the manner
> in which they are held is favourable to unrestricted mental functioning'.
> On this basis he is very often compelled to form an unfavourable opinion
> of traditional religious teaching.[98]

---

[95] Horne, *Young Donald*, p. 178.

[96] See N. McConaghy, 'Maternal deprivation: Can its ghost be laid?',
Australian and New Zealand Journal of Psychiatry 13 (1979): pp. 207–17; with
reply pp. 219–24; A. Manne, 'Electing a new child', *Quadrant* 40 (1-2) (Jan-
Feb 1996): pp. 8–19.

[97] J.J. Walsh, 'Psycho-analysis: A new philosophy of life', *ACR* 2 (1925): pp.
299–311; similar in J.J. O'Brien, 'The Church and hypnotism', *ACR* 1
(1895): pp. 37–49, 283–92; P. O'Farrell, *Documents in Australian Catholic
History* (London, 1969), vol. 2 pp. 293–4; cf. J. Madden, 'The priest and the
neurotic', *ACR* 20 (1943): pp. 179–86; T.A. Johnston, 'Scholasticism and
modern psychology', *Melbourne University Magazine* (1946): pp. 22–4.

[98] R. Want, 'Psychoanalysis and religion', *AJPP* 17 (1939): pp. 241–50, at p.
244; a modern version in S. Mann, *Psychoanalysis and Society* (Sydney, 1994),

Obviously, a proper therapeutic neutrality about a patient's beliefs has here escaped from captivity. It has made the Freudian into a smug Olympian, refusing to inquire into the reasons for a theory (except Freud's), and looking instead at the motives for belief in it.

The actual question of the credibility of psychoanalysis as a theory is a hard problem in the philosophy of science, because of the complexity of the theory and the special nature of the evidence.[99]

PHILOSOPHY concerned with the mind has undergone a revolution in recent years, because of the existence of computers, machines which do a number of mind-like things. At least, that was the plan.[100] The reality has not quite kept up with the vision. It is impressive that a computer can be world chess champion, which might suggest that a machine is thinking,[101] but it is less impressive that the machine can only do so by searching billions of moves a

---

ch. 14; contrary view in P. Lafitte, *The Person in Psychology* (London, 1957), pp. 202–4.

[99] Serious discusion in M. Macmillan, *Freud Evaluated* (Amsterdam, 1991); T. Pataki, 'Psychoanalysis, psychiatry, philosophy', *Quadrant* 40 (4) (Apr 1996): pp. 52–63; also M.P. Levine, ed, *The Analytic Freud: Philosophy and Psychoanalysis* (London, 2000); R. McLaughlin, 'Freudian forces', in *Measurement, Realism and Objectivity*, ed. J. Forge (Dordrecht, 1987), pp. 207–33; J. Resnick, 'Toward a philosophy of science for the art of psychotherapy', *Psychotherapy in Australia* 1 (3) (May 1995): pp. 16–22; J.J. Furedy, 'The scientific status of psychoanalysis', *Pluralist* no. 2 (1963): pp. 4–13; polemic in D. Stove, 'Freud: Business arising out of the minutes', *Quadrant* 32 (9) (Sept 1988): pp. 40–41; replies in 33 (1-2) (Jan-Feb 1989): pp. 58–60; on post-Freudian developments, A. Elliott, *Psychoanalytic Theory: An Introduction* (Oxford, 1994).

[100] P. Slezak & W.R. Albury, eds, *Computers, Brains and Minds* (Dordrecht, 1989); T. Dartnall, ed, *Artificial Intelligence and Creativity* (Dordrecht, 1994); M. Michael & J. O'Leary-Hawthorne, eds, *Philosophy in Mind: The Place of Philosophy in the Study of Mind* (Dordrecht, 1994); *Perspectives on Cognitive Science*, ed. P. Slezak, T. Caelli & R. Clark (Norwood, NJ, 1995), papers 16–23; J. Wiles & T. Dartnall, *Perspectives on Cognitive Science*, vol. 2 (Greenwich, CT, 1999); P. Godfrey-Smith, *Complexity and the Function of Mind in Nature* (Cambridge, 1996), on which symposium in *Metascience* 12 (1997): pp. 7–37; N. Stoljar, 'Churchland's eliminativism', *AJP* 66 (1988): pp. 489–97; various articles in *Mind and Language* 13 (1) (1998); P. Cam, 'Searle on strong AI', *AJP* 68 (1990): pp. 103–8; D.J. Chalmers, 'Does a rock implement every finite-state automaton?', *Synthese* 108 (1996): pp. 309–33; T. van Gelder, 'The roles of philosophy in cognitive science', *Philosophical Psychology* 11 (1998): pp. 117–36; earlier, M. Scriven, 'The mechanical concept of mind', *Mind* 62 (1953): pp. 230–40.

[101] T. van Gelder, 'Into the deep blue yonder', *Quadrant* 42 (1-2) (Jan-Feb 1998): pp. 33–9, with reply in 42 (3) (Mar 1998): pp. 8–9.

second, assisted by hints programmed by human chess experts. The inability of artificial intelligence to achieve thinking in anything like a human way, despite more than forty years of intensive research, has revealed that the mind is much harder to understand than any of the simple theories of the 1950s predicted.

One idea as to what went wrong and how to fix it arises from considering the problem of how a robot could reason about the input from its sensors in order to reach decisions on which to act. The main difficulty lies in how to 'tie' the symbols with which it computes internally to the flow of input — to give the symbols meaning in terms of the robot's 'experience'. The corresponding problem for humans is a long-standing one in philosophy.[102] Sometimes it can seem that for Artificial Intelligence to succeed, it must solve all philosophy's toughest problems first. One approach is to abandon the usual view of reasoning as a process of computation with symbols, as in a computer, and instead to see minds, whether natural or artificial, as more like continuously variable control mechanisms, of the kind that control chemical plants.[103]

A great deal of interest has been aroused by the 'artificial insects' of Rodney Brooks, a South Australian now at Massachusetts Institute of Technology. He agrees with philosophical criticisms of AI as not taking sufficient notice of the fact that human intelligence arises from learning in a body. Intelligence, he agrees, ought to be 'situated' (in an environment) and 'embodied'. So he recommends 'at each step we should build complete intelligent systems that we let loose in the real world with real sensing and real action.'[104] His artificial insects, which learned how to move in a simple environment without any central 'mind', were successful, so much so that Brooks is now collaborating with a leading American philosopher, Dan Dennett, on something

---

[102] M. Davies, *Experience and Content* (Aldershot, 1996); J. Franklin, 'How a neural net grows symbols', Proceedings of the Seventh Australian Conference on Neural Networks, Canberra, 1996, pp. 91–6.

[103] T. van Gelder & R. Port, 'It's about time: An overview of the dynamical approach to cognition', in R. Port & T. van Gelder, eds, *Mind as Motion: Explorations in the Dynamics of Cognition* (Cambridge, Mass, 1995), ch. 1, with symposia in *Metascience* 11 (1997) and *Behavioral and Brain Sciences* 21 (5) (1998); T. van Gelder, 'What might cognition be if not computation?', *Journal of Philosophy* 92 (1995): pp. 345–81; C.A. Hooker, *Reason, Regulation and Realism* (Albany, NY, 1995); W.D. Christensen & C.A. Hooker, 'An interactivist-constructivist approach to intelligence', *Philosophical Psychology* 13 (2000): pp. 5–45.

[104] R.A. Brooks, 'Intelligence without representation', *Artificial Intelligence* 47 (1991): 139–60, at p. 140; R.A. Brooks, *Cambrian Intelligence: The Early History of the New AI* (Cambridge, Mass, 1999); R.A. Brooks, *Flesh and Machines: How Robots Will Change Us* (New York, 2002).

Rodney Brooks and colleague, Massachusetts Institute of Technology, 1998 (Donna Coveney/MIT)

more ambitious — a true humanoid robot that will learn everything from scratch. According to Dennett, they are aiming for a *conscious* robot. Some may think this is a case of the sales department making promises beyond the capacities of the techies in the back room to fulfil, but in any case results are eagerly awaited.[105]

In the meantime, the hoped-for 'cognitive revolution' in the philosophy of mind remains a good deal less overwhelming than promised. Revolutions in philosophy are like that. After them, everything is much the same as before.

---

[105] D. Dennett, 'The practical requirements for making a conscious robot', *Philosophical Transactions of the Royal Society of London*, series *A* 349 (1994): pp. 71–85; reports at www.ai.mit.edu/projects/humanoid-robotics-group .

Chapter 10 The
Inspiration of Youth and the
Pursuit of Virtue

In a Settlement, where the irregular and immoral habits of the Parents are likely to leave their Children in a state peculiarly exposed to suffer from similar vices, you will feel the peculiar necessity that the Government should interfere in behalf of the rising generation and by the exertion of authority as well as of encouragement, endeavour to educate them in religious as well as industrious habits.

— Lord Castlereagh's instructions to Governor William Bligh, 1805[1]

I N A small penal colony, there is room for only one public culture, or public philosophy. The State will decide what it is, as it decides everything else. The locus of conflict about the shape of the State cult will be the 'education question', since there the State will need to provide detail about how the youth are to be instructed in the meaning of life.

The question was, what to inspire the youth with? Who was to exhort the young to virtue and what model of virtue were they to supply? In England, the problem was in principle solved by the existence of an Established Church. The Prime Minister appointed the bishops, the churches were hung with regimental flags and the Tory Party at prayer heard the word of God read in familiar accents. In return, God granted his favoured race dominion over palm and pine. As for transmission to the next generation, the whole package could

---

[1] *Historical Records of Australia*, series 1 vol. 6 p. 18; further, J. Gascoigne, *The Enlightenment and the Origins of European Australia* (Melbourne, 2002), pp. 109–11; G. Nadel, *Australia's Colonial Culture* (Melbourne, 1957), p. 186; J.F. Cleverley, *The First Generation* (Sydney, 1971), pp. 11–12.

be safely left in the hands of schools and their chaplains, and the Anglican clergy who made up the staff of both universities. This happy symbiosis did not transplant well to the Australian colonies. Demographics were against it, for a start: too many Irish, Scots, non-conformists, Jews, virtual atheists, embittered radicals, ticket-of-leave men on the make, bush lawyers and general misfits, 'Germans, Californians, Chartists and Socialists, and all manner of undesirable people';[2] not enough squires. Currents of thought marginal in England could flourish in the colonies like the rabbit and blackberry, unchecked by their natural predators.[3] The Anglican Church was never fully Established in the Australian colonies, in the legal sense, and did not in practice get the help from the State to which it thought it was entitled.[4] According to Governor Bourke,

> In a New Country to which Persons of all religious persuasions are invited to resort, it will be impossible to establish a dominant and endowed Church without much hostility and great improbability of its becoming permanent. The inclination of these Colonists, which keeps pace with the Spirit of the Age, is decidedly adverse to such an Institution; and I fear the interests of Religion would be prejudiced by its Establishment.[5]

The Anglican bishop, Broughton, expressed the opinion that though the Government might tolerate other churches, it should subsidise only the one it believed true.[6] Instead the Government subsidised the clergy and schools of all denominations, leaving an unmistakable impression that it believed none of them. When Broughton demanded that the Governor do something about his Catholic counterpart Polding's styling himself 'Archbishop of Sydney', his pleas were not entertained. The benevolent Government stood above particular warring creeds but underwrote the lowest common denominator that was considered to be essential to the moral welfare of society. Bourke said further:

---

[2] W.C. Wentworth, in *New South Wales Constitution Bill: The Speeches in the Legislative Council*, ed. E.K. Silvester (Sydney, 1853), p. 51; also J. Barrett, *That Better Country* (Melbourne, 1966), ch. 11.

[3] From S. Macintyre, *A Colonial Liberalism* (Oxford, 1991), p. 13; overview in A.G.L. Shaw, 'The old tradition', in *Australian Civilization*, ed. P. Coleman (Melbourne, 1962), ch. 1.

[4] G. Partington, *The Australian Nation: Its British and Irish Roots* (Melbourne, 1994), ch. 2; P. Curthoys, 'State support for churches 1836–1860', ch. 2 of *Anglicanism in Australia: A history*, ed. B. Kaye (Melbourne, 2002).

[5] Bourke to Stanley, 30/11/1833, in *Historical Records of Australia*, series I vol. 17 p. 227; Gascoigne, *The Enlightenment*, ch. 2.

[6] Bourke to Stanley, p. 232.

I cannot conclude this subject without expressing a hope, amounting to some degree of confidence, that, in laying the foundations of the Christian Religion in this young and rising Colony by equal encouragement held out to its Professors in their several Churches, the people of these different persuasions will be united together in one bond of peace, and taught to look up to the Government as their common protector and friend, and that thus there will be secured to the State good subjects and to Society good men.[7]

The character of education, and to a large extent of public life in general, fell instead under the control of the men of the Enlightenment. Much to the distress of the clergy, the ideology that established itself most firmly in the colonies was one that many of them had come to regard as their prime enemy. It was not, indeed, the radical, anti-clerical and materialist thought of the French Enlightenment, but the more benign — or insidious — Enlightenment of England, Scotland and the American colonies, of men like Joseph Banks, Benjamin Franklin, Jefferson and Washington. Its program was anti-sectarianism, toleration as far as possible in religious and political controversy, morality and the 'religion of humanity' against dogma, priestcraft and superstition, classical Rome as an ideal, constitutionalism in government, allied with the development of a virtuous and educated people able to govern themselves and promote Progress.[8]

Several of these Enlightenment themes are clear in W.C. Wentworth's *Statistical, Historical and Political Description of the Colony of New South Wales*, published in London in 1819 to attract settlers and to promote 'liberty' (that is, constitutional development) in the colony.

> The prosperity of nations is not so much the result of the fertility of their soil, and the benignity of their climate, as of the wisdom and policy of their institutions. Decadence, poverty, wretchedness, and vice, have been the invariable attendants of bad governments; as prosperity, wealth, happiness, and virtue, have been of good ones. Rome, once the glory of the world; now a bye-word among the nations: once the seat of civilization, of affluence, and of power; now an abode of superstition, poverty, and weakness, is a lasting monument to the truth of this

[7] Bourke to Stanley, pp. 229–30; cf. *Proclamation: For the encouragement of piety and virtue and for the preventing and punishing of vice, profaneness and immorality* (Sydney, 1837).
[8] J. Gascoigne, *Joseph Banks and the English Enlightenment* (Cambridge, 1994), ch. 2; further in S. Dening, 'Australia 1788(?) — foundling of the Enlightenment', *Meanjin* 47 (2) (Winter 1988): pp. 179–83; G. Melleuish, 'Justifying commerce: The Scottish Enlightenment in colonial New South Wales', *Journal of the Royal Australian Historical Society* 75 (1989): pp. 122–31; missionaries' complaints in F. Crowley, *A Documentary History of Australia*, vol. 1 (Melbourne, 1980), p. 91.

assertion. Her greatness was founded on freedom, and rose with her consulate ... The empires of Persia and Greece, were successively established by the superior freedom and virtue of their citizens; and it was only when the institutions, which were the source of this freedom and virtue, were no longer reverenced and enforced, that each in its turn became the prey of a freer and more virtuous people.[9]

The leading figures in colonial education who followed Wentworth, John Woolley and Sir Henry Parkes and their counterparts in other states, disagreed on many issues, but their vision of a secular yet moral education was substantially a unity, and it was the one eventually implemented in the colonies' system of free, secular and compulsory education. Their success has meant that the core content of Australian education has been much more closely related to philosophy than to religion.

The secularisation of the education system proceeded from the top down. Wentworth's first victory came with the establishment of the secular and state-supported University of Sydney. Wentworth believed contemporary English universities were Anglican in name but Romish and heretical in reality, a lesson 'that the cause of education should be no longer controlled by religious bigotry.'[10] The University was to be 'a fountain of knowledge at whose springs all might drink, be they Christian, Mahomedan, Jew or Heathen.'[11] The Churches were allowed to set up residential colleges, but the University itself was secular and its teaching excluded sectarian and dogmatic theology.[12] Polding objected, 'from the nature of the case, and from what has been the result of similar measures in Europe, that the imagined neutrality in religion of a body of Professors is an impossible thing ... such a body of Teachers must form a sect teaching as effectually religious opinions opposed to those of the vast majority, as if they had an express dogmatic system.'[13] But the Churches had lost the numbers, and the more they protested, the more fear of sectarianism they aroused.

[9] W.C. Wentworth, *Statistical, Historical and Political Description of the Colony of New South Wales* (London, 1819, repr. Adelaide, 1978), pp. 159–61.
[10] *SMH* 7/9/1849, p. 2; see Nadel, *Australia's Colonial Culture*, p. 225.
[11] *SMH* 5/10/1849, p. 2.
[12] F.L. Wood, 'Some early educational problems, and W.C. Wentworth's work for higher education', *Royal Australian Historical Society, Journal and Proceedings* 17 (1931): pp. 368–94; J. Gascoigne, 'The cultural origins of Australian universities', *Journal of Australian Studies* 50/1 (1996): pp. 18–27.
[13] Petition on the Sydney University Bill, *Votes and Proceedings of the Legislative Council*, 1850, vol. 2 p. 573.

Melbourne University, following the same path, went so far as to prevent men in holy orders being professors.[14] Wentworth in Sydney had originally hoped to exclude ordained clergy from both the governance and the teaching of the University, but was happy to choose as Principal John Woolley, who, though ordained, submitted an impressive printed application with 121 testimonials including one from Wordsworth and was regarded as close enough in views to a layman.[15] Woolley's opinions turned out to be all that could have been desired, and set the tone for the University's development. At the inauguration ceremony, he rejoiced that Sydney did not even have London University's vestigial sectarianism, voluntary examinations on the New Testament, and looked forward to the toleration and mutual respect that would result from the mixing of creeds.[16] He espoused a non-dogmatic religion of humanity, to be spread not only by the University but throughout the land via Mechanics Institutes and Schools of Arts.[17] They would become palladia of nationality and give to the colonies what the Greek colonies had but the Australian colonies still lacked: a unifying moral resource, a feeling of fellowship and of assembly for common purposes.

His views had much in common with the later Absolute Idealists, in being religious in general but looking to the supersession of the dogmatic creeds of the present by a higher and more inclusive future synthesis of religions and philosophy.[18] He resembled the Idealists too

---

[14] *Proceedings ...of the Inauguration of the University of Melbourne* (Melbourne, 1855); Nadel, *Australia's Colonial Culture*, pp. 223–5.

[15] W.J. Gardner, *Colonial Cap and Gown* (Christchurch, 1979), pp. 45–54; K.J. Cable, 'John Woolley, Australia's first professor', *Arts* (Sydney) 5 (1968): pp. 47–66; W. Milgate, 'A testimonial from Wordsworth', *Sydney Studies in English* 12 (1986–7): pp. 114–7.

[16] J. Woolley, 'Oration delivered at the inauguration of Sydney University', in *Lectures Delivered in Australia* (Sydney, 1862), pp. 7–8.

[17] On these see P. Candy & J. Laurent, eds, *Pioneering Culture, Mechanics' Institutes and Schools of Arts in Australia* (Adelaide, 1994); S. Petrow, 'The life and death of the Hobart Town Mechanics' Institute 1827–1871', *Tasmanian Historical Research Association, Papers and Proceedings* 40 (1993): pp. 7–18; Gascoigne, *The Enlightenment*, pp. 119–22.

[18] G. Melleuish, 'The theology and philosophy of John Woolley', *Journal of Religious History* 12 (1983): pp. 418–32; G.L. Simpson, 'Reverend Dr John Woolley and higher education', ch. 4 of *Pioneers of Australian Education*, ed. C. Turney, vol. 1 (Sydney, 1969); some papers of Woolley in Sydney University Archives, at www.usyd.edu.au/arms/archives/woolley.htm ; A.-M. Jordens, *The Stenhouse Circle* (Melbourne, 1979), pp. 80–2; similar from an associate of Woolley in D. Green, 'Edward Maitland', in *Between Two Worlds: 'Loss of Faith' and Late Nineteenth Century Australian Literature*, ed. A. Clark, J. Fletcher & R. Marsden (Sydney, 1979), pp. 23–35.

in expressing these uplifting sentiments often and at length in elevated prose. 'The unity of the state is neither police nor force, but the fire which comes down from heaven, kindling every hearth, and burning on the central altar, a visible symbol of inner sacramental brotherhood.'[19] As a teacher, his influence was limited by the fact that the University in his time attracted very few students, though he was remembered with affection by some.[20] He did however lecture widely to the public, though his effect was not always the intended one. His lecture on 'The selfish theory of morals' was attended by an assayer at the Sydney Mint, W.S. Jevons, who came away more impressed with the theory itself than with Woolley's refutation of it. In due course he made it the foundation of the utility theory that made him the leading economic theorist of his time.[21]

Woolley became a friend of Henry Parkes, then beginning to make a name for himself, and together they worked on extending secular education into schools.[22] They were leading figures in the next success, the founding of Sydney's most prestigious school, Sydney Grammar. As with the University, it was set up on strictly unsectarian and classical lines combined with a high sense of moral purpose. The government endowed it and Woolley effectively determined the syllabus.[23]

Then Parkes took up the question of the entire education system. He was for secularised and anti-sectarian, but moral, education, for adults as well as children.[24] The religious denominations, he held,

---

[19] J. Woolley, 'Schools of Art and Colonial Nationality', 1861, quoted in Nadel, *Australia's Colonial Culture*, p. 270.

[20] Recollections by Samuel Griffith, speech in *Record of the Jubilee Celebrations of the University of Sydney* (Sydney, 1902), summary in Melleuish, *Cultural Liberalism*, p. 61; also R.B. Joyce, *Samuel Walker Griffith* (St Lucia, 1984), pp. 9–10; other recollections in 'An Australian', *The Golden Gates of Australia* (London, 1866), pp. 40–48.

[21] *Papers and Correspondence of William Stanley Jevons*, ed. R.D.C. Black & R. Könekamp (London, 1972), vol. 1 pp. 27–8, 132–4; J.A. la Nauze, 'Jevons in Sydney', in *Political Economy in Australia* (Melbourne, 1949), ch. 2; P. Groenewegen & B. McFarlane, *A History of Australian Economic Thought* (London, 1990), pp. 47–9; M.V. White, 'Jevons in Australia: A reassessment', *Economic Record* 58 (1982): pp. 32–45; G. Davison, 'The unsociable sociologist — W.S. Jevons and his survey of Sydney', *Australian Cultural History* 16 (1997/8): pp. 127–50.

[22] A.W. Martin, *Henry Parkes* (Melbourne, 1980), pp. 91–5.

[23] C. Turney, *Grammar* (Sydney, 1989), pp. 29, 34–5; Simpson, 'Reverend Dr John Woolley', pp. 99–100.

[24] G.T. Spaull, *The Educational Aims and Work of Sir Henry Parkes* (Sydney, 1920), pp. 10–11, 34–5; C.M.H. Clark, *A History of Australia*, vol. IV

rightly teach their own opinions, but morality as well as intellectual knowledge are common and therefore the concern of the state.[25] Morality must be explicitly taught:

> The quantity of arithmetic or geometry acquired in a school, or the quantity of language or other branches of study, is far from being the primary consideration. These things should all be so used as to exercise and discipline both the moral and intellectual powers, and to brace up the whole mind for the duties of self-government, the pursuit of noble thoughts, and the maintenance of unflinching virtues. To deem the man well educated who wants these acquirements is to misunderstand his nature and destinies.[26]

Parkes could let fly with Enlightenment anti-clerical rhetoric with the best of them:

> a struggle between Light and Darkness — between the expansion of that glorious intellect which God has given us, and its extinction — between that grovelling superstition which seeks to fetter and degrade and that pure religion which tends to liberate and exalt. Rome has furbished up her rusty arms ... they have sought to hide the real motive by which they are actuated. That motive is not to insure the spread of morality and extend the influence of religion, but *to prevent the multitude from becoming enlightened* ... They are aware that the superstitious fears which give them so mighty an influence over the common people must be dispelled by a sound and rational education. They have therefore systematically opposed every effort which has been made to render such education universal.[27]

Those were views from his early years, but they had changed little by the time of his final victory, when he claimed that Catholic priests were opposed to his bill 'because enlightenment — the rearing of the children in the free exercise of their faculties — is death to their calling. The peculiar genius of the Roman Catholic Church is to thrive

(Melbourne, 1978), pp. 271–86; the same from Woolley in *Lectures Delivered in Australia*, pp. 94, 144.

[25] H. Parkes, 'Intellectual and moral training, the duty of the nation', *Empire* 30/5/1853, p. 2326; further in Partington, *The Australian Nation*, p. 109; D. Morris, ch. 7 of Turney, *Pioneers of Australian Education*, vol. 1.

[26] Parkes, quoted in S.H. Smith & G.T. Spaull, *History of Education in New South Wales* (Sydney, 1925), p. 108.

[27] H. Parkes, 'Darkness or light — which is to conquer?', *Empire* 13/10/1851, p. 250, partly quoted in Martin, *Henry Parkes*, pp. 105–6; discussion in A.W. Martin, 'Henry Parkes and the political manipulation of sectarianism', *Journal of Religious History* 9 (1976): pp. 85–92; Gascoigne, *The Enlightenment*, pp. 106, 114.

upon the enslavement of the human intellect.'[28] These remarks make clear a further reason why the Enlightened took so much interest in the 'education question'. Education just is Enlightenment — or at least it would be, if only control of it could be wrested from the forces of darkness and superstition.

The same views were held by William Wilkins, the energetic public servant in charge of the syllabus and its implementation. He too promoted a generalised religiosity that formed the common core of Christianity as the appropriate foundation for moral education in schools. The differences between sects, he said, are matters for advanced study only, like the conic sections in mathematics, and irrelevant to the basics suitable for children. 'We shall plainly discern the identity of those parts of religion which we have already shown to be the proper and most valuable constituents of the education of children, with those now indicated as the common ground of Christianity.'[29]

The secular victory had come even earlier in Victoria,[30] where the secularists were led by George Higinbotham. The formation of the Australian Church, the embodiment of Absolute Idealism noted in chapter 6, was occasioned by a speech by Higinbotham which urged the laity to revolt against the denominational in-fighting and dogmatic ignorance of their clergy.[31] During the education debate, he too

---

[28] *NSW Parliamentary Debates* 1879–80, vol. 2. p. 1284; discussed in P.F. Cardinal Moran, *History of the Catholic Church in Australasia* (Sydney, 1895), p. 875, cf p. 869.

[29] W. Wilkins, *National Education: An Exposition of the National System of New South Wales* (Sydney, 1865), p. 12; accounts of his work in C. Turney, *William Wilkins: His Life and Work* (Sydney, 1992); C. Linz, *Establishment of a National System of Education in New South Wales* (Melbourne, 1938), ch. 6.

[30] A.G. Austin, *Australian Education, 1788–1900* (2nd ed, Melbourne, 1965), ch. 6, esp. pp. 188–97; A.G. Austin, *George William Rusden and National Education* (Melbourne, 1958); J.S. Gregory, *Church and State* (Melbourne, 1973), ch. 3; D. Grundy, *Secular, Compulsory and Free: The Education Act of 1872* (Melbourne, 1972); R. Ely, 'The background to the "secular instruction" provisions in Australia and New Zealand', *ANZHES Journal* 5 (2) (1976): pp. 33–56; M.R. Leavey, 'The relevance of St Thomas Aquinas for Australian education', *Melbourne Studies in Education*, 1963, pp. 83–200, at pp. 95–132; later philosophical comment on the issues in F. Anderson on State aid, *SMH* 2/10/1909, p. 7; M. Charlesworth, 'The liberal state and the control of education', in *Church, State and Conscience* (St Lucia, 1973), pp. 45–66.

[31] G. Higinbotham, *Science and Religion* (Melbourne, 1883), esp. pp. 4–5, 16, 20; Macintyre, *A Colonial Liberalism*, pp. 124–6.

had promoted 'common Christianity' as a sufficient basis for school education.[32]

The struggle for 'free, secular and compulsory' education and the withdrawal of State aid to Church schools was won in Victoria in 1872, New South Wales in 1880 and in all the colonies by 1895. It defined the shape of Australian education thereafter, dividing Australian youth into three categories: those in private schools, usually run by a Protestant Church, those in Catholic schools, and the majority in the secular State school system, being trained as the men of the Enlightenment wished. The motives behind the struggle included a simple love of education, since the weakness of the earlier Church schools was that their fragmentation prevented them covering the ground in thinly populated regions; only the State could provide universal education. Nevertheless, the widespread suspicion that the movement was an anti-sectarian, and especially anti-Catholic, plot[33] is lent support not only by the expressed views of the leaders like Parkes, but by the fact that complete withdrawal of State aid is not called for by the logic of State education. It did not occur in Britain.

Secular education has been dominant for so long that it is hardly possible any longer to see it as anything but a natural culmination of progressive historical forces assisted by all men of goodwill. To gain a focus on its particular philosophical content, it is, as always, helpful to look at events from the point of view of the opposition.

The Catholic Archbishops Polding and Vaughan, being philosophers themselves, were keenly aware that their opponents were no longer so much rival Christian sects as those who took a wider philosophical view that hoped to transcend sectarian quarrels. They saw also that the crucial arena of the conflict was education, in that secular education inevitably reinforced eclectic opinions. Polding's pastoral letter of 1859 identified the tendencies that would be reinforced by a secular education system:

> One is the presumptuous, but speciously religious, attempt to select certain virtues as the kernel of Christianity: to wit, kindliness, delicacy, charity, unselfishness, &c., ... Many have feared that Free Masonry is partly an attempt to substitute a scheme of benevolence for the Gospel of Christ ... The second characteristic of our day is a quiet, civil infidelity. The Church, and her message, the Gospel, are not now openly blasphemed by those who are the most dangerous infidels. They occupy themselves with mental and physical science, they avoid controversy, they

---

[32] R. Fogarty, *Catholic Education in Australia* (Melbourne, 1959), vol. 1, pp. 155–6; A.G. Austin, *Select Documents in Australian Education, 1788–1900* (Melbourne, 1963), pp. 207–10; Macintyre, *A Colonial Liberalism*, p. 133.
[33] G.V. Portus, *Free, Compulsory and Secular* (London, 1937), pp. 23–6; Gregory, *Church and State*, p. 140.

use even Christian phrases, meaning by them certain amiable and philosophical social virtues.[34]

Vaughan thought Polding had been altogether too accommodating and that it was time to raise the temperature of the fight. The high point of the struggle came with Vaughan's First Pastoral on education, attacking Parkes' plan for free and secular education. Vaughan's position was that secular education is impossible. After some remarks on how the 'hideous blots that disfigure the highest morality of Rome and Athens' — here he responds to the uncritical classicism of the Enlightened — showed the inability of philosophy by itself to underpin civilisation, he concluded that 'it is self-evident that education without Christianity is impossible: you may call it instruction, filling the mind with a certain quantity of secular knowledge, but you cannot dignify it with the name Education'. Then, more controversially, he attacked the secular schools actually in existence: 'a system of practical paganism, which leads to corruption of morals and loss of faith, to national effeminacy and to national dishonour' and — in a phrase that caused particular offence — 'seedplots of future immorality, infidelity and lawlessness, being calculated to debase the standard of human excellence, and to corrupt the political, social and individual life of future citizens.'[35]

These allegations, as was pointed out at the time, implied that the State schools that had already existed for several decades ought to have been turning out youth of exceptional levels of depravity, a prediction not borne out by observation. The political result was that State aid was withdrawn from denominational schools for the next eighty years, and Catholic people had to finance their own system in

---

[34] J.B. Polding, *Pastoral Letter ...on the subject of Public Education* (Sydney, 1859), repr. in P.J. O'Farrell, ed, *Documents in Australian Catholic History*, vol. 1 (London, 1969), p. 210; background in T. Suttor, *Hierarchy and Democracy in Australia, 1788–1970* (Melbourne, 1965), ch. 7; earlier, see Nadel, *Australia's Colonial Culture*, p. 208.

[35] Archbishop and Bishops of N.S.W. Pastoral, *Catholic Education* (Sydney, 1879), repr. in O'Farrell, *Documents*, vol. 1 pp. 386–99, at pp. 388, 390, 393; and also partly in C.M.H. Clark, *Select Documents in Australian History, 1851–1900* (Sydney, 1955), pp. 720–4; see M. Adams, 'Archbishop Vaughan and education', *Journal of the Australian Catholic Historical Society* 8 (1979): pp. 18–35; similar Catholic views in Victoria in Gregory, *Church and State*, p. 177 and J. O'Malley SJ, *Secular Education and Christian Civilisation* (Melbourne, 1875), part III; earlier similar Protestant views in Gascoigne, *The Enlightenment*, p. 110; whether secular education has made Australian historians blind to philosophical and religious questions discussed in P. O'Farrell, 'Historians and religious convictions', *Historical Studies* 17 (1977): pp. 279–98, at p. 297.

addition to, through taxation, the State's. Nevertheless, at a conceptual level, the Archbishop had a point. What system of ideas were the State schools going to use to inspire the youth to virtue, or even inform them as to what was virtuous and what not? There was no thought at that time of abdicating responsibility, by simply confining schooling to instruction in matters of fact.

INTO the great maw of the youth's indifference to virtue was thrown a huge range of solutions. School lessons in civics and morals. Team sports. The Boy Scouts. Cadets. Surf lifesaving. School mottoes. The Empire. The classical languages and the heroes of ancient Rome. The Anzac legend. Wordsworth. Improving literature and literary criticism.

It is worth looking briefly at each of these, since their total effect was to inculcate a thoughtworld now lost, one whose unity was barely acknowledged at the time but which has played a crucial role in making Australia what it is.

The New South Wales Act, following the Victorian, laid down 'the words "secular instruction" shall be held to include general religious instruction as distinguished from dogmatical and polemical theology.'[36] On the one hand, 'No sectarian or denominational publications of any kind shall be used in school, nor shall any denominational or sectarian doctrines be inculcated.' On the other hand, 'It shall be the duty of all teachers to impress on the minds of their pupils the principles of morality, truth, justice and patriotism; to teach them to avoid idleness, profanity and falsehood; to instruct them in the principles of a free Government; and to train them up to a true comprehension of the rights, duties and dignity of citizenship.'[37] Though there were continuing complaints that there was very little moral instruction in fact,[38] moral and basic scriptural lessons were instituted by

[36] Public Instruction Act, 1880, in *Public Statutes of New South Wales, 43 Vic. no. 12–51 Vic. no. 15* (Sydney, 1888), p. 15.
[37] NSW Dept of Public Instruction, *Public Instruction Act of 1880, and Regulations Framed Thereunder* (Sydney, 1886), p. 40; cf. earlier, circular of 1867, in A. Barcan, *Two Centuries of Education in New South Wales* (Kensington, 1988), p. 116; Henry Lawson, 'The "provisional school"', in *Prose Writings*, ed. C. Roderick (Sydney, 1984), p. 250.
[38] G. Sutherland, *Moral Training in Our Public Schools* (Sydney, 1893); similar much later in J.M. Wallis, *Chaos in the Classroom: Free, Compulsory and Secular Education in Australia from the 1870's to the 1980's* (Bullsbrook, WA, 1984), ch. 1.

Wilkins and his colleagues in other states to put these guidelines into effect.[39]

The major reforms in New South Wales education of 1904, instigated by Professor Francis Anderson and carried through by the Director of Education, Peter Board, provided for more emphasis on the freedom, initiative and responsibility of both pupils and teachers. Here Absolute Idealists gave effect to their worship of freedom. This meant, if anything, even more emphasis on moral training on schools. The first words of Board's preface to the new syllabus were:

> The school aims at giving to its pupils the moral and physical training and the mental equipment by which they may qualify themselves to meet the demands of adult life with respect to themselves, the family, society and the State. By its influence upon character it should cultivate habits of thought and action that will contribute to successful work and to upright conduct.[40]

That was not window-dressing. It was implemented by a subject called 'Civics and morals' in the higher primary school years, which incorporated Authorised Scripture lessons and dealt with such subjects as moral courage, pride in thorough work, temperance, the evils of gambling, patriotism, courtesy, kindness to animals and gratitude to parents and teachers. The teacher was advised to use moral examples rather than abstract ethical principles. 'The moral influence of the teacher should be felt in a special manner in the freedom of the playground.'[41]

And the virtues the schools hoped to inculcate were soon seen in behaviour. In the decades up to 1940, there were large falls in the rates of murder and suicide; drunkenness was contained; the age of marriage rose and births fell to levels not seen till decades after the Pill. The story of the spread of restraint in the first half of the twentieth century, when great sections of society pulled themselves out of the cycle of poverty, violence and alcohol addiction through intense

---

[39] Clark, *History of Australia*, vol. IV, pp. 285–9; C.J. Blake, ed, *Vision and Realisation* (Melbourne, 1973), pp. 222–31.

[40] P. Board, Preface, in N.S.W. Department of Public Instruction, *Course of Instruction for Primary Schools* (Sydney, 1905), p. iii; on Board's views on ethics see A.R. Crane & W.G. Walker, *Peter Board* (Melbourne, 1957), pp. 36–9, 53–5; P. Board, 'Australian citizenship', *Journal and Proceedings of the Royal Australian Historical Society* 4 (1919): pp. 196–200; A. Barcan, 'The decline of citizenship as an educational aim', *Quadrant* 16 (2) (Apr 1972): pp. 42–8.

[41] *Course* (1905), pp. 9, 11, 40–1; C.E. Fletcher, 'The teaching of civics in the primary schools', *Public Instruction Gazette* 6 (1913): pp. 57–66.

effort devoted to temperance, thrift, self-control and hard work, has yet to be told.[42]

SPORT was found to have remarkable advantages in supplementing and reinforcing in practice the lessons of the classroom. The immediate contact between thought and action, and the interplay of personal decision with the structure of the rules of playing and scoring, meant that the lessons of sport were not lost in abstract theorising. The nature of sport, especially team sport, meant that the classical virtues of character were the ones naturally instilled: 'physical and moral courage, loyalty and co-operation, the capacity to act fairly and take defeat well, the ability to both command and obey.'[43] That summary is from a modern author, but it agrees with what was said by admirers at the time:

> The recreative effect of games is always of great importance, as through them so much can be done to make the lives of children brighter, more joyful and less monotonous. The educational effect on the mind and character is equally valuable. Children can learn more easily perhaps in this way than in any other the value of co-operation with others, and the need to sacrifice when necessary personal desires and wishes for the common good. The faculty of initiation is at the same time developed, and the habit of obedience is encouraged.[44]

Sport had the additional educational advantage of permitting the great mass of students a share in the excellence and achievement they were manifestly failing to achieve in mathematics and English.

These purposes of sport were associated with Victorian 'muscular Christianity' derived from the tradition of the English 'public' schools[45] — an ideal more muscular than Christian, given the little attention paid in the Bible to Jesus' sporting activities.

---

[42] A modern philosophical treatment of these virtues in J. Kennett, *Agency and Responsibility: A Common-Sense Moral Psychology* (Oxford, 2001).

[43] J.A. Mangan, quoted in G. Sherington, 'Athleticism in the Antipodes', *History of Education Review* 12 (1983): pp. 16–28, at p. 16.

[44] 'Organised games for junior cadets (from notes supplied by the Department of Defence)', *Public Instruction Gazette* (N.S.W.) 5 (1911): pp. 334–6.

[45] D.W. Brown, 'Muscular Christianity in the Antipodes', *Sporting Traditions* 3 (1987): pp. 173–87; D.W. Brown, 'Criticisms against the value claim for sport and the physical ideal in late nineteenth century Australia', *Sporting Traditions* 4 (1988): pp. 150–61; D. Kirk & K. Twigg, 'Civilising Australian bodies: The games ethic and sport in Australian government schools, 1904–1945', *Sporting Traditions* 11 (1995): pp. 3–34; M. Connellan, *The Ideology of Athleticism, its Antipodean Impact, and its Manifestations in Two Elite Catholic Schools* (A.S.S.H. Studies in Sports History no. 5, Adelaide, 1988); I.V.

'Sport had been left out in the genius of Germany, but how magnificently the Australian boys had played up to it',[46] said the Lieutenant-Governor of New South Wales, Sir William Cullen, at Shore school's speech day in 1917. As Chancellor of Sydney University and president of the Boy Scouts' Association, Sir William was on hand to celebrate another way of putting youth on the path to virtue, when the University awarded Baden-Powell an honorary doctorate of laws in 1931 for his work in founding the Boy Scouts. After a speech by the Dean of Law, Professor Peden, praising his service to the Empire, he was presented to the Chancellor. His speech in reply modestly disclaimed any knowledge of law, but surmised that his honour might have something to do with the Scout Law which he had laid down for his organisation. 'The law is that the Scout must not be a fool ... The law of "do" means rendering service and all our law leads up to rendering service to the community and the country.'[47]

What the Scout Law said was more detailed:

1. A Scout's honour is to be trusted.
2. A Scout is loyal to the Queen, his country, his Scouters, his parents, his employers, and to those under him.
3. A Scout's duty is to be useful and to help others.
4. A Scout is a friend to all, and a brother to every other Scout, no matter to what country, class, or creed, the other may belong.
5. A Scout is courteous.
6. A Scout is a friend to animals.
7. A Scout obeys orders of his parents, Patrol Leader, or Scoutmaster, without question.
8. A Scout smiles and whistles under all difficulties.
9. A Scout is thrifty.
10. A Scout is clean in thought, word and deed.[48]

Hansen, *Nor Free Nor Secular* (Melbourne, 1971), pp. 22–4; M. Crotty, 'Making English gentlemen from Australian boys?', *Australian Studies* 13 (1998): pp. 44–67; R. Cashman, *Paradise of Sport* (Melbourne, 1995), pp. 55–7; contemporary protest in J. Lee-Pulling, 'Sport in relation to school life', *Australian Journal of Education* 7 (5) (15/11/1909): pp. 12–3, 18; recent discussion in D.J. Grace, 'Values, sport and education', *Journal of Christian Education* 43 (2) (Sept 2000): pp. 7–11; (English background in J.A. Mangan, *The Games Ethic and Imperialism* (Harmondsworth, 1986)).

[46] G. Sherington, *Shore* (Sydney, 1983), p. 102; on Cullen *ADB* vol. 8 pp. 167–8.

[47] *Speeches by Lord Baden-Powell: His Visit to New South Wales, March, 1931* (pamphlet, Sydney, 1931), pp. 2–3.

[48] *The Policy, Organization and Rules of the Boy Scouts Association* (London, 1959, with amendments of Victorian branch, but dating from 1907), quoted in K. Orr, 'Moral training in the Boy Scout Movement', *Melbourne Studies in Education 1963*: pp. 283–320, at pp. 288–9.

The same law was prescribed by the Guides for girls, in addition to which the primary manual of girl guiding, *How Girls Can Help Build Up the Empire*, has a chapter on morals headed 'When in Doubt — Don't'.[49] Baden-Powell was emphatic that the technical aspects of Scouting — the camping, jamborees and good turns — were simply means to the end of forming character.[50] The purpose of the exercise was to 'seize the boy's character in the red-hot stage of enthusiasm, and to weld it into the right shape and to encourage and develop its individuality, so that the boy may educate himself to become a good man and a valuable citizen for his country.'[51] It is obvious from the Scout Law that the ideal of character in question is a precisely defined one, combining military virtues like loyalty, honour and obedience with what could be considered techniques for surviving a Depression: thrift, combined with self-reliance and aiding others, and forced cheerfulness as a backup.

The details of the Scout Law contain some dubious features. Obedience 'without question' is obviously one, and may account for the brittleness of such a simplistic ideology when confronted by the Andersonian suggestion that questioning is of itself a good thing. But perhaps the cheerful whistling is even more objectionable. In case anyone had not got this message, it was included in the oath of loyalty taken weekly in public schools at various periods:

I love God and My Country
I salute the flag
I honour the King
and cheerfully obey
parents, teachers and the law.[52]

The Anzacs were added to the list of authorities: 'cheerfulness, courage and originality ... in these qualities lie the reason for the appreciative, if impracticable, suggestion that the magpie's borrowed name should be altered to that of "Anzac-bird".'[53] But 'Christian

[49] G.H. Swinburne, *Among the First People: The Baden-Powell Girl Guide Movement in Australia* (Sydney, 1978), p. 41; M. Coleman & H. Darling, *From a Flicker to a Flame: The Story of the Girl Guides in Australia* (Sydney, 1989), pp. 28–9, 3.

[50] Orr, 'Moral training', p. 290.

[51] R. Milne, *Facets of B.-P.* (WASP Committee, Scout Association of Australia, Victoria, 1979), p. 54; recollections in G. McInnes, *The Road to Gundagai* (London, 1965), pp. 157–60, 172.

[52] P. Adam-Smith, *The Anzacs* (Melbourne, 1978), p. 13; B. Dowling, *Mudeye* (Kent Town, SA, 1995), p. 116; B. Hayden, *Hayden: An Autobiography* (Sydney, 1996), p. 26.

[53] A.H. Chisholm, *Mateship with Birds* (Melbourne, 1922), p. 164, also p. 156.

cheerfulness, Church of England fashion', as Manning Clark called it,[54] or the prohibition on 'whingeing',[55] is a deliberate suppression of the tragic in life. It is going to lead to the return of the repressed.

There are indeed larger issues as to whether an ideal like the Scout Law that emphasises the outward-facing human virtues has been in part responsible for the lack of an internal mental and spiritual life that a number of observers have alleged to be typical of Australians: 'they're awfully nice, but they've got no inside to them' (D.H. Lawrence); 'hard-eyed, kindly, with nothing inside them' (McAuley); 'thou shalt not commit any form of introspection whatever' (Conway).[56] If so, the ideal would also have to bear some responsibility for the emotional distance of Australian fathers, widely lamented in recent times.[57] Mass psychoanalysis is a discipline with overwhelming evidentiary difficulties, but it seems as least clear that the ideal in question has a strong tendency towards promoting a lack of inwardness.

The reasons for choosing this particular ideal do not appear, but Scouting does not wholly lack an explicit philosophical basis. The love of the outdoors was associated for Baden-Powell with a touch of pantheism, 'the elemental foundation of all religion',[58] and Scouting ideology promoted a kind of lowest common denominator of faiths, making it acceptable to all religions that did not insist too strongly on dogma. The *Australian Scout Handbook* had this advice on philosophy: There are many questions that arise out of the normal and natural experiences of life — plain human questions. The answers are always of faith. Nobody *knows* what the correct answers really are. They can only be given on the basis of a man's belief — answers of faith. To say, 'I believe there is no meaning in life' is a belief, as surely as the one which says, 'I believe in God who made me and loves me.' But you can never find *proof* of either statement ... Scouting embraces all faiths. Every religious faith has its own particular discipline. Know

---

[54] Manning Clark, *Quest for Grace*, p. 143.

[55] An early example in 'Rural contentment — a pastoral', *Sydney Gazette* 18/9/1808, p. 2; revived in P. Ryan, 'Stress', *Quadrant* 38 (5) (May 1994): pp. 87–8; more generally, H. Caton, 'Whingeing', *Quadrant* 26 (1) (Jan–Feb 1982): pp. 45–9; defence in M. La Caze, 'Envy and resentment', *Philosophical Explorations* 4 (2001): pp. 31–45, with discussion 5 (2).

[56] D.H. Lawrence, *Kangaroo*, ch. 7 (corrected ed, Sydney, 1995, p. 149); J. McAuley, 'Envoi' (*Collected Poems*, Sydney, 1994, p. 7); R. Conway, *The End of Stupor?* (Melbourne, 1984), p. 59; comment in C. Cordner, 'Honour, community and ethical inwardness', *Philosophy* 72 (1997): pp. 401–15.

[57] H. Townsend, *Real Men* (Sydney, 1994), chs 3, 9.

[58] Orr, 'Moral Training', p. 297.

what it is and practise it well, for beneath the outward sign of religion can be a great depth of meaning.[59]

The Scouts came to combine the ideals of bushman, Empire, anti-Communism, mateship and Nature. 'They learn to play the game in Nature's school because they cannot help it.'[60]

Just how much some admirers hoped for from the Scouts appears in an alarming passage written by C.E.W. Bean in 1943 — a rather late date, considering its content:

> The Boy Scout and Girl Guide movements give in many ways ideal character training, with eyes firmly on true values; and many educationists, including the Vice-Chancellor of Melbourne University, believe that we should take a leaf out of the Nazi educational system by adopting the admirable plan of labour camps. These are compulsory for young Germans but their aims are not unlike those of the National Fitness camps established in Australia by Mr Gordon Young and other leaders on the excellent model of those in the United States and Canada. The labour camps, of course, go far beyond these. All classes go into them together. The false values of snobbery are broken down. The six months spent in this way are a source of health and happiness, and even the wealthiest citizen thus experiences, for part of his life, that closeness to nature without which civilized people are apt to become soft and unrealistic, and liable to fall easy prey to the more backward nations whose hard struggle with nature furnishes the material and motive for aggressive soldiery.[61]

The National Fitness movement,[62] school cadets,[63] Outward Bound and the Duke of Edinburgh's Award Scheme were among the imported plans for toughening and uplifting the youth. There were occ-

---

[59] Scout Association of Australia, *Australian Scout Handbook* (Sydney, 1973, repr. 1985), pp. 38–9, cf. p. 21; naturally, the Catholics set up their own scouting movement.

[60] D. Chambers, *'Boss' Hurst* (South Melbourne, 1994), pp. 88–91.

[61] C.E.W. Bean, *War Aims of a Plain Australian* (Sydney, 1943), p. 109; Bean's reference is to J.D.G. Medley, *Education for Democracy* (Melbourne, 1943), p. 19.

[62] T. Irving, G. Sherington & D. Maunders, *Youth in Australia* (Melbourne, 1995), chs 2–3; cf. A.A. Carden-Coyne, 'Classical heroism and modern life: Bodybuilding and masculinity in the early twentieth century', *Journal of Australian Studies* 63 (1999): pp. 138–49.

[63] P.C. Candy, 'Pro Deo et patria: The story of the Victorian cadet movement', *Journal of the Royal Australian Historical Society* 64 (1978): pp. 40–54; J. Barrett, *Falling In: Australia and Boy Conscription, 1911–1915* (Sydney, 1979); D. Kirk & K. Twigg, 'The militarization of school physical training in Australia', *History of Education* 22 (1993): pp. 391–414; G. Sherington & M. Connellan, 'Socialisation, imperialism and war', in *Benefits Bestowed? Education and British Imperialism*, ed. J.A. Mangan (Manchester, 1988), pp. 132–49; Hansen, *Nor Free Nor Secular*, pp. 125–7.

Narrabeen Surf Carnival, Sydney, 1936 (Hood Collection, State Library of NSW)

asional complaints from Labor parliamentarians that young people were quite capable of finding ways of occupying themselves,[64] but the time for such ideas was not ripe.

Australia's special contribution was the Surf Lifesaving Movement, headed for many years by Sir Adrian Curlewis, the man whose inquiry into youth set off the Gough–Kinsella affair described in chapter 5. It is true that the movement had something to do with saving lives in the surf, but that does not explain why there was so much attention paid to marching up and down beaches in lines. A children's novel by Curlewis' sister revels in the spectacle: 'The cobalt sea and tan-gold sand made a brilliant background as the teams came swinging along the beach rank on rank of lithe, well-knit, brown-skinned men marching in perfect rhythm. Each team was preceded by its banner ...'[65] The comparison with the Hitler Youth was more obvious

[64] Irving, Sherington & Maunders, *Youth in Australia*, p. 31.

[65] J. Curlewis, *Beach Beyond* (London & Melbourne, 1923), p. 133; also J. Curlewis, 'Sydney surfing', in *Essays: Imaginative and Critical*, ed. G. Mackaness & J.D. Holmes (Sydney, 1933), pp. 75–82; see Irving, Sherington & Maunders, *Youth in Australia*, pp. 61, 98; E.K.G. Jaggard, 'Saviours and sportsmen: Surf lifesaving in Western Australia, 1909–1930', *Sporting Traditions* 2 (2) (May 1986): pp. 2–22; later developments in L. Stedman,

to outsiders than locals; a German sea-captain, speaking to an English visitor to Sydney in the 1930s, noted the parallel as well as some contrasts: 'Their festivals and drills are a never-to-be-forgotten spectacle. These men are volunteers; here is true discipline with no comic-opera salutes or Strength through Joy uplift. This is life-saving.'[66] The life of the club-house was also part of what the movement was for. Like the government schools, surf club-houses were explicitly non-sectarian, and no political or religious discussion was allowed.[67]

Although Baden-Powell had some success in establishing scouting in European countries, it remained primarily associated with the British Empire. The Empire, as we saw in chapter 6, was pre-eminent as a means to inspire both youth and adults.

The British Empire was often compared to the Roman. The comparison was generally not carried too far, lest scrutiny be invited to the best-known phase of the latter, its Fall. This was only mentioned by those who thought they had a solution for any similar problems that might arise for the British Empire. The first edition of Baden-Powell's manual for scouts ordered, 'don't be disgraced like the young Romans who lost the Empire of their forefathers by being wishy-washy slackers without any go or patriotism in them. Play-up! Each man in his place, and play the game!'[68]

Normally, however, the classical studies that played a central role in education, especially the education of high achievers, concentrated on an earlier period of Rome when admiration for it could be unqualified.

The point of studying the classics was explained in a speech at the inauguration of Sydney University by Sir Charles Nicholson, who had great influence in choosing both the staff and the architecture of the University:

> No better discipline for the intellect of the young can be found than that which is afforded by a careful and thorough initiation into the forms of the Greek and Latin languages. Such a process involves with the learner a practical acquaintance with those fundamental principles of logic of which the grammar of every language is more or less an exemplification. To regard a knowledge of the ancient languages as a mere futile exercise of

'From Gidget to Gonad Man: Surfers, feminists and postmodernisation', *Australian and New Zealand Journal of Sociology* 33 (1997): pp. 75–90.

[66] A.L. Haskell, *Waltzing Matilda: A Background to Australia* (London, 1942), p. 141.

[67] S. Brawley, *Beach Beyond: A History of the Palm Beach Surf Club* (Sydney, 1996), p. 123.

[68] Baden-Powell, *Scouting for Boys* (London, 1909), p. 267, quoted with discussion of British background in J. Springhall, *Youth, Empire and Society* (London, 1977), p. 58.

memory is to betray an ignorance or a perverseness which it is scarcely necessary to attempt either to enlighten or combat ... From whence can the poet, the orator, the statesman draw such pure draughts of inspiration as from the immortal literature of Greece and Rome? As the majesty, the unequalled grace, and unapproachable beauty of the Parthenon have been the envy and admiration of all ages, so will the works of Homer and Aeschylus, of Demosthenes and Plato, be regarded as the archetypes of all that is sublime in poetry, eloquent in oratory, and profound and original in philosophy.[69]

As Nicholson says, the classical texts perform their ennobling task in two ways, through their form and through their content. Logical precision arises from studying the languages themselves, while contact with the sublime thoughts of the classical authors comes from reading their works. After Woolley perished in a shipwreck in 1866 along with the manuscript of his book on logic, the next intellectual leader of the University was Charles Badham, Professor of Classics and Logic and editor of a number of Plato's dialogues. According to Badham, university men mentally trained in the highest discipline, namely the emendation of classical texts, would form a core of society, 'full of reverence, refinement and clear-headedness ... by the very conditions of this discipline temperate in opinion, temperate in measures, temperate in demeanour.' But dry training in logic must be balanced by contact with Absolute Beauty, which alone prevents philosophy becoming 'barren and self-bewildering logic', and turns its attention to 'moral and practical enquiries'.[70] Some students at least, such as Edmund Barton, responded enthusiastically.[71]

The benefits of the classics as a training for the mind, toughening it as sport does the body, were continually pointed to by defenders of

---

[69] H.E. Barff, *A Short Historical Account of the University of Sydney* (Sydney, 1902), p. 26; similar in Woolley's speech, pp. 36–7; and by Woolley and W.S. Macleay in 'Minutes of evidence taken before the Select Committee on the Sydney University', 1859, pp. 29, 77, in *Votes and Proceedings of the Legislative Assembly* 1859–60; C. Mooney, 'Vanquishing the hydra-headed monster: The struggle to establish the classical curriculum in New South Wales schools, 1788–1850', *History of Education* 26 (1997): pp. 335–52; background in P. Ayres, *Classical Culture and the Idea of Rome in Eighteenth Century England* (Cambridge, 1997)

[70] C. Badham, *Speeches and Lectures Delivered in Australia* (Sydney, 1890), pp. 58, 44–5, quoted in Melleuish, *Cultural Liberalism*, pp. 63–4; memoir of him in *Speeches and Lectures*, pp. ix–xxxvi; recollections in A.B. Piddington, *Worshipful Masters* (Sydney, 1929), pp. 6–14, 101–20; *Union Book of 1902*, pp. 246–55; C.J. Brennan, 'Charles Badham', in T. Sturm, ed, *Christopher Brennan* (St Lucia, 1984), pp. 372–3; J.D. Morell, 'Dr Badham and grammatical analysis', *Australian Journal of Education* 3 (1870): pp. 3–5.

[71] J. Reynolds, *Edmund Barton* (Sydney, 1948), pp. 8–9.

compulsory Latin in schools and universities. Sir Mungo MacCallum, Vice-Chancellor and Chancellor of Sydney University, complained that other subjects in Arts are 'very vague, and, especially in the case of the pass student, offer an opportunity to the amateur and the dabbler. It is hard to prevent Literature from fostering in many persons an inclination to vapoury sentiment and fine phrasing; for not a few, History merely means the acceptance of unverified statements; and Philosophy often leads to crude viewiness. The study of the Classics is a useful corrective. In it there must be honest work, independent thought and no make-believe.' Without compulsory Latin, a BA could be made up of English, French, History and a little Botany, 'the sort of subjects that formed the staple for girls' schools in the Early Victorian period before the movement for the higher education of women began. Under these conditions it may be suggested that the style should be altered to B.L.A., *Bachelor of Ladylike Accomplishments.*'[72]

The training of the classics in exactitude of thought was a theme of Sir Owen Dixon, often thought to be Australia's most eminent Chief Justice. 'Whatever else may be the result of a classical training it does implant what is a very useful thing in the law — a fear of error'. He notes a slip by his predecessor, Sir Samuel Griffith, in writing 'fons proxima non remota spectatur': 'In the Privy Council, on reading this, one of their Lordships asked Sir Stanley Buckmaster how it happened that "fons" had lost its gender in its journey to the Antipodes.'[73] The ponderous humour is built on a consensus about a scale of

---

[72] M.W. MacCallum, *Compulsory Latin* (Sydney, 1914), pp. 10–1; also J. Lillie, *Lecture on the Importance of Classical Learning* (Hobart Town, 1840); W. Scott, *What is Classical Study?* (Melbourne, 1885); T.G. Tucker, *The Place of Classics in Education* (Melbourne, 1886); A. Leeper, *A Plea for the Study of the Classics* (Melbourne, 1913); H.K. Hunt, *Training Through Latin* (Melbourne, 1948); C.G. Cooper, *Classics in Modern Education* (Brisbane, 1951); A. Power, 'Classics in education', *ACR* 7 (1901): pp. 14–27; R.G. Menzies, *The Place of a University in the Modern Community* (Melbourne, 1939), pp. 14–15; generally, A. Barcan, 'Latin and Greek in Australian schools', *History of Education Review* 22 (1) (1993): pp. 32–45; R.G. Tanner, 'Latin in Australia', *Romanitas* 5 (1962): pp. 385–98; H. Kingsley, *The Recollections of Geoffry Hamlyn* (Adelaide 1975), pp. 178–9; an overall account of classical scholarship in Australia in E. Morris Miller, *Australian Literature from its Beginnings to 1935* (Melbourne, 1940, repr. Sydney, 1973), pp. 830–4, 838–41, 845–7, 913–27; H.A.K. Hunt, 'Classical studies and archaeology', in *The Humanities in Australia*, ed. A.G. Price (Sydney, 1959), pp. 130–3, 242–7; R.R. Dyer, 'Bibliographical essay on classical studies in Australia since 1958', *Australian Humanities Research Council Annual Report* 9 (1964–5): pp. 44–64.
[73] O. Dixon, 'The teaching of classics and the law', in O. Dixon, *Jesting Pilate* (Melbourne, 1965), pp. 276–8; on T.G. Tucker, Professor of Classics, pp.

values which places exactitude higher than it would be in arrangements of the virtues that might be preferred by religion or philosophy. A concern for applying the rules exactly may be at the expense
of inquiry as to whether those rules are the best ones to apply. Some
wrote forceful letters to the newspapers about split infinitives. We
will see in chapter 15 where Dixon was led on questions of the relation of law to ethics.

A role of the classics arising from their content, possibly their most
important role of all, lay in providing models of civic virtue. As often
observed, Christianity is not an entirely suitable choice as a State religion. Gibbon may have been exaggerating in claiming that the Fall
of the Roman Empire was due to the withdrawal into monasteries of
the men who should have been saving it; still, the injunction of Jesus
to render to Caesar the things that are Caesar's is said without enthusiasm, while the Christian suspicion of 'the world' has the potential to
create difficulties in reconciling Christian principles with a commitment to public life. By contrast, the classical tradition sees civic service as the highest form of life. In addition, it has a positively different
scale of virtues from Christianity's and to some extent also from liberal democracy's. The pagan ideal is more worldly than both, not so
much in concentrating on wealth and status, but in seeing success as
realised in public action, in participation in the civic world, rather
than private intention. Aristotle's 'great-souled' man works hard and
honestly for his position of respect in society, and is not unduly humble about it nor inclined to prefer a transcendent world of values in
comparison to which the standards of this world are as nothing.[74] He
suspects there is truth in the Roman proverb that is the motto of Fort
Street High School, *Faber est suae quisque fortunae* ('each the builder of
his own fortune'). He deserves his knighthood for 'services to the
community'.

Another point of view on the difference is that the religious tradition exalts the 'divine' or 'theological' virtues of Faith, Hope and
Charity (or Love) at the expense of the four 'moral' or human vir-

---

188–9; Dixon's classical education in P. Ayres, *Owen Dixon* (Melbourne,
2003), pp. 9–11.

[74] C. Cordner, *Ethical Encounters* (Basingstoke, 2002), ch. 1; H.J. Curzer,
'Aristotle's much-maligned *megalopsuchos*', *AJP* 69 (1991): pp. 131–51; M.
Stocker, 'Good intentions in Greek and modern moral virtue' *AJP* 57
(1979): pp. 220–4; G. Maddox, 'Civic humanism and republican virtue: An
aristocratic ideal', in *Crown or Country: The Traditions of Australian
Republicanism*, ed. D. Headon, J. Warden & W. Gammage (Sydney, 1994),
pp. 145–60; J. Carroll, *Ego and Soul: The Modern West in Search of Meaning*
(Sydney, 1998), ch. 16; an unsympathetic view in J. Teichman, *Philosophers'
Hobbies and Other Essays* (Melbourne, 2003), ch. 2.

tues, Justice, Prudence, Fortitude (or Courage) and Temperance,[75] while the classical tradition does not. This difference is clearly marked at the institutional level. The churches have a near-monopoly on Faith and Hope — though the Communist Party was a challenger in its day — and most of the larger charities are affiliated with the churches. But the law and the rest of the justice system is secular, as are the official representatives of Courage, the armed services. The Temperance Societies and later anti-drug campaigns had some connections with the churches, but were not run by them. And the Australian Mutual Provident (that is, Prudent) Society and other insurance companies, though full of evangelical fervour in their earlier years ('A poor law degrades the character of a man, but Life Assurance or a Deferred Annuity, exalts and improves it'[76]), became soon enough temples of Mammon.

While the classical and religious streams were generally thought to be compatible, and even at a stretch mutually reinforcing, in that many claimed to be inspired by both simultaneously, the possibilities for conflict are exhibited in Keith Campbell's naming of the 'Christian vices', credulity, self-abasement and self-denial. These create, he says, a passive personality incompatible with the courageous determination to take responsibility for our own lives.[77]

The sacred texts of the classical ideal are the works of Livy and Cicero. Livy treats the history of the rise of Rome as a source of moral examples, 'fine things to take as models, base things, rotten through and through, to avoid.' His ideal, much imitated by Enlightenment political figures like George Washington, is explained by Harry Evans, clerk of the Australian Senate: 'A free country can flourish and remain free only through a virtuous citizenry, by its people exhibiting those qualities which later came to be called republican virtue. The principal ingredients of this virtue are patriotism, devotion to duty, a willingness to rule and be ruled in turn, courage,

---

[75] E.g. M. Sheehan, *Apologetics and Catholic Doctrine*, 2nd ed, Part II (Dublin, 1942), pp. 115–6; *Catechism of the Catholic Church* (Homebush, 1994), pp. 443–50; S. Moore, 'Right and wrong', *IPA Review* 47 (4) (1995): pp. 58–61.
[76] *Australian Mutual Provident Society* (Sydney, 1849), quoted in M. Roe, *Quest for Authority in Eastern Australia, 1835–1851* (Melbourne, 1965), p. 194; see W. Short, *Benjamin Short* (Kensington, 1994); R.K. Nobbs, 'Ventures in Providence: The Development of Friendly Societies and Life Assurance in Nineteenth-Century Australia', PhD, Macquarie University, 1978.
[77] K. Campbell, 'Validating the virtues in a Stoic philosophy', *Proceedings of the Russellian Society* 7 (1982): pp. 14–22, at p. 22; Campbell's alternative in *A Stoic Philosophy of Life* (Lanham, 1986); cf. R.A. Naulty, 'Reflections on a stoic', *ACR* 64 (1987): pp. 182–8.

resolution, fortitude, an incorruptible personal morality, a sense of honour and a contempt for personal gain.'[78] The meaning of Livy is perhaps best caught by the often-repeated story of Cincinnatus, which was widely used even in the 'moral stories' in Australian primary schools, alongside those of British heroes. At a time of crisis in the republic, the envoys of the Senate find Cincinnatus at his plough, and appoint him dictator with absolute power. Having won the necessary military victory and saved the State, he resigns his office and returns to tilling his fields.[79]

A sound training in Livy and Cicero will produce men devoted to the public good, incorruptible and full of gravitas, able to chair commissions of inquiry into more or less anything. Men of this stamp have been leaders of the professions — in law, medicine, engineering — headmasters and generals. Sir Victor Windeyer, Sir Adrian Curlewis, Sir Hermann Black are prototypes. There have been whole dynasties, such as Sir Terence Murray of Yarralumla and his sons Sir Hubert, long lieutenant-governor of Papua, and Sir Gilbert, classical scholar and leading figure in the League of Nations Movement.[80] Politics has been less kind to the type, as the sordid bearpit of democracy is not an ideal milieu for the practice of temperance and honesty, but even there men like Barton, Latham, Casey and Hasluck have approximated the classical ideal. Certain later figures in politics have been touched by a version of the Roman spirit, but perhaps more that of the Imperial 'either Caesar or nothing' than the self-controlled virtues of the early republic.

If a single example of the type were to be taken, the best choice might be Sir John Peden, Challis Professor of Law at Sydney University from 1910 to 1942. Except for being an academic, Peden was a quintessential public figure. He was President of the NSW Legislative Council and led that body in the fight against Lang's attempts to flood it with his appointees.[81] Following Lang's dismissal, he reformed the Council's constitution to make it impossible for a Labor government

[78] H. Evans, 'Lessons from Livy', *Quadrant* 39 (10) (Oct 1995): pp. 27–9.
[79] G.T. Spaull, *History for Fourth Classes with Moral Stories of Great Persons* (Sydney, 1941), pp. 38–42; mentioned in Horne, *Young Donald*, p. 60; Horatius and similar stories in W. Morison, 'Classicism broad and narrow', *Heraclitus* 28 (Sept 1992): pp. 1–5; on W.K. Hancock, Livy and national character, see Melleuish, *Cultural Liberalism*, pp. 120–2.
[80] C. Wilson, *Murray of Yarralumla* (Melbourne, 1968); F. West, *Hubert Murray: The Australian Pro-Consul* (Melbourne, 1968), esp. chs. 1–2; G. Murray, 'Autobiographical fragment', in *Gilbert Murray: An Unfinished Autobiography* (Melbourne, 1960); recent reflections on these virtues in D. Cox, M. La Caze & M. Levine, *Integrity and the Fragile Self* (Aldershot, 2003).
[81] B. Nairn, *The 'Big Fella'* (Melbourne, 1986), p. 214.

to gain control of it without being in office for many years. His interests centred on constitutional law, with a special interest in the Royal Prerogative; Evatt became 'Doc' Evatt by impressing Peden with a thesis on that topic.[82] It was rumoured that he had advised the governor Sir Philip Game to dismiss Lang; the truth seems to be uncertain, but the story was taken seriously by students like Peden's star pupil and protege, John Kerr.[83] He took on the leftist ratbaggery of his fellow Challis Professor, Anderson, by being involved in the moves to secure a second chair of philosophy to 'balance' Anderson. He was the subject of an article 'A Roman character' by his nephew, another figure of the same order, (Sir) Norman Cowper, which expressed unusually clearly what was admirable about such men. After recalling the severity of his Calvinist forebears and describing Peden's education at Sydney Grammar and Sydney University (BA with first-class honours in Latin and Philosophy, University Medal in Law), Cowper constrasted the more philosophical bent of Melbourne Law School with Sydney Law School under Peden: 'He was not interested in clever theorising. He was concerned, not with the law as it ought to be or might be, but with the law as it was.' Though often ferocious with students, 'the simple uprightness of his own character led him to accept without question the reasons proffered for absence from lectures, and some students found this so embarrassing that they resolved that the next time they would tell the truth.' Cowper concluded:

> He never failed anyone who came to him for help. He was punctilious and courteous in the carrying out of his duties, however unimportant. All his successes and dignities had left him unassuming and unaffected.

> While waiting for the ambulance to take him to the hospital after the painful accident which caused his death, he insisted on dictating several letters to his son-in-law. He was a man who derived deep satisfaction from the performance of his duty. At the end he could have had few regrets. He was a citizen of whom any State might be proud.[84]

If success is measured by passing on the torch to the next generation, Peden also rates highly. Norman Cowper, a lieutenant-colonel in the War, became one of Sydney's leading solicitors, making Allens

---

[82] L. Foster, *High Hopes* (Melbourne, 1986), p. 108.

[83] J. Kerr, *Matters for Judgement* (Melbourne, 1978), p. 44; R. Hall, *The Real John Kerr* (Sydney, 1978), pp. 20–3.

[84] N. Cowper, 'A Roman character', *Australian Quarterly* 18 (3) (Sept 1946): pp. 64–8; cf. N. Cowper, 'Sir Galahad, the dauntless imp, and others', *Australian Quarterly* 32 (2) (June 1951): pp. 35–56; confirmed by Bavin and Evatt in *Jubilee Book of the Law School of the University of Sydney*, ed. T. Bavin (Sydney, 1940), pp. 29–37; also *ADB* vol. 11 pp. 190–2.

the pre-eminent firm in the city, and was President of the Law Society of NSW. He chose Barwick as the barrister to defend the banks against Chifley's nationalisation proposals. He was Chairman of Angus and Robertson and other companies, President of the Australian Club and of the Australian Institute of Political Science.[85] Long chairman of trustees of Sydney Grammar, he was recalled from his plough to force the resignation of a headmaster who was creating disharmony in the School.

This classical scene was re-enacted by Sir John Kerr a few years later, at Yarralumla.

IT IS NOT an accident that what Cincinnatus was doing when the envoys of the Senate came upon him was ploughing. This symbolises a last aspect of the classical legacy, which formed the philosophical background to the 'land question' that agitated the colonies in the latter half of the nineteenth century, and more widely, to the place of rural life in the Australian character. James Matra's proposal of 1783 had envisaged New South Wales as a place where convicts would settle on land and be reformed as useful and moral members of society,[86] and Governor Phillip's instructions on the founding of the colony had urged him to settle on farms both convicts of 'good conduct and a disposition to industry', and soldiers.[87] The model stands in contrast to the degeneracy of urban slums from which many convicts came, but also to the ideal of the noble savage, which appealed to some philosophers in Europe but not locally. Watkin Tench, after an account of the Australian Aborigines' mistreatment of their women, concluded:

> A thousand times, in like manner, have I wished, that those European philosophers, whose closet speculations exalt a state of nature above a state of civilization, could survey the phantom, which their heated imaginations have raised: possibly they might then learn, that a state of nature is, of all others, least adapted to promote the happiness of a being, capable of sublime research, and unending ratiocination: that a savage roaming for prey amidst his native deserts, is a creature deformed by all

---

[85] V. Lawson, *The Allens Affair* (Sydney, 1995), ch. 5; obituary in *The Sydneian*, no. 387 (Mar 1988): pp. 20–3.

[86] J.M. Matra, 'Proposal for establishing a settlement in New South Wales', *Historical Records of New South Wales*, vol. 1 part 2, p. 7; also *The Evidence to the Bigge Reports*, ed. J. Ritchie (Melbourne, 1971), vol. 2, pp. 54–5.

[87] *Historical Records of Australia*, series I vol. 1 pp. 14–5; discussion in A. Atkinson, *The Europeans in Australia* vol. 1 (Melbourne, 1997), pp. 68–78, 228; Gascoigne, *The Enlightenment*, ch. 7.

those passions, which afflict and degrade our nature, unsoftened by the influence of religion, philosophy and legal restriction.[88]

In New South Wales, there was to be less passion and more work. 'The soil is capital and the climate delightful', said one of the Scottish political prisoners transported in the 1790s, 'it will soon be the region of plenty, and wants only *virtue* and *liberty* to be another America'.[89] Officialdom was not so sure about liberty, but expressed its commitment to virtue and work in the State's first motto. On 21 September 1791, the colony was delighted by the arrival of His Majesty's Ship *Gorgon*, bearing a quantity of food, fruit trees and cows, and a public seal, extremely well executed in silver. It bore 'a representation of convicts landing in Botany Bay, received by Industry, who, surrounded by her attributes, a bale of merchandize, a beehive, a pickaxe, and a shovel, is releasing them from their fetters, and pointing to oxen ploughing, and a town rising on the summit of a hill ... and for a motto, "Sic fortis Etruria crevit".'[90] The motto, meaning 'Thus Etruria grew strong', was replaced as that of the State but retained by the Bank of New South Wales.[91] As used by the bank, the 'thus' was unexplained because the words appeared alone, and one was no doubt supposed to vaguely associate ancient virtue with the solidity of bank architecture. It is of value to resuscitate the original context, which fills out the suggestions on the seal, since it describes a model of life that has had an enduring success in Australia. The quotation is from the description of the Golden Age in the second book of Virgil's *Georgics*. The farmer is not troubled by the cares of office, the delusions of wealth or the restlessness of travel. In harmony with the rustic gods, he ploughs the earth from year to year, happy to maintain his few acres and herds, and his cottage-home. He encourages his herdsmen in the manly country sports, javelin-throwing and wrestling.

Such was the life the Sabines lived of old:
Such Romulus and Remus: even so

[88] W. Tench, *A Complete Account of the Settlement at Port Jackson* (London, 1793), p. 200, in W. Tench, *Sydney's First Four Years*, ed. L.F. Fitzhardinge (Sydney, 1961), p. 291; discussion in Dixon, *Course of Empire*, ch. 1; a modern version in R. Sandall, *The Culture Cult* (Boulder, 2001), ch. 1.
[89] T.F. Palmer, quoted in M. Masson & J. Jameson, 'The odyssey of Thomas Muir', *American Historical Review* 29 (1924): pp. 49–72, at p. 54; positive outcomes for many convicts in B. Smith, *A Cargo of Women* (Kensington, 1988), pp. 169–74.
[90] D. Collins, *An Account of the English Colony in New South Wales* (London, 1798, repr. Adelaide, 1971), vol. 1 p. 179; cf. P. Carter, *The Road to Botany Bay* (London, 1987), p. xv.
[91] 'The Etruscan', *The Etruscan* 1 (1) (1951): p. 2.

Etruria grew to strength, and Rome surpassed
All other states in glory ...[92]

The model of virtue that Virgil outlines is essentially rural and
strictly democratic. It is the ideal that came to be celebrated as the
'Australian bushman'.

The importation of Virgil's model was taken in hand by Michael
Massey Robinson, Macquarie's secretary and Poet Laureate. Representing himself as Virgil to Macquarie's Augustus, he paints a picture
of sturdy swains filling the Australian landscape with hamlets and
abundant harvests.[93] The verse is execrable. The theme is developed
by W.C. Wentworth in his much better poem, *Australasia*, of 1823.
By discovering the inland grasslands after his crossing of the Blue
Mountains, he could be said to have acquired a certain right to ar-
ticulate a vision of what ought to go there. After an account of Australia's initially savage state, its discovery, and the fine buildings and
industrious comings and goings of Sydney Town, the scene moves
west, and after a few lines that quickly pass over the barrenness of the
Blue Mountains, the new settlements of the West are described. The
'fresh-cultured glade' is said to be already spread with ripening harvests and herds in thousands:

---

[92] Virgil, *Georgics* bk 2 lines 490–536, trans. L.A.S. Jermyn (Oxford, 1947),
pp. 43–4; also in F.J.H. Letters, *Virgil* (Westmead, 1943(?); London, 1946),
pp. 83–4; detailed analysis of the passage in J.R.C. Martyn, 'Vergilius
satiricus', in *Cicero and Virgil*, ed. J.R.C. Martyn (Amsterdam, 1972), pp.
169–91; quoted with a favourable allusion to Mussolini by F.A. Todd in
*Celebration of the Two-Thousandth Anniversary of Virgil's Birth Held by the
University of Sydney* (Sydney, 1930), p. 17; similar in Horace *Odes* III.xvi (in
P.E. Smythe, *A Literal and Explanatory Translation of Horace Odes III* (Sydney,
n.d.)); cf F. Muecke, 'Philosophy at the Sabine farm', *AUMLA* 81 (1994):
pp. 81–92; a similar passage in Horace *Epodes* ii.1 imitated in W. Woolls,
'The country', in *My Country: Australian Poetry and Short Stories*, ed. L.
Kramer (Sydney, 1985), pp. 23–5; Woolls on the *Georgics* and Australia in
Miscellanies (1838), excerpt in *Documents on Art and Taste in Australia: The
Colonial Period,* ed. B. Smith (Melbourne, 1975), p. 52; Sir Thomas Mitchell
on Virgil in *Stapylton with Major Mitchell's Australia Felix Expedition*, ed.
A.E.J. Andrews (Hobart, 1986), pp. 124, 132; T.L. Mitchell, *Journal of an
Expedition into the Interior of Tropical Australia* (London, 1848), p. 295; a more
critical view in C. Brennan, *Prose*, pp. 429–31; also P. McGushin, 'Virgil and
the spirit of endurance', *American Journal of Philology* 85 (1964): pp. 225–53.
[93] *The Odes of Michael Massey Robinson*, ed. G. Mackaness (Sydney, 1946,
repr. Dubbo, 1976), pp. 35, 58, 64–5, 69, 78; discussion in R. Dixon, *The
Course of Empire: Neo-Classical Culture in New South Wales 1788–1860*
(Melbourne, 1986), ch. 2; an earlier parallel in 'The cottager', *Sydney Gazette*
26/5/1805, p. 3.

Soon, Australasia, may thy inmost plains,
A new Arcadia, teem with simple swains.
Soon a Lycoris' scorn again inspire
A Gallus' song to moan his hopeless fire.

The reference is to the pastoral Utopia of Virgil's tenth *Eclogue*. The rise of Rome from humble — even criminal — beginnings is recalled, but it is hoped that Australia's progress will be less bloodstained; the model is Virgil's rural arts of peace, which are contrasted with the devotion of other countries to the goddess of war:

In other climes, Bellona's temples shine,
Ceres', Pomona's, Bacchus', Pan's be thine,
And chaste Minerva's; from thy peaceful plains
May glory's star ne'er charm thy restless swains;
Ne'er may the hope of plunder lure to roam
One Australasian from his happy home;
But rustic arts their tranquil hours employ,
Arts crown'd with plenty, and replete with joy.

The several arts in question are evoked, including forestry, ploughing, and the growing of pears. On this productive superstructure will be built settlement with village spires and crowded cities, graced in due course by academic pursuits of an Enlightenment tinge:

And thou, fair Science! pure ethereal light
Beam on her hills, and chase her mental night;
Direct her sons to seek the perfect day,
Where Bacon trac'd, and Newton led the way;
Till bright Philosophy's full orb arise,
To gild her noon, and cheer her ev'ning skies.[94]

The Australian inland did come to be occupied by prosperous rural communities devoted to the arts of peace. The rise of Philosophy's full orb is still awaited.[95]

Descriptions of Australia produced for the emigrant market — not all written by authors who had actually crossed the equator — claimed that the Golden Age was already in progress in 'an El Dorado and an Arcadia combined ... where every striving man who rears a race of industrious children, may sit under the shadow of his own vine and his own fig tree — not without work, but with little care — living on his own land, looking down the valleys to his herds—towards the hills to his flocks, amid the humming of bees, which know

[94] W.C. Wentworth, *Australasia* (London, 1823, repr. with introduction by G.A. Wilkes, Sydney, 1982), pp. 14–19.
[95] Despite an early start in P. Cunningham, *Two Years in New South Wales* (1827, Sydney, 1966), pp. 87–8.

no winters.'[96] In the colonies themselves, these ideas were given a
political dimension by the belief that the path to the realisation of the
agricultural dream for the common man was blocked by the forces of
evil, namely, the squattocracy. The doctrine of *terra nullius*, which had
deprived the original inhabitants of their land on the grounds that
those who did not work the land had no right to it, now told against
the pioneers; for the squatters, though occupying the land and deriv-
ing profits from it, were not themselves working it with true virtue,
that is, with the plough. As the *Age* said, 'Pan, the god of shepherds,
half-man, half-brute, went before Ceres, the beautiful and beneficent
goddess of corn, but did not stand in her way or dispute her claim to
be considered the parent of civilisation.'[97] The squatters never did
quite achieve total success as a ruling class. Feared by bank managers,
targeted as marital partners, yes, but apotheosised by the bards of the
race, no. The 'land question' was invested with the same agrarian
high-mindedness, even by the rebels of the Eureka Stockade. 'I knew
that hundreds were in great poverty,' said Peter Lalor, 'who would
possess wealth and happiness if allowed to cultivate the wilderness
that surrounded us ... I mounted the stump and proclaimed "Liberty!"'[98]

The political solution was selection, whereby all could choose and
occupy a few acres on which to cultivate wheat and the good life.
This solution is premised on the theory that not only working the
land, but owning it, promotes virtue. 'It is a maxim as old as the
Egyptians', said Woolley, 'that there is no greater teacher of morality
than *property in land*. To pass over the countless merits of a numerous
and independent yeomanry, it will be sufficient to signalise and insist
upon this—that the hope of acquiring land, and of founding a family
of "statesmen" (a race identified with the soil) will supply a motive —
more powerful than any but the best of all — for abstinence, sobriety

---

[96] S. Sidney, *The Three Colonies of Australia* (London, 1852), p. 17, quoted
and discussed in C. Lansbury, *Arcady in Australia* (Melbourne, 1970), p. 75;
also G.A. Wilkes, *The Stockyard and the Croquet Lawn* (Melbourne, 1981), pp.
22–31; a fictional version in C. Koch, *Out of Ireland* (Sydney, 1999), pp.
264–6, 404–5.
[97] *Age*, 6/3/1860, quoted in Macintyre, *A Colonial Liberalism*, p. 98.
[98] *Argus*, 10/4/1855, quoted in D. Goodman, 'Gold fields/golden fields: The
language of agrarianism and the Victorian gold rush', *Australian Historical
Studies* 23 (1988): pp. 19–41, at p. 31; with similar from Raffaello Carboni;
similar in M. Kiddle, *Caroline Chisholm* (3rd ed, Melbourne, 1969), p. 172
and 'Unlock the lands', *Victorian Songster* (Melbourne, 1855), in M. Clark,
Sources of Australian History (Melbourne, 1957), pp. 354–5; P. Ford, *Cardinal
Moran and the A.L.P.* (Melbourne, 1966), p. 132.

Napier Waller, 'The pastoral pursuits of Australia', 1927 (detail) (Art Gallery of South Australia)

and good conduct.'[99] The reality was back-breaking work and failure as often as not, but the darker picture of writers like Henry Lawson does not allow virtue to fade with the Arcadian dream. On the contrary, hardship is taken to be the context of the ethic of mateship in stories like 'The Union buries its dead'.

Books like O'Reilly's *Cullenbenbong* and Facey's *A Fortunate Life* make absolutely clear how hard country life was, but no reader of them can doubt the reality of rural virtue.[100]

The theory of rural virtue has been revived by Les Murray, who posits an eternal conflict between two models of civilisation, Athens and Boeotia. Urban, fashion-conscious and frenetic Athens is always contemptuous of rural Boeotia as rude, boorish, stupid and old-fashioned. The original expression of the Boeotian ideal is the poetry of Hesiod, who celebrated the sacred places of the landscape of the (literal) Boeotia and the rural pursuits of its people.

> By contrast, the only great Athenian poets were dramatists. Athens' glory lay in her drama, her philosophers and her political theorists. All of these are urban and, in our expanded sense, typically 'Athenian' pursuits. Boeotia, in her perennial incarnations, replaces theatre with dance or

---

[99] Woolley, *Lectures Delivered in Australia*, p. 148; on attempts to find virtue also in commerce, Melleuish, *Cultural Liberalism*, pp. 29–32; revived in, e.g., K. Baker, 'Enterprise and virtue', *IPA Review* 45 (4) (1992): 2–3; cf. D. Moore, 'Philosophy of Malcolm Fraser', *Optimism* (Mar 1981): 1, 3.

[100] D. Stove, 'A hero not of our time', in *Cricket Versus Republicanism* (Quakers Hill, 1995), pp. 4–13.

pageant — or sport; philosophy she subordinates to religion and precept, and in politics she habitually prefers *daimon* to *demos*. Mistrustful of Athens' vaunted democracy ... she clings to older ideas of the importance of family and the display of individual human quality under stress. If aristocracy is her besetting vice, that of Athens is probably abstraction. Each has its price, artistically, and it may be that poetry, of all but the dramatic sort, is ultimately a Boeotian art. It often has that appearance, seen over against our modern, increasingly Athenian art. Conflict and resolution take the place, in a crowded urban milieu, of the Boeotian interest in celebration and commemoration, modes that perennially appear in spacious, dignified cultures.[101]

With the exception of Hesiod's imitator, Virgil, says Murray, the Athenian model has been generally in the ascendant, and the balance needs to be restored. The role Murray sees for his own poetry is obvious. 'Athens is lasting, but Boeotia is ever-new, continually recreated, always writing afresh about the sacred places and the generations of men and the gods.'

I F SPORT, the Empire and the classics are powerful ideals individually, together they are unbeatable. The combination is the theme of the most inspirational of all poems for young imperial males, 'Vitaï lampada' by the English poet Sir Henry Newbolt. This is worth quoting in full, as it expresses an ideology in its most concentrated form and with its full emotional charge.

> There's a breathless hush in the Close to-night—
> Ten to make and the match to win—
> A bumping pitch and a blinding light,
> An hour to play and the last man in.
> And it's not for the sake of a ribboned coat,
> Or the selfish hope of a season's fame;
> But his Captain's hand on his shoulder smote:
> 'Play up! play up! and play the game!'
>
> The sand of the desert is sodden red—
> Red with the wreck of a square that broke—
> The Gatling's jammed and the Colonel dead,
> And the regiment blind with dust and smoke.
> The river of death has brimmed his banks,
> And England's far, and Honour a name;
> But the voice of a schoolboy rallies the ranks:

---

[101] Les Murray, 'On sitting back and thinking about Porter's Boeotia', in *The Peasant Mandarin* (St Lucia, 1978), pp. 172–84, at p. 175; and in *A Working Forest* (Sydney, 1997), pp. 121–9; discussion in A. Taylor, *Reading Australian Poetry* (St Lucia, 1987), ch. 11; opposite view in M. Harris, *The Angry Eye* (Sydney, 1973), pp. 70–1.

'Play up! play up! and play the game!'

This is the word that year by year,
While in her place the School is set,
Every one of her sons must hear,
And none that hears it dare forget.
This they all with a joyful mind
Bear through life like a torch in flame,
And, falling, fling to the host behind:
'Play up! play up! and play the game!' [102]

The classical element in the poem is less obvious than the imperial and sporting themes, but it is crucial to the meaning. 'Vitaï lampada tradunt' (the motto of Sydney's Shore school[103]) is from Lucretius' anti-religious philosophical poem *On the Nature of Things*, and gives the poem the image in the last few lines of the 'torch of life', or of tradition, being passed on by each generation to the next. Perhaps it is the best secular substitute for personal immortality that can be had.[104]

The poem had a remarkable penetration throughout the Empire. In Australia, it was distributed to primary schools in the *Commonwealth School Paper* of 1904.[105] In her last major public speech, Oodgeroo Noonuccal recalled that her introduction to poetry in a State School in Queensland in the 1920s was 'Vitaï lampada', which she proceeded to quote from memory.[106] Inspired by Newbolt, a number of schools around Australia adopted 'Play the Game' as their motto.[107]

Newbolt later attempted a poem on an antipodean theme, the sinking of the *Emden* by the *Sydney*, but with unhappy results. It contains the lines:

Their hearts were hot, and as they shot
They sang like kangaroos.[108]

---

[102] H. Newbolt, *The Island Race* (London, 1898), pp. 81–2; (English background on 'Newbolt Man' in P. Howarth, *Play Up and Play the Game* (London, 1973)).

[103] E.R. Holme, *"Shore"* (Sydney, 1951), p. 128.

[104] Gilbert Murray, *Humanist Essays* (London, 1964), p. 15.

[105] *Commonwealth School Paper for Classes V and VI* 1 (4) (Oct 1904), p. 54; also in G.T. Spaull, *British and Australian Poems*, series I (Sydney, 1944(?)), p. 65; its impact in Brown, 'Muscular Christianity in the Antipodes', at p. 173; Bill Gammage & N. Spearritt, eds, *Australians 1938* (Sydney, 1987), p. 183; R. Butler, *A College in the Wattles: Hahndorf and its Academy* (Adelaide, 1989), pp. 90–1.

[106] Oodgeroo Noonuccal, Goossens Lecture, 9/6/1993, in K. Cochrane, *Oodgeroo* (St Lucia, 1994), pp. 212–3.

[107] V. Sigley, *Australian Mottoes* (Canberra, 1989), p. 132.

[108] G. Souter, *Lion and Kangaroo* (2nd ed, Sydney, 1992), p. 218.

His influence on Australia was to be enormous nevertheless.

In the year Newbolt published his book of verse containing 'Vitaï lampada', an Australian student was in his last year at Newbolt's old school, Clifton.[109] C.E.W. Bean was to celebrate the tradition of such schools in one of his last books, *Here, My Son*, a history of Australian private schools. He wrote 'Melbourne Grammar School looking out on its playing fields recalls Clifton and the Close of which Newbolt sang', and the title is also from Newbolt, from his poem on Clifton Chapel which begins, 'Here, my son, your father thought the thoughts of youth.'[110]

Bean's own father, as classics teacher at Sydney Grammar, had been instrumental in introducing Thomas Arnold of Rugby's plan of cadets, organised sport and a prefect system.[111] The first number of the school magazine, established by Bean senior, says 'the object of the Editors will be to exhibit the mental and physical aspects of school life in their proper relations, and, in imitation of the wisest states of antiquity, to hit the golden mean between athletic idiocy and intellectual priggishness.'[112] He then left to become headmaster of All Saints at Bathurst, a boarding school where the Clifton model could be more perfectly realised.

C.E.W. Bean absorbed all this, but his admiration for the English public school system was subject to one important qualification. The system was class-ridden. But since the upper classes had no genetic advantage, it must be possible for self-reliance and honesty to be distributed across the whole of society. 'Australian experience in this matter is decisive. It goes to the heart of our national philosophy, and I believe it gives our nation something worth adding to the world's ideals.'[113] Bean's ideal was Newbolt's, but retooled for democratic Australian conditions.

In the time between his immersion in private schools and his celebration of them, Bean created one of the most enduring and subtle

---

[109] K.S. Inglis, *C.E.W. Bean, Australian Historian* (St Lucia, 1970), p. 6.

[110] C.E.W. Bean, *Here, My Son* (Sydney, 1950), p. 95; further on the ideologies of these schools in G. Sherington, R.C. Petersen & I. Brice, *Learning to Lead: A History of Girls' and Boys' Corporate Secondary Schools in Australia* (Sydney, 1987), chs 7–8.

[111] C. Turney, 'The advent and adaptation of the Arnold public school tradition in New South Wales', *Australian Journal of Education* 10 (1966): pp. 133–44; also Turney, *Pioneers of Australian Education*, vol. 1 ch. 5; 'Bean, E.', *ADB*, vol. 3 pp. 123–4; similar earlier in Tasmania in F.J. Woodward, *The Doctor's Disciples* (Oxford, 1954), ch. 2.

[112] *The Sydneian* no. 1 (1875), preface, repr. in *Sydneian* no. 362 (July 1969), p. 11.

[113] Bean, *War Aims*, pp. 91, 104–7.

adaptations of a myth, when, as official Australian war historian of the First World War, he put into its canonical form the Anzac legend.

After a degree in classics at Oxford, he worked briefly as a teacher at Sydney Grammar and then a journalist. He travelled to the Darling to see whether rural virtues were to be found in the regions where Wentworth had long before predicted their rise, and reported in the affirmative.[114] On the strength of journalism of this sort, he was chosen as official war correspondent. Landing at Anzac Cove on the first day, he saw the situation that 'Vitaï lampada' describes. 'They had come at last to the ancient test; and in the mind of each man was the question — how would they react to it?'[115] Recording how they did react to it became his life work.

The last pages of the first volume of the *Official History* are taken up with a discussion of what it was that made possible the heroism the *History* has described. It was not habit, love of a fight, belief in the rightness of the cause, hatred of the enemy, love of country, or desire for fame. It was character. 'The Australian force contained more than its share of men who were masters of their own minds and decisions. What was the dominant motive that impelled them? It lay in the mettle of the men themselves. To be the sort of man who would give way when his mates were trusting to his firmness ... that was the prospect which these men would not face.'[116] Earlier he had written:

> The big thing in the war for Australia was the discovery of the character of Australian men. It was character which rushed the hills at Gallipoli and held on there during the long afternoon and night, when everything seemed to have gone wrong and there was only the barest hope of success.[117]

The source of the ideal of character that Bean praised was not only poems like Newbolt's, but Plato's *Republic*. An early private notebook of Bean's contains a series of connected essays on the *Republic* and Aristotle's discussion of the virtues. On Plato's plans to reform the State, Bean wrote, 'What he was anxious to improve was really the Greek character; and as he regarded the State as the educating organisation, he was set upon attaining his object by introducing a method of compulsory education on lines which would be calculated

[114] C.E.W. Bean, *On the Wool Track* (1910, 1925, repr. Sydney, 1963), pp. 24, 71, 78, 97, 102; C.E.W. Bean, *Dreadnought of the Darling* (London, 1911, Sydney, 1956), pp. 216–9.

[115] Bean, *Anzac to Amiens* (Canberra, 1946), p. 79.

[116] Bean, *The Story of Anzac* (1921, repr. St Lucia, 1981), vol. 1 pp. 606–7.

[117] Bean, *In Your Hands, Australians* (1918), in Inglis, p. 21.

to make the best, instead of the worst, of the Greek natural genius.'[118] Other points in the notebook of special interest for Bean's work in history are his discussion of Plato's claim that the state or nation can have the same virtues as individuals, but writ large, so to speak, and refined; of Aristotle's view that a trained habit that acts without needing to think can still be called moral; and Aristotle's description of the 'great-hearted' man.[119]

Bean deliberately avoided classical references in his history, to the extent that the only mention of Troy in his volumes is of a private of that name from Western Australia.[120] But the Anzacs, as Bean portrayed them, were uncannily like the ideal Greeks of Plato and Aristotle. The first volume opened with a survey of the character of Australians at the outbreak of the War. The Australians had developed the British character — and indeed only in Australia and New Zealand *were* there British, as opposed to English, Scots, Irish and Welsh — in certain novel directions. Having begun with immigrants, who were naturally more adventurous, and having developed in an active, outdoor and well-fed life, the Australian character was peculiarly independent, able in emergencies, and nearly classless, especially the man of the younger generation 'largely trained in State schools'. 'The only restraint he recognised before the war was self-imposed. This characteristic gave him a reputation for indiscipline, but it endowed him with a power of swift individual decision and, in critical moments, of self-control, which became conspicuous during the war'. Unlike Americans, who admired the strong, the Australian's individualism tended towards protecting the weak. 'These qualities of independence, originality, the faculty of rising to an occasion, and loyalty to a "mate", conspicuous in the individual Australian, became recognisable as parts of the national character.' It was the War that made individual characters into a collective one; before that, there was no recognition of a national character or even a nation.[121]

---

[118] C.E.W. Bean, Notebook on philosophy, c. 1902?, Australian War Memorial series AWM38 item 3DRL 6673/861, p. 45A.

[119] Notebook, pp. 42A, 32, 30A; the same material discussed in R.R.P. Barbour, *Ethical Theory* (Adelaide, 1933), chs 6 & 8; recent revivals in P. Crittenden, *Learning to Be Moral: Philosophical Thoughts about Moral Development* (Atlantic Highlands, 1990), ch. 4; G. Partington, 'Moral education in some English-speaking societies: Antinomian and fundamentalist challenges', *Journal of Moral Education* 19 (1990): pp. 182–91; C. Gleeson, *Striking a Balance: Teaching Values and Freedom* (Sydney, 1993).

[120] Inglis, *C.E.W. Bean*, p. 21.

[121] Bean, *Story of Anzac*, vol. 1 pp. 5–7; further on Bean's intentions in D.A. Kent, 'The Anzac Book and the Anzac legend: C.E.W. Bean as editor and image maker', *Historical Studies* 21 (1985): pp. 376–90; A. Thomson,

Bean's attitude to religion had a close connection with what he chose to praise. A passage in his notebook is interesting as a record of how study of the classics can lead to a scepticism about religious dogmas:

> The Greeks found, as every nation has found, or will find, that the fairy tales and ballads which formed their religion — or upon which it was based, were not compatible with their ideas about the gods. They had begun to speculate about what was right and what was wrong, and why this was virtuous, and that sinful; and so not only was their curiosity stimulated by this inconsistency into a further inquiry; but they began to explain their old fables as allegorical, and as really not being as bad as they appeared to be. This is a state of affairs which always has, and always will cause scepticism; farfetched explanations of timeworn theories are not unheard of in these days; and there is little doubt that they explain a large part of latter day scepticism.[122]

The answer of Plato and Aristotle to the problem, as developed by Bean at some length, was a virtue-based ethics unconnected with religion.

Like Bean himself, the Anzac was apparently 'seldom religious in the sense in which the word is generally used. So far as he held a prevailing creed, it was a romantic one inherited from the gold-miner and the bushman, of which the chief article was that a man should at all times and at any cost stand by his mate. This was and is the one law which the good Australian must never break. It is bred in the child and stays with him through life.'[123]

Some detail was added by Bean in a later book:

> Most nations practice, besides their formally acknowledged religions, the cult of some ideal of manhood or womanhood. With the primitive races it may be that of headhunter. The Japanese 'Bushido' code, that of a warrior devoted to duty, is famous and indeed well-advertised. But history will perhaps judge its influence on mankind to be slight compared with that of the English code of 'gentleman'. This code is based on Christian ethics, but is probably more powerful than formal Christianity in moulding the actions of those nations that it affects. It is clearly derived from the ideal of the knight of chivalry; and its own offspring is the slightly different ideal of 'sportsman', which, transmitted with the spread of games, has become a world-wide standard. It is probably even true to

'"Steadfast until death"'? C.E.W. Bean and the representation of Australian military manhood', *Australian Historical Studies* 23 (1989): pp. 462–78; connections with earlier literature in R. Dixon, *Writing the Colonial Adventure* (Cambridge, 1995), ch. 8.

[122] Bean, Notebook, p. 43A.

[123] *Story of Anzac*, vol. 1, p. 6; earlier in R. Ward, *The Australian Legend* (2nd ed, Melbourne, 1965), p. 170.

C.E.W. Bean lays a wreath on the Stone of Remembrance, Australian War Memorial, Canberra, Anzac Day, 1952 (Australian War Memorial)

say that the average English, American, and Australian youth, involved in a moral problem in civil life or on the battlefield, is more guided in his action by the desire to 'play the game' than by the beliefs of formal religion.[124]

(Also in connection with games, the incident at The Nek where a soldier runs to his death 'like a schoolboy in a footrace', which forms the climax of the film *Gallipoli*, is from Bean's account.[125]) It is not wholly true, however, that Bean reduced all religion to action through character. In a poem of 1915, he did see the possibility of a God who has some beneficent but unknown purpose in destruction.[126] But in general, literal gods were as irrelevant for him as for Plato and Aristotle — and scepticism about morals as unappealing.

Bean permitted himself some allusions to classical themes in the last paragraph of his last volume:

[124] Bean, *War Aims*, pp. 89–90; cf. Notebook, p. 26A.

[125] *Story of Anzac*, vol. 2 pp. 616–8.

[126] Bean, in *The Anzac Book*, ed. C.E.W. Bean (1916, repr. Melbourne, 1975), p. 11.

What these men did nothing can alter now. The good and the bad, the greatness and smallness of their story will stand. Whatever of glory it contains nothing now can lessen. It rises, as it will always rise, above the mists of ages, a monument to great-hearted men; and for their nation, a possession for ever.[127]

Those who understood what Bean had done praised him in the same terms. Sir Keith Hancock, presenting Bean with an honorary degree, said he could associate himself with the aim of Herodotus, 'To preserve from decay the remembrance of what men have done, and to prevent great and wonderful actions ... from losing their due meed of glory.'[128]

Bean's positive vision survived the Great War, which tarnished and even destroyed so many European images of honour.

The philosopher D.H. Monro expressed a conventional view in writing, in 1950, 'One main reason why there has been a moral up-heaval in our time is that the generation which became involved in the 1914–18 war found the *Boys' Own Paper* morality on which most of them had been reared utterly inadequate to the very grim realities which they were called upon to face.'[129] There is at least some truth in such comments with respect to Europe, where there was widespread disillusion with the War and the men who had fought it. The mood was well caught by David Low, the former Sydney *Bulletin* cartoonist, whose invention Colonel Blimp blunders about London's bath houses delivering opinions like 'Bayonets bring out the best of a man — and it stays out' and 'There must be no monkeying with the liberty of Indians to do what they're dashed well told.'[130] But Australia saw little of either pacifism or reactions like the Fascism of Central Europe, the defeatism of France, or British appeasement. Instead, Australia chose to say, 'Lest we forget,' and 'They did not die in vain.'

The peculiarly Australian reaction is evident in the strong memo-ries kept alive in schools of their own war dead,[131] and also in the public war memorials, which were built much more frequently in Australia and New Zealand than in Britain. They were 'sacred places',

---

[127] Bean, *The AIF in France During the Allied Offensive, 1918* (*Official History*, vol. VI) (Sydney, 1942), p. 1096.

[128] Inglis, *C.E.W. Bean*, p. 31.

[129] D.H. Monro, 'Pawns against the devil', *Melbourne Studies in Education 1963*: pp. 23–46, at p. 43 (Monro's early life and pacifism recounted in D.H. Monro, *Fortunate Catastrophes: An Anecdotal Autobiography* (Melbourne, 1991); his papers on the Orr case at National Library of Australia, MS 9643).

[130] D. Low, *Low's Autobiography* (London, 1956), ch. 20.

[131] D.T. Merrett, '"The School at war": Scotch College and the Great War', *Melbourne Studies in Education 1982*: pp. 209–33; G. Dening, *Xavier: A Centenary History* (Melbourne, 1978), pp. 103–7.

a non-denominational, indeed non-Christian, though to a degree religious, commemoration of the fallen.[132] The Hall of Memory in the centre of the Australian War Memorial in Canberra has windows depicting 'what were judged to be the outstanding qualities of the Australian serviceman and woman': West Bay: Social Qualities. Comradeship, Ancestry, Patriotism, Chivalry, Loyalty. South Bay: Personal Qualities. Resource, Candour, Devotion, Curiosity, Independence. East Bay: Fighting Qualities. Coolness. Control, Audacity, Endurance.[133] The windows, and the huge mosaic above them representing the earth surrendering the souls of the dead to the heavens, were the master work of M. Napier Waller, the culmination of a career that included earlier works on such classical themes as 'Virgil' and 'Pastoral'.[134]

John Anderson's view that the war memorials were idols was crude and oversimplified, but not a pure fantasy.

Australia was also unusual in making Anzac Day its main national celebration. And what it celebrates is not military glory; choosing a military failure as the occasion to mark ensures that what is commemorated is what Bean wrote of — sacrifice and character. Its meaning was explained for schools in *New Syllabus English and Australian History for Fifth Classes, with Civics and Moral Stories* of 1937, which has as its last chapter 'The days we celebrate'. The first is Anzac Day, the lesson of which is:

> We can say of these men, what the poet, Henry Newbolt, has said of English youths who died elsewhere:–
> 'Twas the right death to die, lad,
> A gift without regret.

[132] K. Inglis, *Sacred Places: War Memorials in the Australian Landscape* (Melbourne, 1998), especially Introduction and pp. 458–65; also S.P. Kenaelly, 'Anzac memorials', *IPA Review* 43 (4) (Winter 1990): pp. 54–9.

[133] G. Freeland, *Canberra Cosmos* (Sydney, 1995), pp. 64–80; K.S. Inglis, 'The Anzac tradition', *Meanjin* 24 (1965): pp. 25–44, at pp. 43–4; Anon, *Guide to Australian War Memorial* (Canberra, 1959), pp. 2–4; on Bean and the spiritual meanings of the Australian War Memorial, K.S. Inglis, 'A sacred place: The making of the Australian War Memorial', *War and Society* 3 (2) (Sept 1985): pp. 99–126; also Clark, *History of Australia*, vol. 6 p. 307.

[134] G. Fry & A. Gray, *Masterpieces of the Australian War Memorial* (Adelaide, 1982), pp. 124–5; N. Draffin, *The Art of M. Napier Waller* (Melbourne, 1978); *Art in Australia* 3rd series no. 26 (Dec 1928), plates 50–51; 'The Pastoral Pursuits of Australia' (1927) in C. Allen, *Art in Australia* (London, 1997), p. 95; Pythagoreanism in Melbourne classical architecture in G. Pont, 'The cinema as secular temple: ethos, form and symbolism of the Capitol Theatre', *Nexus Network Journal*, 5 (2) (Autumn 2003)

We owe a duty to the fallen Anzacs, and we must see to it that these brave men have not died in vain.[135]

'Without regret' may be an impossible demand, but it is certainly part of the classical legacy. 'Aristotle says that the dying hero is sufficiently rewarded by the intense sense of true honour with which he is inspired in the ecstasy of his noble enthusiasm.'[136] For those left behind, the best that could be done in the way of consolation, short of religion strictly so called, is another story from Livy. An earthquake opens a chasm in the forum, and the soothsayers divine that the city must sacrifice its greatest asset to propitiate the gods. Marcus Curtius, representing the youth of the nation, leaps fully armed into the abyss.[137]

THAT completes an account of the implicit philosophy embodied in secular Australian education, as it stood in its heyday around the 1930s. Before looking at its decay and at attempts to replace it, it is natural to ask whether this ideology had any plan on how to inspire the youth when they grew up. There were several organisations in the field.

The most important was Freemasonry. The story of the Masons and their influence is one of the great untold narratives of Australian history. They were in at the beginning of most of the significant developments in Australia. Joseph Banks was a Mason, and in the early colony, so were Governor Macquarie, Francis Greenway, and the explorers Oxley, Hume and Leichhardt.[138] The first recognised Lodge, the Lodge of Social and Military Virtues, arrived with the regiment it was attached to in 1814,[139] and the Lodges spread widely during the Gold Rushes, during the 1890s, and again between the Wars.[140] Almost all of the conservative Prime Ministers up to 1972 — Barton, Reid, Cook, Bruce, Page, Menzies, Fadden, McEwen, Gorton and

---

[135] G.T. Spaull, *New Syllabus English and Australian History for Fifth Classes, with Civics and Moral Stories* (Sydney, 1937), p. 214; opposite views of these matters in P. Patton & R. Poole, eds, *War/Masculinity* (Sydney, 1985).

[136] Woolley, *Lectures Delivered in Australia*, pp. 383–4; cf. F. Anderson, 'The happy warrior', *AJPP* 9 (1931): pp. 263–8.

[137] Evans, 'Lessons from Livy', at p. 28.

[138] G.H. Cumming, *The Foundations of Freemasonry in Australia* (West Pennant Hills, 1992), pp. 1–10; 'Was Sir Joseph Banks a Mason?', *NSW Freemason* 47 (1952): p. 185; Gascoigne, *The Enlightenment*, pp. 25–6.

[139] Cumming, *Foundations of Freemasonry*, p. 6; earlier, *Historical Records of Australia* series 1 vol. 4 p. 341; K.R. Cramp & G. Mackaness, *A History of the United Grand Lodge of New South Wales* (Sydney, 1938), ch. 4.

[140] M. Hogan, *The Sectarian Strand* (Ringwood, 1987), pp. 197–202, 217; and in many local histories.

McMahon — were Masons,[141] as were such quintessentially Australian heroes as Sir Charles Kingsford Smith, Sir Don Bradman and Sir Edward 'Weary' Dunlop. Freemasonry was particularly strong in the armed forces, the police, banks, AMP, the state and Commonwealth public services and the councils of country towns. Membership increased again after the Second World War, as returned servicemen used the Lodges to continue the mateship of the armed forces. A high point of membership was reached in the mid-1950s, with some 330,000 members in about 2000 Lodges, or one Australian man in sixteen.[142] Since there were virtually no Catholic members and very few blue collar workers, this represents an extraordinary penetration of the target group, the 'managerial classes'.

What did Masonic membership mean? It could, of course, mean nothing, as it seems to have for Menzies, for example. But for those who took membership more seriously, and many did, there was more on offer. Freemasonry is a philosophy.

It is not easy to say precisely what that philosophy is. That is not only because part of it is kept secret, but also because putting 'doctrines' into propositional form is not the preferred method of exposition of the Masonic point of view, even to initiates. Freemasonry is officially 'a system of morality veiled in allegory',[143] and the allegory and symbolism, intended to assist the imagination and memory of the initiate,[144] are the main method of instruction, and the interpretation of the symbols is to some extent left to the individual. But the general outline of the system is not secret. The only Masonic 'dogma', strictly speaking, is the existence of God, belief in which is a condition of entry. Belief in immortality is, however, strongly suggested.[145] Beyond that, religious matters are left to the individual's own sect; a Mason is expected to pursue his own faith, which may be of any Christian or other theistic persuasion.

---

[141] *Freemasonry: Australia's Prime Ministers* (Masonic Historical Society of N.S.W., booklet 2, Sydney, 1994); G.H. Cumming, *Freemasonry and Federation* (Sydney, 2001); some misplaced fears in ASIO file 'Freemasonry: Communist penetration', Australian Archives A6122 item 401.

[142] NSW membership figures in M.H. Kellerman, *From Diamond Jubilee to Centenary: History of Forty Years of the United Grand Lodge of Freemasonry in New South Wales, 1948–1988* (Sydney, 1990), vol. IV, ch. 5.

[143] M.H. Kellerman, 'Freemasonry', in *Australian Encyclopaedia* (4th ed, Sydney, 1983), pp. 241–4; C.D. Morpeth, 'A peculiar system of morality', *NSW Freemason* 30 (2) (Feb 1935): pp. 43–5.

[144] E.A. Hough, 'What is Freemasonry?', *NSW Freemason* 33 (1938): pp. 561–2.

[145] W.C. Bowler, 'Immortality', *NSW Freemason* 22 (1927): pp. 169–70.

The centre of Freemasonry is not doctrinal but moral. 'The whole purpose of Freemasonry is to teach the Moral Law and show that man should live rightly with his fellow man under the all-seeing eye of God.'[146] The normal meanings of the symbols mostly concern morality. The well-known symbols of square and compasses, for example, symbolise respectively rectitude in general and the circle separating right behaviour from wrong. Truth and honesty in dealings are crucial.[147] Men have a 'duty of developing innate powers' and 'bodily and mental functions responsive to our will',[148] and the old image of 'building the temple' is taken to be a symbol of a man's building of his own character; 'in the building of character his greatest work.'[149] The origins of these ideas lie in Freemasonry's being an institutional embodiment of the Enlightenment — not the near-atheist radical Enlightenment of the French *philosophes*, but the tolerant and constitutional English version.[150]

If this ideal is reminiscent of the one traditionally favoured by headmasters, that is no accident. The harmony of the two is the theme of an address given to the Lodge for Sydney Grammar Old Boys in 1935, which expresses concisely and accurately the ideal of character of the Great Public Schools:

> To go 'Forward' requires four qualities, which every Mason must possess, should he desire to answer the challenge to-day, qualities which I believe are those being instilled into the characters of the boys of the G.P.S., viz.:–
>
> (1) Courage
> (2) Energy
> (3) Alertness
> (4) Vision

[146] 'Masonry and the moral law', *NSW Freemason* 42 (1947): p. 185.

[147] F.S. McDowell, 'Masonic philosophy', in K.R. Cramp, *From Jubilee to Diamond Jubilee: History of Ten Years of the United Grand Lodge of Freemasonry in New South Wales, 1938–1948*, pp. 262–4; on the author see K. Henderson, *Masonic Grand Masters of Australia* (Bayswater, 1988), pp. 119–21; also M.H. Kellerman, *Some Words and Thoughts* (Sydney, 1996).

[148] A.R. Wiseman, 'Duty to self', *NSW Freemason* 42 (1947): pp. 33–4.

[149] H.V. Golding, 'Character and conduct: High roads to Masonry', *NSW Freemason* 32 (1937): pp. 145–6; H.O. Wallace, 'The ethics of Masonry', *NSW Freemason* 21 (1926): pp. 465–6.

[150] European background in M.C. Jacob, *Living the Enlightenment: Freemasonry and Politics in Eighteenth-Century Europe* (New York, 1991); Australian knowledge of it in M. Conway, 'Freemasonry and the Age of Enlightenment', *Masonic Research in South Australia* (South Australian Lodge of Research) 1 (1990–4): pp. 19–21; N.J. McDonald, 'Desaguliers', *New South Wales Freemason* 29 (1934): pp. 81–2.

There can be no progress or success without courage. Fear is man's greatest enemy. It destroys his moral fibre and unfits him for the conflicts which must be fought in every human experience ... By 'energy' I mean 'activity', 'work', 'doing things' as compared with idealising, theorising and meditating, which alone cannot drive forward. Masonry is a Life, not only a philosophy and a ritual ... Masonry teaches us, as did our old schoolmasters, the danger of excess in everything, to avoid vice, to curb the aspirations of unbridled ambition, to moderate the ebullitions of wrath, to conquer anger and temper and be not envious and covetous. To do this we must ever be alert and watchful.

Lastly, without a wide, big vision we cannot go forward and answer the challenge. A great prophet truly said, 'Where there is no vision the people perish.' Masonry will give men a wide vision, for it teaches tolerance and sympathy and points out 'the whole duty of man.' It gives him vision not only of this Life, but of that to come. It takes him beyond the narrow confines of this little Life, into that state 'where the blessed ever rest in eternal peace.' Masonry by its ceremonies and its symbols clearly points out to him that path which if followed closely, will lead from birth to boyhood to manhood to Death and then to immortality.[151]

Harmony has not characterised the relations of Freemasonry with the more dogmatic religions, and the reasons for conflict concern basic questions of the relation between philosophy and faith. An Australian article on Masonic philosophy, after invoking Plato and Bacon, says 'The Philosopher-Knight is engaged in a battle, as is every Freemason, the eternal struggle of good and evil, of Light against Darkness, portrayed in the scriptures of the world's faiths.'[152] Freemasonry insists that it is not a religion, but admits to being 'religious', or having something to say in areas already occupied by religion.[153] Its tolerance of all religions — useful in a country with the same ethnic composition as Ulster — can easily give rise to the impression that dogmatic differences do not matter, even though that is never asserted explicitly. These suspicions led to a long-running and well-known conflict between Catholics and Masons. Behind Archbishop Vaughan's intransigence over the education question lay his belief that he was faced with a literal Masonic conspiracy. The campaign for free, secular and compulsory education was, he believed, a plot by 'the Sect, the Church of the Revolution, the International Secret Society, which is weaving its network around the

---

[151] J.L. Cowie, 'The spirit of the Great Public Schools', *NSW Freemason* 30 (1935): pp. 321–2; further in Cowie's books of Masonic addresses: *Facing the East* (Sydney, 1934); *Schools for Freemasons* (Sydney, 1946); *The 24 Inch Gauge* (Sydney, 1956).
[152] E.M. Casperz, 'Why philosophy in a Commandery?', *NSW Freemason* 41 (1946): pp. 165–7.
[153] 'Masonry not a religion', *NSW Freemason* 28 (1933): pp. 208, 223.

world', that is, Freemasonry. Dogmatically opposed to all dogmas, they aimed, he thought, to break down faith by secular schooling, in support of the one dogma of their own, 'that absolute liberty and unlimited freedom to do, say, or think anything he likes, is the natural and inalienable right of every man.'[154] His conspiracy theory was not true (at least of Australia, though something like it was true of France). It was true, though, that the founders of the secular University of Sydney, W.C. Wentworth and Professor Woolley, were Masons, as was the man in charge of the curriculum in the state schools after the Education Act, William Wilkins.[155]

The significance was further heightened by the fact that several other mass organisations imitated or descended from Freemasonry, to varying degrees, and shared some of its moral tendencies. The parallels between Freemasonry and the Boy Scouts were obvious enough. Masons were often surprised to learn that Baden-Powell himself was not one, but his views were close to theirs and the defect was remedied when he was succeeded as Chief Scout by Lord Somers, formerly Governor of Victoria and Masonic Grand Master of that state.[156] In Australia especially, scouting was often run by Masons, who regarded it as an extension of their own ideas.[157]

The benefit societies like the Oddfellows, which together provided assistance to over 40 per cent of the population around 1900, were more concerned with material assistance than the Masons, but in other respects adopted Masonic practices and ideology — ritual, regalia, symbolism such as the all-seeing eye of God, a non-sectarian and international ideal of fraternity, commitment to high ideals of personal behaviour, and a vigorous internal democracy.[158] And these

---

[154] R.B. Vaughan, *Hidden Springs, or the Perils of the Future and How to Meet Them* (Sydney, 1876); J. Franklin, 'Catholics versus Masons', *Journal of the Australian Catholic Historical Society* 20 (1999): pp. 1–15.

[155] 'Woolley, John', *ADB* vol. 6 pp. 435–7; 'Wilkins, William', *ADB* vol. 6 pp. 400–2; 'William Charles Wentworth — certificate of reception into the degree of Rose Croix, presented to him in Paris, 1818', Mitchell Library, MLMSS 6437.

[156] Henderson, *Masonic Grand Masters*, pp. 180–1; A. Gregory, 'Lord Somers' camp: A successful social experiment', *Royal Historical Society of Victoria Journal* 56 (3) (June 1985): pp. 25–32.

[157] 'Freemasonry and scouting', ch. 18 of Kellerman, *From Diamond Jubilee to Centenary*; N. Johnson, 'Scouting and freemasonry', *NSW Freemason* 20 (6) (Apr 1988): pp. 19–20.

[158] D.G. Green & L.G. Cromwell, *Mutual Aid or Welfare State: Australia's Friendly Societies* (Sydney, 1984), ch. 2; G. Blainey, *Odd Fellows: A History of IOOF Australia* (Sydney, 1991), pp. 45, 57, 63; E.R. Guiler, 'Oddfellows at New Norfolk', *Tasmanian Historical Research Association, Papers and Proceedings* 40 (1993): pp. 109–17.

societies shaded into Trade Unions. The Friendly Society of Agricultural Labourers, or Tolpuddle Martyrs, organised itself into Lodges
with a high moral tone and Masonic-style ritual, and it was the oaths
at initiation that were the cause or pretext of their transportation to
Botany Bay.[159]

Perhaps the first workers' association in Australia was the Stone-
mason Benefit Society, formed in Sydney (at the Freemason's Hotel)
in 1828.[160] The tone and symbolism of such early societies are indicated by a medal presented by the Australian Union Benefit Society
in 1834: 'On one side there is, in rich embossed work, the Eye of
Providence, with its rays reflecting on a device of four united hands,
in which are contained the Rose, Shamrock, Thistle and Maize Stalk,
respectively, surrounded by a laurel wreath, and superscribed by the
motto — "United to relieve, not combined to injure."'[161] Later
unionism stems from the unions of skilled workers in the struggle for
the eight-hour day in Victoria in 1850s, the Operative Stonemasons'
Society and the Typographical Society, which were organised into
'Lodges' of 'Brothers', and acted also as friendly societies. Their aims
were not simply better pay and conditions: they were indeed prepared to trade wages for shorter hours, to provide leisure for the
pursuit of moral and intellectual development.[162] Before their
radicalisation in the 1890s, the unions of skilled workers like printers
and Hunter Valley coalminers had an ethos that favoured co-opera-
tives, friendly societies, adult education, thrift and temperance, and
their leaders were prominent in local government and in moves for
constitutional reform.[163] The Unions did not retain Lodge-style ritual,

[159] J. Marlow, *The Tolpuddle Martyrs* (London, 1971), pp. 44–8.
[160] *Monitor* 23/6/1828, p. 1232; *Sydney Gazette* 25/6/1828, p. 1.
[161] *Sydney Gazette* 24/4/1834; these societies described in L. Thomas, *The Development of the Labour Movement in the Sydney District of New South Wales* (MA Thesis, Sydney University, 1919, repr. Canberra, 1962), chs. 3–4; Atkinson & Aveling, *Australians 1838*, pp. 134–5; Gascoigne, *The Enlightenment*, p. 115; *Articles and Rules for the Regulation of the Melbourne Union Benefit Society* (Melbourne, 1839, repr. as *Premier Victorian Pamphlet*, Melbourne, 1937).
[162] H. Hughes, 'The eight-hour day and the development of the labour movement in Victoria in the Eighteen-Fifties', *Historical Studies* 9 (1959–61): pp. 396–412; R. Gollan, *Radical and Working Class Politics* (Melbourne, 1960), pp. 71–3; B. McKinlay, *Australian Labor History in Documents* (Melbourne, 1990), vol. 1 pp. 8–9; J. Hagan, *Printers and Politics* (Canberra, 1966), ch. 2; K.D. Buckley, *The Amalgamated Engineers in Australia, 1852–1920* (Canberra, 1970), ch. 1.
[163] E. McEwen, 'Coalminers in Newcastle, New South Wales: A labour aristocracy?', in *Common Cause*, ed. E. Fry (Sydney, 1986), pp. 77–92; R.

but ideals of brotherhood and solidarity remained, as did practices of democratic internal self-government.[164] W.G. Spence, effectively the founder of the Australian Workers' Union in the 1890s, claimed:

> Unionism has a markedly beneficial effect on character. It inculcates brotherhood. It gives the right to one member of the union to speak to another if he thinks that he is doing or contemplating a wrong act. The effect of discipline is seen at its best, and its effect is to make men better citizens, better husbands, and better fathers ... Unionism came to the Australian bushman as a religion. It came bringing salvation from years of tyranny. It had in it that feeling of mateship which he understood already, and which always characterised the action of one 'white man' to another. Unionism extended the idea, so a man's character was gauged by whether he stood true to Union rules or 'scabbed' it on his fellows.'[165]

It is the union's performance of a Lodge function that Henry Lawson celebrates in his story, 'The Union buries its dead', in which a few Union members pay for the burial of an unknown man found drowned with a Union ticket in his pocket. Lawson has the man belong to a different sect to his buriers to illustrate that 'Unionism is stronger than creed.'[166] Lawson saw unionism as not merely stronger than creed, but itself a 'new and grand religion', which would swallow up all the old 'isms'.[167]

For those excluded by these movements, such as women, but who were still inclined to congregate in the name of virtue, there was the alternative of the temperance movement. Though it did not approve of ritual, it stood for the same virtues of self-control and moral enlightenment as the Lodges, and also transcended sects. It too gave its members practice in the running of affairs, and was thus a seedbed of women's suffrage.[168] When the temperance movement faded, it was in some ways replaced by the Country Women's Association.[169]

Gollan, *The Coalminers of New South Wales* (Melbourne, 1963), p. 28; 'Estell, John', *ADB* vol. 8 pp. 441–2.

[164] Bob James, 'Benefit societies and freemasons in labour history', *Illawarra Unity* 1 (3) (1998): pp. 5–21 (www.takver.com/history/tragedy.htm with further articles at www.takver.com/history/benefit).

[165] W.G. Spence, *Australia's Awakening* (Sydney, 1909), pp. 524, 78; cf. C. Lansbury, 'The miner's right to mateship', *Meanjin* 25 (1966): pp. 435–43.

[166] *Henry Lawson: Prose Writings*, ed. Roderick, pp. 81–4.

[167] H. Lawson, 'A new religion' (1890), in *Henry Lawson: Autobiographical and Other Writings*, ed. C. Roderick (Sydney, 1972), pp. 16–18.

[168] Roe, *Quest for Authority*, pp. 165–74; E. Windschuttle, 'Women, class and temperance: Moral reform in Eastern Australia 1832–1857', *Push from the Bush* 3 (1979): pp. 5–21; A. Hyslop, 'Temperance, Christianity and feminism: The Women's Christian Temperance Union of Victoria, 1887–97', *Historical Studies* 17 (1976): pp. 27–49; J. Luxton, 'The Women's

In the same way that the CWA was a modernised version of the Victorian moral organisations, the lodges were to some extent replaced by the 'service clubs' like Rotary, Lions and Apex. They abandoned ritual and secrecy, but retained the outward-looking ideals of fellowship and practical 'service to the community'.[170]

B Y THE 1950s, at the latest, the philosophy or ideology summed up in Empire, Scouts, Lodge and playing the game was beginning to look moth-eaten, pompous and narrow-minded. Traditional thinking was running on empty. The certainties of Absolute Idealism had faded, and the ideals of the founders of secular education had been lost, or at least the reasons for them had been.

When this ideology attempted to explain itself in the public arena, the effect was ridiculous. The most public expression of the old ways was the extraordinary 'Call to Australia' issued by leading Australian churchmen and judges on Remembrance Day, 1951. The twelve signatories included Cardinal Gilroy, the Anglican Primate of Australia, Sir Mellis Napier, then Chief Justice of South Australia and former Masonic Grand Master, and Sir John Morris, Chief Justice of Tasmania and the man chiefly responsible for appointing Sydney Sparkes Orr over more-qualified but less Christian candidates. If there was ever a moment when the traditional order was secure, it was 1951. The Menzies era was just beginning, and even the defeat of his anti-Communist referendum appeared to be a victory for Australian decency; the King whose simple courage had seen the Empire through the War was still on the throne; traditional religion was expanding;[171] radicalism of all kinds was in retreat. Constitutional forms had sur-

Christian Temperance Union of South Australia', *Cabbages and Kings* 16 (1988): pp. 124–32; J. Pixley, 'Wowser and pro-woman politics: Temperance against Australian patriarchy', *Australian Journal of Sociology* 27 (1991): pp. 293–314; I.R. Tyrrell, *Woman's World, Woman's Empire* (Chapel Hill, 1991); J.B. Hirst, *The World of Albert Facey* (Sydney, 1992), pp. 39–47; N.J. Kyle, 'Give us the franchise ... [and] ... we will show how we will use it', *Journal of the Royal Australian Historical Society* 84 (1998): pp. 56–67; 'McLean, M.', *ADB* vol. 10 p. 331.

[169] H. Townsend, *Serving the Country: The History of the Country Women's Association of New South Wales* (Sydney, 1988), pp. 15–18, 111–2; E.K. Teather, 'The Country Women's Association of New South Wales in the 1920s and 1930s as a counterrevolutionary organisation', *Journal of Australian Studies* 41 (1994): pp. 67–78.

[170] H. Hunt, *The Story of Rotary in Australia 1921–1971* (Sydney?, 1971); R.A. Wild, *Bradstow* (Sydney, 1974), pp. 86–8; Henderson, *Masonic Grand Masters*, p. 120.

[171] D. Hilliard, 'God in the suburbs: The religious culture of Australian cities in the 1950s', *Australian Historical Studies* 24 (1991): pp. 399–419.

vived even socialist government. There was indeed an external threat from the spread of Communism in East Asia, but the mood of the leaders of society was instead of grave concern about the internal forces of evil:

> There are times in the histories of peoples when those charged with high responsibilities should plainly speak their minds.
>
> Australia is in danger. We are in danger from abroad. We are in danger at home. We are in danger from moral and intellectual apathy, from the mortal enemies of mankind which sap the will and darken the understanding and breed evil dissensions. Unless these are withstood, we shall lack moral strength and moral unity sufficient to save our country and our liberties ...
>
> The dangers demand of all good Australians community of thought and purpose. They demand a restoration of the moral order from which alone true social order can derive ...
>
> THEREFORE
>
> we call for a new effort from all Australians to advance moral standards ...
>
> We call for an adequate understanding of the nature of law and of its necessity as the principle of order in a free society.
>
> We call on all Australians to take the active concern in public affairs proper to citizens of a free society ...
>
> We call on our people to think now of the future into which our children go, that we may shape it well and wisely for them.
>
> We call on our people to remember those whose labours opened this land to the uses of mankind; those who bore and reared the children of a new nation; those who died in battle for us, bringing splendour to Australian arms; those who worked with mind and muscle for the heritage which we, please God, shall hold and enlarge for our children and their children.
>
> And that this may be so, we ask that each shall renew in himself the full meanings of the call which has inspired our people in their highest tasks and in their days of danger:
>
> FEAR GOD, HONOUR THE KING.

The Call was printed in every daily newspaper, with favourable editorial comment, and also the *Times*, and broadcast on almost all radio stations. Each state had Call to Australia Standing Committees for several years. Three and a half million copies were printed nationwide, and the Call was the topic of thousands of sermons and talks in schools, Scout groups, Lodges and CWA rooms. A special effort was made at the time of the Coronation, when 'a tastefully de-signed poster in colour directing attention to Her Majesty's personal dedication of herself to the service of her peoples was produced and

6,325 copies were displayed on railway stations, in shop windows and business premises.'[172]

This is an ideology that has over-extended itself. Menzies himself saw the writing on the wall, and his lament is more than a simple repetition of the classical theme of the decay of modern times. He quoted a remark of General Smuts, philosopher and Prime Minister,[173] which he 'would like to hang in every Parliament and Party room, and preach in every school and university': 'There is today a decay of the individual's responsibility and share in government which seems to strike at the roots of our human advance ... The sturdy individualism which inspired progress in the past, which made Rome, which made Scotland, which has created all our best human values, seems to be decaying in the atmosphere of confusion and disillusion of our day.'[174]

But one person's confusion and disillusion is another's excitement and opportunity.

The easier times for youth were certainly part of what caused the change, since a set of ideals (thrift, for example) appropriate to a depression and earlier hard times were not necessarily so evidently useful thereafter. The ideology distressed the children of many parents of the time. Jill Ker Conway writes, 'My mother's code of thrift, sobriety and industry had served her well growing up in a simpler Australian society, but it had little appeal for her children, hungry for excitement and experience, and made aware of a more complex society by their urban schooling.'[175]

Equally unbearable for the more intellectual of the new generation was the unwillingness of the old to engage in argument, and the association of the old order with anti-intellectualism and censorship. Shirley Hazzard recalls, 'the battle against knowledge was fought from an emotional and incoherent concept of "morality".'[176]

It was no match for Anderson and his destructive and relentless criticism. 'Tradition itself invites criticism', he said, 'because it represents certain things as worth while but is unable to give any account

---

[172] Call to the People of Australia — NSW Standing Committee, Annual Report, 1952–1956.

[173] See W.K. Hancock, *Smuts*, vol. 2 (Cambridge, 1968), pp. 176–97; P.H. Partridge, 'Logic and evolution', *AJPP* 12 (1934): pp. 161–72.

[174] Menzies, *Speech is of Time*, pp. 219–20.

[175] J. Ker Conway, *The Road from Coorain* (London, 1989), p. 109; cf. R. Gaita, *Romulus, My Father* (Melbourne, 1998), pp. 103–4.

[176] S. Hazzard, *Coming of Age in Australia* (Sydney, 1985), p. 16; something more hostile in J. Rutherford, *The Gauche Intruder: Freud, Lacan and the White Australian Fantasy* (Melbourne, 2001).

of their value.'[177] Efforts like those of Bruxner and Macdonald, discussed in chapter 1, made some sense to those who shared the loyalties of their own generation, but cut no ice with the contemporaries of the Push.

From the other direction, the gap between the generations was widened by the impression of parents that their offspring were taking from their university education a mere ability to shuffle words, unconnected with the emotional realities that the words should have meant.[178]

But one should not underestimate the ability of an unexpressed tradition to survive as a pattern of actions, however comprehensively it may be mocked by the chattering classes. It is a recurrent theme of classical literature that the last exemplar of true republican values died some time ago, but perhaps, if we care to look, it will not prove that virtue was last seen down the Lachlan years ago.

The biography of Mr Justice Wood, Royal Commissioner into the New South Wales Police Force, is a recognisable one. With a family background where he 'learnt responsibility and self-sufficiency early on', he was a sergeant in the cadets at Knox Grammar, and a useful cricketer and distance runner. A member of the Newport surf lifesaving club, he was injured by his board, and legend has it that he sat stoically while his lip was stitched without anaesthetic. After a university medal in law at Sydney University, he rose to become one of the youngest judges of the Supreme Court, while maintaining a commitment to triathlons and trekking. His work as Royal Commissioner in the mid-1990s was characterised by courageous, intelligent and unrelenting pursuit of the corruption that proved to have been ingrained in many parts of public life.[179]

There was one aspect of the old world order that did survive the acid of the 1960s, at least in part. The last and possibly most widespread idea on how to inspire the youth was to teach them literature. Peter Board's reforms particularly emphasised it, and under the heading, 'General aim in teaching literature', the New South Wales English syllabus of 1911 said, 'The special educating power in Literature lies in its effect in developing the mind, filling it with high ideals, and in its influence in refining and ennobling character.'[180]

---

[177] J. Anderson, 'Socrates as an educator', *Studies in Empirical Philosophy*, p. 207.

[178] E.g. A. Seymour, *The One Day of the Year* (Sydney, 1962), p. 94.

[179] M. Safe, 'The untouchable', *Australian*, magazine 13–14/1/1996, pp. 14–19; J.R.T. Wood, 'Police corruption', *Australian Journal of Forensic Sciences* 32 (1) (2000): pp. 3–10.

[180] NSW Department of Public Instruction, *Courses of Study for High Schools* (Sydney, 1911), p. 18.

We are speaking here of a somewhat more highbrow product than poems like '*Vitaï lampada*', and the philosophy implicit in it is more subtle than the one so far discussed. It is not opposed to what has gone before, but it has a different tone. Where the classical model is stoical in the face of adversity rather than consolatory, masculine, and partaking of the impersonality of antique statuary, the tendency of the kind of literature favoured by teachers of English is to the effusive, the emotional and the colourful. It is Romantic rather than classical. The Romantic view envisages a communion of mind with the world, through which the mind takes on the noble and spiritual qualities actually present in Nature. The faculty that apprehends these qualities is not reason but imagination, and the natural mode of expression of the outcome is not argumentative prose or speeches but odes and sonnets. The favoured seers of the Romantics were Shelley, Keats and most especially, the one we saw Bob Menzies reading as he tramped the sacred Romantic sites of England, Wordsworth.

Wordsworth had a view of the world not unlike that of modern enthusiasts for the environment. It is a 'philosophy of "natural religion" ... in brief it amounts to examples of the way in which Nature, unsophisticated and uncontaminated ... can instruct us "seriously and sweetly, through the affections; melting the heart, and through that instinct of tenderness, developing the understanding."'[181] 'Nature' in Wordsworth — or at least in the popular understanding of him — means especially the English landscape. A reader of his works in Australia was either an English emigrant, for whom his poetry poignantly recalled the 'Home' that had lain about him in his infancy, or an Australian native, for whom England was in effect a construct out of Wordsworth and similar authors.

The Australian landscape, however, was not at all co-operative. Bare and dry, usually silent, it showed little inclination either to instruct the affections or to melt the heart. Barron Field, Judge-Advocate in Macquarie's time, apparently the first to rhyme 'Australia' with 'failure' ('having been born within the sound of Bow Bells, he pro-

---

[181] T.G. Tucker, 'How to read great authors: Wordsworth', *Life* (Aug 1907): pp. 132–4; also explained in B. Spurr, *Literature and Spirituality* (Sydney, 1993), pp. 14–17; A.L. French, 'The "fair seed-time" in Wordsworth's *Prelude*', *Critical Review* 17 (1974): pp. 3–20; W.J.T., 'Some aspects of Wordsworth', *Austral Light* 17 (1916): pp. 538–48; on earlier similar ideas, J. Wall, 'Poetry and Bonaventure's theory of perception', *Parergon* 23 (1979): pp. 29–33; on Wordsworth and rural virtue, M. Keay, *William Wordsworth's Golden Age Theories During the Industrial Revolution in England* (Werribee, 1996); on the development of Romanticism, *Studies in the Genesis of Romantic Theory in the Eighteenth Century* (Cambridge, 1923), by J.G. Robertson, Henry Handel Richardson's husband.

nounces Australia as if it ended with an *r*, and makes it rhyme with *failure*, shrewdly considering the kangaroo a failure on the part of Australian Nature in her awkward attempts to make a proper quadruped for that country'[182]) and later biographer of Wordsworth, attempted to cast the mantle of Wordsworthian sublimity over the Blue Mountains, but the landscape defeated him.[183] Though some of the colonial poets, like Harpur and Kendall, were partly Wordsworthian in their approach to nature,[184] there was little development in this direction. It is notable that Australia's most famous nature poem, Dorothea Mackellar's 'My Country', is utterly un-Wordsworthian. She makes clear her love for the harsh brown land, but there is no suggestion it will reciprocate.

But those of a strong imaginative bent are not ones to be discouraged by an unprepossessing here and now, since they are quite capable of living their mental life in more pleasant surroundings. For such people, Wordsworthianism fulfilled the same role that Absolute Idealism did for those of a more propositional cast of mind — it was a kind of natural religion, free of uncomfortable dogmas but representing the universe as congenial.

Wordsworth was a favourite of Australia's best attempt at a prime ministerial philosopher. Alfred Deakin was always scribbling his thoughts on spiritualism, unsectarian religion, theosophy and so on. President of the Victorian Association of Spiritualists at twenty-two, he widened his views through a huge range of reading, in the search for communion with the 'Infinite Spirit of Unity, Order and Harmony', whose instrument he might be.[185] He produced a book-length manuscript, thankfully unpublished, on 'The Gospel according to Wordsworth' ('the keynote of Wordsworthianism is that Nature is

---

[182] J.D. Lang, *An Historical and Statistical Account of New South Wales* (4th ed, London, 1875), p. 157.

[183] B. Field, *Geographical Memoirs*, quoted in B. Smith, *European Vision and the South Pacific* (2nd ed, Sydney, 1985), p. 241; G. Little, *Barron Field's Memoirs of Wordsworth* (Sydney, 1975); A.D. Cousins, 'Barron Field and the translation of Romanticism to colonial Australia', *Southerly* 58 (4) (Summer 1998–9): pp. 157–74.

[184] J. Wright, *Preoccupations in Australian Poetry* (Melbourne, 1965), pp. 6–9, 23–4, 41; M. Ackland, 'Innocence at risk: Charles Harpur's adaptation of a romantic archetype to the Australian landscape', *AUMLA* 70 (1988): pp. 239–59; E. Perkins, 'The religious faith of Charles Harpur', in *Between Two Worlds*, ed. Clark *et al.*, pp. 3–22; Taylor, *Reading Australian Poetry*, ch. 3; E. Morris Miller, 'O'Dowd's "The Bush": An exposition', *Diogenes* 3 (1957): pp. 18–40; D. Haskell, 'Landscape at the edge of a promise: Neilson and Australian Romanticism', *Meridian* 9 (1990): pp. 133–42.

[185] G. Partington, 'Alfred Deakin and the significant past', *Journal of the Royal Australian Historical Society* 78 (3/4) (1992): pp. 108–19.

active, positive, vital, formative and beautiful — in a word, that Nature is *living*.')[186]

Christopher Brennan gives an unusually clear statement of what the imagination does, as conceived by the poetic tradition. It is not a frenzy, or creative, as widely thought, but 'perceptive', in that it acquaints us with an aspect of reality, an aspect not accessible by sensation and intellect alone. 'Imagination, then, by its own nature, is a symbol of unity which is our true spiritual being: by that scheme of correspondences which is the law of its activity, it symbolizes for us our living relation to that true being, and makes plain to us, but through delight and not through demonstration, the ideal kinship and unity of all things.'[187]

Not long afterwards, Wordsworth's ability to paint the mundane world in idealist colours caught the fancy of the young Menzies when, almost sixteen, he received a copy of Wordsworth's *Poetical Works* as a prize for bible knowledge. His poem three years later, 'To Wordsworth', got to the point of what the poet had to offer:

> Great Master, let us sit and learn of thee!
> Give us the sense of glory that was thine!
> Show us the visions that we do not see,
> Of Nature's wonders, and of things Divine!
>
> ...
>
> Then teach us, guide us ere our faith grow weak,
> Show us the sunset ere its hues depart![188]

Ere we dismiss Ming as a harmful eccentric, we need to recall that the education of almost all Australian pupils introduced them to what one called 'a remarkably disembodied world' of skylarks and haw-

---

[186] J.A. La Nauze, *Alfred Deakin* (Melbourne, 1965), ch. 3; A. Gabay, *The Mystic Life of Alfred Deakin* (Cambridge, 1992); quote from W. Murdoch, *Alfred Deakin* (London, 1923), p. 137; on Deakin's friendship with the American idealist philosopher Josiah Royce, see La Nauze, pp. 123–6, Murdoch, pp. 126–30; letters of Royce to Deakin in *Letters of Josiah Royce*, ed. J. Clendenning (Chicago, 1970), pp. 218, 227, 521, 569; Royce on Australia in 'Reflections after a wandering life in Australasia', *Atlantic Monthly* 63 (May 1889): pp. 675–86, (June 1889): pp. 813–28 and 'Impressions of Australia', *Scribner's Magazine* 9 (Jan 1891): pp. 75–87; F.M. Oppenheim, *Royce's Voyage Down Under* (Lexington, 1980).

[187] C. Brennan, 'Vision, imagination and reality' (1901), in *the Prose of Christopher Brennan*, ed. A.R. Chisholm & J.J. Quinn (Sydney, 1962), pp. 38–9; discussion in Taylor, *Reading Australian Poetry*, ch. 4.

[188] *Melbourne University Magazine* 7 (2) (1913), p. 57, quoted in Brett, *Robert Menzies' Forgotten People*, p. 129; similar from Deakin in Murdoch, pp. 29–30; Sydney parallels in Melleuish, *Cultural Liberalism*, p. 96.

thorn,[189] mediated by English poetry. Andrew Riemer, a Jewish immigrant child with no natural ties to either the physical or cultural environment, recalls:

> [Tennyson's] poetry, and that of Wordsworth, Keats and Shelley ... provided an escape from and a consolation for the ugliness and meanness of the world in which we were forced to live. Neither the physical world we inhabited, nor any of the poetry produced by it, could provide such escape or consolation. The windows of my classroom did not give onto a sylvan glade, but looked out on a busy thoroughfare where lorries laboured up a hill past the garish bunting of second-hand car yards. The literature of England conducted us into the world of the romantic imagination which served one of the essential needs of adolescence. It also catered generously for others: a heroic or noble past in which we could participate, and ethical structures to provide models for fantasies, if not for actual life.

> These are contentious issues to raise in the current climate of cultural nationalism. The literature we were required to read at school — and those other books to which we were gradually drawn after many of us started to discard our infatuation with a philistine way of life — provided models of loyalty, altruism, courage and perseverance which, once again, appealed to our adolescent need for imaginative structures that seemed to avoid the compromises we were instinctively making in our daily lives. Literature gave us heroes to worship. It gave us, for instance, Henry V, whom many of us got to know by way of Olivier's stirring film, this leading us, in turn, to reconsider our scorn for Shakespeare. It gave us Sidney Carton; it gave us some of Scott's noble and romantic creatures. It gave us, on a more familiar and domestic level, Jane Austen's characters and the world in which they lived, a cosy rural England, where the values of good breeding, politeness, and consideration for others were mixed with the art of conversation and other civilised accomplishments.[190]

The loss of those models is lamented by A.D. Hope in his poem 'The Sacred Way':

> I wake in the night. I turn and think of the age.
> What image has it of man; what roots for the mind?
> What names now does imagination find
> To fix our heritage?

---

[189] H. Harris, *The Balance of Improbabilities* (Oxford, 1987), p. 3; cf. Horne, *Education,* p. 161.

[190] A. Riemer, *Inside, Outside* (Sydney, 1992), p. 157; quoted and discussed in R. Hughes, *The Culture of Complaint* (New York, 1993), p. 90; similar in M. Boyd, *Day of My Delight* (Melbourne, 1965), pp. 27–31; Souter, *Idle Hill of Summer,* pp. 116–7; C. Veliz, 'A world made in England', *Quadrant* 27 (3) (Mar 1983): pp. 8–19; exactly as intended by earlier education reformers: F. Tate, *Literature as a Study for the Teacher* (Melbourne, 1893), quoted in R.J.W. Selleck, *Frank Tate* (Melbourne, 1982), pp. 74–6.

The world I grew up in now belongs to the past;
Round my cradle, behind my pillow there stood
Hercules, Samson, Roland, Robin Hood,
To say: Stand firm, stand fast!

My unripe soul, groping to fill its need,
Found in those legends a food by which it grew.
Whatever we learned, the heroes were what we knew.
We were fortunate indeed.

To have lost that world. How shall my son go on
To form his archetypal image of man?
Frankenstein? Faust? Dracula? Don Juan?
O Absolom, my son![191]

It is a training in the imagination, certainly, with the promise of stocking the internal cinema with a rich supply of images. At least, the first half of Riemer's quote concentrates on the pictorial aspect of the imagination, its role as a storehouse and organ of recombination of visual images, where planning and design take place.[192] The second half of the quote, and Hope's poem, develop the other role of the imagination, the one especially relevant to ethics and literature. This is the possibility of imagining ourselves in the place of a literary or real character. Seen from this point of view, the important genre of literature is not the ode or the epic, but the novel, which can develop character as fully and naturalistically as possible.

The novel is, in general, about ethics in the sense of characters debating how to live, in their situation, and the novelist manipulating our praise and blame. It is surely impossible, for example, to read Jane Austen at all without a reasonably developed ethical understanding.[193] And one can hardly understand the development of the English novel without taking note of the fact that when it comes to the moral virtues of prudence, temperance, justice and fortitude, Austen is for them and Lawrence against.[194]

Greg Currie argues that fiction can provide moral knowledge in a direct way, through its forcing the reader to imagine himself in situations that will test values. The reader is required to imaginatively

[191] A.D. Hope, *A Late Picking* (Sydney, 1975), p. 22.

[192] See J. Passmore, 'Educating for the twenty-first century', *Quadrant* 29 (8) (Aug 1985): pp. 11–19.

[193] E.g. E.B. Moon, '"A model of female excellence": Anne Elliot, persuasion and the vindication of a Richardsonian ideal of the female character', *AUMLA* 67 (1987): pp. 25–42; J. Ely, 'Jane Austen: A female Aristotelian', *Thesis Eleven* 40 (1995): pp. 93–118.

[194] E.g., N. Brown, 'Ethics and literature', *ACR* 72 (1995): pp. 399–408.

project himself into the situations of others — not as in fantasy, but in situations that are distillations of fact. The writer's task is to present more complex and inventive situations than one could easily imagine oneself. The reader then imagines himself in the character's position, and can test his own values in that imagined situation.[195] Naturally, problems can arise if the writer represents one character's point of view in heroic terms and reduces another character to the whites of his eyes. And there can be moral objections when the situation represented is not of the kind that actually happened, or where too much is conceded to an evil point of view — or both, as in the case of Helen Demidenko.

A novel may, indeed, undertake a moral task by representing evil,[196] but it is likely to be concerned also with examining the good and casting it in realistic colours. James McAuley wrote:

> If a true morality is based, as it is, on the truth about human nature and human relations, and if great literature needs a considerable measure of the same truth, then great literature will tend to be morally sound. By the same token, perversity and sophisticated silliness may be morally offensive, but they also offend artistically; they limit very drastically the sort of achievement that is possible and preclude real greatness because they preclude depth of insight and respect for human realities.[197]

This is why a novel needs to portray characters that 'matter', that the reader cares about. A.D. Hope's famous review of Patrick White's *Tree of Man*, which ended with an Andersonian flourish by calling it 'pretentious and illiterate verbal sludge', also said, 'He has what the

---

[195] G. Currie, 'The moral psychology of fiction', *AJP* 73 (1995): pp. 250–9; also G. Currie, *The Nature of Fiction* (Cambridge, 1990), ch. 5; G. Currie & I. Ravenscroft, *Recreative Minds: Imagination in Philosophy and Psychology* (Oxford, 2002); J. Kennett, 'Autism, empathy and moral agency', *Philosophical Quarterly* 52 (2002): pp. 340–57; G.P. Gleeson, 'The value of reading fiction', *Literature and Aesthetics* 2 (1992): pp. 67–81; A. Hyslop, 'Emotions and fictional characters', *AJP* 64 (1986): pp. 289–97; D. Mannison, 'On being moved by fiction', *Philosophy* 60 (1985): pp. 71–87; R. Brown, 'Imaginative performances', *Critical Review* 24 (1982): pp. 37–45.

[196] A. Boyce Gibson, 'Hell lies about us', *Meanjin* 5 (1946): pp. 285–97.

[197] J. McAuley, 'Literature and morality', in *The End of Modernity* (Sydney, 1959), pp. 48–54, at p. 51; similar in J.P. Kenny, 'Art and morality', *ACR* 21 (1944): pp. 75–83 (further, see *The Humanities in Australia*, p. 312); S. Moore, 'The dragon on the road: Reflections on the novel', *Quadrant* 33 (5) (May 1989): pp. 59–61; P. Hunt, 'Will English survive?' *Quadrant* 29 (1-2) (Jan-Feb 1985): pp. 129–32; J. Wiltshire, 'What is "English" for?', *Meridian* 2 (1983): pp. 152–4; criticism of these opinions of McAuley in D. Robinson, 'The traditionalism of James McAuley', *Australian Literary Studies* 11 (1983): pp. 205–15.

Australian novel largely lacks, the power to present people who are important to us in themselves, chief characters who impress us by something out of the common order — in this case integrity.'[198]

If ethical questions are as much philosophy's province as literature's, it must be admitted that philosophy in the mid-century had largely abandoned the field. Authors like Judith Wright and Morris West were right to complain that the philosophers of their time had nothing to say about the important questions of life, and to suggest that literature had no choice but to fill the gap.[199] (Though as we will see in chapter 16, philosophers have fought back since then.)

That is all very well, but from the school-teaching point of view, literature is a problem because it is hard to know how to examine it. If it is supposed to develop taste, or virtue, or discrimination, how can it be examined by asking a student to write down a list of sentences? The problem was made more acute because the most noble writers, the English Romantic poets and Shakespeare, did not condescend to argue. The poets, as we saw, consciously preferred imagination to reason, while Shakespeare, compared to the greats of other languages like Dante or Dostoevsky, is notoriously imprecise and inconsistent about matters philosophical. Alfred Deakin extracted a supposed 'Gospel According to Shakespeare' from the works,[200] but few others have felt so confident. He is, however, usefully strong on character, and his works have supported many a diverting school essay on the subject. A superior example of the genre is Henry Lawson's 'Mateship in Shakespeare's Rome', which analyses the relationship between Brutus and Cassius with considerable insight.[201]

The plan in Australian schools was the same as that adopted in England as a result of the 1921 Newbolt report, through which Sir Henry had his last and possibly greatest impact on Imperial education. The Greek and Roman classics were replaced with the 'classics' of English literature. The logic formerly implicit in Latin grammar was now to be learned through a study of the English language by means of a Latinate grammar, while the English classics, chosen for their Romantic qualities as counters to the spirit of scientific rationality,

---

[198] A.D. Hope, 'The bunyip stages a comeback', *SMH* 16/6/1956, p. 15, repr. in A.D. Hope, *Native Companions* (Sydney, 1974), pp. 75–9.
[199] V. Vallis, 'Doing philosophy's job', *Times Literary Supplement* 3865 (9/4/1976): p. 432; Morris West, 'An absence of philosophers', *Australian Author* 16 (2) (June 1984): pp. 1–2, 8; generally M. Spies, 'Religion and philosophy in Australian literature', *Antipodes* 11 (1) (June 1997): pp. 17–23.
[200] Murdoch, *Alfred Deakin*, pp. 135–6.
[201] H. Lawson, 'Mateship in Shakespeare's Rome', *Prose Writings*, ed. Roderick, pp. 701–13; generally in M.W. MacCallum, *Shakespeare's Roman Plays* (1910, repr. London, 1967), pp. 212–54.

were studied through the production by the student of something called 'literary criticism'.[202] There is a difficulty with this scheme, in that the Romantic souls capable of inspiring students with a love of literature are not, in general, the same ones who would enjoy teaching grammar. Despite that, English on this plan has been the most studied of all school subjects.

Generations of students found difficulties in understanding what literary criticism actually was, or on what principles one was expected to discuss and judge literary works. The effective official answer was that one should refer to the works of Matthew Arnold, T.S. Eliot and F.R. Leavis, and imitate them. On doing so one found a strongly moral element to the process, but one was not supposed to write that down in the finished product. The activity of criticism leads to 'improvement', through developing the student's powers of discriminating between good and bad literature. 'Good' means partly, though not solely, morally good: Leavis refers to the 'moral preoccupations that characterise the novelist's peculiar interest in life.'[203] Unfortunately — or, as experts in the subject believe, fortunately — this still gives no actual criteria for evaluating novels or poems. Leavis was notably, and in principle, anti-philosophical in explaining his criteria. In his school, the flow of words allegedly explaining why one work, author or period is better than another, seems to be grounded in the

---

[202] P. Brock, 'The struggle for curriculum development in English studies, with special reference to New South Wales', *Journal of the Australian and New Zealand History of Education Society* 11 (1) (Aug 1982): pp. 18–33.
[203] C. Cordner, 'F.R. Leavis and the moral in literature', in R. Freadman & L. Reinhardt, eds *On Literary Theory and Philosophy* (Basingstoke, 1991), pp. 60–81; *Renegotiating Ethics in Literature, Philosophy and Theory* ed. J. Adamson, R. Freadman & D. Parker (Melbourne, 1999); V. Buckley, *Poetry and Morality: Studies in the Criticism of Matthew Arnold, T.S. Eliot and F.R. Leavis* (London, 1959), on which see T.L. Suttor, 'Poetry and morality', *Twentieth Century* 14 (1959–60): pp. 47–60 & 160–74; A. Boyce Gibson, 'Education, culture and elites', *Melbourne Studies in Education 1965*: pp. 3–20; S.L. Goldberg, 'F.R. Leavis', *Current Affairs Bulletin* 36 (3) (1965); S.L. Goldberg, *Agents and Lives: Moral Thinking in Literature* (Cambridge, 1993); papers in *Critical Review* 33 (1993); I. Saluszinsky, 'Deconstruction in the classrooms', *Meridian* 10 (2) (1991): pp. 108–16; opposite view in P. Gilbert, *Writing, Schooling and Deconstruction* (London, 1989); history of Leavisism in Australia in J. Docker, *In a Critical Condition* (Ringwood, 1984), chs 2, 4, 7; C. Wallace, *Greer: Untamed Shrew* (Sydney, 1997), pp. 59–64; A. Riemer, *Sandstone Gothic* (Sydney, 1998), pp. 116–22, 131–78; Arnold's philosophy in Francis Anderson, 'The poetry of Matthew Arnold', *Centennial Magazine* 1 (1888): pp. 114–7.

sensitivity of the critic's antennae rather than in anything factual about the work, or what the work describes.[204]

Departments of English made the most of the opportunity, becoming often the largest in their faculties on the strength of their possession of rights to the imagination, Shelley's 'great instrument of moral good'. A 'failure of imaginative response' to literature was the stock in trade when other literary critics were to be fought or students to be failed.[205] There is no answer to that charge, and the only defence is to counter-attack in the same style, but louder. The procedure of literary criticism of this sort is neatly described by Anderson in his early paper 'Romanticism and classicism': 'condemnation of a work — refusal to read wonderful meanings into the drivellings of Wordsworth, for instance — is taken as a sign of the inadequacy of the critic's spiritual resources. Works of art, then, merely serve as texts for vague and arbitrary moralising, and strict analysis is frowned upon as calculated to "spoil" appreciation of the work.'[206]

Nevertheless, Leavis did stand for a commitment to the morally serious in literature,[207] and there is cause to regret its passing in favour of debased philosophies like post-structuralism and deconstruction, Marxist and feminist approaches, and the like.[208] In their different ways, they replaced attempts to understand what an author was saying with some form of the 'hermeneutics of suspicion', or the 'sociopoliticization of the ethical',[209] undermining the author's voice and trying to find a higher ground from which to fire at him. It is not clear why anyone with these views would bother studying literature, except perhaps to acquire an academic position that might be difficult to obtain in a real subject.

---

[204] T.L. Suttor, 'Dogma, literary judgement, liberal education', *Twentieth Century* 15 (1960–1): pp. 69–80, at pp. 73–4.

[205] I. Read, '"The great instrument of moral good": English at Melbourne University', *Typereader* 4 (Spring 1990): pp. 39–45.

[206] J. Anderson, *Art & Reality* (Sydney, 1982), p. 56; cf. J. Maze, 'Wordsworth! Stop that drivelling', *SMH* 31/7/1982, p. 38.

[207] D. Parker, 'Leavisophobia and the return of ethics in literary studies', *Quadrant* 40 (6) (June 1996): pp. 61–66.

[208] R. Freadman, 'Literary studies and philosophy', *Meridian* 10 (2) (1991): pp. 24–35; R. Freadman & S. Miller, *Re-Thinking Theory* (Cambridge, 1992), ch. 2, 'Literary theory and the problem of ethics'; S.L. Goldberg, 'The deconstruction gang', *London Review of Books* 2 (10) (22/5/1980): pp. 14–16; C. Maslen & L. Slattery, *Why Our Universities Are Failing* (Melbourne, 1994), ch. 5; D. Parker, *Ethics, Theory and the Novel* (Cambridge, 1994).

[209] C.A.J. Coady & S. Miller, 'Literature, power, and the recovery of philosophical ethics', *Critical Review* 33 (1993): pp. 55–77.

Anderson's remarks recall the fact that there has been a long-running conflict between philosophy and literature. The feeling of literary folk that philosophy deals in a world of spectral abstractions, somehow divorced from their meanings in real life, is a cause of some of the anti-Andersonian feeling among his students who pursued literature. According to James McAuley,

> My own first resistances centred on one of the outlying parts of Anderson's work, which he himself acknowledged contained unresolved difficulties: the field of aesthetics. One could not even begin to apply Anderson's view to arts other than literary, and when applied to literature it had the effect of a bath of acid, dissolving the corpus until only one tell-tale relic was left, Joyce's 'Ulysses'.[210]

Another of Anderson's students, the novelist Peter Shrubb, attacks Anderson's reduction of the literary criticism of works to finding their 'themes' and listing the illusions they expose, and speaks of 'the arrogance of the intellect which, finding an idea to nestle under, knows no more the heat of the sun.'[211] These charges are correct in Anderson's case. Nonetheless, literary minds tend to find such criticisms decisive, while philosophers cannot see what reasons have been given for them.

The philosophically inclined, for their part, are apt to be impatient with the litterateurs' insistence on dressing up everything in rhetoric. Why not the bare facts or arguments, without all the clutter? Why does 'literature' mean fiction, as if non-fiction is beyond the pale, and does not acquire literary merit until the true propositions are filleted out?[212] How can the *Oxford History of Australian Literature* say without irony that non-fiction is not included, since it could not be done 'without serious distortion'?[213] And why do people not read straightforward introductions to philosophy, but instead buy by the millions Gaarder's *Sophie's World*, a not very well written introductory philosophy text dressed up as a novel?[214]

---

[210] J. McAuley, in *Bulletin* 30/6/1962, p. 29; also in J. McAuley, 'Symbolism: An Essay in Poetics', MA Thesis, Sydney University, 1940, discussed in G. Balzidis, 'James McAuley's radical ingredients', *Meanjin* 39 (1980): pp. 374–82.

[211] P. Shrubb, 'John Anderson as literary critic', *Quadrant* 27 (1) (Jan-Feb 1983): pp. 43–9; cf. P. Shrubb, *Family Matters* (Sydney, 1988), pp. 213–4.

[212] J. Franklin, 'Lit crit and non-fiction', *Quadrant* 28 (10) (Oct 1984): pp. 41–4; D. Green, *Writer, Reader, Critic* (Sydney, 1991), pp. 4–5.

[213] *Oxford History of Australian Literature*, ed. L. Kramer (Melbourne, 1981), p. v; H.M. Green's *History of Australian Literature*, however, is strong on non-fiction, including philosophy.

[214] W. Tarrant, review of *Sophie's World*, *Philosopher* 1 (1) (Autumn 1995): pp. 47–8.

And why, for that matter, if moral characters in novels and plays are a good influence on youth, aren't real heroes even better? Biography is not part of the high school syllabus. 'The large question, "Which qualities confer upon heroic men and women the authority which all of them must have to act wisely?" not only isn't asked in our schools; it isn't asked in our culture.'[215] Yet there remains a strong innate response to real heroes like 'Weary' Dunlop and Mary McKillop.[216]

These conflicts resurfaced in the debate over Helen Demidenko, where those with a background in literature generally argued that Ms D, as an imaginative writer, was free to re-imagine history however she wished. Those in the opposite camp, mostly from philosophical, political and other social science areas, took this to be a sign of the frivolity of litterateurs concerning matters of fact.[217] These questions are important, not only in themselves, but because of the victory of literature over philosophy in school education. English, including some study of literature, is a compulsory subject almost everywhere; unlike in, say, France, philosophy is rarely studied in school at all. The youth receive a body of opinion on literature, but are left to pick up philosophical ideas at random.

BY THE 1960s, the moral consensus presumed by 'secular, moral' education had evaporated. That was true in high schools, especially, where all the teachers had a defined sphere of technical expertise to teach and anything else fell through the cracks. Margaret Mackie's 1966 book on the philosophy of education, a kind of benign Andersonianism adapted to the classroom,[218] described accurately

---

[215] S. Moore, 'The clean sea breeze of the centuries', *IPA Review* 44 (1) (Spring 1990): pp. 57–9.

[216] G. Davison, 'The last hero and the first saint', *Quadrant* 39 (12) (Dec 1995): pp. 19–25; P. Martyr, 'Dunlop and MacKillop', *Quadrant* 40 (3) (Mar 1996): pp. 59–60; cf. Manning Clark, 'Heroes', in *Australia: The Daedalus Symposium*, ed. R. Graubard (Sydney, 1985), pp. 57–84.

[217] A. Riemer, *The Demidenko Debate* (St Leonards, 1996), ch. 4 versus R. Manne, *The Culture of Forgetting* (Melbourne, 1996), ch. 7; philosophers' comments in R. Gaita, 'Literary and public honours', *Quadrant* 39 (9) (Sept 1995): pp. 32–6; R. Shapiro, 'Ethics, the literary imagination and the other', *Journal of Australian Studies* 50/1 (1996): pp. 42–50; S. Moore, 'Home truths', *Quadrant* 39 (10) (Oct 1995): pp. 10–17; A. Heathcote, 'The Demidenko affair', *Philosopher* 1 (3) (1996): pp. 31–7.

[218] On Margaret Mackie and Anderson, M. Mackie, 'Anderson as I saw him', *Heraclitus*, 47 (Feb 1996): pp. 12–13, 48 (Apr 96): pp. 8–9 & 49 (June 96): p. 12; on philosophy of education more generally: B.S. Crittenden, 'Philosophy of education in Australia', in *Australian Education*, ed. J. Keeves (Sydney, 1987), pp. 3–28; C. Beck, 'North American, British and Australian

enough the 'many teachers who avoid as far as possible, on principle, introducing ethical considerations into their discussions with the pupils. This is sometimes because the teacher believes it is wrong to influence immature pupils in this matter. It is ironical that, while ethics is being avoided as controversial and unsuitable for dogmatic (or, for that matter, any) treatment, the argument that working hard at school is desirable because this leads to getting on in the world and making money is often used without any awareness that it raises a moral issue. It is assumed, without question, that "getting on" is good.'[219] It was what the Catholics had predicted as the result of secular education: 'Wealth, justly or even dishonestly acquired, is the idol of the multitude ... Compared with it, honour, virtue, public and private worth are antiquated titles to the reverence of the multitude. Money, the divinity of the age, alone receives homage.'[220] It is no surprise that the moral sense of the Sixties generation who rejected 'getting on' turned out to be based on the more unformed and immature moral emotions, such as indignation.[221]

In more recent times, there have been some serious attempts to revive at least a skeleton of basic moral education and to state the principles that are to be inculcated. The New South Wales Department of Education and Training divides the values to be 'fostered' into three categories: those relating to education (curiosity, logical and critical thinking, among others), those relating to self and others

---

philosophy of education from 1941 to 1991', *Educational Theory* 41 (1991): pp. 311–20; J.S. Kaminsky, 'Philosophy of education in Australasia: A definition and a history', *Educational Philosophy and Theory* 20 (1988): pp. 12–26; C.D. Hardie, *Truth and Fallacy in Educational Theory* (Cambridge, 1942); D.H. Rankin, *The Philosophy of Australian Education* (Melbourne, 1941); J. Anderson, *Education and Inquiry,* ed. D.Z. Phillips (Oxford, 1980), J. Passmore, *The Philosophy of Teaching* (London, 1971); C.D. Hardie, *Truth and Fallacy in Educational Theory* (Cambridge, 1942).

[219] M. Mackie, *Education in the Inquiring Society* (Hawthorn, 1966), p. 76; cf. B.V. Hill, *Values Education in Australian Schools* (Melbourne, 1991), esp. pp. 16–19; A. Boyce Gibson, *Towards an Australian Philosophy of Education* (Sydney, 1962), lecture 3; M. Raphael, 'The philosophical vacuum in Australian education', *Dialogue* 1 (1) (Spring 1967): pp. 4–12; A. Barcan, 'The decline of citizenship as an educational ideal', *Quadrant* 16 (2) (Mar-Apr 1972): pp. 42–7; G. Partington, '(Im)moral and moral education', *Journal of Moral Education* 13 (1984): pp. 90–100; G. Partington, 'Morals and education', *Quadrant* 35 (4) (Apr 1991): pp. 54–9.

[220] 'Junius', 'Secular education, the hereditary enemy of true progress', *ACR* 4 (1898): pp. 447–59, at p. 450.

[221] See S.P. Kenaelly, 'What happened to my school', *IPA Review* 42 (2) (Aug 1988): pp. 45–9; also L. Hemingway, *The Modern World and Self-Control* (Melbourne, 1968).

(accepting one's own worth, being honest, caring and punctual, and 'accepting the importance of developing a positive personal belief and value system'), and those relating to citizenship (including being in favour of democracy, liberty, economic development and conservation, and conforming to the school rules). A primary school subject, 'General Religious and Moral Education', helps students to understand these matters through a 'study that is objective and non-sectarian', but it is much less clear what is to happen in high school.[222] And as for the universities having a beneficial effect on the character of their students, the last person to have suggested that seems to have been Menzies, in 1939.[223]

In the end, though, it has to be doubted whether training in values without education in the reasons for them is a credible plan. Doubt-less it will work well enough for a proportion of the population, but that proportion may be smaller than is realised, because of the phi-losophical crisis of puberty. Typically, younger children take rather naturally to the more abstract areas of philosophy like metaphysics and logic, as the now popular 'philosophy for children' movement has found.[224] But during the teen years most of the population loses a large part of its curiosity about the abstract, including both mathe-

---

[222] NSW Dept of School Education, *The Values We Teach* (Revised, 1991, Sydney); various similar ideas in A.J. Watt, *Rational Moral Education* (Melbourne, 1976); B. Crittenden, *Bearings in Moral Education* (Melbourne, 1978); C.W. Evers, ed, *Moral Theory for Educational Leadership* (Melbourne, 1987); E. Burman *et al*, eds, *Values in Education* (London, 1997); S. Pascoe, ed, *Values in Education: College Yearbook 2002* (Deakin West, 2002); complaints that 'values' do not help 'character' in M. Freakley, 'The values cop-out and the case for character development in moral education', *Educational Practice and Theory* 18 (2) (1996): pp. 29–37.

[223] Menzies, *Place of a University*, pp. 12–3; 25–6.

[224] P. Cam, *Thinking Together: Philosophical Inquiry for the Classroom* (Sydney, 1995); P. Cam, ed, *Thinking Stories: Philosophical Inquiry for Children* (Sydney, 1993); C. de Haan, S. MacColl & L. McCutcheon, *Philosophy With Kids* (3 books, South Melbourne, 1995); A.B. Gibson & A.A. Phillips, *Thinkers at Work* (2nd ed, Melbourne, 1951); L. Splitter & A.M. Sharp, *Teaching for Better Thinking* (Hawthorn, Vic, 1995); L. Splitter, 'Every child a philosopher', *Education News* 19 (2) (Mar 1985): pp. 35–8; L. Splitter, 'Philosophy and democracy in Asia and the Pacific: Philosophy and civic education', *Thinking* 13 (3) (1997): pp. 6–16; T.V. Daly, 'Eleven-year-olds and philosophy', *Catholic School Studies* 62 (2) (Oct 1989): pp. 50–4; R. Laird, 'Philosophy for children in remote Aboriginal classrooms', *The Aboriginal Child at School* 20 (4) (Aug 1992): pp. 27–36; S. Moore, 'Philosophy in schools', *Education Monitor* 6 (1) (1995): pp. 1–2; articles in *Thinking* 13 (2) (1997); and the journal *Critical & Creative Thinking;* FAPCA website, www.uq.edu.au/~pdgburgh/FAPCA; also www.vaps.vic.edu.au .

matics and philosophy, and acquires the fetishism for the 'practical' that is characteristic of adulthood. At the same time, however, there can be a sudden demand for meaning, as parental values are no longer treated as self-evident; the phenomenon is seen in both the idealism and the cynicism of youth.[225] The brief interval between the onset of the search for meaning and the loss of interest in the abstract is a period in which philosophical views can be set for life, never to be re-examined beyond some minor softening in the light of 'experience'. A sudden accession of the feeling that life must have meaning can spur an enthusiasm for the religion closest to hand, or the need to establish a separate identity can produce the opposite. In this window of vulnerability, the youth is susceptible to purveyors of mechanistic theories of reality, such as Calvinists, socialist agitators, and those whose business it is to recruit Jihad-crazed suicide bombers.[226] The more precocious may even think up something dangerous for themselves. Donald Horne, on a walk in the Blue Mountains shortly before he went to University — before knowing anything about Anderson — discovered, as he remembers it, 'I was finally able to think a thought':

> If I didn't believe in God and I didn't believe in life after death why was I always worrying about everything? What did it matter what I was? If there was no good and no bad why didn't I just be bad if I wanted to? I could be as selfish as I liked, plan everything just to please myself, be unscrupulous, just take what I wanted. What was the point of believing in anything? Everything is meaningless. Why should I act according to beliefs if I didn't believe in them and they got in my way? Beliefs were a lot of bullshit. There was no reason whatsoever why I should act one way or the other. What did should mean? Nothing. I was going to die. There was no God to punish me. Nothing meant anything. But I would have to be careful. Other people expected you to have beliefs. You should act as if you had them. That would be smart. You could act as if you believed in honesty and so forth, and all the time you were lying.

---

[225] R. Conway, 'The search for meaning, the dilemma of the adolescent student', *Quadrant* 25 (1-2) (Jan-Feb 1981): pp. 14–17; M. Charlesworth, 'The future of youth — a moral perspective', *Australian Journal of Forensic Sciences* 19 (1987): pp. 55–61; P. Cantwell, 'Counselling and man's search for meaning', *Compass* 6 (1) (Mar/Apr 1972): pp. 27–32; Carroll, *Ego and Soul*, p. 1.

[226] E. Mayo, *Psychology and Religion* (Melbourne, 1922), discussed in Melleuish, *Cultural Liberalism*, pp. 156–7.

I considered these thoughts so important that I kept on repeating them for the rest of the walk, so that I would remember them. Now I felt optimistic about the future.[227]

Horne gives the reader to understand that these views are some-how connected with special circumstances resulting from his father's breakdown.

Nevertheless, the problem is perennial. A system of ideas with moral and inspirational content is a necessity for the youth. Someone will have to come up with something.

---

[227] Horne, *Young Donald*, 2nd ed, p. 168; recalled in D. Horne, *Confessions of a New Boy* (Ringwood, 1986), p. 55 and *Portrait of an Optimist* (Ringwood, 1988), p. 166.

PART THREE:
SPECIAL INTERESTS

Chapter 11　　The Sydney Disturbances

DURING the twenty years from 1965, the philosophy department at Sydney University was rent by a series of bitter left-right disputes. Such fights — or rather, the same fight in many instantiations — were common enough in humanities departments in the period. The unique virulence of the one at Sydney, which eventually led to a split into two departments, was due not only to the strength of the left, which was a frequent occurrence elsewhere, but to the determination not to give way of the leading figures of the right, David Armstrong and David Stove.

Armstrong and Stove, as we saw in chapter 2, were students of John Anderson in the late 1940s, and ones of unusually independent mind. Armstrong had early success. He went for postgraduate work to Oxford, where the linguistic philosophy then current made only a limited impression on his Andersonian interest in the substantial questions of classical philosophy. He recalled attending a seminar by the leading linguistic philosophers Strawson and Grice.

> Grice, I think it was, read very fast a long paper which was completely unintelligible to me. Perhaps others were having difficulty also because when the paper finished there was a long, almost religious, hush in the room. Then O.P. Wood raised what seemed to be a very minute point even by Oxford standards. A quick dismissive remark by Grice and the room settled down to its devotions again. At this point a Canadian sitting next to me turned and said, 'Say, what is going on here?' I said, 'I'm new round here, and I don't know the rules of this game. But I think Strawson and Grice are winning.'

The story of the brash young colonial passed round Oxford. As an examiner of Armstrong's thesis, Grice later explained why the arguments of the thesis involved a contradiction — this counts as a knockdown win in the philosophical world — but the examiners graciously allowed him to pass anyway. After some years in Melbourne writing successful books on perception, Armstrong became Challis Professor of Philosophy at Sydney University in 1964, at the age of 37.[1]

Stove, on the other hand, only just scraped into academic life. In 1951, Anderson proposed to appoint his son Alexander (Sandy) to a teaching fellowship in his department. Sandy was widely regarded as having few talents other than a fine baritone voice, and the University determined to stand up to Anderson's attempted nepotism. A committee was set up and recommended the appointment of someone else. Anderson appealed to the Senate against this encroachment on his academic freedom, and Stove was appointed as a compromise candidate.[2] The next year, a job opportunity arose through the general studies program at the new University of New South Wales. In an attempt to make science students aware of the humanities and humanities students aware of the sciences, the program taught large numbers of students the philosophy of science.[3] The selection committee placed Stove second, but through a clerical error both of the top two candidates were sent letters of offer. Stove proved to have received his letter by the time the mistake was discovered, and the University decided its projected expansion made possible the appointment of both candidates.[4] He moved back to Sydney University in 1960.

[1] R. Bogdan, *D.M. Armstrong* (Dordrecht, 1984), pp. 3–27, Oxford at p. 11; *Bulletin* 29/2/1964, pp. 3–4; Interview, in *Matters of the Mind: Essays and Interviews in Honour of Leonie Kramer*, ed L. Jobling & C. Runcie (Sydney, 2001), pp. 322–32 (text at www.ditext.com/armstrong/kramer.html); Armstrong's papers are in National Library, MS 9363 (index at www.nla.gov.au/ms/findaids/9363.html).

[2] B. Kennedy, *A Passion to Oppose* (Melbourne, 1995), pp. 170–1; on his earlier life, G. Harrison, *Night Train to Granada* (Sydney, 2002), pp 19–23, 132–3; G. Harrison, 'Living on the edge', *Heraclitus* 81 (June 2000): pp. 8–12; 83 (Nov 2000): pp. 10–13.

[3] D. Oldroyd, *Student Attitudes Towards Courses in History and Philosophy of Science at the University of New South Wales* (Kensington, 1974), pp. 1–11; B.N. Kaye, 'Cardinal Newman at the University of New South Wales', *ACR* 68 (1991): pp. 72–9; J.B. Thornton, 'The courses in scientific thought', *Technology* 8 (1963): pp. 44–5 (Anderson himself taught in the program after his retirement from Sydney.)

[4] Anderson to Ruth Walker, 25/4/1952, in Walker papers, Sydney University Archives, P.158 series 2; Anderson's rude song about UNSW, 'Philosophical blues', composed for Stove's farewell, in G. Pont, 'Don Laycock: Collector and creator of dirty songs', in T. Dutton et al, eds, *Pacific Linguistics* series C no. 110 (1992), pp. 635–44, at pp. 643–4.

Armstrong and Stove should have acquired at least a minor degree of fame from the 'Bertrand Russell, Andersonian' affair, recounted in chapter 2, but as we saw, the truth was not revealed until decades later. By the mid-1960s, though, the time for such innocent pleasures as exposing Bertrand Russell was fast coming to a close, as was the happy seclusion of philosophy from the public eye. There was no shortage of the glare of publicity in the Knopfelmacher affair, one of the top news stories of 1965.

Dr Frank Knopfelmacher had for some years been one of the most controversial figures in the University of Melbourne, where he was a lecturer in psychology. Foreseeing the Holocaust, he had escaped Czechoslovakia in 1939, and again bribed his way out of Czechoslovakia after the Communist coup of 1948. Naturally, he took a more alarmist view of totalitarian threats than was common in Australia, and regarded Australians in general and Australian intellectuals in particular as dangerously naive when it came to the designs of Communism.[5] He harangued, organised and made sarcastic jokes without pause, and a generation of Melbourne University students split into pro- and anti-Knopfelmacher camps.[6] In 1965, Knopfelmacher was an applicant for a senior lectureship in political philosophy in the Philosophy Department at Sydney University. With the strong support of Armstrong, he was chosen by the selection committee, and the appointment went forward to the Professorial Board for approval.

Normally committee recommendations were unanimous and Board approval a formality. But there was dissatisfaction from one member of the selection committee, Charles Birch, the professor of biology, a Christian of 'progressive' views and later author of a number of books on philosophy. He called to the attention of W.N. Christiansen, the Professor of Electrical Engineering, the existence of one of Knopfelmacher's occasional writings, one he had not submitted in his application. Christiansen hurriedly looked through 'The situation at the University of Melbourne', published in the Jesuit

---

[5] F. Knopfelmacher, 'My political education', *Quadrant* 39 (7–8) (July–Aug 1995): pp. 34–41; F. Knopfelmacher, 'The unquiet life of Sydney Hook', *Quadrant* 21 (8) (Aug 1987): pp. 8–14; obituary in *Australian* 18/5/1995, p. 13.

[6] V. Buckley, *Cutting Green Hay* (Melboune, 1983), pp. 207–218; P. O'Brien, 'Dr Knopfelmacher and university Catholics', *Twentieth Century* 25 (1971): pp. 358–71; J. Carroll & R. Manne, 'Homage to Knopfelmacher', *Quadrant* 33 (3) (Mar 1989): pp. 10–14; P. Monk, 'Memories of Santa and Franta', *Quadrant* 46 (7–8) (July–Aug 2002): pp. 53–55; Germaine Greer and Knopfelmacher in B. Faust, 'My friend Germs', in *Ferretabilia*, ed. R. Walsh (St Lucia, 1993), pp. 80–1.

magazine *Twentieth Century* in 1964, and read selected passages to the Professorial Board.[7] The offending passages included the following:

> At the time when the Communist Party constituted the nucleus of intellectual and social life at the University of Melbourne, it operated through a system of concentric circles of sympathizers entrenched in academic organizations which it either created, captured or influenced ... the Old Melbourne Left continues to wield the whip-hand, or at least to exercise significant veto powers in matters of academic preferments and sinecures ... The tactic chosen [by the left] was internal disruption and the devices were sectarianism and sex. They were cleverly selected; the organizers of the Hitler Youth had shown the way.

It concluded:

> Like rats, they wish to operate in the dark. Their aim is, therefore, total intellectual *stagnation*, certainly not 'dissidence' or 'rebellion'. Their wish is to eliminate altogether intelligent discussions of political issues from the campus. The outspoken command is — be a fellow-traveller, or a neutralist, or keep quiet. The fact that the struggle for academic freedom has to be waged not against oppressive governments and an obscurantist clergy, but against an academic junta whose members have been corroded by totalitarianism and against their psychologically disturbed and delinquent student progeny is very damning. It must lead, sooner or later, to a fundamental re-examination of our current notions about the structural guarantees of academic freedom in Australia.[8]

The Board, especially its scientific members, were not used to that sort of thing. They were appalled at the tone of voice and agreed to Christiansen's proposal that the appointment not go through until they had had the opportunity to acquaint themselves with more of Dr K's writings. Further research turned up nothing worse, though there was one more article that caused offence. One sentence in a short piece on state aid to Church schools was, 'The notion that Catholic education produces a thing called "an authoritarian personality" filled with murderous and aggressive prejudices is a myth based on a discredited psychological theory which maintains its hold among Australian psychologists by suppression and falsification of research findings.'[9] The reference was to, among others, the Sydney University Andersonian psychologist John Maze,[10] but the Board's objection was not so much to Knopfelmacher's attack on any particular person as to

---

[7] W.N. Christiansen to author, 27/7/1996.

[8] F. Knopfelmacher, 'The situation at the University of Melbourne', *Twentieth Century* 18 (1964): pp. 196–207; similar in F. Knopfelmacher, 'The threat to academic freedom', *Quadrant* 2 (2) (Autumn 1958): pp. 17–26.

[9] F. Knopfelmacher, 'State aid', *Bulletin* 8/6/1962: pp. 28–9.

[10] J.R. Maze, 'Catholicism and the authoritarian personality', in *Catholics and the Free Society*, ed. H. Mayer (Melbourne, 1961), ch. 7.

Frank Knopfelmacher, 1990 (Newspix)

his attacking the bona fides of academics without giving specific evidence. There was also some question as to whether Knopfelmacher had adequate formal qualifications in political philosophy, but it is clear that this consideration did not play a significant part in the controversy. The Professorial Board did not want someone who spoke like that on their patch.[11]

Knopfelmacher and his friends of course saw the incident as proof of everything he had been saying about the infiltration of universities by Communists. From the point of view of the press[12] and of federal

---

[11] D.M. Armstrong & R.N. Spann, 'The Knopfelmacher case', *Minerva* 3 (1964–5): pp. 538–55; A.K. Stout, 'On university appointments: Thoughts after Knopfelmacher', *Minerva* 4 (1965–6): pp. 55–72, further, Stout papers, Fisher Library, Sydney University, items 188, 953–69; *Bulletin* 25/12/1965 pp. 27–9; C. Pybus, *The Devil and James McAuley* (Melbourne, 1999), pp. 205–7; W.F. Connell *et al.*, *Australia's First: A History of the University of Sydney*, vol. 2, pp. 165–6, 294.

[12] S. Lipski & D. Horne in *Bulletin* 1/5/1965, pp. 37–42; *Bulletin* 11/12/1965, pp. 41–3; 26 articles listed in *Bulletin Index* 1965, p. 277; bibliography in R.M. Scoble, 'The Knopfelmacher case', *Quadrant* 15 (5) (Sept-Oct 1971): pp. 72–82; W.G. Smith, 'Dr Knopfelmacher and Sydney University', *Twentieth Century* 19 (1965): pp. 358–64; J. Curtis, 'The Sydney University branch of the Communist Party of Australia', *Twentieth Century* 20 (1966): pp. 261–71, at p. 269; *Honi Soit* 38 (8) (28/4/1965); *Australian*

and state parliaments, where the matter was debated extensively, it was a simple matter of left versus right. The counterattack centred on the person of Professor Christiansen. As pointed out by W.C. Wentworth in federal Parliament,[13] Christiansen had appeared in the documents Petrov had brought with him on his defection, under the code-name 'Master', though there was no suggestion he had done anything improper.[14] Soviet intelligence regarded him as part of their ring of Australian spies, which included his brother-in-law Jim Hill, but there seems to be no evidence that he passed any information.[15] A brief exchange in his appearance before the Petrov Royal Commission is interesting as evidence of the connection often seen in 'internationalist' scientific circles between certain philosophical views and leftist opinions:

> Commissioner: I gather that although you are not a member of the Communist party, you subscribe to the Communist doctrine?
>
> Christiansen: Yes, I feel that the materialist concept of history is the one which fits in best with scientific thinking, and it is the one that I favour.[16]

The efforts to reverse the Professorial Board's decision were unavailing. The Senate confirmed it, the position was readvertised, and a selection committee of almost the same composition as before met to consider the matter. It was decided to ask the opinion of Charles Martin,[17] who was about to succeed Alan Stout as Professor of Philosophy. Though he had been worried by Knopfelmacher's rudeness, he had been convinced by the weight of philosophical opinion that his appointment was desirable, and it was hoped that his support would convince the committee to vote again for Knopfelmacher. He travelled to Sydney via Melbourne, where he was presented with

---

4/5/1965, p. 8; R. W(alsh), 'The great Fred controversy', *Oz* no. 25 (Jan 1966): p. 17; B.A. Santamaria, *Point of View* (Melbourne, 1969), pp. 235–41; J. McLaren, *Writing in Hope and Fear* (Cambridge, 1996), pp. 90–3.

[13] *Commonwealth of Australia, Parliamentary Debates, House of Representatives* 12–13/5/1965 (vol. HofR 46, pp. 1445–9).

[14] *Report of the Royal Commission on Espionage* (Sydney, 1955), pp. 218–9; ASIO file on Christiansen, Australian Archives series A6119/78 items 863–4, A6119/83 items 1486–7; also Petrov documents under Christiansen W., A6201 items 376, 377, 379.

[15] D. Ball & D. Horner, *Breaking the Codes: Australia's KGB Network, 1944–1950* (Sydney, 1998), pp. 247–51; Christiansen's reply in *Quadrant* 43 (Mar 1999): pp. 5–6.

[16] *Royal Commission on Espionage, Transcript of Proceedings* (Canberra, 1955), vol. 4 p. 1972.

[17] See J.J.C. Smart, 'C.B. Martin: A biographical sketch', in J. Heil, ed, *Cause, Mind and Reality: Essays Honouring C.B. Martin* (Dordrecht, 1989), pp. 1–3.

"'incontrovertible evidence" of conduct by Dr K which made it now impossible for him to support the appointment.'[18] The conduct in question was Knopfelmacher's persistent bad-mouthing of the left-wing philosophy lecturer Don Gunner in an attempt to have him dismissed.[19] With Martin's opinion being negative, and with Stout being unwilling to foist on his successor someone he did not want, the committee changed its mind. As it did not disclose its reasons, public controversy continued.[20] Armstrong wrote years later,

> In the course of his political controversies he quite often used intemperate, not to say ungentlemanly language in writing about his opponents. In this he was a man fatally ahead of his time by a few years. A short time afterwards academic rebels were saying pretty much anything they liked, how they liked, about their opponents. If anyone tried to censure them or impede their careers as a result of this, the shouts that their academic freedom had been violated were deafening. To Knopfelmacher, however, the novelist Saki's saying applied: it is the first Christian martyr who gets the hungriest lion.[21]

The job left vacant by the affair eventually went to the Sydney libertarian George Molnar, prominent in later disturbances. The Professorial Board apparently did not read any of his articles, so the author of 'Sexual freedom in the Orr case', 'The sexual revolution' and 'The nature of moralism' was employed to lecture first-year philosophy. Naive female first-year students had little representation on the Professorial Board.

In 1968 Armstrong's *A Materialist Theory of the Mind* (considered in chapter 9) was published. It had great international success, and established him as the country's most eminent philosopher. This was useful later when he was outnumbered in political fights, as the University was prepared to take a certain amount of action to avoid losing him.

B ETWEEN the Knopfelmacher affair and the next round of the left-right fight a great deal happened. The major US and European campus disruptions of 1968 and the Vietnam demonstrations came and (up to a point) went. The old order put on its ugliest faces — Askin, McMahon, Bolte, Nixon — and did its best to 'ride over

---

[18] Stout statement, 18/9/1976, in Stout papers, item 967.

[19] C.B. Martin to author, 23/2/1998; also Stout papers, item 964; recollection of Gunner in *Eureka Street* 11 (10) (Dec 2001): pp. 16–17.

[20] 'The Knopfelmacher case', *Minerva* 4 (1965–6): pp. 287–99; Clyde Packer in *NSW Parliamentary Debates* 3rd series, vol. 56 pp. 5–6, 59 pp. 2289–95, 61 pp. 3570–84 & 4070–74; John Gorton in the Senate, *Commonwealth of Australia, Parliamentary Debates, Senate* 17/11/1965 and 8/12/1965 (vol. S 30, pp. 1557, 2106).

[21] D.M. Armstrong, in Bogdan, *D.M. Armstrong*, p. 29.

the bastards', in Askin's famous words to LBJ.[22] True, there were plenty of places in Australia where these changes were almost invisible — country towns, banks and RSL clubs were disturbed by no more than an occasional miniskirt. It was universities, as everyone knew, that were at the centre of the trouble. One factor was the conscription ballot, which concentrated the minds of many who would never have bothered to analyse society otherwise.[23] Another factor was the huge expansion of universities during the 1960s, named by B.A. Santamaria as Menzies's worst mistake. Apart from admitting to academic positions certain individuals with little talent or interest in matters intellectual, there were problems arising from expansion without much increase in the number of professors. 'Junior' staff who would once have been professors of minuscule departments at 30 seethed. Even David Armstrong agreed that the power of professors should be reduced.[24] But even in universities, there was little sign of disturbance in many areas — in engineering faculties, for example. For obvious reasons, connected both with the content of the disciplines and the kind of students they attracted, arts and social science departments were the centres of activism. To its central position among those disciplines, philosophy added a tradition of intransigence on matters of principle. Principles are, after all, what philosophy is about. Practical consequences are not.

Philosophers of conservative views thus had a box seat view of the coming wave. They were not happy. Armstrong recalled being with John Searle, the noted philosopher who was an early leader of demands for change at Berkeley, the centre of American campus protest, though later a critic:

> A phone rang. It was a lieutenant of Searle's from the campus. The first 'Filthy Speech Movement' posters were being paraded about the campus. The open writing up of four-letter words still had the power to shock in those days. As John started shouting back at his aide, I thought I had been privileged to witness a historic moment. It must have been thus when the Gironde first began to realize that the Jacobins were not simply people a

---

[22] D. Hickie, *The Prince and the Premier* (Sydney, 1985), pp. 66–7.

[23] See J. Burnheim, 'The morality of conscientious objection', in *Catholics in Revolution*, ed. P. Ormonde (Melbourne, 1968), pp. 119–24; C.F. Bowers, 'The Catholic Church in Sydney and the Vietnam conflict', *Australian Left Review* 71 (Oct 1979): pp. 30–7; D.H. Monro, 'Civil rights and conscription', in *Conscription in Australia*, ed. R. Forward & B. Reece (St Lucia, 1968), pp. 1–21; Knopfelmacher's view in *Age* 30/6/1966, p. 7.

[24] D.M. Armstrong, 'Student activism in a free society', *Vestes* 11 (1968): pp. 138–40.

bit to their left, but that they wanted the overthrow of all who were not as radical as they.[25]

Stove too was disturbed by the Berkeley events and was among the first to accuse the Australian university authorities of 'caving in'.[26] As violent demonstrations and sit-ins multiplied, he spoke of 'the end of my own love affair with the University of Sydney. Less than five years ago it was to me the most agreeable place in the world, and I could hardly believe my own good fortune in being allowed to work in it. I looked forward to the time when my children could share it with me. How very remote all that seems now!'[27]

In academic philosophy itself, people began to wonder if too much attention to the meaning of words had rendered the profession 'irrelevant'. 'To the basic questions which the times thus posed — questions about the dis-ease of bourgeois culture, the forms of possible alternatives, the strategies and tactics of the path from one to the other — there came no answers from the thin voice of analytic philosophy quavering on heedlessly in university mausoleums.'[28] Surely something was called for from the supposed experts in ethics, when commitment was spreading abroad? Tweed coats were put away and afros grown. Pipes were replaced by microphones. Minds were expanded by the works of Marx and Mao, and by mind-expanding substances of a more physical kind. The Sydney University Philosophy IV students of 1970 included a dope-smoking group and a heroin-shooting group.[29]

The early leader in the 'red shift', however, was not Sydney University but Flinders University in Adelaide. The Professor of Philosophy there, Brian Medlin, had worked on conventional philosophical

---

[25] Bogdan, *D. M. Armstrong*, p. 28.

[26] D. Stove, 'The revolution at Berkeley', roneoed, 1966; 'The Berkeley affair', *Vestes* 10 (1967): pp. 38–9; 'University Letter: "The Humphreys Affair"', *Quadrant* 11 (3) (May-June 1967): pp. 54–56; other refs in D.W. Rayment, 'The Philosophy Department Split at Sydney University 1964–1973', BA Hons thesis, History Dept, Sydney University, 1999, p. 14; also F. Moorhouse, 'The importance of the word "Berkeley"', *Sydney Libertarians Broadsheet* 50 (Nov 1966): pp. 1–6, with reply by Stove 51 (May 1967): 9; R. Smilde, 'Sydney University suspends a student', *SLB* 52 (Aug 1967): pp. 1–6; A. Stout, 'Academic freedom and the student revolution', in *Liberty and Politics*, ed. O. Harries (Sydney, 1976), pp. 61–80.

[27] D. Stove, 'University notes: Sydney', *Quadrant* 14 (2) (Mar-Apr 1970): pp. 37–39.

[28] W. Suchting, 'Philosophy', in *Paper Tigers*, ed. R. O'Donnell *et al.* (Sydney, 1978), pp. B67–B78, at p. B69.

[29] Analysis in J. Curthoys, 'The head scene', *Old Mole* no. 7 (26/10/1970), p. 9.

topics, but changed direction completely. His best-known article had begun, 'I believe that it is now pretty generally accepted by professional philosophers that ultimate ethical principles must be arbitrary,'[30] a view with evident tendencies to encourage the substitution for morality of either total inaction or politics. Medlin's choice was politics. He was one of the leaders in Adelaide of the Vietnam protests, which he continually pushed in a more radical direction.[31] 'With his long, straight black hair,' burbled the papers, 'he looks like a cross between Che Guevara and Tariq Ali.' He was known also for readings of his poems, many of them not published because of the 'Lawrentian use of Anglo-Saxon words'.[32] He succeeded in being gaoled for five days in 1971 after resisting arrest during the Moratorium demonstration and refusing to pay the fine.[33] Four of the five members of the Flinders philosophy department converted to revolutionary socialism. A subject on 'Vietnam, imperialism and the nature of man' was the harbinger of a total transformation of the department's courses to Marxism, especially Maoism.[34]

An article by Medlin of the time, 'Strategy for the revolution', explains why action is needed to break up the complacency of the people. 'Most of the deprivation is unapparent to the deprived,' so the populace are not going to start the revolution spontaneously. But the revolutionary will not initiate violence. He will provoke the system with apparently respectable actions, staying just ahead of the liberals, who must be kept on side. The system will then be goaded into violent repression, which will induce *and justify* revolutionary violence:

> In case my doctrine should strike some as timid, I wish to make it clear that I would not regard the wholesale assassination of the Australian cabinet, in defence of the Vietnamese revolution, as an act initiating violence. Provided that such an action would bring to an end Australia's aggression in Indo-China, it would be entirely justified as a reasonable, though vio-

---

[30] B. Medlin, 'Ultimate principles and ethical egoism', *AJP* 35 (1957): pp. 111–18.

[31] M. Saunders, 'The campaign for peace in Vietnam (S.A.) 1967–1973', *Flinders Journal of History & Politics* 4 (1974): pp. 117–23.

[32] 'A rare Australian bird on the banks of the Thames', *SMH* 28/6/1968; 'A book of poems', *On Dit* 38 (9) (13/7/1970): p. 7, 'Medlin replies', 38 (11) (31/7/1970): p. 2; 'Three poems', *Quadrant* 12 (4) (July-Aug 1968): pp. 9–11; 'The argument from evil', *Southern Review* 3 (1969): p. 218; see 'To Brian Medlin', in J.J. Bray, *Poems 1961–1971* (Milton, Qld, 1972), p. 27; Pybus, *The Devil and James McAuley*, p. 224; earlier protest in *Australian* 5/1/1966; debate on 2FC, 26/5/1971.

[33] *SMH* 25/3/1971, p. 2; 2/4/1971, p. 1.

[34] *Australian* 16/12/1970, p. 13; also 18/12/1970, p. 3; D. Hilliard, *Flinders University: The First Twenty-Five Years* (Adelaide, 1991), pp. 57–8.

lent, response to the violence of the Australian Government. What would
be wrong with such an action is that it would be worse than ineffective: it
would strengthen the Australian counter-revolution. This is because it
would be *seen* as initiating violence ... Killing the Australian cabinet
would be bad tactics. There are two reasons for this. In the first place, a
number of men would be killed to no good end. For this reason alone,
then, the action would be a bad one — however agreeable some of us
would find it to throttle cabinet ministers with our bare hands. In the second place, forgetting the fate of the cabinet ministers, the action would be
a disaster for the Australian revolution. Hence it would strengthen the
bourgeoisie and so generally increase human misery. Bad tactics in a good
cause are bad morality.[35]

Good news for the cabinet, but not so encouraging for softer targets such as philosophy departments. As large street demonstrations
became rare after 1971, leftist agitation concentrated on smaller and
more focused campaigns. As long as the left could keep small numbers of committed students 'confronting' authority, university ad-
ministrations were faced with the dilemma of failing to react, leading
to contempt for their gutlessness and to further demands, or reacting
firmly, causing radicalisation of a wider body of students.[36]

The high point of philosophical 'action' came at the Australasian
philosophy conference of 1970, when Medlin draped a red flag over
the lectern before giving his talk on 'The onus of proof in political
argument'. The conference passed the resolution 'that the United
States and Australia are engaged in a senseless and inhuman struggle in
Indo-China and affirms that Australians are justified in opposing
Allied military involvement in the Indo-China war and conscription
for that war by non-violent acts of civil disobedience.' (Eighteen for,
twelve against, six abstaining.)[37]

There was a danger — or opportunity, depending on one's point
of view — of philosophy being swallowed by politics. David Stove,
seeing Sydney University as on a pre-Flinders stage on a slippery
slope, wrote:

> For the essence of totalitarianism is contained in the great helmsman's in-
> junction to 'put politics in command'. This is not just Communist-Chi-

[35] B. Medlin, 'Strategy for the revolution', *Dialectic* (Newcastle University) 7
(1972): pp. 46–65, at p. 51.
[36] D.M. Armstrong, 'The nature of our democracy', *Dialectic* 7 (1972): pp. 1–
9, at p. 4.
[37] *AJP* 48 (1970): p. 420; Santamaria in *News Weekly* no. 1378 (9/9/1970): p.
16; G. Molnar, 'Mr Santamaria and the philosophers', *Honi Soit* 43 (29)
(8/10/1970): pp. 6–7, 12; earlier, G.P. Molnar, 'The mania for action',
Quadrant 12 (4) (July-Aug 1968): pp. 25–6; G. Molnar, 'Rights and freedom
in a University', *Sydney Libertarians Broadsheet* 52 (Aug 1967): pp. 9–12.

nese baby-talk. What it means is this: that you are to take over every institution, whatever it may be, and empty out everything which distin-
guishes it from other institutions, and turn it into yet another loudspeaker
for repeating 'the general line'. Destroy the specific institutional fabric of
— a University, a trade-union, a sporting body, a church — and give
them all the same institutional content, viz. a political one. Contraposi-
tively, the essence of resistance to this process by liberal-democrats must
consist in trying to maintain the specific institutional integrity of different
institutions.[38]

Stove and Armstrong were not, however, skilful in gaining support
among the student body. Dr Knopfelmacher's abilities in that area
were sorely missed.

Was resistance to extend to opposing the appointment to academic
positions of candidates committed to revolution? David Armstrong
announced that he would not vote on a selection committee for a
candidate who was 'not prepared to work within the institutional
framework of the University, e.g. if he was associated with sit-ins and
disruption as opposed to due process. DMA emphasised that he saw
this not as a punitive action, but as a matter of protecting the institution against known dangers.'[39] Staff who did want to politicise the
University thus saw Armstrong as a known danger to their careers.

By contrast, the other side argued that there was no standpoint
outside the political. According to John Burnheim, among the least
radical of those who came to form the Department of General Philosophy, this was supported by the nineteenth-century European tradition, which emphasised the historical situatedness of all beliefs:

> The philosopher, like it or not, must take a position that rests not on
> ultimate truths, but on a reading of our specific historical situation.
> Inevitably it will be a partisan reading, since our situation is one of deep
> conflicts that we are certainly not in a position to resolve on a neutral or
> impartial basis. Recognising this point engenders the fear that philosophy
> will degenerate into mere politics. It may indeed. But the appropriate
> response is not an attempt to withdraw to untenable 'olympian' positions,
> but to attempt to arrive at a more adequate understanding of the situation
> and the choices it imposes on us. We might even emerge in the twentieth
> century.[40]

---

[38] D. Stove, 'Santamaria and the philosophers', *Honi Soit* 43 (32)
(29/10/1970): p. 11, similarly Armstrong in *Australian* 18/12/1970, p. 11.

[39] Staff meeting 27/5/1971, summary of proceedings (Devitt Documents:
hereafter 'DD': a collection kept by Michael Devitt, to whom I am grateful
for supplying them. Most of them are also in the Armstrong papers, National
Library MS 9363, series 6).

[40] J. Burnheim, '"Profound crisis" in philosophy', *University of Sydney News* 8
(11/10/1976): p. 200; on this topic, J.E. Grumley, *History and Totality:*

D.M. Armstrong, "the Beast", attempts to seize back the microphone, 24 June 1971 (Fairfax Photos)

In June 1971, David Armstrong chaired a lunchtime talk by the First Secretary of the South Vietnamese Embassy. A student formerly expelled from the University[41] took the microphone at the end of the talk and began abusing the speaker. Armstrong tried to seize the microphone back, and a scuffle ensued while he was restrained. The incident is remembered for a spectacular photograph taken of an enraged Armstrong trying to grab the microphone.[42] People had the picture blown up and took to referring to Armstrong as 'the Beast'.

By this time, the challenge long feared by Armstrong and Stove had arrived in their own department. Wal Suchting and Michael Devitt proposed for 1972 and 1973 courses in Marxism-Leninism (options for second and third year, in consecutive years, so that a student

Radical Historicism from Hegel to Foucault (London, 1989); also J. Burnheim, 'After religion — reflections on the post-Christian situation', *Quadrant* 16 (1) (Jan-Feb 1972): pp. 38–44; J. Burnheim, 'The destruction of philosophy', *Quadrant* 43 (7-8) (July-Aug 1999): pp. 20–23; M. Deutscher, *Subjecting and Objecting* (St Lucia, 1983), p. 2.

[41] M. Bloom, 'The ASIO–Hall Greenland affair', *On Dit* 38 (11) (31/7/1970): 12; *Honi Soit* 43 (20) (16/7/1970): p. 1; *Old Mole* no. 1 (1/6/1970): p. 1.

[42] *SMH* 25/6/1971, p. 3; *Australian* 25/6/1971, p. 3.

could take both). The outline of the courses included mention of the ideas of Stalin, Ho Chi Minh, Mao and Che Guevara, though these were to take up only a small proportion of the courses. Armstrong was willing to agree to a certain amount of teaching on Marx ('not a major philosopher ... but a major thinker'), but jibbed at the other names. 'These men have no place in the history of *thought*. They were engaged exclusively in political activity.' He also objected to the total weight that would be given to Marxism and doubted the objectivity of the lecturers, who made no secret of their left-wing commitments. Suchting and Devitt said Che and Mao had a few interesting ideas, and claimed their course would be 'objective' but of course not 'neutral'. 'Neutrality means not espousing a position ... [it] is neither desirable in theory nor realisable in practice.'

Matters came to a head at a departmental meeting on 7 June 1971. Suchting, Devitt and Armstrong reiterated their positions. Stove suggested that the reference to 'theory and practice' in the course outline ought to be interpreted in the Leninist sense. 'He alleged that the courses were an imposture and that they must be regarded as the first step in the process of complete politicisation.' The proposers agreed to remove the word 'Leninism' from the title, and voting was then ten to three in favour of the proposed courses. Armstrong as head of department vetoed them. The meeting carried eight-to-four a motion of censure against Armstrong for his veto.[43] The issues of Marxism, democratisation of departments and 'academic freedom' were thus rolled into one and the fight was on. The battle lines of the era, normally dividing parties who had never met each other, were drawn across a department of a dozen people sharing a common room. A moderate, Keith Campbell, urged a conciliatory style, given that victors and vanquished would have to go on living and working together.[44] It was not going to happen. Armstrong, Suchting and Molnar belonged to the crash-through-or-crash school of politics.

After negotiations in higher university bodies and press comment, a compromise was patched up, with one course going ahead under the name 'Marxism'.[45] It was obvious that the next conflict could not be far off.

---

[43] Armstrong to Suchting and Devitt, 3/6/1971, reply of same date (DD); 'Staff meeting of 7th June, 1971, summary of proceedings', (DD).
[44] Campbell to Devitt, 14/9/1971 (DD).
[45] *Nation* no. 319 (26/6/1971): pp. 7–10; *University of Sydney News* 3 (7) (16/6/1971): pp. 1, 7; 3 (10) (28/7/1971): pp. 1–2; 'The philosophy dispute: An interview with Wal Suchting and Michael Devitt', *Honi Soit* 8/7/1971, pp. 8–9; Bogdan, *D.M. Armstrong*, p. 36; press comment listed in C. Green, *Disputes within the Department of Philosophy at the University of*

Michael Devitt (left) and Wal Suchting, 8 June 1971 (Fairfax Photos)

In 1972, Professor Graham Nerlich had the unenviable job of Head of Department. Democratisation proceeded apace. A meeting that included postgraduate and undergraduate representatives recommended the appointment as a tutor of a Marxist[46] whom Armstrong did not regard as the best candidate. He complained to the administration about such a wide suffrage being allowed in matters of appointments, and tensions exceeded their previous maximum. Devitt wrote an enraged private note to Nerlich, suggesting tactics for dealing with the situation. He added a postscript: 'It is now clear that the Beast will not leave any of us in peace. It seems necessary therefore that he be discredited and driven from the University. I shall henceforth support any tactic (within certain limits) that seems likely to help the achievement of this end.'

Sydney 1971–1973 (School of Social and Policy Studies in Education, University of Sydney, paper, 1991), pp. 5–6.

[46] Rayment, 'The Philosophy Department Split', pp. 47–50; P. Flanagan, 'Chomsky and his critics', *Old Mole* no. 3 (29/6/1970): pp. 14–15; P. Flanagan & W. Suchting, 'Radical literature in university libraries in Sydney', *Australian Library Journal* 21 (1972): pp. 49–51.

Nerlich proposed to take no notice of it ('Look, I have people bursting into my office all the time saying wild and inflammatory things', he said later), but the note somehow fell into Armstrong's hands. Here, it seemed, was Marxist-Leninist praxis, red in tooth and claw, not only on the doorstep but inside it. Armstrong felt it necessary to publish the note 'in self-defence'. Peter Coleman took the matter up in state Parliament, reading the offending sections of Devitt's letter and arguing, 'If academic self-government is to be used as an excuse for left-wing McCarthyites to smear responsible professors, responsible educators, and to drive them out of education institutions, then there is something wrong either with the doctrine of academic self-government, or with the practice of it.' Santamaria urged Armstrong to demand Devitt's dismissal, but it was felt more advantageous to take the rare opportunity for the right to enjoy underdog status.[47] Devitt denied there had been any actual plot; earlier and later evidence makes it clear that that was true, but some recalled the Orr and Knopfelmacher cases as warnings that threats to destroy academic careers were not to be taken lightly. The Vice-Chancellor rejected Armstrong's appeal, and the tutor chosen by the departmental meeting was appointed.[48]

As expected, 1973 was not a year of peace and harmony. In late 1972, a departmental meeting widened suffrage to all philosophy students including those in first year, thus delivering control to those radical enough to keep turning up.[49] Philosophy was the only department to go as far as that. A subsequent meeting allowed the teacher of any option to decide how students were to be passed and graded, meaning that exams and assignments could be dispensed with. By this time, feminism had appeared as an organised force, and was demanding a place in university courses. It was unclear where it should fit, as the then new theory of feminism could as easily be called anthropology, sociology or political theory as philosophy. The lack of a place for theory about the private sphere or 'politics of experience' was one

[47] W.H.C. Eddy to Stove, 30/8/1972.
[48] G. Harris, ed, 'Quadrangle papers' issue of *Honi Soit* 45 no. 20 (14/9/1972); Rayment, 'The Philosophy Department Split', pp. 51–6, with a different opinion on the 'plot'; *Nation Review* 26/8/1972; *Australian* 23/8/1972, p. 3; Coleman in Legislative Assembly, 23/8/1972 (*NSW Parliamentary Debates* 3rd ser vol 99 pp. 243–4, 803); Clyde Packer question, Legislative Council 5/9/1972 (p. 579); B. Williams, then VC, to author, 25/12/2002, on the need for any appeal to go to Academic Board; other documents listed in Green, pp. 8–12.
[49] Bogdan, *D.M. Armstrong*, p. 38; Rayment, 'The Philosophy Department Split', p. 56.

of the phenomena whose analysis was promised.[50] In February 1973, two graduate students took up a trouble-making idea from Suchting.[51] Jean Curthoys and Liz Jacka proposed a course on 'The politics of sexual oppression', to run as an option in philosophy in the second half of the year. Apart from the content, the proposal was unusual in being put forward six months later than normal, and in being offered by graduate students — though investigation did turn up a few other courses being given by similarly qualified postgraduates.

The old issues of objectivity and bias were raised in a radio interview in which Jacka and Curthoys outlined their plans:

Jacka: ... and finally we hope to discuss how women may liberate themselves. Whether it will be by conventional, political action, by raising their consciousness or by other methods including revolution.

Interviewer: Is it a political propaganda course then?

Jacka: Not necessarily. We don't pretend to be neutral. We are committed to women's liberation. But we hope to maintain objectivity and philosophical rigour in our discussion.

Interviewer: Jean, is this the new phase in the women's lib movement?

Curthoys: In my personal opinion, yes. I think that up until now, although women's liberation has been very effective, that it has suffered from a lack of theory and in a sense a lack of direction. I hope that our course will help remedy this. I personally think the future of the women's lib movement lies in tying itself up with Marxist movements.[52]

Curthoys was later to surmise that the explosion in women's studies courses in universities in 1974 was a sign that women were becoming content to work within universities, instead of radically transforming their function.[53] Her views on the need for radical transformation were far from Devitt's 'no threat' scenario. Her radical views stemmed from her descent from Communist royalty and her long involvement in Sixties protest.[54]

---

[50] Curthoys speech of 26/6/1973, summarised in 'Strike: Sydney University', *Scrounge* no. 3–4 (June 1973), pp. 13–18.
[51] Rayment, 'The Philosophy Department Split', p. 64.
[52] P. Westmore, 'The strike at Sydney University', *Quadrant* 17 (4) (July–Aug 1973): pp. 23–9, at p. 25.
[53] J. Curthoys, 'Political challenge or co-opted movement?', in *Guide to Women's Studies in Australia*, ed. P. Ryan (Melbourne, 1975), pp. 6–8; also J. Curthoys, 'Memoirs of a feminist dinosaur', *Australian Feminist Studies* 13 (1998): pp. 55–61.
[54] *SMH* 8/4/1966, p. 1; *Daily Telegraph* 3/11/1965; NSW Special Branch file 24/66; family background in B. Curthoys, 'International Women's Day in Newcastle in the Fifties and Sixties: A personal account', *Labour History* 66 (1994): pp. 122–8.

The department voted overwhelmingly for the course, although the minority voting against it included the four most senior members. The Faculty of Arts also approved it, though only on the casting vote of the chairman. The Professorial Board rejected the proposed course, and a strike of staff and students began, spreading to several arts and social science departments and disrupting lectures in them for weeks. Students attending the lectures of Armstrong and other non-striking philosophers faced pickets outside and inside the lectures. Tents were pitched on the quadrangle lawn. Jack Mundey appeared on campus and promised a Builders Labourers Federation ban on work at the University.[55]

After various negotiations and inquiries, the University's governing bodies agreed to the course, under the title 'Philosophical aspects of feminist thought', and with a more or less nominal supervision by John Burnheim. In effect, it was an outright win for the strikers.[56]

A visitor described the victory party:

> They were singing sentimental Irish songs under the banner 'Philosophers hitherto have only interpreted the world — the point now is to change it.'

> They had two four-gallon casks of wine — which is counter-culturally acceptable alcohol; spirits and beer are frowned upon, spirits because of their upper-income connotations and beer because it is associated with the worst kinds of Australian male behaviour.

> We talked briefly with George Molnar, a lecturer in philosophy who had been centrally active in the strike. He was making the 'goodies' in the kitchen (not savouries).

> 'Tomorrow the world', he said.[57]

From the other side, the outlook was gloomy. Armstrong wrote: 'In the immediate aftermath of the strike, things seemed very bleak.

---

[55] Rayment, 'The Philosophy Department Split', p 66; M. & V. Burgmann, *Green Bans, Red Union* (Sydney, 1998), p. 144.

[56] Westmore, 'The strike'; A. Bashford, 'The return of the repressed: Feminism in the Quad', *Australian Feminist Studies* 13 (1998): pp. 47–54; M.D. Jones, Remembering Academic Feminism, PhD thesis, University of Sydney, 2003; 'Proposed appointment of two part-time lecturers in philosophy', *University of Sydney News* 5 (9) (4/7/1973): pp. 1–2; 'Special report on philosophy dispute', *USN* 25/7/1973: pp. 87–94; Bogdan, *D.M. Armstrong*, pp. 38–40; Connell, *Australia's First*, vol. 2, pp. 167–8, 388–9; 115 documents listed in Green, pp. 14–27.

[57] F. Moorhouse, 'For the course, for the strike — and for the party', *Bulletin* 4/8/1973, repr. in *Days of Wine and Rage* (Ringwood, 1980), pp. 43–5; opposite view in P. Shrubb, 'Meeting life', *Quadrant* 17 (4) (July-Aug 1973): p. 5; see G. Molnar, 'Drugs and freedom' *Tharunka* 16 (3) (18/3/1970): p. 9.

The radicals had effective control of the department, and there seemed to be no future in it for the rest of us. Some older members of staff planned to retire early, others started to look for jobs elsewhere. It did not seem that it would be possible for philosophy as we understood it to go on being practised and taught at Sydney University.[58] Nerlich did leave, taking a chair in Adelaide. Stove had applied for positions elsewhere but without success. But salvation, of a kind, was at hand. Campbell, who had been a moderate and was grossly insulted by the radicals for it, got together a proposal to split the department. Faced with the probable loss of the philosophers of repute, the Vice-Chancellor agreed. Armstrong and six others formed the Department of Traditional and Modern Philosophy. It became 'the pleasantest environment for teaching philosophy that I have ever experienced', Armstrong says, while David Stove said in 1991, 'the first twenty years of the new Department of Traditional and Modern Philosophy have been fertile in good philosophy, to a degree unparalleled in any similar period in this or any other Australian university. The department has also enjoyed a rare freedom from internal disharmony. As I have often said, it is the best club in the world, and to be or have been a member of it is a pleasure as well as a privilege.'[59] The resulting philosophy is described elsewhere, mostly in chapter 12.

The atmosphere was not so tranquil in the other department, which was allowed to get away with the name General Philosophy. Animosity had already run high in the strike itself between feminists and the unreconstructed Marxist males who regarded the women's course merely as a pretext for another fight about democratisation and self-management.[60] The course went ahead laden with Marxist concepts like the mode of production and the ideology of bourgeois science[61] but the search was on for more authentically feminist replacements. The appearance of the phrase 'transcending the Aristotelian subject/object distinction' heralded the strange future of feminist theory, to be described in chapter 14.

[58] Bogdan, *D.M. Armstrong*, p. 39; Rayment, 'The Philosophy Department Split', pp. 63, 72–3.
[59] D. Stove, 'David Armstrong, Challis Professor of Philosophy', speech for Armstrong's retirement, 14/11/1991.
[60] A. Neale, 'The philosophy strike', *Refractory Girl* 3 (Winter 1973): pp. 28–9; D. McKnight, 'Red letter: Successful uni strike', *Tribune* 31/7/1973, p. 5; D. Payne, 'Victory for women's course', *Direct Action* 44 (19/7/1973), p. 9.
[61] E. Jacka, 'Philosophical aspects of feminist thought', *Refractory Girl* 4 (Spring 1973): p. 51; J. Curthoys in 'Sexism in the university', pamphlet, July(?) 1973 (DD).

The Department of General Philosophy was fully democratic, with all staff and students having the right to speak and vote on matters of course content, assessment and appointments. Meetings of up to 500 were known, though student apathy kept most down to 20 or so. Formal exams were eliminated[62] and in some subjects students assessed themselves. Enrolments were much larger than for the Trad and Mod Department — in 1978, GP had about 750 to T & M's 200. But all was not sweetness and light. For one thing, the Administration played hard ball. Though they never had the stomach to 'clean up' GP, they did fail to provide extra resources to cope with the extra students, and periodically threatened to forcibly amalgamate the two departments. They also refused to allow the Department a full Professor, as would have been normal, which permitted David Armstrong, as 'Professor most concerned', to interfere to some degree in various matters, especially appointments. But the more important source of trouble was a series of internal disputes, splits and scandals. They mostly arose from the domination of departmental meetings by a group led by Wal Suchting and calling itself the 'Marxist caucus'.[63] It was regarded by others as ruling by vigorous meeting attendance, humiliation and ridicule. Wal was, according to outsiders then and insiders since, in his element.

Devitt, who wanted to get on with mainstream philosophy, found himself increasingly isolated. A tutor was appointed in logic who thought logic played a reactionary role in maintaining bourgeois philosophical ideology.[64] Devitt failed in an attempt to have a permanent position that had been vacated by a specialist in logic and language filled by someone in the same area. A tutor not in the ruling group, who had been persuaded to come from the US by Burnheim with a written offer of a job for three years, found himself out of a job after two, courtesy of a departmental meeting.[65] Some bravely urged that promises created a moral obligation. Devitt recalls that the Caucus were not impressed by this piece of bourgeois morality. 'I attended a Caucus meeting (although not a member) where the whole matter was discussed. Someone asked what Burnheim's position was. I viv-

[62] See G. Molnar, 'The examined life is not worth living', *Radical Philosophy* 8 (Summer 1974): pp. 2–6.

[63] *Honi Soit* 29/6/1976, p. 13.

[64] R. Archer to Devitt, 4/6/1976 (DD).

[65] G. Molnar, 'Sydney University's second philosophy department — appearance and reality', *Sydney Libertarians Broadsheet* 92 (Sept 1977): pp. 6–10; B. Neilson, 'To all students of general philosophy', June 1976 (DD).

idly remember Wal's reply: he chuckled cynically and simply went through the motions of washing his hands.'[66]

Jean Curthoys, then much under Suchting's influence, openly defended the political nature of the decision at the meeting: 'It is important to be clear on two things: (1) That all appointments are political appointments and (2) that part of the case against Bryan and for Julie and Dick is quite frankly political.' Since the whole point of the department is 'a critique of all the practices of other departments in the University, as well as of society at large', 'the reason that Bryan cannot assist the particular school of philosophy we think it is important to develop is that his whole philosophical approach is the orthodox one it is our object to criticise.'[67] If those were the chances of a candidate actually present, the prospects of anyone absent were even less. Over many years, the determination of GP to appoint only its own candidates to positions became an ever better-known scandal.

Marks as well as appointments were handed out for political rather than intellectual performance.[68] Even Suchting, who certainly took scholarship seriously, regarded the department's inflated marks for poor work as indefensible.[69] 'It is well known,' he wrote a few years later, 'if perhaps seldom (very seldom) noted and discussed, that a student can pass a course in GP by attending next to no classes in that course, so long as s/he puts in an essay of a very minimum standard of merit on some subject more or less connected with the course, at some time or other ... I personally find it very demoralising to give a reasonable course to such and such a number of more or less regularly attending students (classes tend to be treated like lengthy TV movies that one watches off and on during the evening, with breaks for a drink and a snack, a game of chess, etc.) and then find submitted at the end a number of scripts far more numerous than that, most of which I am more or less obliged to pass, though they bear no impress of the course at all ... This sort of assessment very largely ... accounts for the size of our enrolment.'[70] At one point, it was discovered that the department was giving a course without official approval — on

---

[66] Devitt to author, 1/1/1998; cf. J. Burnheim, 'Public morality and structures of decision making', *Bulletin of the Australian Society of Legal Philosophy* 16 (1991): pp. 24–36.

[67] 'Appointments are a political issue', *Honi Soit* 29/6/1976, p. 13.

[68] Molnar, 'Sydney University's second philosophy department'; Devitt to VC, 22/12/1976 (DD); J. Curthoys, 'The loyalty requirement', *Quadrant* 43 (10) (Oct 1999): pp. 5–6.

[69] W. Suchting, Memo to all members of GP, 16/12/1975 (DD).

[70] W. Suchting, 'A modest proposal regarding assessment in GP', 25/9/1983 (DD).

anarchism, appropriately enough — and allowing self-assessment in it.[71]

Devitt denounced the Caucus:

> What is disturbing, and, in a way, more relevant, is the typical practice of (small) Marxist groups in capitalist countries. Bourgeois critics refer to them as 'dogmatic', 'ruthless', 'fanatical', etc. It seems to me that these labels are unpleasantly close to the truth. Their approach to theory tends to be narrow-minded and inflexible. At their best such groups are simply insensitive to outsiders; at their worst they treat them with a relentless inhumanity, intolerance and contempt. Warmth, kindness and generosity are more despised than admired (unless the beneficiary is a 'comrade'). What is strikingly lacking is an appropriate degree of *scepticism* about themselves, their theories, and their actions; a *sense of proportion*. Indeed the atmosphere is more religious than scientific; converts struggling to learn the new theology ... advocating the 'tough' line is psychologically and socially (within the group) rewarding ... and the same grounds are readily available, of course, to dismiss criticisms of the sort to be found here.[72]

These views on Marxist sects were hardly original, but few have had the opportunity to observe their truth so closely.

Devitt and two others had had enough, and began negotiating secretly with the Vice-Chancellor with a view to re-amalgamation. 'The VC puffed smoke, made encouraging noises, and did nothing. (It was often hard to tell if he was breathing.)'[73] When it became clear nothing was going to happen, they quit General Philosophy, again denouncing the intimidation, insults, ostracising and hectoring there. They joined the Traditional and Modern Department, becoming known as the first wave of 'boat people'.[74] The remaining members were rocked. The radicals wanted to keep up the fight: 'Certainly the department may be destroyed, but better it be destroyed than it evolve into a Traditionalist department.'[75] Burnheim, as usual, and Suchting, unusually, and others in receipt of salaries advised caution. The 'period of easy offensives is over', Wal announced.[76]

---

[71] 'Gee, I'm good!', *Bulletin* 24/7/1979, p. 140; Devitt to VC Ward, 24/7/1979 (DD).

[72] M. Devitt, 'Some thoughts on being asked to join the Marxist Caucus', 24/6/1976 (DD); Curthoys, 'The loyalty requirement'.

[73] Devitt to author, 1/1/1998.

[74] *Honi Soit* 14/9/1976, p. 8; 5/10/1976, pp. 10–11; 19/10/1976, p. 22; *University of Sydney News* 9 (18/4/1977), pp. 51, 53.

[75] Ted Sadler, 'General Philosophy: One step forward, two steps back', *Honi Soit* 5/4/1977, p. 7; M. Campioni, 'To the curriculum committee/appointments committee', 8/12/1977 (DD).

[76] W. Suchting, 'A letter from afar', 16/4/1977 (DD); J. Burnheim, 'The future of the Department of General Philosophy', 1977 (DD).

What the department was teaching its students in these early years can be gathered from the 1978 anthology *Paper Tigers*, which arose out of the first-year General Philosophy 'Counter-ideology' course. The anthology gives a good insight to the general thought-world that spread in the social sciences as the expansion of the Whitlam years delivered control in those disciplines to the Marxist scholars called by their enemies the 'tenured radicals'. Much of it is concerned with attacking what is taught in other disciplines in the University. 'In practice, the process of *de*mystifying what is offered to us as objective knowledge, and of offering an alternative, has been inseparable from struggle against the educational practices and authoritarian organisation of the university itself.'[77] It was hoped that the 'bourgeois' departments being attacked would respond by trying to suppress the course, leading to some useful action.[78]

The volume is especially interesting because, in contrast to the general run of Marxist philosophy,[79] the authors have taken seriously the introductory nature of the exercise, and the result is by and large coherent and free from obscure jargon. This makes all the stronger its inescapable air of a floating world. Everything is to be analysed without residue in terms of 'class conflict': what people do is to be explained in terms of their class interest. No attempt is made to present evidence that that is the only, the best, or even a possible explanation. Nor is there any effort to ground concepts of mass psychology like 'class' in individual psychology. It is explicitly denied that the capitalist class literally conspire (usually) to advance their class interest, and it is suggested that by and large they do not even consciously recognise

[77] Ted Sadler, Preface, *Paper Tigers*, ed. R. O'Donnell, P. Stevens & I. Lennie (Sydney, 1978), p. vii; another intoduction in M. Harnecker, *The Basic Concepts of Historical Materialism* trans. E. Sadler & W. Suchting (Sydney, 1976).

[78] Ted Sadler, 'Discussion document: The role of counter-ideology in General Philosophy', 7/10/1975 (DD).

[79] Historical overview in A.R. Giles-Peters, 'The Marxist tradition', in *Essays on Philosophy in Australia*, ed. J.T.J. Srzednicki & B. Wood (Dordrecht, 1992), pp. 153–68; W. Hudson, *The Marxist Philosophy of Ernest Bloch* (London, 1982); the older party view in Education Committee of the Central Committee, Communist Party of Australia, *Philosophy: A Guide to Action for the Working Man* (Sydney, 1965); E. Aarons, *Philosophy for an Exploding World* (Sydney, 1972); later in J. Allen & P. Patton, eds, *Beyond Marxism?* (Sydney, 1983); A. Gare, *Beyond European Civilization: Marxism, Process Philosophy and the Environment* (Bungendore, 1993); I. Hunt, *Analytical and Dialectical Marxism* (Aldershot, 1993); consequences for school education in M.R. Matthews, *The Marxist Theory of Schooling* (Brighton, 1980), p. 200; K. Harris, *Education and Knowledge: The Structured Misrepresentation of Reality* (London, 1979).

it.[80] As a result, how class interest acts causally on anything is left as magic.

It is apparently the need to keep the theory floating unsupported that causes so much of the effort in the book to be devoted to explaining why empirical support for theories is a bad thing (this is denounced as the error of 'empiricism', which is criticised with much reference to work in the philosophy of science on the supposed impossibility of distinguishing between observations and theories). The lack of evidence is in one way just as well, as the rare excursions into matters of fact are not happy ones: 'Despite their defects in other areas, such as political liberties, the U.S.S.R, the Chinese People's Republic, and others, have made considerable progress in the elimination of poverty, unemployment, anarchic production and so on, by ending the capitalist economic system.'[81] Further, any demand that mass terms like classes should be explained in terms of people is put down to the bourgeois error of 'individualism'.

In his contribution, Suchting maintains the Marxist dogma that all opponents are infected with 'idealism'. Thus analytic philosophy is supposed to be confined to the analysis of concepts. That may have had some truth as applied to Melbourne Wittgensteinianism — paradoxically far left politically — but was obviously untrue of Sydney philosophy, as in Armstrong's *A Materialist Theory of the Mind*. Suchting simply labels Armstrong an idealist.[82]

Study of this material would tend to rot the critical faculties, if someone enrolling in General Philosophy had any left. As to the moral faculties, the effect would seem to be the same.[83] The only sin mentioned is oppression, which is committed by classes, not individuals. It appears to follow that the only virtue is solidarity and that personal morality is a leftover of bourgeois individualism that is a mere cloak for class interest and is best abandoned. This consequence is not explicitly drawn out. Indeed, the whole point is to avoid talking about any such personal issues and to replace morality with political commitment.

It is customary for philosophers of a continental bent to declare themselves for one or other European author, commentary on whose

---

[80] O'Donnell, Stevens & Lennie eds, *Paper Tigers*, p. 7; for a serious treatment of the issue see C.B. McCullagh, 'How objective interests explain actions', *Social Science Information* 30 (1991): pp. 29–54.

[81] O'Donnell, Stevens & Lennie eds, *Paper Tigers*, p. 12.

[82] W. Suchting, 'Philosophy', in O'Donnell, Stevens & Lennie eds, *Paper Tigers*, pp. B67–B80, at B70; further W. Suchting, 'On materialism', *Radical Philosophy* 31 (Summer 1982): pp. 1–9.

[83] Polemic along these lines in P. Shrubb, 'Down at the Works: Pure Mind', *A List of All People and Other Stories* (Sydney, 1982), pp. 211–6.

works provides the mass of the scholars' own output. In General Philosophy, first choice of guru was Louis Althusser, author of *For Marx, Reading Capital, Lenin and Philosophy*, etc.[84] Embarrassingly, Geoffrey Harris, a student of both the Sydney University Philosophy Department and the Aquinas Academy, visited Paris, secured an interview with Althusser, and brought back bad news for his Australian disciples. He had never heard of them, and when their interpretation of his work was explained he denounced it as a travesty. The movement of his thought, he said, was away from ideology, and he had this message: 'Go and tell the comrades down there, on my behalf, not to confuse philosophy with ideology nor to reduce philosophy to political agitation.'[85] But the Althusserian message that one might be just as good a revolutionary by producing dense theory as by agitating in the streets had already sunk in, so much so that some began complaining that real activists were becoming intimidated by theory.[86] 'As we all know', George Molnar said, 'Althusser himself stayed in bed during the Paris student uprising in 1968.'[87] In any case, a few years later Althusser suffered a recurrence of mental illness and murdered his wife. It was time to move on.

There were plenty more gurus where Althusser came from. An early favourite was Michel Foucault.[88] A faction that eventually over-

[84] W. Suchting, 'Louis Althusser's theory of history', *Arena* 20 (1974): pp. 22–8; Ted Sadler, 'Aspects of Althusser's epistemology', *Working Papers on Sex, Science and Culture* 1 (2) (Nov 1976): pp. 61–71; P. Patton, 'Althusser's epistemology', *Radical Philosophy* 19 (Spring 1978): pp. 8–18; earlier H. McQueen, 'Marx for himself', *Old Mole* no. 5 (31/8/1970): pp. 8–9; K. Gooding, 'Reading *Reading Capital*', *Australian Left Review* 31 (July 1971), 39 (Mar 1973), 40 (May 1973); Editorial, *Intervention* 1 (Apr 1972): pp. 3–8; J. Althofer, 'Activist and theoretical Marxism: Early receptions of Althusser in Australia', *Overland* 155 (Winter 1999): pp. 56–61.

[85] G. Harris, 'Burnheim's historicism', *University of Sydney News* 8 (15/11/1976): p. 222.

[86] T. Brennan, 'On academic Marxists', *Intervention* 10/11 (Aug 1978): pp. 69–75.

[87] Molnar, 'Sydney University's second philosophy department', p. 8.

[88] M. Morris & P. Patton, eds, *Michel Foucault: Power, Truth, Strategy* (Sydney, 1979); B. Hindess, *Discourses of Power: From Hobbes to Foucault* (Oxford, 1996); C. O'Farrell, *Foucault: Historian or Philosopher?* (Basingstoke, 1989); C. O'Farrell, ed, *Foucault: The Legacy* (Kelvin Grove, 1997); D. Williamson, *Authorship and Criticism* (Sydney, 1989); A. McHoul & W. Grace, *A Foucault Primer* (Melbourne, 1993); P. Barker, *Michel Foucault: Subversions of the Subject* (Sydney, 1994); C. Falzon, *Foucault and Social Dialogue* (London, 1998); J. Frow, 'Some versions of Foucault', *Meanjin* 47 (1988): pp. 144–56, 353–65; P.J. Dwyer, 'Foucault, docile bodies and post-compulsory education in Australia', *British Journal of Sociology of Education* 16 (1995): pp. 467–77; D.

threw the Marxist Caucus leaned towards French authors who combined Marxism, feminism and psychoanalysis — Irigaray, Lacan, Derrida, Lyotard, Baudrillard, Deleuze and so on.[89] 'The new wave is Freudo-semiotics etc,' said Wal gloomily.[90] The local impact of the feminists among these is described in chapter 14, that of the postmodernists in chapter 15.

In the face of student disillusionment with Marxism, *Paper Tigers* proving too hard for first-year students, and above all the loss of the numbers by the Marxist ruling staff faction, the acting head of the department in 1979, Alan Chalmers, suspended the democratic constitution and assumed the traditional powers of a head of department.[91] As Stove put it, 'General Chalmers has overthrown the government of General Philosophy. He has promised that free elections will be held *after order has been restored.*'[92] The promised restoration of democracy never took place. The department also increased its respectability by the appointment of a leading Hungarian Marxist forced to leave his own country, George Markus.[93]

Willett, 'Foucault and the history of homosexuality', *Melbourne Historical Journal* 24 (1996): pp. 10–25; C. Colebrook, 'Ethics, positivity and gender', *Philosophy Today* 42 (1998): pp. 40–52; M. Clinton & M. Hazelton, 'Towards a Foucauldian reading of the Australian mental health nursing workforce', *International Journal of Mental Health Nursing* 11 (2002): pp. 18–23; also D. Altman, *Defying Gravity* (Sydney, 1997), p. 96.

[89] E. Gross, 'Lacan, the symbolic, the imaginary and the real', *Working Papers in Sex, Science and Culture* 1 (2) (Nov 1976): pp. 12–32; later comment in E. Grosz, 'Identity and difference: A response', in *Critical Politics*, ed. P. James (Melbourne, 1994), pp. 29–33; M. Campioni, 'Psychoanalysis and Marxist feminism', pp. 33–59; T. Brennan, M. Campioni & M. Jacka, 'One step forward, two steps back', *Working Papers* 1 (1) (Jan 1976): pp. 15–45; R. Albury, 'Two readings of Freud: Juliet Mitchell and Luce Irigaray', pp. 4–14; M. Campioni & E. Gross, 'Little Hans: The production of Oedipus', in *Language, Sexuality and Subversion*, ed. P. Foss & M. Morris (Sydney, 1978), pp. 99–122; M. Campioni, 'The phenomenon of feminism in general philosophy', *Random Issue* 2 (June 1980): pp. 13–19; later T. Brennan, *History after Lacan* (London, 1993); P. Patton, *Deleuze and the Political* (London, 2000); C. Colebrook, *Understanding Deleuze* (London, 2002).

[90] Suchting to Molnar, 11/7/1978, in Molnar papers, Mitchell Library MLMSS 6978, box 1.

[91] A. Chalmers, announcement, 1979; 'Honest Al's philosophy department', poem (DD); earlier, *Honi Soit* 23/7/1979, p. 6.

[92] D.M. Armstrong to author, 3/3/1998.

[93] G. Bence & J. Kis, 'On being a Marxist: A Hungarian view', *Socialist Register* 1980, pp. 263–97, at pp. 288–94; G. Markus, *Marxism and Anthropology* (Assen, 1978); G. Markus, *Language and Production* (Dordrecht, 1986); G. Markus, 'Ferenc Feher, 1933–1994', *Thesis Eleven* 42 (1995): pp.

Meanwhile there were parallel developments at the pioneering university, Flinders. It had instituted a women's studies course in philosophy in 1973, the same year as Sydney. There was less trouble over it, though the usual reactionary academics had the usual complaints about matters such as group assessment and the policy of giving people 'the grade they feel they need'.[94] Medlin was appointed nominal co-convenor to keep the administration happy. Philosophy staff and students were prominent in the occupation of the administration buildings of 1974. In a probably unique development, the occupation was ended through spontaneous direct action by lackeys of the ruling class, when University staff who had been excluded from their offices for three weeks stormed the building and threw out the students.[95] The department continued its radical course on a track similar to Sydney's General Philosophy. No other major Australian philosophy department became primarily radical, but many acquired radical factions, necessitating a lot of exhausting organisational activity on all sides.[96]

Back at Sydney University, a new Vice-Chancellor found himself deluged by complaints about the doings of General Philosophy. In 1984, he was finally willing to grasp the nettle. After secret discussions with Traditional and Modern Philosophy, he announced, on a Friday, a coup giving control of a united School of Philosophy to Keith Campbell. It was to be effective immediately. Burnheim and GP worked furiously over the weekend to round up support. By Monday, the VC had caved in.[97] The result was that GP then had effective control of its appointments. They proceeded to use it, in securing the appointments of two internal feminist candidates, Denise Russell and Elizabeth Grosz, over outsiders regarded by T & M as obviously superior.

---

vi–vii; J. Grumley, P. Crittenden & P. Johnson, eds, *Culture and Enlightenment: Essays for Gyorgy Markus* (Aldershot, 2002).

[94] Ryan, *Guide to Women's Studies*, pp. 39–43; R. Helling, *The Politics of Women's Studies* (Adelaide, 1981), pp. 166–8; S. Sheridan, '"Transcending tauromachy": The beginnings of women's studies in Adelaide', *Australian Feminist Studies* 13 (1998): pp. 67–73.

[95] Hilliard, *Flinders University,* pp. 66, 68.

[96] Connections between GP and UTS in E. Morris, 'Report from the front', *Sydney Libertarians Broadsheet* 94 (Jan 1978): pp. 8–10; A. Curthoys, *For and Against Feminism* (Sydney, 1988), pp. 54–6; H. Wilson, 'Afterword' in H. Wilson, ed, *Australian Communications and the Public Sphere* (Melbourne, 1989), pp. 277–86; M. Wark, *The Virtual Republic* (Sydney, 1997), pp. 75–83.

[97] Devitt to author, 1/1/1998.

The Grosz case in particular showed the stark contrast between practice in General Philosophy and the standards applying in the rest of the Australian philosophical community. When Dr Grosz's appointment as lecturer was under consideration, eleven of the seventeen permanent members of the School of Philosophy conveyed to the selection committee their view that her appointment would be 'unacceptable in any circumstances.'[98] It was leaked that a moderate outside feminist was likely to be appointed, whereupon 60 members of the Faculty of Arts signed a petition in Grosz's favour, and further references were allowed for Grosz but not for the other candidates. Specious reasons were thought up to eliminate the strongest of the 55 external candidates. Charges against Grosz's teaching and assessment were ignored.[99] Grosz was appointed. Another wave of three 'boat people' left GP for T & M. They included Jean Curthoys.

In 1984–5 David Stove protested publicly that the Faculty of Arts was favouring women in appointments.[100] It appeared that the figures the administration had supplied him with were not accurate, which was a cause of embarrassment, but he relied also on information about individual cases such as those of Russell and Grosz. *Playboy* invited him to write, and 'Willesee' and 'Nationwide' suggested he appear on TV, but he declined his opportunity for fifteen minutes as performing seal.[101] Susan Ryan, the federal minister largely responsible for the Affirmative Action Act, embroidering on Stove's claim that contrary to there having been discrimination against women, philosophers would appoint a broomstick if it was the best philosopher, told the Senate, 'I will not extrapolate on the broomstick analogy and suggest that in the appointment of Professor Stove there was perhaps something other than total adherence to the merit principle ... The fact that Professor Stove was so outrageously wrong in his claims about the percentage of women appointed to the philosophy department does more to undermine confidence in the employment practices of Sydney University than the appointment of women.'[102] At the same time, Stove

---

[98] Devitt to VC Ward, 20/10/1985.

[99] 'General Philosophy during 1985', briefing note for meeting of Armstrong with Ward, 18/2/1986 (DD).

[100] D. Stove, 'The feminists and the universities', *Quadrant* 28 (9) (Sept 1984): p. 8; 'Universities and feminists once more', *Quadrant* 28 (11) (Nov 1984): p. 60; 'Jobs for the girls: Feminist vapours', *Quadrant* 29 (5) (May 1985): pp. 34–35; *SMH* 10/5/1985, p. 3; 11/4/1986, p. 2; comment in P. Shrubb, 'Jobs for the girls', *Quadrant* 29 (7) (July 1985): pp. 14–16.

[101] Stove to author, 1/10/1984.

[102] *Commonwealth of Australia, Parliamentary Debates, Senate* vol. S 105, p. 887 (12/9/1984), Stove defended by P. Coleman in House of Representatives, vol. HofR 139 pp. 1048–9 (11/9/1984).

wrote an article arguing that women are on average intellectually inferior to men. His colleagues persuaded him that the time for its publication was not opportune, and it did not surface until after his retirement.[103] When he wrote to the Vice-Chancellor threatening to name those responsible if Denise Russell were to be appointed to the lectureship in General Philosophy over stronger candidates, the University of Sydney was finally moved to action. The Registrar wrote to Stove in the following terms:

> The Vice-Chancellor considers that your letter of 29 May 1985 to Professor Dunston may be cause for disciplinary action against you in that the letter may constitute an improper attempt to influence some members of the Committee which will consider applications for the advertised lectureship in General Philosophy.
>
> In accordance with Section 4 of Chapter XXXVI of the By-laws I am writing to inform you that the Vice-Chancellor has decided to have this matter investigated to determine whether disciplinary proceedings should be taken against you.[104]

No more came of it, but the threat of disciplinary action for such an 'offence' is a rare one.

Later in the same year the University of New South Wales advertised its only chair in philosophy. There had been no other professorial appointment in philosophy since 1966, so it was an important event for the direction of philosophy there. The advertisement said, 'The School of Philosophy has a particular interest in developing teaching and research relating to women and philosophy and in extending its participation in the Women's Studies program.'[105] On the face of it, this was not wholly consistent with Senator Ryan's affirmative action policy, 'Employers should ensure that job advertisements are classified by the type of occupation under which they fall rather than by pre-conceived ideas of what sex the person should be.'[106] Some exceptionally strong male candidates applied, but, needless to say, were unsuccessful. The woman appointed — not, it was said, the woman desired by the writers of the ad — was Genevieve Lloyd, author of *The Man of Reason: 'Male' and 'Female' in Western Philosophy.*

---

[103] D. Stove, 'The intellectual capacity of women', *Proceedings of the Russellian Society* 15 (1990): pp. 1–16, repr. in D. Stove, *Cricket Versus Republicanism* (Sydney, 1995), pp. 27–48 and in D. Stove, *Against the Idols of the Age* (New Brunswick, 1999), pp. 113–36 .

[104] K. Jennings, Registrar, to Stove, 27/6/1985.

[105] *SMH* 30/11/1985, p. 79.

[106] S. Ryan & G. Evans, *Affirmative Action for Women: A policy discussion paper* (Canberra, 1984), p. 44.

Stove's last word on the question, before he took early retirement, was his 1986 *Quadrant* article, 'A Farewell to Arts'. 'The Faculty of Arts at the University of Sydney', he wrote, 'is a disaster-area, and not of the merely passive kind, like a bombed building, or an area that has been flooded. It is the active kind, like a badly-leaking nuclear reactor, or an outbreak of foot-and-mouth disease in cattle.' The centre of these developments, he said, was General Philosophy. 'The Department of English may have more feminists, French may have semioticians still more impenetrable, Anthropology or Fine Arts may have even stupider Marxists, but you cannot go past General Philosophy for solid *all-round* disaster.' As evidence, he offered three passages from writings in the Faculty. The most offensive of them was from a paper, 'What is feminist theory?', by Elizabeth Grosz:

> Feminist theory cannot be accurately regarded as a *competing* or rival account, diverging from patriarchal texts over what counts as true. It is not a true discourse, nor a more objective or scientific account. It could be appropriately seen, therefore, as a *strategy*, a local, specific intervention with definite political, even if provisional, aims and goals. In the 1980s, feminist theory no longer seems to seek the status of unchangeable, trans-historical and trans-geographic truth in its hypotheses and propositions. Rather, it seeks effective forms of intervention into systems of power in order to subvert them and replace them with others more preferable.

Stove comments that the value of the passage 'lies in proving that nowadays the Faculty of Arts has philosophy lecturers who frankly avow that their "philosophy" has nothing to do with an interest in truth and everything to do with an interest in power.' The only solution, Stove suggested, was the imposition of fees, at least for Arts students, and the diversion of resources from Arts to the scientific faculties.[107]

Reaction was predictable. 'Little more than a gross display of bigotry', wrote an Arts academic from another university, while ANU's Humanities Research Centre wrote to cancel its *Quadrant* subscription.[108]

Michael Devitt and Jean Curthoys in large part repented of their earlier radicalism. Devitt became well known in the US as a philosopher of language, and Curthoys wrote a book attacking radical femi-

---

[107] D. Stove, 'A farewell to arts: Marxism, semiotics and feminism', *Quadrant* 30 (5) (May 1986): pp. 8–11, repr. In Stove, *Cricket Versus Republicanism*, pp. 14–24; Grosz's text reprinted in C. Pateman & E. Gross, eds, *Feminist Challenges* (Sydney, 1986), p. 196; also in H. Crowley & S. Himmelwait, eds, *Knowing Women* (Oxford, 1992), pp. 355–69.

[108] *Quadrant* 30 (7-8) (July-Aug 1986): pp. 9–15; also P. Stavropoulos, 'Conservative intellectuals and feminism', *Australian Journal of Political Science* 25 (1990): pp. 218–27.

nist 'theory', to be considered in chapter 14 (Professor Elizabeth Grosz's subsequent career will be noticed there as well). George Molnar left academic philosophy and became a public servant, though he continued to do serious work on laws of nature up to his death in 1999.[109] Wal Suchting remained an unreformed old-style Marxist until his death in 1997.[110] David Armstrong, by then the University's longest-serving professor, retired in 1991;[111] his 1997 book, *A World of States of Affairs*, which sums up over twenty years of work on universals and laws of nature, is described in chapter 12. He was succeeded as Challis Professor by Keith Campbell. Brian Medlin made legal history when injuries in a car accident led to his early retirement on the grounds that he felt a lack of 'intellectual energy' and concentration, and the resulting loss of earnings was held to entitle him to compensation.[112] David Stove died in 1994. He is best known for his two books of philosophical polemics, *Popper and After* (first published 1982, reprinted in Australia in 1998 under the title *Anything Goes* and in the United States in 2001 as *Scientific Irrationalism*), and *The Plato Cult* (1991) an attack on the persistent idealist currents in philosophy. His prose style has made his books of essays widely read in Australia and overseas.[113]

As for the disaster in Arts faculties complained of by Stove, its spread has been unstoppable.[114]

It is sometimes presumed that after the early 1980s the department of General Philosophy settled down and became a respectable enough outfit, at least by the standards of Arts faculties. Doubts about whether the leopards had really changed their spots were raised by the Stephen Buckle case in 1998. Buckle had been a member of the Department of General Philosophy for over five years with a very good publication record, in more traditional areas of philosophy than those of the

---

[109] Obituaries in *SMH* 10/9/1999, *Australian* 15/9/1999; *AJP* 78 (2000): p. 595; G. Molnar, *Powers* (Oxford, 2003).

[110] W. Suchting, *Marx: An Introduction* (Brighton, 1983); W. Suchting, *Marx and Philosophy: Three Studies* (Basingstoke, 1986); obituary in *Australian* 19/2/1997, p. 12.

[111] 'The passionately rational professor retires', *SMH* 20/12/1991, p. 3.

[112] *Medlin v SGIC*, *Australian Law Reports* 127 (1995): pp. 180–96; *Commonwealth Law Reports* 182 (1994–5): pp. 1–25.

[113] D. Stove, *Cricket Versus Republicanism* (Sydney, 1995); *Against the Idols of the Age* (New Brunswick, 1999), with introduction 'Who was David Stove?', by R. Kimball; see S. Campbell, 'Defending common sense', *Partisan Review* 67 (3) (Summer 2000): pp. 500–3; D. Stove, *On Enlightenment*, ed. A. Irvine (Somerset, NJ, 2002).

[114] J. Franklin, 'The Sokal hoax', *Philosopher* 1 (4) (1996): pp. 21–4; see also Franklin's internet site, Australia's Wackiest Academic Websites, www.maths.unsw.edu.au/~jim/wackiest.html .

General Philosophy majority. In 1995, he published in *Philosopher* magazine a vigorous attack on the misuse of statistics by a number of academic feminists. Feminist illusions, he wrote, 'fed by an inappropriate and melodramatic vocabulary, and embedded in an interpretation of history which verges on paranoia, are the main cause of feminism's present impasse', and so on.[115] Unfortunately for him, he had neglected to obtain tenure before committing these observations to print. After some rewriting of his position description, his contract came up for renewal; no-one was surprised to hear that his job had gone to a Canadian political theorist, whose writings on Mabo and sovereignty are more or less identical in content to the writings on Mabo and sovereignty of two GP insiders. They were even less surprised when it turned out that the Dean of Arts, whose work on feminist statistics had been attacked years before in terms similar to those of Buckle's article, had chaired Buckle's selection committee. The Vice-Chancellor showed himself of similar quality to earlier VCs. Buckle left and took a position at the Australian Catholic University.[116] His well-received later work in Enlightenment thought[117] did not qualify him for the lectureship in that area advertised in Sydney University Philosophy in 2003.

The end came for T&M over the summer of 1999/2000. The head of the philosophy school declared that on the last day of the old century the department had ceased to exist, and hence was no longer able to vote to prolong its existence. The wishes of the majority of remaining T&M members were otherwise, but the struggle had become impossible.[118]

Sydney University has recently gained a well-funded centre in the philosophy of time, but its activities are closer to physics than philosophy. Apart from that, philosophy remains in decline. The Challis Chair of Philosophy once graced by Anderson and Armstrong has stayed vacant for years without explanation. Since the other universities in Sydney have never taken philosophy very seriously, Sydney is no longer a city where a student can find a respectable course of study in philosophy.

---

[115] S. Buckle, 'Feminism at the crossroads', *Philosopher* 1 (2) (Winter 1995): pp. 51–59.

[116] J. Franklin, 'The Sydney philosophy disturbances', *Quadrant* 43 (4) (Apr 1999): pp. 16–21; further in 43 (5) (May 1999): pp. 7–8, 43 (10) (Oct 1999): pp. 6–7.

[117] S. Buckle, *Hume's Enlightenment Tract* (Oxford, 2001), reviewed in *Times Literary Supplement* 5176 (14/6/2002): pp. 8–9.

[118] *SMH* 21/2/2000; *Australian* 1/3/2000, p. 35; *Honi Soit* 8/3/2000, pp. 1, 4; J. Franklin, 'T&M Philosophy: The end', *Quadrant* 44 (5) (May 2000): p. 51.

Chapter 12   Science, Anti-Science and Australian Realism

CITATIONS. That word strikes fear into the heart of the average academic. To deflate all but the most robust intellectual ego, it is only necessary to ask innocently, 'How are you going in the Citation Indexes, mate?' These Indexes, of which the *Arts and Humanities Citation Index* is the one relevant to philosophy, list under each author's name all citations to his work in the current year, that is, all the papers that year which have cited his previous productions in a footnote. The purpose of the exercise is to allow research topics to be followed up: find an old paper on a topic and look it up in the Citation Indexes and you have a start on current research in the area. A by-product is that every academic can see how many people are taking notice of his work. Or not, as the case may be.

Another by-product is the possibility of tracking large-scale trends in academic fashion. A considerable study was made on the *Arts and Humanities Citation Index* for the period 1976 to 1983, and the results include a list of the works of the twentieth century most cited worldwide. The most cited *author* of the century was Lenin, which confirmed a number of right-wing suspicions about the humanities industry. But the most cited single book, on any subject, was Thomas Kuhn's *The Structure of Scientific Revolutions*. Sir Karl Popper's major works on the philosophy of science, *The Logic of Scientific Discovery* and *Conjectures and Refutations*, were both among the top fifty.

The naive observer might draw the conclusion that scholars in the humanities were at last taking an interest in science and were keen to understand it. Nothing could be further from the truth. Popper and

Kuhn do not explain science, scientific truth or the methods by which science reaches truth. They explain them away.

The main idea of Popper, the founder of the central school of twentieth-century philosophy of science, was that observations and experiments do not, as most people believe, *support* scientific theories. The ultimate virtue for theories, he said, is falsifiability: a good theory is one that sticks its neck out and makes definite predictions that can be checked. Falsifiable theories include 'All ravens are black' and Einstein's theory of relativity. Popper had in mind as unfalsifiable the theories of Marx and Freud, which always seemed to have the ability to give some plausible explanation of any recalcitrant observation. The crucial point which Popper's opponents objected to was his answer to the question: what should we think about a theory that has successfully withstood rigorous tests designed to falsify it? Is it then worthy of belief, or probable, or reliable as a basis for action? Popper's answer was no. To admit otherwise would be to fall back into 'inductivism', the belief that observations do (probabilistically) support conclusions.

'Inductivism' here refers to the ancient 'problem of induction'. How can one ever be sure of the truth of an 'all' statement like 'All swans are white', when the evidence for it can only be that all of the swans observed so far have been white? Surely, however many have been observed, the next one *could* be non-white? Undoubtedly, logicians in past centuries were excessively sanguine on the question, and Australia's first contribution to world philosophy was its well-known criticism of the standard logicians' example, 'All swans are white.' In a strategy that has been used on criticism from Australia more than once since, the logicians simply substituted 'all ravens are black', and carried on regardless.[1] But the 'black swan of trespass' of which Ern Malley speaks[2] was on the wing, and it was only a matter of time before it came home to roost. John Stuart Mill wrote that the inference from the whiteness of European swans to the whiteness of all swans 'cannot have been a good induction, since the conclusion turned out to be erroneous'.[3] This is a remark so patently wrong as to suggest the depth of the underlying problem, which is that of conceiving of a logical argument that is worthwhile, although fallible. Mill's extreme reaction was also that of Popper, in the Vienna where extreme reac-

---

[1] F. Burgersdijk (Burgersdicius), *Institutionum logicarum,* bk. 1, ch. 31 (Cambridge, 1666, p. 97).
[2] Ern Malley, *Collected Poems* (Sydney, 1993), p. 25.
[3] J.S. Mill, *A System of Logic* bk III ch. III sect. 3 (8th ed, repr. London, 1941), p. 205, quoted and discussed in D. Stove, *The Plato Cult* (Oxford, 1991), p. 39; on Mill's failure to incorporate probability, H. Laurie, 'Methods of inductive inquiry', *Mind* 2 (1893): pp. 319–38.

tions were a way of life, and it became the orthodoxy of the turbulent and sceptical times that followed. Popper and his followers, believing there could be no such thing as a *logic* of probability, concluded from 'observations can't make you certain of a generalisation' to 'observations can't give you any good reason at all for believing a generalisation.'

Sir Karl was showered with all the honours he could have wished for. Except a job in Australia. He applied for the chair in philosophy at the University of Queensland just before the Second World War but was not short-listed, the successful candidate possessing 'the special advantages of long and responsible experience in this university and of experience in the service of the Queensland Department of Public Instruction.'[4] Popper spent the War in New Zealand, and in 1945 was offered a position at Sydney University. His autobiography implied that he refused the offer as a result of anti-semitic sentiment in Sydney. It is true that a question was asked in Parliament complaining about his appointment because he was an alien, and the fuss prompted him to withdraw. John Anderson persuaded him to withdraw his withdrawal, but he soon received a better offer from the London School of Economics and went there instead.[5] In 1950–1, he was considered for a chair at ANU, but lost out to Percy Partridge.[6]

Kuhn agreed with Popper's anti-inductivism, and added the notion of 'incommensurability of paradigms'. According to this view, epochs of 'normal science' are punctuated by sudden changes of paradigm, such as the change from Ptolemy's to Copernicus' theory of the solar system. Paradigms cannot be rationally compared, since the very concepts involved in two different paradigms are quite different. Lakatos

---

[4] M.I. Thomis, *A Place of Light and Learning: The University of Queensland's First Seventy-Five Years* (St Lucia, 1985), p. 115; brief biography of the successful candidate: 'W.M. Kyle', in H. Gregory, *Vivant Professores* (St Lucia, 1987), pp. 72–6.

[5] K. Popper, *Unended Quest* (London, 1976), p. 120; *NSW Parliamentary Debates* 15 Mar 1945 (2nd series, vol. 177 pp. 2691–2); *SMH* 8/3/1945, p. 4; A.K. Stout, 'Popper and Stone', *Bulletin* 15/5/1965, p. 46; Popper to Anderson, 12/3/1945, in Anderson papers, Sydney University Archives, P.42 series 20; Anderson to Ruth Walker, 14/2/1952, in Walker papers, Sydney University Archives, P.158 series 2; Anderson's 'Ballad of the Open Society, or Wheeze Goes the Popper' in M. Weblin, 'The flea on the sands', *Quadrant* 46 (7–8) (July-Aug 2002): pp. 72–3; W.F. Connell *et al.*, *Australia's First: A History of the University of Sydney*, vol. 2 (Sydney, 1995), pp. 28–9; J. Passmore, *Memoirs of a Semi-Detached Australian* (Melbourne, 1997), pp. 238–9; A.J. Baker in *Heraclitus* 38 (Nov 1994): p. 12; P. Biskup, 'Popper in Australasia, 1937–1945', *Quadrant* 44 (6) (June 2000): pp. 20–28; 'Karl Popper passing', *Nation Review* 16–22/3/73, p. 653.

[6] W.G. Osmond, *Frederic Eggleston* (Sydney, 1985), pp. 273–4.

applied these ideas to mathematics, the central bastion of scientific rationality. His presentation is notable for its continual use of scare quotes around words like 'knowledge', implying that what is normally taken to be 'known' or 'proved' is not really so. Feyerabend took this line of thought to its logical conclusion with his dictum, 'Anything goes.' Voodoo is as good as science, logically speaking.[7] The essence of these thinkers' views can best be appreciated from the caricature of them in David Stove's *Anything Goes*, perhaps the best Australian work of philosophical polemic. As Stove explains, authors who do not think evidence can give us any rational confidence in theories must forever be undermining the ordinary words that attribute *success* to scientific endeavours:

HELPS TO YOUNG AUTHORS

NEUTRALISING SUCCESS WORDS, AFTER THE MANNER OF THE BEST AUTHORITIES

HOW TO REWRITE THE SENTENCE: COOK DISCOVERED COOK STRAIT.

Lakatos: Cook 'discovered' Cook Strait.

Popper: Among an infinity of equally possible alternatives, one hypothesis which has been especially fruitful in suggesting problems for further research and critical discussion is the conjecture (first 'confirmed' by the work of Cook) that a strait separates northern from southern New Zealand.

Kuhn: It would of course be a gross anachronism to call the flat-earth paradigm in geography mistaken. It is simply incommensurable with later paradigms: as is evident from the fact that, for example, problems of antipodean geography could not even be posed under it. Under the Magellanic paradigm, however, one of the problems posed, and solved in

---

[7] Summary accounts of all four in D. Oldroyd, *The Arch of Knowledge* (Sydney, 1986), chs. 8–9; M. Charlesworth, *Science, Non-Science and Pseudo-Science* (Geelong, 1982); P.J. Riggs, *Whys and Ways of Science* (Melbourne, 1992); expositions of Popper in C. Simkin, *Popper's Views on Natural and Social Sciences* (London, 1993); G. Stokes, *Popper: Philosophy, Politics and Scientific Method* (Cambridge, 1998); R. Champion, 'Popper's philosophy of science', *The Skeptic* 13 (1) (Autumn 1993): pp. 36–40; support for Popper from scientists in H. Messel, *Highlights in Science* (Sydney, 1987), pp. 8, 22; S.J. Baker, 'A history and philosophy of pharmaceutical research, I: some thoughts on Popper, Kuhn and other philosophers', *Australian Journal of Hospital Pharmacy* 26 (1996): pp. 331–5; also in D. Wishart, 'Resuscitating Popper: Critical theory and corporate law', *Canberra Law Review* 3 (1996): pp. 99–103; R.W. Young, 'Paradigms in geography', *Australian Geographical Studies* 17 (1979): pp. 204–9; J. Fox, 'Appraising Lakatos', *AJP* 59 (1981): pp. 92–103.

the negative, was that of whether New Zealand is a single land mass. That this problem was solved by Cook is, however, a vulgar error of whig historians, utterly discredited by recent historiography. Discovery of the Strait would have been impossible, or at least would not have been science, but for the presence of the Royal Society on board, in the person of Sir Joseph Banks. Much more research by my graduate students into the current sociology of the geographical profession will be needed, however, before it will be known whether, under present paradigms, the problem of the existence of Cook Strait remains solved, or has become unsolved again, or an un-problem.

Feyerabend: Long before the constipated and bone-headed Cook, whose knowledge of the optics of his telescopes was minimal, rationally imposed, by means of tricks, jokes, and non-sequiturs, the myth of Cook Strait on the 'educated' world, Maori scientists not only 'knew' of the existence of the Strait, but often crossed it by turning themselves into birds. Now, however, not only this ability but the very knowledge of the 'existence' of the Strait has been lost forever. This is owing to the malignant influence exercised on education by authoritarian scientists and philosophers, especially the LSE critical rationalists, who have not accepted my criticisms and should be sacked. 'No doubt this financial criticism of ideas would be more effective than ... intellectual criticism, and it should be used.' (*Boston Studies in the Philosophy of Science*, Vol. LVIII, 1978, p. 144.)[8]

A caricature, but the reality is only too close. The popular Australian textbook, Alan Chalmers' *What is This Thing Called Science?* contained (in the first edition, though not the second) the Feyerabendian thought, 'In medieval Europe, witches really inhabited the commonsense world while in modern times they do not.'[9]

---

[8] D.C. Stove, *Anything Goes: Origins of the Cult of Scientific Irrationalism* (Sydney, 1998), repr as *Scientific Irrationalism* (Piscataway, 2000), pp. 49–50; originally in *Popper and After: Four Modern Irrationalists* (Oxford, 1982), pp. 19–20, repr. in D.C. Stove, *Cricket Versus Republicanism* (Quakers Hill, 1995), pp. 25–6.

[9] A. Chalmers, *What Is This Thing Called Science?* (St Lucia, 1976), p. 131; (translations in Italian, German, Spanish, Dutch, Japanese, Indonesian, etc; 3rd ed, 1999, with symposium in *Metascience* 9 (2) (July 2000)); sequel in A. Chalmers, *Science and its Fabrication* (Milton Keynes, 1990); further pro-Feyerabendian work in Australia in G. Couvalis, *Feyerabend's Critique of Foundationalism* (Aldershot, 1991); D. Russell, 'Anything goes', *Social Studies of Science* 13 (1983): pp. 437–64; and (up to a point) H. Sankey, *The Incommensurability Thesis* (Aldershot, 1994) and *Rationality, Relativism and Incommensurability* (Aldershot, 1997); and (to an even lesser degree) G. Couvalis, *The Philosophy of Science: Science and Objectivity* (London, 1997); S. Clarke, *Metaphysics and the Disunity of Scientific Knowledge* (Aldershot, 1998); see A. Lucas, 'How did philosophy of science produce anything so peculiar as Feyerabend's methodological anarchism?', *Scientia Essays* 3 (1994): pp. 90–

David Stove, c. 1990 (D.M. Armstrong)

Stove's point is that the 'four irrationalists' are using a variety of underhand techniques to undermine the ability of science to come up with at least well-supported theories. Some are just tricks, like neutralising success words by enclosing them in inverted commas. More central is their 'deductivism', the thesis that all logic is strictly deductive, so that there can be no relations of partial support between evidence and hypothesis. This is true even of Popper, who at least claimed to be on the side of science and gave his work the comparatively upbeat title *The Logic of Scientific Discovery* — despite the fact that, according to the contents, there is no such thing as a logic of scientific discovery. It is, Stove says, 'one kind of reaction to the disappointment of extreme expectations: that kind of reaction, namely, of which the best epitome is given in Aesop's fable of the fox and the grapes. The parallel would be complete if the fox, having become convinced that neither he nor anyone else could ever succeed in tasting grapes, should nevertheless write many long books on the progress of viticulture.'[10]

111; R. Nola & H. Sankey, eds, *After Popper, Kuhn and Feyerabend* (Dordrecht, 2000).

[10] Stove, *Popper and After*, p. 52; similar in A. Heathcote, 'Method and madness', *Proceedings of the Russellian Society* 14 (1989): pp. 23–37; A. Olding, 'Popper for afters', *Quadrant* 43 (12) (Dec 1999): pp. 19–22.

The reasons for Popper and Kuhn's huge popularity among the Humanities Crowd are clear. They provide a science substitute, a ready-made theory *about* science which means never having to say you're sorry about your ignorance of science itself. It licenses you to avoid studying any real science, while still allowing you to speak in a superior tone about the supposed objectivity of science and lacing your talk with the names of the scientific greats.[11] The irrationalists' success is a symptom of the uncomfortable position of philosophy astride the great fault line of the academic world, the one that separates the sciences and the humanities, the famous 'Two Cultures'. Philosophy has been nurtured in the humanities, and has absorbed basic humanist ways of thinking and expressing itself. Nevertheless, one of its ambitions is to explain to scientists what they are really doing, and to make real contributions on matters like the logical structure of theories. Conflict between the scientific and philosophical points of view has been inevitable. Anderson was an example. Despite his avowed interest in the 'ways of working' of things in the world, he took virtually no interest in the natural sciences, while being free with his criticism of them:

> The intellectual weakness of 'science' comes out particularly in the neglect of the true intellectual tradition (going back to the Greeks) of systematic philosophy and the amateurish substitution therefore of a mixture of professional devices (tricks of the trade) with philosophical odds and ends.[12]

The big four 'irrationalists' took very little notice of the shouting from distant Australia. When one of Stove's articles attacking him appeared in a leading English journal,[13] Popper did send a brief not-for-publication letter to the editor along the lines of 'more in sorrow than in anger ... sad that a journal such as yours ...', but did not reply publicly. The one Australian attack that did provoke a response was an article on Feyerabend by the Sydney Marxist philosophers Jean Curthoys and Wal Suchting, well-remembered for their role in the

---

[11] J. Franklin, 'Thomas Kuhn's irrationalism', *New Criterion* 18 (10) (June 2000): pp. 29–34; 'Last bastion of reason', *New Criterion* 18 (9) (May 2000): pp. 74–8.

[12] J. Anderson, review of *The Western Intellectual Tradition*, by J. Bronowski & B. Mazlish, *Australian Journal of Politics and History* 7 (1961): pp. 178–84, at p. 184; similar in *Studies in Empirical Philosophy*, p. 184. Anderson's alleged description of Einstein's Relativity as 'utterly illogical' in S. Grave, *A History of Philosophy in Australia* (St Lucia, 1984), pp. 47, 50, with reference to *Studies in Empirical Philosophy*, p. 9.

[13] D. Stove, 'Karl Popper and the Jazz Age', *Encounter* 65 (1) (June 1985): pp. 65–74, repr. in D. Stove, *Against the Idols of the Age* (New Brunswick, 1999), pp. 3–32.

Sydney split. Feyerabend, they said, was still 'immersed in the empiricist problematic', and was no better than a liberal, that is, virtually a class enemy:

> In the hands of class-peripheral, parasitic intellectuals, liberalism becomes stripped to its bare constituent atom, the single individual, posturing about in despair or self-congratulation (or different mixtures of both), often spouting *enfant-terrible*-ish pseudo-radical rhetoric the while.[14]

Persistent criticism of Feyerabend on the grounds that his views were not true had washed off him like water off a duck's back, but being accused of ethico-political deviation was hitting where it hurt. He replied with an article, 'Marxist fairytales from Australia':

> Sydney has one opera house, one Arts centre, one zoo, one harbour, but two philosophy departments. The reason for this abundance is not any overwhelming demand for philosophy among the antipodes but the fact that philosophy has party lines ... our two southern rhapsodists have studied the Marxist vocabulary well. They are not too original and there are certainly better stylists even among contemporary Marxists. Still, they know the right words and they know how to put them together. But Marxism is not just an inventory of phrases, it is a *philosophy* and it demands from its practitioners a little more than a pure heart, strong lungs, and a good memory ... No doubt they first made up their mind that I was a no-good, big-mouthed liberal-empiricist bum and then adapted their mental reactions to this image. But I am astonished to find two philosophers so unfamiliar with elementary principles of the art of argumentation.[15]

Behind this smokescreen of vocabularies in collision is a recognition by the Old Left of the grave danger to themselves in the migration of leftist intellectuals into regions like scientific irrationalism, idealism and post-modernism. If the point is not to examine the world but to change it, as Marx has it, then it helps to believe the world is there, and that one's plans might have a real impact on it.

---

[14] J. Curthoys & W. Suchting, 'Feyerabend's Discourse Against Method: A Marxist critique', *Inquiry* 20 (1977): pp. 243–371, at p. 338; discussion in A.R. Giles-Peters, 'The Marxist tradition', in *Essays on Philosophy in Australia*, ed. J.T.J. Srzednicki & B. Wood (Dordrecht, 1992), pp. 153–68, at pp. 160–6; on Marxism and philosophy of science, also A. Theophanous, 'The philosophy of Marx's science', *Politics* 14 (1979): pp. 19–28 (the author's bribery conviction in *SMH* 23/5/2002, p. 2); G. Kitching, *Marxism and Science* (University Park, 1994).

[15] P. Feyerabend, 'Marxist fairytales from Australia', *Inquiry* 20 (1977): pp. 372–97, at pp. 372–3; repr. in P. Feyerabend, *Science in a Free Society* (London, 1978), p. 155; reply in W. Suchting, 'Rising up from downunder', *Inquiry* 21 (1978): pp. 337–61; the whole debate translated into Italian in *Metodo scientifico tra anarchismo e marxismo* (Rome, 1982).

Popper, Kuhn and company, and the issues they considered, are now regarded as more than a little *passé*. Needless to say, that does not mean that the rationality of science is now orthodoxy among philosophers. On the contrary, the 'social construction of science' movement that is now all the rage maintains that science is now even more irrational than previously thought. A descendant of Kuhn's talk of the non-rational conflict of paradigms, it maintains that science is a yarn got up to reflect the needs of the scientists' society or his patrons. The overseas leaders of this field, such as Bruno Latour, recommended a host of sociological studies that would actually show how the content of scientific theories does reflect the interests of their proponents. One attempt to carry through this program was in Melbourne. Four philosophers led by Max Charlesworth lived with a group at the Walter and Eliza Hall Institute that worked on malaria vaccine and observed their behaviour from an anthropological point of view. The resulting book, *Life Among the Scientists*, did not work out quite according to plan. Some of the group thought the scientists were engaged in exactly the construction of fictions expected, but others came away with the impression that the researchers were actually discovering things about immunology and malaria. The book had to go to print with a disappointingly non-committal conclusion.[16]

There were soon educationists keen to share these new insights with the young, especially science students who might be acquiring reactionary opinions in class. The Victorian educationist Noel Gough, writing in the *Australian Science Teachers Journal*, took Latour and Charlesworth to have established that there is no special or rational method to science. It follows that school laboratories are 'mythic spaces' promoting the politically objectionable fantasy that chemicals and solutions are really there and have the properties science claims they do. He recommended that schools stop what they are doing at once and replace it with 'the kinds of activities through which learners might come to understand science as "politics continued by other means".'[17] And a Sydney University mathematics educa-

---

[16] M. Charlesworth, L. Farrall, T. Stokes & D. Turnbull, *Life Among the Scientists* (Geelong, 1989); a similar position in D. Broderick, *The Architecture of Babel: Discourses of Literature and Science* (Melbourne, 1994).

[17] N. Gough, 'Laboratories in schools: Material places, mythic spaces', *Australian Science Teachers Journal* 39 (2) (June 1993): pp. 29–33; more of the same in N. Gough, 'Environmental education, narrative complexity and postmodern science fiction', *International Journal of Science Education* 15 (1993): pp. 607–625; similar in R. Albury, 'Science teaching or science preaching?' in *Science under Scrutiny*, ed. R.W. Home (Dordrecht, 1983), pp. 159–72, section 6; L. Pereira, 'Stepping out with the constructivists', *ASTJ* 42 (2) (June 1996): pp. 26–8; J.E. Butler, 'Radical philosophy and history of

tion 'expert' recommended various changes in the way mathematics is taught on the basis that it is 'now generally accepted by researchers' that 'Coming to know is an adaptive process that organizes one's experiential world; one does not discover an independent, pre-existing world outside the mind of the knower.'[18]

By this stage, we know where we are. The wheel has turned full circle and we have come round to idealism again.

While the education system has not actually capitulated yet, thanks to a reservoir of good sense in that much maligned profession, school-teaching, there is obviously a need to do something about the problem. One rational response is to say that there is no point in arguing with people who do not accept the rationality of logic. As Stove said about all authors who say things so bizarre even they must know to be false, they are 'beneath philosophical notice and unlikely to benefit from it.'[19] Unfortunately, ignoring the blight does not make it go away. Somebody ought to explain clearly what has gone wrong. It's a dirty job, but somebody's got to do it, and as usual there is an Australian at the front line. Peter Slezak, of the University of New South Wales, observes that a lack of respect for finding the truth does mean that *anything* goes, including some very unpleasant items. To put it bluntly, 'for educators the grounds for concern are seen clearly enough by reflecting on the fact that the sociology of scientific knowledge could have offered no principled objection to teaching the racial theories of *Mein Kampf* when they were believed by a majority.'[20] Those kind of regimes are in a position to give you the

science', *ASTJ* 23 (2) (1977): pp. 39–42; K. Harris, *Education and Knowledge: The Structured Misrepresentation of Reality* (London, 1979), ch. 2; R.S. Laura, 'The philosophical foundations of science education', *Educational Philosophy and Theory* 13 (1981): pp. 1–13; D.C. Phillips, 'Can scientific method be taught?', *ASTJ* 14 (2) (1968): pp. 32–41; discussion in *Science and Education*, special issue on philosophy and constructivism in science education, 6 (1–2) (Jan 1997); P.G. Cole, 'Constructivism or scientific realism?' *Australian Journal of Teacher Education* 22 (1) (1997): pp. 41–48.
[18] K. Crawford, 'The context of cognition: The challenge of technology', in P. Ernest, ed, *Constructing Mathematical Knowledge* (London, 1994), pp. 92–106, at p. 96; similar in M. Barnes, 'Constructivist perspectives on mathematics learning', *Reflections* 19 (4) (Nov 1994): 7–15.
[19] Stove, *Plato Cult*, p. 30.
[20] P. Slezak, 'Sociology of scientific knowledge and scientific education: part I', *Science and Education* 3 (1994): pp. 265–94, at p. 270; also P. Slezak, 'The social construction of social constructionism', *Inquiry* 37 (1994): pp. 139–57; earlier debate on the same theme in F.C. White, 'Knowledge and relativism III: The sciences', *Educational Philosophy and Theory* 16 (1984): pp. 1–29; F.C. White, *Knowledge and Relativism* (Assen, 1983); P. Pettit, 'The strong sociology of knowledge without relativism', in R. Nola, ed, *Relativism and*

choice of having your compliance extracted, or your teeth. In Australia, though, it is more likely that minority science would assert its right to a fair go. Helen Verran of Melbourne, praised by Latour as the world leader in 'symmetric anthropology', argues that Aboriginal science which lacks numbers and the concept of prediction is something we ought to learn a lot from.[21]

Slezak adds an interesting anti-idealist argument, arising from the fact that there are computer programs that can do a certain amount of science, such as finding laws in data. Since computer programs are not members of society, at least not yet, they show that the content of science can be independent of society. Since the laws that the programs discover are the same as the ones humans discover, there is good reason to believe that humans too are applying discovery methods that are not mere reflections of society's wants.[22]

While disputes over the ability of science to reach the truth give rise to entertaining polemics in the style of a Punch and Judy show, there is perhaps more genuine interest in the investigations of philosophers on what kinds of truths exactly science has arrived at, and what kinds of entities science has discovered.

Among the more abstract disputes that true philosophers love are those on what kinds of things exist. Are there gods, or not? Is there such a thing as moral worth? Are there minds over and above brains? Even if we keep to the purely scientific world, there is a lot of doubt about which of the various items mentioned in scientific writings should be interpreted literally as referring to real things. At a general level, realism confronts 'instrumentalism', the theory that the unobservable entities of science, like electrons, force fields, and so on are not to be taken as literally existing, but are only mental 'instruments' that help us in inferring from one observed state of the world to another. Obviously, instrumentalism is essentially the same thought as

Realism in Science (Dordrecht, 1988), pp. 81–91; M. Matthews, ed, *Constructivism in Science Education: A Philosophical Critique* (Dordrecht, 1998); P. Davson-Galle, 'Constructivism, "a curate's egg"', *Educational Philosophy and Theory* 31 (2) (1999): pp. 205–19; objections in D. Mercer, 'The higher moral panic: Academic scientism and its quarrels with science and technology studies', *Prometheus* 17 (1) (Mar 1999): pp. 77–85.

[21] M. Wertheim, 'The way of logic', *New Scientist* 2/12/1995, pp. 38–41; H. Watson-Verran & D. Turnbull, 'Science and other indigenous knowledge systems', in *Handbook of Science and Technology Studies*, ed. S. Jasonoff *et al.* (Thousand Oaks, 1995), pp. 115–39.

[22] P. Slezak, 'Scientific discovery by computer as empirical refutation of the Strong Programme', *Social Studies of Science* 19 (1989): pp. 563–600, with replies pp. 671–95; also P. Slezak, 'Artificial experts', *Social Studies of Science* 21 (1991): pp. 175–201.

idealism, but applied in a piecemeal way: idealism denies the reality of everything outside the mind, while one may be instrumentalist about just this or that kind of entity. Since Jack Smart's commitment to the realist position in the 1950s,[23] Australians have been in the forefront in defending realism about scientific entities against the instrumentalism prevalent in, especially, the universities in the eastern United States.[24] Michael Devitt summarises the argument for realism:

> The basic argument for the unobservable entities is simple. By supposing they exist, we can give good explanations of the behaviour and characteristics of observed entities, behaviour and characteristics which would otherwise remain completely inexplicable. Furthermore, such a supposition leads to predictions about observables which are well confirmed; the supposition is 'observationally successful'.[25]

That is not to say one should be excessively fundamentalist about scientists' language, since scientists explicitly use certain language, such as complicated pieces of mathematics like the Hilbert spaces of quantum mechanics, as devices for calculation, not as names of proposed entities. Scientific realism must be selective.[26] Therefore, some

---

[23] Overview in B. Maund, 'History and philosophy of science in Australia', in *Essays*, ed. Srzednicki & Wood, pp. 231–60, especially pp. 232–4; J.J.C. Smart, 'The reality of theoretical entities', *AJP* 34 (1956): pp. 1–12; J.J.C. Smart, *Philosophy and Scientific Realism* (London, 1963), ch. 2; J.J.C. Smart, 'A form of metaphysical realism', *Philosophical Quarterly* 45 (1995): pp. 301–15; P. Dowe, 'Jack Smart and the rise of scientific realism', in *Australian Philosophers*, ed. P. Dowe, M. Nicholls & L. Shotton (Hobart, 1996), pp. 25–37; contrary views in J.B. Thornton, 'Scientific entities', *AJP* 31 (1953): pp. 1–21, 73–100; J.P. McKinney, 'The status of theoretical entities', *AJP* 34 (1956): pp. 207–13.

[24] M. Devitt, *Realism and Truth* (2nd ed, Oxford, 1991), ch. 7; B. Ellis, *Truth and Objectivity* (Oxford, 1990), Part I; P. Forrest, 'Why most of us should be scientific realists', *Monist* 77 (1994): pp. 47–70; C.A. Hooker, *A Realistic Theory of Science* (Albany, NY, 1987); S. Clarke & T.D. Lyons, ed, *Recent Themes in the Philosophy of Science: Scientific Realism and Commonsense* (Dordrecht, 2002); F.J. Clendinnen, 'Realism and the underdetermination of theory', *Synthese* 81 (1989): pp. 63–90; J. O'Leary-Hawthorne, 'What does van Fraassen's critique of scientific realism show?', *Monist* 77 (1994): pp. 128–45; S. Clarke, 'Defensible territory for entity realism', *British Journal for the Philosophy of Science* 52 (2001): pp. 701–22; papers in special issue of *Revue internationale de philosophie* 41 (1987) on 'Nouvelles tendances du réalisme: La perspective australienne'.

[25] Devitt, *Realism and Truth*, p. 108; M. Devitt, 'Scientific realism', in *Oxford Handbook of Contemporary Analytic Philosophy*, ed. F. Jackson & M. Smith (to appear).

[26] K. Campbell, 'Selective realism in the philosophy of physics', *Monist* 77 (1994): pp. 27–46.

of the most interesting questions concern the existence of particular sorts of entities. What about forces, for example? Are they just ways of talking about accelerations, or are they real entities that cause movement and that we experience directly when we feel pressure or push something?[27] What about space? It is easy to suppose that there are physical things and distances between them, but no actual *thing* or stuff, 'space'. But modern physics speaks of the curvature of space, which has causal effects related to gravity, and talks of empty space supporting gravitational and electrical fields. It is a big job for something that doesn't exist, and one may be tempted by the opposite theory, that space is more like a stuff or ether. This is the view ably defended in *The Shape of Space*, by the Adelaide philosopher Graham Nerlich.[28] There is also the problem of the structure of space at the sub-microscopic level — on present scientific theory, it is uncertain whether space is continuous (infinitely divisible) or discrete (that is, atomic, so that a cubic metre of space would consist of a finite though large number of points).[29] It is hard to believe the question makes sense for something that does not really exist. Then there are the 'secondary qualities', like colour and taste. Even if physical things really have shape and size, perhaps colour and taste are in the eye, or mind, of the beholder? Even here, Australian philosophers have been more prepared than most to defend a realist position.[30]

[27] Ellis, *Truth and Objectivity*, pp. 67–70; J.J.C. Smart, 'Heinrich Hertz and the concept of force', *AJP* 29 (1951): pp. 36–45, with discussion by P. Foulkes and Smart, 29 (1951): pp. 175–80 & 30 (1952): pp. 124–32; J.C. Bigelow, B.D. Ellis & R.J. Pargetter, 'Forces', *Philosophy of Science* 55 (1988): pp. 614–30; earlier [A.I. Clark?], 'Force and motion: a prediction', *Quadrilateral* (Hobart) 1 (1874): pp. 53–6.

[28] G.C. Nerlich, *The Shape of Space* (2nd ed, Cambridge, 1994); also G.C. Nerlich, *What Spacetime Explains* (Cambridge, 1994); C. Mortensen & G. Nerlich, 'Physical topology', *Journal of Philosophical Logic* 7 (1978): pp. 209–23; J.R. McKie, 'Conventionalism, realism and spacetime structure', *Theoria* 54 (1988): pp. 81–101; contrary in I. Hinckfuss, *The Existence of Space and Time* (Oxford, 1975); a middle view in D.G. Londey, 'The concept of space', *Philosophical Review* 64 (1955): pp. 590–603.

[29] P. Forrest, 'Is space-time discrete or continuous? — an empirical question', *Synthese* 103 (1995): pp. 327–54; R. Jozsa, 'An approach to the modelling of the physical continuum', *British Journal for the Philosophy of Science* 37 (1986): pp. 395–404; J. Franklin, 'Achievements and fallacies in Hume's account of infinite divisibility', *Hume Studies* 29 (1994): pp. 85–101.

[30] B. Maund, *Colours: Their Nature and Representation* (Cambridge, 1995); D.M. Armstrong, 'The secondary qualities', *AJP* 46 (1968): pp. 225–41; D.M. Armstrong, 'Smart and the secondary qualities', in *Metaphysics and Morality: Essays in Honour of J.J.C. Smart*, ed. P. Pettit, R. Sylvan & J. Norman (Oxford, 1987): pp. 3–15; J. Bigelow, J. Collins & R. Pargetter,

For those who think of themselves as 'philosophers' philosophers', the central question of the 'What exists?' family is the problem of universals. According to both common sense and advanced science — in agreement for once — physical things act in virtue of the *properties* they have. A table looks as it does because of the colour and shape it has. A sun attracts a planet because of the mass it has. Another table with the same colour and shape (and texture: whatever properties contribute to looks) would look the same; another body with the same mass would attract the planet in the same way. It is these repeatable properties like blue, being cubic, and having a mass of one kilogram, traditionally called 'universals', whose existence is in question. Should we say that the colours, shapes and so on really exist, or only the things that have them?[31]

David Armstrong's defence of the realist position on universals is one of the high points of Australian philosophy. In a series of books over the last twenty-five years,[32] he argues that the opposite 'nominal-

'Colouring in the world', *Mind* 99 (1990): pp. 279–88; K. Campbell, 'David Armstrong and realism about colour', with reply, in *Ontology, Causality and Mind: Essays in Honour of D.M. Armstrong*, ed. J. Bacon, K. Campbell & L. Reinhardt (Cambridge, 1993), pp. 249–73; M. Johnston, 'Are manifest qualities response-dependent?', *Monist* 81 (1998): pp. 3–43; M. Johnston, 'How to speak of the colors', *Philosophical Studies* 68 (1992): pp. 221–63; A. Olding, 'The ontological status of secondary qualities', *AJP* 46 (1968): pp. 52–64; W. Joske, *Material Objects* (New York, 1967), ch. 4; J.J.C. Smart, '"Looks red" and dangerous talk', *Philosophy* 70 (1995): pp. 545–54; F. Jackson, 'Philosophizing about color', in *Color Perception: Philosophical, Psychological, Artistic and Computational Perspectives*, ed. S. Davis (New York, 2000); D. McFarland & A. Miller, 'Disjunctions, programming and the Australian view of colour', *Analysis* 60 (2) (2000): pp. 209–12.
[31] A. Donagan, 'Universals and metaphysical realism', *Monist* 47 (1963): pp. 211–46, repr. in *Philosophical Papers of Alan Donagan*, ed. J.E. Malpas (Chicago, 1994), vol. 1, pp. 210–34; H.J. McCloskey, 'The philosophy of linguistic analysis and the problem of universals', *Philosophy and Phenomenological Research* 24 (1964): pp. 329–38; J. Bigelow, 'Universals', *Routledge Encyclopedia of Philosophy*, vol. 9, pp. 539–44.
[32] D.M. Armstrong, *Universals and Scientific Realism* (2 vols, Cambridge, 1978); *What Is a Law of Nature?* (Cambridge, 1983); *Universals: An Opinionated Introduction* (Boulder, Co, 1989); *A Combinatorial Theory of Possibility* (Cambridge, 1989); *A World of States of Affairs* (Cambridge, 1997), on which see symposium in *Metascience* 8 (1) (Mar 1999); Armstrong's intellectual autobiography in *D.M. Armstrong*, ed. R. Bogdan (Dordrecht, 1984); bibliography of Armstrong's works in *Ontology, Causality and Mind*, ed. Bacon, Campbell & Reinhardt, pp. 275–83; summary of his philosophy in preface to same work; basic argument about whether the question of universals makes sense in M. Devitt, '"Ostrich nominalism" or "mirage

ist' position, which holds that universals are mere names or concepts, is unable to give an account of laws of nature. What is the difference between a true law of nature, like 'all bodies attract one another' and a mere cosmic coincidence?[33] Surely the reason that the law supports predictions — that two new bodies would also attract — is that there is some real connection in things between having mass and attracting other bodies. That 'real connection' is a law of nature, and the aspect of things, such as mass, that it connects must also be real.[34]

While making sense of science is Armstrong's main basis for realism about universals, he also has some sympathy for the more classical route to universals via the meaning of words.[35] Do we not all come to agree on the meaning of 'yellow' because all yellow things have some character in common which affects different observers' vision in the same way? Armstrong insists, however, that universals are not something 'postulated' for the purpose of giving words meaning, much less somehow created by language or thought. It is for science, not linguistics, to discover what universals there are. The word 'lightning' has a different meaning to the phrase 'electrical discharge in the clouds', but scientific investigation shows they are the same thing.

realism"?', *Pacific Philosophical Quarterly* 61 (1980): pp. 433–9; D.M. Armstrong, 'Against "ostrich" nominalism', *PPQ* 61 (1980): pp. 440–9.

[33] This question also discussed earlier in R.S. Walters, 'The problem of counterfactuals', *AJP* 39 (1961): pp. 30–46; R.S. Walters, 'Laws of science and law-like statements', in *Encyclopedia of Philosophy*, ed. P. Edwards (New York, 1967), vol. 4, pp. 410–4; G. Nerlich & W. Suchting, 'Popper on law and natural necessity', *British Journal for the Philosophy of Science* 18 (1967): pp. 233–5; G. Molnar, 'Kneale's argument revisited', *Philosophical Review* 78 (1969): pp. 79–89; D.M. Armstrong, 'C.B. Martin, counterfactuals, causality and conditionals', in J. Heil, ed, *Cause, Mind and Reality: Essays Honouring C.B. Martin* (Dordrecht, 1989), pp. 7–15; C.A. Hooker, 'Laws, natural', *Routledge Encyclopedia of Philosophy*, vol. 5, pp. 470–5; older views of the question in B. Quaife, *The Intellectual Sciences* (Sydney, 1872), vol. 1, pp. 163–5.

[34] Also in M. Tooley, 'The nature of laws', *Canadian Journal of Philosophy* 7 (1977): pp. 667–98; B. Taylor, 'On natural properties in metaphysics', *Mind* 103 (1993): pp. 81–100; D. Hodgson, 'Constraint, empowerment and guidance: A conjectural classification of laws of nature', *Philosophy* 76 (2001): pp. 341–70; D. Braddon-Mitchell, 'Lossy laws', *Nous* 35 (2001): pp. 260–77; B. Ellis, *Scientific Essentialism* (Cambridge, 2001); B. Ellis, *The Philosophy of Nature: A Guide to the New Essentialism* (Montreal, 2002).

[35] Also L. Goddard, 'The existence of universals', in R. Brown & C.D. Rollins, eds, *Contemporary Philosophy in Australia* (London, 1969), pp. 31–51; J. Teichmann, 'Universals and common properties', *Analysis* 29 (1969): pp. 162–5; B. Taylor, *Modes of Occurrence* (Oxford, 1985); C. Legg, 'Predication and the problem of universals', *Philosophical Papers* 30 (2001): pp. 117–43.

David Armstrong answering questions, Catholic University of Lublin, 1995

Armstrong calls his realism 'scientific' because it leaves to science all such questions as which universals exist, which differently described universals are actually the same, which are basic and what the laws connecting them actually are. Philosophical investigation does, however, establish certain more general truths. For example, it finds that the basic furniture of the world is 'states of affairs' — a particular thing's having a certain universal, such as this table's being square.

These are the basic objects that act on one another causally, and that act on us in that particular causal process, perception.

As soon as one admits the existence of properties, a host of questions crowd in. Perhaps what really exists is not just 'blue' in the abstract, but the individual bluenesses of this and that?[36] If things have properties, how many do they have? Is a physical thing just the 'bundle' of its properties (as Bertrand Russell thought); if not, what is there to it other than its properties? What about relations? 'Being two metres apart' is a repeatable, but applies to two things, rather than being a property in either one.[37] What should be said about tendencies or dispositions, like solubility?[38] Are they a different kind of universal and one of the fundamental kinds of things in the world, or are they eliminable in favour of laws? What about active dispositions — powers?[39] What about higher-order universals, such as the resemblance between ordinary universals such as red and orange, or the ratio of two kilograms to one kilogram?

One question much studied is the notion of cause. If laws of nature are interpreted realistically, then causality can be explained in terms of the operation of universals.[40] But there remain many issues needing treatment, such as when to infer a cause from co-occurrences, and what connection cause has with the pushes and pulls one experiences directly.[41] Another question concerns what science has actually shown

---

[36] K. Campbell, *Abstract Particulars* (Oxford, 1990); on which J.P. Moreland, 'A discussion of Campbell's refurbished nominalism', *Southern Journal of Philosophy* 35 (1997): pp. 225–46; J. Bacon, *Universals and Property Instances: The Alphabet of Being* (Cambridge, 1995).

[37] See R. Langton & D. Lewis, 'Defining "intrinsic"', *Philosophy and Phenomenological Research* 58 (1998): pp. 333–45.

[38] E. Prior Jonson, *Dispositions* (Aberdeen, 1985); J. Franklin, 'Are dispositions reducible to categorical properties?' *Philosophical Quarterly* 36 (1986): pp. 62–4, with discussion *Philosophical Quarterly* 38 (1988): pp. 84–7; R.J. Pargetter & E.W. Prior, 'The categorical and the dispositional', *Pacific Philosophical Quarterly* 63 (1982): pp. 366–70; J.J.C. Smart, 'Dispositional properties', *Analysis* 22 (1961–2): pp. 44–6; D.M. Armstrong, C.B. Martin & U.T. Place, *Dispositions: A Debate*, ed. T. Crane (New York, 1996); G. Molnar, 'Are dispositions reducible?', *Philosophical Quarterly* 49 (1999): pp. 1–17.

[39] G. Molnar, *Powers: A Study in Metaphysics* (Oxford, 2003).

[40] D.M. Armstrong & A. Heathcote, 'Causes and laws', *Nous* 25 (1991): pp. 63–73; P.J. Riggs, ed, *Natural Kinds, Laws of Nature and Scientific Methodology* (Dordrecht, 1996); B. Ellis, 'Causal laws and singular causation', *Philosophy and Phenomenological Research* 61 (2000): pp. 329–51.

[41] M. Tooley, *Causation: A Realist Approach* (Oxford, 1987); P. Menzies, 'Probabilistic causation and causal processes', *Philosophy of Science* 56 (1989): pp. 642–63; P. Menzies, 'A unified account of causal relata', *AJP* 67 (1989):

about the nature of causality, given that it is conceived of in realist terms. In defending the theory that science has found that causality essentially involves transfers of energy, Phil Dowe pulled off one of the rarest of philosophical successes. He expressed his theory in terms of criticism of the reigning account of the American philosopher Wesley Salmon. In philosophy, even more than in other disciplines, the young are always out to make their name by attacking those in power; but in this case, the result was altogether unexpected. The great man not only admitted Dowe's criticisms were right, but changed his own theory completely to agree with Dowe's.[42]

The problem of universals was central to scholastic philosophy in the middle ages, but was commonly treated as a pseudo-problem thereafter. The Australian Catholic scholastics, as we saw, believed that a realist theory of universals was essential to the defence of objective morality. Anderson was one of the few other philosophers of the early or mid-century to have the question on the agenda. What Anderson's view on the matter was is controversial, with writers of differing views attributing their own opinions to him. In his only substantial treatment of the subject, Anderson was emphatically against universals, but meant by this only that they should not be thought of as things in their own right, somehow separate from what they are characters of. On the other hand, he admitted a kind of propositional structure to reality: the subject-predicate structure of sentences is not merely a fact about language, but reflects how reality is: 'the subject is the region within which the occurrence takes place, the predicate is the sort of occurrence it is.'[43] This is why logic was so

pp. 59–83; P. Menzies & H. Price, 'Causation as a secondary quality', *British Journal for the Philosophy of Science* 44 (1993): pp. 187–203; K.B. Korb, 'In search of the philosopher's stone', *BJPS* 48 (1997): pp. 543–53; A. Heathcote, 'A theory of causality', *Erkenntnis* 31 (1989): pp. 77–108; M. Colyvan, 'Can the Eleatic Principle be justified?', *Canadian Journal of Philosophy* 28 (1998): pp. 313–36; earlier, J. Anderson, 'The problem of causality', repr. in *Studies in Empirical Philosophy* (Sydney, 1962), pp. 126–36; J. Mackie, 'Causes and conditions', *American Philosophical Quarterly* 2 (1965): pp. 245–64; J. Mackie, *The Cement of the Universe* (Oxford, 1974); an anti-realist theory in D. Gasking, 'Causation and recipes', *Mind* 64 (1955): pp. 479–87.

[42] P. Dowe, 'Wesley Salmon's process theory of causality and the conserved quantity theory', *Philosophy of Science* 59 (1992): pp. 195–216; W.C. Salmon, 'Causality without counterfactuals', *Philosophy of Science* 61 (1994): pp. 297–312; later in P. Dowe, *Physical Causation* (Cambridge, 2000).

[43] J. Anderson, '"Universals" and occurrences', *AJPP* 7 (1929): pp. 138–45, repr. in *Studies in Empirical Philosophy*, pp. 115–21; analysed in A.J. Baker, *Australian Realism: The Systematic Philosophy of John Anderson* (Cambridge, 1986), ch. 5.

central to Anderson's system: his logic was a theory of reality as much as a theory of reasoning or language. So Anderson was certainly also against nominalism, the theory that universals are 'mere names' (or mere concepts), imposed by us on the world. According to A.D. Hope,

> He [Anderson] stopped my attempt to write a thesis on the theories of William Occam by declaring that there was nothing worth while in the whole of medieval philosophy. I was amazed for it seemed to me that Occam had anticipated Anderson's own objections to the modern nominalist schools he so brilliantly combated. I even ventured to ask, 'Have you read any medieval philosophers?' 'No', he said, ...[44]

To confuse the situation further, G.F. Stout, the eminent English psychologist and father of Alan Stout, accompanied his son to Sydney and brought yet another opinion. His theory was that it is primarily the *individual* characters of things — this rock's whiteness — that exist. He attributed this theory to Anderson, though apparently wrongly.[45] And David Armstrong credits Anderson as the source of his own realist theory of universals.

Among more strictly scientific topics, a favourite among philosophers is quantum mechanics. The German founders of this theory had studied rather too much idealist philosophy, and imposed a philosophical gloss on the equations with vague talk of 'the observer', in a way that has led to widespread anti-realist talk in Humanities Departments along the line of 'Even science now admits that reality depends on the observer.'[46] As one would expect, Australians have been among those arguing for more realist interpretations; they include Peter Forrest and the Melbourne Jesuit John Honner.[47] Still, as most

---

[44] A.D. Hope, *Chance Encounters* (Melbourne, 1992), p. 52; on Anderson and nominalism, T.A. Rose, 'The nominalist error', *AJP* 27 (1949): pp. 91–112 (obituaries of Rose in *Australian* 20/11/1997, p. 16; *Heraclitus* 62 (Jan 1998): pp. 2–3; his papers in Sydney University Archives P.198).

[45] G.F. Stout, 'Things, predicates and relations', *AJPP* 18 (1940): pp. 117–30; D.J. O'Connor, 'Stout's theory of universals', *AJP* 27 (1949): pp. 46–69.

[46] See also F. Mathews, *The Ecological Self* (London, 1991), pp. 55–7; Stove, *Plato Cult*, pp. 99–100; other supposed implications in R.S. Laura & S. Heaney, *Philosophical Foundations of Health Education* (London, 1990), ch. 3.

[47] P. Forrest, *Quantum Metaphysics* (Oxford, 1988); P. Forrest, 'In defence of the phase space picture', *Synthese* 119 (1999): pp. 299–311; J. Honner, *The Description of Nature: Niels Bohr and the Philosophy of Quantum Physics* (Oxford, 1987); H. Krips, *The Metaphysics of Quantum Theory* (Oxford, 1987); H. Krips, 'The objectivity of quantum probabilities', *AJP* 67 (1989): pp. 423–31; H. Krips, 'Quantum mechanics and the postmodern in one country', *Cultural Studies* (London) 10 (1996): pp. 78–114; A. Heathcote, 'Unbounded operators and the incompleteness of quantum mechanics',

of the realist authors note, there may be certain costs in realism about quantum mechanics, possibly including causation backwards in time.[48] But that is still much cheaper than idealism, which costs the earth. Sceptical outsiders hold the opinion that quantum mechanics is in such a conceptual mess that there is no point in a philosopher touching it until the scientists sort it out. The case of quantum mechanics provides a good answer to the question John Passmore asks: 'Why bother with philosophy of science, and not just let the scientists get on with the real science?'[49] Taking that position will result in the scientists doing the philosophy instead, but badly, and possibly without even realising it is philosophy they are doing.

Evolution is another old favourite. It is the perfect scientific theory for philosophers: it is a brilliant idea on how to explain a great deal with very little. Using only natural selection on random mutations, one can explain everything from why people look like apes to why gentlemen prefer blondes. Or so it would seem; give any philosopher a phenomenon of living things to explain, and he will construct an evolutionary scenario for it within seconds. It allows plenty of in-principle chat and conceptual distinctions, without needing too much attention to details. It is an infinitely flexible tool for adding a 'scientific' 'foundation' to speculations on literature, women, social planning, nature versus nurture, the liberation of science from theology, and a host of similar topics.[50] Surely such a good idea *must* be right?

Philosophy of Science 57 (1990): pp. 523–34; also in *AJP* 72 (1994): pp. 236–45.

[48] H. Price, *Time's Arrow and Archimedes' Point: New Directions for the Physics of Time* (Oxford, 1996), on which symposium in *Metascience* 11 (1997); H. Price, 'A neglected route to realism about quantum mechanics', *Mind* 103 (1994): pp. 303–36; P. Dowe, 'The anti-realism of Costa de Beauregard', *Foundations of Physics Letters* 6 (1993); pp. 469–75; P. Dowe, 'Backwards causation and the direction of causal processes', *Mind* 105 (1996): pp. 227–48.

[49] J. Passmore, 'Why philosophy of science?', in *Science under Scrutiny*, ed. R.W. Home (Dordrecht, 1983), pp. 5–29.

[50] D. Oldroyd & I. Langham, eds, *The Wider Domain of Evolutionary Theory* (Dordrecht, 1983); A. Olding, *Modern Biology and Natural Theology* (London, 1991); (review by Stove in *AJP* 69 (1991): pp. 360–2; obituaries of Olding in *Quadrant* 45 (10) (Oct 2001): pp. 36–8, *Heraclitus* 91, (Oct 2001): 16); P. Singer, *A Darwinian Left: Politics, Evolution and Cooperation* (New Haven, 1999); C.D. Goodwin, 'Evolution theory in Australian social thought', *Journal of the History of Ideas* 25 (1964): pp. 393–416; on what it can explain see K. Neander, 'Pruning the tree of life', *British Journal for the Philosophy of Science* 46 (1995): pp. 59–80; also K. Sterelny & P.E. Griffiths, *Sex and Death: An Introduction to Philosophy of Biology* (Chicago, 1999); K. Sterelny,

On the other hand, evolution is a theory logically rather distant from the evidence on which it rests, and subject to a large number of qualifications, extensions and excuses. So it suits the purely logical inquiries that sceptical philosophers revel in. Two of the best anti-Darwinian books have come from Sydney, Michael Denton's *Evolution: A Theory in Crisis* and David Stove's *Darwinian Fairytales*.[51] Denton argues that evolutionary theory has not coped with the classic problems that have dogged it since the time of Darwin: the gaps in the fossil record, or 'missing links', the uselessness of incipient structures like half-wings, and the difficulty of a random search process producing the observed complexity in the time available. Stove's objections are quite different. He claims that time and again evolutionists try to have their cake and eat it. Darwin's theory, he argues, postulated a relentless struggle for life in all species, and then, to explain why humans were not observed struggling, had to postulate an unobserved Cave Man age when they did struggle. Dawkins' *Selfish Gene*, the modern 'sociobiological' version of evolutionary theory, is falsified in its few predictions, such as that an animal will sacrifice itself for three siblings, but has an endless supply of logical patches to explain away its errors. Both old and new Darwinism, Stove says, offend logic as much as common decency, by picturing the life of humans and other species as either a constant struggle, or a struggle under a veneer of respectability.

Correspondingly, philosophers have generally not wanted to know about areas of science where the truth has been fully established. There is not enough to argue about. There are two such areas. One comprises disciplines like physiology and chemistry where there are well-established generalisations close to experience. No amount of juggling about the tentativeness of conceptual schemes or the underdetermination of theory by observation is going to make the theory of the circulation of the blood doubtful. As Sir Henry Harris magis-

---

The Evolution of Agency and Other Essays (Cambridge, 2001); J.S. Chisholm, *Death, Hope and Sex* (Cambridge, 1999).

[51] M. Denton, *Evolution: A Theory in Crisis* (Bethesda, Md, 1986); M. Denton, *Nature's Destiny* (New York., 1998); D.C. Stove, *Darwinian Fairytales* (Aldershot, 1995), on which see J. Franklin, 'Stove's anti-Darwinism', *Philosophy* 72 (1997): pp. 133–6; also H. Caton, 'The biology battlefield', *Quadrant* 31 (5) (May 1987): pp. 64–8; M. Stuart-Fox, 'Evolution, meaning and the humanities', *Meanjin* 47 (1988): pp. 762–8; on the debate in Darwin's day, see A. Mozley, 'Evolution and the climate of opinion in Australia 1840–76', *Victorian Studies* 10 (1966–7): pp. 411–20; W. Philips, 'The defence of Christian belief in Australia 1875–1914: The responses to evolution and higher criticism', *Journal of Religious History* 9 (1977): pp. 402–23.

terially wrote, in a useful corrective to the one-sided diet of examples that feeds the stranger denizens of the philosophy of science zoo, 'I do not believe that it will ever be shown that the blood of animals does not circulate; that anthrax is not caused by a bacterium; that proteins are not chains of amino acids. Human beings may indeed make mistakes, but I see no merit in the idea that they can make nothing but mistakes.'[52] Harris, Regius Professor of Medicine at Oxford, had had the advantage of a dose of Andersonian realism in Sydney in the 1940s.[53]

The other area where scientific knowledge is secure is in mathematics and related sciences, where proof is available to back up claims to certainty.[54] Philosophy of mathematics in the early twentieth century was inclined to explain away the certainty of mathematics as being about 'merely' logic, or some purely abstract entities like sets. Australians have been in the forefront of recent realist attempts to explain what genuine aspects of the world mathematics is about. The central idea is to revive the theory of the scholastics and Newton that numbers are essentially ratios, which are real repeatable properties. 'Being double' is a relation that really holds between certain pairs of weights, and also certain pairs of lengths; likewise, the same relation holds between a heap of four parrots and a heap of two parrots.[55] For the same reason, there has been attention to the notion of measure-

---

[52] H. Harris, 'Rationality in science', in *Scientific Explanation*, ed. A.F. Heath (Oxford, 1981), pp. 36–52, at p. 40.
[53] H. Harris, *The Balance of Improbabilities: A Scientific Life* (Oxford, 1987), pp. 27–30.
[54] J. Franklin & A. Daoud, *Introduction to Proofs in Mathematics* (Sydney, 1988).
[55] J. Bigelow, *The Reality of Numbers: A Physicalist's Philosophy of Mathematics* (Oxford, 1988); P. Forrest & D.M. Armstrong, 'The nature of number', *Philosophical Papers* 16 (1987): pp. 165–86; J. Bigelow & R. Pargetter, *Science and Necessity* (Cambridge, 1990), sections 2.5, 8.2, 8.3; J. Franklin, 'Mathematical necessity and reality', *AJP* 67 (1989): pp. 286–94; D.M. Armstrong, 'Classes are states of affairs', *Mind* 100 (1991): pp. 189–200; A.D. Irvine, 'Nominalism, realism and physicalism in mathematics', in A. Irvine (ed), *Physicalism in Mathematics* (Dordrecht, 1990), pp. ix–xxvi; C. Mortensen, 'On the possibility of science without numbers', *AJP* 76 (1998): pp. 182–97; earlier, B. Quaife, *The Intellectual Sciences* (Sydney, 1872), vol. 1 pp. 196–206; D.K. Picken, *The Number System of Arithmetic and Algebra* (Melbourne, 1923); L. Goddard, 'Counting', *AJP* 39 (1961): pp. 223–40; a more Platonist realism in M. Colyvan, *The Indispensability of Mathematics* (Oxford, 2001); contrary view in D.A.T. Gasking, 'Mathematics and the world', *AJP* 18 (1940): pp. 97–116, repr. in P. Benacerraf & H. Putnam, eds, *Philosophy of Mathematics* (Oxford, 1964), pp. 390–403; also W. Doniela, 'John Anderson and mathematics', *Heraclitus* 75 (July 1999): pp. 1–4.

ment, since 'measurement is the link between mathematics and science.'[56]

A growing point in the philosophy of science concerns the 'formal sciences' or 'mathematical sciences' — subjects like operations research, control theory and computer science which have come to prominence, or even come into existence, only in the last sixty years. While they are outside mathematics proper, they rely on pure reasoning, but also apply to the world directly, by studying the interactions of parts of real complex systems like traffic flow, job allocation and scheduling, and network design. Theorists of science have almost ignored them, despite the remarkable fact that, if the practitioners are to be believed, they seem to have come upon the 'philosophers' stone', a way of converting knowledge about the real world into certainty, merely by thinking. They cater well, too, for the word-oriented aspect of philosophy. If one aim of studying philosophy is to be able to speak plausibly on all subjects, as Descartes says, then the formal sciences can be of assistance. They supply a number of concepts, like 'feedback', 'bottleneck' and 'self-organization' which permit 'in principle' explanatory talk about complex phenomena, without demanding too much technical detail. It is just this feature of the theory of evolution that has provided a century of delight to philosophers, so the prospects for the formal sciences must be bright. [57]

Do the social sciences, like sociology, economics and history, pose different problems to the natural sciences? It is often maintained that the fact that they deal with human creations makes them essentially different. As might be expected, sceptical attacks on knowledge that remain marginal in science are orthodoxy in the humanities. According to the feminist historian Ann Curthoys, 'Most academics in the humanities and social sciences, and as far as I know in the physical and natural sciences as well, now reject positivist concepts of knowledge, the notion that one can objectively know the facts ... Many take this even further, and argue that knowledge is entirely an effect of power, that we can no longer have any concept of truth at all.'[58] A

---

[56] J.J.C. Smart, 'Measurement', *AJP* 27 (1959): pp. 1–22; B. Ellis, *Basic Concepts of Measurement* (Cambridge, 1966); J. Forge, ed, *Measurement, Realism and Objectivity* (Dordrecht, 1987); J. Forge, *Explanation, Quantity and Law* (Aldershot, 1999).

[57] J. Franklin, 'The formal sciences discover the philosophers' stone', *Studies in History and Philosophy of Science* 25 (1994): pp. 513–33; further in *Studies in History and Philosophy of Science* 30 (1999): pp. 721–3; cf. M. Colyvan, 'The miracle of applied mathematics', *Synthese* 127 (2001): pp. 265–77.

[58] A. Curthoys, 'Unlocking the academies: Responses and strategies', *Meanjin* 50 (2–3) (1991): pp. 386–93, at p. 391; further debate in A. Curthoys & J. Docker, 'Is history fiction?', *UTS Review* 2 (1) (1996): pp. 12–37.

number of Australian books, from Quentin Gibson's *Logic of Social Inquiry* and Robert Brown's *Rules and Laws in Sociology*[59] to Keith Windschuttle's *The Killing of History* and Behan McCullagh's *Justifying Historical Descriptions*,[60] have defended the social sciences as rational enterprises in which generalisations may be supported with good evidence in the same way as in other sciences. Any such attempt faces the difficulty that it is very hard to make people listen to defences of rationality. 'Hero's Feet Found Not Of Clay After All': what kind of a headline is that? Compared to the fashionably shocking productions of the postmodernists, the profile of these books in the Citation Indexes is, in the old Australian metaphor, 'lower than a black snake's armpit'.

It is obvious from the above that the various defences of rational thinking in science depend on logic itself being accepted as sound. There is no point in scrabbling for the logical high ground if that itself is going to crumble under one's feet.

Fortunately, there is a core of logic, developed by Frege and Russell based on Aristotle's works, that has proved resistant to all attacks on it, and is accepted by everybody. Not so fortunately, the core is

---

[59] Q. Gibson, *The Logic of Social Inquiry* (London, 1960); R. Brown, *Rules and Laws in Sociology* (London, 1973); both summarised in Grave, *History*, pp. 196–7; also R. Brown, *The Nature of Social Laws: Machiavelli to Mill* (Cambridge, 1984); S.I. Benn & G.W. Mortimore, eds, *Rationality and the Social Sciences* (London, 1976); J. Azevedo, *Mapping Reality: An Evolutionary Realist Methodology for the Natural and Social Sciences* (Albany, NY, 1997); contrary views in H. Stretton, *The Political Sciences* (London, 1969).

[60] K. Windschuttle, *The Killing of History* (Sydney, 1995; New York, 1997), ch. 7; C.B. McCullagh, *The Truth of History* (London, 1998); also C.B. McCullagh, *Justifying Historical Descriptions* (Cambridge, 1984); C.A.J. Coady, *Testimony: A Philosophical Study* (Oxford, 1992), ch. 13; F.J. Clendinnen, 'The rationality of method versus historical relativism', *Studies in History and Philosophy of Science* 14 (1983): pp. 23–38; C.B. McCullagh, 'Metaphor and truth in history', *Clio* 23 (1993): pp. 23–49; M. Levine & J.E. Malpas, '"Telling it like it was": History and the ideal chronicle', *AJP* 72 (1994): pp. 151–72; earlier in J. Passmore, 'The objectivity of history', *Philosophy* 33 (1958): pp. 97–111; A. Donagan, 'Historical explanations: The Popper–Hempel theory reconsidered', *History and Theory* 4 (1964): pp. 3–26; M. Scriven, 'Truisms as grounds for historical explanations', in *Theories of History*, ed. P. Gardiner (New York, 1959), pp. 443–75; K. Milanov, 'Knowledge in history', *Tasmanian Historical Association Papers and Proceedings* 5 (1) (1956); J. Mackie, 'Scientific method in textual criticism', *AJP* 25 (1947): pp. 53–80; W.K. Hancock, 'Jane Austen, historian', *Historical Studies* 10 (1963): pp. 422–30; opposite views in R. Campbell, *Truth and Historicity* (Oxford, 1992) (Campbell biography at arts.anu.edu.au/philosophy/academic/campbell/campbell.htm).

not nearly extensive enough to cover much of the serious arguing that one wishes to do. It is adequate, more or less, for proof in mathematics, but woefully insufficient to evaluate arguments in science, history, law or philosophy, not to mention in real life. Further, if one asks questions in the philosophy of logic, such as why logic works, what counts as logic and what not, whether logic has limits to its applicability, what exactly are the 'propositions' that logic discusses, and so on, one is again in uncharted, or at least disputed, territory.[61]

One main source of the trouble is that the core of logic is deductive, whereas most real arguments are not. Consider, for example, the two arguments,

> All men are mortal
> Socrates is a man
> Therefore Socrates is mortal

and

> 99 per cent of men are mortal
> Socrates is a man
> Therefore Socrates is mortal

The first is a part of core deductive logic, in that if the premises are true, the conclusion *must* also be true. The second is not, despite its obvious close resemblance to the first. In the second argument, the premises *could* be true but the conclusion false. The premises of the second give, at best, good though inconclusive reason for believing the conclusion. The question is, whether this good reason is a matter of pure logic, or whether it depends on some contingent feature of the world such as the laws of nature. Could the world be different in such a way that the information '99 per cent of men are mortal and Socrates is a man' (just by itself and in the absence of further relevant evidence) was *not* a good reason to believe 'Socrates is mortal'?

---

[61] J. Bacon, 'The reality of logic', *Monist* 69 (1986): pp. 153–62; L. Goddard & R. Routley, *The Logic of Significance and Context* (Edinburgh, 1973); G. Priest, *Beyond the Limits of Thought* (Cambridge, 1995); G. Restall, 'Logical laws', *Routledge Encyclopedia of Philosophy*, vol. 5, pp. 785–9; G. Restall, *An Introduction to Substructural Logics* (New York, 2000); W.R. Boyce Gibson, *The Problem of Logic* (London, 1908); J. Teichmann, 'Propositions', *Philosophical Review* 70 (1961): pp. 500–17; G. Priest, *Logic: A Very Short Introduction* (Oxford, 2000).

The heat generated by this question is extraordinary, despite the fact that the issue is hardly ever joined directly.[62] As we saw, it was a central plank in Popper's system that there could be no probabilistic support of theory by observations, so the debate is crucial for the philosophy of science. But most logicians have regarded the matter as not on their turf, while unsympathetic philosophers of science have taken it to be a matter of logic that there can be no such thing as non-deductive logical support.

This brings us to the problem of induction. What is the bearing of 'all observed ravens have been black' on the theory 'all ravens are black'? Generally, can one learn about the unobserved from the observed? Stove's answer, based on an idea of the American philosopher Donald Williams, is to reduce inductive inference to the inference from proportions in a population described above. It is a purely mathematical fact that the great majority of large samples of a population are close to the population in composition. For example, in opinion polling on voting intentions, most of the large — say of 1000 people — samples that one could take from the whole population are representative of the population, in that the proportions of those voting for the various parties are very close to those of the whole population. The observed, in other words, is probably a fair sample of the unobserved. This applies equally in the case where the sample is of past observations, and the population includes future ones. The sample is probably still a fair one, and one can make a probable inference (unless, of course, one has further reason not to: probable inferences are always relative to the evidence at hand). [63]

---

[62] D. Stove, 'Deductivism', *AJP* 48 (1970): pp. 76–98; also D. Gasking, 'Subjective probability', c. 1970, and 'Inductive and deductive arguments', c. 1972, in *Language, Logic and Causation*, ed. I.T. Oakley & L.J. O'Neill (Melbourne, 1996), pp. 42–57 and 69–84; survey in A. Hájek, 'Probability, logic and probability logic', in *Blackwell Guide to Philosophical Logic*, ed. L. Goble (Oxford, 2001), pp. 362–84; some technical work on probability logic in P. Roeper & H. Leblanc, *Probability Theory and Probability Logic* (Toronto, 1999); historical aspects in J. Franklin, *The Science of Conjecture: Evidence and Probability before Pascal* (Baltimore, 2001).

[63] D.C. Stove, *The Rationality of Induction* (Oxford, 1986); defended in S. Campbell, 'Fixing a hole in the ground of induction', *AJP* 79 (2001): pp. 553–63; S. Campbell & J. Franklin, 'Randomness and the justification of induction', *Synthese* 138 (2004); some less ambitious thoughts along the same lines in F.J. Clendinnen, 'Induction, indifference and guessing', *AJP* 64 (1986): pp. 340–4; B. Langtry, 'Popper on induction and independence', *Philosophy of Science* 44 (1977): pp. 326–31; P. Edwards, 'Russell's doubts about induction', *Mind* 58 (1949): pp. 141–63; G.N. Schlesinger, *The Sweep of Probability* (Notre Dame, 1991), ch. 4.

One reason for believing that Stove was right in thinking induction is purely a matter of logic is that it works in mathematics. The decimal expansion of the number π begins:

3.141592653589793238462643383279502884197169399375105820974944592 ...

It can be seen that this sequence of digits is random, in the sense of lacking any patterns such as repetition of digits or predominance of one particular digit. It can be confirmed with statistical tests that the same is true for any longer part of the decimal expansion of π that has so far been calculated, though there is no proof that π must continue like this. But it would be extremely surprising if it did not: the inductive argument, 'the first million digits of π are patternless, so the next million probably are too' is a good one. But the digits of π are what they are in all worlds, irrespective of the laws of nature. It would seem, then, that inductive inference must be a matter of logic rather than depending on any assumptions about nature, since it works irrespective of any facts about one particular world.[64]

The defence of rationality through the logic of probability does, however, have an Achilles heel. As we saw also, the chief arguments for realism, against both idealism in general and instrumentalism in science, required a particular kind of probabilistic argument: inference to the best explanation. The existence of an external world was said to be the best explanation of appearances, and that was taken to be a good reason for believing in its existence. Armstrong too notes that he relies crucially on such an argument, in saying that laws of nature are the best explanation of observed regularities.[65] Such arguments are necessary also for inferring the existence of other minds.[66] And inference to the best explanation, unfortunately, is one of the worst understood kinds of argument. It has so far proved impossible to say what makes one explanation better than another, or to measure how much better. Several authors have made progress in discussing whether one scientific theory is better than another by being simpler, or by explaining the behaviour of wholes in terms of the properties of parts, or by lacking *ad hoc* twiddles and kludges,[67] but even on those

[64] J. Franklin, 'Non-deductive logic in mathematics', *British Journal for the Philosophy of Science* 38 (1987): pp. 1–18.

[65] Armstrong, *What is a Law of Nature?*, pp. 53, 59; A. Heathcote, 'Abductive inference and invalidity', *Theoria* 61 (1995): pp. 231–60; C. Legg, 'Naturalism and wonder: Peirce and the logic of Hume's argument against miracles', *Philosophia* 28 (2001): pp. 297–318.

[66] R.J. Pargetter, 'Scientific inference to other minds', *AJP* 62 (1984): pp. 158–63.

[67] G. Schlesinger, *Method in the Physical Sciences* (London, 1963); J. Wright, *Science and the Theory of Rationality* (Aldershot, 1991); McCullagh, *Justifying*

more definite issues, a good deal of mystery remains. Simplicity might seem a simple enough concept, but there is no good way to measure it, in general, nor is there any convincing reason known why simpler theories are better than complex ones.[68]

Non-deductive logic is far from the only area of logic that causes difficulties of principle. Within deductive logic itself, many problems concern, one way or another, 'if'. 'If' is a word subject to extraordinary difficulties of interpretation, especially for its size. Some of them are explained by David Lewis. Lewis was an eminent American philosopher who regularly visited Australia to take in the realist air, and was known more widely for his conjecture that Ern Malley was named after the Austrian philosopher of the non-existent, Ernst Mally.[69] The Australian flavour of his example is a tribute to his hosts. He analyses 'If kangaroos had no tails, they would topple over', to mean, 'In all possible worlds close to the present one, in which the antecedent holds, the consequent also holds.' There is more than in this analysis than meets the eye:

> *'If kangaroos had no tails, they would topple over'* is true (or false, as the case may be) at our world, quite without regard to those possible worlds where kangaroos walk around on crutches, and stay upright that way. Those worlds are too far away from ours. What is meant by the counterfactual is that, things being pretty much as they are — the scarcity of crutches for kangaroos being pretty much as it actually is, the kangaroos' inability to use crutches being pretty much as it actually is, and so on — if kangaroos had no tails they would topple over.

> We might think it best to confine our attention to worlds where kangaroos have no tails and *everything* else is as it actually is; but there are no such worlds. Are we to suppose that kangaroos have no tails but that their tracks in the sand are still as they actually are? Then we shall have to suppose that these tracks are produced in a way quite different to the actual way. Are we to suppose that kangaroos have no tails but that their genetic makeup is as it actually is? Then we shall have to suppose that

Historical Descriptions, ch. 2; cf. W. Leatherdale, *The Role of Analogy, Model and Metaphor in Science* (Amsterdam, 1974) (obituary of Leatherdale in *Metascience* 3 (1985): pp. 71–2); W.M. O'Neil, *Fact and Theory: An Aspect of the Philosophy of Science* (Sydney, 1969).

[68] Schlesinger, ch. 1; Wright, ch. 3; F.J. Clendinnen, 'Rational expectation and simplicity', in R. McLaughlin, ed, *What? Where? When? Why?* (Boston, 1982), pp. 1–26; G.I. Webb, 'Further experimental evidence against the utility of Occam's Razor', *Journal of Artificial Intelligence Research* 4 (1996): pp. 397–416.

[69] D. Lewis, 'Ern Malley's namesake', *Quadrant* 39 (3) (Mar 1995): pp. 14–5; reply in 39 (4): p. 5; obituaries in *Eureka Street* 11 (10) (Dec 2001): p. 17; *Quadrant* 46 (1-2) (Jan-Feb 2002): pp. 21–3; also G. Priest, 'David Lewis: A view from down under', *Nous* 36 (2002): pp. 351–8.

genes control growth in a way quite different from the actual way (or else that there is something, unlike anything there actually is, that removes the tails). And so it goes; respects of similarity and difference trade off. If we try too hard for exact similarity to the actual world in one respect, we will get excessive differences in some other respect.[70]

Frank Jackson confused library cataloguers everywhere by producing two books on the subject of 'if' with the same title, and plenty of others, from Anderson on, have tried their hand as well.[71]

One approach to taming 'if' that has been popular in Australia is 'relevant logic', a project pursued by a group of logicians first collected in Armidale in the 1960s.[72] It was admitted by the mathemati-

---

[70] D. Lewis, *Counterfactuals* (Oxford, 1973), pp. 8–9; also D.P. Nolan, *Topics in the Philosophy of Possible Worlds* (New York, 2002); J. Collins and A. Hájek, articles 'Counterfactuals: Philosophical aspects', in *International Encyclopedia of the Social and Behavioral Sciences*, ed. N. Smelser & P. Baltes (Amsterdam, 2001), vol. 4 pp. 2869–74.

[71] F. Jackson, *Conditionals* (Oxford, 1987); F. Jackson, ed, *Conditionals* (Oxford, 1991); J. Anderson, 'Hypotheticals', *AJP* 30 (1952): pp. 1–16, repr. in *Studies in Empirical Philosophy*, pp. 137–47, comment in J. Bennett, 'The number of logical forms', *AJP* 30 (1952): pp. 177–87; also V.H. Dudman, 'On conditionals', *Journal of Philosophy* 91 (1994): pp. 113–28 and many other articles (see A.J. Dale & A Tanesini, 'Why are Italians more reasonable than Australians?', *Analysis* 49 (1989): pp. 189–94); D. Gasking, 'Hypotheticals, recipes and causation', c. 1955, in *Language, Logic and Causation*, pp. 116–31; K.K. Campbell, 'Definitions of entailment', *AJP* 43 (1965): pp. 353–9; J. Bacon, 'The subjunctive conditional as relevant implication', *Philosophia* 1 (1971): pp. 61–80; L. Chipman, 'Material and illative implication', *Mind* 80 (1971): pp. 179–93; R. Routley & R.K. Meyer, 'The semantics of entailment (I)', in *Truth, Syntax and Modality*, ed. H. Leblanc (Amsterdam, 1973), pp. 199–243; B.D. Ellis, 'A unified theory of conditionals', *Journal of Philosophical Logic* 7 (1978): pp. 107–24; A. Hazen, 'Even if', *Analysis* 39 (1979): pp. 35–8; F.C. White, 'If ... then', *International Logic Review* 3 (1972): pp. 124–5; R.K. Meyer, 'Entailment is not strict implication', *AJP* 52 (1974): pp. 212–31; S.J. Barker, 'The consequent-entailment problem for even if', *Linguistics and Philosophy* 17 (1994): pp. 249–60; S.J. Barker, 'Towards a pragmatic theory of if', *Philosophical Studies* 79 (1995): pp. 185–211; B.H. Slater, 'Conditional logic', *AJP* 70 (1992): pp. 76–81; B.H. Slater, 'Non-conditional "If"'s, *Ratio* 9 (1996): pp. 47–55; G. Restall, 'Truthmakers, entailment and necessity', *AJP* 74 (1996): pp. 331–40; M. McDermott, 'On the truth conditions of certain "If"-sentences', *Philosophical Review* 105 (1996): pp. 1–37; M. McDermott, 'Counterfactuals and access points', *Mind* 108 (1999): pp. 291–334.

[72] L. Goddard, 'A personal view of the development of deductive logic in Australia', in *Essays*, ed Srzednicki & Wood, pp. 169–85; E.P. Martin, 'Logic in Australia', *Essays*, pp. 187–230; Grave, *History*, pp. 182–90; R.K. Meyer & E.P. Martin, 'Logic on the Australian plan', *Journal of Philosophical*

cal logicians who followed the standard formalism of Frege and Russell that explaining 'if' was one of the more awkward problems. The standard formalism has a surrogate for 'if', according to which 'if *p* then *q*' is true whenever *p* is false. This inconveniently makes 'If the moon is made of green cheese then everything is permitted' true, contrary to the usual requirement of English that in 'if *p* then *q*' there ought to be some connection between *p* and *q*, or *relevance* of *p* to *q*. This was one of Anderson's objections to Russell's logic, and it is one of the cases where Anderson's ideas, regarded at his death as antediluvian, have proved more long-lived than those of his rivals. One of those to maintain Anderson's ideas on the subject through the intervening period was Paul Foulkes, author of 'Russell's' *Wisdom of the West*.[73] Relevant logicians have developed mathematical systems to overcome this difficulty,[74] and the Automated Reasoning Project at ANU has developed software to implement the results and exhibit the power of relevant logics.[75]

More alarmingly, a few hardy souls have gone much further in their divergence from the trodden paths of logic; indeed, have gone as far as it is possible to go. Graham Priest quotes Wittgenstein, 'I predict a time when there will be mathematical investigations of calculi containing contradictions, and people will actually be proud of having emancipated themselves from consistency',[76] and joyfully fulfils that prediction, defending the thesis that some contradictions are true.

Logic 15 (1986): pp. 305–32; R. Sylvan, 'Significant movements in the development of Australian logic', *Logique et Analyse* 137–8 (1992, in fact 1995): pp. 5–44; D. Hyde, 'Richard (Routley) Sylvan: Writings on logic and metaphysics', *History and Philosophy of Logic* 22 (2001): pp. 181–205; obituary of Sylvan in *Bulletin of Symbolic Logic* 4 (1998): pp. 338–40.

[73] P. Foulkes, 'What is deduction?', *International Logic Review* 3 (1972): pp. 64–72.

[74] J. Norman & R. Routley, eds, *Directions in Relevant Logic* (Dordrecht, 1989); R. Routley, R. K. Meyer, V. Plumwood & R.T. Brady, *Relevant Logics and Their Rivals* (Atascadero, Ca, 1982; vol. 2, Aldershot, 2002); R. Sylvan, *Ventures in Epistemology* (Aldershot, 2000); R. Sylvan, *Sociative Logics and Their Applications* (Aldershot, 2000); E.D. Mares & R.K. Meyer, 'Relevant logics', in *Blackwell Guide to Philosophical Logic*, ed. L. Goble (Oxford, 2001), pp. 280–308.

[75] cslab.anu.edu.au/ar .

[76] G. Priest, *In Contradiction* (Dordrecht, 1987), p. 65; also G. Priest, R. Routley & J. Norman, eds, *Logic: Essays on the Inconsistent* (Munich, 1989), pp. 55–7, 107–10; C. Mortensen, *Inconsistent Mathematics* (Dordrecht, 1995); earlier, L. Goddard, 'Laws of thought', *AJP* 37 (1959): pp. 28–40; also special issue of *AJP* on logic, 78 (4) (Dec 2000).

At least Australia can take the credit for some of the objections to this push.[77]

The concentration on logic as a fiercely technical science of relations between propositions tended to obscure the older view of logic as the art of reasoning correctly. Even in the heyday of mathematical logic, it was realised that informal reasoning, or the methodology of live argument, was a much wider subject that needs its own investigations.[78] This view has been revived more fully in recent decades, thanks to the attempt by Artificial Intelligence to imitate human reasoning by computer. Or more exactly, by the failure of AI to succeed in that project. It looked easy, but it wasn't, and the reasons why not involved a failure to understand how humans reason. If the way the mind does inference were really understood fully, it ought to be possible to program its secrets into a computer, and hence come up with, for example, computer systems for medical diagnosis that are as good as the best human experts. Having to program a working system is the severest possible critic of any fuzziness in one's understanding, and will rigorously expose the smallest shortcoming. Once the early optimistic promises of Artificial Intelligence proved to be nowhere near what was achievable, it became clear that there were many basic logical issues still to be sorted out before it was possible to imitate human reasoning mechanically.

Once this was understood, the way was open for a close and productive relationship between science and philosophy.

One framework for solving some of these problems is the 'belief revision' promoted by the philosophers Brian Ellis and Peter Forrest.[79]

---

[77] B.H. Slater, 'Paraconsistent logics', *Journal of Philosophical Logic* 24 (1995): pp. 451–4; B.H. Slater, 'Thought unlimited', *Mind* 101 (1992): pp. 347–54; his opposing view in detail in B.H. Slater, *Prolegomena to Formal Logic* (Aldershot, 1989); *Intensional Logic* (Aldershot, 1994); *Against the Realisms of the Age* (Aldershot, 1995).

[78] C. Hamblin, *Fallacies* (London, 1970), on which J. Mackenzie & P. Staines, 'Hamblin's case for commitment', *Philosophy and Rhetoric* 32 (1999): pp. 14–39; C. Hamblin, *Imperatives* (New York, 1987); 'Mathematical models of dialogue', *Theoria* 27 (1971): pp. 130–55; 'Quandaries and the logic of rules', *Journal of Philosophical Logic* 1 (1972): pp. 74–85; (on Hamblin's contribution to reverse Polish notation in computing, see obituary in *Australian Computer Journal* 17 (4) (1985): pp. 194–5 and www.csc.liv.ac.uk/~peter/hamblinbio.html); I. Tammelo, *Outlines of Modern Legal Logic* (Wiesbaden, 1969) (obituary in *Sydney Law Review* 10 (1983): pp. 128–42); T.J. Richards, *The Language of Reason* (Sydney, 1978); P.B. Bell & P.J. Staines, *Reasoning and Argument in Psychology* (Kensington, NSW, 1979). J.S. & J.M. Rybak, *Map Logic* (Sydney, 1973).

[79] B. Ellis, *Rational Belief Systems* (Oxford, 1979); P. Forrest, *The Dynamics of Belief: A Normative Logic* (Oxford, 1986); J. Collins, 'Belief, desire and

One thinks of one's beliefs as forming a network. The nodes are propositions, each labelled with one's degree of belief in it. The connections represent the logical relations between them. The problem is to calculate how the degrees of belief should adjust when one comes to believe something new. If, for example, one learns something incompatible with one's present beliefs, how do the adjustments to degrees of beliefs flow through the network to restore equilibrium? The problem is purely logical, but is much closer to implementations than purely formal logical investigations.

Perhaps the most hopeful approach, and one in which Australians have been leaders, is 'machine learning', or 'inductive learning', which concerns the automatic extraction of knowledge from large amounts of raw data. Given many results of suites of pathology tests, tagged with their correct diagnosis by experts, how can one extract rules for diagnosis which will generalise to new cases? Given second-by-second logs of how pilots use their controls to land planes, how can one use the data to train a computer to land a plane?[80]

It is a project where the most abstract concepts of philosophy, logic, mathematics and computer science combine to attack the most practical problems. Artificial Intelligence, or any half-way reasonable imitation of it, is a goal worth achieving, considering the shortage of the natural article. The way to get it, if it is possible at all, lies in bridging the gap between philosophy and science.

revision', *Mind* 97 (1988): pp. 333–42; A.C. Nayak & N.Y. Foo, 'Abduction without minimality', *Lecture Notes in Artificial Intelligence* no. 1747 (1999): pp. 365–77; K.R. Korb, 'Inductive learning and defeasible inference', *Journal of Experimental and Theoretical Artificial Intelligence* 7 (1995): pp. 291–324; G. Antoniou, *Nonmonotonic Reasoning* (Cambridge, Mass, 1997).

[80] J.R. Quinlan, *C4.5: Programs for Machine Learning* (San Mateo, CA, 1993); C. Sammut, 'Using background knowledge to build multistrategy learners', *Machine Learning* 27 (1997): pp. 241–57; D. Richards & P. Compton, 'Generalising ripple-down rules', *Lecture Notes in Artificial Intelligence* no. 1937 (2000): pp. 380–6; T. Caelli, 'Learning paradigms for image interpretation', *Spatial Vision* 13 (2000): pp. 305–14; W. Buntine, 'A guide to the literature on learning probabilistic networks from data', *IEEE Transactions on Knowledge & Data Engineering* 8 (1996): pp. 195–210.

Chapter 13   I Love a Sunburnt Environment

THE environment is like the Empire used to be. It adds moral tone to what could otherwise look like a pretty ordinary pile of rocks. It is continuous with daily life — you're standing in it — but the best parts of it are somewhere else. Constant vigilance is needed against its many enemies. All-embracing yet uncontroversial, it is the perfect devotional object for schools.

Surveys tend to show that the 'environment' is the only public issue considered important by adolescents.[1] It is not hard to get 70 per cent of schoolchildren to disagree with the statement, 'Humans have the right to modify the natural environment to suit their needs', though it is harder to motivate them to learn any of the scientific facts involved,[2] and other surveys seem to suggest that real concern is more characteristic of Whitlamite baby-boomers than the jaded youth.[3]

The more extreme environmentalist educators have made the most of the opportunity, and their enthusiasm rivals the Protestant recruiting sermonisers of the First World War.[4] They have not been shy of

---

[1] *Australian* 28/11/1995, p. 1.

[2] B. Clarke, 'Environmental attitudes and knowledge of year 11 students in a Queensland high school', *Australian Journal of Environmental Education* 12 (1996): pp. 19–26; similar in S. Connell *et al.*, 'Young people and the environment in Australia', *Australian Journal of Environmental Education* 14 (1998): pp. 39–48.

[3] N.W.H. Blaikie, 'The nature and origins of ecological world views: An Australian study', *Social Science Quarterly* 73 (1992): pp. 144–65.

[4] M. May, 'Towards a new cosmology of the earth', *Australian Journal of Environmental Education* 4 (1988): pp. 9–21; K. Dyer & P. Gunnell, 'Humans and nature: A spectrum not a dichotomy', *Australian Journal of Environmental Education* 9 (1993): pp. 53–70; K. Dyer, 'Environmentalism as social purpose

advocating major changes in philosophy. 'A shift towards an ecological paradigm for education does not simply mean more environmental education, peace studies, development education and women's studies on school timetables. A paradigm shift involves changes in our *total* world view.'[5] Education must 'encourage the kind of storytelling which "transcends the proclamation of difference" between ourselves and the earth.'[6] 'A poststructuralist position in science and environmental education would encourage an understanding of "reality" that I once saw encapsulated in the words of a poster in an English (language) classroom: "the universe is not made of atoms — it is made of stories."'[7]

Even a sympathetic observer says, 'As rightful heirs to the 1960s counterculture, contemporary greens affect a certain studied looniness.'[8] Though these views are not shared by the mainstream of educators concerned about the environment, there is certainly some basis at least for the charges of critics like the former Finance Minister Peter Walsh, who accused the Government of appeasing a 'gaggle of kindergarten Marxists, secular religion zealots and new-class freeloaders who comprise Australia's green extremists.'[9] Another writer sees the extremists as reviving Wordsworth: mining is not seen as working with nature, but as desecration; nature should be an untouched spectacle.[10] It may be going too far to accuse the fringe of the green movement of reviving a pagan religion whose worship of nature may require human sacrifice in the form of a culling of the over-

in higher education', *Australian Journal of Environmental Education* 13 (1997): pp. 37–47.
[5] N. Gough, 'Greening education', in *Green Politics in Australia*, ed. D. Hutton (Sydney, 1987), pp. 173–202, at p. 181.
[6] N. Gough, 'Healing the earth within us: Environmental education as cultural criticism', *Journal of Experiential Education* 13 (1990): pp. 12–17, at p. 14; also N. Gough, 'From epistemology to ecopolitics', *Journal of Curriculum Studies* 21 (1989): pp. 225–41; Gough's Eureka Prize for Environmental Education in *SMH* 27/11/1997, p. 8.
[7] N. Gough, 'Environmental education, narrative complexity and postmodern science/fiction', *International Journal of Science Education* 15 (1993): pp. 607–25, at p. 615; also N. Gough, 'Playing at catastrophe: Ecopolitical education after poststructuralism', *Educational Theory* 44 (1994): pp. 189–210, at p. 210.
[8] R. Goodin, 'A green theory of value', in D.J. Mulvaney, ed, *The Humanities and the Australian Environment* (Canberra, 1991): pp. 61–86, at p. 61.
[9] *Sun-Herald* 24/2/1991, p. 3.
[10] R. Sworder, 'Where man is not, nature is barren', *IPA Review* 45 (3) (1992): pp. 36–9.

prolific human species,[11] but even in this case there is some evidence. As one environmental educator put it, humans have 'no more right to exist than any other species'.[12]

Of course, there *is* an environment, and there are many threats to it. Attitudes to environmental questions divide into two philosophical camps: the 'shallow' and the 'deep' (the words are meant as description, not evaluation). The shallow view, which appeals especially to those with a scientific orientation, is concerned about threats to the environment and recommends research to understand and counter them, but does not see any need for fundamental changes in world views or ethics. The shallow view is unappealing to visionaries, who generally argue that we need to see the natural world in a completely different way, one that recognises it as having an intrinsic value independent of human interests — perhaps as having a right to remain undisturbed.

Shallow and proud of it is John Passmore, author of one of the first books on environmental philosophy, the widely read *Man's Responsibility for Nature*. Passmore was one of the first of Anderson's disciples to become a professional philosopher.[13] His first extensive works were on the relation of Andersonian views to the then-new philosophy of logical positivism,[14] and he then worked on the history of philosophy, in which his *A Hundred Years of Philosophy* and its sequel, *Recent Philosophers*,[15] summarised the opinions of a large number of philosophers that few other people had the energy to read. He wrote on public issues before it was fashionable for philosophers to do so,[16] discussing

---

[11] J.K. Williams, 'The religion of environmentalism', *Economic Witness* no. 50 (6/7/1990); M. Drummond, 'Australians finding a new religion in environmentalism', *Rural Business* 2 no. 22 (1990): pp. 8, 10.

[12] T. Trainer, 'Towards an ecological philosophy of education', *Discourse* 10 (1990): pp. 92–117, at p. 104.

[13] J. Passmore, *Memoirs of a Semi-detached Australian* (Melbourne, 1997), ch. 7.

[14] S. Grave, *A History of Philosophy in Australia* (St Lucia, 1984), pp. 85–9; J. Passmore, 'Philosophy and science', *AJPP* 17 (1939): pp. 193–207; 'Logical positivism', *AJPP* 21 (1943): pp. 65–92; 22 (1944): pp. 129–43, 24 (1948): pp. 1–19.

[15] J. Passmore, *A Hundred Years of Philosophy* (London, 1957, 2nd ed, London, 1966); *Recent Philosophers* (London, 1985); also *Ralph Cudworth* (Cambridge, 1951); *Hume's Intentions* (rev. ed., London, 1968); his account of Australian philosophy in *The Pattern of Australian Culture*, ed. A.L. McLeod (Ithaca, NY, 1963), pp. 131–68.

[16] J. Milliken, 'John Passmore: A very Australian intellectual', *National Times* 30/8–5/9/1981: p. 27; 'John Passmore', in M. Thomas, *Australia in Mind* (Sydney, 1989), pp. 194–206; F. Jackson, 'Passmore, John' in *Routledge Encyclopedia of Philosophy*, vol. 7, pp. 247–8; his papers in National Library MS 7613.

in substantial books art, education, the impact of science and environmental issues. His work is interdisciplinary in a way that is accessible to the general public but sometimes raises suspicions among specialists. He remarks in his memoirs that though his works are at 'too high a level of generality to suit environmentalists, educators, art critics, they are too concrete in their references for philosophers. And, one can add, too historically-minded for either, although not enough for historians.'[17] The philosophy of these books is Andersonianism at a lower emotional temperature. Though there are things that make him angry — Catholicism, for example[18] — the general tenor is an even-handed distribution of praise and blame, combined with an opposition to any views that smack of irrationalism or mysticism. Thus his *Science and its Critics* agrees that modern science is to blame for some technological disasters, but argues against the more extreme humanist views that science is bad in itself. *The Perfectibility of Man* is a historical account of attempts to aim at human perfection. It is deeply suspicious of utopians and visionaries, from the ancients to the drug gurus of the Sixties. His book on the environment, *Man's Responsibility for Nature*, is similar. It admits there are environmental problems which require urgent research and action, but argues that more hard scientific thinking is needed, not less. It has no sympathy with those who demand a totally new, mystical ethic:

> It is at this point, indeed, that the cry grows loudest for a new morality, a new religion, which would transform man's attitude to nature, which would lead him to believe that it is intrinsically wrong to destroy a species, cut down a tree, clear a wilderness. As I have already suggested, these demands strike one, at a certain level, as merely ridiculous. One is reminded, indeed, of the exchange between Glendower and Hotspur in Henry IV Pt. I (III.i.53):
>
>> Glendower: I can call spirits from the vasty deep.
>>
>> Hotspur: Why so can I, or so can any man,
>>
>> But will they come when you do call for them?
>
> A morality, a religion, is not, as I have already argued, the sort of thing one can simply conjure up. It can only grow out of existing attitudes of mind, as an extension or development of them.[19]

Passmore is firmly against any attribution of rights to nature. Bacteria and men do not have any common interests, he says, therefore they do not form a community and so there cannot be any mutual

---

[17] Passmore, *Memoirs*, p. 132.

[18] Passmore, *Memoirs*, pp. 115–6; Passmore, *Man's Responsibility for Nature* (2nd ed, London, 1980), p. 131 fn; cf. p. 162.

[19] Passmore, *Man's Responsibility*, p. 111.

obligation between them. 'The idea of "rights" is simply not applicable to what is non-human.'[20]

At the time Passmore was writing, the early 1970s, apocalyptic predictions about the fate of the earth — spectacularly unrealised — and the general utopianism of the times prompted rethinking of the whole framework in which discussions had so far taken place.[21] The Norwegian philosopher Arne Naess promoted the notion of 'deep ecology', which attributed to nature intrinsic values and rights of exactly the kind Passmore found incoherent.[22]

Australia was among the first centres of interest.[23] The early leaders were Richard and Valerie Routley, who were also Canberra environmental activists, especially in opposition to woodchipping.[24] Richard Routley (later Sylvan) hoped environmental philosophy would give Australian philosophy as a whole a distinctive cast, making it something different from a collection of imports from the northern hemisphere.[25] In line with Peter Singer's attempt in *Animal Liberation* at about the same time to break down the moral division between

---

[20] Passmore, *Man's Responsibility*, p. 116; similar in B. Maley, *Ethics and Ecosystems* (Sydney, 1994), ch. 2; S. Waight, B. Tapp & D. Brooks, 'Ecophilosophies: Exercises in irrelevance', in *Ecopolitics V Proceedings*, ed. R. Harding (Kensington, 1992), pp. 460–4; objections in V. Routley, Critical notice of Passmore, *Man's Responsibility*, *AJP* 53 (1975): pp. 171–85; other 'shallow' theories in H.J. McCloskey, *Ecological Ethics and Politics* (Totowa, NJ, 1983); D.H. Monro, *Ethics and the Environment* (Melbourne, 1984); C.A. Hooker, 'On deep versus shallow theories of environmental pollution', in *Environmental Philosophy*, ed. R. Elliot & A. Gare (St Lucia, 1983), pp. 58–84; B. Medlin, *Human Nature, Human Survival* (Adelaide, 1992).

[21] C. Ware, 'Some considerations for an ethic of ecology', *Dialectic* (Newcastle University) 8 (1972): pp. 39–48.

[22] Account in W. Fox, *Towards a Transpersonal Ecology* (Totnes, 1995), part 3; N. Witoszek & A. Brennan, eds, *Philosophical Dialogues: Arne Naess and the Progress of Ecophilosophy* (Lanham, Md, 1999); also *The Deep Ecologist* newsletter, Ballarat, 1982–91.

[23] D. Mannison & M. McRobbie, Introduction, in D. Mannison, M. McRobbie & R. Routley, eds, *Environmental Philosophy* (Canberra, 1980), pp. 1–7; (obituary of Mannison in *AJP* 68 (1990): p. 131).

[24] R. & V. Routley, *The Fight for the Forests* (2nd ed, Canberra, 1974); R. Routley & V. Plumwood, 'The *Fight for the Forests* affair', in *Intellectual Suppression*, ed. B. Martin (Sydney, 1986), pp. 70–3; V. Plumwood, 'The struggle for environmental philosophy in Australia', *Worldviews* 3 (1999): pp. 157–78.

[25] R. Sylvan, 'Prospects for regional philosophies in Australasia', *AJP* 63 (1985): pp. 188–204; R. Sylvan, 'Issues in regional philosophy: Austrian philosophy? And its Austral image?', in *Austrian Philosophy Past and Present*, ed. K. Lehrer & J.C. Marek (Dordrecht, 1997), pp. 147–66; Sylvan papers are in University of Queensland Library.

human and non-human, the Routleys proposed to extend the sphere of environmental moral concern to all sentient beings, that is, beings which could have interests. 'Human chauvinism' would thus be overturned.[26] Their 'deep-green theory' was unlike deep ecology in being against new-age sloganising with tinges of pagan spirituality. They approved of argument to establish a coherent ethical (rather than spiritual) theory.[27] Their position was that the well-being of whatever is capable of well-being (that is, animate beings) may not be jeopardised without good reason.

In any of its versions, deep ecology must answer the question, what properties exactly make something have intrinsic value? And if one airily and democratically proposes to extend value to *all* life — to speak of an 'equal right to live and blossom' as early formulations of deep ecology did — why stop there? Why not rocks as valuable? And if so, why not as *equally* valuable? At that point, the theory becomes vacuous, since there are no remaining gradations in value. Surely, as Routley puts it, value is more patchily distributed in the universe, like yellow.

Further, one can apparently have too much of what would other-wise be a good thing, like plagues of rats: 'there is a principle (a sort of inverse of rarity) of *diminishing value* with increasing numbers, ap-plying also to humans'.[28]

---

[26] R. & V. Routley, 'Human chauvinism and environmental ethics', in Mannison, McRobbie & Routley, pp. 96–189; earlier partial versions in 'Is there a need for a new, an environmental ethic?', in *Proceedings of the XVth World Congress of Philosophy* (Sofia, 1973), vol. 1 pp. 205–10; 'Against the inevitability of human chauvinism', in *Ethics and Problems of the 21st Century*, ed. K.E. Goodpaster & K.M. Sayre (Notre Dame, 1979), pp. 36–59; summary in Grave, *History*, pp. 223–5; replies in S.I. Benn, 'Personal freedom and environmental ethics: The moral inequality of species', in *Equality and Freedom* ed. G. Dorsey (New York, 1977), vol. 2, pp. 401–24; J. Begley, 'Do we need a new ecological ethics?', *Compass Theology Review* 25 (1990): pp. 28–36; discussion in McCloskey, *Ecological Ethics and Politics,* pp. 57–61.

[27] Emphasised in R. Sylvan & D. Bennett, *The Greening of Ethics: From Human Chauvinism to Deep-Green Theory* (Cambridge, 1994), ch. 5; survey of positions on breadth of moral community: introduction to A. Brennan, ed, *The Ethics of the Environment* (Aldershot, 1995); A. Brennan, 'Environmental ethics', *Routledge Encyclopedia of Philosophy*, vol. 3, pp. 333–6; N. Low & B. Gleeson, *Justice, Society and Nature: An Exploration of Political Ecology* (London, 1998), ch. 6.

[28] R. Sylvan, 'A critique of deep ecology', *Radical Philosophy* 40 (Summer 1985): pp. 2–12 & 41 (Autumn 1985): pp. 10–22; discussion in W. Fox, *Approaching Deep Ecology: A response to Richard Sylvan's Critique of Deep Ecology* (Hobart, 1986).

If value is unevenly distributed, it is up to environmental philosophers to explain what properties of things confer these degrees of
value. There are two main suggestions, both of some intuitive appeal
but both with certain conceptual problems, and not easily combined,
nor easily justified as criteria. The first is 'naturalness', the second
'diversity' or 'complexity'.

Elliot and Goodin suggest that the property of being naturally
evolved (as opposed to made) is crucial to what gives a wilderness, for
example, its unique value.[29] The value of a part of the environment
thus depends on its history, in much the same way as the value of a
work of art can depend on its genuineness: something really made by
Leonardo is more valuable than a modern reproduction, even a perfect reproduction. This makes the value of environmental restoration
tricky, and also means that a divinely created universe would have a
different kind of value (though possibly an equal one).

The other possible source of value lies in aesthetic properties, of
'diversity, stability, complexity, beauty, grandeur, subtlety, harmony,
creativity, organisation, intricacy, elegance and richness'.[30] On the
value of diversity, Passmore quotes Aquinas: 'Although an angel,
considered absolutely, is better than a stone, nevertheless a Universe
containing angels and other things is better than one containing angels only.'[31] As Passmore points out, this raises a problem with the
invasion of exotic species, which increases diversity but conflicts with
the value of naturalness. The cane toad and the prickly pear, however
beautiful in themselves, are not welcome in the Australian ecosystem
and do not add value to it, while the wallabies of Derbyshire have
been little loved despite their contribution to England's impoverished
biodiversity. The problem is made worse by the fact that intuitions
were apparently different in the nineteenth century, when
Acclimatisation Societies busily transferred species both ways.[32] And if
exotic species are a pest and restoration to the pristine state is desirable, should we take advantage of advances in cloning to resuscitate
the Tasmanian tiger?[33] Or the Tasmanian Aborigines?

[29] R. Elliot, 'Intrinsic value, environmental obligation and naturalness',
Monist 75 (1992): pp. 138–60; R. Elliot, *Faking Nature: The Ethics of
Environmental Restoration* (London, 1997); R.E. Goodin, *Green Political Theory*
(Cambridge, 1992), ch. 2; cf. W. Godfrey-Smith, 'The value of wilderness',
Environmental Ethics 1 (1979): pp. 309–19.

[30] Elliot, 'Intrinsic value', at p. 151.

[31] Passmore, *Man's Responsibility*, p. 119.

[32] L. Gillbank, 'The origins of the Acclimatisation Society of Victoria',
Historical Records of Australian Science 6 (1986): pp. 359–74.

[33] P. Bagust, 'The end of extinction?', *Australian Journal of Communication* 28
(1) (2001): pp. 1–81.

'Diversity' is a good that attaches more to species than individuals. So the more that value attaches to such large abstractions as natural ecosystems, the less there is for individual animals: if cruelty and predation are natural to an ecosystem, should the value of the individual or that of the ecosystem take precedence?[34] 'Complexity' as a good produces other problems. Individual life forms and perhaps ecosystems are not the only things with complexity or purposiveness. Should we not assign value to kidneys, even if they are not inside organisms? Or for that matter, to machines (which are exactly what the environmentalists wanted to disvalue)?[35] Indeed, should we not praise the engineer, who brings into being new ceramics and organic molecules with marvellous properties, which nature herself has left in the sphere of the merely possible? If natural evolution of complex life forms is good, is not speeding it up through biotechnology better?

Those thoughts may encourage a renewed emphasis on naturalness as a good. But the very effort to find non–human–centred criteria of goodness (like diversity, complexity and naturalness) and to see humanity as simply 'part of the universe' tends to destroy the distinction between natural and artificial and induces a kind of quietism. If one species has the habit of covering the earth with concrete jungles, why worry? That is just its nature. And too easy an acceptance of what happens naturally may deny us reason to object to asteroid strikes, ice ages or HIV mutations, which are certainly natural and may well clear the earth for a wealth of new evolutionary opportunities.[36]

Obviously, it is not easy for environmentalists to get straight what they really mean to say. It is very hard, especially, to make sense of deep ecological ideas as an add-on to our usual views of the way the world is. Philosophical foundations for environmental philosophy *need* not be half-baked, but to bake the whole cake will take some intellectual effort. Passmore's claim that rights and values are not the kind of things nature can have need not be accepted, but if those ideas are to make sense at all, it seems they will need to be situated in a much larger metaphysical reorientation which will reveal the world to be rather different from the way the mainstream of Western thought has taken it to be. Some environmental thinkers have therefore looked for resonances between what they believe and older phi-

---

[34] L.E. Johnson, *A Morally Deep World: An Essay on Moral Significance and Environmental Ethics* (Cambridge, 1991), pp. 4–5, 242–3.

[35] J. Thompson, 'A refutation of environmental ethics', *Environmental Ethics* 12 (1990): pp. 147–60.

[36] W. Grey, 'Anthropocentrism and deep ecology', *AJP* 71 (1993): pp. 463–75; also W. Grey, 'A critique of deep green theory', in *Beneath the Surface*, ed. E. Katz et al (Cambridge, Mass, 2000), pp. 43–58 (biography at www.uq.edu.au/~pdwgrey).

losophical traditions. Two leading candidates are Aboriginal philosophy and the pantheism of Spinoza.

Despite some misappropriations by environmentalists — Aborigines are not 'conservationist' in the contemporary sense[37] — there is something in the claim that Aboriginal world views incorporate a kind of ecological philosophy. Though there is a danger of falsifying Aboriginal thought by trying to express it in English, by and large experts have been happy to systematise and describe what Aboriginal views are in the area occupied in Western thought by philosophy. Anderson's associate A.P. Elkin arranged Aboriginal opinions on the workings of nature under the headings of space, time, causation and number, and was happy to compare the dwelling of Dreamtime spirits with Leibniz's monads.[38] It is agreed that the Dreaming is not a simple matter of feeling, or myth (in the Western sense), but an expression of an understanding of how reality is, and proof that 'the blackfellow ... shares with us "the metaphysical gift"'.[39] It has definite content, corresponding with the eternal realities that Western religious traditions believe underlie the visible world.[40] The landscape has been

[37] L. Sackett, 'Promoting primitivism: Conservationist depictions of Aboriginal Australians', *Australian Journal of Anthropology* 2 (1991): pp. 233–46; J.L. Kohen, *Aboriginal Environmental Impacts* (Kensington, 1995); R. Sworder, *Mining, Metallurgy and the Meaning of Life* (Quakers Hill, 1995), pp. 11–13; B.J. Coman, 'Environmental primitivism and the noble savage', *Quadrant* 47 (3) (Mar 2003): pp. 38–43.

[38] A.P. Elkin, 'Elements of Australian Aboriginal philosophy', *Oceania* 40 (1969): pp. 85–98, at p. 89; 'Berkeleian' in B. Chatwin, *The Songlines* (London, 1987), p. 14; annotated bibliography on Aboriginal philosophy and totemism in T. Swain, *Aboriginal Religions in Australia* (Westport, CT, 1991), pp. 79–87.

[39] W.E.H. Stanner, 'The Dreaming', in *Reader in Comparative Religion*, ed. W.A. Lessa & E.Z. Vogt (3rd ed, New York, 1972), pp. 269–77; comment in S. Muecke, 'Travelling the subterranean river of blood: Philosophy and magic in cultural studies', *Cultural Studies* 13 (1) (1999): pp. 1–17.

[40] T. Swain, 'Dreaming, whites and the Australian landscape: Some popular misconceptions', *Journal of Religious History* 15 (1989): pp. 345–50; T. Swain, *A Place for Strangers* (Cambridge, 1993), pp. 22–36; K. Maddock, *The Australian Aborigines* (Melbourne, 1974), pp. 27–8, 109–10; L.R. Hiatt & R. Jones, 'Aboriginal conceptions of the workings of nature', in *Australian Science in the Making*, ed. R.W. Home (Cambridge, 1988), pp. 1–22, part II; review in J.B. Callicott, *Earth's Insights: A Survey of Ecological Ethics from the Mediterranean Basin to the Australian Outback* (Berkeley, 1994), pp. 172–84; D.B. Rose, *Nourishing Terrains: Australian Aboriginal Views of Landscape and Wilderness* (Canberra, 1996); D.L. Morgan & M.D. Slade, 'Aboriginal philosophy and its impact on health care outcomes', *Australian and New Zealand Journal of Public Health* 21 (1997): pp. 597–601; discussion of later

fashioned by totemic ancestors,[41] and hence special or sacred sites, the transformed bodies of timeless ancestral beings, are places of unusually close connection with the eternal.[42]

The most hopeful Western philosophical tradition as a foundation for environmental philosophy is that of Spinoza. It emphasises the interconnections between humans and nature and conceives of nature itself as having ethical properties. It is often regarded as a version of pantheism, the view that the whole universe is God, or at least has divine attributes,[43] though the 'divinity' envisaged is far from a personal one. There has been an enduring stream of Spinozism in Australia — or perhaps one should rather say a recurrent rediscovery of the Spinozist option, since the thinkers involved very rarely mention their predecessors. There has probably been more writing by Australians on Spinoza than on any of the other classical European philosophers,[44] and many other thinkers who do not specifically mention Spinoza have developed similar theories.

developments in K. Maddock, 'Metamorphosing the sacred in Australia', *Australian Journal of Anthropology* 2 (1991): pp. 213–32.

[41] T.G.H. Strehlow, *Aranda Traditions* (Melbourne, 1947), pp. 25–33.

[42] R.M. Berndt, *The Sacred Site: The Western Arnhem Land Example* (Australian Aboriginal Studies no. 29, Canberra, 1970), pp. 1–10; also T.G. Thomas, 'The land is sacred', in *The Gospel Is Not Western*, ed. G.W. Trompf (Maryknoll, NY, 1987), pp. 90–4; B. Neidjie, *Kakadu Man* (Queanbeyan, 1985), pp. 46–9 (discussion in V. Plumwood, 'Plato and the bush', *Meanjin* 49 (1990): pp. 524–36); S. Muecke, 'Towards an Aboriginal philosophy of place', in *Speaking Positions*, ed. P. van Thoorn & D. English (Melbourne, 1995), pp. 167–79; M. Slade & D. Morgan, 'Aboriginal philosophy in Australian higher education', in *Local Knowledge and Wisdom in Higher Education*, ed. G.R. Teasdale & Z. Ma Rhea (Oxford, 2000), pp. 51–78; some white attempts to populate the bush with spiritual entities in L.H. Allen, *Gods and Wood-Things* (Sydney, 1913).

[43] M.P. Levine, 'Pantheism, ethics and ecology', *Environmental Values* 3 (1994): pp. 121–38; M.P. Levine, *Pantheism* (London, 1994); G. Oppy, 'Pantheism, quantification and mereology', *Monist* 80 (1997): pp. 320–36; P. Forrest, 'Pantheism and science', *Monist* 80 (1997): pp. 307–19.

[44] J.A. Gunn, *Benedict Spinoza* (Melbourne, 1925); J.A. Gunn, 'Spinoza', *AJPP* 2 (1924): pp. 23–42; J.A. Gunn, *Spinoza, the maker of lenses: A play* (London, 1932); (Gunn's papers are in Melbourne University Archives); R. Jackson, 'The doctrine of substance in Descartes and Spinoza', *AJPP* 4 (1926): pp. 205–11; K. Hart, *The Departure* (St Lucia, 1978), pp. 33–4; A.C. Fox, *Faith and Philosophy: Spinoza on Religion*, ed. A.J. Watt (Nedlands, 1990); A. Donagan, *Spinoza* (Chicago, 1989); G. Lloyd, *Part of Nature: Self-Knowledge in Spinoza's Ethics* (Ithaca, NY, 1994); G. Lloyd, *Routledge Philosophy Guidebook to Spinoza and the Ethics* (London, 1996); M. Gatens & G. Lloyd, *Collective Imaginings: Spinoza, Past and Present* (London, 1999); G. Lloyd, ed, *Spinoza: Critical Assessments* (London, 2001).

A theory of this kind was maintained by Samuel Alexander, the first famous Australian-born philosopher. Alexander was born in Sydney and grew up in Melbourne, but left for England at the age of eighteen in 1877 and never returned.[45] He maintained that space-time, existing entirely independently of thought, was the fundamental stuff out of which things and events were made. The evolution of the universe leads to the gradual emergence of more complex and higher levels of reality — life, and later consciousness. In due course, deity will evolve.[46] Alexander's main book, *Space, Time and Deity*, was based on lectures he delivered in Glasgow in 1918. They were attended by the young John Anderson, and their impact was a crucial event in his reorientation from the idealism of his teachers to his distinctive realism.[47] Of course he discarded Alexander's views that some levels of reality were higher than others. He characteristically said that *Space, Time and Deity* 'has given us the fullest and most logical statement of realism yet presented, but with such concessions to idealism as to render it ineffective.'[48]

Alexander, like many of the school, was more concerned to present and develop his theory than to argue for it. Those who have looked for supporting arguments have often found something helpful in the strange world of modern physics. One obvious area worth mining is quantum mechanics, whose account of the nature of reality is unusual — on some interpretations, at least. This line of thought was pursued

---

[45] Alexander's recollections of Australia in S. Alexander, *Philosophical and Literary Pieces* (London, 1939), pp. 1–3; further in H. Munz, 'Professor Samuel Alexander', *Australian Jewish Historical Society Journal and Proceedings* 1 (6) (1941): pp. 171–8; *ADB*, vol. 7, pp. 133–4; his contributions to Zionism in C. Weizmann, *Trial and Error* (New York, 1949), pp. 152, 117–8.

[46] Summary of his philosophy in C.R. Goodwin, 'On rediscovering Alexander', *Twentieth Century* 21 (1966): pp. 62–9; A. Boyce Gibson, 'Samuel Alexander: An appreciation', *AJPP* 16 (1938): pp. 251–4; Passmore, *A Hundred Years of Philosophy*, 2nd ed, pp. 266–78; criticism in H.B. Loughnan, 'The empiricism of Dr Alexander', *AJPP* 9 (1931): pp. 91–102; H.B. Loughnan, 'Emergence and the self', *Monist* 46 (1936): pp. 211–27; (Fr Loughnan's book on Bradley, Bosanquet and Alexander, *Metaphysics and Ethics: A Scholastic Study of Three English Monists*, remains unpublished: D. Strong, *Australian Dictionary of Jesuit Biography* (Sydney, 1999), pp. 198–9); G.F. Stout, 'A criticism of Alexander's theory of mind and knowledge', *AJPP* 22 (1944): pp. 15–54; D.C. Stove, 'Two problems about individuality', *AJP* 33 (1955): pp. 183–8.

[47] B. Kennedy, *A Passion to Oppose* (Melbourne, 1995), pp. 47, 61, 117–9.

[48] J. Anderson, 'The non-existence of consciousness', *AJPP* 7 (1929): pp. 68–73 (repr. in *Studies in Empirical Philosophy* (Sydney, 1962), pp. 60–7); see also the index to *Studies* under 'Alexander'; Anderson's lectures on Alexander at setis.library.usyd.edu.au/oztexts/lectures.html .

in the 1950s by the freelance philosopher Jack McKinney, Judith Wright's husband.[49] He proposed to take literally the language of quantum physicists when they described reality as made up of events, indeterminacies and probabilities, 'waves of knowledge', and other ultimately non-physical constituents, all with a close relationship to consciousness.[50] He hoped such ideas would spontaneously lead to a change of heart that would turn humanity away from the destructive tendencies evident in the World Wars and the atomic bomb. Judith Wright recalls that meeting him 'set me, too, off on new tracks of thinking and put those years of Andersonian philosophy in quite new lights. The thinkers most people revered were being turned upside down ...'[51] His ideas formed the basis of her later environmental activism.[52] When asked by an interviewer, 'What are you trying to do in your poetry?', Wright answered, 'The job philosophy has opted out of.'[53]

The clearest and best-argued presentation of a Spinozist philosophy, and also the one that connects it most closely to environmental philosophy, is Freya Mathews' *The Ecological Self.*[54] She argues that Einstein's General Relativity is best seen as showing that the basic

[49] J. Wright, *Half a Lifetime* (Melbourne, 1999), ch. 8; V. Brady, *South of My Days* (Sydney, 1998), pp. 113–22, 126–8, 163, 170–1; Wright in *ADB,* vol. 15, p. 252.

[50] J.P. McKinney, *The Challenge of Reason* (Brisbane, 1950); 'Philosophical implications of the modern revolution in thought', *Philosophy and Phenomenological Research* 18 (1957): pp. 35–47; 'Experience and reality', *Mind* 67 (1958): pp. 386–93; *The Structure of Modern Thought* (London, 1971); articles in *Meanjin* 1–3 (1942–4); *Language* 1 (1952); on these publications, Wright, *Half a Lifetime,* pp. 224–5, 261, 276.

[51] Wright, quoted in Brady, pp. 116–7; also M. Noonan, 'A leap to air: The evolution of Judith Wright's thinking on the mystery of creation', *Compass* 30 (Winter 1996): pp. 7–14.

[52] J. Wright, 'Conservation as a concept', *Quadrant* 12 (1) (Jan-Feb 1968): pp. 29–33; J. Wright, 'The principles of conservation', *Wildlife Newsletter* 17 (Nov 1968): pp. 4–6.

[53] V. Vallis, 'Doing philosophy's job', *Times Literary Supplement* 3865 (9/4/1976), p. 432.

[54] F. Mathews, *The Ecological Self* (London, 1991); also F. Mathews, 'Conservation and self-realization: A deep ecology perspective', *Environmental Ethics* 10 (1988): pp. 347–55; and briefly in F. Mathews, '*Terra incognita*: Carnal legacies', in L. Cosgrove, D. Evans & D. Yencken, eds, *Restoring the Land* (Melbourne, 1994), pp. 37–46; F. Mathews, 'Ecological philosophy', *Routledge Encyclopedia of Philosophy,* vol. 3 pp. 197–202; some other partly similar works: W. Fox, 'Deep ecology: A new philosophy for our time?', *Ecologist* 14 (1984): pp. 194–200; W. Fox, *Towards a Transpersonal Ecology* (Totnes, 1995); A. Gare, *Postmodernism and the Environmental Crisis* (New York, 1993).

furniture of the universe is force-fields and their variations, and what appear to be substantial things are only semi-permanent fluctuations in the basic fields.[55] As to quantum mechanics, she does not accept idealist interpretations according to which reality is dependent on 'the observer', but argues that non-classical principles like 'non-locality and intrinsic dynamism' again suggest a holistic view of the universe.[56] Certain parts of the world, though, such as living organisms, have an internal organisation that tends to keep them in existence; they have an integrity that makes them 'matter to themselves', whether or not they are conscious of it. This confers on them an intrinsic value, independent of any valuation of them by anything external.[57] Rocks are different: they are only stuck together by external forces: 'A rock is no way self-affirming, demarcating and preserving its own identity; a rock is just a lump of matter, arbitrarily hewn out, waiting to be worn away by wind and rain.'[58] (Here Mathews comes close to Alfred Deakin's words of a century earlier: 'if the unity of the universe were merely the unity of a rock, which might be more properly styled homogeneity, or the unity of an arch or of a circle, it could not inspire feeling of any kind. The vital factor in Wordsworth is that he holds the universe to be a *living* unity, which therefore inspires faith.'[59])

Mathews does not exactly hold the universe to be a living unity, but grants it a low level of self-organisation and hence a kind of 'background value', like the cosmic background radiation.[60] That has no bearing on our actions, since we cannot affect the existence or non-existence of the whole universe. But particular living things that do have value to themselves, and strive to maintain their existence against difficulties, deserve our respect and our recognition of their vital needs, to the extent that they do not conflict with the vital needs of other selves.

There have been attempts to work out a Christian philosophy of the environment,[61] though they face suspicion from the orthodox as

---

[55] Mathews, *Ecological Self*, pp. 50–60.

[56] Mathews, *Ecological Self*, pp. 54–7.

[57] Mathews, *Ecological Self*, pp. 104–5.

[58] Mathews, *Ecological Self*, p. 104.

[59] A. Deakin, *The Gospel According to Wordsworth* (1884), quoted in K. Murdoch, *Alfred Deakin* (London, 1923), p. 137.

[60] Matthews, *Ecological Self*, p. 118.

[61] J. Scullion, A. Hamilton, T. Daly & W. Daniel, *God's Creation and Human Responsibility for the Earth* (Melbourne, 1981); P. Collins, *God's Earth* (Melbourne, 1995); R.M. Gascoigne, *The History of Creation: A Christian View of Inorganic and Organic Evolution* (Sydney, 1993) (obituary of Gascoigne

probably pagan and from the actual pagans as futile exercises in me-tooism. The most noted such attempt is by Charles Birch, for many years Professor of Biology at Sydney University. The first version appeared in 1965, the year in which Birch was engaged in nobbling Knopfelmacher's application to Sydney University.[62] 'The Universe', he says, 'turns out to be less like a machine and more like a life.'[63] Where materialists argue that since everything other than minds is material, so some way will be found to show minds too are reducible to brains, Birch argues in reverse: other parts of the universe have the purposiveness of minds, but to lesser degrees. 'Atoms resemble human experience in the sense of taking account of their environment without being totally determined by it.'[64] God is the Life of the World, literally.

The later chapters of Paul Davies' books on popular science may contain a similar view, but they are so vague philosophically that it is hard to tell.[65]

These somewhat colourless abstractions about the nature of the universe are altogether too blokey for some. According to ecofeminists, the rape of nature is intimately connected with the rape of women. They find deep ecology too abstract, alien, cognitive, positivist and generally too focused on the evils of humanity, rather than of men, and not political enough.[66]

---

in *Australasian Association for the History, Philosophy and Social Studies of Science Newsletter* no. 48 (Aug 1994)).

[62] C. Birch, *Nature and God* (London, 1965).

[63] C. Birch, *On Purpose* (Kensington, 1990), p. xi.

[64] Birch, *On Purpose*, p. xii; also C. Birch & J.B. Cobb, *The Liberation of Life* (Cambridge, 1981), summary in Collins, *God's Earth*, pp. 138–41; interview in C. Jones, *The Search for Meaning* (Sydney, 1989), pp. 63–75; '"Heretic" scoops religion's richest prize', *SMH* 7/3/1990, p. 1; Birch papers in Sydney University Archives, P.131; cf. P. Edwards, 'Panpsychism' in *Encyclopedia of Philosophy*, vol. 6, pp. 22–31; similar views in W.E. Agar, *A Contribution to the Theory of the Living Organism* (Melbourne, 1943, 2nd ed, 1951), ch. 3; R. Eckersley, *Environmentalism and Political Theory* (London, 1992), ch. 3; papers in *Concrescence: The Australasian Journal of Process Thought* 1 (June 2000) (www.alfred.north.whitehead.com/AJPT/ajpt_home.htm); a version closer to Spinoza in J. Evans, *Theistic Monism* (London, 1928).

[65] P. Davies, *The Mind of God* (Melbourne, 1992), chs 7–8, etc; analysis by J. McCaughan reported in M. Kay, 'On Paul Davies and *The Mind of God*', *Creation Ex Nihilo Technical Journal* 10 (1996): pp. 188–93; Davies' prize for Progress in Religion, *SMH*, 9/3/1995, p. 3.

[66] P. Hallen, 'Reawakening the erotic: Why the conservation movement needs ecofeminism', *Habitat Australia* 22 (1) (Feb 1994): pp. 18–21; A. Salleh, 'The ecofeminism/deep ecology debate: A reply to patriarchal reason', *Environmental Ethics* 14 (1992): pp. 195–216; A. Salleh, *Ecofeminism*

These themes appear in the later work of Val Plumwood (formerly Routley).[67] She has the advantage of being able to draw on her experience of a close and nearly fatal encounter with the forces of nature, when a canoe trip alone in Kakadu led to an attack by a crocodile. The crocodile attacked the canoe several times. Plumwood managed to jump from the canoe into the lower branches of a paperbark tree beside the river. At the same moment the crocodile grabbed her legs and rolled her into the water. She writes of her near-death experience:

> In its final, frantic attempts to protect itself from the knowledge of vulnerability and impending death that threatens the normal, subject-centred framework, the mind can instantaneously fabricate terminal doubt of extravagant, Cartesian proportions: *this is not really happening, this is a nightmare, from which I will soon awake.* This desperate delusion split apart as I hit the water. In that flash, when my consciousness had to know the bitter certainty of its end, I glimpsed the world for the first time 'from the outside', as no longer *my* world, as raw necessity, an unrecognisably bleak order which would go on without me ...

The water however was not deep, and at the end of the roll, Plumwood was able to draw breath. A second roll had the same result, and finding herself near an overhanging branch, she hung onto it. The crocodile let her go and she was able to climb into the paperbark. But the crocodile again leapt out and seized her by the thigh and a third roll ensued. At the end of it, the crocodile had tired and Plumwood was able to crawl slowly up a mudbank. Despite her severe injuries, she was able to travel some distance and was found in time by rangers. She eventually made an almost full recovery in hospital.

She later meditated on what the experience of being prey showed about human vulnerability. Referring to a strange rock formation that had given her a sense of unease shortly before the incident, she wrote:

> The wisdom of the rock formation draws a link between my inability to recognise my vulnerability and the similar failure of my culture in its occupation of the planetary biosystem. The illusion of invulnerability is typical of the mind of the coloniser; and as the experience of being prey is eliminated from the face of the earth, along with it goes something it has to teach about the power and resistance of nature and the delusions of

as Politics: Nature, Marx and the Postmodern (London, 1997); C.J. Mews & K. Rigby, eds, *Ecology, Gender and the Sacred* (Clayton, 1999); reply in W. Fox, 'The deep ecology-ecofeminism debate and its parallels', *Environmental Ethics* 11 (1989): pp. 5–25; R.S. Laura & R. Buchanan, 'Towards an epistemology of ecofeminism', *Education Research and Perspectives* 28 (1) (2001): pp. 57–90.
[67] V. Plumwood, *Feminism and the Mastery of Nature* (London, 1993); V. Plumwood, *Environmental Culture* (London, 2002)

human arrogance. In my work as a philosopher, I now tend to stress our failure to perceive human vulnerability, the delusions of our view of ourselves as rational masters of a malleable nature ... Let us hope it does not take a similar near-death experience to instruct our culture in the wisdom of the rock.[68]

[68] V. Plumwood, 'Human vulnerability and the experience of being prey', *Quadrant* 39 (3) (Mar 1995): pp. 29–34; also *SMH* 25/2/1985, p. 3.

Chapter 14 — This Space Intentionally Left Blank: Francofeminism

THERE is a dilemma at the heart of feminism. Should women get into shoulder pads, think rationally, break through the glass ceiling and take on the boys on the level playing field? That would be to fall for gung-ho masculist criteria of success. Or would it be better to play up the traditionally feminine, get in touch with emotions and bodies, and transform the world with quilting and yoga? That would be to accept the old masculine definitions of what is women's business, and end up in ghettoisation and irrelevance, leaving the public realm to men.[1]

Those outside philosophy will naturally think of a dilemma as in some way a bad thing. If politics is one's concern, a dilemma *is* a bad thing. It causes splits, enmities, loss of zeal, as activists and potential activists take up their positions. In philosophy, it is the opposite. There is nothing that feeds philosophy like a good dilemma, and a truly irresolvable one is a philosophical Magic Pudding. The more monographs, critiques, PhD theses and talkfests that have been carved out of it, the more there are left.

Feminism's dilemma can spawn fierce debate on virtually any issue. Fat is a feminist issue, but it is undecided whether slimming is an approved taking of one's destiny into one's own hands or a capitulation to male conceptions of female beauty. Women philosophers can either join in the disputes of traditional philosophy, or set up a 'feminist philosophy' sub-industry at the risk of diverting their graduate students into an intellectual sheltered workshop. But the

---

[1] M. Gatens, *Feminism and Philosophy: Perspectives on Difference and Equality* (Bloomington, Ind, 1991), pp. 4–5.

most distinctively philosophical debate concerns the relation of women and 'reason'.

Descartes and many other philosophers have praised reason at length and regarded it as one of the supreme attributes of humanity. They have spoken of the faculty of reason almost as if it were disembodied, and as if it is threatened by too close association with the passions and the body. Genevieve Lloyd, in her much cited book, *The Man of Reason*, and many other feminist thinkers, are against this image of reason and believe it has contributed to women's oppression.[2]

Why exactly does a view of reason as independent of the body contribute to the oppression of women? A naive view might hold the opposite: that the more independent reason is from the body, the less that bodily differences between men and women should matter to it, and hence the more opportunity there would be for women to simply pursue science and reason on the same terms as men. It is admitted that this is what Descartes intended.[3] Feminist philosophers are not impressed. They object to 'a "sexlessness" which, as many feminists have pointed out, is often a covert way of privileging maleness.'[4] Why does it privilege maleness? The idea is that our ideals of ration-

---

[2] G. Lloyd, *The Man of Reason: 'Male' and 'Female' in Western Philosophy* (London, 1984; 2nd ed, London, 1993); earlier in 'The man of reason', *Metaphilosophy* 10 (1979): pp. 18–37; later in G.M. Lloyd, 'Maleness, metaphor and the "crisis" of reason', in *A Mind of One's Own*, ed L. Antoy & C. Witt (Boulder, 1993), pp. 69–83; *A Companion to Feminist Philosophy*, ed. A.M. Jaggar & I.M. Young (Oxford, 1998), ch. 16; summary in M. Nicholls, 'Genevieve Lloyd and contemporary feminism', in *Australian Philosophers*, ed. P. Dowe, M. Nicholls & L. Shotton (Hobart, 1996), pp. 97–120; similar in J. Thompson, 'Women and the high priests of reason', *Radical Philosophy* 34 (Summer 1983): pp. 10–14; D. Russell, 'Women and reason', *Hecate* 14 (1) (1988): pp. 40–50; E.J. Porter, *Women and Moral Identity* (Sydney, 1991), ch. 4; V. Kirby, 'Viral identities: Feminisms and postmodernisms', in N. Grieve & A. Burns, eds, *Australian Women: Contemporary Feminist Thought* (Melbourne, 1994), pp. 120–32; Gatens, *Feminism and Philosophy*, ch. 5; C. Colebrook, 'Feminist philosophy and the philosophy of feminism: Irigaray and the history of Western metaphysics', *Hypatia* 12 (1) (Winter 1997): pp. 79–98; R.W. Connell, *Masculinities* (Sydney, 1995), ch. 7; objections in K. Green, *The Woman of Reason* (Cambridge, 1995), ch. 1; S.C. Hetherington, 'Dispensing with (men of) reason', *Reason Papers* 24 (Fall 1999): pp. 57–72; T. van Gelder, 'Heads I win, tails you lose', *Quadrant* 43 (7-8) (July-Aug, 1999): pp. 15–19; a middle view in R. Langton, 'Feminism in epistemology: Exclusion and objectification', in *The Cambridge Companion to Feminist Philosophy*, ed. M. Fricker & J. Hornsby (Cambridge, 2000).

[3] Lloyd, *The Man of Reason*, 2nd ed, p. 45.

[4] Lloyd, *The Man of Reason*, p. xi.

ality have been symbolised in ways that are traditionally associated with the male. The main evidence provided for this assertion is a list of dualities attributed to the ancient Pythagoreans: light versus darkness, right versus left, mind versus body, odd versus even, male versus female. The first of each pair is said to be valued over the second.[5] Not much evidence has been supplied for the prominence of these dualities in Western thought between the time of Pythagoras and women's studies courses in the 1980s, but they are presumed to have somehow infected Western thought at a deep level. The other evidence is that some men in several past centuries sometimes used masculine metaphors like 'conquest' in talking about the advance of reason.

Despite the tenuousness of the evidence, later and more radical feminists take these conclusions to have been firmly established, and assert without further argument: 'Within philosophy, for example, the presumedly timeless values of the discipline — Truth, Reason, Logic, Meaning, Being — have been shown by feminists (such as Lloyd, Irigaray) to be based on implicit but disavowed relations to their "others" — poetry, madness, passions, body, non-sense, non-existence. These "others" are defined as feminine ...'[6]

Not all feminists were happy with demonising logic. Some noticed the awkward fact that showing that pursuing a norm of reason harms women does not thereby prove there is anything mistaken with it. Instead it invites the question, what is wrong with women that norms of reason are a problem for them?[7] The assault on reason was especially trying to those feminists capable of writing intelligible prose. Kate Jennings says, 'Here I was wanting "to know more than I did yesterday", lead a sane life, and write lucidly, and my feminist peers were deeming all knowledge suspect and finding rationality to be "complicitous with male privilege" and clarity "a male strategy" ... It has been a jolting experience to be repudiated by my peers; to be bundled up in a job lot with Margaret Thatcher and Leonie Kramer.'[8]

[5] Lloyd, *The Man of Reason*, p. 3.
[6] E.A. Grosz, 'The in(ter)vention of feminist knowledges', in *Crossing Boundaries: Feminisms and the Critique of Knowledges*, ed. B. Caine, E.A. Grosz & M. de Lepervanche (Sydney, 1988), pp. 92–104, at p. 96; similar agreed to by Gatens, *Feminism and Philosophy*, ch. 5; R. Braidotti, *Patterns of Dissonance* (Cambridge, 1991), pp. 185–90, etc.
[7] R. Langton, 'Beyond a pragmatic critique of reason', *AJP* 71 (1993): pp. 364–84.
[8] K. Jennings, *Bad Manners* (Melbourne, 1993), p. 64; cf. pp. 80, 43–5; cf. A. Summers, *Ducks on the Pond* (Melbourne, 1999), p. 284. (Leonie Kramer's evil is taken as read among feminists; one writes that she is 'seeming proof that gender is socially constructed rather than biologically determined': P.

Nevertheless, in feminist philosophy the debate has moved on. If it is agreed that reason is a bad thing, what is the alternative? There are two possible moves to make. The first is to find out something about logic and make some alternative suggestions. The second is to change the question altogether, and praise some opposite of reason. The first alternative has been taken by some unusual work by the ecofeminist Val Plumwood, who had earlier done some work on alternative logics. Writing on 'Classical logic as the logic of domination', she objects to the way in which logic defines the negation of a proposition p, not-p (symbolised ¬ p) in terms of p:

> Such an account of ¬ p specifies ¬ p in relation to p conceived as the controlling centre, and so is p-centred. The very features of simplicity which have helped to select classical logic over its rivals are implicated here. In the phallic drama of this p-centred account, there is really only one actor, p, and ¬ p is merely its receptacle.[9]

But, she says, there are non-classical logics available which are not so arrogantly dualistic.

This plan, whatever may be said for or against it, at least requires some knowledge of logic, which arguably involves too much of a concession to reason. A purer, not to say easier, strategy is to simply attack an undifferentiated reason and talk about some opposite of it. Since reason is done by the mind, the opposite of it must be 'the body'. There is a whole Australian school of 'corporeal feminism'.[10]

Gilbert, 'Personal growth or critical resistance? Self-esteem in the English curriculum', in *Hearts and Minds*, ed. J. Kenway & S. Willis (Lewes, 1990), pp. 173–89, at p. 184.)

[9] V. Plumwood, 'The politics of reason: Towards a feminist logic', *AJP* 71 (1993): pp. 436–62 at p. 454; also in V. Plumwood, *Feminism and the Mastery of Nature* (London, 1993), pp. 56–7; cf. R. Ferrell, 'Copula: The logic of the sexual relation', *Hypatia* 15 (2) (2000): pp. 100–14.

[10] M. Gatens, *Imaginary Bodies* (New York, 1995), on which interviews in *Polemic* 7 (1) (1996): pp. 11–15; *Bulletin*, 9/1/2001, pp. 48–50; R. Diprose, *The Bodies of Women: Ethics, Embodiment and Sexual Difference* (London, 1994); R. Ferrell, *Passion in Theory: Conceptions of Freud and Lacan* (London, 1996); R. Diprose, *Corporeal Generosity* (Albany, NY, 2002); V. Kirby, *Telling Flesh: The Substance of the Corporeal* (London, 1997); A. Cranny-Francis, *The Body in the Text* (Melbourne, 1995); N. Sullivan, *Tattooed Bodies: Subjectivity, Textuality, Ethics and Pleasure* (Westport, Conn, 2001); M. Davies & N. Naffine, *Are Persons Property?* (Aldershot, 2001); various papers in *Australian Feminist Studies* 5 (Summer 1987) and *Hypatia* 6 (3) (Fall 1991); C. Colebrook, 'From radical representations to corporeal becomings: The feminist philosophy of Lloyd, Grosz and Gatens', *Hypatia* 15 (2) (2000): pp. 76–93; P.M. Rothfield, 'A conversation between bodies', *Melbourne Journal of Politics* 22 (1994): pp. 30–44; A. Caddick, 'Feminism and the body', *Arena* 74 (1986): pp. 60–88; M. la Caze, 'Simone de Beauvoir and female bodies',

What 'the body' means in this discourse is, needless to say, problematic. Someone actually asked one of the school at a Canberra conference whether 'the body' as here spoken of had anything to do with actual biological bodies. 'Deciding that I must still be immersed in a precritical notion of the body, the speaker dismissed me with a revealing theatrical gesture. As if to underline the sheer absurdity of my question, she pinched herself and commented, "Well, I certainly don't mean *this* body.""[11] This no doubt explains why the 'body' of feminist discourse never seems to be sick or old, much less newborn, or unborn. Nor does it seem to have as many parts as real bodies: 'there is surprisingly little feminist criticism', writes one author, 'on the nature of the stomach, the bowels, or the internal cavity of the mouth.'[12] One point of the exercise is explained thus: 'It is an unavoidable (and welcome) consequence of constructing an *embodied* ethics that ethics would no longer pretend to be universal.'[13] (That is, what's not all right for men is all right for women.) Another outcome is that it saves learning anything about biology — any suggestion that biological differences between men and women may have any relevance can be met with a smokescreen of abusive words like 'biolo-

---

Australian Feminist Studies 20 (Summer 1994): pp. 91–105; J. Wright, 'A feminist poststructuralist methodology for the study of gender construction in physical education', *Journal of Teaching in Physical Education* 15 (1) (Oct 1995): pp. 1–24; M. Paech, 'Sex or gender? A feminist debate for nurses', *Contemporary Nurse* 5 (4) (Dec 1996): pp. 149–56; M. Maddox, 'Bodies, equality and truth', *Alternative Law Journal* 21 (1996): pp. 168–72; E. McWilliam, 'Gender (im)material: Teaching bodies and gender education', *Australian Journal of Education* 41 (1997): pp. 48–58; P. Cheah, D. Fraser & J. Grbich, eds, *Thinking Through the Body of the Law* (Sydney, 1996); I. Karpin, 'Reimagining maternal selfhood: Transgressing body boundaries and the law', *Australian Feminist Law Journal* 2 (1994): pp. 36–62; M.B. Walker, *Philosophy and the Maternal Body* (London, 1998); C. Vasseleu, *Textures of Light* (London, 1998), ch. 3; M. Negus, 'Corporeal architecture', *Architectural Theory Review* 3 (2) (Nov 1998): pp. 112–22; S. Sandford, 'What is entitlement?', *Radical Philosophy* 90 (July/Aug 1998): pp. 54–6; P. Deutscher, 'The body', in *Australian Feminism: A Companion* (Melbourne, 1998), pp. 11–19; S. Squire, 'The personal and the political: Writing the theorist's body', *Australian Feminist Studies* no. 37 (2002): pp. 55–64; survey in Kwok W.L., 'New Australian feminism', *Antithesis* 7 (1) (1995): pp. 47–63.

[11] V. Kirby, '*Corpus delicti*: the body at the scene of writing', in *Cartographies: Poststructuralism and the Mapping of Bodies and Spaces*, ed. R. Diprose & R. Ferrell, pp. 88–100, at p. 91; cf. M. Gatens, 'Towards a feminist philosophy of the body', in *Crossing Boundaries*, pp. 59–70, at p. 62.

[12] E.A. Wilson, *Neural Geographies* (London, 1998), p. 52.

[13] Gatens, 'Towards a feminist philosophy of the body', at p. 67; similar in Diprose, *The Bodies of Women*, p. vi.

gism', 'reductionism', 'essentialism' and so on.[14] This in turn explains the strange absence in the debate of any mention of the nature-nurture question. Whether men and women have biological differences that cause psychological differences in, for example, their intellectual skills, is a question that is not allowed on the table. The scientific evidence on the question is indeed not always clear, and it is possible to argue about its meaning — but feminist thought is so constructed that it is a thought-crime to examine it.[15] Meanwhile, feminist theorists are always on the lookout for such scientific 'discoveries' as that lactation is not the sole prerogative of the female.[16]

Corporeal feminism is a part of a wider movement that calls itself the feminism of 'difference'. The notion of difference as used here is a product of the original dilemma of feminism. The older feminism which demanded equal rights for women is condemned as a 'feminism of equality', where equality is identified with uniformity, and uniformity in a male mould at that ('the right to be the same as men'[17]). 'Difference', by contrast, is intended to have the cachet of an openness to diversity, in the way 'multiculturalism' does. It is not supposed to be a simple denial of the demand for equality, since that would be to accept the terms of the debate given by earlier male thinkers. Since there is not in fact much conceptual room between equality and non-equality, it is necessary to develop the complicated conceptions of various continental thinkers to resolve the dilemma — or if not to resolve it, at least to keep the debate going between the two sides of the apparently immortal dichotomies of Western thought, like sameness and difference, male and female, mind and body, and so on.[18]

---

[14] Wilson, *Neural Geographies*, pp. 14–16.

[15] D. Stove, 'The intellectual capacity of women', *Proceedings of the Russellian Society* 15 (1990): pp. 1–16, repr. in D. Stove, *Cricket Versus Republicanism* (Quakers Hill, 1995), pp. 27–48; also F. Mora, 'Metaphysical purdah', *Philosophy* 55 (1980): pp. 377–85; D. Stove, 'The subjection of John Stuart Mill: The intellectual capacity of women and equality between the sexes', *Philosophy* 68 (1993): pp. 5–13; replies in I. Thiel, 'On Stove on Mill on Women', *Philosophy* 69 (1994): pp. 100–1; J. Teichman, 'The intellectual capacity of David Stove', *Philosophy*, 76 (2001): pp. 149–57; some actual feminist examination of the question in L. Rogers, 'Biology: Gender differentiation and sexual variation', in *Australian Women: Feminist Perspectives*, ed. N. Grieve & P. Grimshaw (Melbourne, 1981), ch. 5.

[16] B. Davies, 'A feminist poststructuralist analysis of discursive practices in the classroom and playground', *Discourse* 13 (1) (Oct 1992), pp. 49–66, at p. 49.

[17] E. Gross [later Grosz], 'Women's studies: Feminism and the University', *Hermes* N.S. 1 (1) (1985): pp. 29–31.

[18] Gatens, *Feminism and Philosophy*, pp. 92–4; Braidotti, *Patterns of Dissonance*, pp 128–30, 141, etc; P. Deutscher, *A Politics of Impossible Difference* (Ithaca,

The Australian leader of the school of corporeal feminism is Professor Elizabeth Grosz.[19] We saw in chapter 11 that her initial appointment at Sydney University provoked complaints about her assertion that feminist theory was a strategy aimed at gaining power, not an attempt to say something true. In later work, she has emphasised this theme several times. She begins one article with a quote from Nietzsche, 'A woman does not *want* the truth; what is truth to women?' She agrees:

> Lloyd, Le Doeff, Irigaray, Daly and others have questioned philosophy's commitments to the following patriarchal beliefs.
>
> 1. The belief in a single, eternal, universal truth independent of the particularities of observers, history, or social conditions. In aiming towards a truth based on correspondence between a proposition and a part of reality, philosophy seeks a position outside of history, politics and power.
>
> 2. The belief in objective, that is, in observer-neutral, context-free knowledge ...
>
> 3. The belief in a stable, reliable, transhistorical subject of knowledge, that can formulate true statements and construct objective knowledge.[20]

(Nevertheless, feminism has the right to judge and supersede patriarchal beliefs.[21]) 'Rather, instead of aspiring to the status of truth, a feminist philosophy prefers to see itself as a form of *strategy* ... To deny that a feminist philosophy aspires to truth is not to claim that it is content with being regarded as false; rather, the opposition between truth and falsity is largely irrelevant for a strategic model'.[22]

Naturally, Grosz is against science. In her contribution to *Crossing Boundaries*, the 1988 book that represents the Australian founding of the 'francofeminist' school based on Parisian high theory, she takes it that philosophers of science like Popper and Kuhn have done away with 'naive adherences to a notion of science as pure truth'.[23] Science

---

NY, 2002); how 'equality' and 'difference' work in such debates analysed in S. Buckle, 'Same difference!', *Philosopher* 6 (1998): pp. 3–6.

[19] Bibliography at www.cddc.vt.edu/feminism/Grosz.html ; earlier partial bibliography in 'Theorizing corporeality: Interview', *Melbourne Journal of Politics* 22 (1994): pp. 3–29.

[20] E. Grosz, 'Philosophy', in S. Gunew, ed, *Feminist Knowledge: Critique and Construct* (London, 1990), pp. 147–74, at pp. 165–6, also in E. Grosz, 'Bodies and knowledges: Feminism and the crisis of reason', in L. Alcoff & E. Potter, eds, *Feminist Epistemologies* (London, 1993), pp. 187–215.

[21] Grosz, 'Philosophy', p. 167

[22] Grosz, 'Philosophy', p. 168.

[23] E.A. Grosz & M. de Lepervanche, 'Feminism and science', in *Crossing Boundaries: Feminisms and the Critique of Knowledges*, ed. B. Caine, E.A. Grosz & M. de Lepervanche (Sydney, 1988), pp. 5–27, at pp. 17–19; later on

is masculine, and the mark of its coming from a masculine point of view is its pretence of not coming from a point of view: 'Irigaray suggests that man effaces his masculinity and particularity to proclaim instead the global relevance and *perspectivelessness* of his construct.'[24]

Some of Grosz's analysis of science does however lack a certain intimacy of acquaintance with the originals. She says of James Watson's view of Rosalind Franklin, his colleague and rival in the DNA research that led to the discovery of the double helix: 'Watson even speculates that she was "the product of an unsatisfactory mother who unduly stressed the desirability of professional careers that could save bright girls from marriages to dull men".'[25] That is not quite what Watson says. In fact, it is the opposite. The quotation from Watson's book actually reads, 'So it was quite easy to imagine her the product of an unsatisfactory mother ... But this was not the case. Her dedicated, austere life could not be thus explained — she was the daughter of a solidly comfortable, erudite banking family.' On the same page, Grosz presents Watson's criticism of Franklin's boss for forcing her to go elsewhere as Watson's own attempt to get rid of her. And the whole DNA project is taken to be a search by men for reproduction without women. Grosz, it is true, has not made up these misunderstandings herself. They are taken uncritically from another feminist 'scholar'.[26] As the postmodernists say, texts refer only to other texts.

In any case, having rejected science, Grosz is not shy about suggesting alternatives. In a remarkable piece of prose, she writes:

> To formulate different conceptions of corporeality, it may be necessary to:
>
> 1. Explore non-Euclidean and non-Kantian notions of space. If Euclidean, three dimensional space organises hierarchised perspective according to the laws of point-for-point projection, then different 'pre-oedipal' or infantile non-perspectival spaces, for example, may provide the basis for alternatives to those developed in dominant representations of corporeality. This may entail research in post-Einsteinian concepts of space-time; or, in an altogether different vein, psychological or fantasmatic concepts of space, for example, the kind experienced by the infant before vision has been hierarchically privileged and coordinated the information provided by the other senses into an homogeneous totality. This is necessary if the

---

feminism and science in special issue of *Australian Feminist Studies* 14 (no. 29) (Apr 1999).

[24] Grosz & de Lepervanche, 'Feminism and science', p. 25; analysis in J. Curthoys, *Feminist Amnesia* (London, 1997), pp. 93–9.

[25] Grosz & de Lepervanche, 'Feminism and science', p. 15.

[26] J.D. Watson, *The Double Helix* (London, 1968), p. 17; exposed by A. Olding, as reported in Curthoys, *Feminist Amnesia*, p. 181 n. 47; later on the same topic in E. Grosz, 'Darwinism and feminism', *Australian Feminist Studies* 14 (no. 29) (Apr 1999): pp. 31–45.

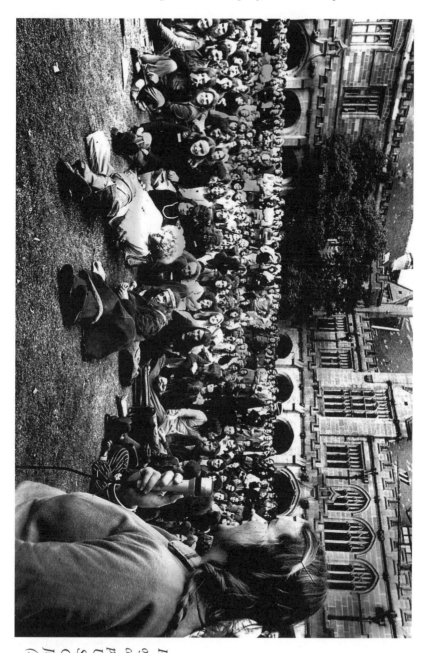

Protest in favour of the feminist course in philosophy, University of Sydney Quadrangle, 28 June 1973 (Newspix)

representational grid which produces conventional patriarchal representations of the body is to be superseded. Exploring other conceptual schemas which rely on different initial premises and different forms of argument prove useful in showing at the least, that Euclidean/Cartesian conceptions are not the only possibilities.[27]

Grosz has been at the forefront of corporeal feminism, especially in her 1994 book *Volatile Bodies*. The 'bodies' here are, of course, not the natural objects sometimes called by that name: 'the body, or rather bodies, cannot be adequately understood as ahistorical, precultural, or natural objects in any simple way; they are not only inscribed, marked, engraved, by social pressures external to them but are the products, the direct effects, of the very social constitution of nature itself.'[28] Her special contribution to the theory of corporeality lies in her lengthy discussions of bodily fluids, which are ideologically sound because they transgress the boundaries between the body and the outside: 'The tactile is related by Irigaray to the concept of the mucus, which always marks the passage from inside to outside, which accompanies and lubricates the mutual touching of the body's parts and regions. The mucus is neither the subjective touching of the toucher nor the objectivity of the touched but the indeterminacy of any distance between them.'[29] 'What is disturbing about the viscous or the fluid is its refusal to conform to the laws governing the clean and proper, the solid and the self-identical, its otherness to the notion of an entity — the very notion that governs our self-representations and understanding of the body. It is not that female sexuality is like, resembles, an inherently horrifying viscosity. Rather, it is the production of an order that renders female sexuality and corporeality marginal, indeterminate, and viscous that constitutes the sticky and the viscous with their disgusting, horrifying connotations.'[30]

If fluids are politically correct, it follows that organs, which insist on maintaining a fixed shape, are incorrect. Grosz's praise of Deleuze and Guattari's concept of the 'body without organs' is another high point of her work:

[27] E. Grosz, 'Notes towards a corporeal feminism', *Australian Feminist Studies* no. 5 (Summer 1987); cf. E. Grosz, 'Lived spatiality: Insect space/virtual sex', *Agenda* nos 26/7 (1992–3): pp. 5–8.

[28] E. Grosz, *Volatile Bodies: Toward a Corporeal Feminism* (Sydney, 1994), p. x; discussion in T. Welton, 'Grosz's corporeal feminism and standpoint epistemology', *Political Theory Newsletter* 8 (1) (Aug 1996): pp. 40–8; gay objections in R. Schubert, 'Helen Reddy, *ergo sum*', *Meanjin* 55 (1996): pp. 64–75.

[29] Grosz, *Volatile Bodies*, p. 107; cf. p. 194; similar in Vasseleu, *Textures of Light*, pp. 67–8.

[30] Grosz, *Volatile Bodies*, p. 195, also p. 203.

The BwO is a tendency to which all bodies, whatever their organization, aspire. Deleuze and Guattari speak of it as an egg, which instead of being composed of three kinds of substances is fluid throughout (neither Lacan's scrambled egg of a subject, the 'hommelette,' nor the egg in its differential properties, hard shell, clear white and yellow yolk), an unimpeded flow: ... 'That is why we treat the BwO as the full egg before the extension of the organism and the organization of the organs' ... it refuses the sedimentation and hierarchization required for the movement of transcendence, resists the stratifications and layerings and overcodings that produce the three great strata or identities: the union constituting the organism, the unification that constitutes the subject, and the structure of significance. It refuses all propriety.[31]

There is more to Grosz's philosophy than that, but it would take too long to give attention to her aperçus like 'philosophy is best undertaken dancing'[32] and 'Power can be thought of as running around and through us, like honey, in various degrees of fluidity and sticky congealment',[33] to her objections to AIDS advertising on the grounds that it encourages women to look after themselves,[34] to her love of plurals,[35] and to her many articles on such subjects as hermaphroditism, the necessity of lesbianism, lesbian fetishism, the fascination of men [*sic*] with animal and insect sex, freaks and so on.[36]

As early as 1989, the *Bulletin* included her in an article on six of 'Australia's top thinkers'.[37] From Sydney she moved to Monash University, becoming Professor and Director of the Institute for Critical and Cultural Studies. *Volatile Bodies* won a (New South Wales) Premier's Literary Award, being praised by the judges for its 'strong contribution to intellectual thought in the area of philosophy,

---

[31] Grosz, *Volatile Bodies*, pp. 169–70.

[32] E. Grosz, *Space, Time and Perversion* (London, 1995), p. 214.

[33] Grosz, reported in *Transitions: New Australian Feminisms,* ed. B. Caine & R. Pringle (St Leonards, 1995), p xi.

[34] Grosz, *Volatile Bodies*, p. 197.

[35] *Crossing Boundaries: Feminisms and the Critique of Knowledges*, ed. B. Caine, E.A. Grosz & M. de Lepervanche (Sydney, 1988); E. Grosz, 'A thousand tiny sexes: Feminism and rhizomatics', *Topoi* 12 (1993): pp. 167–79.

[36] E. Gross [later Grosz], 'Foucault, Herculine Barbin and the truth of sex', *Gay Information* 8 (1982): pp. 16–23; E.A. Grosz, 'The hetero and the homo: The sexual ethics of Luce Irigaray', *Gay Information* 17/18 (1988): pp. 37–44, at p. 44; E. Grosz, 'Lesbian fetishism?', in E. Apter & B. Pietz, eds, *Fetishism as Cultural Discourse* (Ithaca, 1993), pp. 101–15; E. Grosz, 'The labors of love: analyzing perverse desire', *Differences* 6 (2) (Summer 1994): pp. 274–95; E. Grosz, 'Animal sex' in *Sexy Bodies: The Strange Carnalities of Feminism*, ed. E. Grosz & E. Probyn (London, 1995), pp. 278–99; E. Grosz, 'Freaks', *Social Semiotics* 1 (2) (1991): pp. 22–38.

[37] 'What the top thinkers think', *Bulletin* 16/5/1989: pp. 48–55, at pp. 50–1.

feminisms, and cultural studies'.[38] She has moved on to a prestigious appointment in the United States.

It is not easy to understand either why anyone would write such things as Grosz, or why anyone who did would be taken seriously. Grosz is not given to revealing personal detail about her motives, though there is perhaps evidence of a misunderstanding of more common experiences than hers in her remark that the space of heterosexuality is 'where it's hardest to imagine an actual coming together of the two sexes in a mutually rewarding context ... certainly your average normative heterosexuality.'[39] She does however reveal the image she has of her own work. She contrasts a paper she regards as more experimental with her usual writings:

> I figured that at least once in my professional life I could — indeed I must — take the risk of being totally wrong, of committing some heinous theoretical blunder, of going way out on a limb, instead of being very careful, covering myself from rearguard criticism, knowing in advance that at least some of my claims have popular support or general credibility.[40]

The question of why Grosz's views do have so much popular support or general credibility is no easier. It is like trying to explain the Children's Crusade or any other outbreak of mass irrationalism: ultimately, there is nothing to explain it in terms of. Nevertheless, it is not hard to see in general terms what interests are served by such work. In politics, there is a permanent tension between reform and revolution. Revolution is simpler, purer, easier to explain and express in slogans. But there is pressure against it, in that one aim of politics is to get things done, and everyone understands that that needs compromise. In philosophy, it is the other way round. 'Radical critique' is what one goes to philosophy for, in much the same way as some churchgoers feel purified by listening to hellfire preachers whose views they do not literally agree with.

What exactly Grosz's work offers to the appetite for purity of critique can probably best be seen by noticing what things stand as unexamined presumptions for her. One is that 'transgression' as such is something one can congratulate oneself on. Whenever Grosz uses words like 'problematise', 'unsettle', 'destabilise' and so on, there is always an unargued-for payoff, a buzz of naughtiness which the reader is invited to share. (*I* question, *you* are complicit, *he* privileges.)

---

[38] *SMH* 16/9/1995, p. 11.

[39] 'Volatile bodies: Elizabeth Grosz in volatile conversation with Dianne Chisholm', *Mattoid* 50 (1996): pp. 37–62, at p. 59.

[40] E. Grosz, 'Refiguring lesbian desire', in *The Lesbian Postmodern*, ed. L. Doan (New York, 1994), pp. 67–84, at p. 68.

When 'unquestioned' is a term of insult, there is no space left in the discourse for the possibility that something should be questioned, and found to hold up pretty well. 'Questioning' is a process with a pre-determined answer; it is 'no'. Anyone who grew up in the Sixties will understand.

The other unquestioned assumption of Grosz's work, which gives it an appeal in some quarters, is that everything is to be evaluated according to whether it is useful to feminism (not useful to *women*; useful to *feminism*). Her attitude is the direct opposite of the one well expressed by Helen Garner: 'The struggle for women's rights is ... not a matter of gender loyalty. It is a matter of ethical principle, and as such, it does not dictate automatic allegiance to the women's side in any given argument.'[41]

BUT WHILE francofeminism has been hogging into the trough, a spectre has appeared at the feast. It is the spectre of Women's Liberation. This ghost from the past has found its voice in Jean Curthoys' book, *Feminist Amnesia*. Curthoys was one of the founders of academic feminism in the days when it was still Women's Liberation, and before it got 'theory'. Her book breathes the spirit of a member of Cromwell's New Model Army who has seen the revolution taken over by careerists and bureaucrats, or one of the idealistic men of 1917 about to be shipped off to the Gulag. Postmodernist academic feminism, she says, has suppressed the moral force that drove Women's Lib and buried it under a mountain of garbled theory. It has caricatured earlier feminists as enmeshed in simplistic liberal demands for equality for women, which is taken to be a position hopelessly naive and superficial. Yet it depends for its appeal on presenting itself as radical, as challenging power, questioning boundaries, and so on; that is, it is parasitic on the morality of liberationism. Curthoys finds the development of feminist theory beyond comprehension:

> [The book] developed out of a curiosity about the kind of thinking which, as a university teacher, I saw all around me and which seemed to more than accidentally involve conceptual muddles and basic ignorance. I was deeply puzzled about how my peers could think that way, how they could present such thinking as profound, innovatory and involving great learning and about how such thinking could have appeal for keen, intelligent and apparently genuinely 'socially concerned' young students.[42]

---

[41] H. Garner, *The First Stone* (Sydney, 1995), front matter.

[42] J. Curthoys, *Feminist Amnesia* (London, 1997), p. viii; denunciation in V. Plumwood, 'Feminist betrayals', *Arena Journal* 13 (1999): pp. 143–63.

Keen young students are always ready to be corrupted by high-sounding theory, so there is nothing hard to understand there. But as to why those teaching them should also fall for it, the simple answer, Curthoys says, is that the 'surrationalism' of writers like Grosz is 'a means for acquiring power which is appropriate to a movement whose moral credibility depends on the perception that it opposes power.'[43] Francofeminism pretends to be the heir to the high moral hopes of Women's Liberation, while actually denying there are any of the universal moral values like equality that Women's Liberation depended on; at the same time it purports to add profundity to its analysis by concentrating on alleged deep 'dualisms' of Western thought (mind/body, same/different, male/female and so on).[44] The interests served by the work of feminists like Grosz are those of radical feminist bureaucracy, which it protects from accountability to the claims of both reason and humanity.

Curthoys develops the parallel between francofeminism and the Lysenkoist biology imposed by Stalin. According to Lysenko, there were two sciences, bourgeois and proletarian. Like Grosz, Lysenko criticised the philosophical form of bourgeois (that is, orthodox) genetics. As Curthoys explains, 'This will turn out to be the necessary ideological move because it will enable ideas to be rejected ("dismantled") without any critical discussion which even pretends to meet them in their own terms. This is because once such a thesis is accepted it is no longer the content of ideas which is at issue but their form ... It is then only necessary to ... identify this form of ideas as intellectually and politically pernicious and we have at hand an easy means for rejecting and denouncing ideas, one which requires no demanding critical engagement at all, at the same time as it could, to those new to theoretical discussion, have the appearance of theoretical sophistication.'[45] She adds, 'I am not sure that it is in fact much less crazy to think of political conflicts taking place between categories of "sameness" and "difference" or between "bourgeois formal logic" and "proletarian dialectical thought" than it is, say, to believe that one

---

[43] Curthoys, *Feminist Amnesia*, p. 56; also 'The corruption of feminism: An interview with Jean Curthoys', *Philosopher* 6 (Summer 1998): pp. 7–10; cf. Wilson, *Neural Geographies*, p. 40.

[44] Curthoys, *Feminist Amnesia*, p. 107; also J. Curthoys, 'Do men and women live in the same world?', *Quadrant* 42 (4) (Apr 1998): pp. 9–16; similar in M. Tapper, '*Ressentiment* and power: Some reflections on feminist practices', in *Nietzsche, Feminism and Political Theory*, ed. P. Patton (Sydney, 1993), pp. 130–143, at p. 134.

[45] Curthoys, *Feminist Amnesia*, p. 70; on Diprose and Ferrell's evaluation of DNA as politically incorrect, pp. 87–92.

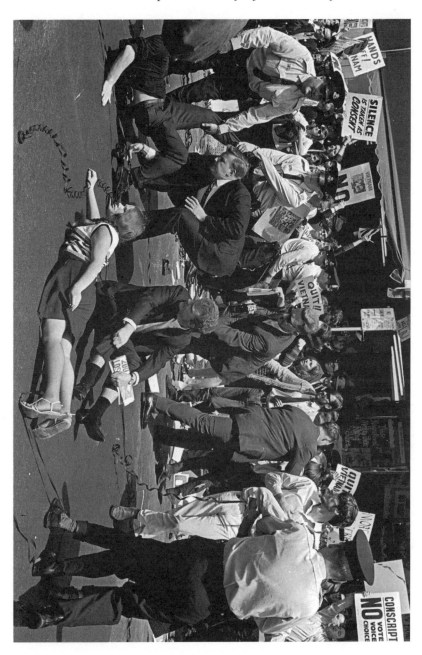

Jean Curthoys (front) about to be dragged from the path of President Johnson's motorcade, Sydney, 22 October 1966 (Fairfax photos)

is being pursued by Hitler around one's local neighbourhood. But it does look a lot less crazy.'[46]

A remarkable feature of Curthoys' book, and one which contrasts greatly with most feminist writers, is its robustly objectivist account of the morality of the liberation movements of the Sixties: 'It can be shown that the morality as such is objectively grounded with reference to a conception of the intrinsically or essentially human. In other words, it can be shown that the idea of irreducible respect for people is not good because it is the only one which might work, but that it might work because it is morally sound.'[47] Liberation theory in this sense, she says, is an answer to Socrates' ancient quest for the virtuous life. 'If we do regard liberation theory in this way as a modern response to this ancient philosophic quest, the simultaneous appropriation and denial of its truths by what now passes as sophisticated "theory" would count as the kind of ignorance parading as wisdom which Socrates understood as a part of the inevitable attempt to suppress philosophy.'[48] The re-appearance of objective moral values and quests for virtue is certainly a surprise. It is easy to see why Curthoys calls herself a dinosaur.[49]

Feminists outside philosophy who are interested in projects like recovering the female voice in history or restraining male violence should listen carefully to these warnings. It is tempting to give an easy solidarity to sisters who are working on 'deep' theory that one does not really understand. But the truth is that feminist philosophical 'theory' is anti-women because it is anti-human. Any feminists who feel their maternal instincts being tweaked by this strange growth in their nest should remember: it's a full egg the cuckoo lays.

---

[46] Curthoys, *Feminist Amnesia*, p. 117.
[47] Curthoys, *Feminist Amnesia*, pp. 41–2; cf. Green, *The Woman of Reason*, pp. 167–8.
[48] Curthoys, *Feminist Amnesia*, p. 32.
[49] J. Curthoys, 'Memoirs of a feminist dinosaur', *Australian Feminist Studies* 13 (1998): pp. 55–61.

Chapter 15 The Return of the Repressed

EXTINCTION in philosophy is not forever. Any opinion or argument, no matter how finally it seems to have been hunted down and refuted into oblivion, has the chance of being rediscovered by a new generation eager for novelties. In this chapter, we examine the revival of two old philosophies once thought well off the agenda: idealism and Catholic natural law philosophy. They have not been seen much in philosophy departments, but have flourished in, respectively, literature departments and the High Court of Australia.

As we saw in chapter 6, David Stove wrote that idealism, the doctrine that everything is mind-dependent, was sustained by what he identified as the 'Worst argument in the world': We can know things only as they are related to us/under our forms of perception and understanding/in so far as they fall under our conceptual schemes, etc, so, we cannot know things as they are in themselves. In Berkeley's version, 'we cannot have trees-outside-the-mind in mind without them being in mind, so there cannot be trees outside the mind (or if there could be, they could not be thought of). That argument did not vanish with the 1890s. We saw in chapter 11 that John Burnheim adopted an 'inevitably partisan' reading of the Sydney disturbances on the grounds that philosophy 'rests not on ultimate truths, but on a reading of our specific historical situation' (that is, we cannot know things except through our specific historical situation, therefore we cannot know things as they are in themselves). In the last chapter, we saw that Elizabeth Grosz 'questioned' the 'patriarchal belief' in a 'single, eternal, universal truth independent of the particularities of observers, history, or social conditions.' And it is the argument that drives the 'linguistic idealism' known as postmodernism that festers dankly in all too many corners of the humanities world of the present. How can we talk about anything outside texts — truth in history or science, or what authors really intended by their writings — since that is just more text? How can there be texts about what-is-outside-texts, without them being just more text? Therefore, there cannot be (or cannot be talked-about, at least) things outside texts. As one admirer explains it,

> Based on the Saussurean principle of the sign, which is that the relationship between the signifier ... and the sign ... is arbitrary, the structure of language for Lacan is such that 'language' is already cut off from 'reality'. What is taken as the meaning ... of any word, for example, is always going to be the result of that word's *difference* from all other words within a particular language. ... Consequently the Saussurean-based theory of language ... is radical because it erases 'reality' from the system: reality is never present 'in' or 'to' the system of language ... The gap between word and thing ... is a necessary one inasmuch as language can never be identical with what it names, for example, and vice versa ... From this it follows that presence (truth, reality, self-identity) is an effect of a system that is constituted by absence and separation. The very lack within language and the very gap between word and thing is what makes reality possible, making it seem present.[1]

The last part of this is a 'Worst Argument'. The apparent preceding reasoning from Saussure's view of linguistic structure is no more than a softening-up operation: while you're cowering in your foxhole disoriented from hearing that 'cat' gets its meaning merely by contrast with 'dog' and not from any connection with your experience of cats, the real Worst Argument is coming across the wire at you. It is just a linguistic version: we cannot speak about things except through the forms of language, therefore we cannot speak about things as they are in themselves.

The argument is, in short, of the same form as 'We have eyes, therefore we cannot see.'[2] The parallel makes it clear what is wrong with all such arguments: the fact that knowledge has to be implemented in brains, or cultures, or languages, is not a reason in itself for doubting it, or regarding it as cut off from reality. Just as the electronic insides of a calculator are not cut off from the laws of arithmetic, but instead implement them, so the knowledge processes in brains can track reality. There may be reasons for thinking they are sometimes in error, but the mere fact that they are implemented in brains

---

[1] N. Lucy, *Postmodern Literary Theory: An Introduction* (Oxford, 1997), p. 23; cf. p.42.
[2] A. Olding, 'Common sense and uncommon nonsense', unpublished; A. Olding, 'Religion as smorgasbord', *Quadrant*, 42 (5) (May 1998), pp. 73–5.

is not such a reason.[3] To think it is is to revert to Stove's caricature of the typical products of a modern high school:

> Their intellectual temper is (as everyone remarks) the reverse of dogmatic, in fact pleasingly modest. They are quick to acknowledge that their own opinion, on any matter whatsoever, is only their opinion; and they will tell you, too, the reason why it *is* only their opinion. This reason is, that it is *their* opinion.[4]

And was the same argument behind the excesses of feminism, seen in the last chapter? Stove suggests it was:

> The cultural-relativist, for example, inveighs bitterly against our science-based, white-male cultural perspective. She says that it is not only injurious but cognitively limiting. Injurious it may be; or again it may not. But why does she believe that it is cognitively limiting? Why, for no other reason in the world, except this one: that it is ours.[5]

Throwing a dart anywhere in the humanities in the 1990s would be very unlikely to have missed an example of the effects of these arguments. Let us look at just one area, 'media studies'. Somewhere back in the Seventies, the (then) Colleges of Advanced Education saw the opportunity to offer courses for students hoping to become journalists. They employed some ex-journos with ten or twenty years' experience in the industry to teach the students what they wanted to know. Then a dilemma arose. These lecturers could not be appointed heads of department, since they only possessed BAs. And the courses could not count as 'respectable' university courses because they lacked theory. The void was filled in the traditional way, by importing from the Old Country the latest in ideological technology — in this case the graduates of the 'Cultural Studies' movement associated with Birmingham University.[6] It is all linguistic idealism:

> Understood this way, language does not describe reality, it actually constitutes it. Our language system determines, delimits and shapes the way in

[3] J. Franklin, 'Stove's discovery of the worst argument in the world', *Philosophy* 77 (2002): pp. 615–24; A. Musgrave, 'Conceptual idealism and Stove's Gem', in A. Musgrave, *Essays on Realism and Rationalism* (Amsterdam, 1999), pp. 177–84..

[4] D.C. Stove, *The Plato Cult and other Philosophical Follies* (Oxford, 1991), p. 168.

[5] Stove, *The Plato Cult,* p. 167.

[6] K. Windschuttle, 'The poverty of media theory', *Quadrant* 42 (3) (Mar 1998): pp. 11–18.

which we understand the world. Therefore, to examine the structures of our language is to examine the structures of culture in general.[7]

Naturally, a theory like that gives endless scope to fill up courses with 'deconstructions' of the guile of media tycoons, the self-deception of readers and so on. But surely the public demands that the media tell in reasonably plain English what actually happened? There is an official answer to that naive realist thought: according to one Professor of Media Studies, the reading public is made up too:

> the invisible fictions that are produced institutionally in order for various institutions to take charge of the mechanisms of their own survival. Audiences may be imagined empirically, theoretically or politically, but in all cases the product is a fiction that serves the need of the imagining institution. In no case is the audience 'real' or external to its discursive construction.[8]

It is a perfect example of the ability of philosophical errors, nailed time and again centuries ago, to ooze out of their sarcophagi, clothe themselves with a local habitation and a name, and stalk the earth seeking a *tabula rasa* to colonise.

Media studies was not the only discipline in the 1980s on the lookout for a bit of theory. Nursing studies, for example, had to change quickly from hands-on training in hospitals to serious study in Colleges of Advanced Education, soon renamed universities. So it too needed some theory, any theory, in a hurry. So it has had to take on wads of prose like: 'Post structuralist feminist processes of deconstruction remind us that the world is a place of multiple and contradictory views'; 'Feminist and other scholars are showing that this ideal person (who may not exist!) who derives from European Protestantism and capitalism is epistemologically androcentric rather than a truly abstract objective individual.'[9] No doubt graduates of such courses find emptying bedpans a relief.

---

[7] G. Turner, 'Media texts and messages', in S. Cunningham & G. Turner, eds, *The Media in Australia: Industries, Texts, Audiences* (Sydney, 1993), p. 219, quoted in Windschuttle, 'Poverty'; further in K. Windschuttle, 'Cultural studies versus journalism', *Quadrant* 43 (3) (Mar 1999): pp. 11–20; similar in I. Marshall & D. Kingsbury, *Media Realities* (South Melbourne, 1996), pp. 38–40.

[8] J. Hartley, 'Invisible fictions', in J. Frow & M. Morris, eds, *Australian Cultural Studies: A Reader* (Sydney, 1993), p. 166, quoted in Windschuttle, 'Poverty'.

[9] A. Street, *Nursing Replay* (South Melbourne, 1995), p. xv; J. Horsfall, *Social Constructions in Women's Mental Health* (Armidale, 1994), p. 2; also A. Street, *Nursing Practice* (Geelong, 1990), pp. 5, 10; A.J. Walters, *Caring as a Theoretical Construct* (Armidale, 1994); C. Cheek & T. Rudge, 'Nursing as textually mediated reality', *Nursing Inquiry* 1 (1) (Nov 1994): pp. 15–22;

There is even postmodern Australian history. Paul Carter's *The Road to Botany Bay*, widely noticed in Australia and New York, dismisses all earlier writing on Australian history thus: 'We are well-supplied with historical geographies, but these share the diorama mentality: they take it for granted that the newcomers travelled and settled a land *which was already there* [his emphasis]. Geomorphologically, this was perhaps so — although even the science of landforms evolved as a result of crossing the country — but historically that country remained to be described. The diorama model shows us the river on the hill's far side; it shows us hills. But it was precisely such features which spatial history had to constitute.'[10] Of course there can be histories of such matters as how the colonists saw the landscape, but that is not what writers like Carter are doing. They are dressing up phenomenology as idealism to make it look shocking. One is intended to think, 'I might not go as far as that, but it is certainly good to see writers being bold, stimulating and transgressive.' Their rhetorical strategy seems to have been successful in every case, so far.

Writers such as these are best known to the public through the caricature in David Williamson's *Dead White Males*. Dr Grant Swain, lecturer in literary theory at 'New West University', is a composite caricature of a number of vogue ideologues. His belief that 'there are no absolute "truths", there is no fixed "human nature" and what we think of as "reality" is always and only a manufactured reality' is, as we have seen, mild enough in comparison with what is actually out there.[11] The main problem with the caricature is that the playwright has to compress Swain's views into a short space, lest the audience drift off. As a result, Swain's views are a good deal more coherent than those of the originals.

Any suspicions that Swain is an exaggeration are easily refuted by attention to the article 'Monstrous knowledge', by Bob Hodge,

A.M. Evans, 'Philosophy of nursing: Future directions', *Australian and New Zealand Journal of Mental Health Nursing* 4 (1) (1995): pp. 14–21; N. Glass & A. Davis, 'An emancipatory impulse: A feminist postmodern integrated turning point in nursing research', *Advances in Nursing Research* 21 (1) (1998): pp. 43–52; a reply in J. Solas, 'The poverty of postmodern human services', *Australian Social Work* 55 (2002): pp. 128–35.

[10] P. Carter, *The Road to Botany Bay* (London, 1987), p. xxi; similar in S. Ryan, *The Cartographic Eye* (Cambridge, 1996), pp. 121–4; discussion in K. Windschuttle, *The Killing of History* (Sydney, 1995), ch. 4; more on 'calling space into being' in R. Barcan & I. Buchanan, *Imagining Australian Space* (Nedlands, 1999), pp. 8–9.

[11] D. Williamson, *Dead White Males* (Sydney, 1995), p. 2; a reply in M. Morris, '"The truth is out there ..."', *Australian Book Review* no. 181 (June 1996): pp. 17–20.

Foundation Professor of Humanities at the University of Western Sydney, Hawkesbury, and co-author of *Language as Ideology, Myths of Oz, Children and Television: A Semiotic Approach*, etc.[12] After running through the views of the usual revolutionary thinkers like Kuhn and Foucault, he gives a picture of the type of PhD which will dominate in the postmodern regime. The student will be anarchist and oppositional, be forever immersed in CD-ROMs and image packages, welcome discontinuities, and draw on 'a long tradition of experimental avant-gardism, with its breaks with the modernist values of realism, transparency of text, linear logic ...' Hodge casually mentions that he has supervised or examined thirty-seven PhD theses in the last five years, so we are in for many decades of reconceptualising yet.

Postmodernism is a form of the French movement known as post-structuralism, and it inherits from structuralism the particularly *linguistic* cast of its idealism. The Australian philosophers Devitt and Sterelny, in their introductory book on the philosophy of language, put their finger on the weak point in Saussure, the founder of structuralism and hence father of the linguistic phase of idealism. Saussure compares language to a chess game, in which the 'meaning' of any piece, or move, arises solely through its place in the matrix of other moves. Similarly, he says, the meaning of words is constituted by their relation to other words. It is essential to the meaning of 'white', for example, that it is the opposite of 'black'. It is 'the view of language with each of its signs "defined" in terms of "pure difference" from all other signs; which is a bit like geography based on the generalization of Lennie Lower's dictum that "Chatswood is one of those places that are a stone's throw from some other place".'[13] What is missing from this picture is any relation between 'white' and white things, between language and the reality it is supposed to be about. That is what makes it a form of idealism.[14] It should have been pinned down in Saussure's time, but it wasn't, and the result is summed up in the much-quoted aphorism of Derrida, 'There is no outside-the-

[12] Bob Hodge, 'Monstrous knowledge: Doing PhDs in the new humanities', *Australian Universities' Review* 38 (2) (1995): pp. 35–9; see J. Franklin, 'The Sokal hoax and postmodernist embarrassment', *Continuum: Journal of Media and Cultural Studies* 14 (3) (Dec 2000): pp. 359–62.
[13] A. Olding, 'The law of the exclusive muddle: Categories and social theory', *Australian Journal of Anthropology* 3 (1992): pp. 43–54, at p. 51.
[14] M. Devitt & K. Sterelny, *Language and Reality* (Oxford, 1987), ch. 13; also P. Godfrey-Smith, 'Towards a sensible semiotics', *Arts* (Sydney) 14 (1989): pp. 22–37; J. Maze, 'A realist view of deconstruction', *Heraclitus* 65 (May 1998): pp. 2–9.

A simulacrum of Jacques Derrida impresses a youthful audience, University of New South Wales, 13 Sept 1996. (Newspix)

text.'[15] At least some of Derrida's local followers agree that this denial of 'reference' to language is his key achievement. John Hay, later Vice-Chancellor of the University of Queensland, writes, 'the tenacious notion that scientific and philosophical discourse is referential, mimetically reflecting a verifiable reality, seems often to have exempted it from the suspicion that, quite as much as literature, its

[15] See R. Freadman & S. Miller, *Re-Thinking Theory* (Cambridge, 1992), ch. 5; C.R. Pigden, 'Est-ce qu'il y a de hors texte? — On a defence of Derrida', *Critical Review* 30 (1990): pp. 40–62; J. Passmore, *Recent Philosophers* (London, 1985), pp. 29–33; G. Matte, 'Derrida, Foucault and the real estate market', *Australian Journal of Comedy* 5 (1) (1999): pp. 149–86; more sympathetic accounts in D. Buchbinder, *Contemporary Literary Theory and the Reading of Poetry* (South Melbourne, 1991), ch. 4; K. Hart, 'Differant curioes', *Southerly* 49 (1989): pp. 182–96; T. Thwaites, L. Davis & W. Mules, *Tools for Cultural Studies* (South Melbourne, 1994), pp. 26–31; N. Lucy, *Debating Derrida* (Melbourne, 1995), ch. 1; deeper analyses in J. Curthoys, *Feminist Amnesia* (New York, 1997), ch. 6 and J. Teichman, 'Deconstruction and aerodynamics', *Philosophy* 68 (1993): pp. 53–62; on Derrida and Mabo, see P. Patton, 'Mabo, freedom and the politics of difference', *Australian Journal of Political Science* 30 (1995): pp. 108–19; on Derrida's 1999 Australian visit, *SMH* 12/8/1999, p. 19, 13/8/1999, p. 7; D. McQueen-Thomson, 'Derrida comes to town', *Arena Magazine* 44 (1999): pp. 13–14; texts of his 1999 Australian talks in *Jacques Derrida: Deconstruction Engaged*, ed. P. Patton & T. Smith (Sydney 2001).

procedures are tropical and metaphoric. For many, Paul de Man and Jaques [*sic*] Derrida have decisively set aside this view of scientific and philosophical discourse that has lasted from the time of Plato to that of Lévi Strauss.'[16]

Postmodernism in the Parisian style is a perfect candidate for deflation by Australian realism, which would do something to redress the shocking disproportion in the French-Australian balance of intellectual trade. Australian computer scientists have already made a contribution, with the Monash Postmodern Essay Generator, a computer program that randomly generates a new postmodern essay each time you log in.[17]

A special place in the story is held by Jean Baudrillard, the French philosopher whose theory that everything is a media construct caused widespread offence after the publication of his book *The Gulf War Did Not Take Place*.[18] Baudrillard chose to comment on (to the extent that his works could be said to be 'on' anything) art, so that he soon enough found himself in the sights of one of the masters of aggressive Australian prose, Robert Hughes. Hughes is not a professional philosopher, but then, idealism is not a very subtle doctrine, and it only needs a basic intelligence and a readiness to wade through some jargon to sort it out. Hughes writes:

> Baudrillard is something of a McLuhanite: not only is the medium the message, but the sheer amount of traffic has usurped meaning. 'Culture' — he is fond of those snooty quotation marks — is consigned to the endless production of imagery that has no reference to the real world. There *is* no real world. Whether we go to Disneyland, or watch the Watergate hearings on TV, or follow highway signs while driving in the desert, or walk through Harlem, we are enclosed in a world of signs. The signs refer just to one another, combining in 'simulacra' (Baudrillardese for 'images') of reality to produce a permanent tension, an insatiable wanting, in the audience ... It lets him take a wonderfully lofty view of

[16] J. Hay, 'Deconstructing Utopia: The blind metaphors of colonial painters and diarists', in *The Writer's Sense of the Past*, ed K. Singh (Singapore, 1987). p. 133; cf. J. Hay, 'Canonical and colonial texts', in *A Sense of Exile*, ed. B. Bennett (Perth, 1988), pp. 15–21.

[17] www.elsewhere.org/cgi-bin/postmodern , based on TR 96/264: 'On the Simulation of Postmodernism and Mental Debility Using Recursive Transition Networks'. Compare with the 'real' thing available on the Australia's Wackiest Academic Web Sites page, www.maths.unsw.edu.au/~jim/wackiest.html .

[18] J. Baudrillard, *The Gulf War Did Not Take Place*, trans. P. Patton (Sydney, 1995); similar but less extreme analysis in M. Wark, *Virtual Geography: Living with Global Media Events* (Bloomington, Ind, 1994), chs 1–2; *Australian* 5/6/1996, p. 28.

the relations between fact and illusion, for it denies the possibility of experiencing anything *except* illusion.

The accusation that this or that philosopher hides meaninglessness behind high-sounding jargon is a common one in the trade, so much so that professional philosophers have more or less agreed to a moratorium on it. Not so outsiders, and Hughes on Baudrillard is one of the best examples of the genre:

> Jargon, native or imported, is always with us; and in America, both academe and the art world prefer the French kind, a thick prophylactic against understanding. We are now surfeited with mini-Lacans and mock Foucaults. To write direct prose, lucid and open to comprehension, using common language, is to lose face. You do not make your mark unless you add something to the lake of jargon to whose marshy verge the bleating flocks of post-structuralists go each night to drink, whose waters (bottled for export to the States) well up between Nanterre and the Sorbonne. Language does not clarify; it intimidates. It subjects the reader to a rite of passage and extorts assent as the price of entry. For the savant's thought is so radically original that ordinary words will not do. Its newness requires neologism; it seeks rupture, overgeneralization, oracular pronouncements and a pervasive tone of apocalyptic hype.

The corollaries for the art world hardly need to be stated:

> If all signs are autonomous and refer only to one another, it must seem to follow that no image is 'truer' or 'deeper' than the next, and that the artist is absolved from his or her struggle for authenticity — an ideal proposition for dealers with a lot of product to shift and a clientele easily snowed by jargon.[19]

An unfair parody? Baudrillard himself said, when interviewed for a Brisbane art magazine, 'Simulation refers to a world without reference, from which all reference has disappeared ... I have rather a primitive knowledge of the fine arts, and I've deliberately maintained this slightly primitive attitude. I'm instinctively suspicious of everything which is aesthetic or part of culture as a whole. I'm something of a peasant or a barbarian at heart, and I do my best to stay that way.'[20]

Baudrillard visited Sydney University in 1984 as the star turn at a conference 'Futur★Fall: Excursions into Post-Modernity'. His paper 'The year 2000 will not take place' was received with acclaim. In fact, a thousand people turned up, so that many had to listen to him, appropriately enough, on closed-circuit television. Other papers with

[19] R. Hughes, 'Jean Baudrillard: *America*', in R. Hughes, *Nothing If Not Critical* (London, 1990), pp. 375–87.
[20] N. Zurbrugg, Interview with Jean Baudrillard, *Eyeline* (Brisbane) no. 11 (1990): pp. 4–7.

titles like 'Humour/Perversity/And Other Shit' completed the program.[21]

A number of Australian tertiary courses in art theory then fell into the hands of Baudrillardian and allied forces, with what effect on students' appreciation of quality in art may be imagined.[22] Meanwhile, Baudrillard's theory that Disneyland is a plot to hide the real America ('presented as imaginary to make us believe that the rest is real') had a role in inspiring some of his Australian followers to hold a conference on the relevance of French theory to Bugs Bunny. It resulted in what claimed to be the world's first book of 'scholarly essays theorizing animation'.[23]

Needless to say, outpourings like Hughes's were taken by Baudrillard's Australian admirers to be as ignorant as they were tasteless. Their continued support for the master was expressed by their invitation to him to revisit Australia. The result was an unexpected media circus, variously describable as a stunning confirmation of Baudrillardian media theory, or Brisbane's best literary beat-up before Helen Demidenko. A collection of photographs by Baudrillard — announced as 'a sort of Elvis Presley of science-fiction theory'[24] — was to be exhibited at Brisbane's Institute of Modern Art, sponsored by the French Ministry for Foreign Affairs. When the philosopher and his photographs arrived, Customs demanded excise of $16,000 because *they were not art.* 'As Griffith University's Dr Nicholas Zurbrugg, who is researching M. Baudrillard's legacy for the 90s, said: "The man who said art was dead then became (a photographic) artist, but when his art got to Australia the Customs said, 'Your art isn't art', Perhaps they've read him".' Desperate negotiations between Queensland's Minister for the Arts and the Federal Minister for Customs

[21] C. Ferrall, 'Simulating post-modernity', *Arena* no. 68 (1984): pp. 20–2; G. Gill, 'Post-structuralism as ideology', *Arena* 69 (1984): pp. 60–96; the papers are in *Futur*Fall: Excursions into Post-Modernity*, ed. E. Grosz (Sydney, 1986); further in A. Frankovits, ed, *Seduced and Abandoned: The Baudrillard Scene* (Glebe, 1984); something more critical in B.S. Turner, 'Baudrillard for sociologists', in *Forget Baudrillard?*, ed. C. Rojek & B.S. Turner (London, 1993), pp. 70–87; a later visit, *SMH* 27/3/2001, p. 14, 29/3/2001, p. 16, *Australian* 11/4/2001, p. B3.

[22] J. McDonald, 'The failure of art schools', *Independent Monthly* (Mar 1991): pp. 37–8; less rudely in C. McAuliffe, 'Jean Baudrillard', in *The Judgement of Paris: Recent French Theory in a Local Context*, ed. K.D.S. Murray (North Sydney, 1992), pp. 97–111.

[23] A. Cholodenko, ed, *The Illusion of Life* (Sydney, 1991), pp. 34, 9.

[24] *Courier-Mail* 20/4/1994, p. 22.

secured the release of the photographs hours before the exhibition opened.[25]

Baudrillard then visited Sydney. His talks were booked out. He told reporters, 'The kind of thing I bring to fruition is a simulation — it's neither true nor false. We can't therefore be wrong ... art has already disappeared without us noticing it ... There's no denial of reality. Rather my discourse goes beyond reality.'[26] That certainly explains why anyone trying to refute Baudrillard on his own terms will experience not so much confusion as vertigo; if he hasn't denied or asserted anything, where could you possibly start? What would count as evidence against him? As one who valiantly made the attempt found, 'It is dizzy torture indeed to stabilize, for security's sake, some sense of what Baudrillard means, and when, by *meaning, reality, the real, representation, reference, referent,* or "a" *referential.*'[27]

One of Baudrillard's most ardent local admirers has been Julian Pefanis, senior lecturer in Visual Culture of the Twentieth Century at Sydney University, who went to the trouble of translating his *Revenge of the Crystal* and editing Lyotard's *The Postmodern Explained to Children*.[28] His own prose style has become something of a legend. An admiring reader submitted a selection of it to the first Bad Writing Contest, run in 1994 by the PHIL-LIT electronic discussion forum on philosophy and literature. Against ferocious international competition across all disciplines, it took off second prize. This is the entry:

> The libidinal Marx is a polymorphous creature, a hermaphrodite with the 'huge head of a warlike and quarrelsome man of thought' set atop the soft feminine contours of a 'young Rhenish lover'. So it is a strange bi-sexed arrangement giving rise to a sort of ambivalence: the Old Man and the Young Woman, a monster in which femininity and virility exchange indiscernibly, 'thus putting a stop to the reassuring difference of the sexes.' Now the Young Woman Marx, who is called Alice (of Wonderland fame), is obfuscated by the perverse body of Capital because it simultane-

---

[25] *Australian* 22/4/1994, p. 6; cf. N. Zurbrugg, *The Parameters of Postmodernism* (Carbondale, Ill, 1993), pp. 21, 150; obituary of Zurbrugg in *Australian* 9/1/2002, p. 31; agreement with Baudrillard's 'art is dead' in P. Hutchings, 'Once more with feeling: Art and disappearance', *Art & Text* no. 36 (1990): pp. 36–44, at p. 36.

[26] *SMH* 4/5/1994, pp. 29–30.

[27] M. Morris, 'Room 101 or a few worst things in the world', in M. Morris, *The Pirate's Fiancee* (London, 1988), ch 10, at p. 195; also D. Broderick, *Theory and its Discontents* (Geelong, 1997), pp. 29–32.

[28] J. Baudrillard, *Revenge of the Crystal*, ed. & trans. P. Foss & J. Pefanis (London, 1990); J. Lyotard, *The Postmodern Explained to Children*, ed. J. Pefanis & M. Thomas (Sydney, 1992); also J. Pefanis, *Heterology and the Postmodern: Bataille, Baudrillard and Lyotard* (Durham, NC, 1991).

ously occasions in her a revulsion and a strange fascination. She is the Epicurean Marx, the Marx of the doctoral thesis, the aesthetic Marx. She claims a great love for this man of thought who offers to act as the Great Prosecutor of the crimes of Capital. He is 'assigned to the accusation of the perverts' and entrusted with the invention of a suitable lover, the proletariat, for the little Alice.[29]

If that excursion into Looking Glass Land couldn't pull off first prize, we was robbed.

What makes them do it? David Stove remarks:

> Defects of empirical knowledge have less to do with the ways we go wrong in philosophy than defects of *character* do: such as the simple inability to shut up; determination to be thought deep; hunger for power; fear, especially the fear of an indifferent universe.[30]

NOW for something completely different.

A previous chapter left Catholic philosophy in an apparently decrepit state. The scholastic philosophy descended from the middle ages came to be thought a hopelessly antiquated embarrassment, both inside and outside Catholic circles. But in the legal world the middle ages are only yesterday. There, the scholastic method of arguing for and against propositions with the citation of learned authorities is fully preserved.[31] So are practices like wearing robes and hiring champions to fight one's case. The scholastic natural law philosophy of ethics, stressing objective principles of justice, has also survived and flourished in the nourishing habitat of the Australian courts.

Consequently, the most dramatic outcome of Catholic philosophy in recent times has been the High Court's Mabo judgment on Aboriginal land rights. The fundamental issue in the case was the conflict between the existing law based on the principle of *terra nullius*, and what the judges took to be objective principles of justice.

The relation between law and morality is a question on which Catholic philosophy is dramatically opposed to traditional legal theories. On one older view of the relation between the two, 'the King can do no wrong': the law simply is whatever is laid down by properly constituted authority. A less extreme position holds that there

---

[29] J. Pefanis, 'Jean-François Lyotard', in *The Judgement of Paris: Recent French Theory in a Local Context*, ed. K.D.S. Murray (North Sydney, 1992), pp. 113–129, at pp. 122–3; on the libidinal, see also 'Author, lover lose the plot', *Daily Telegraph* 1/6/1996, p. 1.

[30] D. Stove, *The Plato Cult and Other Philosophical Follies* (Oxford, 1991), p. 188.

[31] J. Franklin, *The Science of Conjecture: Evidence and Probability before Pascal* (Baltimore, 2001), pp. 17, 345.

may be moral constraints on law as on any other human activity, but that law is still not especially connected with morality. Instead it is a set of customs that have arisen to allow society to become organised. They could have been different, but once they arise they are fixed so that everyone can get on with life, knowing what is expected of themselves and others.[32] It is hard to see what other view is possible for those who lack the scholastic view that morality is somehow founded on the objective facts of human nature. At the opposite extreme, the scholastics hold that law and morality are so closely related as to be almost the same thing. The whole point of law, they say, is to implement the demands of justice, whose standards are external and objective. Or rather, one should not think of the standards of justice as external to law, since the aim is that law should realise and internalise the principles of justice: 'the precepts of law are designed to be the precepts of justice.'[33] Father Farrell, the Dominican who denounced university philosophy in 1961, was one of the most active in promoting this view, and many other Australian Catholics have defended it.[34]

[32] M. Krygier, 'Law as tradition', *Law and Philosophy* 5 (1986): pp. 237–62; M. Krygier, 'Julius Stone: Leeways of choice, legal tradition and the declaratory theory of law', *UNSW Law Journal* 9 (1986): pp. 26–38; summary in article 'Common law/custom' in *Routledge Encyclopedia of Philosophy*; an ethical defence in T. Campbell, *The Legal Theory of Ethical Positivism* (Aldershot, 1996); T. Campbell & J. Goldsworthy, eds. *Judicial Power, Democracy and Legal Positivism* (Aldershot, 2000); a more nuanced view in M. Krygier, 'Ethical positivism and the liberalism of fear', in Campbell & Goldsworthy, pp. 59–87; further in J. Finnis, 'The truth in legal positivism', in *The Autonomy of Law*, ed. R.P. George (Oxford, 1996), pp. 195–214; defence of similar view by former logic lecturer and Chief Justice of the High Court, Sir John Latham, in Latham papers, National Library of Australia, series 12; J.G. Latham, 'Law and the community', *Australian Law Journal* 9 Supplement (1935): pp. 2–8.

[33] F.G. Brennan & T.R. Hartigan, *An Outline of the Powers and Duties of Justices of the Peace in Queensland* (Brisbane, 1967), p. 200; discussion of such views G. Sawer, 'The administration of morals', in *Legal Change: Essays in Honour of Julius Stone*, ed. A.R. Blackshield (Sydney, 1983), pp. 88–99; the topic avoided in *Bulletin of the Australian Society of Legal Philosophy* special issue on justice and legal reasoning (1981); other views of the question in M.J. Detmold, *The Unity of Law and Morality* (London, 1984); E. Kamenka & A.E.-S. Tay, eds, *Justice* (London, 1979); P. Cane, *Responsibility in Law and Morality* (Oxford, 2002).

[34] P.M. Farrell, *Sources of St. Thomas' Concept of Natural Law* (pamphlet, Melbourne, 1957), reprinted from *The Thomist* 20 (1957): pp. 237–94; 'The theological context of law', *ACR* 32 (1955): pp. 319–25; 'The location of law in the moral system of Aquinas', *Australian Studies in Legal Philosophy*, ed. I. Tammelo *et al.* (Berlin, 1963), pp. 165–94; earlier, J.G. Murtagh, *Australia:*

The two views come into conflict over the issue of whether a precedent should be followed even when it is unjust. Generations of lawyers absorbed the fundamental doctrine of precedent: a precedent cannot be overthrown in favour of some abstract conception of 'justice'; there is to be no private revelation of justice, since that would make the law unstable, as each new judge imposed his own opinions or the changeable opinions of society. Sir Owen Dixon, often regarded as Australia's most eminent Chief Justice of the High Court, expressed the old consensus in 1956:

> But in our Australian High Court we have had as yet no deliberate innovators bent on express change of acknowledged doctrine. It is one thing for a court to seek to extend the application of accepted principles to new cases, or to reason from the more fundamental of settled legal principles to new conclusions, or to decide that a category is not closed against unforeseen instances which in reason might be subsumed thereunder. It is an

The Catholic Chapter (New York, 1946), pp. 252–3; M.V. McInerney, 'Natural law', *Twentieth Century* 1 (4) (June 1947): pp. 58–68; D.P. O'Connell, 'The natural law revival', *Twentieth Century* 7 (4) (Winter 1953): pp. 35–44; Anon, 'The natural law and Catholic social principles', *Social Survey* 3 (7) (July 1954): pp. 13–17; later in 'The natural law as a basis of social justice', Australian Catholic Bishops' Social Justice Statement, 1959, in *Justice Now!*, ed. M. Hogan (Sydney, 1990), pp. 206–12; R.D. Lumb, 'The scholastic doctrine of natural law', *Melbourne University Law Review* 2 (1959/60): pp. 205–21; R.D. Lumb, 'Natural law — an unchanging standard?', *Catholic Lawyer* 6 (1960): pp. 224–33; B. Miller, 'Being and the natural law', *Australian Studies*, ed. Tammelo, pp. 219–35; F.A. Mecham, 'Philosophy and law', *ACR* 46 (1969): pp. 137–46; and *Australian Society for Legal Philosophy, Preliminary Working Papers*, 1972; D.W. Skubik, 'The minimum content of natural law', *Bulletin of the Australian Society of Legal Philosophy* 12 (1988): pp. 101–46; J. Finnis, *Natural Law and Natural Rights* (Oxford, 1980); on which V. Kerruish, 'Philosophical retreat: A criticism of John Finnis's theory of natural law', *University of Western Australia Law Review* 15 (1983): pp. 224–44; J. Finnis, 'Natural law and legal reasoning', *Cleveland State Law Review* 38 (1990): pp. 1–13; also in *Natural Law Theory*, ed. R.P. George (Oxford, 1992), pp. 134–57; an unsympathetic view in M. Davies, *Asking the Law Question* (North Ryde, 1994), pp. 59–74; Andersonian objections in W.L. Morison, 'Anderson and legal theory', *Sydney Law Review* 8 (1977): pp. 294–304, at pp. 302–3; see also on earlier history, G.P. Shipp, 'Divine and natural law in Greece', in *For Service to Classical Studies*, ed. M. Kelly (Melbourne, 1966), pp. 149–52; D. Grace, 'Natural law in Hooker's *Of the Laws of Ecclesiastical Polity*', *Journal of Religious History* 21 (1997): pp. 10–22; L. Chipman, 'Grotius and the derivation of natural law', *Bull. ASLP* no. 26 (1993): pp. 66–78; H. Ramsay, 'William Blackstone's natural law', *Bull. ASLP* 20 (1995): pp. 58–70; T.J.F. Riha, 'Natural law and the ethical content of economics', *Australian Journal of Legal Philosophy* 22 (1997): pp. 15–50.

entirely different thing for a judge, who is discontented with a result held to flow from long accepted legal principles, deliberately to abandon the principle in the name of justice or of social necessity or of social convenience ... The latter means an abrupt and almost arbitrary change. The objection is not that it violates Aristotle's precept 'that the effort to be wiser than the laws is what is prohibited by the codes that are extolled.' The objection is that in truth the judge wrests the law to his authority. No doubt he supposes that it is to do a great right. And he may not acknowledge that for the purpose he must do more than a little wrong ... It is for this reason that it has been said that the conscious judicial innovator is bound under the doctrine of precedents by no authority except the error he committed yesterday.[35]

This means, in plain terms, that if the legal system as a whole falls into a mistake, it can never dig itself out.

One will not find in Dixon's works a discussion of such matters as whether there is or could be any such thing as an abstract standard of justice. His view on such large philosophical issues is clear, though, from his remark, 'An enquiry into the source whence the law derives its authority in a community, if prosecuted too far, becomes merely metaphysical.'[36]

Such inquiries were pursued nonetheless, by those less shy of metaphysics. Besides the work of Catholics, the massive volumes and long years of teaching of Julius Stone, Professor of Jurisprudence at Sydney University, served to bring questions about the source of legal authority to the fore. Though he did not precisely agree with the view that there are moral principles that the law must implement, that view was one he took seriously and expounded sympathetically. His students, who included three of the Mabo judges, were introduced to a range of opinions on the matter and a habit of looking for the principles that informed the law.[37]

Dixon's view was upheld by his immediate successors as Chief Justice, Barwick and Gibbs.[38] Barwick did indeed allow that there is a community sense of justice and fairness that may occasionally be

---

[35] O. Dixon, 'Concerning judicial method', reprinted in *Jesting Pilate and Other Papers and Addresses* (Melbourne, 1965) pp. 152–65, at pp. 158–9; P. Ayres, *Owen Dixon* (Melbourne, 2003), pp. 251–4; some doubts as to whether Dixon's practice accorded with his pronouncement, K. Mason, *Continuity and Change* (Leichhardt, 1990), pp. 38–9.

[36] O. Dixon, 'The Statute of Westminster 1931', *Australian Law Journal* 10 (Supplement) (1936): pp. 96–112, at p. 96.

[37] J. Stone, *Human Law and Human Justice* (London, 1965), pp. 249–52; J. Stone, *Precedent and Law* (Sydney, 1985), pp. 238–9; see L. Star, *Julius Stone: An Intellectual Life* (Sydney, 1992), pp. 176–9.

[38] G. Barwick, *A Radical Tory* (Sydney, 1995), pp. 224, 274–5; H. Gibbs, 'Law and government', *Quadrant* 34 (10) (Oct 1990): pp. 25–9, at p. 28.

'pandered to' when interpreting ambiguous laws, but went on to say, 'it is not for the individual judge or judges to express his or their own views as to the law, views perhaps tinged by a philosophy of one kind or another. Such a course would, it seems to me, be a complete deviation from the judicial tradition of the common law. It would lead to a rule by men rather than a rule by law.'[39] But by the 1980s, doubts had set in at the highest level. Sir Anthony Mason, Chief Justice at the time of the Mabo decision, wrote of Dixon's passage, 'Yet in some respects his Honour's outline resembles an elegantly constructed mansion in which some of the windows have been deliberately left open.'[40] He means that Dixon has neglected the possibility of inconsistency among precedents, or between precedents and principles. 'If applied too rigidly, the doctrine of precedent produces both injustice and lack of rationality — the very flaws whose purpose it is to expel. Thus adherence to a past decision which reflects either a principle undermined by subsequent legal development or the values of a bygone era, will produce an unjust result, judged by the standards of today.'[41] Mason thus emphasised the conflict an outdated precedent may have with 'community values' rather than with an abstract standard of justice, but the recognition that a precedent may conflict with something more basic was the major step away from Dixon's reasoning.

The most detailed and explicit answer to Dixon, in terms of the conflict between precedent and absolute standards of justice, came from Sir Gerard Brennan, the writer of the first Mabo judgment and Mason's successor as Chief Justice. His theory of the relation of morality and law is that of the Catholic natural law school. In earlier works he had praised such Catholic legal heroes as Thomas More, well known for his stand on the conflict of law and morality, and the colonial Irish lawyers Therry and Plunkett, whose 'impartial enforcement of the law' secured the convictions of the perpetrators of the Myall Creek massacre. He also commented favourably on Hig-

---

[39] G. Barwick, 'Judiciary law: Some observations thereon', *Current Legal Problems* 33 (1980): pp. 239–53, at pp. 243–4; G. Barwick, 'Courts, lawyers and the attainment of justice', *Tasmanian University Law Review* 1 (1958): pp. 1–19, at pp. 3–7; criticism in M. Atkinson, '*Trigwell* in the High Court', *Sydney Law Review* 9 (1982): pp. 541–67.

[40] A. Mason, 'Future directions in Australian law', *Monash University Law Review* 13 (1987): pp. 149–63, at pp. 155, 159.

[41] A. Mason, 'The use and abuse of precedent', *Australian Bar Review* 4 (1988): pp. 93–111, at p. 94; also A. Mason, 'Courts and community values', *Eureka Street* 6 (9) (Nov 1996): pp. 32–4; Lionel Murphy's view in G. Sturgess & P. Chubb, *Judging the World* (Sydney, 1988), p. 362; cf. pp. 346, 351.

gins's adoption in the Harvester judgment of the phrase 'reasonable and frugal comfort', as the standard which a basic wage ought to support, from an outside moral source, an encyclical of Pope Leo XIII.[42] Lawyers, he also said, have moral duties beyond simply applying the law they find in place. 'If the law itself is an obstacle to justice, the duty of a Christian lawyer extends to seeking its reform.'[43] Most remarkably, in a speech on 'Commercial law and morality', he said:

> Moral values can and manifestly do inform the law ... The stimulus which moral values provide in the development of legal principle is hard to overstate, though the importance of the moral matrix to the development of judge-made law is seldom acknowledged. Sometimes the impact of the moral matrix is obvious, as when notions of unconscionability determine a case. More often the influence of common moral values goes unremarked. But whence does the law derive its concepts of reasonable care, of a duty to speak, of the scope of constructive trusts — to name but a few examples — save from moral values translated into legal precepts?[44]

The complex maze of rules that makes up commercial law may seem an inhospitable domain for moral imperatives, but the opposite is true, according to Brennan. It is for the commercial lawyer to discern the moral purpose behind each abstruse rule, and advise his client's conscience of what is just in the circumstances, not merely what he can legally get away with.

So when he comes to the specific matter raised by Dixon, whether a precedent can be overturned for conflicting with justice, it is no surprise to find him agreeing that it can: 'The existing body of law may yield no relevant legal rule, or, in rare cases, may yield a legal rule which is offensive to basic contemporary conceptions of justice.'

---

[42] G. Brennan, 'The peace of Sir Thomas More', *Queensland Lawyer* 8 (1985): pp. 51–66; G. Brennan, 'The Irish and law in Australia', in *Ireland and Irish Australia*, ed. O. MacDonagh & W.F. Mandle (London, 1986), pp. 18–32; Higgins and Leo XIII from J. Rickard, *H.B. Higgins: The Rebel as Judge* (Sydney, 1984), pp. 173–4; on which see also J. Dynon, 'The social doctrine of Leo XIII and Australia', *Twentieth Century* 6 (1) (Spring 1951): pp. 12–21; full details in K. Blackburn, 'The living wage in Australia: A secularization of Catholic ethics on wages, 1891–1907', *Journal of Religious History* 20 (1996): pp. 93–113.

[43] G. Brennan, 'The Christian lawyer', *Australian Law Journal* 66 (1992): pp. 259–61; cf. G. Brennan, 'Pillars of professional practice: Function and standards', *Australian Law Journal* 61 (1987): pp. 112–8.

[44] G. Brennan, 'Commercial law and morality', *Melbourne University Law Review* 17 (1989): pp. 100–6, at p. 101; see also G. Brennan, 'The purpose and scope of judicial review', *Australian Bar Review* 2 (1986): pp. 93–113, at pp. 104–5; P. Finn, 'Commerce, the common law and morality', *Melbourne University Law Review* 17 (1989): pp. 87–99.

In overturning it, however, the judge does not simply impose his private morality. 'The reasons for judgment in the higher appellate courts increasingly look behind the legal rule to discover the informing legal principle and behind the informing principle to discover the basic value.'[45] The answer of the innovators to Dixon's charge that judges who upset a precedent are imposing their idiosyncratic notions of morality is thus a cunning one. Overturning an unjust precedent need not be a matter of judges implementing their personal morality, but instead (in Dixon's own words) 'to reason from the more fundamental of settled legal principles to new conclusions.' It is simply that the judges now perceive that the offending precedent conflicts with more fundamental legal principles or values. Brennan's successor as Chief Justice, Murray Gleeson, asserts that all judges must be for Dixon's 'strict and complete legalism'; what this means, however, is not an adherence to the letter of the law but that judges are appointed to 'interpret and apply the values inherent in the law.'[46]

In the Mabo case, such a conflict was found between the existing law, which justified the dispossession of the Aborigines by the doctrine of *terra nullius*, and principles of justice which, the judges held, conflicted with that precedent. *Terra nullius* is not a phrase of English law, but its substance is contained in a judgment of the Privy Council in 1889 according to which New South Wales in 1788 was 'a colony which consisted of a tract of territory practically unoccupied, without settled inhabitants or settled law, at the time when it was peacefully annexed to the British dominion.'[47] Aborigines, in other words, have no more rights to the land they walk over than tourists. To explain what is wrong with this, the Court needed first to adopt a theory of native title. Obviously, this cannot be part of the existing (British) law, and must be found in more general principles of justice. An explanation close to that adopted by the Court is found in a 1988 article by Frank Brennan, Jesuit, barrister, son of Sir Gerard and adviser to the Catholic bishops on Aboriginal affairs:

[45] G. Brennan, 'A critique of criticism', *Monash University Law Review* 19 (1993): pp. 213–6.
[46] M. Gleeson, *The Rule of Law and the Constitution* (Sydney, 2000), p. 134; cf. p. 98; similar in M.H. McHugh, 'The judicial method', *Australian Law Journal* 73 (1999): pp. 37–51, esp. p. 46; some backsliding from Dixon himself in *Jesting Pilate*, p. 165.
[47] *Cooper* v. *Stuart* (1889) 14 AC at p. 291, per *Finding Common Ground*, ed F. Brennan *et al.* (2nd ed, Melbourne, 1986), p. 13; other philosophical perspectives in D. Ivison, P. Patton & W. Sanders, eds, *Political Theory and the Rights of Indigenous Peoples* (Melbourne, 2000); G. Lloyd, 'No one's land: Australia and the philosophical imagination', *Hypatia* 15 (2) (Spring 2000): pp. 26–39 .

Where a traditional tribal community has continued to reside on its traditional land, discharging its spiritual obligations with regard to that land, and that land has never been occupied by any other persons, that community is entitled to a legal title to that land in *legal recognition* of the fact that they have always lived on that land, land to which no other persons have any moral claim. To deny legal title to that land would be to complete the act of dispossession commenced 200 years ago, or else it would be to deny the rule of law operation with respect to these citizens and their most precious possession.[48]

Insiders of scholastic philosophy will notice that the judges' theory of native title is even closer to one of the scholastic classics, and a founding work of modern international law, Francisco de Vitoria's *De Indis*. It was written in 1539 in response to the original question of this kind, the rights of the American Indians to their land.[49]

Having established that native title exists, the question of its conflict with precedent arises. Both of the two main Mabo judgments, the first written by Gerard Brennan and the second by Justices Deane and Gaudron, admit that to achieve justice in the case, the existing law will have to be overturned. Brennan writes, 'According to the cases, the common law itself took from indigenous inhabitants any right to occupy their traditional land, exposed them to the deprivation of the religious, cultural and economic sustenance which the land provides, vested the land effectively in the control of the Imperial authorities without any right to compensation and made the indigenous inhabitants intruders in their own homes and mendicants for a place to live. Judged by any civilised standard, such a law is unjust and its claim to be part of the common law to be applied in contem-

---

[48] F. Brennan, 'The absurdity and injustice of terra nullius', *Ormond Papers* 5 (1988): pp. 51–5, at p. 54; see also F. Brennan, 'Aboriginal aspirations to land' in *Finding Common Ground*, pp. 11–49.

[49] Original in F. de Vitoria, *Political Writings* ed. A. Pagden & J. Lawrance (New York, 1991), pp. 231–92, especially pp. 239–40 and 264–5; see J. O'Rorke, 'Francis de Vitoria', *ACR* 17 (1940): pp. 308–20; Stone, *Human Law and Human Justice*, p. 62; mentioned in H. Wootten, 'Mabo and the lawyers', *Australian Journal of Anthropology* 6 (1/2) (1995): pp. 116–133, at p. 123 and in J. Thompson, 'The loss of Aboriginal sovereignty', *Res Publica* 2 (2) (1993): pp. 1–8; similar in F. Brennan, *Land Rights: The Religious Factor* (Adelaide, 1993), p. 5; J. Malbon, 'Natural and positive law influences on the law affecting Australia's indigenous people', *Australian Journal of Legal History* 3 (1997): pp. 1–39; G. Marks, 'Law, theology and justice in the Spanish colonies', *Australian Journal of Legal History* 4 (1998): pp. 163–73; a slightly different discussion also from scholastic principles in E. Azzopardi, *Human Rights and Peoples* (Drummoyne, 1988), pp. 131–2, 159–64.

porary Australia must be questioned.'[50] Both judgments treat the overturning of precedent that this circumstance renders necessary as a
serious matter, needing careful justification. Not any unjust law whatever can be overturned, they hold. 'In discharging its duty to declare
the common law of Australia, this court is not free to adopt rules that
accord with contemporary notions of justice and human rights if their
adoption would fracture the skeleton of principle which gives the
body of our law its shape and internal consistency.'

To overturn a law like that of *terra nullius*, it must be found inconsistent with one of the basic underlying principles of the law. That
principle is a simple one: equality before the law. 'No case can command unquestioning adherence if the rule it expresses seriously of-
fends the values of justice and human rights (especially equality before
the law).'[51] Even if there is such an inconsistency, one must weigh
whether the disturbance to the settled rule of law would be 'dispro-
portionate to the benefit flowing from the overturning.' (Even this
last point, which appears at first sight to be a modern and sophisticated concession to the Dixonian view, can be found in Aquinas.[52])
One must also consider international law. While the English legal
system is not strictly bound by outside decisions, an influence from
them is legitimate, 'especially when international law declares the existence of universal human rights.'[53]

The same views are crucial to the other Mabo judgment, that of
Deane and Gaudron. In writing of the natural law basis of international law, as founded by Aquinas and Vitoria, Deane had earlier said
that 'This basis gave international law a rich philosophical foundation
which was a source of unlimited development. In it there is a reservoir of rules for all situations and cases. A law based on natural law
can never grow out of touch with the current needs of nations.'[54] The
legal principle drawn out of the reservoir for Mabo is again that of
equality before the law, on which he had written more explicitly in
an earlier case:

> For one thing, there is the conceptual basis of the Constitution. As the
> preamble and s. 3 of the *Commonwealth of Australia Constitution Act 1900*

---

[50] G. Brennan in *The Mabo Decision with Commentary by Richard H. Bartlett*
(Sydney, 1993), p. 18.

[51] *The Mabo Decision*, p. 19.

[52] Thomas Aquinas, *Summa Theologiae* I-II q. 97 art. 2.

[53] *The Mabo Decision*, p. 29.

[54] W.P. Deane, 'Crisis in the law of nations', *Social Survey* 6 (1957): pp. 8–15,
at p. 12; also briefly in W. Deane, review of Oppenheim & Lauterpacht,
International Law, *Sydney Law Review* 2 (1957): pp. 382–4; W. Deane,
'Vatican diplomacy', *Twentieth Century* 15 (1960–1): pp. 347–52; cf. W.P.
Deane, 'An older Republic', *Hermes* 1950, pp. 5–10.

(Imp.) (63) make plain, that conceptual basis was the free agreement of 'the people' — all the people — of the federating peoples ... At the heart of that obligation [to act judicially] is the duty of a court to extend to the parties before it equal justice, that is to say, to treat them fairly and impartially as equals before the law and to refrain from discrimination on irrelevant or irrational grounds.[55]

The intrinsic equality of all people, he said, 'might sound a bit wet, but it is just basic to the whole of my thinking.'[56] Deane acknowledges the role of Catholic natural law philosophy in his Mabo judgment. 'The basis of natural law', he says, 'is the belief that some things are innately right and some innately wrong, flowing from the nature of things, including our nature as human beings. That approach provides a philosophical basis for seeing such things as human rights as going deeper than any particular act of Parliament or what have you. That is not exclusively Catholic. It runs through Christian belief.'[57] Similarly, Mary Gaudron writes that 'equality' means more than a purely formal requirement that there be no irrelevant discriminations among litigants. The High Court, she says, has been embedding in constitutional interpretation a theory of equality 'not dissimilar to that propounded by Aristotle.' This theory, as she explains it, involves an active taking into account of relevant differences, so that true equality between persons is preserved; it implies, for example, the provision of legal aid and interpreter services in court to prevent discrimination by default.[58]

The inevitable outcome of this philosophical orientation was the rejection of the law's unjust past, in the passage of great moral force that became the most quoted part of the Mabo decision:

[55] Deane J. in *Leeth* v. *The Commonwealth*, *Commonwealth Law Reports* 174 (1991–2), pp. 486–7; cf. *CLR* 168 (1980), p. 522; I am grateful to George Winterton for calling these passages to my attention.

[56] T. Stephens, *Sir William Deane: The Things That Matter* (Sydney, 2002), p. 94.

[57] W. Deane to author, 14/5/1996; Stephens, *Sir William Deane*, p. 100.

[58] M. Gaudron, 'Equality before the law with particular reference to Aborigines', *Judicial Review* 1 (1992–4): pp. 81–9; implications in *Dietrich v. The Queen*, *Commonwealth Law Reports* 177 (1992): p. 292; similar in Gleeson, *The Rule of Law and the Constitution*, pp. 61–3; opposite view in Barwick, *A Radical Tory*, p. 274; bibliography of philosophy of law and equality in A.E.-S. Tay, *Human Rights for Australia* (Canberra, 1986), pp. 173–5; also H.J. McCloskey, 'A right to equality?', *Canadian Journal of Philosophy* 6 (1976): pp. 625–42; K. Dunn, '"Yakking giants": Equality discourse in the High Court', *Melbourne University Law Review* 24 (2000): pp. 427–61.

If this were any ordinary case, the court would not be justified in re-opening the validity of fundamental propositions which have been endorsed by long-established authority ... Far from being ordinary, however, the circumstances of the present case make it unique. As has been seen, the two propositions in question [that Australia was *terra nullius*, and that full ownership vested in the Crown] provided the legal basis for the dispossession of the Aboriginal peoples of most of their traditional lands. The acts and events by which that dispossession in legal theory was carried into practical effect constitute the darkest aspect of the history of this nation. The nation as a whole must remain diminished unless and until there is an acknowledgement of, and retreat from, those past injustices. In these circumstances, the court is under a clear duty to re-examine the two propositions. For the reasons which we have explained, that re-examination compels their rejection.[59]

For giving effect to philosophical principles, the law is supreme.

Naturally, there were complaints from those who abhorred such judicial 'activism'. The complaints entirely ignored the careful arguments of the Mabo judges concerning the basic principles of the law. Instead they returned to Owen Dixon's jibes about the personal standards of judges. The 'activists' were said to replace 'strict rules with flexible standards based on their own notions of reasonableness, fairness and efficiency.'[60] In assuming there were no objective standards and moving discussion instead to the sociological entity 'their own standards', the conservative commentators were making the same move as the postmodernists in replacing objective standards of truth with relations of power and rhetoric. Why should we accept our laws as they stand? For no other reason than this, that they are ours.

---

[59] Deane and Gaudron, in *The Mabo Decision*, p. 82; reflections in R. Gaita, *A Common Humanity* (Melbourne, 1999), pp. 73–86, cf J. Thompson, *Taking Responsibility for the Past: Reparation and Historical Injustice* (Cambridge, 2002)

[60] J. Gava, 'The rise of the hero judge', *UNSW Law Journal* 24 (2001): pp. 747–59; D. Heydon, 'Judicial activism and the death of the rule of law', *Quadrant* 41 (1) (Jan-Feb 2003): pp. 9–22.

Chapter 16   *Last Rights:*
Applied Ethics

'I BELIEVE that it is now pretty generally accepted by professional philosophers that ultimate ethical principles must be arbitrary',[1] wrote Brian Medlin in 1957. That may have been a slight exaggeration, but the tendency of philosophy in the mid-century was certainly towards an extreme minimalism in ethics. Mackie, as we saw, agreed with Medlin and denied that there was any such thing as ethics. He argued that moral properties would be 'queer' ones, from a scientific point of view. Where is the cruelty of an act, he asks, over and above the pain it causes and the subjective responses in the observers?[2] David Armstrong spoke for many philosophers who were not primarily interested in ethics when he claimed that objective value is not the kind of thing that can be causally efficacious — it would be a kind of metaphysical superfluity to the world revealed by science.[3]

In Melbourne, they did not go quite as far as that. Philosophers there agreed in part, but believed there were ways of refuting selfishness without the need to suppose there were any really *moral* values. There was, they thought, plenty of scope for reason in ethics, and its

[1] B. Medlin, 'Ultimate principles and ethical egoism', *AJP* 35 (1957): pp. 111–8, repr. in W.P. Alston & R.B. Brandt, eds, *The Problems of Philosophy: Introductory Readings* (Boston, 1967), pp. 229–35.

[2] J. Mackie, *Ethics: Inventing Right and Wrong*, pp. 38–41; similar in P. Godfrey-Smith, 'No, Virginia, there is no right or wrong', *Proceedings of the Russellian Society* 10 (1985): pp. 1–13; I. Hinckfuss, *The Moral Society* (www.uq.edu.au/philosophy/morsoc); reply in J. Finnis, *Fundamentals of Ethics* (Oxford, 1983), pp. 57–60.

[3] D.M. Armstrong, 'A search for values', *Quadrant* 26 (6) (June 1982): pp. 65–70.

purpose was to achieve co-ordination of interests.[4] Kurt Baier's *The Moral Point of View*, the most famous work of this school, emphasised that moral rules function to resolve conflicts between individuals by adopting a non-person-relative perspective.[5]

Outside professional philosophy, meanwhile, the social sciences tended to take for granted a relativism about ethics, with anthropology especially concentrating on the *differences* between the mores of cultures. Philosophers impressed with these currents have produced a stream of books dominated by the thought that valuation needs a valuer, and are inclined to see moral value as nothing over and above what valuers do; relativism is suggested by the fact that there are disagreements among valuers.[6]

Until about 1970, such general questions about the nature of ethics dominated philosophical work in the subject. Philosophers (except Catholics) didn't *take sides*, or tell people what to do. They only clarified the principles.

If one asked mainstream philosophers for advice as to what one should actually do, the main suggestion they had to offer was utilitarianism. Its standard version, 'hedonistic act utilitarianism', claims that

[4] S. Grave, *A History of Philosophy in Australia* (St Lucia, 1984), ch. 7; B. Scarlett, 'Moral philosophy 1945–1980', in *Essays on Philosophy in Australia*, ed J.T.J. Szrednicki & D. Wood (Dordrecht, 1992), pp. 53–79.

[5] K. Baier, *The Moral Point of View: A Rational Basis of Ethics* (Ithaca, 1958) (summary in F.N. Magill, *World Philosophy: Essay Reviews of 225 Major Works* (Englewood Cliffs, 1982), vol. 5, pp. 2478–89) (p. 299 of Baier's book has occasioned comment from logicians); later, K. Baier, *The Rational and the Moral Order* (Chicago, 1995); K. Baier, *Problems of Life and Death* (New York, 1997); *Reason, Ethics and Society: Themes from Kurt Baier, with His Responses*, ed. J.B. Schneewind (Chicago, 1996); also P. Edwards, *The Logic of Moral Discourse* (Glencoe, Ill, 1955; New Delhi, 1971); D.H. Monro, *Empiricism and Ethics* (Cambridge, 1967); J. Kovesi, *Moral Notions* (London, 1967); similar later in M. Smith, *The Moral Problem* (Oxford, 1994), on which symposium in *Ethics* 108 (1) (Oct 1997); M. Smith, *Selected Essays on Moral Psychology and Metaethics* (Cambridge, to appear); M. Smith, 'Moral realism', ch. 1 of *Blackwell Guide to Ethical Theory*, ed. H. LaFollette (Malden, Mass, 2000); F. Jackson, *From Metaphysics to Ethics* (New York, 1998), ch. 5; similar but more Hobbesian in R.E. Ewin, *Co-operation and Human Values* (Brighton, 1981).

[6] G. Gaus, *Value and Justification* (Cambridge, 1990); F. Snare, *Morals, Motivation and Convention* (Cambridge, 1991); F. Snare, *The Nature of Moral Thinking* (London, 1992); T. Trainer, *The Nature of Morality: An Introduction to the Subjectivist Perspective* (Aldershot, 1991); discussion in N. Levy, *Moral Relativism: A Short Introduction* (Oxford, 2002); relevance to education in D.N. Aspin, 'The nature of values and their place and promotion in schemes of values education', *Educational Philosophy and Theory* 31 (1999): pp. 123–43.

the right action in any circumstance is the one that (most likely) leads to maximisation of happiness.[7] The theory has a definite appeal. Happiness is something everyone is in favour of, and it is remarkable how often the aim of maximising happiness results in recommendations that agree with normal moral intuitions.

Nevertheless, the theory has some well-recognised problems. Firstly, why maximise just happiness, as opposed to other goods that could be thought of? The main Australian defender of utilitarianism, Jack Smart, defends happiness as the sole aim of ethics thus: 'What could be better than to maximize happiness? Any theory that was not equivalent to hedonistic act utilitarianism would imply that on occasion one should make the world less happy than it would otherwise be.'[8] And again, 'The chief persuasive argument in favour of utilitarianism has been that the dictates of any deontological [i.e., rule-based] ethics will always, on some occasions, lead to the existence of misery that could, on utilitarian principles, have been prevented.'[9] That is the only justification he offers. He does not mean that the theory of utilitarianism is *correct* — much less that he has proved it correct. He believes, like Mackie and others, that there are no genuine moral facts, but he himself recommends utilitarianism and hopes others too will find it preferable as a guide to action.

Difficulties for utilitarianism arise from its commendation of the total quantity of happiness, as opposed to its distribution. It is not exactly true that utilitarianism prefers the situation with the least misery. If in some case we have a choice between distributing a burden to many, who suffer mild discomfort, and heaping it all on a scapegoat whose life becomes a torture, utilitarianism recommends the latter if the total unhappiness is less, however slightly. That is, utilitarianism recommends more misery, since in the equal distribution there is none — no real *misery*, that is, only a widely distributed discomfort.[10]

A problem of this kind arises especially over the possible conflicts between happiness maximisation and justice. Consider the case of a sheriff in a town of the old South who is faced with a choice between

---

[7] Early discussion in J. Anderson, 'Utilitarianism', *AJPP* 10 (1932): pp. 161–72, repr. in *Studies in Empirical Philosophy* (Sydney, 1962), pp. 227–37; A.K. Stout, 'But suppose everyone did the same?', *AJP* 32 (1954): pp. 1–29; Grave, *History*, pp. 148–54; also R. Goodin, *Utilitarianism as a Public Philosophy* (Cambridge, 1995).

[8] J.J.C. Smart, 'Utilitarianism and its applications', in *New Directions in Ethics*, ed. J.P. DeMarco & R.M. Fox (New York, 1986), pp. 24–41, at p. 24.

[9] J.J.C. Smart & B. Williams, *Utilitarianism: For and Against* (Cambridge, 1973), p. 62.

[10] J.J.C. Smart, 'Utilitarianism and punishment', *Israel Law Review* 25 (1991): pp. 360–75.

executing an accused black he knows is innocent, and allowing a white mob to riot and kill many.[11] According to utilitarianism, he must kill the innocent man to prevent the greater evil. Smart accepts that utilitarianism does recommend unjust killing in such cases, though he hopes they are rare.[12] But the problem is not merely that this is a difficult case, but that utilitarianism gives no weight at all to the injustice. Even someone who thinks the sheriff ought to hang the black if the riot will be bad enough feels there is some problem of injustice that the size of the catastrophe must outweigh.

Utilitarianism is a harsh doctrine for those whose desires for themselves are at odds with what many others want them to do.

THE counterattack on behalf of objective ethics has included three Australians among its leaders — Alan Donagan, John Finnis and Raimond Gaita.

Donagan, a Melbourne graduate who unusually included studies in law in his undergraduate degree, was for many years Professor of Philosophy at the University of Chicago.[13] The definite article in the title of his book *The Theory of Morality* is important. He argued that there is a coherent theory underlying the general moral outlook and behaviour of all (normal) people, though it is not necessarily consciously expressed. *Rules* of ethics are not basic. Instead, they are generated by a more fundamental assumption, that persons are valuable in themselves. Thus, the reason why murder is wrong is not anything to do with the co-ordination of society or the maximisation of happiness, much less the command of a deity. Nor are rights basic: a right to life is simply the wrongness of destruction of a life, from the point of view of the person living the life.[14] What is wrong with murder is

---

[11] Originally in H.J. McCloskey, 'An examination of restricted utilitarianism', *Philosophical Review* 66 (1957): pp. 466–85; also McCloskey, *Meta-Ethics*, ch. 7; further in C.L. Ten, 'Jim's utilitarian mission', *Philosophy* 54 (1979): pp. 221–2; C.L. Ten, *Crime, Guilt and Punishment* (Oxford, 1987), ch. 2.

[12] Smart in *Utilitarianism: For and Against*, pp. 70–2; 'Utilitarianism and punishment', at pp. 365–6.

[13] B. Donagan, 'Alan Donagan: A memoir', *Ethics* 104 (1993): pp. 148–53; bibliography pp. 154–60; S. Toulmin, 'Alan Donagan and Melbourne philosophy', in A. Donagan, *Philosophical Papers*, ed. J.E. Malpas (Chicago, 1994), vol. 1, pp. vii–xiii; J.E. Malpas, 'Donagan, Alan', in *Encyclopedia of Ethics*, 2nd ed (New York, 2001), vol. 1 pp. 416–18.

[14] Debate on rights in H.J. McCloskey, 'Rights: Some conceptual issues', *AJP* 54 (1976): pp. 99–115; H.J. McCloskey, 'The right to life', *Mind* 84 (1975): pp. 403–25; R. Young, 'Dispensing with moral rights', *Political Theory* 6 (1978): pp. 63–74; D. Oderberg, *Moral Theory: A Non-Consequentialist Approach* (Oxford, 2000), chs 7–10 .

that it results in the destruction of something intrinsically valuable, a human life. He writes:

> I take the fundamental principle of that part of traditional morality which is independent of any theological presupposition to have been expressed in the scriptural commandment, 'Thou shalt love thy neighbour as thyself', understanding one's neighbour to be any human being, and love to be, not a matter of feeling, but of acting in ways in which human beings as such can choose to act. The philosophical sense of this commandment was correctly expressed by Kant in his formula that one act so that one treats humanity always as an end and never as a means.[15]

All moral rules, he maintained, even very detailed ones about specific cases, should be deducible from this general principle with some thought. He argued further that it is possible to say exactly what it is about humans that makes them valuable. It is their rationality. He defined rationality rather narrowly, as 'a capacity to perform acts whose contents belong to the domain of logic'.[16] He was less than clear on why this aspect of human nature alone is the one that confers worth.

Plainly, Donagan's theory was in many ways a revival of the Catholic natural law theory described in chapter 4. Donagan admitted as much, though he believed that there was a systematic distortion of natural law theory in Aquinas. Donagan objected to Aquinas' view that lying is wrong because it contravenes the 'natural purpose' of speech, to express the truth; such an argument, Donagan says, does not rest on the basic worth of persons and cannot be sustained.[17] He objected, that is, to the kind of argument from 'what is natural' that can lead to saying things like, 'If God had meant us to fly, he would

---

[15] A. Donagan, *The Theory of Morality* (Chicago, 1977), pp. 65–6; M. Reichlin, 'Alan Donagan e la crisi dei fondamenti dell'etica', *Rivista di filosofia neo-scolastica* 92 (2000): pp. 59–107; similar in N. Brown, *The Worth of Persons* (Manly, 1983).

[16] Donagan, *Theory of Morality*, p. 235.

[17] A. Donagan, 'The scholastic theory of moral law in the modern world', in A. Kenny, ed, *Aquinas: A Collection of Critical Essays* (New York, 1969), pp. 325–39; similar in M. Charlesworth, 'Questions about the natural law', *Australian Biblical Review* 14 (1966): pp. 9–23; other criticism of 'the natural' in ethics in W.D. Falk, 'Morality and nature', *AJP* 28 (1950): pp. 69–92; discussion in R. Gascoigne, *Freedom and Purpose: An Introduction to Christian Ethics* (Sydney, 1993), pp. 23–6; also E. D'Arcy, 'Natural law', *Encyclopedia of Bioethics*, ed. W.T. Reich (New York, 1978), vol. 3, pp. 1131–7; other realist views in M. Devitt, 'Moral realism', *Croatian Journal of Philosophy* 2 (2002): pp. 1–15; J. Franklin, 'On the parallel between mathematics and morals, *Philosophy* 79 (2004).

have given us wings'. Such arguments are not justified by an ethics based on natural intrinsic worth.

A more explicit revival of Catholic natural law theory is the influential *Natural Law and Natural Rights* by John Finnis, originally a South Australian, later Professor of Law and Legal Philosophy at Oxford. Finnis summarises the aspects of human nature that are especially relevant to ethics in a list of things that are self-evidently 'basic aspects of my well-being', or 'the basic forms of good for us': life (including health), knowledge, play, aesthetic experience, friendship, practical reasonableness and religion.[18] ('Practical reasonableness' covers the ability to think intelligently about how to live one's life, and the freedom to do it.) These goods, Finnis maintains, are all equally fundamental and none are superior to others. He emphasises that these goods are not supposed to be deduced from a pre-existing concept of human nature; if anything, what human nature is is to be understood by a practical investigation of what is fulfilling for people.[19] These considerations are intended to fill out the traditional conception of human nature. His ethical conclusions are in keeping with traditional morality.

Neither Donagan nor Finnis gives in his writings any strong impression of a personality different from that of other philosophers. Their conclusions are opposite to those of the subjectivists and utilitarians, but their style of expressing them is much the same. It is otherwise with Raimond Gaita. Gaita's book on his childhood, *Romulus, My Father*, is one of the most gripping of Australian autobiographies.

---

[18] J. Finnis, *Natural Law and Natural Rights* (Oxford, 1980), pp. 87–97, repr. in P. Singer, ed, *Ethics* (Oxford, 1994), pp. 229–35; a similar list in H.J. McCloskey, *Meta-Ethics and Normative Ethics* (The Hague, 1969); earlier, J.M. Finnis, 'The value of the human person', *Twentieth Century* 27 (1972): pp. 126–37; later J. Finnis, *Fundamentals of Ethics* (Oxford, 1983); summary in J. Begley, 'A new approach to natural law and natural right — the writings of John Finnis', *Catholic Theological Review* 5 (1983): pp. 33–42; Finnis, 'Natural law', *Routledge Encyclopedia of Philosophy,* vol 6, pp. 685–90; discussion in R. Campbell, 'Natural law as practical reasonableness', *ACR* 63 (1986): pp. 416–25; N. Brown, 'The basic principles of Christian ethics', *ACR* 64 (1987): pp. 167–81; M.C. Sayers, 'Knowledge as a self-evident good in Finnis and Aquinas', *Australian Journal of Legal Philosophy* 23 (1998): pp. 92–101, with reply in 25 (2000): pp. 111–19.

[19] J. Finnis & G. Grisez, 'The basic principles of natural law', *American Journal of Jurisprudence* 26 (1981): pp. 21–31; G. Grisez, J. Boyle & J. Finnis, 'Practical principles, moral truths and ultimate ends', *AJJ* 32 (1987): pp. 99–151; discussion in J. Goldsworthy, 'Fact and value in the new natural law theory', *AJJ* 41 (1996): pp. 21–46; I. Gold, 'Does natural law have non-normative foundations?', *Sophia* 41 (1) (2002): pp. 1–17.

Gaita was born in Cologne in 1946, the son of a Romanian black-smith who was one of the millions of Eastern Europeans working in Germany as virtual slave labour. The family soon escaped to rural Victoria. Gaita's childhood was overshadowed by the serious mental illnesses of both his parents, and his powers of survival are by impli-cation enormous. One understands why a life as a moral philosopher would seem the only possible one after such a beginning. The ill-nesses were balanced, when his father was well, by a solidity in his father's life that is the foundation of what Gaita writes on ethics.

> The philosopher Plato said that those who love and seek wisdom are clinging in recollection to things they once saw. On many occasions in my life I have had the need to say, and thankfully have been able to say: I know what a good workman is; I know what an honest man is; I know what friendship is; I know because I remember these things in the person of my father, in the person of his friend Hora, and in the example of their friendship.[20]

The result is something that has struck everyone who reads or hears Gaita, or at least those who have any sympathy for his views. Robert Manne recalls encountering him at a Melbourne University forum on existentialism, where he spoke along with a philosopher and a flam-boyant student personality. 'His talk made the speech of the philoso-pher seem superficial and the speech of the famous undergraduate unbearably frivolous. I was drawn to something in his manner — a seriousness, a kind of genuine openness to experience, a purity of spirit.'[21] The theme of Gaita's *Good and Evil: An Absolute Conception* is not so much an attempt to say what it is that founds the objectivity of good, as a concentration on the seriousness of moral evil, and the way in which sceptical philosophies of ethics like those of Medlin and Mackie would undermine it. What is most wrong with moral scepti-cism is not its falsity, he says, but its evil; it is 'to be rejected, not be-cause it is false or muddled or incoherent, but because it is an invita-tion to wickedness ... the fear of losing our sense of the reality of good and evil [is] a fear internal to a serious understanding of good and evil ... there are some things it is evil even to believe, and that good and evil may be an illusion is one of them.'[22] Characteristically, he develops this thought by having moral scepticism of the kind dis-cussed in professional philosophy confront the reality of evil, and his condemnation of it is moral before it is intellectual:

---

[20] R. Gaita, *Romulus, My Father* (Melbourne, 1998), p. 74.
[21] R. Manne, 'Robert Manne's speech at the launch of Raimond Gaita's *Romulus, My Father*', *Australian Book Review* (Feb/Mar 1998): pp. 10–11; also S. Moore, 'Reflections on *Romulus*', *AQ* 71 (1) (Jan/Feb 1999): pp. 6–9.
[22] R. Gaita, *Good and Evil* (Basingstoke, 1991), pp. 330–1, 21.

The fraudulent kind [of moral scepticism] which titillates itself with the pretence of thinking dangerous thoughts, is a tasteless form of intellectual and moral irresponsibility. If it were not fraudulent it would be evil, for it would question the reality of the evil that people have suffered in a way which is itself a form of evil. To see this quite clearly one need only imagine a tutorial in which one of its members had been a victim of terrible evil of which all the other members were aware, and in which the tutor invited them to consider whether our sense of the terribleness of evil was not an illusion. Everyone would be outraged if their tutor was not serious and struck by unbelieving horror if he was.

The example brings out that scepticism of this kind is itself an act against those who have been the victims of evil. The victim need not be directly before us as in the example. If people find themselves thinking that Jews are swines who deserved what the Nazis did to them, then that is itself something for which they should be ashamed, not merely because of what it shows about them, but also for the sake of those who suffered under the Nazis; for in thinking what they did they placed themselves in a concrete moral relation with them. If they said that it was, after all, *merely a thought,* they would betray their moral coarseness.[23]

Gaita suggests that we start our ethical reflection not from abstract questions about foundations or from attempts to resolve conflicts between moral intuitions, but from our most serious moral experiences, like remorse. His willingness to use in all seriousness — with the seriousness of common speech — moral concepts like remorse, guilt and corruption sets him off from the great majority of moral philosophers. He is of course hostile to modern tendencies to see guilt as a bad thing, to be remedied perhaps by psychoanalysis. He says simply, 'The modern hostility to guilt and guilt feelings threatens a proper understanding of good and evil, and proper sense of our humanity and of the independent reality of others, in one of the most fundamental ways possible.'[24]

His emphasis on the moral before (though not in exclusion to) the intellectual leads him to doubt whether the intellectual skills of philosophers are an advantage in thinking about ethics. He writes:

It is not accidental that there are no moral whizz-kids. That is partly because we cannot acquire moral knowledge in any sense that would make us morally *knowledgeable* ... It is more natural to speak of a depth of moral

---

[23] Gaita, *Good and Evil*, p. 319; also R. Gaita, 'Remembering the Holocaust: Absolute value and the nature of evil', *Quadrant* 39 (12) (Dec 1995): pp. 7–15; applications to social work in M. Gray & J.A. Stofberg, 'Respect for persons', *Australian Social Work* 53 (2) (Sept 2000): pp. 55–61.
[24] Gaita, *Good and Evil*, p. 50; cf. J. Carroll, *Guilt: The Grey Eminence behind Character, History and Culture* (London, 1985).

Rai Gaita and Gypsy, 2002 (Konrad Winkler)

understanding or of wisdom, and it is not accidental to these that their achievement takes time.[25]

[25] Gaita, *Good and Evil*, p. 270.

It is for this reason that he rejects Donagan's attempt to found the worth of persons on their possession of rationality, conceived narrowly as an ability to think logically. Such a conception, he argues, would trivialise remorse. 'Remorse often presents itself in the accents of a horrified discovery of the significance of what we did but it is trivialised if we express a murderer's horrified realization of what he did in terms such as these: "My God what have I done. I have been a traitor to reason. I have violated rational nature in another!"'[26]

Indeed, Gaita does not approve of founding ethics on any properties of humans at all, or on any view of reality outside ethics. 'There cannot be an independent metaphysical inquiry into the "reality of good and evil which would underwrite or undermine the most serious of our ways of speaking.'[27] In particular, questions of the existence of God can have no bearing on the foundations of ethics. That does make it difficult for him to explain whether the different ways we treat humans, dogs and insects is a result of the objective differences between them.[28] However, he does agree with the central thrust of Donagan's and Finnis's ideas, that the rules of ethics are only an effect of something more basic about the value of human nature:

> If the insistence on exceptionless principle is not to appear merely lunatic — an instance of what Jack Smart called 'rule worship' — then it will have to make clear its relationship to a sense of the meaning of wrongdoing that is interdependent with the sense that each human being is unconditionally precious.[29]

I F GAITA was opposed to the main trends of the mid-century in thinking about ethics, he was no happier with the direction the subject has taken since. For good or ill, the fastidiousness of philosophy in the face of practical problems did not last. Casuistry is back, and the public have more and more accepted the *relevance* of philosophy to decision-making in real life — public life, at least. A great number of philosophers have gained employment in a large industry providing ethics courses to professionals. The excesses of the

---

[26] Gaita, *Good and Evil*, p. 33; R. Gaita, *A Common Humanity* (Melbourne, 1999), introduction.

[27] Gaita, *Good and Evil*, p. 192; discussed in R. Blackford, 'The inward journeys of Raimond Gaita', *Quadrant* 44 (9) (Sept 2000): pp. 46–52.

[28] R. Gaita, *The Philosopher's Dog* (Melbourne, 2002), pp. 37, 153, 161, 170, 180, 197; debate on whether God can be kept out of ethics in P. Forrest, 'The mystery of secular ethics', *Australian Religion Studies Review* 7 (2) (Autumn 1995): pp. 1–8.

[29] R. Gaita, 'Reflections on the euthanasia debate', *Eureka Street* 5 (10) (Dec 1995): pp. 22–7.

business world in the 1980s created a demand for business ethics,[30] and parallel scandals led to demands for police ethics,[31] public service ethics,[32] computer ethics,[33] and professional ethics generally.[34]

[30] D. Grace & S. Cohen, *Business Ethics: Australian Problems and Cases* (2nd ed, Melbourne, 1998) (Cohen 'is ranked #34 on the basis of the number of business ethics articles published by an individual author between 1995–99': UNSW Philosophy website); R.E. Ewin, *Why Worry About Business Ethics?* (West Perth, 1992); C.A.J. Coady & C.J.G. Sampford, *Business, Ethics and the Law* (Sydney, 1993); R.D. Francis, *Business Ethics in Australia: A Practical Guide* (Melbourne, 1994); R.D. Francis, *Ethics and Corporate Governance: An Australian Handbook* (Sydney, 1999); P. Brokensha, *Corporate Ethics* (Wentworth Falls, 1993); P.H. Northcott, *Ethics and the Accountant* (Sydney, 1994); G.L. Clark & E.P. Jonson, eds, *Management Ethics* (Sydney, 1995); D. Massey, *The Ethics of Management and Managing Ethics* (Brisbane, 1995); K. Woldring, ed, *Business Ethics in Australia and New Zealand* (Melbourne, 1996); P. Costello, 'Restoring confidence in corporate morality', *Quadrant* 34 (9) (Sept 1990): pp. 20–22; K. Woldring, 'The ethics of Australian executive remuneration packages', *Journal of Business Ethics* 14 (1995): pp. 937–47, and articles in special issue of *Journal of Business Ethics* on 'Research on business and public sector ethics: An Australasian perspective', 14 (8) (Aug 1995); J.M. Smith, 'Ethics as excellence: A strategic management perspective', *Journal of Business Ethics* 14 (1995): pp. 683–93; J. Milton-Smith, 'Business ethics in Australia and New Zealand', *Journal of Business Ethics* 16 (1997): pp. 1485–97; J. Batten, S. Hettihewa & R. Mellor, 'The ethical management practices of Australian firms', *Journal of Business Ethics* 16 (1997): pp. 1261–71; R.E. Ewin, 'The moral status of the corporation', *Journal of Business Ethics* 10 (1991): pp. 749–56; C. O'Leary & R. Radich, 'An analysis of Australian final year accountancy students' ethical attitudes', *Teaching Business Ethics* 5 (2001): pp. 235–49; J. Franklin, 'Accountancy as computational casuistics', *Eureka Street* 9 (1) (Jan/Feb 1999): pp. 2, 43–6; earlier, H.T. Lovell, 'The ethics of advertising', *AJPP* 4 (1926): pp. 18–26; D.S. Waller, 'Ethics, education and self-regulation: The 1920 Sydney Advertising Convention', *Journal of the Royal Australian Historical Society* 81 (1995): pp. 99–107.

[31] S.R.M. Miller, J. Blackler & A. Alexandra, *Police Ethics* (Sydney 1997); J. Kleinig, *The Ethics of Policing* (Cambridge, 1996); K.M. McConkey, G.E. Huon & M.G. Frank, *Practical Ethics in the Police Service* (Payneham, 1996).

[32] N. Preston, ed, *Ethics for the Public Sector* (Sydney, 1994); G.L. Clark, E.P. Jonson & W.C. Caldow, eds, *Accountability and Corruption: Public Sector Ethics* (Sydney, 1997); Royal Institute of Public Administration (Queensland Branch), *Do Unto Others: Ethics in the Public Sector* (Brisbane, 1990); Management Advisory Board, *Ethical Standards and Values in the Australian Public Service* (Canberra, 1996); N. Preston & C. Sampford, *Encouraging Ethics and Challenging Corruption* (Sydney, 2002).

[33] T. Forester & P. Morrison, *Computer Ethics* (2nd ed, Cambridge, Mass, 1994); J. Weckert & D. Adeney, *Computer and Information Ethics* (Westport,

There has not been much about academic ethics[35] (except perhaps for the books on the Orr case). One perennial issue in academic ethics is plagiarism. Strangely, applied ethics itself provided the most notable plagiarism accusation in Australian philosophy. In 1984 the philosopher Suzanne Uniacke published in the little-read American journal *The Thomist* an article on the 'doctrine of double effect' (of which more later).[36] She was surprised to read a very lightly retouched version of a considerable quantity of her own words in the 1987 book *The Sanctity-of-Life Doctrine in Medicine*, by Dr Helga Kuhse, Deputy Director of Monash University's Centre for Human Bioethics. The words were not in quotation marks, and there were only two or three brief footnotes to her article. When she complained to the publishers, Oxford University Press, the Press issued, with Kuhse's agreement, a special announcement that Kuhse had 'insufficiently acknowledged' her debt to Uniacke's paper, and supplied a corrigenda list of eleven new footnotes acknowledging the debt. Kuhse still denied any suggestion of plagiarism.[37] Various Melbourne philosophers issued statements about how unimportant the whole matter was; Max Charlesworth, who had been unworried by plagiarism of his own work, and as acting Vice-Chancellor of Deakin University did little

Conn, 1997); S. Miller, ed, *Issues in Computer Ethics* (Wagga Wagga, 1996); E. Rooksby, *E-mail and Ethics* (London, 2002).

[34] *Australian Journal of Professional and Applied Ethics*; M. Coady & S. Bloch, *Codes of Ethics and the Professions* (Melbourne, 1996); J. Lawrence, *Argument for Action: Ethics and Professional Conduct* (Aldershot, 1999); S.R.M. Miller, ed, *Professional Ethics* (Wagga Wagga, 1995); J. Oakley & D. Cocking, *Virtue Ethics and Professional Roles* (Cambridge, 2001); C. Lowy, *Agents: The Philosophical Dimensions of Third Party Decision Making* (Aldershot, 2000); papers in *Professional Ethics* 6 (3–4) (1998); S. Johnston, P. Gostelow, E. Jones & R. Fourikis, *Engineering and Society: An Australian Perspective* (Melbourne, 1995), chs 11–12; S. Beder, *The New Engineer* (Melbourne, 1998); B.J. Farrell & D.M. Cobbin, 'A content analysis of codes of ethics in Australian enterprises', *Journal of Managerial Psychology* 11 (1) (1996): pp. 37–55; G.J. Syme & B.E. Nancarrow, 'The determinants of perceptions of fairness in the allocation of water to multiple uses', *Water Resources Research* 33 (1997): pp. 2143–52.

[35] But something in R. Gaita, 'Goodness and truth', *Philosophy* 67 (1992): pp. 507–21; R. Gaita, 'Intellectuals: The examined life', *Quadrant* 36 (12) (Dec 1992): pp. 37–9; J. Teichman, *Social Ethics: A Student's Guide* (Oxford, 1996), pp. 113–9; D. Lewis, 'Academic appointments: Why ignore the advantage of being right?' *Ormond Papers* 6 (1989): pp. 80–89.

[36] S. Uniacke, 'The doctrine of double effect', *The Thomist* 48 (1984): pp. 188–218; her later work in S. Uniacke, *Permissible Killing* (Cambridge, 1994).

[37] 'Academic admits book insufficiently acknowledged another's work', *Age* 14/7/1989, p. 3.

about (subsequently proved) accusations of faked research against his Dean of Science,[38] advised the *Age* that since Plato most philosophical writing had involved little more than 'remanipulating' the ideas of others. What Kuhse had done was, he said, not 'a scholarly crime in the usual sense', but more 'a matter of bad manners or inadvertence.'[39] Monash University looked into the matter of Kuhse's PhD thesis, of which the book was a slightly revised version, but they did not do so very vigorously, choosing as an 'independent investigator' a philosopher who had been effusively thanked in the preface to the original book.[40] Sydney philosophers took the matter more seriously and arranged for *Quadrant* to print several pages of parallel quotations from the two works.[41] There the matter rested.

MEDICAL ethics, or 'bioethics', has been at the forefront of applied ethics. An interest in health is reasonably objective, and it has proved possible, to a considerable extent, to achieve agreement on particular cases, even among philosophers who disagree on matters of ethical principle.[42]

---

[38] G. Maslen & L. Slattery, *Why Our Universities Are Failing* (Melbourne, 1994), p. 112.

[39] *Age* 17/7/1989, p. 13.

[40] *Herald* 4/10/1990, p. 3; comment in *Quadrant* 34 (12) (Dec 1990): p. 3 and 35 (1-2) (Jan-Feb 1991): p. 4.

[41] 'Bad manners? The case of Helga Kuhse', *Quadrant* 34 (10) (Oct 1990): pp. 65–9; also K. Campbell in *Age*, 4/8/1989, p. 10; other plagiarism accusations in Australian philosophy: A. Olding, 'MacColl on Keller on McClintock', *Quadrant* 36 (6) (June 1992): pp. 64–6, with rejoinder 36 (7-8) (July-Aug 1992): pp. 105–6; J.A. Stewart, *Drifting Continents and Colliding Paradigms* (Bloomington, Ind, 1990), p. 261.

[42] J. Oakley, 'Medical ethics, history of: Australia and New Zealand', *Encyclopedia of Bioethics*, ed. W.T. Reich (New York, 1995), vol. 3 pp. 1644–6; M. Charlesworth, 'Bioethics in Australia', *Bioethics Yearbook*, vol. 4, ed. B.A. Lustig (Boston, 1995), pp. 377–92; L. Gillam, 'Bioethics and public policy in Australia', *Politics & the Life Sciences* 13 (1994): pp. 87–88; J. Oakley, 'Applied ethics', *Routledge History of Philosophy*, vol. 10 (London, 1997), ch. 12; J.D. McCaughey, 'The newfound interest in medical ethics', in *Tradition and Dissent* (Melbourne, 1997), pp. 99–111; M. Charlesworth, *Bioethics in a Liberal Society* (Cambridge, 1993); L. Shotton, ed, *Health Care Law and Ethics* (Katoomba, 1997); K.J. Breen, V.D. Plueckhahn & S.M. Cordner, *Ethics, Law and Medical Practice* (Sydney, 1997); C.A. Berglund, *Ethics for Health Care* (Melbourne, 1998); K.R. Mitchell, I.H. Kerridge & T.J. Lovatt, *Bioethics and Clinical Ethics for Health Care Professionals* (2nd ed, Wentworth Falls, 1996); on particular issues, E. Prior Jonson, *AIDS: Myths, Facts and Ethics* (Sydney, 1988); J.W. Smith, *Aids, Philosophy and Beyond* (Aldershot, 1991); P.M. McNeill, *The Ethics and Politics of Human Experimentation* (Cambridge, 1993); S. van Hooft, L. Gillam & M. Byrnes,

Bioethics was driven not so much by scandals like those that gave rise to business ethics as by the remarkable advances in medical technologies, such as test–tube babies. Victoria had the world's first legislation on in vitro fertilisation in 1984. It provided for a philosopher to be included on the committee overseeing research and practice in the field. Max Charlesworth was appointed, and soon found himself advising on such matters as whether embryos could be created specially for research or had to be 'spare' ones, and whether an 'ovum in the process of being fertilised' was an embryo.[43] Ethical philosophers had often been criticised for concentrating on 'unrealistic' imaginary cases, but now they found it hard to keep up with reality. B.A. Santamaria was quick to warn that the cases were likely to become bizarre, with scientists freezing embryros and mixing human sperm with rat ova.[44] His predictions were quickly overtaken by events when two embryos in a Melbourne refrigerator became 'orphans' after their parents were killed in a South American plane crash, leaving an estate of $8 million. It was a legal mess spectacular even by Australian standards.[45] By 1998, there were 8000 frozen embryos in Melbourne whose par-

Facts and Values: An Introduction to Critical Thinking for Nurses (Sydney, 1995); H. Kuhse, *Caring: Nurses, Women and Ethics* (Oxford, 1997); P. Bowden, *Caring: Gender-Sensitive Ethics* (London, 1997); M.A. Birch, *Conscientious Objection and Clinical Nursing Practice* (Deakin, 1998); A.M. Evans, 'Philosophy of nursing: Future directions', *Australian and New Zealand Journal of Mental Health Nursing* 4 (1) (Mar 1995): pp. 14–21.

[43] M. Charlesworth, 'Bioethics and the limits of philosophy', *Bioethics News* 9 (1) (1989): pp. 9–25; N. Tonti-Filippini & T.V. Daly, *Experimenting with the Origins of Human Lives* (Melbourne, 1985); F. Harman, 'A Christian philosophy on experimenting with life', *Australian Journal of Forensic Sciences* 17 (1985): pp. 131–40; M.D. Kirby, 'Bioethics of IVF', *Journal of Medical Ethics* 10 (1984): pp. 45–8; feminist objections in R. Rowland, *Living Laboratories: Women and Reproductive Technology* (Sydney, 1992); debate promised in the forthcoming *Australian Journal of Emerging Technologies and Society*.

[44] B.A. Santamaria, *Test Tube Babies?* (Melbourne, 1984), with reference to P. Quinn, 'Polyethylene glycol-induced attachment of human spermatozoa to zona-free rat ova', *Australian Journal of Biological Science* 35 (1982): pp. 179–86; later B. Tobin, 'Challenging our inventiveness: Ethics today', *ACR* 77 (2000): pp. 148–58.

[45] *Bulletin* 3/7/1984, pp. 22–4; G.P. Smith, 'Australia's frozen "orphan" embryos', *Journal of Family Law* 24 (1) (1985–6): pp. 27–41; C. Corns, 'Deciding the fate of frozen embryos', *Law Institute Journal* 64 (1990): pp. 273–6; R.F. Atherton, 'Between a fridge and a hard place: The case of the frozen embryos or children en ventre sa frigidaire', *Australian Property Law Journal* 6 (1998): pp. 53–60.

ents could not be traced. Thawing and destruction of them was begun.[46]

Bioethics is the field of Peter Singer, undoubtedly Australia's most famous philosopher — he has been described as 'the most influential philosopher alive'.[47]

Singer, like Gaita, is informed by the sense of a close personal relation to the European past, but the tradition he comes from could hardly be more different from that of Romulus Gaita. Singer's maternal grandfather, whose biography he has recently written, was a classical scholar of Enlightenment views and a close associate of Freud in Vienna. In 1911 he co-authored with Freud an article on erotic dreams in folklore, unpublished at that time because of a dispute between the co-authors.[48] He died in the Holocaust, as did both Singer's paternal grandparents.[49] His grandmother survived the camps and brought to Australia the manuscript of the then unknown work by Freud and her husband.

Singer was a philosophy student at Melbourne University in the Sixties. Like many, he turned away from 'rather fruitlessly analyzing the meaning of words' to involvement in Vietnam and other issues of the time.[50] He wrote a thesis on 'Why should I be moral?' before leaving for Oxford.[51] He soon achieved fame with his argument that as long as people in the Third World are starving, it is immoral to buy ourselves new clothes and cars.[52] At Oxford he fell in with

[46] *SMH* 8/12/1997, p. 5; ethical debate in B.F. Scarlett, 'The moral status of embyros', *Journal of Medical Ethics* 10 (1984): pp. 79–81, with reply by Kuhse and Singer pp. 80–1, further pp. 217–8; an account of taking Peter Singer's advice in M. Hogben, 'What size is an embyro's soul?', *Human Life Review* 24 (3) (Summer 1998): pp. 88–93.

[47] 'Living and dying, with Peter Singer', *Psychology Today* 32 (1) (Jan/Feb 1999): pp. 56–9, 78–9, at p. 56; list of his publications in D. Jamieson, *Singer and His Critics* (Oxford, 1999) and at www.princeton.edu/~uchv/faculty/CV91802.htm; links to many online articles at www.petersingerlinks.com .

[48] S. Freud & D.E. Oppenheim, 'Dreams in folklore', in *The Standard Edition of the Complete Psychological Works of Sigmund Freud*, vol. 12 (London, 1958), pp. 177–203; Singer's account: *Pushing Time Away: My Grandfather and the Tragedy of Jewish Vienna* (Pymble, 2003).

[49] P. Singer, *How Are We To Live?* (Melbourne, 1993), pp. 158–9.

[50] 'A conversation with Peter Singer, part II', *The Animals' Agenda* 14 (3) (May 1994): pp. 30–1; Singer on the Whitlam years in *SMH* 1/12/1982, p. 7.

[51] Brief autobiography in *SMH* 22/2/1997, p. 2s.

[52] P. Singer, 'Famine, affluence and morality', *Philosophy and Public Affairs* 1 (1971/2): pp. 229–43; P. Singer, 'Reconsidering the famine relief argument', in *Food Policy* ed. P.G. Brown & H. Shue (New York, 1977), pp. 36–53; and P. Singer, *Practical Ethics* (2nd ed, Cambridge, 1993), ch. 8; also on this

vegetarians, and finding he could not answer their arguments, became one. He then wrote his hugely successful book *Animal Liberation*,[53] which has sold some half a million copies and been translated into most major languages.[54] He conceives animal liberation as a successor to the liberation movements of blacks and women. Why not for animals as well? He wrote: 'A liberation movement demands an expansion of our moral horizons and an extension or reinterpretation of the basic principle of equality'. Equality of what? Not of objective characteristics: just as differences in IQ among people do not license differences in moral consideration, so the undoubted differences between animals do not imply they should be treated unequally. 'Equality is an ideal, not a simple assertion of fact ... not a description of an alleged actual equality between humans; it is a prescription of how we should treat humans.' Equality of moral consideration does not imply exactly equal rights; pigs will not be given the right to vote, because they can't vote. But in explaining why moral consideration does not extend beyond animals to, say, stones, Singer asserts that equality of consideration requires the possession of an objective property, namely sentience. 'Capacity for suffering is the vital characteristic that gives a being the right to equal consideration.'[55]

---

issue, J. Begley, 'World hunger: Moral aspects', *Catholic Theological Review* 5 (1983): pp. 78–86; B. Opeskin, 'The moral foundations of foreign aid', *World Development* 24 (1996): pp. 21–44.
[53] P. Singer, *Animal Liberation* (London, 1976, 2nd ed, London, 1991); P. Singer, ed. *In Defense of Animals* (New York, 1986); P. Singer, *Ethics into Action: Henry Spira and the Animal Rights Movement* (Melbourne, 1999), ch. 3; survey of Singer's ethics in J. Colman, 'Peter Singer: On behalf of animals', in *Australian Philosophers*, ed. P. Dowe, M. Nicholls & L. Shotton (Hobart, 1996), pp. 121–38; P. Singer, 'The Animal Liberation movement', *Current Affairs Bulletin* 60 (3) (Aug 1983): pp. 15–21; L. Munro, 'A decade of animal liberation', *CAB* 70 (7) (Dec 1993): pp. 12–19; P. Singer, 'Neither human nor natural: Ethics and feral animals', *Reproduction, Fertility and Development* 9 (1997): pp. 157–62; Singer's inspiration of Animal Liberation in Australia: C. Townend, *A Voice for the Animals* (Kenthurst, 1981), pp. 7–8.
[54] *SMH* 10/6/1995, Spectrum p. 3; on the effects of the book in the US, R. Usher, 'Saintly or satanic?', *Time Australia* 4 (47) (20/11/1989): pp. 88–9; P. Singer, 'Unkind to animals', *New York Review of Books* 2/2/1989, pp. 36–8.
[55] P. Singer, 'All animals are equal', *New York Review of Books* 5/4/1973, expanded in P. Singer, ed, *Applied Ethics* (Oxford, 1986), ch. 13; also in *Practical Ethics*, 2nd ed, ch. 3; comment in L.E. Johnson, 'Do animals have an interest in life?', *AJP* 61 (1983): pp. 172–84; arguments to the contrary: A. Townsend, 'Radical vegetarians', *AJP* 57 (1979): pp. 85–93; H.J. McCloskey, 'The moral case for experimentation on animals', *Monist* 70 (1987): pp. 64–82; J. Thompson, [J.L. Arbor], 'Animal chauvinism, plant-regarding ethics and the torture of trees', *AJP* 64 (1986): pp. 335–9; R.

Peter Singer campaigning against animal experiments, 1988 (Newspix)

If there is a choice between killing an animal and killing a human, we may prefer to save the human, Singer says, but the reason for this is simply that humans have more preferences: 'taking the life of a person will normally be worse than taking the life of some other being, since persons are highly future-oriented in their preferences. To kill a person is therefore, normally, to violate not just one but a wide range of the most central and significant preferences a being can have.'[56] (This argument seems to be vulnerable to research that might discover a cat could foresee dinner and plan to arrive at dinnertime.)

Singer wonders, as well he might, whether the carnivores might not be better eliminated. He rejects the proposal, but only because he lacks confidence in the capacity of humans to manage the ecology.[57]

Elliot, 'Moral autonomy, self-determination and animal rights', *Monist* 70 (1987): pp. 83–97; P. Harrison, 'Do animals feel pain?', *Philosophy* 66 (1991): pp. 25–40.

[56] Singer, *Practical Ethics*, 2nd ed, p. 95.

[57] Singer, *Animal Liberation*, 2nd ed, pp. 225–6; on sex with animals, P. Singer, 'Heavy petting', www.nerve.com/Opinions/Singer/heavyPetting .

The impact of *Animal Liberation* on farming practice and medical research on live animals has been substantial, and this is what is meant by the claim that Singer is the most influential philosopher alive. The bona fides of the research in *Animal Liberation* were attacked much later by some California biologists, who claimed that the chapter dealing with research on animals presented misreferenced and distorted views of that research.[58] US researchers in pediatric surgery, which is particularly dependent on animal experiments, asked about the ethics of the alternative, experimenting directly on children.[59] But it was far too late to shut the stable door.

On the strength of the success of *Animal Liberation*, Singer became Professor of Philosophy at Monash University in 1977 at the age of 30. He became a well-known public figure, especially in Melbourne, and showed a certain flair for publicity by getting himself arrested at the piggery formerly part-owned by Paul Keating[60] and standing as a Senate candidate for the Greens[61] (though he received only 2.8 per cent of the vote). He founded and became first Director of the Monash Centre for Human Bioethics. The Centre took advantage of the upsurge of interest in bioethics created by the new medical techniques like in vitro fertilisation, in which Monash University doctors were world leaders.[62] The researchers at the cutting edge found the

---

[58] S.M. Russell & C.S. Nicoll, 'A dissection of the chapter tools for research in Peter Singer's *Animal Liberation*', *Proceedings of the Society for Experimental Biology & Medicine* 211 (1996): pp. 109–38; Singer's response, pp. 139–46; authors' response, pp. 147–54; comment in A.R. Morrison, 'Animal-rights movement's "Bible" contains distorted revelations', *The Scientist* 10 (16) (19/8/1996): p. 11.

[59] R.E. Sonnino & R.E. Banks, 'Ethical issues: Impact of the animal rights movement on surgical research', *Pediatric Surgery International* 11 (1996): pp. 438–43, also R.P. Vance, 'An introduction to the philosophical presuppositions of the animal liberation/rights movement', *Journal of the American Medical Association* 268 (1992): pp. 1715–19.

[60] *SMH* 22/11/1995, p. 7; 'Pigs in the limelight', *Animal Liberation* 44 (Apr/June 1993): p. 16; further on his animal liberation activism in the journal *Animal Liberation* 24 (Apr/June 1988): p. 8; 25 (July/Sept 1988): pp. 9–11; 27 (Jan/Mar 1989): pp. 4–7, 27; 35 (Jan/Mar 1991): pp. 4–8.

[61] Bob Brown and P. Singer, *The Greens* (Melbourne, 1996); *SMH* 14/2/1996, p. 14; P. Singer, 'Standing for the Greens', *Generation* 6 (1–2) (Oct 1996): pp. 3–6.

[62] W. Walters & P. Singer, *Test Tube Babies* (Melbourne, 1982) (see review by B. Scarlett in *Australian Book Review* 44 (Sept 1982): p. 32); P. Singer & D. Wells, *The Reproduction Revolution* (Oxford, 1984) (on Wells' activities as Queensland Attorney-General, see D. van Gend, 'On the "sanctity of human life"', *Quadrant* 39 (9) (Sept 1995): pp. 57–60); P. Singer et al., eds, *Embryo Experimentation* (Cambridge, 1990); R.M. Albury, 'Challenges to

support of philosophers a comfort. One said, 'I had to sort myself out in the early days just like anyone who works in a new area involving something like human embryos. If we hadn't had Peter Singer around in those days I think we might not have pursued some things to the extent that we have.'[63]

The basis of Singer's ethics is very clear, as he explains in his immensely successful textbook, *Practical Ethics*. He is a 'preference utilitarian', meaning that he holds that what is right is what maximises the satisfaction of preferences (or interests). All interests are equal; 'an interest is an interest, whoever's interest it may be.'[64] Thus, an animal's pain is entitled to equal consideration to an equal pain in a human,[65] but since trees do not have feelings or sufferings they do not have to be taken into moral account. This principle may, as Singer explains, conflict with a principle of equality of the organisms that have the pain. For example, if we are faced with a choice of helping only one of two earthquake victims, one of whom has lost a leg and will lose another toe if we do not help, and the other who has lost no leg but will lose one leg if we do not help, then we should help the less seriously injured victim, since losing a leg is worse than losing a toe.[66] Equality of preferences explains why differences in IQ or race, for example, are not morally relevant: 'the most important human interests — such as the interest in avoiding pain, in developing one's abilities, in satisfying basic needs for food and shelter, in enjoying warm personal relationships, in being free to pursue one's projects without interference, and many others — are not affected by differences in intelligence.'[67] Singer does not discuss the case of mental patients and Buddhists who have transcended these interests, but, as we will see, he does have some conclusions to draw about infants.

Naturally, this theory leads to the usual problems for utilitarians over whether the preferences of many override the preferences of one. Singer was tackled about this is an interview:

> Interviewer: There's something I don't understand about preference utilitarianism. Let's say there are 11 beings, and 10 of those beings want to kill one of those beings. Do the intense preferences of those 10 outweigh the intense preference of that one?

common sense: Debates about the status of human embryos outside women's bodies', *Journal of Australian Studies* 59 (1998): pp. 129–38.
[63] M. Duffy, 'The vegetarian philosopher', *Independent Monthly,* (Sept 1990), pp. 37–8.
[64] Singer, *Practical Ethics*, 2nd ed, p. 21.
[65] Singer, *Practical Ethics*, p. 58.
[66] Singer, *Practical Ethics*, p. 25.
[67] Singer, *Practical Ethics*, p. 31.

Singer: Numbers matter, but I'd assume the preference of that one being not to die is much more intense than the preferences of the other ten to kill it. You'd have to actually live all 11 of those lives to know for certain.

Interviewer: Right — so how can you evaluate the intensity of a preference from the outside?

Singer: It's very hard. You can't actually go around living a moral life by doing those calculations all the time. That's why we have moral rules of thumb. In general, most people have a very serious, intense preference to live that outweighs almost any other preference. But these rules don't have absolute moral status.[68]

Of the many novel and controversial doctrines advanced by Singer, none has created more anger than his assertion that babies up to about the age of four weeks have no right to life. He is not here dealing with the genuine problem of severely deformed babies,[69] but is speaking of normal babies. He writes in *Practical Ethics*:

In thinking about this matter we should put aside feelings based on the small, helpless and — sometimes — cute appearance of human infants. To think that the lives of infants are of special value because infants are small and cute is on a par with thinking that a baby seal, with its soft white fur coat and large round eyes, deserves greater protection than a whale [2nd ed: gorilla], which lacks these attributes. If we can put aside these emotionally moving but strictly irrelevant aspects of the killing of a baby we can see that the grounds for not killing persons do not apply to newborn infants. The indirect, classical utilitarian reason does not apply, because no one capable of understanding what is happening when a newborn baby is killed could feel threatened by a policy which gave less protection to the newborn than to adults. In this respect Bentham was right to describe infanticide as 'of a nature not to give the slightest inquietude to the most timid imagination'. Once we are old enough to comprehend the policy, we are too old to be threatened by it.

Similarly, the preference utilitarian reason for respecting the life of a person cannot apply to a newborn baby. A newborn baby cannot see itself as

[68] 'Living and dying, with Peter Singer', p. 79.
[69] H. Kuhse & P. Singer, *Should the Baby Live?* (Oxford, 1985); H. Kuhse, 'Quality of life and the death of "Baby M"', *Bioethics* 6 (1992): pp. 233–250; B. Teo, 'Sanctity of life and the case of the death of "Baby M": A response to Helga Kuhse', *Pacifica* 7 (1) (1994): pp. 233–50; R.B. Young, 'Infanticide and the severely deformed infant', in R. Laura, ed, *Problems of Handicap* (Melbourne, 1986), pp. 126–35; N. Tonti-Filippini, 'The status of anencephalics', *ACR* 63 (1986): pp. 169–78; M. Charlesworth, 'Disabled newborn infants and the quality of life', *Journal of Contemporary Health Law and Policy* 9 (1993): pp. 129–37; D. Sinclair, 'Birthrights', *Southern Cross University Law Review* 1 (1997): pp. 52–74; earlier, G. Hawkins, 'Thoughts on mercy killings', *Bulletin* 18/4/1964, pp. 15–16.

a being which might or might not have a future, and so cannot have a desire to continue living ... If there were to be legislation on this matter, it probably should deny a full legal right to life to babies only for a short period after birth — perhaps a month ... If these conclusions seem too shocking to take seriously, it may be worth remembering that our present absolute protection of the lives of infants is a distinctively Judaeo-Christian attitude ... None of this is meant to suggest that someone who goes around randomly killing babies is no worse than a woman who has an abortion, or a man who thinks it fine sport to shoot ducks. We should certainly put very strict conditions on permissible infanticide; but these restrictions might owe more to the effects of infanticide on others than to the intrinsic wrongness of killing an infant.[70]

It is here that the consequences of preference utilitarianism, with its doctrine that all preferences are equal whoever or whatever has them, become most obvious. As Singer puts it under the heading, 'Does a person have the right to life?', 'the wrong done to the person killed is merely one factor to be taken into account, and the preference of the victim could sometimes be outweighed by the preferences of others.'[71] Since the utilitarian values happiness or preference fulfilment in abstraction from the people who have the happiness or preferences, he has no objection in principle to the painless killing of one being and its replacement by another with similar happiness.[72]

Naturally, one would like someone to ask Singer about his own children. A recent interviewer did so and Singer was happy to answer:

> Interviewer: Do you have children yourself? Everyone says that however you feel about kids in the abstract, it changes when you're confronted with critical decisions regarding your own. How would you behave given a dire situation involving your own offspring?
>
> Singer: I have three grown daughters. It is important to remember that I have never said that it is OK, or a trivial matter, to kill newborn infants in normal circumstances, that is, when they have loving parents who care for them. My point is that the wrong done is really, at that stage, a wrong to the parents rather than to the infant who has no awareness of its own ex-

---

[70] Singer, *Practical Ethics* (Cambridge, 1979), pp. 123–6 (2nd ed, 1993, pp. 170–3); again in P. Singer, 'Killing babies isn't always wrong', *Spectator*, 16/9/1995, pp. 20–2; similar earlier arguments criticised in S. Benn, 'Abortion, infanticide and respect for persons', in *The Problem of Abortion*, ed. J. Feinberg (Belmont, Ca, 1973), pp. 92–104.

[71] Singer, *Practical Ethics*, 2nd ed, p. 95.

[72] S. Uniacke, 'Replaceability and infanticide', *Journal of Value Inquiry* 31 (1997): pp. 153–66; S. Uniacke, 'A critique of the preference utilitarian objection to killing people', *AJP* 80 (2002): pp. 209–17; older views in G. Cowlishaw, 'Infanticide in Aboriginal Australia', *Oceania* 48 (1978): pp. 262–83.

istence. So, of course, I cared for and loved my children, and would have been deeply upset if they had died, but that is really because of my feelings, and those of my wife, not because of what they were at that moment. So I don't think it is true that I don't take emotions into account.[73]

A remarkable number of commentators have accepted at least Singer's assertion that babies are not rational and that they have no awareness of their own existence. Of course they can't talk or write books, but a baby learns more in a day than a philosophy professor does in a year, and at birth is already remembering, expressing surprise, reacting with pleasure and displeasure to different things, and so on.[74] Why is that not enough to be 'rational and self-conscious',[75] in the words Singer chooses to describe things that may not be killed? He does not say. His claim that 'Killing a snail or a day-old infant does not thwart any desires of this kind [for the future], because snails and newborn infants are incapable of having such desires'[76] is, on the face of it, simply false, and he does not defend it with any evidence. He does know, of course, that the potentialities of snails and babies are different, but that is not relevant, according to him: only properties a thing *actually* has now can be relevant to its rights. As Jacqueline Laing points out, this is a worry for anyone in a temporary coma, or even asleep.[77] She wonders, too, if the only reason Singer gives for not growing deliberately brain-damaged babies for organ harvesting — that it would damage our "attitude of care and protection for in-

[73] 'Living and dying, with Peter Singer', p. 78.

[74] B.F. Scarlett, 'The moral uniqueness of the human animal', in *Human Lives*, ed. D.S. Oderberg & J.A. Laing (New York, 1997), pp. 77–95, at pp. 91–2; other debate on innate mental abilities in F. Cowie, *What's Within: Nativism Reconsidered* (Oxford, 1999).

[75] Singer, *Practical Ethics*, 2nd ed, p. 181, cf. p. 169.

[76] Singer, *Practical Ethics*, 2nd ed, p. 90; cf. pp. 182, 191; on Singer's redefinition of 'person' in this context see J. Teichman, 'The definition of person', *Philosophy* 60 (1985): pp. 175–85; Teichman, *Social Ethics*, ch. 4; also N. Ford, 'Different concepts of the person employed in bioethics', *ACR* 75 (1998): pp. 255–63; on the 'personhood' of great apes, P. Singer, *Rethinking Life and Death: The Collapse of Our Traditional Ethics* (New York, 1994), p. 182; on which T. Kelly, 'Seesaw on the slippery slope?', *Quadrant* 39 (10) (Oct 1995): pp. 7–8.

[77] J.A. Laing, 'Innocence and consequentialism: Inconsistency, equivocation and contradiction in the philosophy of Peter Singer', in *Human Lives*, ed. Oderberg & Laing, pp. 196–224, at pp. 203–7; a reply in Singer, *Practical Ethics*, 2nd ed, pp. 98–9, also S. Buckle, 'Arguing from potential', *Bioethics* 2 (1988): pp. 227–53; questions on Singer's spending money on his Alzheimer's-afflicted mother in 'Mum tests professor of death' *Herald Sun* (Melbourne) 15/9/1999.

fants" — is quite in logical accord with the rest of his pronounce-
ments.

Still, that sort of point-scoring is not going to make much impact
on Singer's position. If he is wrong, a moral revulsion must be more
relevant than fancy intellectual footwork. Gaita holds that the act of
discussing seriously the permissibility of infanticide is itself corrupt:

> Only twenty years ago it was believed that the conclusion that infanticide
> was permissible was a *reductio* of any argument that led to it. In particular,
> it was agreed by all that abortion would be inconceivable if it were shown
> to be (morally) the same as infanticide. Today there are philosophers who
> believe that infanticide is permissible under much the same conditions as
> is abortion; and philosophy students the Western world over who are
> taking courses in practical ethics, think that it is at least arguable. Amongst
> philosophers it is thought to be perfectly proper to argue that infanticide is
> an evil but it is thought to be improper to say that conjecturing whether it
> is permissible is itself an evil to be feared. If a philosopher were to say that
> students were liable to be corrupted by those who invite them to seriously
> consider whether they may kill six-week-old babies for the same kinds of
> reasons that will procure an abortion, then most of his colleagues would
> judge that he had shown himself to be less than a real philosopher, less
> than a real thinker.[78]

These considerations lead up to the most savage of Gaita's condemnations of the kind of applied ethics that Singer and his colleagues
pursue:

> Those practical philosophers who have been in the forefront of the argu-
> ment to relax the conditions under which it is permissible to kill people
> and who have created a new genre called 'practical ethics' have not made
> academic philosophy less insular. Quite the contrary: they have extended
> the arrogance and insularity of the worst kind of academic professionalism
> beyond the academy. Generally they show no fear or even slight anxiety
> at the responsibility they have assumed; they have no sense of awe in the
> face of the questions they have raised, and no sense of humility in the face
> of the traditions which they condescendingly dismiss. They are aggres-
> sively without a sense of mystery and without a suspicion that anything
> might be too deep for their narrowly professional competence. They
> mistake these vices for the virtues of thinking radically, courageously and
> with an unremitting hostility to obscurantism.[79]

Singer has shown no tendency to acknowledge that kind of attack,
or any evidence of understanding it. His opponents have wondered if

[78] Gaita, *Good and Evil*, pp. 315–6.
[79] Gaita, *Good and Evil*, p. 326; further in 'The good life', interview with
Gaita, *Eureka Street* 4 (5) (1994): pp. 34–41; opposite in P. Singer, 'Moral
experts', in *Writings on an Ethical Life* (New York, 2000), pp. 3–6.

he was perhaps lacking something in the area of emotions.[80] The relation of the emotions to ethics is a vexed issue[81] (Gaita complains of 'a distinction between reason and emotion that distorts our understanding of one of the most important facts about the ethical — that we often learn by being moved by what others say or do'[82]) but it certainly seems that anyone who does not have an immediate emotional reaction to pictures of Belsen is lacking a perception of something important to ethics. It is strange that Singer goes out of his way, in the passage quoted above about infanticide and seals, to recommend the putting aside of the 'emotionally moving but strictly irrelevant aspects' of killing babies. Nor does he notice that seals are cute because they look like babies. At one point, he almost admits to a lack of relevant emotions, at least in the past; the total effect of his admission is decidedly odd:

> Interviewer: What do you think has been added to the animal rights movement by the feminist critique of animal oppression?

> Singer: The feminist critique has, perhaps, made some of us who are inclined to look at things in a rational way realize that we have not given enough attention to emotional connections to animals and to caring attitudes towards them. We should try to extend people's emotional attachment and commitment to animals, and we ought to try to get people to empathize more with the less charismatic, less attractive animals.[83]

Opposition to Singer's views has taken the form of more than mere words. In 1989/90, a philosophy professor at the University of Duisberg offered a course based on Singer's *Practical Ethics*, which by then had been translated into German, Spanish, Italian and Swedish as well as being widely used in philosophy courses in English-speaking countries. The course was subjected to repeated protests over the book's advocacy of active euthanasia for disabled newborn infants. In late 1990 Helga Kuhse was unable to deliver a lecture in Vienna because of protests from the disabled. The prestigious International Wittgenstein Symposium for 1991 invited Singer to speak, but the president of the Austrian Ludwig Wittgenstein Society decided that protesters had a case and that the invitation should be cancelled. The

---

[80] 'The man in the black plastic shoes', *HQ* (Winter 1992): pp. 54–61.

[81] J. Oakley, *Morality and the Emotions* (London, 1992); C. Taylor, *Sympathy*, (New York, 2002); L. Reinhardt, 'Morality: Vision or feeling', *Critical Philosophy* 2 (1986): pp. 65–86; R. Langton, 'Duty and desolation', *Philosophy* 67 (1992): pp. 481–505; M. Johnston, 'The authority of affect', *Philosophy and Phenomenological Research* 63 (2001): pp. 181–214.

[82] R. Gaita, 'Reflections on the euthanasia debate', p. 22.

[83] 'A conversation with Peter Singer, part II', *The Animals' Agenda* 14 (3) (May 1994): pp. 30–1.

organising committee cancelled the entire symposium instead. The weekly *Die Zeit* published two articles on Singer's views and the leader of Germany's 'Cripples Movement' chained his wheelchair to the doors of the editorial office. When Singer rose to speak on animal rights in Zürich, part of the audience began to chant 'Singer *raus!* Singer *raus!*'. He writes, 'As I heard this chanted, in German, by people so lacking in respect for the tradition of reasoned debate that they were unwilling even to allow me to make a response to what had just been said about me, I had an overwhelming feeling that this was what it must have been like to attempt to reason against the rising tide of Nazism in the declining days of the Weimar Republic. The difference was that the chant would have been, not "Singer *raus*", but "*Juden raus*"'. One protester tore Singer's glasses off, throwing them on the floor and breaking them.[84]

In his account, Singer speaks throughout as if his opponents are in favour of the absolute sanctity of life of all human beings, while he is in favour merely of killing severely deformed babies. This is disingenuous, to say the least,[85] even though it was principally disabled babies that were the concern of the German adult disabled. Singer also says that euthanasia as he understands it has nothing to do with the Nazi murder of 'people considered unworthy of living from the racist

---

[84] P. Singer, 'On being silenced in Germany', *New York Review of Books* 15/8/1991: pp. 36–42, repr in *Practical Ethics,* 2nd ed, pp. 337–59; P. Singer, 'Bioethics and academic freedom', *Bioethics* 4 (1990): pp. 33–44; P. Singer, 'A philosopher among the test tubes', *Meanjin* 50 (1991): pp. 493–500; P. Singer, 'A German attack on Applied Ethics: A statement by Peter Singer', *Journal of Applied Philosophy* 9 (1992): pp. 85–91; B. Schöne-Seifert & K.-P. Rippe, 'Silencing the Singer: Antibioethics in Germany', *Hastings Center Report* 21 (6) (Nov-Dec 1991): pp. 21–7; documentation in C. Anstötz, R. Hegselmann & H. Kliemt, eds, *Peter Singer in Deutschland* (Frankfurt, 1995); also J. Stenzel, *Kein Recht auf Leben: Peter Singers Kritik des Lebensrechtes im Lichte der Philosophie Constantin Brunners* (Essen, 1993); A. Leist, 'Bioethics in a low key', *Bioethics* 7 (1993): pp. 271–9; P. Singer & H. Kuhse, 'Bioethics and the limits of tolerance', *Journal of Medicine and Philosophy* 19 (1994): pp. 129–45; later in *SMH* 6/5/1996, p. 10; opinions of the Australian disabled in J. Fitzgerald, 'Legalizing euthanasia', *Australian Disability Review,* no. 2 of 1996, pp. 3–14 and C. Newell, 'Medical killing and people with disability', pp. 28–37; I. Parsons & C. Newell, *Managing Mortality: Euthanasia on Trial* (Geelong, 1996); H. Ramsay, 'Distinctive moralities: The value of life and our duties to the handicapped', *Journal of Value Inquiry* 32 (1998): pp. 507–17.

[85] S. Uniacke & H.J. McCloskey, 'Peter Singer and non-voluntary "euthanasia": Tripping down the slippery slope', *Journal of Applied Philosophy* 9 (1992): pp. 203–19.

viewpoint of the German *Volk*.'[86] That is true, but a dangerous thing for a preference utilitarian to call attention to, given that his theory implies that sufficiently strong desires by sufficiently many Nazis would make the genocide of a sufficiently small Jewish race right.

Singer compares himself, of course, not to Hitler but to Socrates.[87] The wounded tone of his complaints about the suppression of free speech and his attacks on defenders of 'the conventional doctrine of the sanctity of life' prompt Jenny Teichman to wonder if Singer 'adheres to the conventional doctrine of the sanctity of free speech,' and to add 'if *human life itself* has only conventional importance it becomes terribly hard to see how Singer's wish to speak at conferences could have any importance whatsoever.'[88] Gaita writes, 'some of the people in wheelchairs may have had a point. They must have realised that if their mothers had believed what Singer does, then they would almost certainly be dead.'[89]

The controversies have not died down. Singer's appointment in 1998 as Ira W. DeCamp Professor of Bioethics at Princeton University's Center for Human Values sparked more protests from the disabled.[90] There were more protests at his first lectures and a major donor threatened to withdraw funding.[91]

---

[86] Singer, *Practical Ethics*, 2nd ed, p. 356; 'Euthanasia: Emerging from Hitler's shadow', in P. Singer, *Writings on an Ethical Life* (New York, 2000), pp. 201–8.

[87] Singer, 'A German attack on applied ethics', p. 89.

[88] J. Teichman, 'Humanism & personism', *Quadrant* 36 (12) (Dec 1992): pp. 26–9, repr. in J. Teichman, *Polemical Papers*, pp. 87–95; replies in *Quadrant* 37 (6) (June 1993): pp. 33–8; also D.S. Oderberg, 'The Singer controversy', *Quadrant* 37 (9) (Sept 1993): pp. 74–6; J. Teichman, 'Dr Jekyll & Mr Hyde', *New Criterion* 19 (2) (Oct 2000): pp. 64–7, (some biography of Teichman in J. Jorgensen, *More Hats* (Melbourne, 2002)); G. Preece, ed, *Rethinking Peter Singer: A Christian Critique* (Downers Grove, Ill, 2002).

[89] R. Gaita, 'Some questions for Peter Singer's admirers', *Arena Magazine* 21 (Feb/Mar 1996): pp. 25–8, infanticide defended in H. Brent, 'Questions for Gaita', *Arena Magazine* 23 (June 1996): pp. 15–16; Gaita's reply in 24 (Aug 1996): pp. 13, 53–4.

[90] 'A messenger of death at Princeton', *Washington Times* 30/6/1998; *New York Times* 10/4/1999, p. 1; *Boston Globe* 27/7/1999, p. A01; various articles in *Human Life Review* 24 (4) (Fall 1998): pp. 30–67; J. Sharlet, 'Why are we afraid of Peter Singer?', *Chronicle of Higher Education* 10/2/2000; D.K. Hainsworth, 'Mr Singer goes to Princeton', *Zadok Perspectives* 65 (Spring/Summer 1999–2000): pp. 11–16; www.welcome.to/PSAI .

[91] *Times* (London), 18/10/1999, p. 14; student reaction in *Daily Princetonian* 26/5/2000.

A MINORITY of deaths are now due to acute events, so most readers will need to consider, sooner or later, the decisions to be made at the end of their lives. Euthanasia is an ethical issue that most will not be able to avoid.

The majority of print expended on the subject deals with side issues like slippery-slope arguments, worries about emotional blackmail of the frail elderly, the adequacy of safeguards, State rights, the rights or otherwise of some people to impose their moral views on others, whether legalising euthanasia will create a 'culture of death' which will impact badly on palliative care, and so on. These are important issues in themselves — few issues are more serious — but everyone knows they are not the central ones. Neither are the very real issues that arise in decisions about borderline cases, like patients in persistent vegetative states.[92] With respect to the euthanasia debate itself, those are no more than debating points. Positions are taken first and foremost on the raw issue: is the intentional ending of innocent life permitted?

While philosophers like Singer are 'for' euthanasia, and those like Finnis and Gaita are 'against' it, it is extraordinarily difficult to discover what the real positions of both sides on this basic question are. Both sides speak in ways that are misleading. It seems at first glance that those against euthanasia maintain there is a 'sanctity of life', an irreducible worth of life that may not be intentionally violated, while those for euthanasia generally believe in some naturalist world view which does not include any such metaphysical entities, and take their stand on liberty: 'Whose life is it anyway?' If that were the situation, it would be an example of how philosophical clarification revealed a basic clash of metaphysical beliefs behind a mass of rhetoric. It does reveal that, but the philosophical situation turns out to be much more complicated. On the one hand, supporters of euthanasia do not usually believe in a general right to suicide, as is implied by the stand for arbitrary liberty; normally, they would not assist a healthy teenager planning suicide,[93] and many would be unhappy about assisting in the

---

[92] B. Scarlett, 'On the death of Tony Bland', *Res Publica* 3 (2) (1994): pp. 14–17, and in *Arena* 17 (1995): pp. 37–9; N. Ford, 'Moral dilemmas in the care of the dying', *ACR* 73 (1996): pp. 474–90; J. Finnis, 'Bland: Crossing the Rubicon?', *Law Quarterly Review* 109 (1993): pp. 329–37; J. Finnis, 'The "value of human life" and "the right to death"', *Southern Illinois University Law Journal* 17 (1993): pp. 559–71; Singer's interpretation in *Rethinking Life and Death*, ch. 4.

[93] Cf. D.S. Oderberg, 'Voluntary euthanasia and justice', in *Human Lives*, ed. Oderberg & Laing, pp. 225–40; at p. 135; further in D. Oderberg, *Applied Ethics: A Non-Consequentialist Approach* (Oxford, 2000), part II; an

deaths of old people who requested death while suffering nothing worse than loneliness.[94] They require at least a serious illness to justify euthanasia, apparently implying some weighty preference for life which the seriousness of the illness may balance. On the other hand, opponents of euthanasia almost always permit the administration of drugs to ease pain for dying people, even if they will hasten death. A few opponents of euthanasia do adhere strictly to the absolute sanctity of life,[95] but that is not the traditional opinion held by, for example, Catholic moralists.[96] The traditional view has survived nearly unchanged from the older Catholic casuists, one of whom explained it thus:

> The last moments of our conscious life are most precious. The eternal salvation of a sinful man who has not made his peace with God depends on how he makes use of them ...

> Nevertheless it is sometimes lawful to relieve the extreme suffering of a dying person by the administration of a drug which deprives him of consciousness from which he never recovers. The conditions under which such a procedure may be permitted are as follows:–

> (a) The consent of the patient must be freely given ...

> (b) It must be morally certain that the sick man has made every preparation for death ...

> (c) The suffering he has to undergo must be more than he can be expected reasonably to tolerate. While there would be an obligation to bear ordinary pain and discomfort, especially when it is soon to come to an end in death, there is no clear obligation to endure what is morally beyond the limits of human fortitude. It is true that the dying man's conscious life is shortened, but conscious life is shortened by a narcotic administered at any other time during life, and the shortening of conscious life for the relief of unsupportable pain is justified by the principle of totality. The good of the whole man is the first consideration, and if he is better in a narcotic sleep than suffering excruciating pain, may he not

'autonomy'-based approach in Charlesworth, *Bioethics in a Liberal Society*, ch. 3.

[94] B. Tobin, 'Did you think about buying her a cat? Some reflections on the concept of autonomy', *Journal of Contemporary Health Law and Policy* 11 (1995): pp. 417–28.

[95] G. Brennan, 'Evil in man', *Australian Journal of Forensic Sciences* 15 (1982): pp. 4–16, at p. 14; B. Pollard, *The Challenge of Euthanasia* (Crows Nest, 1994), ch. 4, on which H. Brent, 'Dr Brian Pollard and euthanasia', *Monash Bioethics Review* 17 (4) (Oct 1998): pp. 11–21, reply pp. 21–5.

[96] Emphasised in E. Hepburn, *Of Life and Death: An Australian Guide to Catholic Bioethics* (Melbourne, 1996), pp. 46–8, and in N. Ford, 'Ethical dilemmas in treatment decisions at the end of life', in N. Ford, ed, *Ethical Aspects of Treatment Decisions at the End of Life* (Melbourne, 1997), pp. 65–86.

submit to the drug? It is only *per accidens* that on this occasion he will never awake from it, but the principle which permits the administration of a narcotic applies essentially in the same way for every period of life. This reservation, however, should be made: The last moments of our earthly existence are of the greatest value, and so a more serious cause is required to justify passing into unconsciousness, artificially and deliberately induced, at that crisis than on an occasion when the danger of death does not enter the consideration.

(d) Finally, it is usually laid down that the drug administered to a sick person must not notably shorten his life, though some slight abbreviation of life may be permitted as an effect proportionate to the good result which is sought, i.e., relief from pain. In this case, however, the patient is at death's door, independent of human interference. What must be guarded against is a dose out of proportion to his condition, which would in itself be sufficient to cause death. All that is permitted is sufficient to relieve the pain. This may be the occasion of death sooner than would otherwise happen; but the dose given must never be lethal, in all the circumstances of the case.[97]

In short, both sides allow the administration of drugs that will certainly shorten the patient's life, if the patient's condition is sufficiently bad (but not otherwise). What then is it that they are arguing about, exactly?

Most of the attempted explanation of this question has focused on the notion of intention. What is wrong, according to the proponents of the 'anti' side like Finnis, is the *intentional* ending of (innocent) human life.[98] The 'pro' side, especially utilitarians like Singer, have argued that intention is irrelevant to deciding whether an action is good or bad: instead, they say, one should look only at the goodness of the total situation that the action brings about, the consequences of the action.[99] Supporters of intention argued with some conviction that

---

[97] J. Madden, 'The use of narcotics', *ACR* 35 (1958): pp. 140–4; similar in Vatican Declaration of 1980, repr. in P. Singer, ed, *Ethics* (Oxford, 1994), pp. 253–6; on Madden see L.J. Ansell, *Shepherd Amid Shepherds: The Life of Monsignor James Cole Madden DD* (Toowoomba, 1982); K.J. Walsh, *Yesterday's Seminary* (Sydney, 1998), pp. 237–52, 269–76, 304–15; C. Geraghty, *The Priest Factory* (Melbourne, 2003), pp. 59-62, 68-72, 103-6; a fictionalised version in T. Keneally, *The Place at Whitton* (London, 1964), ch. 9.

[98] J. Finnis, 'A philosophical case against euthanasia', in J. Keown, ed, *Euthanasia Examined* (Cambridge, 1995), pp. 23–35, further pp. 46–55, 62–71; N. Brown, 'The "harm" in euthanasia', *Australian Quarterly* 68 (3) (Spring 1996): pp. 26–35.

[99] Singer, *Practical Ethics* (2nd ed), ch. 7; I. Hunt, 'Is euthanasia wrong in itself?', in I. Hunt & L. Burns, ed, *The Quality of Death: Euthanasia in Australia* (Bedford Park, 1996), pp. 81–96.

there was a meaningful distinction in general between what one directly intends, and side-effects of one's action that one foresees but regrets — it is important in distinguishing murder from manslaughter, for example, and the deliberate terror bombing of civilians from the unfortunate side-effects of bombing military targets.[100] The distinction is expressed in traditional Catholic ethics as the 'principle of double effect': a regrettable side-effect may be permissible, provided that it is not intended in itself, that the good effect cannot be obtained without it, that the good effect is the direct result of the act and not of the side-effect, and that the bad effect is not out of proportion to the good one.[101]

The distinction between intention and side-effects may be meaningful, and even morally relevant, but it is hard to see that it has answered the primary question about the ethics of euthanasia: when can the needle go in? Rules about intentions say nothing about where that point is. The difficulty is to explain why the intention of others should be the deciding factor in what can happen to the victim. To decide on whether to discontinue aggressive treatment, or increase the dose of painkillers to a level that would hasten death, one must reach the conclusion that death is a more desirable state of affairs than the alternative, in all the circumstances of the case. If it is, how can it be wrong to bring about that state of affairs? The talk about intentions and double effects is no help in answering that question. Doubtless, if the victim is beyond the allowed point, the doctor can and should compose his intention so as to have pain relief and not death directly in mind, while if the victim is not yet at that point, the doctor may not so compose his intention. (The fact that intention will naturally follow a decision on the facts of the case is what makes it hard to interpret the many surveys that show most doctors and nurses 'favour

---

[100] J. Finnis, 'Intention and side-effects', in R.G. Frey & C.W. Morris, eds, *Liability and Responsibility* (Cambridge, 1991), pp. 32–64; J. Finnis, 'Euthanasia, morality and law', *Loyola of Los Angeles Law Review* 31 (1998): pp. 1123–45, at p. 1129; D. Kelly, 'Treating the dying: Emerging issues', *Bioethics News* 12 (3) (Apr 1993): pp. 37–46; J. Oakley & D. Cocking, 'Consequentialism, moral responsibility and the intention/foresight distinction', *Utilitas* 6 (1994): pp. 201–16; generally in Oderberg & Laing, eds, *Human Lives*.

[101] Uniacke, *Permissible Killing*, ch. 3; S. Uniacke, 'Double effect', *Routledge Encyclopedia of Philosophy*, vol. 3, pp. 130–2; J. Madden, 'The principle of double effect', *ACR* 38 (1961): pp. 211–9; A. Donagan, 'Moral absolutism and the double-effect exception', *Journal of Medicine and Philosophy* 16 (1991): pp. 495–509; Oderberg, *Moral Theory*, ch. 11.

euthanasia'[102] — whether what they favour satisfies the rules about intention is generally impossible to tell.) The question still is, how is that point to be decided?

On this question, Singer does offer an answer, though it is an alarming one. Being a preference utilitarian, he believes that where the line should be drawn depends heavily on the preferences of people other than the sufferer. If the sufferer has many heirs who greatly covet his fortune, that will move the line earlier. On the other hand, if the Queen of Australia's late daughter-in-law had survived the crash in the Pont d'Alma tunnel, the wishes of her billions of fans to have her kept alive would override any sufferings of hers. *Any* kind of utilitarianism is a harsh doctrine, because of the weight it gives to the happiness or preferences of those other than the individual who has to suffer the consequences of its recommendations.

The other side at least agrees that the question, 'When can the needle go in?' ought to depend principally on the degree of suffering of the victim. It is all a matter of proportion, of drawing a line on a continuum by determining whether further life and further treatment are 'excessively' burdensome. The patient can forgo 'treatment which either involves an imbalance between probable benefits to and burdens on the patient or is clearly therapeutically useless.'[103] It is a humane approach, but one that makes a good deal of the existing debate on philosophical principles beside the point. It is not even clear, for example, whether the much fought-over Northern Territory Rights of the Terminally Ill Act, the first legislation in the world to allow euthanasia, did or did not satisfy these conditions.[104] Cer-

---

[102] C.A. Stevens & R. Hassan, 'Management of death, dying and euthanasia: Attitudes and practices of medical practitioners in South Australia', *Journal of Medical Ethics* 20 (1994): pp. 41–6; R. Hassan, 'Euthanasia and the medical profession: An Australian study', *Australian Journal of Social Issues* 31 (1996): pp. 239–252; H. Kuhse & P. Singer, 'Voluntary euthanasia and the nurse: An Australian study', *International Journal of Nursing Studies* 30 (1993): pp. 311–22; H. Kuhse, P. Singer *et al.*, 'End-of-life decisions in Australian medical practice', *Medical Journal of Australia* 166 (17/2/1997), pp. 191–96, on which W. Uren, 'Life and death matters', *Eureka Street* 7 (4) (May 1997): pp. 18–19; comment in *Australian Nursing Journal* 3 (3) (1995): p. 26; opinions of the prominent in *The Last Right?*, ed. S. Chapman & S. Leeder (Melbourne, 1995); of Bill Hayden in *SMH* 22/6/1995, p. 1; comment in *SMH* 23/6/1995, p. 8, 26/6/1995, p. 2; S. Leys, *The Angel and the Octopus* (Sydney, 1999), pp. 239–41.

[103] B. Tobin, 'Guidelines: Dying with dignity', *Medical Journal of Australia* 159 (1993): p. 358.

[104] P. Singer, 'The legalisation of voluntary euthanasia in the Northern Territory', *Bioethics* 9 (1995): pp. 419–24, text of bill pp. 425–36; 'Why I wanted to die: Bob Dent's last words', repr. in W. Grey, 'Right to die or

tainly, it is an approach far removed from the apparent stark simplicity of a conflict of world views and basic ethical principles. In a matter of such importance, it is deeply disturbing that both sides have so seriously failed to explain their positions.

duty to live? The problem of euthanasia', *Journal of Applied Philosophy* 16 (1999): pp. 19–32; I.H. Kerridge & K.R. Mitchell, 'The legalisation of active voluntary euthanasia in Australia', *Journal of Medical Ethics* 22 (1996): pp. 273–8; C.J. Ryan & M. Kaye, 'Euthanasia in Australia: The Northern Territory Rights of the Terminally Ill Act', *New England Journal of Medicine* 334 (1996): pp. 326–8; reply p. 1668.

Epilogue   Stove on Why Have Philosophers?

This is David Stove's review of Selwyn Grave's History of Philosophy in Australia (1984)

THE author of this book was Professor of Philosophy at the University of Western Australia from 1961 to 1981. He is so absurdly modest a man that his own name is not mentioned once in the book, although he gives space to scores of lesser lights than himself. Never mind: his name will not be forgotten now, at least while philosophy survives in Australia. For philosophy feeds constantly on its own history, and Selwyn Grave has written a splendid history of philosophy in this country up to 1980. How this feat was possible in a book of 252 pages, I do not understand. Grave combines institutional and individual history with detailed accounts of many hundreds of articles, books and conversations. He leaves out very little of importance, and is always accurate and fair, and still contrives at the same time to be readable. Since he has done it, it would be idle to brood over how he could possibly have done it. But the labour entailed by first surveying, and then organising and compressing the material of this book, can have been nothing short of colossal.

What impression such a book must make on non-philosophers, I tremble to think. All these inexpressibly weird questions, about numbers, properties, individuals, space, time, causation, minds, possibility, probability, necessity, obligation, reasons, laws, God ... Not only are the questions weird individually, but collectively they form a mere chaos, defying all attempts to reduce them to a rational sequence. And then, none of the questions ever seem to get finally answered. It *is* a distressing scene, when you stand back and look at the whole of it. What is most painful about it is, the contrast it presents with science, looked at as a whole. In fact it is scarcely possible for anyone, reading a book like this, not to wonder why there should be such things as philosophers at all; or at least to wonder why there should be so many of them, all paid huge amounts of money taken from other and more useful people.

The latter question is absolutely unanswerable, in my opinion. But the former I believe I can answer. The vital clue to keep hold of is that people, and that includes all scientists, are only people after all: poor forked complicated creatures like yourself. Take Professor AB, our distinguished geneticist, member of the such-and-such, winner of the so-and-so: what a very clever man *he* must be! Well, so he is, in a way, but he is no glassy essence of genetic knowledge; he is lots of other things as well, and one of them is, that he happens to be a Methodist half-wit. Or take CD, a top physicist; but he also happens to take Uri Geller seriously, or believes that the latest physics vindicates Berkeley's spiritualistic philosophy. Professor EF of pure mathematics, approaching retirement, begins to drive his busy colleagues wild by asking questions like 'What the hell are numbers, anyway?' GH finished up as an economist but the mainspring of his life was a vision he picked up from some 19th century philosophers, of a paradise in which 'the toiling masses' come into their own. (He hasn't noticed that, where he lives, they knocked off toiling long ago.)   The Professor of History, IJ, cannot always silence his own perplexities about historical inevitability, and finds himself asking, as philosophers do, what the truth-conditions are of a statement like 'Hitler would have won the war, if he had not attacked Russia'. KL, the Professor of Medicine, is drawn by his own new technology, if by nothing else, into agonised deliberations about the duties of a doctor to his patients. And so on.

In other words, intelligent people, left to themselves, will philosophise anyway, late or soon, whatever special field of intellectual work they are engaged in, or even if they are engaged in none. The impulse to philosophy is in fact so natural and so strong that nothing is known, short of totalitarian terror, which can absolutely repress it. In a non-totalitarian society, then, philosophy *will* be done, and the only remaining practical question is how, or by whom, it is likely to be done best.

And here comes in the final fact. There are philosophers who have thought longer and better about the ethics of medicine than the professor of medicine ever had time to do. There are philosophers who have thought longer and better about the two-slit experiment than physicists have. There are philosophers who have thought longer and better about the foundations of mathematics than a mathematician is ever likely to do. And so on. I am conscious that a philosopher cannot say this of his profession without betraying a certain arrogance. Nevertheless it is literal truth. And it is a sufficient justification for the existence of a class of persons especially trained in philosophy.

As a class, philosophers are never well-regarded by their university colleagues. The charge against us used to be, that we were lost in cloudy generalities. Nowadays it is usually the reverse: that we neglect 'the great questions' in favour of minute and pointless technicalities. This charge is not true, but it is entirely understandable that it should be made. The standard of rigour in philosophy has risen very steeply in the present century, and this fact on its own is sufficient to account for the breaking-up of single big questions into many smaller ones, and the consequent slowing down of the whole process.

To the outsider, who cannot see the wood for the trees, the business naturally looks as though it could never have the remotest connection with anything that matters, so a theoretical chemist, for example, is apt to look at you and think, 'There goes another blasted philosopher: what *do* we feed those fellows for?' Well, such thoughts are not irrational; but they are wrong. At the same time as they despise us, our colleagues are also rather afraid of us. This too is not without a rational foundation! In argument of any kind, philosophers are *hard men* (some of whom are women), and most people do not care to tangle with us more than once or twice. In our company, as in another and more famous company of which the national poet sang, 'The man that holds his own is good enough'.[1]

[1] D. Stove, 'Why have philosophers?', *Quadrant* 29 (7) (July 1985): pp. 82–3; other philosophers on philosophy in B. Muscio, 'Our philosophical heritage', *AJPP* 2 (1924): pp. 153–63; H. Laurie, 'A plea for philosophy', *Victorian Review* 5 (Nov 1881): pp. 76–89; D. Braddon-Mitchell & J. Thomas, 'I earn therefore I am', *Australian Society* 8 (8) (Aug 1989): pp. 28–31; D.M. Armstrong, 'Continuity and change in philosophy', *Quadrant* 17 (5-6) (Dec 1973): pp. 19–23; J.J.C. Smart, 'Why philosophers disagree', in *Méta-philosophie: Reconstructing Philosophy?*, ed. J. Couture & K. Nielsen (Calgary, 1993), pp. 67–82; J. Passmore, 'Demarcating philosophy', in *Méta-philosophie*, pp 107–25; A.B. Palma, 'Philosophizing', *Philosophy* 66 (1991): pp. 41–51.

Bibliographies and Guides to Further Reading

History of Philosophy

SCIENTISTS, mathematicians and doctors regard the history of their subject as merely of curiosity value, fit for pottering around in after one's retirement. The history of philosophy is taken much more seriously, as a part of philosophy itself. Because of what the outsider would see as a lack of forward movement in the subject, the arguments and points of view of the great figures of the past do not become obsolete, and meditation on them continues to be worthwhile. The most ambitious Australian work in the field was John Passmore's *A Hundred Years of Philosophy*, which aimed to survey all the main writers in philosophy from about 1850 to 1950. Some were offended that Anderson and his school were relegated to a single footnote.[1] Most of the Dead White Overseas Males have their Australian interpreters, listed here in chronological order of their subjects:

P.F. O'Grady, *Thales of Miletus* (Aldershot, 2002).
R. Sworder, *Parmenides of Elea* (Bendigo, 1993).
I.F. Helu, *Herakleitos of Ephesos* (Nuku'alofa, 1995).
H.D. Rankin, *Plato and the Individual* (London, 1964).
E. Benitez, *Forms in Plato's Philebus* (Assen, 1989).
E. Benitez, ed, *Dialogues with Plato* (special issue of *Apeiron* 29 (4) (1996)).
F.C. White, *Plato's Theory of Particulars* (New York, 1981).
K. Lycos, *Plato on Justice and Power* (London, 1987).

---

[1] J. Passmore, *A Hundred Years of Philosophy*, p. 267 n. 1; sequel in J. Passmore, *Recent Philosophers* (London, 1985).

P. Thom, *The Syllogism* (Munich, 1981).

P. Thom, *The Logic of Essentialism* (1996).

H. Tarrant, *Plato's First Interpreters* (London, 2000).

H. Tarrant, *Scepticism or Platonism? The Philosophy of the Fourth Academy* (Cambridge, 1985).

H. Tarrant, *Thrasyllan Platonism* (Ithaca, NY, 1993).

H.A.K. Hunt, *The Humanism of Cicero* (Melbourne, 1954).

D.G. Londey & C. Johanson, *The Logic of Apuleius* (Leiden, 1987).

R. Mortley, *Désir et différence dans le tradition platonicienne* (Paris, 1988).

L. Alston, *Stoic and Christian in the Second Century* (London, 1906).

D. Baltzly, D. Blyth & H. Tarrant, eds, *Power and Pleasure, Virtues and Vices: Essays in Ancient Moral Philosophy* (Auckland, 2001).

E.F. Osborn, *The Beginning of Christian Philosophy* (Cambridge, 1981).

E.F. Osborn, *The Philosophy of Clement of Alexandria* (Cambridge, 1957).

M. Charlesworth, *St Anselm's Proslogion* (Oxford, 1965).

R.J. Campbell, *From Belief to Understanding: A Study of Anselm's Proslogion Argument on the Existence of God* (Canberra, 1976; New York, 1987).

C.J. Mews, *Reason and Belief in the Age of Roscelin and Abelard* (Aldershot, 2002).

C.J. Mews, *Abelard and His Legacy* (Aldershot, 2001).

R.P. Prentice, *Psychology of Love According to St Bonaventure* (St Bonaventure, NY, 1951, 1957).

J. Finnis, *Aquinas: Moral, Political and Legal Theory* (Oxford, 1998).

A. Donagan, *Human Ends and Human Actions: An Exploration of St Thomas' Treatment* (Milwaukee, 1985).

S. Day, *Intuitive Cognition: A Key to the Significance of the Later Scholastics* (St Bonaventure, NY, 1947).

R. Brown, *The Nature of Social Laws: Machiavelli to Mill* (Cambridge, 1984).

B. Mansfield, *Phoenix of His Age: Interpretations of Erasmus c. 1550–1750* (Toronto, 1979).

S. Gaukroger, *Francis Bacon and the Transformation of Early Modern Philosophy* (Cambridge, 2001).

A. Boyce Gibson, *The Philosophy of Descartes* (London, 1932).

W.A. Merrylees, *Descartes* (Melbourne, 1934).

H. Caton, *The Origin of Subjectivity: An Essay on Descartes* (New Haven, 1973).

S. Gaukroger, *Cartesian Logic* (Oxford, 1989).

S. Gaukroger, *Descartes: An intellectual biography* (Oxford, 1995).

S. Gaukroger, *Descartes' System of Natural Philosophy* (Cambridge, 2002).

S. Gaukroger, J. Schuster & J. Sutton, eds, *Descartes' Natural Philosophy* (London, 2000).

P. MacDonald, *Descartes and Husserl: The Philosophical Project of Radical Beginnings* (New York, 1999).

S. Gaukroger, ed, *The Soft Underbelly of Reason: The Passions in the Seventeenth Century* (London, 1998).

J. Sutton, *Philosophy and Memory Traces: Descartes to Connectionism* (Cambridge, 1998).

J. Broad, *Women Philosophers of the Seventeenth Century* (Cambridge, 2002).

S. Gaukroger, ed, *The Uses of Antiquity: The scientific Revolution and the Classical Tradition* (Dordrecht, 1991).

B. Brundell, *Pierre Gassendi* (Dordrecht, 1987).

J.A. Passmore, *Ralph Cudworth* (Cambridge, 1951).

R.E. Ewin, *Virtue and Rights: The Moral Philosophy of Thomas Hobbes* (Boulder, 1991).

J.A. Gunn, *Benedict Spinoza* (Melbourne, 1925).

G. Lloyd, *Part of Nature: Self-Knowledge in Spinoza's Ethics* (Ithaca, NY, 1994).

G. Lloyd, *Routledge Philosophy Guidebook to Spinoza and the Ethics* (New York, 1996).

M. Gatens & G. Lloyd, *Collective Imaginings* (London, 1999).

A.C. Fox, *Faith and Philosophy: Spinoza on Religion*, ed. A.J. Watt (Nedlands, 1990).

A. Donagan, *Spinoza* (Chicago, 1989).

S. Buckle, *Natural Law and the Theory of Property: Grotius to Hume* (Oxford, 1991).

K. Haakonssen, *Natural Law and Moral Philosophy: From Grotius to the Scottish Enlightenment* (Cambridge, 1996).

J. Kilcullen, *Sincerity and Truth: Essays on Arnauld, Bayle and Toleration* (Oxford, 1988).

P. Anstey, *The Philosophy of Robert Boyle* (London, 2000).

J. Mackie, *Problems from Locke* (Oxford, 1976).

U. Thiel, *John Locke* (Reinbek, 1990).

U. Thiel, ed, *Locke: Essay über den menschlichen Verstand* (Berlin, 1997).

U. Thiel, ed, *Locke: Epistemology and Metaphysics* (Aldershot, 2002).

J. Colman, *John Locke's Moral Philosophy* (Edinburgh, 1983).

S.A. Grave, *Locke and Burnet* (Perth, 1981).

J.A. Cover & J. O'Leary-Hawthorne, *Substance and Individuation in Leibniz* (Cambridge, 1999).

I. Hunter, *Rival Enlightenments: Civil and Metaphysical Philosophy in Early Modern Germany* (Cambridge, 2001).

D.H. Monro, *The Ambivalence of Bernard Mandeville* (Oxford, 1975).

D.H. Monro, *A Guide to the British Moralists* (London, 1972).

D.M. Armstrong, *Berkeley's Theory of Vision* (Melbourne, 1960).

J.A. Passmore, *Hume's Intentions* (rev. ed., London, 1968).

D.C. Stove, *Probability and Hume's Inductive Scepticism* (Oxford, 1973).

J. Mackie, *Hume's Moral Theory* (London, 1980).

M.P. Levine, *Hume and the Problem of Miracles* (Dordrecht, 1989).

S. Buckle, *Hume's Enlightenment Tract* (Oxford, 2001).

K. Haakonssen, *The Science of a Legislator: The Natural Jurisprudence of David Hume and Adam Smith* (Cambridge, 1981).

K. Haakonssen, ed, *Traditions of Liberalism: Essays on John Locke, Adam Smith, and John Stuart Mill* (St Leonards, 1988); (Haakonssen also edited the *Cambridge History of Eighteenth Century Philosophy*, which has several Australian contributors).

D.H. Monro, *Godwin's Moral Philosophy* (London, 1953).

S.A. Grave, *The Scottish Philosophy of Common Sense* (Oxford, 1960).

H. Laurie, *Scottish Philosophy in its National Development* (Glasgow, 1902).

M. McCloskey, *Kant's Esthetic* (Albany, NY, 1987).

J.T.J. Srzednicki, *The Place of Space and Other Themes: Variations on Kant's First Critique* (The Hague, 1983).

E. Morris Miller, *Moral Action and Natural Law in Kant* (Melbourne, 1911).

E. Morris Miller, *Kant's Doctrine of Freedom* (Melbourne, 1913).

E. Morris Miller, *The Basis of Freedom: A Study of Kant's Theory* (Sydney, 1924).

E. Morris Miller, *The Moral Law and the Highest Good: The Study of Kant's Doctrine of the Highest Good* (Melbourne, 1928).

P. Hutchings, *Kant on Absolute Value* (London, 1972).

F.C. White, *Kant's First Critique and the Transcendental Deduction* (Aldershot, 1996).

R. Langton, *Kantian Humility* (Oxford, 1998).

P. Singer, *Hegel* (Oxford, 1983).

P. Redding, *Hegel's Hermeneutics* (Ithaca, 1996).

P. Redding, *The Logic of Affect* (Ithaca, 1999).

R. Gascoigne, *Religion, Rationality and Community: Sacred and Secular in the Thought of Hegel and His Critics* (Dordrecht, 1985).

T. Nicolacopoulos & G. Vassilacopolous, *Hegel and the Logical Structure of Love* (Aldershot, 1999).

J. Watkin, *Kierkegaard* (London, 1997).

J. Watkin, *A Historical Dictionary of Kierkegaard's Thought* (Lanham, Md, 2001).

F.C. White, *On Schopenhauer's Fourfold Root of the Principle of Sufficient Reason* (Leiden, 1992).

E. Kamenka, *The Philosophy of Ludwig Feuerbach* (London, 1970).

J.A. Gunn, *Modern French Philosophy* (London, 1922).

E. Kamenka, *Ethical Foundations of Marxism* (London, 1962, 2nd ed, 1972).

E. Kamenka, *Marxism and Ethics* (London, 1979).

W.H.C. Eddy, *Understanding Marxism* (Oxford, 1979).

P. Singer, *Marx* (Oxford, 1980).

M.A. Rose, *Marx's Lost Aesthetic* (Cambridge, 1984).

S.A. Grave, *Conscience in Newman's Thought* (Oxford, 1989).

J.T.J. Srzednicki, *Franz Brentano's Analysis of Truth* (The Hague, 1965).

H.J. McCloskey, *John Stuart Mill* (London, 1971).

C.L. Ten, *Mill on Liberty* (Oxford, 1980).

N. Thornton, *The Problem of Liberalism in the Thought of John Stuart Mill* (New York, 1987).

E.E. Sleinis, *Nietzsche's Revaluation of Values* (Urbana, 1994).

T. Sadler, *Nietzsche: Truth and Redemption* (London, 1995).

R. Small, *Nietzsche in Context* (Aldershot, 2001).

G. Currie, *Frege* (Brighton, 1982).

J. Hill, *The Ethics of G.E. Moore* (Assen, 1976).

J. McKellar Stewart, *A Critical Exposition of Bergson's Philosophy* (London, 1911, 1913).

J.A. Gunn, *Bergson and His Philosophy* (London, 1920).

L. Goddard & B. Judge, *The Metaphysics of Wittgenstein's Tractatus* (Melbourne, 1982).

L.E. Johnson, *Focusing on Truth* (London, 1993).

A. Donagan, *The Later Philosophy of R.G. Collingwood* (Oxford, 1962).

T. Sadler, *Heidegger and Aristotle: The Question of Being* (London, 1996).

M. Charlesworth, *The Existentialists and Jean-Paul Sartre* (St Lucia, 1975).

N. Levy, *Sartre* (Oxford, 2002).

N. Levy, *Being up to Date: Foucault, Sartre and Postmodernity* (New York, 2001).

(Other work on Foucault was listed at ch. 11, fn. 88.)

D. Roberts, ed, *Reconstructing Theory: Gadamer, Habermas, Luhmann* (Melbourne, 1995).

R. Mortley, *French Philosophers in Conversation* (London, 1991).

D. Grosz, *Jacques Lacan: A Feminist Introduction* (Sydney, 1990).

J. Begley, *The Descriptive Metaphysics of P.F. Strawson* (Rome, 1964).

J.E. Malpas, *Donald Davidson and the Mirror of Meaning* (Cambridge, 1992).

F. D'Agostino, *Chomsky's System of Ideas* (Oxford, 1985).

K. Green, *Dummett: Philosophy of Language* (Cambridge, 2001).

N. Lucy, *Debating Derrida* (Melbourne, 1995).

P. Patton, *Deleuze and the Political* (London, 2000).

B. Colebrook, *Understanding Deleuze* (London, 2002).
C. Freundlieb, *Dieter Henrich and Contemporary Philosophy* (Aldershot, 2003).

I am grateful to Udo Thiel for help with this bibliography.

FOR a quicker run through the most famous of the DWOMs, one could try Hector Monro's *Sonneteer's History of Philosophy* (Melbourne, 1981). There are also a few books that survey particular themes over long periods of time:
R. Campbell, *Truth and Historicity* (Oxford, 1992).
G. Lloyd, *The Man of Reason* (2nd ed, London, 1993).
D.C. Stove, *The Plato Cult and Other Philosophical Follies* (Oxford, 1991).
Philosophical Papers of Alan Donagan, vol. 1: Historical Understanding and the History of Philosophy, ed. J.E. Malpas & A. Donagan (Chicago, 1994).
J. Franklin, *The Science of Conjecture: Evidence and Probability before Pascal* (Baltimore, 2001).
R. Ferrell, *Genres of Philosophy* (Aldershot, 2002).
P.S. MacDonald, *History of the Concept of Mind* (Aldershot, 2003).

Australian Philosophy

FOR further information on the history of Australian philosophy, Selwyn Grave's *History of Philosophy in Australia* (St. Lucia, 1984) is excellent within its scope, which is philosophy in the analytic style done in universities up to 1983. The same can be said of its continuation by Bob Brown (R. Brown, 'Recent Australian work in philosophy', *Canadian Journal of Philosophy* 18 (1988): pp. 545–78). *Essays on Philosophy in Australia*, ed. J.T.J. Srzednicki & D. Wood (Dordrecht, 1992) and *Australian Philosophers*, ed. P. Dowe, M. Nicholls & L. Shotton (Hobart, 1996) survey developments in various particular fields. C.A.J. Coady offers a brief overview in 'Australia, philosophy in', *Routledge Encyclopedia of Philosophy*, ed. E. Craig (London, 1998), vol. 1 pp. 574–84. An encomium of Australian philosophy is at www.humanities.org/review/b22_gaukroger.html and rankings at www.philosophicalgourmet.com .

  More biographical in style are Cassandra Pybus's book on the Orr case, *Gross Moral Turpitude* (Melbourne, 1993), renamed *Seduction and Consent* (Melbourne, 1994), Brian Kennedy's biography of John Anderson, *A Passion to Oppose* (Melbourne, 1995), and the biography of E. Morris Miller, J. Reynolds & M. Giordano, *Countries of the Mind* (Hobart, 1985). W. Martin Davies' *The Philosophy of Sir William*

Mitchell (1861–1962): A Mind's Own Place appeared in 2003, while Mark Weblin's account of John Anderson, *A Passion for Thinking*, is completed. The first volume of Weblin's edition of Anderson's papers, *A Perilous and Fighting Life*, was published in 2003.

Some recollections of Australian philosophy by its leaders are D. Armstrong, 'Black swans: The formative influences in Australian philosophy', in *Rationality and Irrationality*, ed. B. Brogaard & B. Smith (Vienna, 2000), pp. 11–17 (text at www.ditext.com/arm-strong/swans.html) and J.J.C. Smart, 'Australian philosophers of the 1950s', *Quadrant* 33 (6) (June 1989): pp. 35–9. On the earliest period, E. Morris Miller, 'The beginnings of philosophy in Australia and the work of Henry Laurie', *AJPP* 7 (1929): pp. 241–51 and 8 (1930): pp. 1–22 is informative.

The *Australasian Journal of Philosophy* has been the flagship journal of academic philosophy since its foundation (as the *Australasian Journal of Psychology and Philosophy*) in 1923. More specialist journals include *Sophia* (on the philosophy of religion), the *Australian Journal of Professional and Applied Ethics*, *Res Publica*, *Monash Bioethics Review*, *Bioethics Outlook*, the *Journal of Political Philosophy*, *Metascience*, *Educational Philosophy and Theory*, the *Australian Journal of Legal Philosophy, Critical & Creative Thinking: The Australasian Journal of Philosophy for Children*, *Contretemps* (online journal of the Australasian Society for Continental Philosophy) and *Concrescence: The Australasian Journal of Process Thought*. The demise of the lively popular magazine *Philosopher* (1995–98) has left a gap in the market.

The website of the Australasian Association of Philosophy www.uq.edu.au/hprc/aap has recent information on events. It includes a link to, among other things, the valuable though now somewhat outdated guide to Internet philosophy resources, 'Philosophy in cyberspace', compiled by Dey Alexander of Monash University.

R ECOMMENDED reading in Australian philosophy: the following are simply my favourites, and no litigation will be entered into.

For readability, it is impossible to go past David Stove's stylish polemics in *Popper and After: Four Modern Irrationalists* (Oxford, 1983, repr. as *Anything Goes*, Sydney, 1998, and as *Scientific Irrationalism*, New Brunswick, 2001), (on the philosophy of science); *The Plato Cult, and Other Philosophical Follies* (Oxford, 1991), (on philosophical errors in general) and in the collections of essays, *Cricket versus Republicanism* (Quakers Hill, 1995), *Against the Idols of the Age* (New Brunswick, 1999) and *On Enlightenment* (New Brunswick, 2002).

For abstract argument at the highest level, but still written comprehensibly, there are D.M. Armstrong's books on metaphysics: *Universals and Scientific Realism* (Cambridge, 1978), *What is a Law of Nature?*

(Cambridge, 1983), *Universals: An Opinionated Introduction* (Boulder, 1989), and *A World of States of Affairs* (Cambridge, 1997).

On a different science-related topic is Graham Nerlich's *The Shape of Space* (2nd ed, Cambridge, 1994).

Excellent books on the basic questions of ethics are Raimond Gaita, *Good and Evil: An Absolute Conception* (Basingstoke, 1991) and Alan Donagan, *The Theory of Morality* (Chicago, 1977).

On the philosophy of religion, old issues are treated in a new way in Peter Forrest, *God Without the Supernatural* (Ithaca, NY, 1996).

For a small amount of political philosophy, M. Krygier, 'In praise of conservative-liberal-social democracy', *Quadrant* 36 (5) (May 1992): pp. 12–23.

A good introduction to philosophy of language is M. Devitt & K. Sterelny, *Language and Reality* (Oxford, 1987).

Some interesting attempts at introductions to philosophy via popular culture are R. Hanley, *The Metaphysics of Star Trek* (New York, 1997) and C. Falzon, *Philosophy Goes to the Movies* (London, 2002).

Political and Social Philosophy

APOLOGIES are in order for the absence of political and social philosophy in this book. They are very large and valuable topics in themselves, but they have a very different character from the more abstract philosophical topics treated here. To deal with them would require another book of the same size. The following surveys provide starting points for further research:

D. Muschamp, 'Political philosophy in Australia', in *Essays on Philosophy in Australia*, ed. J.T. Srzednicki & D. Wood (Dordrecht, 1992), pp. 81–96.

C. Condren, 'Political theory', in *Surveys of Australian Political Science*, ed. D. Aitkin (Sydney, 1985).

G. Stokes, 'Conceptions of Australian political thought — a methodological critique', *Australian Journal of Political Science* 29 (1994): pp. 240–258.

R.E. Goodin & P. Pettit, eds, *Companion to Contemporary Political Philosophy* (Oxford, 1995).

R. Brown, 'Social philosophy', in Academy of the Social Sciences in Australia, *Challenges for the Social Sciences and Australia* (Canberra, 1998), pp. 209–13.

There is a strong Australian presence in the *Journal of Political Philosophy*.

Monty Python's Philosophers Song

THE Bruces from Monty Python Live at City Center and Monty Python Live at the Hollywood Bowl, etc. [courtesy Python (Monty) Pictures Ltd]

Bruce: How are you, Bruce?
Bruce: G'day Bruce.
Bruce: Gentlemen, I'd like to introduce a man from Pommyland who is joinin' us this year in the philosophy department at the University of Woolloomooloo.
Everybruce: G'day!
Michael: Hello.
Bruce: Michael Baldwin, Bruce. Michael Baldwin, Bruce. Michael Baldwin, Bruce.
Bruce: Is your name not Bruce?
Michael: No, it's Michael.
Bruce: That's going to cause a little confusion.
Bruce: Mind if we call you 'Bruce' to keep it clear?
Bruce: Gentlemen, I think we better start the faculty meeting. Before we start, though, I'd like to ask the padre for a prayer.
Bruce: Oh Lord, we beseech Thee, Amen!!
Everybruce: Amen!
Bruce: Crack tube! *(Bottles opening)*
Bruce: Now I call upon Bruce to officially welcome Mr Baldwin to the philosophy faculty.
Bruce: I'd like to welcome the pommy bastard to God's own Earth, and remind him that we don't like stuck-up sticky-beaks here.
Everybruce: Hear, hear! Well spoken, Bruce!
Bruce: Bruce here teaches classical philosophy, Bruce there teaches Hegelian philosophy, and Bruce here teaches logical positivism. And is also in charge of the sheep dip.
Bruce: What's New-Bruce going to teach?
Bruce: New-Bruce will be teaching political science, Machiavelli, Bentham, Locke, Hobbes, Sutcliffe, Lindwall, Miller, Hassett and Benaud.
Bruce: Those are all cricketers!
Bruce: Aww, spit!
Bruce: Howls of derisive laughter, Bruce!
Everybruce: Australia, Australia, Australia, Australia, we love you, amen!
Bruce: Another tube! *(Bottles opening)*
Bruce: Any questions?
Bruce: New-Bruce, are you a Poofter?

Bruce: Are you a Poofter?

New-Bruce: No!

Bruce: No. Right, I just want to remind you of the faculty rules: Rule One!

Everybruce: No Poofters!

Bruce: Rule Two, no member of the faculty is to maltreat the others in any way at all — if there's anybody watching. Rule Three?

Everybruce: No Poofters!!

Bruce: Rule Four: now this term, I don't want to catch anybody not drinking. Rule Five?

Everybruce: No Poofters!

Bruce: Rule Six, there is NO ... Rule Six. Rule Seven?

Everybruce: No Poofters!!

Bruce: Right, that concludes the readin' of the rules, Bruce.

Bruce: This here's the wattle,

> The emblem of our land.
> You can stick it in a bottle,
> Or you can hold it in your hand.

Everybruce: Amen!

(Now all four Bruces launch into the Philosopher's Song.)

> Immanuel Kant was a real piss-ant who was very rarely stable.
> Heidegger, Heidegger was a boozy beggar who could think you under the table.
> David Hume could out-consume Schopenhauer and Hegel,
> And Wittgenstein was a beery swine who was just as sloshed as Schlegel.
> There's nothing Nietzsche couldn't teach ya 'bout the raising of the wrist.
> Socrates, himself, was permanently pissed.
> John Stuart Mill, of his own free will, after half a pint of shandy was particularly ill.
> Plato, they say, could stick it away, 'alf a crate of whiskey every day.
> Aristotle, Aristotle was a bugger for the bottle,
> And Hobbes was fond of his dram.
> And Rene Descartes was a drunken fart:
> "I drink, therefore I am."
> Yes, Socrates himself is particularly missed;
> A lovely little thinker, but a bugger when he's pissed.

Index